Sociology
The Core

eighth edition

Michael Hughes
Virginia Polytechnic Institute and State University

Carolyn J. Kroehler

McGraw Hill **Higher Education**

Boston   Burr Ridge, IL   Dubuque, IA   New York   San Francisco   St. Louis
Bangkok   Bogotá   Caracas   Kuala Lumpur   Lisbon   London   Madrid   Mexico City
Milan   Montreal   New Delhi   Santiago   Seoul   Singapore   Sydney   Taipei   Toronto

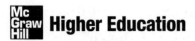
SOCIOLOGY: THE CORE, EIGHTH EDITION

Published by McGraw-Hill, an imprint of The McGraw-Hill Companies, Inc., 1221 Avenue of the Americas, New York, NY 10020.

1 2 3 4 5 6 7 8 9 0 DOC/DOC 0 9 8 7 6

ISBN: 978-0-07-110176-9
MHID: 0-07-110176-4

www.mhhe.com

We dedicate this edition to Walter R. Gove, sociologist and mountain climber.

about the authors

Michael Hughes is Professor of Sociology at Virginia Polytechnic Institute and State University (Virginia Tech). He received his Ph.D. in sociology from Vanderbilt University in 1979 and has taught introductory sociology over the past 34 years. He also regularly teaches courses in minority group relations, deviant behavior, the sociology of mental illness, and data analysis. From 2000 to 2004, he served as editor of the *Journal of Health and Social Behavior.* He has held positions as research fellow at the University of Michigan's Institute for Social Research (1992–1994) and research associate at Vanderbilt University (1980–1982). With Walter R. Gove he is the author of the book *Overcrowding in the Household.* His research interests in mental health and mental illness, race and ethnicity, and crowding and living alone have resulted in over 60 professional articles published in a variety of journals. In 2004–2005, he served as president of the Southern Sociological Society.

Carolyn J. Kroehler is a professional writer and editor who has received her sociological education "on the job." Before her work on *Sociology: The Core,* she contributed to criminology and criminal justice textbooks. She edited and helped with the writing of a guide to academic success for college students, *Straight A's: If I Can Do It, So Can You.* At the Virginia Water Resources Research Center, she wrote public education and technical materials about water quality and other environmental issues, including a book on drinking water standards. Her writing experience also includes several years in a college public relations office and writing and editing for the *Lancaster Independent Press.* She earned her Ph.D. in botany at Virginia Tech and has published in the *Canadian Journal of Botany, Plant and Soil,* and *Oecologia.*

Mike and Carrie live in Blacksburg, Virginia, with their children Edmund and Camilla.

contents in brief

contents

chapter five   132

Deviance and Crime   132

5.1 Students Doing Sociology
*Spit, Saliva, and the Social Construction
of Deviance   136*

5.2 Doing Social Research
*Drink 'Til You're Sick: What Explains
College Binge Drinking?   146*

5.3 Social Inequalities
*Being Black Brings Extra Punishment
for Crime   163*

chapter six   174

Social Stratification   174

6.1 Sociology Around the World
*Is Race the Basis for an American
Caste System?   178*

6.2 Doing Social Research
*Income Inequality within Societies:
A Look around the World   184*

6.3 Social Inequalities
Why Do Doctors Deliver Babies?   202

chapter twelve   394
Population and Environment   394

chapter thirteen   428
Social Change   428

13.1 Students Doing Sociology
The Un-TV Experiment   433

13.2 Doing Social Research
Blogging Our Way to Intimacy   439

13.3 Social Inequalities
*When Will Same-Sex Marriages Become
"the Norm"?   454*

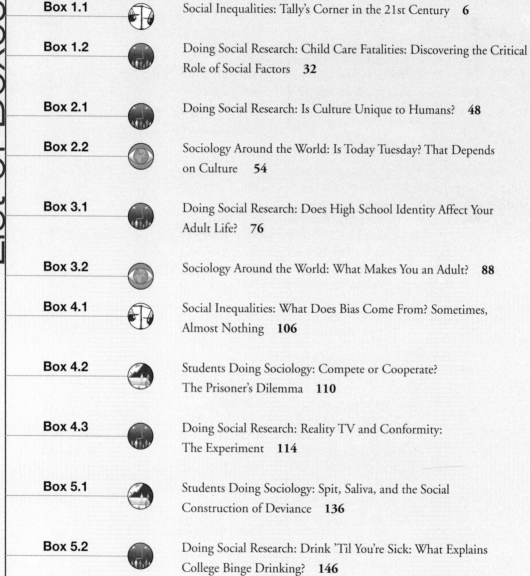

The education that students receive should allow them to live fuller, richer, and more fruitful lives. Such a goal is ultimately the bedrock upon which we build and justify our careers as educators and sociologists. Students today face the challenges presented by the transformation to an information and global economy, the growth of biotechnology and cloning, the ever-expanding human population, and the environmental problems associated with population growth. To understand and live in this rapidly changing social environment, they need a solid foundation in sociological concepts and perspectives.

Sociology encourages us to examine aspects of our social environment that we might otherwise ignore, neglect, or take for granted, and it allows us to look beneath the surface of everyday life. The introductory course in sociology gives students the opportunity to use this sociological imagination in understanding and mastering their social world, and *Sociology: The Core* provides the information they need to do so.

Providing the Core

A course in sociology should broaden students' horizons, sharpen their observational skills, and strengthen their analytical capabilities. *Sociology: The Core* aims to make the introductory course manageable for instructors and students alike. The eighth edition retains the core concept with a tight, readable text that provides the essentials. It includes all the major sections of the seventh edition, with streamlined feature boxes, figures that present data critical to an introductory text, and a stick-to-the-basics approach. It provides the core of sociology—the basic foundations of the discipline.

The coverage of many key topics in *Sociology: The Core*—theory, culture, socialization, groups, formal organizations, deviance, social stratification, race, gender, power, the family,

religion, and social change—is equal to, and in many cases exceeds, that found in most other introductory textbooks. The **functionalist, conflict**, and **interactionist perspectives** are introduced in the first chapter and applied throughout the book. This helps students to develop a solid understanding of these major sociological perspectives and their contributions to the topics covered here, and it provides something for everyone in departments where all faculty members are required to use the same introductory textbook.

It would be presumptuous for any sociologist to program another sociologist's course. Instead, we hope that *Sociology: The Core* provides a solid resource—a common intellectual platform—that each instructor can use as a sound foundation in developing an introductory course. As a coherent presentation of sociological materials, a core text is an aid to pedagogy. Instructors can supplement the text with papers, readers, or monographs that meet their unique teaching needs. Likewise, students can use *Sociology: The Core* as a succinct source of information.

Bringing Students In

In *Sociology: The Core*, we seek to make sociology come alive as a vital and exciting field, to relate principles to real-world circumstances, and to attune students to the dynamic processes of our rapidly changing contemporary society. The study of a science can captivate students interest and excite their imaginations. In this edition, we capitalize on students' desires to read about issues of interest to them with **feature boxes on reality TV, Blogs, becoming an adult, binge drinking, high school identities, campus rape, and affirmative action in college admissions.** Because students live and will work in an increasingly diverse and global world, we have **increased coverage of global**

issues with boxes on exporting toxic trash and cultural variation in marking time as well as integrating **cross-cultural comparisons** in various chapters. Our box series "Social Inequalities" enhances our **emphasis on issues of race, ethnicity, class, and gender** as a regular part of most topics in sociology.

Pedagogical Aids

In selecting pedagogical aids for the text, we decided to use those that provide the most guidance with the least clutter and to focus on those that students are most likely to actually use.

Chapter Outline

Each chapter opens with an outline of its major headings; this allows students to preview at a glance the material to be covered.

Cross-Reference Icons

Referrals to material in other chapters are highlighted with cross-reference icons that provide specific page references, making it easy for students and instructors to find such material.

Questions for Discussion

Each feature box includes two or three questions geared toward linking the box material to core concepts and toward getting students thinking about the issues raised.

Key Terms

The terms most essential to the core of sociology are set in boldface type and are defined as they are presented in the text. These key terms appear in the chapter summaries, again in boldface type to emphasize their importance and to reinforce the student's memory. At the end of each chapter, a **Glossary** lists the key terms included in the chapter and provides their definitions. All key terms appear in the index, along with an indication of where they are first defined.

Chapter Summary

Each chapter concludes with a **Chapter in Brief** summary that uses the same outline of major headings used in the chapter outline. The summary recapitulates the central points, allowing students to review in a systematic manner what they already have read. The use of major headings allows students to return to the appropriate section in the chapter for more information. The Chapter in Brief includes all of the glossary terms, boldfaced to remind students that they are key terms.

Review Questions

Each chapter concludes with a list of review questions on the central ideas presented in the chapter.

Internet Exercises

The end-of-chapter feature **Internet Connection** provides students with an opportunity to explore sociological data and information on the Internet and hone their critical thinking abilities.

Boxes

The eighth edition includes four types of boxes, all of which add to the concepts and theories discussed in the chapter in which they appear, and many of which add insights to other chapters as well.

Social Inequalities boxes explore inequalities of race, ethnicity, class, or gender from a sociological perspective. Topics include race, crime, and punishment; geographical variation in gender inequality; same-sex marriage; affirmative action; disenfranchisement; and unequal childhoods.

Doing Social Research boxes focus on how social scientists approach various research problems; topics discussed have been chosen to illustrate or enhance the topics discussed in the chapter.

Sociology Around the World boxes focus on sociological research that extends beyond the United States, on research done with subjects from outside the United States, on cross-cultural sociological research, and on illustrations of sociological concepts in a variety of cultural settings.

Students Doing Sociology boxes summarize the experience of students who were asked to think like sociologists: to interpret certain events with sociological concepts and principles or to perform sociological research.

Additional *Students Doing Sociology* boxes are available in the Instructor's Manual. Instructors may wish to use them to create their own classroom exercises or assignments.

Figures and Tables

The data presented in the figures and tables throughout *Sociology: The Core* are as up to date as possible—and as user-friendly and accessible as we could make them. Whenever possible, we have created figures from published data instead of simply presenting percentages and numbers from statistical sources. In many cases, we have generated original analyses from publicly available data sets. Sources for figures and tables include the U.S. Census Bureau, the National Center for Health Statistics, the General Social Survey, the *Statistical Abstract of the United States*, and the Survey of Consumer Finances.

Photographs and Cartoons

Photographs and cartoons serve both to draw the students in and to illustrate important concepts and principles. The eighth edition includes new and bigger photos and new cartoons. Photo captions tie the photographs to the text, and cartoons, in addition to adding a light touch to the text and reinforcing important ideas, make points that can't be made any other way.

References

The eighth edition of *Sociology: The Core* presents new data and references throughout,

including major updates in race and ethnicity; gender inequality; welfare reform and poverty; crime; wealth and income; and more. It includes 135 new references, including articles from the major sociological journals, books, government documents and data sets, and popular media, most published in 2003, 2004, 2005, and 2006. Full citations appear at the end of the text.

Changes in the Eighth Edition

While the eighth edition retains all the core information of the seventh edition, there are a number of significant additions and enhancements. The eighth edition:

- Completely updates data and figures throughout the book wherever possible.

- Incorporates new examples relevant to students, including Hurricane Katrina, the tsunami, and the Pakistani earthquake; stem cell research fraud; global warming; contemporary movies; and the Bin Laden Itch.

- Uses a new chapter opener on the over-representation of male characters in kids' movies for the **gender** chapter.

- Adds a discussion of racial formation as well as new data and figures in the **race and ethnicity** chapter.

- Updates the global gender picture; presents new data on labor force participation, sexual harassment, wage parity, occupations, and political leadership; and provides a new section on gender differences based on Janet Shibley Hyde's meta-analysis of diffences in the **gender** chapter.

- Includes a new section on race and crime and a new box on the extended punishment for crime that African Americans suffer in U.S. society in the **deviance and crime** chapter.

- Updates the debate on marriage and the traditional family with new figures and data about family arrangements in the United

States, labor force participation, living alone, divorce, age of marriage, and household income as related to race, ethnicity, and gender, as well as revisions of the section on same-sex unions in the **family** chapter.

- Reviews new data on the state of public **education** in the U.S. and presents TIMSS international rankings of educational achievement.

- Updates the discussion of **stratification** with new wealth data from the most recent Federal Reserve Survey of Consumer Finances and new survey information about poverty and about the American dream.

- Discusses the current **health care** crisis in the United States and includes new data on the uninsured.

- Streamlines and updates discussions, provides contemporary examples, and updates voting participation and political action committee figures in the **political and economic power** chapter.

- Substantially revises the discussion of the **environment** to focus on global warming, adds new material on **urban sprawl** and on sex ratios in developing countries, and provides the newest **population** and life expectancy data.

- Presents new examples, a revised section on mass hysteria, updated data and figures on computer and Internet use, and a discussion of Friedman's "flat world" idea in the **social change** chapter.

Sociology: The Core was originally conceived and written by James W. Vander Zanden, and some of his work is retained in this eighth edition. However, he did not participate in this revision and is not responsible for any new material, changes, or additions in the eighth edition. Michael Hughes and Carolyn J. Kroehler are responsible for all of the revisions and changes in the fifth through the eighth editions.

Ancillary Materials

The eighth edition of *Sociology: The Core* is accompanied by a number of supplementary learning and teaching aids.

For the Student

Student's Online Learning Center (OLC)

The Online Learning Center website that accompanies this text offers a variety of resources for the student. In addition to various study tools, students will find chapter objectives, chapter outlines, and overviews, interactive chapter quizzes, annotated lists of weblinks, Internet exercises, census updates, and flashcards of key terms. Please visit the *Sociology: The Core* OLC at www.mhhe.com/Hughes8.

Reel Society Interactive Movie CD-Rom

Available as a separate package option, this professionally produced movie on CD-Rom demonstrates the sociological imagination using actors in campus life scenarios. Each viewer influences key plot turns by making choices for them. Through it all, a wide variety of issues and perspectives are addressed relating major sociological concepts and theories to students' lives. Please go to www.mhhe.com/reelsoc for further details.

For the Instructor

Instructor's Manual

The Instructor's Manual provides chapter summaries, chapter outlines, learning objectives, teaching suggestions and discussion questions, student exercises and projects, and suggested films/videos. The Instructor's Manual can also be downloaded from the Instructor's Online Learning Center.

Test Bank

The Test Bank offers 75 multiple-choice, 25 true-false, and 10 essay questions for each chapter in the text. The Test Bank can be downloaded as a Word file from the Instructor's Online Learning Center. It is **also available as a computerized test bank.**

PowerPoint Slides. A collection of tables and figures from the text, augmented by additional graphics, allows instructors to add visual content to their lectures. The PowerPoint files can be downloaded from the Instructor's Online Learning Center.

Instructor's Online Learning Center (OLC)

Password-protected, the Instructor's side of the OLC contains a variety of resources, activities, and classroom tips. The Instructor's Manual, PowerPoint slides, and Test Bank can be accessed electronically on this site, www.mhhe.com/hughes8.

The Classroom Performance System (CPS)

This revolutionary wireless response system gives the instructor immediate feedback from every student in the class. CPS units include easy-to-use software for creating and delivering questions and assessments to your class. Each student simply responds with their individual wireless response pad, providing instant results. Suggested CPS questions specific to *Sociology: The Core*, 8/e, are available on the Instructor's

Online Learning Center. CPS is the perfect tool for engaging students while gathering important assessment data. Go to www.mhhe.com/einstruction for further details.

PageOut: The Course Website Development Center

Online content for *Sociology: The Core* is supported by WebCT, eCollege.com, Blackboard, and other course management systems. Additionally, McGraw-Hill's PageOut service is available to help instructors get their course up and running online in a matter of hours, at no cost. [No programming knowledge is required.] When you use PageOut, your students have instant, 24-hour access to your course syllabus, lecture notes, assignments, and other original material. Students can even check their grades on-line. Material from the Online Learning Center (OLC) can be pulled into your website. PageOut also provides a discussion board where you and your students can exchange questions and post announcements. To find out more about PageOut, ask your McGraw-Hill representative for details, or fill out the form at www.mhhe.com/pageout.

Videos

Please contact your McGraw-Hill sales representative to learn about videos that are available to adopters of McGraw-Hill introductory sociology textbooks.

acknowledgments

We would like to thank James W. Vander Zanden, who originally conceived of *Sociology: The Core*, and who authored the first four editions. We still follow his organization of basic concepts, and many of his other contributions remain. We also would like to thank the McGraw-Hill team that worked to make *Sociology: The Core* a reality, including editorial director Phil Butcher and sponsoring editor Sherith Pankratz. Many people worked to transform a pile of paper into an attractive and user-friendly textbook: project manager Ruth Smith, designer Laurie Entringer, production supervisor Janean Utley, and photo research coordinator Nora Agbayani. We would also like to express our appreciation to our marketing manager, Dan Loch, for his efforts to promote this book. Special thanks go to developmental editor Craig Leonard, who kept us on track through thick and thin and without whose friendly reminders we might have missed most of our deadlines.

We would like to thank the many students who have provided feedback on the textbook over the years. Particularly helpful in the past two revisions was Tarek Turaigi, who provided comments that enlightened us and considerably improved the text. Mike is very thankful to recent and current graduate students at Virginia Tech, including Ian Lovejoy, Peter Mateyka, and Tugrul Keskin for intellectually stimulating conversations that have improved his focus on core issues dealt with in the text.

Many thanks also go to Mike's colleagues at Virginia Tech who, through many and varied discussions and suggestions, have directly or indirectly made substantial contributions to this work: Carol Bailey, Alan Bayer, Cliff Bryant, Toni Calasanti, Peggy DeWolf, Jay Edwards, Skip Fuhrman, Ted Fuller, Ellington Graves, Kwame Harrison, Jim Hawdon, Brad Hertel, Terry Kershaw, Jill Kiecolt, Paulo Polanah, Chishamiso Rowley, John Ryan, Don Shoemaker, Bill Snizek, Bob Turner, Stacy Vogt-Yuan, and Dale Wimberly. We would also like to particularly thank Keith Durkin, of Ohio Northern University, for comments that have been helpful to us in making revisions over the years.

We are also very grateful to the following reviewers for their many helpful comments and suggestions: Edward Albert, Hofstra University; Betty L. Alt, University of Southern Colorado; Mark Austin, University of Louisville; Susan L. Brown, Bowling Green State University; Erica Childs, Eastern Connecticut State University; Keith Durkin, Ohio Northern University; Michael C. Kanan, Northern Arizona University; Donna King, University of North Carolina-Wilmington; Kathleen E. Miller, George Washington University; Michael Plekon, Baruch College-CUNY; Tom Shannon, Radford University; Tim Sullivan, Cedar Valley College; Suzanne Tallichet, Morehead State University; Bob Thaler, Saginaw Valley State University; Nathan Weinberg, California State University-Northridge; and C. Ray Wingrove, University of Richmond.

Finally, we'd like to thank our children, Edmund and Camilla, for their patience, love, and sociological insights; and our "families of orientation" for launching us on our careers.

Michael Hughes
Carolyn J. Kroehler

visual preview

Sociology encourages us to examine aspects of our social environment that we might otherwise ignore, neglect, or take for granted and allows us to look beneath the surface of everyday life. The introductory course in sociology gives students the opportunity to use the sociological imagination in understanding and mastering their social world, and *Sociology: The Core* provides the information they need to do so.

The eighth edition continues to adhere to the core concept, offering a compact, accessible, and affordable text that presents the essentials. It provides the core of sociology—the basic foundations of the discipline—for the student.

Chapter Opener and Outline

Each chapter opens with an outline of its major headings, allowing students to preview at a glance the material to be covered.

Chapter 2

CULTURE AND SOCIAL STRUCTURE

Components of Culture
Norms
Values
Symbols and Language

Cultural Unity and Diversity
Cultural Universals
Cultural Integration
Ethnocentrism
Cultural Relativism
Subcultures and Countercultures

Social Structure
Statuses
Roles
Groups
Institutions
Societies

Box 2.1   *Doing Social Research: Is Culture Unique to Humans?*
Box 2.2   *Sociology around the World: Is Today Tuesday? That Depends on Culture*

In 1789 mutineers led by Fletcher Christian seized control of the ship *Bounty* shortly after it had departed from Tahiti, an island in the South Pacific. They set William Bligh, the ship's captain, and 18 of his men adrift. The mutineers returned to Tahiti, where some of the men decided to remain. Nine men elected to seek another island and induced 6 Tahitian men and 12 Tahitian women to sail with them to Pitcairn Island.

The story of the mutiny on the *Bounty* and the subsequent settlement on Pitcairn Island is a perennial favorite. For sociologists, Pitcairn Island—where descendants of the first settlers still live today—offers a unique social experiment in the founding of a society and the fashioning of a new culture. Imagine the problems that confronted the English and Tahitian colonists when they arrived on this tiny, uninhabited South Pacific island. How would they find food? How would they protect themselves from the elements? How would they maintain order? How would they manage their sexual relationships, a matter of no small concern in a community of 15 men and 12 women? How

would they provide for any children born on the island?

In finding solutions to their problems, the English and Tahitian colonists could not fall back on the sorts of genetic adaptations such as those that permit insects to live a group existence. They lacked the built-in behavioral responses and highly specialized appendages that would prepare them for a particular environmental niche. An ability to adapt is not found in human's genetic heritage, but in culture and society, the topics of this chapter.

Culture refers to the social heritage of a people—those learned patterns for thinking, feeling, and acting that are transmitted from one generation to the next, including the embodiment of these patterns in material items. It includes both *nonmaterial culture*—abstract creations like values, beliefs, symbols, norms, customs, and institutional arrangements—and *material culture*—physical artifacts or objects like stone axes, computers, loincloths, tuxedos, automobiles, paintings, electric guitars, hairstyles, and domed stadiums. **Society** refers to a group of people who live within the same territory and

42

43

Cross-Reference System

References in the text to concepts discussed in previous chapters are highlighted with cross-reference icons with page numbers, making it easy for students and instructors to find and review the earlier material.

of perfection. In fact, Weber was quite critical of bureaucracy as an organizational form. Instead, Weber used the term *ideal type* to p. 13–14 refer to a concept constructed by sociologists to portray the principal characteristics of a phenomenon. The ideal type of the bureaucracy abstracts common elements from organizations as diverse as a government agency, the Roman Catholic

to be able to take for granted. Though we dislike bureaucracy and can feel alienated by it, most of us expect that the organizations we encounter will work the way Weber described, and we feel mistreated if they do not.

For example, we wish those holding positions in our schools, government, and corporations to gain these offices and exercise power

How Does Weber's Ideal Bureaucracy Work?

1. Each office or position has clearly defined duties and responsibilities. In this manner, the regular activities of the organization are arranged within a clear-cut division of labor.
2. All offices are organized in a hierarchy of authority that takes the shape of a pyramid. Officials are held accountable to their superiors for subordinates' actions and decisions in addition to their own.
3. All activities are governed by a consistent system of abstract rules and regulations that define the responsibilities of the various offices and the relationships among them. They ensure the coordination of essential tasks and uniformity in performance regardless of changes in personnel.
4. All offices carry with them qualifications and are filled on the basis of technical competence, not personal considerations. Presumably, trained individuals do better work than those who gain an office on the basis of family ties, personal friendship, or political favor. Competence is established by certification (e.g., college degrees) or examination (e.g., civil service tests).
5. Incumbents do not "own" their offices and cannot use offices for personal ends. Positions remain the property of the organization, and officeholders are supplied with the items they require to perform their work.
6. Employment by the organization is defined as a career. Promotion is based on seniority or merit, or both. After a probationary period, individuals gain the security of tenure and are protected against arbitrary dismissal. In principle, this feature makes officials less susceptible to outside pressures.
7. Administrative decisions, rules, procedures, and activities are recorded in written documents preserved in permanent files.

Thematic Boxes

The eighth edition includes four box categories, all of which add to the concepts and theories discussed in the chapter in which they appear, and many of which add insights to other chapters as well: *Doing Social Research*; *Sociology Around the World*, *Students Doing Sociology*, and *Social Inequalities*. Each box concludes with questions for discussion.

6.1 Sociology around the World

Is Race the Basis for an American Caste System?

Americans often are fascinated by India's traditional caste system. The idea of groups of people having special status and performing only certain jobs seems very undemocratic. The Brahmins, the most pure caste, serve as priests and have special privileges. The Kshatriyas protect society, holding top military and political positions. The Vaisyas fill farming, livestock production, and commerce jobs, and the last caste, the Sudras, serves those above it. The untouchables, not strictly a part of the caste system, do those jobs Hindus consider to be the most polluting: working with body parts, excrement, and dead bodies.

Does the United States have a caste system? We have said that in some ways the United States provides a good example of an open system of stratification. But we will

person with "one drop of black blood" was black. This idea translated into the practice of classifying a person as black if he or she had any known black ancestors (Davis, 1991).

Does the "one drop" rule still hold today? Professional U.S. golfer Tiger Woods has a mother from Thailand and a father with African, European, and Native American ancestors (Page, 1997), and he has described himself as "Cablinasian" (for Caucasian, black, Indian, and Asian), yet he is widely regarded as African American in the United States (Nolan, 1997; Foster, 1997; Brand-Williams, 1997).

The second basic characteristic, that marriage within one's caste is mandatory, is not true in the legal sense; there are no longer any laws in the United States that

The fourth characteristic, that occupation is strongly related to caste, also describes American society to a substantial degree. Occupations that can be held by blacks or whites are not dictated by law. But in the 19th and 20th centuries, African-American physicians, dentists, engineers, and corporate executives were nearly nonexistent, and nearly all agricultural field workers in the South were black. By now, there has been substantial occupational mobility for African Americans, just as there has been for lower-caste persons in India in the late 20th century. But the occupational distribution in the United States retains significant castelike properties. African Americans are substantially overrepresented in low-status service and manufacturing jobs and underrepresented

3.1 Doing Social Research

Does High School Identity Affect Your Adult Life?

Think back to your high school days. Were you ever the president of Student Council? Did you perform in school plays, play sports, party a lot, regard all organized activities with suspicion, or spend most of your time studying? Which crowd did you hang with?

Adolescents' crowd identities serve not only as labels for others but as public identities for themselves (Barber, Eccles, and Stone, 2001). But do such identities have any impact on our later lives?

In a long-term study of 900 young people who were in high school in the 1980s, researchers Bonnie Barber, Jacquelynne Eccles, and Margaret Stone investigated the impact of social (or "crowd") identity in adolescence on adult outcomes. As an indicator of identity, they used categories borrowed from the well-known and then popular 1985 film about

- Prosocial activities (church attendance, community service).

In the first part of their analysis, Barber and her colleagues discovered that the social identity categories were linked to 10th grade activity participation, with Jocks and Criminals most strongly represented in sports, Basket Cases and Princesses in performing arts, and Brains in prosocial activities. Princesses also were well represented in school involvement activities. But did their high school social identities predict what sorts of young adults they would become?

It turns out that for a number of measurements taken in 1996 when the respondents were around 24 years old, the answer was yes. High school identities predicted adult substance use,

sophomores. Why do the crowd identities and activities of 10th graders predict adult outcomes? Barber and her colleagues have some guesses (2001:450–451):

> Perhaps adolescents make use of the formal activities and the informal social organizations of the high school to negotiate and formalize their identities. The patterns of behavior expressed, solidified, and formalized first in high school organizations may carry forward, providing continuity in connection to others with similar values and backgrounds as well as ongoing validation of the social identity established in adolescence.

Questions for Discussion

1. Identities of adolescents today may be different from those in 1987. If you were designing a replication of this study and

8.3 Students Doing Sociology

"There's a Totally Cute Girl Smoking a ———ing Cigar!"

Many—perhaps most—college students today believe that gender inequality is pretty much a thing of the past. Because they grew up in a time when women could vote, work outside the home, run for office, go to college, and the like, some students find feminist ideology—well, extreme. So complacent are many students that they are quick to reject arguments of feminist sociologists that our culture promotes gender inequality through its "compulsory heterosexuality." But the results of more than 650 field observations recorded by sociology students over a 15-year period offer substantial evidence that compulsory heterosexuality is deeply embedded in American culture (Nielsen, Walden, and Kunkel, 2000).

Students were assigned to

crocheted in public, bought sanitary napkins, wore women's clothes or shoes, cried, carried purses, tried out "women's occupations," painted their fingernails, and read romance novels. One even threw a Tupperware party. Female students opened doors for men, smoked cigars and pipes, chewed tobacco, sent men flowers, went shirtless while doing sports activities, bought condoms, and read *Playgirl*. Some displayed knowledge about "guy stuff," such as cars and sports.

And what were the reactions to these norm violations? Surprisingly, especially given the wide variety of projects, the reactions were easily categorized—and completely different depending on whether the norm violator was a woman or a man. Men were

married because she probably wouldn't get any dates," "Is this any way for two pretty young girls to behave?" and "There's a totally cute girl smoking a ———ing cigar!"

The experiences of the hundreds of students involved in this study clearly demonstrate the power of gender expectations. Gender-role norms function as a signal of the willingness of those adhering to them to be part of the heterosexual world, and they provide sanctions for those who would violate them. Feminist sociologists argue that compulsory heterosexuality is deeply embedded in our culture and in the demands it makes on us in our everyday lives. This study supports that argument.

9.1 Social Inequalities

What Oppression Teaches—The Long Reach of Disenfranchisement

Why don't people long oppressed by authoritarian regimes create effective democracies as soon as authoritarianism is lifted? Why, for example, has it not been easy to establish democracy in Afghanistan and Iraq after the demise of authoritarian regimes in the two countries in 2002 and 2003? Social structures teach people patterns of behavior that are not quickly and easily changed when the rules and laws governing political participation are changed. Though not as drastic as a change in regime, American women gaining the right to vote provides a focused example of this effect in action.

In 1920, the Nineteenth

up after the Nineteenth Amendment was passed and voting for women had become an "inalienable right," were the first group to go out and vote in equal numbers.

Sociologists Glenn Firebaugh and Kevin Chen (1995) showed that the oppression people experience during their early years can continue to affect their behavior long after the oppression itself is lifted. Using postelection survey data gathered from 1952 to 1988, Firebaugh and Chen found that the odds of women born in 1896 voting in any election were less than half as great as the odds of men voting. This disenfranchisement effect—women failing to vote despite having gained the right to

these researchers used were based on elections beginning *30 years* after women gained the right to vote in the United States, yet women born and socialized during and immediately after the period when women could *not* vote continued to vote at lower rates than men. Voting rates for men and women have now converged; women socialized in an era during which women have the right to vote are just as likely to vote as men are. As Firebaugh and Chen put it (1995:978): "After passage of the Nineteenth Amendment, historical conditions no longer 'taught' young women the impropriety of voting."

Chapter in Brief

Each chapter concludes with a summary that uses the same outline of major headings used in the chapter opener, recapitulating the central points and allowing students to review in a systematic manner what they have read.

Glossary

Each chapter includes a Glossary of the key terms. In addition, to reinforce the importance of these terms, the Chapter in Brief includes all of the Glossary terms in bold face.

Review Questions

At the end of each chapter there is a list of review questions that focus on the central ideas presented in the chapter.

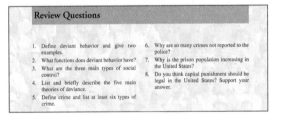

Internet Connection

An exercise at the end of each chapter encourages students to go online to analyze topics and issues relevant to the chapter content.

media resources

Online Learning Center

The Online Learning Center (OLC) is a text-specific website that offers students and instructors a variety of resources and activities. Material from this website can be used in creating the PageOut website. To learn more about *Sociology: The Core's* OLC, go to www.mhhe.com/hughes8.

PowerWeb

Developed by McGraw-Hill/Dushkin, PowerWeb is a resource for the introductory course that is password-protected on the Online Learning Center. It allows students to supplement their learning experience using Internet-based course materials. It includes refereed course-specific weblinks and articles, student study tools, weekly updates, and additional resources. For further information about PowerWeb, go to www.dushkin.com/powerweb.

Reel Society Interactive Movie CD-Rom

Available as a separate package option, this professionally produced movie on CD-Rom demonstrates the sociological imagination using actors in campus life scenarios. Each viewer assumes the role of one of the characters and influences key plot turns by making choices for them. A wide variety of issues and perspectives are addressed relating major sociological concepts and theories to students' lives. For further details, go to www.mhhe.com/reelsoc.

PageOut: The Course Website Development Center

PageOut ®

Create a custom course website with **PageOut**, free to instructors using a McGraw-Hill textbook.

To learn more, contact your McGraw-Hill publisher's representative or visit www.mhhe.com/solutions.

Online content for *Sociology: The Core* is supported by WebCT, eCollege.com, Blackboard, and other course management systems. Additionally, McGraw-Hill's PageOut service is available to help instructors get their course up and running online in a matter of hours, at no cost. No programming knowledge is required. When you use PageOut, your students have instant, 24-hour access to your course syllabus, lecture notes, assignments, and other original material. They can even check their grades. Material from the OLC can be integrated with your website. To find out more about PageOut, ask your McGraw-Hill representative for details, or go to www.mhhe.com/pageout.

DEVELOPING A SOCIOLOGICAL CONSCIOUSNESS

Each of us is a social being. We are born into a social environment; we fully develop into human beings in a social environment; and we typically live out our lives in a social environment. What we think, how we feel, and what we say and do all are shaped by our interactions with other people. The scientific study of these social interactions and of social organization is called **sociology.**

Why are some people wealthy and others poor? What causes war? Why do people violate social rules? How do revolutions occur? What causes mass hysteria? We know from ancient folklore, myths, and archeological remains that humans have long had an interest in understanding themselves and their social arrangements. Yet it has been only in the past 175 years or so that human beings have sought answers to these and related questions through science. This science—sociology—pursues the study of social interaction and group behavior through research governed by the rigorous and disciplined collection of data and analysis of facts.

Many of us are not only interested in understanding society and human behavior. We also would like to improve the human condition so that we might lead fuller, richer, and more fruitful lives. To do this we need knowledge about the basic structures and processes underlying our social lives. Sociology, through its emphasis on observation and measurement, allows us to bring rigorous and systematic scientific thinking and information to bear on difficult questions associated with social policies and choices, including those related to poverty, health, immigration, crime, and education. Many people interested in these issues do not realize that more than concern is needed to solve problems. Action must be informed by knowledge.

3

Sociological research often is applied to practical matters. For example, the U.S. Supreme Court relied heavily upon social science findings regarding the effects of segregation on children in reaching its historic 1954 decision declaring mandatory school segregation unconstitutional (Klineberg, 1986; Jackson, 1990). Social and behavioral sciences also are central to the world's health and science agenda. A 2002 study showed that human behaviors—including smoking, drinking, practicing unsafe sex, and eating improperly—are major contributors to death and disease around the world (Ezzati et al., 2002). Other major factors in global mortality and disease stem from societal problems: air pollution, unsafe drinking water, poor sanitation, and inadequate nutrition.

Recent data show that nearly 18 percent of America's children live in poverty (DeNavas-Walt, Proctor, and Lee, 2005). Certainly no society would be proud that so many of its children have inadequate housing, food, and other resources. But there's another reason to be concerned. Sociological research has shown that socioeconomic conditions have a lasting influence: People who grow up in disadvantaged families have worse cardiovascular health, worse dental health, and higher rates of substance abuse than those from families of high socioeconomic status, even if they are no longer poor as adults (Poulton et al., 2002).

The Indian Ocean tsunami, Hurricane Katrina, and the Pakistan earthquake killed nearly 300,000 people and left millions homeless in 2004 and 2005 (Bohannon, 2005). Analyses done in the aftermath of these events show clearly that social organization and social policy are critical factors that can either increase or decrease the impact of natural disasters (Stone and Kerr, 2005).

Insurance companies classify such events as "acts of God": misfortunes for which no one is at fault. But in their aftermath, many scientists are pointing out that natural disasters are anything but natural: Societies can mitigate their impacts by making the right decisions about where and how people live, how information is shared, and what kind of research to invest in. (Bohannon, 2005:1883)

Natural disasters directly cause great damage, but social factors such as government policy and the effectiveness of response agencies affect the severity of their impact.

Sociologists may do basic research, seeking to better understand social interaction and group behavior, or they may design studies deliberately to evaluate public policies or to inform us about social conditions, including assessments of criminal justice programs, the social consequences of unemployment, and the effects of family structure on children and their future. The collection of census and other national statistical data, which is the foundation of many federal and state policies on health, education, housing, and welfare, is based on sample survey and statistical techniques developed by sociologists and other social scientists. Sociology, then, is a powerful scientific tool both for acquiring knowledge about ourselves and for intervening in social affairs to realize various goals.

The Sociological Perspective

The sociological perspective invites us to look beyond what we take for granted about our social lives and examine them in fresh and creative ways (Berger, 1963). There are many layers of meaning in the human experience. Networks of invisible rules and institutional arrangements guide our behavior. We continually evolve, negotiate, and rework tacit bargains with family members, friends, lovers, and work associates. As we look beyond outer appearances at what lies beneath, we encounter new levels of social reality. This approach to reality is the core of the sociological perspective.

In this section we will see how sociology uncovers new levels of reality, discuss the sociological imagination, and define microsociology and macrosociology.

New Levels of Reality

Tally's Corner, a classic study by social scientist Elliot Liebow (1967/2003) in a downtown Washington, D.C., African-American neighborhood, shows us how sociology can reveal new levels of social reality. In the early 1960s, our nation's concern about poverty led Liebow to involve himself in a unique study of low-income urban black men. Of course, most African Americans are not poor; today, for example, more than 75 percent live above the poverty line (DeNavas-Walt, Proctor, and Lee, 2005), and African-American men are typically employed and live respectable, conventional lives (Duneier, 1992). Nonetheless, most of the problems of poverty that Liebow observed 40 years ago are still with us today, and his findings continue to provide insight into this major U.S. social problem. Perhaps more importantly for us, his study provides an excellent example of how sociological research allows us to go beyond outward appearances and simplistic explanations.

Liebow conducted his study by hanging out on a corner in front of the New Deal Carry-out Shop, where he won the trust of 20 or so African-American men. The men Liebow got to know came to the corner shop, not far from the White House in a blighted section of the city, to eat, to enjoy easy talk, and in general to pass the time. The following excerpt relates what Liebow observed one weekday morning (Liebow, 1967/2003:19):

A pickup truck drives slowly down the street. The truck stops as it comes abreast of a man sitting on a cast-iron porch and the white driver calls out, asking if the man wants a day's work. The man shakes his head and the truck moves on up the block, stopping again whenever idling men come within calling distance of the driver. At the Carry-out corner, five men debate the question briefly and shake their heads no to the truck. The truck turns the corner and repeats the same performance up the next street.

The white truck driver viewed the African-American streetcorner men as lazy and irresponsible, unwilling "to take a job even if it were handed to them on a platter." Like many

Tally's Corner in the 21st Century

Are Elliot Liebow's conclusions still valid? The republication in 2003 of his 1967 book *Tally's Corner*, which had sold more than a million copies, is an indication of its value to social scientists, teachers, students, and others. In introducing the new edition, sociologist William Julius Wilson commented, "[Liebow's] arguments concerning the work experience and family life of black street-corner men in a Washington, D.C., ghetto still ring true today" (Wilson, 2003:xxxiii). Indeed, Wilson says, job market prospects for low-skilled black men are worse now than they were when Liebow conducted his research. He explains that structural factors continue to prevent inner city black men from finding work that allows them to support themselves and their families: "The computer revolution . . . is displacing low-skilled workers and rewarding the more highly trained; and the growing internationalization of economic activity . . . has increasingly pitted low-skilled workers in the United States against low-skilled workers around the world" (Wilson, 2003:xxxiv).

As when Liebow wrote his book, there are those who argue today that young African-American males are without jobs because they refuse to accept low-paying jobs. But sociologist Stephen M. Petterson found "no race differences in the wages sought by young jobless men" (1997:605). In fact, black men's reports of the lowest wage they would accept and wages at last employment were *lower* than those of white men. As Liebow found in the 1960s, joblessness is not necessarily related to a lack of willingness to work for low wages, and social programs designed in ignorance of that fact are doomed to failure.

Both Liebow and Wilson acknowledge that urban black men may give up looking for work—*after* experiencing the fruitlessness of searching for decent work at a decent rate of pay. "Liebow was perhaps the first scholar to place appropriate emphasis on the fact that ongoing lack of success in the labor market lowers one's self-confidence and gives rise to feelings of resignation that frequently result in a temporary, or even permanent, abandonment of the job search," comments

Wilson. The fundamental problem of male joblessness contributes to many problems of the inner city: high rates of welfare dependency, teenage pregnancy, drug abuse, and crime. Can anything be done to attack the problem at its roots? Wilson suggests that programs must "address attitudes, norms, and behaviors in combination with local and national attempts to improve job prospects. Only then will fathers have a realistic chance to adequately care for their children and envision a better life for themselves" (Wilson, 2003:xxxix).

Questions for Discussion

1. Think about the life problems faced by your family, friends, or self. Are any of them attributable to structural factors as opposed to individual characteristics?

2. More than 40 years is a long time for a problem to persist. Can you think of other social problems that have been around for a considerable length of time?

middle-class Americans then and today, he believed that inner-city African-American men live only for the moment with little thought for long-term consequences. The truck driver assumed that all the streetcorner men were able-bodied men with no means of support—and no desire to take the work he offered them. Like many Americans, he assumed that the job problems of inner-city men resulted from the men themselves—from their lack of willingness to work.

Liebow's relationship with the men at the New Deal allowed him to look beyond the stereotyped images of African-American men to find another level of reality. Liebow found that most of the men who turned down the truck driver's offer had jobs but, for various reasons, were not at work that particular morning. A few did not have jobs, but with reason; the man on the porch, for example, had severe arthritis. Liebow also discovered that streetcorner men and middle-class men differed not so much in their values and their attitudes toward the future as in the different futures they saw ahead of them. Middle-class men have incomes high enough to justify long-term investments, and they hold jobs that offer the promise of career advancement. Like middle-class men, the men on the corner wanted stable jobs and marriages. However, in their world, jobs were only intermittently available, almost always menial, often hard, and invariably low paying. The day jobs offered by such as the driver of the pickup truck usually involved back-breaking labor at heart-breakingly low wages. Even the jobs held by the men that day did not offer them much hope for the future. As Liebow observed, "A man's chances for working regularly are good only if he is willing to work for less than he can live on, sometimes not even then" (Liebow, 1967/2003:32).

Social policy based on the truck driver's interpretations would be directed toward changing the motivations of streetcorner men and encouraging them to develop those values and goals that lead to occupational achievement. But such social programs would have no chance of succeeding; the men were already willing to work and did not need to have their values and goals redirected. What they needed were jobs that provided wages they could live on.

In seeking an explanation for their behavior, Liebow looked beyond the individual men and the outward appearances of streetcorner life. He turned his investigative eye upon the social arrangements that are external to individuals but that nonetheless structure their experiences and place constraints on their behavior.

The Sociological Imagination

A basic premise underlying sociology is the notion that only by understanding the society in which we live can we gain a fuller insight into our lives. Sociologist C. Wright Mills (1959) termed this quality of the discipline the **sociological imagination:** the ability to see our private experiences, personal difficulties, and achievements as, in part, a reflection of the structural arrangements of society and the times in which we live. We tend to go about our daily activities thinking only about school, job, family, and neighborhood. The sociological imagination allows us to see the relationship between our personal experiences and broader social and historical events.

Mills, an influential but controversial sociologist, pointed out that our personal troubles and public issues "overlap and interpenetrate to form the larger structure of social and historical life." The job difficulties recently experienced by many young Americans provide an example. The restructuring and downsizing of corporate America in the early 1990s compounded the effects of economic recession. This economic malaise had a devastating effect on the employment ranks of the nation's youth: According to the Department of Labor, more than 1 million fewer young people were employed in 2005 than in 2000 (http://www.bls.gov/cps/cpsatabs.htm). Clearly, the work values and attitudes of 1 million young Americans did not change so drastically that by 2003 they were unwilling to work. Mills's (1959) point is that in situations of this kind we cannot simply look to the personal character of individuals to explain changes in their employment circumstances. Rather, we need to focus on our economic and political institutions for a definition of the problem, for an understanding of its causes, and for a range of possible solutions. The sociological imagination allows us to place the private job frustrations of many Americans into the context of the structural factors operating in the larger society and the workplace.

We see the usefulness of the sociological imagination in other spheres of life as well. Mills (1959:9) was especially concerned with issues of war and peace:

The personal problems of war, when it occurs, may be how to survive it or how to die in it with honor; how to make money out of it; how to climb into the higher safety of the military apparatus; or how to contribute to the war's termination. . . . But the structural issues of war have to do with its causes; with what types of men it throws up into command; with its effects upon economic and political, family and religious institutions, with the unorganized irresponsibility of a world of nation-states.

In sum, the sociological imagination allows us to identify the links between our personal lives and the larger social forces of life—to see that what is happening to us immediately is a minute point at which our personal lives and society intersect.

Microsociology and Macrosociology

Sociologists seek to extend Mills's insight by distinguishing between the micro, or small-scale, aspects of the social enterprise and the macro, or large-scale, structural components. When we focus on the micro elements, we examine behavior close-up and observe what happens as people interact on a face-to-face basis. Sociologists term this level microsociology— micro meaning "small" as in the word "microscope." **Microsociology** entails the detailed study of what people say, do, and think moment by moment as they go about their daily lives. Liebow's study of the African-American men on the Washington street corner provides an illustration of microsociology. Liebow wanted to find out how the men saw themselves, how they

dealt with one another in face-to-face encounters, and how they balanced their hopes and aspirations with their real-world experiences. Microsociology, then, deals with everyday life: a woman and a man initiating a conversation on a bus, several youngsters playing basketball on an inner-city playground, guests at a baby shower, a police officer directing traffic at a busy intersection, or students and their teacher interacting after class.

Sociologists also turn an investigative eye upon "the big picture" and study social groups and societies. This approach is termed macrosociology—macro meaning "large." **Macrosociology** focuses upon large-scale and long-term social processes of organizations, institutions, and broad social patterns, including the state, social class, the family, the economy, culture, and society. At this level sociologists may direct their attention to the changes in the structure of a religious sect, the impact of population dynamics and computer technologies on the workforce, shifts in the racial and ethnic composition of a city, or the dynamics of intergroup competition and conflict. When we examine the lives of Liebow's streetcorner men from a macrosociological perspective, we gain a picture of the institutional constraints that minority and economically disadvantaged men face and that limit their job opportunities.

The microsociological and macrosociological levels are not independent of one another (Ritzer and Goodman, 2004; House, 1995). The circumstances of the streetcorner men Liebow studied testify to this fact. We can most appropriately think of the distinction between "micro" and "macro" as one of degree (Lawler, Ridgeway, and Markovsky, 1993). Macro structures, such as organizations or the hierarchy of social classes, are composed of routine patterns of interaction on the micro level. Macro structures provide the social contexts in which people encounter one another at the micro level. Micro structures, such as friendship relations and work groups, form out of these encounters and provide a link from individuals to macro structures. Micro structures also may cause change and evolution in macro structures. For example, the macro structure of education and an organization embedded in it, your high school, may have provided the social context from which your group of best friends—a micro structure—emerged. Such a group of students, through letter-writing campaigns, sit-ins, formation of clubs, and other means, can cause a high school and education in general—macro structures—to adapt and change. In sum, complex webs of relationship between the micro and macro levels contribute to an ever-changing and diverse social order (Móuzelis, 1992).

The Development of Sociology

Sociology, too, is a product of micro and macro forces. The political revolutions ushered in by the French Revolution in Europe in 1789 and continuing through the 19th century provided a major impetus to sociological work (Ritzer and Goodman, 2004). At the same time, the Industrial Revolution that swept many Western nations resulted in large numbers of people leaving a predominantly agricultural setting for work in factories. New social and economic arrangements arose to provide the many demands of emergent capitalism. These major changes in the way society was organized led some of the thinkers of the day to turn their attention to the study of social organization and social interactions, resulting in the founding of the science we now call sociology (Ritzer and Goodman, 2004).

In this section we will consider the contributions of six particularly influential sociologists, the emergence of sociology in the United States, and contemporary sociology.

Auguste Comte: The Founder of Sociology

Auguste Comte (1798–1857) is commonly credited with being the founder of sociology and as having coined the name "sociology" for the new science. He was also an advocate of a philosophical system, positivism, that argues that abstract laws govern the relationships among phenomena in the world, including its social elements, and that these laws could be tested using empirical data (Ritzer and Goodman, 2004). As a part of this, he emphasized that the study of society must be scientific, and he urged sociologists to use systematic observation, experimentation, and comparative historical analysis as their methods.

Comte divided the study of society into social statics and social dynamics, a conceptual distinction that is still with us. **Social statics** involves those aspects of social life that have to do with order, stability, and social organization that allow societies and groups to hold together and endure. **Social dynamics** refers to those processes of social life that pattern institutional development and have to do with social change. Although his specific ideas no longer direct contemporary sociology, Comte created the intellectual foundation for a science of social life and exerted enormous influence on the thinking of other sociologists, particularly Herbert Spencer, Harriet Martineau, and Émile Durkheim.

Harriet Martineau: Feminist and Methodologist

While Comte was laying the theoretical foundations for sociology, the English sociologist Harriet Martineau (1802–1876) was paving the way for the new discipline through her observations of social behavior in the United States and England. Like Comte, she insisted that the study of society represents a separate scientific field.

Among her contributions was the first book on the methodology of social research, *How to Observe Manners and Morals,* published in 1838. She also undertook the comparative study of the stratification systems of Europe and the United States. Martineau showed how the basic moral values of the young American nation shaped its key institutional arrangements. Throughout her career Martineau was an ardent defender of women's rights. She showed the similarities between the position of women in Western societies and that of American slaves, and called for freedom and justice for all in an age in which they were granted only to white males (Rossi, 1973; Deegan, 1991).

Though Harriet Martineau was a popular and influential intellectual and author during her lifetime, her contributions to sociology were marginalized by the men who dominated the discipline during its early years and kept women like Martineau out of powerful academic positions (Ritzer and Goodman, 2004). Consequently, Martineau's significance in the early development of sociology has only recently been fully recognized (Deegan, 2003; Hoecker-Drysdale, 1994; Lengermann and Niebrugge-Brantley, 2000a).

Herbert Spencer and Social Darwinism

Herbert Spencer (1820–1903), an English sociologist, shared Comte's concern with social statics and social dynamics. He compared society to a biological organism and depicted it as a system, a whole made up of interrelated parts. Just as the human body is made up of organs, so society is made up of institutions (e.g., the family, religion, education, the state, and the economy). In his description of society as an organism, Spencer focused on its structures and the functional contributions these structures make to its survival. This image of society is in line with what sociologists now call structural-functional theory.

Spencer viewed static social institutions as the organs of society, but he had an even greater interest in social dynamics. He proposed an evolutionary theory of historical development, one that depicted the world as growing progressively better. Intrigued by the Darwinian view of natural selection, Spencer applied the

The conflict perspective argues that the structure of our society is powerfully affected by conflicts such as that between New York transit workers and the city of New York in 2005.

concept of survival of the fittest to the social world, an approach termed **Social Darwinism.** He sought to demonstrate that government should not interfere with the natural processes going on in a society. In this manner, he argued, people and social patterns that were "fit" would survive and those that were "unfit" would die out. If this principle were allowed to operate freely, human beings and their institutions would progressively adapt themselves to their environment and reach higher and higher levels of historical development (Ritzer and Goodman, 2004).

Spencer's Social Darwinist ideas were used extensively within England and the United States to justify unrestrained capitalism. John D. Rockefeller, the American oil tycoon, would echo Spencer and observe: "The growth of a large business is merely a survival of the fittest. . . . This is not an evil tendency in business. It is merely the working out of a law of nature" (quoted by Lewontin, Rose, and Kamin, 1984:26).

Karl Marx: The Role of Class Conflict

Although Karl Marx (1818–1883) considered himself a political activist and not a sociologist, in truth he was both—and a philosopher, historian, economist, and political scientist as well. He viewed science not only as a vehicle for understanding society but also as a tool for transforming it. Marx was especially eager to change the structure of capitalist institutions and to establish new institutions in the service of humanity. Although born in Germany, authorities there viewed Marx as politically dangerous, and he was compelled to spend much of his adult life as a political exile in London.

Marx tried to discover the basic principles of history. He focused his search on the economic environments in which societies develop, particularly the current state of their technology and their method of organizing production, such as hunting and gathering, agriculture, or industry. At each stage of history these factors dictate the group that will dominate society and the groups that will be subjugated. He believed that society is divided into those who own the means of producing wealth and those who do not, which gives rise to **class conflict.** All history, he said, is composed of struggles between classes. In ancient Rome the conflict was between patricians and plebeians and between masters and slaves. In the Middle Ages it was a struggle between guildmasters and journeymen and between lords and serfs. In contemporary Western societies, class antagonisms revolve about the struggle between the oppressing capitalist class or bourgeoisie and the oppressed working class or proletariat. The former derive their income through their ownership of the means of production, primarily factories, which allows them to exploit the labor of workers. The latter own nothing except their labor power and, because they are dependent for a living on the jobs provided by capitalists, must sell their labor power in order to exist.

Marx's perspective is called **dialectical materialism,** the notion that development depends on the clash of contradictions and the subsequent creation of new, more advanced structures. The approach depicts the world as made up not of static structures but of dynamic processes, a world of becoming rather than of being. In the Marxian view of history, every economic order grows to a state of maximum efficiency; at the same time, it develops internal contradictions or weaknesses that contribute to its decay. The roots of a new order begin to take hold in the old order. In time the new order displaces the old order while absorbing its most useful features. Marx depicted slavery as being displaced by feudalism, feudalism by capitalism, capitalism by socialism, and ultimately socialism by communism, the highest stage of society.

In Marx's theory, political ideologies, religion, family organization, education, and government make up what he called the *superstructure* of society. This superstructure is strongly influenced by the economic base of society—its mode of producing goods and its class structure. When one class controls the critical means whereby people derive their livelihood, its members gain the leverage necessary to fashion other aspects of institutional life—the superstructure—in ways that favor their class interests. However, the economic structure does not only shape the superstructure; aspects of the superstructure act upon the economic base and modify it in a reciprocal relationship. Marx thought that if a revolutionary ideology emerged to mobilize the working class in pursuit of its class interest, the existing social order would be overturned and replaced by one that would pursue more humane goals (Boswell and Dixon, 1993). In Marx's view, economic factors—whether one owns and controls the means of production—are primary. For this reason, he is viewed by many as an **economic determinist.**

Though Marx is often identified with the communist revolutions and socialist governments that appeared in many nations in the 20th century, Marx actually had little to say about communism or socialism. Marx was a utopian who centered his attention on capitalism and its internal dynamics, assuming that when socialism replaced capitalism many of the world's problems would disappear.

Marx is now recognized by most sociologists as a major figure in sociological theory (Ritzer and Goodman, 2004; Pampel, 2000). Today he is better known and understood, and more widely studied, than at any time since he began his career in the 1840s. Much of what is valuable in his work has now been incorporated into mainstream sociology, particularly as it finds expression in the conflict perspective. In sum, for most sociologists as for most historians and economists, Marx's work is too outdated to follow in its particulars, but it remains theoretically important and animates much contemporary research and theory (e.g., Wright, 2000).

Émile Durkheim: Social Integration and Social Facts

While Marx saw society as a stage upon which classes with conflicting interests contested with one another, the French sociologist Émile Durkheim (1858–1916) focused his sociological eye on the question of how societies hold together and endure. The principal objections Durkheim had to Marx's work were that Marx attributed too much importance to economic factors and class struggle and not enough to social solidarity (Turner, 1990) and that Marx did not recognize the capacity of modern society to reform itself (Pampel, 2000).

Central to Durkheim's (1897/1951) sociology is the concept of *social integration.* Social integration refers to the density of social relationships, literally the number of relationships that exist among a collection of people. The more people are connected to one another, the stronger and more meaningful are the sentiments that emerge out of these relationships (Pope, 1976). Durkheim argued that social integration is necessary for the maintenance of the social order and for the happiness of individuals. In particular, he suggested that happiness depends on individuals' finding a sense of meaning outside themselves that occurs within the context of group involvement. Durkheim sought to demonstrate that the destruction of social bonds (e.g., divorce) has negative consequences and under some circumstances can increase the chance that people will commit suicide. Other sociologists picked up on this central idea and showed how the breakdown of group bonds can contribute to deviant behavior (Merton, 1968) and participation in social movements (Kornhauser, 1959). Like Marx, Durkheim continues to influence modern sociology, stimulating research, tests of his ideas, and theoretical change (Bergesen, 2004; Moody and White, 2003; Stockard and O'Brien, 2002).

In *The Division of Labor in Society* (1893/1964), Durkheim examined social solidarity, the tendency of people to maintain social relationships. He distinguished between the types of solidarity found in early and modern societies. In early societies such as hunting and gathering or agrarian societies, the social structure was relatively simple, with little division of labor. People were knit together by their engagement in similar tasks. They derived a sense of oneness from being so much alike, what Durkheim termed *mechanical solidarity*. Modern societies, in contrast, are characterized by complex social structures and a sophisticated division of labor. People perform specialized tasks in factories, offices, and schools. No one person is self-sufficient, and all must depend upon others to survive. Under these circumstances, society is held together by the interdependence fostered by the differences among people, what Durkheim labeled *organic solidarity*.

In examining social solidarity and other sociological questions, Durkheim believed that we should focus on the group, not the individual. He contended that the distinctive subject matter of sociology should be the study of social facts. **Social facts** are aspects of social life that cannot be explained in terms of the biological or mental characteristics of the individual. People experience social facts as external to themselves in the sense that facts have an independent reality and form a part of people's objective environment. As such, social facts serve to constrain their behavior and include not only legal and moral rules in society, but also relationships and behavior patterns of others that affect our day-to-day lives.

Material social facts include society itself, its major institutions (the state, religion, family, education, etc.) and the various forms that underlie society (housing patterns, the crime rate, population distributions, etc.). *Nonmaterial social facts* are the social rules, principles of morality, meanings of symbols, and the shared consciousness that results from these.

Durkheim insisted that the explanation of social life must be sought in society itself. Society, he said, is more than the sum of its parts; it is a system formed by the association of individuals that comes to constitute a reality with its own distinctive characteristics.

Durkheim convincingly demonstrated the critical part social facts play in human behavior in his book *Suicide* (1897/1951), a landmark study in the history of sociology. Whereas earlier sociologists were given to armchair speculation, Durkheim undertook the painstaking collection and analysis of data on suicide. He found that suicide rates were higher among Protestants than Catholics, higher among the unmarried than the married, and higher among soldiers than civilians. Moreover, suicide rates were higher in times of peace than in times of war and revolution, and higher in times of economic prosperity and recession than in times of economic stability. He concluded that different suicide *rates* are the consequence of variations in social solidarity. Individuals enmeshed in a web of social bonds are less inclined to suicide than individuals who are weakly integrated into group life.

Durkheim was the first major sociologist to face up to the complex problems associated with the disciplined and rigorous empirical study of social life. He challenged the idea that suicide was the result of purely individual factors. As an alternative, he proposed that suicide is a social fact: a product of the meanings, expectations, and structural arrangements that evolve as people interact with one another. As such, suicide is explainable by social factors.

Max Weber: Subjectivity and Social Organization

No sociologist other than Marx has had a greater impact on sociology than the German sociologist Max Weber (1864–1920). Over the course of his career, Weber left a legacy of rich insights for a variety of disciplines, including economics, political science, and history. Among sociologists, he is known not only for his theoretical contributions but also for a number of specific ideas that have generated considerable interest and research in their own right. Many common but important ideas that we use to understand social life have their origin in the work of Weber, including *bureaucracy, lifestyle,* the *Protestant ethic,* and *charisma.* His sociological work covered a wide range of topics, including politics, organizations, social stratification, law, religion, capitalism, music, the city, and cross-cultural comparison, and it continues to influence sociological scholarship today (e.g., Swedberg, 2003; Wright, 2002).

Weber contended that a critical focus for sociology is the study of human subjectivity: the intentions, values, beliefs, and attitudes that underlie people's behavior. Weber employed the German word **Verstehen**—meaning "understanding" or "insight"—in describing this approach for learning about the subjective meanings people attach to their actions. In using this method, sociologists mentally attempt to place themselves in the shoes of other people and identify what they think and how they feel.

Another notable sociological contribution Weber made is the concept of the ideal type. An *ideal type* is a concept constructed by sociologists to portray the principal characteristics of something they want to study. It is a tool that allows sociologists to generalize and simplify data by ignoring minor differences in order to accentuate major similarities. For example, a police department and a hospital differ in many obvious respects, but they share many attributes under the heading "bureaucracy." In Chapter 4 we will see how Weber employed ◄── pp. 117–118 the notion of the ideal type to devise his model of bureaucracy. The ideal type serves as a measuring rod against which sociologists can evaluate actual cases. For example, if sociologists determine, on the basis of historical and contemporary evidence, that the ideal type of bureaucracy has a specific set of characteristics, they can compare this ideal type with actual bureaucracies and then develop explanations for why some of the characteristics of actual

bureaucracies deviate from the ideal type. In this way we can learn much about causes of variation in how organizations function.

In his writings Weber stressed the importance of a **value-free sociology.** He emphasized that sociologists must not allow their personal biases to affect the conduct of their scientific research. Weber recognized that sociologists, like everyone else, have individual biases and moral convictions regarding behavior. But he insisted that sociologists must cultivate a disciplined approach to the phenomena they study so that they may see facts as they are, not as they might wish them to be. By the same token, Weber recognized that objectivity is not neutrality or moral indifference. *Neutrality* implies that a person does not take sides on an issue and *moral indifference* that one does not care; *objectivity* has to do with the pursuit of scientifically verifiable knowledge. Though he promoted objectivity as an important goal in social science, he did not take a neutral stance as an intellectual or as a citizen. He was not afraid to express a value judgment or to tackle important issues of the day (Ritzer and Goodman, 2004).

American Sociology

The sociologists we have considered thus far have been of European origin. Were sociologists to establish a sociological Hall of Fame, Comte, Martineau, Spencer, Marx, Durkheim, and Weber would unquestionably be among its first inductees. Yet, as sociology entered the 20th century, Americans assumed a critical role in its development. In the period preceding World War I, an array of factors provided a favorable climate for sociology in the United States (Fuhrman, 1980; Hinkle, 1980). As in Europe, the Industrial Revolution and urbanization gave a major impetus to sociological study. An added factor was the massive immigration of foreigners to the United States and the problems their absorption and assimilation posed for American life. Further, both sociology and the modern university system arose together. In Europe, by contrast, sociology had a more difficult time becoming established because it had to break into an established system of academic disciplines.

Early American sociology was optimistic, forward-looking, and rooted in a belief in progress, the value of individual freedom and welfare, and a confidence that, though there might be some flaws, American society was basically sound. Some early American sociologists, like Lester Ward (1841–1918), believed that sociologists should identify the basic laws that underlie social life and use this knowledge to reform society. Others, like William Graham Sumner (1840–1910), adapted a survival-of-the-fittest approach derived from Spencer, believing that society's problems would work themselves out if left alone.

An exception to such optimism is the work of W. E. B. Du Bois (1868–1963), a leading African-American intellectual and one of the founders of the National Association for the Advancement of Colored People, who analyzed racial inequality and advocated radical changes to eliminate it (Du Bois, 1903/1990; Blau and Brown, 2001). Du Bois also took sociology out of the ivory tower and did investigative fieldwork, gathering material on the African-American community of Philadelphia, which appeared as *The Philadelphia Negro* in 1900. Between 1896 and 1914, Du Bois led the annual Atlanta University Conferences on Negro Problems that produced the first reliable sociological research on the South.

Contributions of considerable significance to sociology were also made by sociologists at the University of Chicago, where the first department of sociology in the United States was established in 1893. Here, in the first 30 years of the 20th century, a number of sociologists carried out work that remains influential in sociology today. The city of Chicago was viewed as a "social laboratory," and it was subjected to intense and systematic study. Included in this research were investigations of juvenile

W. E. B. Du Bois conducted path-breaking research on African-American life, developed a theoretical understanding of racial inequality, and advocated radical social change to eliminate racism.

gangs, immigrant ghettos, wealthy Gold Coast and slum life, taxi-dance halls, prostitution, and mental disorders.

During this period, Chicago sociologists trained an estimated half of the sociologists in the world. Significantly, a number of the world's most capable female social scientists were among the university's graduates. But its department of sociology was largely a male world, one that afforded a hostile environment to the political activism espoused by many of the women. The women's world of sociology was centered at Hull House, a Chicago settlement house cofounded in 1889 by Jane Addams and Ellen Gates Starr. Settlement houses were charitable establishments set up in poor neighborhoods to provide services to the urban poor, particularly immigrants. Hull House served as a model for the social reform activities and the civic, recreational, and educational programs that came to be identified with the settlement houses that were established throughout the nation. The juvenile court system and workers' compensation were products of the two women's efforts. Addams and Starr also pioneered campaigns for woman suffrage, better housing, improvements in public welfare, stricter child-labor laws, and the protection of working women. The women of Hull House are credited with inventing the research procedures of community case studies and of demographic mapping—showing on city maps the distributions of people with respect to income, age, ethnicity, language, levels of education, and other characteristics—that would later become hallmarks of Chicago sociology (Deegan, 1988; Fitzpatrick, 1990; Lengermann and Niebrugge-Brantley, 2000a).

During the 1940s and until the mid-1960s, sociologists at Columbia, Harvard, and the University of California at Berkeley took the lead and established the major directions for sociological research and theory, crafting techniques for surveying public attitudes and refining models that portrayed society as a system made up of parts with interrelated functions. Leading American sociologists believed that sociology should be a science concerned with pursuing knowledge for its own sake, so they insisted that the discipline not be focused directly on solving social problems.

However, the social turmoil of the 1960s and early 1970s brought to sociology many students who were activists for civil rights, student power, and peace. These young "new breed" sociologists contended that the doctrine of sociological neutrality was a cloak concealing moral insensitivity. In their reaction against the neutrality of previous decades, they also broke with established sociological theory and sought new directions in theory and research grounded in the work of Karl Marx and C. Wright Mills (see Lemert, 2002; Ritzer and Goodman, 2004).

Contemporary Sociology

The evolution of sociology continues. Among the many theoretical developments that have occurred, three influential and related frameworks stand out: critical theory, feminism, and postmodernism.

▲ Critical Theory

Critical theory grew out of a dissatisfaction with 20th-century sociology in general and Marxism in particular (Ritzer and Goodman, 2004). Early critical theorists were German sociologists who fled the Nazi regime in the 1930s and came to the United States, where some remained. These critical theorists and their followers criticized sociology for having a scientific approach that viewed individuals as passive and helpless entities locked in social structures, and for analyzing societies without detecting social problems or envisioning what societies should be. They criticized Marxism because they believed it denied the importance of culture by viewing it as part of the "superstructure," largely determined by economic forces. Critical theorists argue that mass culture (e.g., television, film, popular music), a product of a capitalist media industry, cannot be a true reflection of people's beliefs, tastes, values, ideas, and lifestyles. Instead, mass culture pacifies, represses, and controls people who might otherwise recognize important contradictions and inequalities in their social lives. Critical theorists claim that mass culture makes the political system seem to be a benign entity, supporting the status quo, that benefits all.

Critical theory is both an outgrowth of and a contributor to conflict theory, which we will discuss in the next section. It has also had a major influence on two other contemporary movements in sociology: feminism and postmodern social theory.

▲ Feminism

Feminism is an intellectual movement in the humanities and social sciences that is currently having a profound impact on the nature and direction of sociology (e.g., Thistle, 2000). Sociological feminism begins with the observation that for most of the history of sociology, women hardly appear in social theory and research. Men's experiences have been viewed as universal and women's activities and experiences have been hidden. When women have been studied and theorized about, it is in marginal and secondary roles such as housewife or workers in other low-status occupations. Feminism explicitly examines women's roles and experiences in society, working to fully uncover women's contributions to social life and the nature of the structures and processes that maintain gender inequality. At the same time, sociological feminism has worked to develop theories grounded in the experiences and situations of women that can be used to criticize oppressive social relations and produce social transformation for the betterment of all humankind (Lengermann and Niebrugge, 2007).

Feminism is not a single theory but an evolving set of theoretical perspectives, including liberal feminism, Marxian feminism, psychoanalytic feminism, radical feminism, and socialist feminism, all of which focus on women's experiences and on gender inequality (England, 1993) and which have recently begun to significantly impact mainstream sociological theory (Chafetz, 1997; Tong, 1998).

The latest major developments in feminist theory and research grow out of the realization that the social experience of gender is not universal (e.g., Beisel and Kay, 2004; Browne and Misra, 2003). Women's and men's experiences are strongly influenced by social class, race, ethnicity, nationality, age, and sexual preference and by their social positions in the family, the labor force, and the world economic system. For example, the experience of gender for a young white middle-class Episcopalian woman is fundamentally different from that of an elderly woman who is a Cuban immigrant living in poverty. Sociological feminism places much emphasis on different forms of oppression, on how these forms intersect with gender and with each other, on the resulting diversity of experience, and on the implications such an orientation has for the elimination of all forms of exploitation and oppression (Richardson, Taylor, and Whittier, 1997; Lengermann and Niebrugge, 2007).

▲ Postmodernism

Like feminism, postmodernism (Ritzer and Goodman, 2004; Best and Kellner, 1991; Ritzer, 1997) is an intellectual movement that has influenced scholarship in literature, art, politics, communications, and other disciplines, as well as sociology. Postmodernists are deeply distrustful of science and the principle of objectivity, arguing that scientific knowledge is as much a product of the socially determined interests and biases of investigators as it is of facts, which

According to postmodernism, we have entered an age in which human society is dominated by images and information disseminated through advertising and mass media.

themselves are products of social processes. In addition, postmodernists point out that scientific knowledge has failed to solve social problems or to prevent war and genocide.

At the core of postmodern social theory is the assumption that the modern period of history is coming to an end. That period, which began with the Enlightenment and the end of the medieval period, included industrialization, urbanization, colonialism, and the ideologies of democracy, individualism, and secularism. According to postmodernists, we are now entering an age dominated not by the goods-producing economy of modernity but by the production and dissemination of images and information through mass media and advanced computer technology. If societies are based on ever-changing signs, codes, and models presented in the media, they have no basic structure, and the grand abstract social theories of Marx, Durkheim, Weber, and others discussed above can be of little use in understanding them. In the world of postmodern theory, culture is an amalgamation of images, symbols, and ideas from television programs, MTV, commercials, magazines, and other sources and conveys no essential, enduring meanings. Social divisions, where they exist, thus have no legitimacy and should be removed, eliminating barriers between races, ethnic groups, genders, cultures, nations, and academic disciplines.

In its most extreme formulations (e.g., Baudrillard, 1983, 1990), having no confidence that any social and moral principles exist to give meaning to people's lives and no hope that human beings can control the processes that oppress them, postmodernism is a very pessimistic framework (Adam and Allan, 1995; see also Sica, 1996), arguing that there is no foundation for objective, reliable knowledge about social life.

Though postmodernism has no coherent set of theoretical principles, it does point to some of the ways that contemporary societies constrain and control people, particularly through media and advertising (Ritzer, 1995, 1997, 2007), and it suggests ways people can liberate themselves. Postmodernism has also broadened sociology through its emphasis on the multidisciplinary nature of social inquiry, revitalized sociology's debunking function through the method of deconstructing texts to show their hidden assumptions, and encouraged continuous reexamination of basic theoretical assumptions (Ritzer and Goodman, 2004).

Theoretical Perspectives

As we have seen, sociologists have asked fundamental questions about social life throughout the history of sociology: Why does social inequality exist? How do people learn to interact with each other and be effective participants in society? How and why do societies change? Sociologists have answered these and many more by developing social theories. No one social theory has been so successful that it has been able to eliminate its competitors and dominate the field.

There now exist many different social theories to explain many different facets of our social lives. To reduce complexity, we can combine theories with similar approaches into theoretical perspectives. A *theoretical perspective* provides a set of assumptions, interrelated concepts, and statements about how various social phenomena are related to one another.

An important development of 20th-century sociology was the emergence of three general theoretical perspectives. The adherents of each perspective ask somewhat different questions about society and provide different views of social life. We do not need to accept only one model and reject all the others; rather, theoretical perspectives are tools—mental constructs—that allow us to visualize something. Any model necessarily limits our experience and presents just one angle on a concept, but a good model also *increases* what we can see by providing rules of inference through which new relationships can be discovered and suggestions about how the scope of a theory can be expanded.

The three contemporary theoretical perspectives in sociology are: *functionalism,* which emphasizes order and stability; *conflict theory,* which focuses on inequality, exploitation, oppression, social turmoil, and social change; and *symbolic interactionism,* which argues that society emerges from and is changed by the process of human beings interacting with one another using symbols based in shared meanings. Together, these three perspectives form the theoretical background of most current sociological work. We will be returning to them throughout the book. For now, let us briefly examine each in turn.

The Functionalist Perspective

The structural-functional—or, more simply, functionalist—perspective draws substantially upon the ideas of Auguste Comte, Herbert Spencer, and Émile Durkheim. Its theorists take a broad view of society and focus on the macro aspects of social life. In the 1950s and early 1960s the functionalist theories of Talcott Parsons (1949, 1951) and his students occupied center stage in American sociology. Indeed, some proponents such as Kingsley Davis (1959) argued that the approach was essentially synonymous with sociology.

▲ Society as a Social System
Functionalists take as their starting point the notion that society is a *system,* a set of elements or components that are related to one another in a more or less stable fashion through a period of time. Functionalists focus on the parts of society, particularly its major institutions, such as the family, religion, the economy, the state, and education. They identify the structural characteristics of each part much as biologists describe the principal features of the body's organs. They then determine what the functions of each part are.

One of the features of a system stressed by functionalists is its tendency toward equilibrium, or balance, among its parts and among the forces operating on it. Change in one part has implications for other parts and for the community or society as a whole, with change and adaptation being a continuous process. Some parts may also change more rapidly than others, contributing to social dislocations. For example, as increasing numbers of mothers with preschool children enter the paid labor force, new arrangements are required to take care of their children during the day. Yet licensed day care facilities are currently available for fewer than one-third of the children with mothers in the labor force. Research shows that many children—as many as 75 percent of those from low-income homes—receive inadequate care (U.S. National Center for Educational Statistics, 1995).

▲ Functions and Dysfunctions
Within system analysis, functionalists pay particular attention to the **functions** performed by a system's parts, especially organizations, groups, institutions, and cultural patterns. Functionalists say that if a system is to survive, certain essential tasks must be performed; otherwise, the system fails to maintain itself and perishes. If society is to exist, its members must make provision for certain functional requirements. Institutions, to be discussed in more detail in Chapter 2, are the principal structures ◄ p. 61 whereby these critical tasks for social living—functions—are organized, directed, and executed. Each institution, such as education, the economy, and the family, is built around a standardized solution to a set of problems. Functions are the observed consequences of the existence of institutions, groups, and other system parts that permit the adaptation or adjustment of a system (Merton, 1968).

Robert K. Merton (1968) pointed out that just as institutions and the other parts of society can contribute to the maintenance of the social system, they can also have negative consequences. Those observed consequences that lessen the adaptation or adjustment of a system he terms **dysfunctions.** Poverty, for example, has both functional and dysfunctional properties (Gans, 1972). For example, it is functional because it ensures that the nation's "dirty work" is done—those jobs that are physically dirty, dangerous, temporary, dead-end, poorly paid, and menial. However, poverty is dysfunctional because it intensifies a variety of social problems, including those associated with health, education, crime, and drug addiction.

▲ Manifest and Latent Functions

Merton (1968) also distinguished between manifest functions and latent functions. **Manifest functions** are those consequences that are intended and recognized by the participants in a system; **latent functions** are those consequences that are neither intended nor recognized. Some ceremonials of the Hopi Indians of the Southwest, for example, are designed to produce rain. Though these rituals do not actually produce rain, their latent function is to produce a collective expression by which the Hopi people achieve a sense of social solidarity. What outsiders may see as irrational behavior (performing a rain ceremony) is actually functional for the group itself.

▲ Social Consensus

Functionalists also assume that most members of a society agree on what is desirable, worthwhile, and moral, and what is undesirable, worthless, and evil. Through a social learning process, they come to share a consensus regarding their core values and beliefs. For example, most Americans accept the values and beliefs inherent in democracy, the doctrine of equal opportunity, and the notion of personal achievement. Functionalists say that this high degree of consensus on basic values provides the foundation for social integration and stability in U.S. society.

▲ Evaluation of the Functionalist Perspective

The functionalist perspective is a useful tool for describing society and identifying its structural parts and the functions of these parts at a particular point in time. It provides a "big picture" of the whole of social life, particularly as it finds expression in patterned, recurrent behavior and institutions. For some purposes, it is clearly helpful to have a clear description of the parts that make up society and how they fit together.

However, such an approach does not provide us with the entire story of social life. The functionalist approach has difficulty dealing with history and processes of social change. In the real world, societies are constantly changing, but functionalism has done a poor job of accounting for the never-ending flow of interaction that occurs among people. Moreover, the functionalist perspective tends to exaggerate consensus, integration, and stability while disregarding conflict, dissent, and instability. The problems that structural-functional theory has in dealing with change, history, and conflict have led critics to charge that it has a conservative bias and that it tends to support existing social arrangements.

The Conflict Perspective

Conflict theorists, like functionalists, focus their attention on society as a whole, studying its institutions and structural arrangements. Yet the two perspectives are at odds on a good many matters. Where functionalists depict society in relatively static terms, conflict theorists emphasize the processes of change that continually transform social life. Where functionalists stress the order and stability to be found in society, conflict theorists emphasize disorder and instability. Where functionalists see the common interests shared by the members of a society, conflict theorists focus upon the interests that divide. Where functionalists view consensus as the basis of social unity, conflict theorists insist that social unity is an illusion resting on coercion. Finally, where functionalists often view existing social arrangements as necessary and justified by the requirements of group life, conflict theorists see many of the arrangements as neither necessary nor justified.

▲ Diversity of Approaches

Although conflict theory derives much of its inspiration from the work of Karl Marx, it has many other sources as well, including the work of such sociologists as Georg Simmel (1908/1955, 1950), Lewis Coser (1956), Randall Collins (1975), and Eric Olin Wright (1985, 2000). Although class conflict was the core of Marx's theory, many contemporary sociologists view conflict as occurring among many groups and interests—religion versus religion, race versus race, consumers versus producers, taxpayers versus welfare recipients, sunbelt versus snowbelt states, central city residents versus suburbanites, the young versus the elderly, and so on.

▲ Sources of Conflict

The main source of conflict in human societies is scarcity of social and material resources. Wealth, prestige, and power are always in limited supply, so that gains for one individual or group are usually associated with losses for others. **Power**—the ability to control the behavior of others, even against their will—determines who will gain and who will lose (Lasswell, 1936). Power also determines which group will be able to translate its preferences for behavior (its values) into the operating rules for others. Conflict theorists ask how it is that some groups acquire power, dominate other groups, and effect their will in human affairs. In so doing, they look at who benefits and who loses from the way society is organized.

▲ How Society Is Possible

If social life is fractured and fragmented by confrontations between individuals or groups, how is a society possible? Functionalists say society is held together primarily by a consensus among its members regarding core values and norms, but conflict theorists reject this view. They maintain that society is often held together in spite of conflicting interests.

When one group enjoys sufficient power, it makes and enforces rules and shapes institutional life so that its interests are served. Many conflict theorists regard the state—government and the rules it creates and enforces—as an instrument of oppression employed by ruling elites for their own benefit; functionalists tend to view the state as an organ of the total society, functioning to promote social control and stability.

Many divided but overlapping interest groups generate a large number of crosscutting conflicts. People who are opponents in one conflict are allies in another. Society persists because no one conflict can become so great as to tear the society apart (Coser, 1956). For example, an African-American woman at odds with her white neighbor over affirmative action policy may agree with her about increasing funding for their neighborhood schools.

▲ Evaluation of the Conflict Perspective

The conflict perspective complements functionalist theory. The functionalist approach has difficulty dealing with history and social change; the conflict approach makes these matters its strength. The conflict approach has difficulty dealing with some aspects of consensus, integration, and stability; the functionalist approach affords penetrating insights.

Some sociologists contend that the functionalists and conflict theorists are simply studying two aspects of the same reality. They note that both consensus and conflict are central features of social life. In addition, both approaches have

LIB

traditionally taken a holistic view of social life, portraying societies as systems of interrelated parts (van den Berghe, 1963).

Other sociologists such as Lewis Coser (1956), drawing upon the seminal work done by Georg Simmel (1908/1955), suggested that under some circumstances conflict is functional for society; it prevents social systems from becoming rigid and fixed by exerting pressure for change and innovation. The civil rights movement, although challenging established interests and racist patterns, may have contributed to the long-term stability of American institutions by bringing African Americans into the "system."

However, it is clear that conflict is often dysfunctional for an existing system. There are many destructive conflicts around the world that are preventing societies and nations from fully developing socially and economically, such as those between the Israelis and Palestinians in the Middle East and between Catholics and Protestants in Northern Ireland. The potential for civil war in Iraq among the Shia, Sunni, and Kurdish populations is a serious problem for those who wish to develop a fully functioning, inclusive democracy in Iraq (Packer, 2005).

The Interactionist Perspective

The functionalist and conflict perspectives take a big-picture approach to sociology, focusing on the macro or large-scale structures of society. In contrast, the interactionist perspective is more concerned with the micro or small-scale aspects of social life. Sociologists like Charles Horton Cooley (1902/1964), George Herbert Mead (1934/1962), Manford Kuhn (1964), and Herbert Blumer (1969) turned their attention to the individuals who make up society and asked how social interaction is possible. Answers to this question focus on individuals' subjective experiences and understandings, and especially on how shared understandings of the world emerge from social interaction and form the basis for social life. As with the functionalist and conflict perspectives, a number of themes recur in the various formulations of interactionist thought.

▲ Symbols

Interactionists emphasize that we are social beings who live a group existence. However, we possess few, if any, innate behaviors for relating to one another. Whatever inborn capacities we have seem to require exposure to others to fully develop; we will discuss this further ◀ pp. 70–72 in Chapter 3. If we are largely lacking in such inborn mechanisms, how is society possible? Interactionists find the answer in the ability of human beings to communicate by means of symbols. A symbol is something that stands for something else. That something else is its *meaning*. Social interaction, and therefore society itself, is possible because people share meanings. The combined emphasis on symbols and interaction gives this perspective its name: *symbolic interactionism.*

▲ Meaning: Constructing Reality

Symbolic interactionism is based on three core assumptions (Mead, 1934/1962; Blumer, 1969; Fine, 1993). First, we respond to things in our environment on the basis of their meanings— that is, the understandings we have of them. Our responses differ if we see people swinging bats as playing a baseball game or as trying to hit us. Second, meanings are not inherent in things, but emerge from social interaction. Turning 16 years of age is no more meaningful than turning 15, except for the social conventions (e.g., obtaining one's driver's license) that make this a particularly meaningful birthday. Third, because we are continually interacting, shared cultural meanings are continually emerging and changing. The world we live in, therefore, is largely a social reality, manufactured by people as they intervene in the world and interpret what is happening there using the symbols and meanings available to them.

Accordingly, symbolic interactionists say that we experience the world as a **constructed reality.**

Everyday fashion is a good example. When we encounter a person dressed in a certain way, the reaction we have to the clothes they wear is not to the clothes per se, but to the meanings they symbolize. High-topped black tennis shoes, hiking boots, wing-tips, flip-flops, and Birkenstocks each have a different meaning, and the meaning shifts depending on other characteristics of the wearer, including age, gender, and race.

Symbolic interactionists also emphasize how symbols and meanings emerge to provide a more concrete reality to things that are abstract and elusive, such as societies and nations. Though it is difficult to point to a society the way we can point to a chair or a tree, we give our society a name ("the United States," "Canada," or "India"), we draw borders between our society and others, and we come to treat the United States, Canada, and India as objects. By acting and interacting with others as if the United States is real, we make it real. By treating society and its parts as "things," we give them existence and continuity (Hewitt, 2003).

All this leads symbolic interactionists to say that if sociologists are to understand social life, they must understand what people actually say and do from the viewpoint of the people themselves. Put another way, sociologists must "get inside people's heads" and view the "world" as it is seen, interpreted, acted upon, and shaped by the people themselves. This orientation is strongly influenced by Max Weber's concept of *Verstehen.*

▲ Fashioning Behavior

Symbolic interactionists portray us as creatively constructing our actions in accordance with the meanings we attribute to a situation. In fashioning our behavior we use symbols to define our perceptual inputs, mentally outline possible responses, imagine the consequences of alternative courses of action, eliminate unlikely possibilities, and finally select the optimal mode of action (Stryker, 1980). We mentally rehearse our actions before we actually act and, upon acting, serve as audiences to our own actions. As a result, our behavior is improvised and unpredictable; we must continually create meanings and devise ways to fit our actions together (Manis and Meltzer, 1994).

Symbolic interactionists argue that we are at least as likely to shape "social structure" as to be shaped by it. Think of the social structure that is your relationship with your roommate(s). It's unlikely that you were handed a list of rules for coexisting; rather, you have negotiated agreements, spoken and unspoken, about how to do so. Your relationship shifts and changes as you encounter problems and solve them. It is a circular process, in which social structure influences individuals and individuals influence social structure.

▲ Evaluation of the Interactionist Perspective

The interactionist perspective has the advantage of bringing "people" into the panorama of sociological investigation. From interactionists we gain an image of human beings as active agents who fashion their behavior, as opposed to an image of individuals who simply respond passively in a manner prescribed by social rules and institutional arrangements. This perspective directs our attention to the activities of individuals as they go about their everyday lives. Through interaction they acquire the symbols and the meanings that allow them to interpret situations, assess the advantages and disadvantages of given actions, and then select one of them.

However, the interactionist perspective has its limitations. First, there is the temptation to conclude that because social reality is constructed, there is no reality independent of social constructions. For example, because mental illness is a construction that emerges from a social process of diagnosis based on socially constructed categories of illness, one may wish to argue that mental illness is not "real." However, as philosopher John R. Searle (1995) made clear, we can understand social reality as constructed without rejecting the idea that there is a reality totally independent of us that may affect our social constructions. Second, in their everyday lives people do not enjoy total flexibility in shaping their actions. Although interactionists acknowledge that many of our actions are guided by systems of preestablished meanings, including culture and social order, many interactionists downplay the parts these larger elements play in our lives. And third, research by symbolic interactionists has often focused on narrow aspects of social life, such as nude beaches, the relationships between prostitutes and truck drivers, and the role of odors in social life.

To rectify some of these problems a number of sociologists (Collins, 2000; Fine, 1993; Stryker, 1980, 1987) have introduced structural and large-scale components into interactionist thought by linking social structure to the individual and by showing how the intertwined patterns of action and interaction form the foundation for groups and societies.

Using the Three Perspectives

The details of and contrasts among the three sociological perspectives will become clearer as we see how they operate in the chapters to come. As we noted, each theoretical approach has its advantages and its disadvantages. (Table 1.1 is a summary of the major theoretical perspectives.) Each portrays a different aspect of reality and directs our attention to some dimension of social life that the other neglects or overlooks.

Let's look at how each perspective might describe poverty. As we discussed earlier, functionalism highlights the functions and dysfunctions of poverty in terms of the operation of the larger society. Conflict theorists portray the inequalities that flow from the way society is organized and show who gains and who loses

Table 1.1	Major Theoretical Perspectives in Sociology		
	Functionalist	Conflict	Interactionist
Primary level of analysis	Macro	Macro	Micro
Nature of society	A set of interacting parts	A set of competing interest groups	A social reality that is created and recreated in social interaction
Foundations of social interaction	Consensus of shared beliefs and values	Conflict, coercion, and power	Shared meanings
Focus of study	Social order	Social conflict and social change	The dynamic interplay between the individual and society
Advantages	An understanding of social structure and social stability	Uncovers historical processes that lead to social change	An understanding of human beings as active agents in social life
Disadvantages	Ineffective in dealing with social change	A weak understanding of social consensus and social stability	Has difficulty dealing with social structure

from these arrangements. Interactionists suggest that people define certain circumstances as deviating from what they perceive to be an ideal standard of living, assign an unfavorable meaning to these conditions, and apply the label "poverty" to them. Each approach offers a somewhat different insight.

Further, each perspective affords a more effective approach, a better "fit," to some kinds of data—some aspects of social life—than other perspectives do. Each approach need not preclude the accuracy of another perspective in explaining given data or predicting particular outcomes. Indeed, each approach is useful precisely because it provides us with some piece of information regarding the exceedingly complex puzzle of social life. All three perspectives are useful sociological tools for describing and analyzing human behavior.

Conducting Research

The sociologists we have considered have provided us with important theories regarding the nature and workings of social life. A *theory* is a general framework or perspective that provides an explanation for a specific social phenomenon. However, as most sociologists would agree, theory unconfirmed by facts has little solid value. We require both theoretical understanding *and* facts; for this reason, both theory and research are essential components of the sociological enterprise. Theory inspires research that can verify or disprove it. Research provides findings that permit us to accept, reject, or modify our theoretical formulations, while simultaneously challenging us to craft new and better theories.

Research also provides the information needed to formulate public policy. Many basic human problems are products of social relations and human behavior. For example, about 70 percent of the premature deaths in the United States are caused by individual behaviors and environmental factors (U.S. Department of Health and Human Services, 2000). Sociological research can provide citizens, policy makers, and public officials with basic knowledge to fashion solutions to social problems such as poverty, drug abuse, gender inequality, and racism.

In this section we will discuss the logic of science, define a number of research methods, list the steps in the scientific method, and consider research ethics.

The Logic of Science

Science makes the assumption that every event or action results from an antecedent cause. Indeed, a primary objective of science is to determine what causes what. Sociologists assume that crime, racism, social inequality, and marriages do not simply happen, but that they have causes. Moreover, they assume that under identical conditions, the same cause will always produce the same effect.

Scientists also assume that truth can be empirically tested; data can be gathered and objectively analyzed by means of careful observation and measurement, and the facts discovered by one scientist can be verified by other scientists. For example, if it is true that people behave differently in the presence of others than when alone, then any social scientist who investigates this using careful observation and measurement will obtain the same results.

However, science is not simply a collection of research findings; science is produced through a set of complex social processes. The people who practice science are products of their own societies and of the groups to which they belong. As a result, scientists are subject to a variety of social influences in addition to their core scientific values and principles. These other factors, self-interests, and biases may shape a scientist's research design, collection of data, and interpretation of results. However, the importance of objectivity is not that it is always realized in science, but that it is an important goal toward which all scientists are committed to working.

How Do Sociologists Collect Data?

Sociologists must collect facts to support or dispute theories and to answer questions about social life. They employ four major techniques of data collection: experiments, surveys, observation, and archival research. Before describing each of these, let's define some important scientific terms.

▲ Basic Concepts in Research

Scientists look for relationships among variables. A **variable** is a concept that can take on different values. Scientists use this term to refer to something that they think influences (or is influenced by) something else. The variables sociologists typically study have to do with social statuses, conditions, attitudes, and behaviors. In studying political behavior, for example, sociologists might examine variables such as differences in race, gender, age, religion, and socioeconomic standing.

In investigating cause-and-effect relationships, scientists distinguish between the independent and the dependent variable. An **independent variable** is one that *causes* an effect. The **dependent variable** is the variable that *is affected.* The causal variable (the independent variable) precedes in time the phenomenon it causes (the dependent variable). For example, as the education level of women (independent variable) increases, the mortality rate of their infants decreases (dependent variable). In their research, scientists attempt to predict the relationship they will find between the independent and dependent variables. Such a statement—or **hypothesis**—is a proposition that can then be tested to determine its validity.

In testing a hypothesis, scientists try to determine the degree of association that exists between an independent and a dependent variable. If the variables are causally related, then they must be correlated with one another. A **correlation** exists if a change in one variable is associated with a change in the other variable. Because the mortality rate of infants decreases as the education level of women increases, for example, the two variables are said to be *correlated.*

Correlation, however, does not establish causation (Cole, 1972). For example, the death rate is considerably higher among hospitalized individuals than among nonhospitalized individuals. Yet we would be wrong to conclude on the basis of this correlation that hospitals cause death. Likewise, the amount of damage resulting from a fire is closely associated with the number of fire engines that are on the scene. Again, we would be wrong to conclude that fire engines cause greater fire damage. The latter two examples are cases of a **spurious correlation**—the apparent relationship between the two variables is produced by a third variable that influences the original variables. Severe sickness is associated both with admission to hospitals and with death; similarly, a large, uncontrolled fire is associated both with extensive damage and the mobilization of multiple firefighting units. To reduce the likelihood that their research will be contaminated by third variables, scientists employ *controls,* a matter we will discuss below when we deal with experimentation.

▲ Methods of Research

Experiments. The experiment is the ideal design for scientific research because it best provides researchers with data that enable them to accept or reject a hypothesis. To obtain such data, scientists must try to control all the relevant variables to eliminate other explanations for their findings. Though not perfect, the **experiment** best meets this requirement. In an experiment, researchers work with two groups that are made to be identical in all relevant respects through a process of random assignment. For example, in an experiment on voter

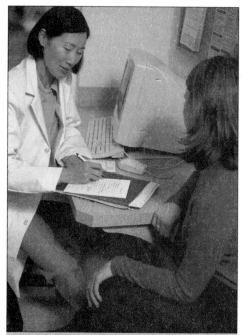

The survey researcher depicted here is gathering data from the respondent through an interview.

time watching videos unrelated to voting. The effects of television commercials (independent variable) on voter preference (dependent variable) could then be measured.

We commonly think of experiments as being performed in a laboratory setting, which is the case for much medical research and for a good deal of the research done by psychologists and social psychologists. However, sociologists also do *field experiments* in which the independent variable is manipulated in a natural setting rather than in a laboratory. This enables researchers to observe various forms of social behavior under conditions in which they normally occur. In a laboratory study, subjects know they are being observed and thus may display the behavior they believe is desirable. This makes studying some social responses such as helping behavior difficult in the laboratory.

Although the field experiment combines the strict rules of experimentation with a natural setting, it does have disadvantages (Deaux and Wrightsman, 1984). In the field, researchers have no control over unexpected intrusions that may reduce or destroy the effectiveness of the changes they make in the independent variable. Further, it is often difficult to use random assignment in field experiments to ensure that the control group and experimental group are identical.

Surveys. Some objects of study, such as people's values, beliefs, attitudes, perceptions, motivations, and feelings, are not directly accessible to observation. Others, such as sexual activity, health, religious practices, and drug use, are often sensitive, private matters. Under these circumstances the **survey** is a valuable tool in the researcher's arsenal.

Survey data are typically gathered in one of two ways. Researchers interview people by reading them questions from a prepared questionnaire, or people can receive a questionnaire in the mail, fill it out, and return it by

preferences, the two groups studied would need to be of the same size, and their members should reflect a similar socioeconomic, gender, and racial mix. Researchers introduce a change in one group—the **experimental group**—but not in the other group—the **control group.** The two groups are identical except for the factor that the researchers introduce in the experimental group. The control group affords a neutral standard against which the changes in the experimental group can then be measured.

Experiments allow sociologists to test the effects of an independent variable on a dependent variable. In our voter preference example, one group might be asked to watch a series of television commercials on candidates, while the other would spend the same amount of mail. In either case, *self-reports* are the source of data.

In both interview and questionnaire surveys, sampling procedures are critical. If researchers need information about a large population, they do not need to contact every member of that population. Instead, they can draw on a small but *representative sample,* a sample that accurately reflects the composition of the general public. Public opinion pollsters such as the Gallup and Harris organizations often employ a small sample of no more than 1,500 individuals to tap the opinions of nearly 300 million Americans. Similarly, physicians need only a small sample of your blood to run tests and draw conclusions about the composition of all your blood and thus about your health.

Sociologists typically employ either a random sample or a stratified random sample in their research. In the **random sample,** researchers select subjects on the basis of chance so that every individual in the population has the same opportunity to be chosen. A **stratified random sample** provides greater precision. Researchers divide the population into relevant categories, such as age, gender, socioeconomic level, and race, and draw a random sample from each of the categories. If African Americans constitute 12 percent of the population and Hispanics 9 percent, African Americans will comprise 12 percent of the sample and Hispanics 9 percent.

Designing good questionnaires is not easy. The wording of the questions, their number, and the format in which they appear are all critical matters (Fowler, 2001; Schaeffer and Presser, 2003). For example, the wording of a question may systematically bias the answers. A New York Times/CBS News survey found that only 29 percent of respondents said they favored a constitutional amendment "prohibiting abortions." But in response to a later question in the same survey, 50 percent said they favored an amendment "protecting the life of an unborn child"—which amounts to the same thing (Dionne, 1980).

Politicians have tried to use this tactic to their advantage (Bradburn and Sudman, 1988). For example, a survey item that begins "I agree that Candidate X" is more likely to produce a positive response than a question that begins "Does Candidate X." Pretesting is required to ensure that questions are understandable, unbiased, and specific enough to elicit the desired information.

Probably the major difficulty with self-report information has to do with the issue of its accuracy (Stone et al., 1999). Because individuals are involved in the data they are reporting, they may intentionally or unwittingly supply biased reports. They may withhold or distort information because, even though many surveys are anonymous, telling the truth can cause people to feel threatened or embarrassed. In addition, many people lack the insight required to provide certain kinds of information. And at least 10 percent of the population lacks the literacy necessary to comprehend even the simplest question.

An increasing problem with survey research is the difficulty in finding respondents (Groves et al., 2002). From 20 to 70 percent of the people who receive a questionnaire in the mail fail to complete or return it, distorting the sample's representativeness. More and more Americans are refusing to answer surveys (Dillman, 2000; Dillman and Carley-Baxter, 2001).

Observation.   As baseball's Yogi Berra once observed, "You can observe a lot just by watching." Observation—watching—is a primary tool of sociological inquiry. Observation becomes a scientific technique when it (1) serves a clear research objective, (2) is undertaken in a systematic rather than haphazard manner, (3) is carefully recorded, (4) is related to a broader body of sociological knowledge and theory, and (5) is subjected to the same checks and controls applied to all types of scientific evidence (Selltiz, Wrightsman, and Cook, 1981).

Sociologists typically observe people in one of two ways. They may observe the activities of people without intruding or participating in the activities, a procedure termed **unobtrusive observation.** Or sociologists may engage in activities with the people that they are studying, a technique called **participant observation.** Elliot Liebow's (1967/2003, see pp. 5–7) study of the African-American streetcorner men, which we discussed earlier in the chapter, involved participant observation. Liebow, a white, began his study by striking up a friendship with an African-American man, Tally Jackson, at the New Deal Carry-out Shop. Over the next several weeks Liebow often ate at the Carry-out. The streetcorner men were at first suspicious of Liebow, but Tally eased their distrust by, in effect, sponsoring Liebow as his friend.

Within a few months Liebow was well enough known and accepted by the streetcorner men to go to their rooms or apartments, needing neither an excuse nor an explanation for doing so. Clearly an outsider, Liebow (1967:164/2003) reflected on his acceptance by the group:

[B]ut I also was a participant in a full sense of the word. The people I was observing knew that I was observing them, yet they allowed me to participate in their activities and take part in their lives to a degree that continues to surprise me.

In many situations observation is the only way to gather data (Anderson, 2001). At times people are unable or unwilling to tell about their behavior: As we have said, they may lack sufficient insight to report on it or, because their behavior is illicit, taboo, or deviant, they may be reluctant to do so. For instance, we may wish to get answers to such questions as, Why and how are people drawn to crack and heroin? How is the drug market structured? How does drug use affect the social and economic life of the community? What is its role in crime and violence? Some of the most informative answers to these questions have come from researchers who have undertaken unobtrusive observation

while living and working in drug-ridden communities (Anderson, 1990, 1999). But observation has limitations similar to those for field experiments: Researchers have no control over unexpected intrusions, and groups or individuals observed may not be representative of others. Additionally, there is the practical problem of applying observational procedures to phenomena that occur over a long period, such as a certain historical era. For these types of investigation, archival data are particularly useful.

Comparative and Historical Research.
We may learn a good deal about work, sexual behavior, family life, leisure, and other matters within the United States and other Western societies. But do these insights hold for non-Western peoples? And do they hold for earlier historical periods? To answer these sorts of questions, sociologists need to look to other societies and other historical periods to test their ideas. Comparative and historical research is well suited to the task (Mahoney, 2004). One approach involves archival research. **Archival research** refers to the use of existing records that have been produced or maintained by persons or organizations other than the researcher. Census data, government statistics, newspaper reports, books, magazines, personal letters, speeches, folklore, court records, works of art, and the research data of other social scientists are all sources for archival research (e.g., Ruef, 2004; Budro, 2004). A new utilization of data already collected for some other purpose may have considerable value and merit.

Comparative and historical materials have provided us with valuable insights on issues relating to the nation-state. A good illustration is sociologist Theda Skocpol's landmark study, *States and Social Revolution* (1979). In this study Skocpol looked for similarities in the societal conditions that existed at the time of the French (1787–1800), Russian (1917–1921), and Chinese (1911–1949) revolutions, comparing them with conditions in nations where revolutions failed or did not take place. Skocpol's comparative historical analysis led her to conclude that successful social revolutions pass through three stages: An old regime's state apparatus collapses; the peasantry mobilizes in class-based uprisings; and a new elite consolidates political power.

Archival research has the advantage of allowing researchers to test hypotheses over a wider range of time and societies than would otherwise be possible. We gain greater confidence in the validity of a hypothesis when we can test it in a number of cultures and historical periods rather than restrict ourselves to a single group in the present time and place. However, the technique also has its disadvantages. The major problem is that missing or inaccurate records often prevent an adequate test. And when material is available, it is frequently difficult to categorize in a way that gives an answer to a research question (Deaux and Wrightsman, 1984).

Feminist Research Methods.   Feminism not only is having a strong impact on contemporary social theory, as noted earlier in this chapter, but it also is having an important influence on how sociologists do research. Feminist methodology includes a commitment to three goals: (1) to include women's lives in social research and reveal the diversity in the way women actually live their lives, uncovering what has previously been ignored, censored, and suppressed; (2) to minimize harm by avoiding exploitation of research subjects and by limiting the negative consequences of research; and (3) to focus research efforts so that results will promote social change, reduce inequality, and be of value to women (DeVault, 1996).

Though many feminist researchers have done important and influential research using observational methods to examine women's experiential, subjective, and emotional lives, Joey Sprague and Mary K. Zimmerman (1993) stressed that the important contributions of feminist methodology are:

1.   To create an objective account of social life while being sensitive to the subjective experience of those we study.
2.   To develop abstract theories without losing sight of the real concrete lives of people.
3.   To recognize the importance of rationality in social life without ignoring the importance of emotion.
4.   To realize that both statistical analysis of quantitative data and qualitative observation can reveal important insights about women's and men's social lives.

In sum, feminist methodology is not a particular method of doing research but an approach that emphasizes inclusion, fairness, and humaneness, as well as the pursuit of all evidence that can be used to transform society and women's lives.

Multiple Methods.   Many methods are used to gather data in sociology, some radically different from others. Some research problems can be studied only with certain methods. The study of sociocultural change over hundreds of years, for example, requires the use of comparative historical analysis of archival data. But if we want to know how employment affects the mental health of U.S. women in the paid labor force today, we would use field observation and survey methods. Using multiple methods, each with its own strengths and weaknesses, can give us a more complete answer to our research question; different methods provide different windows on reality. As Peggy Thoits (1995) showed in her study, what we find with one method may be made understandable by examining data collected using another method. For her study of stresses and psychological symptoms, simply examining the average symptom level associated with each stressor was not enough; she needed to know the context in which stresses had occurred. Divorce, for example, might come as a devastating shock to one person and as a welcome relief to another, depending on each person's particular situation, and only Thoits's qualitative analysis of more extended comments from respondents and interviewers allowed her to interpret her data accurately. Box 1.2 provides a more detailed look at how a researcher selects research methods.

Steps in the Scientific Method: A Close-up Look

The *scientific method,* a series of steps that seeks to ensure maximum objectivity in investigating a problem, allows researchers to pursue answers to their questions by gathering evidence in a systematic manner. Although no single method can eliminate uncertainty, the steps embodied in the scientific method maximize the chances for deriving information that is relevant, unbiased, and economical. The scientific method relies on the rigorous and disciplined collection of facts and on the logical explanation of them. Its steps include selecting a researchable problem, reviewing the literature, formulating a hypothesis, choosing a research design, collecting the data, analyzing the data, and stating conclusions.

Ideally sociological research follows this step-by-step procedure, although in practice it is not always possible. Let's examine each step in Figure 1.1 (p. 34) as we follow a study of adolescents' first experience of sex, their religiosity, and their attitudes about sex (Meier, 2003).

1. Selecting a Researchable Problem.
The range of topics available for social research is as broad as the range of human behavior. Sociologists focus on research problems that merit study and that can be investigated by the methods of science. Ann M. Meier was intrigued by the fact that over recent decades, more American teenagers have become sexually active at increasingly younger ages. Most high school graduates today are not virgins. She decided to do a study to uncover social factors that would help explain sexual behavior among contemporary adolescents. She suspected that teenagers' attitudes about sexual behavior and their religiosity might be important determinants of their sexual activity.

2. Reviewing the Literature.
Meier surveyed the research literature dealing with religiosity, attitudes, and first sex to find out what had been discovered in previous research. What she found suggested a variety of leads and saved her from duplicating the work of other researchers. Studies uncovered by her search showed that *having more permissive attitudes* about sexual activity and *being less religious* were each related to a higher likelihood of adolescents having sex. This body of research suggested that adolescents' attitudes about sexual behavior and their religiosity might be important influences on sexual behavior. However, evidence in these studies also supported another possibility—that adolescents might develop more permissive attitudes about sex and become less religious as a consequence of having sex.

When sociologists discover an association, or *correlation,* between variables, they have not established *causation.* Do low religiosity and more permissive attitudes about having sex lead to more sexual behavior among teenagers? Or does having sex lead teenagers to be more permissive about sex and to be less religious?

3. Formulating a Hypothesis.
After reviewing the literature, researchers form a hypothesis regarding the relationship they believe exists between variables. A hypothesis can take the form of a predictive statement or of a question. Meier hypothesized that there were causal processes going in both directions: that permissive attitudes about having sex and low religiosity would both increase the likelihood of sexual behavior among adolescents, and that having sex would increase permissive attitudes about having sex and would decrease religiosity.

Child Care Fatalities: Discovering the Critical Role of Social Factors

While fatalities among the nearly 8 million U.S. children in child care are rare, approximately 75 such deaths occur each year, and each one is a tragedy. News stories about these incidents highlight negligence, misbehavior, or aggression by child care workers; and cases are followed avidly on TV news and Court TV. What viewers want to know is this: How could anyone let a child die or, worse yet, kill a child? What sociologists want to know is this: Do social factors play an important role in child care fatalities? Are some care situations safer than others? And if so, why? Sociologists Julia Wrigley and Joanna Dreby (2005) thought these were questions worth asking.

It was not easy to find answers. National data on fatalities and serious injuries in child care do not exist, and state data are limited. There is no one agency to which child care providers must report injuries or deaths. In many states, family day care homes are not regulated at all. In fact, Wrigley and Dreby's study was the first systematic national study of child care fatalities. How did they go about it?

The researchers used multiple methods for counting cases of child care fatalities and serious injuries. First, they used online search engines, the electronic archives of individual newspapers, and a clipping service to search for newspaper accounts of such incidents from 1985 to 2003. In addition, they used legal cases involving "caregiving failures"— cases in which a caregiver was found to be responsible for the death or serious injury of a child. And third, in seven states, they used information from state child care licensing agencies, child protective agencies, child death review boards, and licensing case decisions.

The dataset that Wrigley and Dreby assembled covers all types of non-family-provided child care: child care centers, in-home care (nannies and babysitters), and family day care situations. It provides information about both accidental and violent fatalities. For each fatality or serious injury, the database includes the age and sex of the child as well as the caregiver, whether the death was a homicide or an accident, how and where the death occurred, what kind of child care was involved, and whether the caregiver had a record of abuse or neglect. Further, the records they collected often provided detailed accounts of the case, allowing them to learn more about how deaths can occur in child care settings.

What did they find? First of all, as noted above, fatalities in young children in child care are rare. Secondly, child care centers, which provide care for about 66 percent of the nation's children in out-of-family care, protect children almost completely from death and

Before undertaking their research, however, researchers must define their variables. In developing **operational definitions,** scientists take abstract concepts and put them in a form that permits their measurement. In this case Meier specified how she would measure adolescents' religiosity, sexual attitudes, and sexual behavior. Religiosity was measured by asking respondents how important religion was to them and how frequently they attended church, prayed, and participated in church youth groups. Responses to these questions were combined into a single index of religiosity. Similarly, the degree of respondents' permissive attitudes about sexual behavior was measured by seven questions that asked about the perceived benefits and costs of having sex. Sexual behavior was measured by asking respondents whether they had had sexual intercourse. Meier's *operational hypotheses,* stated in terms of measurable variables, were as follows:

- More permissive attitudes toward having sex will increase the probability of having sex.

- Higher levels of religiosity will decrease the probability of having sex.

- Having sex will result in adolescents having more permissive attitudes about having sex.

- Having sex will result in lower levels of religiosity.

serious injury. Fatalities and serious injuries occur almost entirely among the 7 percent of child care recipients who are cared for in their own homes by nannies and babysitters or among the 27 percent enrolled in family day care.

The differences are especially dramatic for infants. Between 1993 and 2003, 130 infants in family day care and 24 infants receiving in-home care suffered violent deaths; during the same time, there were no infant deaths from violence in child care centers. During the entire period of their study, Wrigley and Dreby found only a single infant fatality from violence in a child care center. For any age child, only five violent fatalities occurred in centers, compared to 507 fatalities in home-based care. Similarly, deaths from accidental causes (drowning, suffocation, fire, strangulation, and poison) occurred far more frequently in home-based care than in center care.

What Wrigley and Dreby concluded is that the *social organization* of child care is the critical element in protecting children from fatal accidents or fatal violence in child care situations. Severely injuring or killing an infant takes only a few moments of shaking or other violent behavior by a caregiver overwhelmed by anger or frustration. Accidental deaths similarly occur very quickly, requiring only a few moments of inattention. Such behavior—either inattention or violence—is much less likely to occur in a child care center, where multiple caregivers, professional staff, safety checklists, and physical and social environments arranged specifically for the safety of children all work to provide multiple safeguards against personal failures.

Interestingly, Wrigley and Dreby did not uncover evidence that workers in child care centers avoid feelings of frustration, anger, and hostility on the job. These feelings do occur in child care centers. The critical difference, however, is that these emotions are less likely to lead to violence against the children in child care centers than they do in other forms of care. Why does this difference occur? Child care centers are organized, provide training for workers, follow routine procedures, and, most importantly, employ mechanisms of social control that prevent negative emotions from resulting in violence toward children.

Questions for Discussion

1. In what ways does the problem of sexual victimization and harassment of high school students by teachers parallel the problem discussed here? How might you study this problem? What would your hypotheses be? Do you think that social organization would emerge as a critical factor? Why or why not?

2. Think of a situation in which you felt frustrated or angry, but social control factors were more important determinants of your behavior than these emotions were. What were the social control factors? How did they affect your behavior?

4. Choosing a Research Design. Once researchers have formulated their hypotheses, they have to decide how they will collect the data that will provide a test of each hypothesis. The private and sensitive nature of sexual behavior ruled out observation and experimentation as appropriate research methods. Instead, Meier used a survey design in which people were asked questions to measure the concepts in the study. The survey data she used were collected by other researchers as part of a larger project, the National Longitudinal Study of Adolescent Health (Add Health). In this study, measurements were taken through interviews with 15,000 adolescents at two different points in time, 1995 and 1996. The longitudinal nature of the study allowed Meier to employ a quasi-experimental design, with some of the subjects being exposed to the "treatment" (first sex) between 1995 and 1996, and others not. Of course, this was not a true experiment; students were not randomly assigned to an experimental group in which having sex was the treatment condition.

5. Collecting the Data. For some researchers, collecting the data is a critical and time-consuming part of the research process. Because Meier's project was a **secondary data analysis** (analysis of data collected by others), she did not have to worry about conducting this phase of the study herself. As part of the Add

Selecting a Researchable Problem
Finding a problem that merits study and that can be investigated by the methods of science

Reviewing the Literature
Surveying the existing theory and research on the subject

Formulating a Hypothesis
Arriving at a statement that specifies the relationship between the variables and developing an operational definition that states the variables in a form that permits their measurement

Choosing a Research Design
Determining whether to test the hypothesis by designing an experiment, conducting interviews, observing the ways people behave in particular situations, examining existing records and historical evidence, or combining these procedures

Collecting the Data
Gathering the data and recording it in accordance with the specifications of the research design

Analyzing the Results
Searching for meaningful links between the facts that emerged in the course of the research

Stating Conclusions
Indicating the outcome of the study, extracting the broader meaning of the work for other knowledge and research, and suggesting directions for future research

Figure 1.1   **The Steps in the Scientific Method**
The chart shows the steps researchers commonly follow in investigating a problem.

Health project, other researchers had already conducted in-home interviews with a sample of adolescents and included all the measures needed in Meier's study. Her subset of this larger sample included 15- to 18-year-old never-married adolescents, all of whom were virgins at the first interview and none of whom had experienced forced sex by the time of the second interview. Some of these adolescents had sex for the first time between the first and second waves of data collection, and others did not.

Respondents are not always honest in face-to-face interviews about private matters such as sexual behavior. For this reason, sexual behavior was measured using a computer-assisted self-interview, in which the respondents answered questions on a computer in a private setting.

6. Analyzing the Data.

Once researchers have their data, they must analyze them to find answers to the questions posed by their research project. Analysis involves a search for meaningful links among the facts that have emerged in the course of the research. Meier chose methods of data analysis that would show two things: (1) whether attitudes and religiosity expressed in the first interview (that is, in 1995) were correlated with having sex between the first interview and the second interview (in 1996), and (2) whether having sex between the first and second interviews was related to a change in religiosity and/or attitudes between the two interviews.

In the first analysis, Meier found that lower religiosity and more positive attitudes about having sex (as measured in the first interview) were both related to having sex between the two interviews. In the second analysis she found that having sex between the two interviews did not result in lower religiosity in the second interview, but it did result in more positive attitudes about sex among females in the second interview. For males, who on average had more positive attitudes about sex to begin with, having sex between the interviews did not significantly change their attitudes about sex.

7. Stating Conclusions.

After completing their analysis of the data, researchers are ready to state their conclusions. They typically accept, reject, or modify their hypothesis. Additionally, researchers usually seek to extract broader meaning from their work by linking it to other knowledge and theory. Meier's findings support two of her hypotheses—students who have more positive attitudes about having sex and those who are less religious are more likely to engage in sexual activity. A third hypothesis, that having sexual activity results in more positive attitudes about having sex, is supported only for females. And the findings indicate that we should reject the fourth hypothesis—having sex did not result in lower levels of religiosity. Religious students are apparently less likely to have sex, but students who have sex do not therefore become less religious.

In a broader context, Meier's study provides a method for other researchers to use when there is concern about the direction of causation. By looking at interviews with respondents conducted a year apart, she was able to determine the effects of religiosity and attitudes on first sex *and* the effects of first sex on religiosity and attitudes. Without two sets of data at two separate times, our knowledge about how attitudes and religiosity are related to sexual behavior would be incomplete.

Research Ethics

Though scientific research on human beings is potentially valuable and important, it also can be dangerous and harmful to the people who are studied. Such harm is described in *Darkness in El Dorado: How Scientists and Journalists Devastated the Amazon* (Tierney, 2000), which accuses anthropologists of conducting unethical research among the Yanomami Indians of Venezuela (Holden, 2002). As a result of this and other controversies, sociologists have become increasingly sensitive and committed to ethical considerations in their research.

Yet sociologists confront a dilemma in conducting research. On the one hand, they must not distort or manipulate their findings to serve untruthful, personal, or institutional ends. On the other hand, they are obligated to consider people as ends and not means.

Because of the possible conflicts between these various responsibilities, the American Sociological Association (1989), the major professional organization for the discipline in the United States, has provided a code of ethics to govern the behavior of its members. Among these principles are the following:

- *Sociologists should not misuse their positions as professional social scientists for fraudulent purposes or as a pretext for gathering intelligence for any organization or government. Sociologists should not mislead respondents involved in a research project as to the purpose for which that research is being conducted.*

- *The process of conducting sociological research must not expose respondents to substantial risk of personal harm. Informed consent must be obtained when the risks of research are greater than the risks of everyday life. Where modest risk or harm is anticipated, informed consent must be obtained.*

- *Sociologists must not coerce or deceive students into serving as research subjects.*

- *No sociologists should discriminate in hiring, firing, promotions, salary, treatment, or any other conditions of employment or career development on the basis of sex, sexual preference, age, race, religion, national origin, handicap, or political orientation.*

In sum, because sociological knowledge can be a form of economic and political power, sociologists must exercise care to protect their discipline, the people they study and teach, and society from abuses that may stem from their professional work.

The Chapter in Brief: *Developing a Sociological Consciousness*

The Sociological Perspective

Sociology is the scientific study of social interaction and social organization.

■ *New Levels of Reality*   The sociological perspective encourages us to examine aspects of our social environment in ways that delve beneath the surface. As we look beyond the outer appearances of our social world, we encounter new levels of reality.

■ *The Sociological Imagination*   The essence of the **sociological imagination** is the ability to see our private experiences and personal difficulties as entwined with the structural arrangements of our society and the times in which we live.

■ *Microsociology and Macrosociology*
Microsociology is the detailed study of what people say, do, and think moment by moment as they go about their daily lives. **Macrosociology** focuses upon large-scale and long-term social processes of organizations, institutions, and broad social patterns.

The Development of Sociology

■ *Auguste Comte: The Founder of Sociology*   Auguste Comte is commonly credited as being the founder of sociology. He emphasized that the study of society must be scientific, and he urged sociologists to employ systematic observation, experimentation, and comparative historical analysis as their methods. He divided the study of society into **social statics** and **social dynamics.**

▮ *Harriet Martineau: Feminist and Methodologist*   Harriet Martineau wrote the first book on social research methods and was among the first to do systematic, scientifically based, social research. Her comparative analysis of slavery and the position of women in the Western world paved the way for feminist scholarship and the further pursuit of gender equality.

▮ *Herbert Spencer and Social Darwinism*   Herbert Spencer depicted society as a system, a whole made up of inter-related parts. He also set forth an evolutionary theory of historical development. **Social Darwinism** is Spencer's application of evolutionary notions and the concept of survival of the fittest to the social world.

▮ *Karl Marx: The Role of Class Conflict*
Karl Marx focused his search for the basic principles of history on the economic environments in which societies develop. He believed that society is divided into those who own the means of producing wealth and those who do not, giving rise to **class conflict. Dialectical materialism** is Marx's theory that development depends on the clash of contradictions and the creation of new, more advanced structures out of these clashes.

▮ *Émile Durkheim: Social Integration and Social Facts*   Émile Durkheim was especially concerned with social solidarity, distinguishing between mechanical and organic solidarity. He contended that the distinctive subject matter of sociology should be the study of **social facts.**

▮ *Max Weber: Subjectivity and Social Organization*   Max Weber said that a critical aspect of the sociological enterprise is the study of the intentions, values, beliefs, and attitudes that underlie people's

behavior. He used the word *Verstehen* in describing his approach and contributed his notions of the ideal type and a **value-free sociology.**

▮ *American Sociology*   In the United States, sociology and the modern university system arose together. The first department of sociology was established at the University of Chicago in 1893, and Chicago served as a "social laboratory" at the beginning of the century. Midcentury sociologists crafted survey techniques and refined models of society. "New breed" sociologists in the 1960s and 1970s refined Marxism and established new research approaches and perspectives.

▮ *Contemporary Sociology*   Contemporary movements in sociology include critical theory, feminism, and postmodern social theory.

Theoretical Perspectives
Contemporary sociologists acknowledge three general theoretical perspectives, or ways of looking at how various social phenomena are related to one another. These are the functionalist, the conflict, and the symbolic interactionist perspectives.

▮ *The Functionalist Perspective*   The structural-functional—or, more simply, functionalist—perspective sees society as a system. Functionalists identify the structural characteristics and **functions** and **dysfunctions** of institutions, and distinguish between **manifest functions** and **latent functions.** Functionalists also typically assume that most members of a society share a consensus regarding their core beliefs and values.

▮ *The Conflict Perspective*   The conflict approach draws much of its inspiration from the work of Karl Marx and argues that the structure of society and the nature of social relationships are the result of past and ongoing conflicts.

■ *The Interactionist Perspective*

Symbolic interactionists contend that society is possible because human beings have the ability to communicate with one another by means of symbols. They say that we act toward people, objects, and events on the basis of the meanings we impart to them. Consequently, we experience the world as **constructed reality.**

Conducting Research

■ *The Logic of Science*

Sociology is a social science. Science assumes that every event or action results from an antecedent cause—that is, cause-and-effect relationships prevail in the universe. These causes and effects can be observed and measured, and sociologists look for **correlations** among **variables** as a way of doing so.

■ *How Do Sociologists Collect Data?*

Four major techniques of data collection are available to sociologists: experiments, surveys, observation, and archival research. In the **experiment,** researchers work with an **experimental group** and a **control group** to test the effects of an **independent variable** on a **dependent variable.** Interviewing and questionnaires constitute the primary techniques used in **surveys,** using **random** or **stratified random samples.** Observation can take the form of **participant observation** or **unobtrusive observation.** Other techniques include **archival research** and feminist methodology.

■ *Steps in the Scientific Method: A Close-up Look*

The scientific method includes selecting a researchable problem, reviewing the literature, formulating a **hypothesis,** creating an **operational definition,** choosing a research design, collecting the data, analyzing the data, and stating conclusions.

■ *Research Ethics*

It is important that sociologists observe the ethics of their discipline in carrying out research. They have an obligation not to expose their subjects to substantial risk or personal harm in the research process and to protect the rights and dignity of their subjects.

Glossary

archival research   The use of existing records that have been produced or maintained by persons or organizations other than the researcher.

class conflict   The view of Karl Marx that society is divided into those who own the means of producing wealth and those who do not, giving rise to struggles between classes.

constructed reality   Our experience of the world. Meaning is not something that inheres in things; it is a property that derives from, or arises out of, the interaction that takes place among people in the course of their daily lives.

control group   The group that affords a neutral standard against which the changes in an experimental group can be measured.

correlation   A change in one variable associated with a change in another variable.

dependent variable   The variable that is affected in an experimental setting.

dialectical materialism
The notion in Marxist theory that development depends on the clash of contradictions and the creation of new, more advanced structures out of these clashes.

dysfunctions   Observed consequences that lessen the adaptation or adjustment of a system.

economic determinist   A believer in the doctrine that economic factors are the primary determinants of the structure of societies and social change.

experiment   A technique in which researchers work with two groups that are identical in all relevant respects. They introduce a change in one group, but not in the other group. The procedure permits researchers to test the effects of an independent variable on a dependent variable.

experimental group   The group in which researchers introduce a change in an experimental setting.

functions   Observed consequences that permit the adaptation or adjustment of a system.

hypothesis   A proposition that can be tested to determine its validity.

independent variable   The variable that causes an effect in an experimental setting.

latent functions
Consequences that are neither intended nor recognized by the participants in a system.

macrosociology   The study of large-scale and long-term social processes.

manifest functions
Consequences that are intended and recognized by the participants in a system.

microsociology   The detailed study of what individuals say, do, and think moment by moment as they go about their daily lives.

operational definition
A definition developed by taking abstract concepts and putting them in a form that permits their measurement.

participant observation
A technique in which researchers engage in activities with the people that they are observing.

power   The ability to control the behavior of others, even against their will.

random sample   A sampling procedure in which researchers select subjects on the basis of chance so that every individual in the population has the same opportunity to be chosen.

secondary data analysis
Analysis of data collected by others.

Social Darwinism   The application of evolutionary notions and the concept of survival of the fittest to the social world.

social dynamics   Those aspects of social life that pattern institutional development and have to do with social change.

social facts   Those aspects of social life that cannot be explained in terms of the biological or mental characteristics of the individual. People experience the social fact as external to themselves in the sense that it has an independent reality and forms a part of their objective environment.

social statics   Those aspects of social life that have to do with order and stability and that allow societies to hold together and endure.

sociological imagination
The ability to see our private experiences and personal difficulties as entwined with the structural arrangements of our society and the historical times in which we live.

sociology   The scientific study of social interaction and social organization.

spurious correlation
The apparent relationship between two variables produced by a third variable that influences the original variables.

stratified random sample
A sampling procedure in which researchers divide a population into relevant categories and draw a random sample from each of the categories.

survey   A method for gathering data on people's beliefs, values, attitudes, perceptions, motivations, and feelings. The data can be derived from interviews or questionnaires.

unobtrusive observation
A technique in which researchers observe the activities of people without intruding or participating in the activities.

value-free sociology   The view of Max Weber that sociologists must not allow their personal biases to affect the conduct of their scientific research.

variable   A concept that can take on different values; the

term scientists apply to something they think influences (or is influenced by) something else.

Verstehen   An approach to the study of social life developed by Max Weber in which sociologists mentally attempt to place themselves in the shoes of other people and identify what they think and how they feel; translates roughly as "understanding."

Review Questions

1. What is the sociological imagination?
2. Define microsociology and macrosociology.
3. Name four major figures from the history of sociology and briefly describe their contributions to the field.
4. What are the three major sociological perspectives? Give a brief description of each.
5. How do sociologists collect data? Use either the study on nannies or the report on age at first sex to discuss sociological research.

Internet Connection

 www.mhhe.com/hughes8

Open the Web page for the American Sociological Association, **http://www.asanet.org/.** Information is provided for sociologists, students, and the public. Click on "students" and follow the link to "Careers in Sociology." Based on what you learn about sociology and sociological careers, think about whether you would be interested in pursuing a career in sociology. Why or why not? Write a short report on the careers that are available to people who study sociology and your thoughts about these careers.

Chapter 2

CULTURE AND SOCIAL STRUCTURE

Components of Culture

Norms
Values
Symbols and Language

Cultural Unity and Diversity

Cultural Universals
Cultural Integration
Ethnocentrism
Cultural Relativism
Subcultures and Countercultures

Social Structure

Statuses
Roles
Groups
Institutions
Societies

In 1789 mutineers led by Fletcher Christian seized control of the ship *Bounty* shortly after it had departed from Tahiti, an island in the South Pacific. They set William Bligh, the ship's captain, and 18 of his men adrift. The mutineers returned to Tahiti, where some of the men decided to remain. Nine men elected to seek another island and induced 6 Tahitian men and 12 Tahitian women to sail with them to Pitcairn Island.

The story of the mutiny on the *Bounty* and the subsequent settlement on Pitcairn Island is a perennial favorite. For sociologists, Pitcairn Island—where descendants of the first settlers still live today—offers a unique social experiment in the founding of a society and the fashioning of a new culture. Imagine the problems that confronted the English and Tahitian colonists when they arrived on this tiny, uninhabited South Pacific island. How would they find food? How would they protect themselves from the elements? How would they maintain order? How would they manage their sexual relationships, a matter of no small concern in a community of 15 men and 12 women? How

would they provide for any children born on the island?

In finding solutions to their problems, the English and Tahitian colonists could not fall back on the sorts of genetic adaptations such as those that permit insects to live a group existence. They lacked the built-in behavioral responses and highly specialized appendages that would prepare them for a particular environmental niche. An ability to adapt is not found in human's genetic heritage, but in culture and society, the topics of this chapter.

Culture refers to the social heritage of a people—those learned patterns for thinking, feeling, and acting that are transmitted from one generation to the next, including the embodiment of these patterns in material items. It includes both *nonmaterial culture*—abstract creations like values, beliefs, symbols, norms, customs, and institutional arrangements—and *material culture*—physical artifacts or objects like stone axes, computers, loincloths, tuxedos, automobiles, paintings, electric guitars, hairstyles, and domed stadiums. **Society** refers to a group of people who live within the same territory and

43

share a common culture. Very simply, culture has to do with the customs of a people, and society has to do with the people who are practicing the customs. Culture provides the meanings that enable human beings to interpret their experiences and guide their actions, whereas society represents the networks of social relations that arise among a people.

In fashioning a new society, the Pitcairn Islanders had the combined heritage of two cultures to draw on, and the cultural patterns they evolved were a blend of their different backgrounds. Because Pitcairn ecologically resembles Tahiti, their food patterns consisted principally of Tahitian items. However, their tools—metal hoes, spades, and mattocks—were of English origin. Because the women took responsibility for the preparation and cooking of food, the nonmaterial aspects of Tahitian culture came to dominate in household arrangements; as in Tahiti, the Pitcairn Islanders ate their meals in the late morning and in the early evening. And Pitcairnese language evolved as a stew of 18th-century English, Polynesian, and seafaring terms.

Serious conflicts over women in the early years were eventually overcome. An 1833 visitor, Captain Freemantle, found the residents to be "a well-disposed, well-behaved, kind, hospitable people." They had developed a culture that promoted deep attachments to their island and strong bonds of social unity. Social rules evolved to discourage close interpersonal relations, even romantic ones, out of concern that such relations weaken commitment to the group. A late 20th-century visitor to the island found a social order where the interests of individuals are second to the interests of the community. Culture and society on Pitcairn today, as at its founding, are both affected significantly by its isolation from other cultures and societies (Birkett, 1997).

In this chapter we will discuss components of culture, consider cultural unity and diversity, and introduce a number of key concepts related to social structure.

Components of Culture

When some people hear the word *culture,* they think of the opera, the ballet, the art museum, or the symphony. But when social scientists use the term, they have in mind something more comprehensive and consequential. They mean something that provides individuals with a set of common understandings used to fashion behavior. Culture allows us to "know" in rather broad terms what we can expect of others and what they can expect of us. For example, Pitcairn Islanders visiting other Pitcairn Islanders can expect meals in the late morning and early evening (Birkett, 1997); Pitcairn Islanders visiting the United States might be surprised to be served breakfast, lunch, and dinner.

Simultaneously, culture affords a kind of map or a set of guideposts for finding our way about life. It provides a configuration of dos and don'ts, a complex of patterned mental stop-and-go signs that tell us about the social landscape: "Notice this," "Ignore that," "Avoid this action," and "Do that" (Kluckhohn, 1960:21). If we know a people's culture—their design for living—we can understand and predict a good deal of their behavior. Why are the Washington beltways crammed with cars early in the morning and again in the late afternoon? Such a pattern of traffic might be mysterious to visitors from another country but an accepted way of life to citizens here.

In providing common understandings, culture binds the separated lives of individuals into a larger whole, making society possible by providing a common framework of meaning. Only by sharing similar perspectives with one another—designs and ways of life—can we weave integrated webs of ongoing interaction. Let us examine more carefully some of the key components of culture that make these shared understandings possible: norms, values, and symbols and language.

Norms

To live with others in a group setting, we must share understandings that tell us which actions are permissible and which are not. For example, unless we have a prior understanding, we cannot take something from a neighbor's yard; the difference between borrowing and stealing is based on shared understandings. These understandings give our daily lives order and allow us to determine which behaviors we can legitimately insist others perform and which they can legitimately insist we perform. When we enter a clothing store, begin a college course, get married, or start a new job, we understand at least some of the expectations that will hold for us and others in these settings. Such expectations are norms. **Norms** are social rules that specify appropriate and inappropriate behavior in given situations. They tell us what we "should," "ought," and "must" do, as well as what we "should not," "ought not," and "must not" do. In all cultures the great body of these social rules deal with matters involving sex, property, and safety.

But norms are not just moral rules. They provide guidance so that we can align our actions with those of others when situations are unclear or ambiguous, and they provide standards by which we judge other people and make decisions about how we will interact with them. Faculty at your college or university provide an example. Inappropriate behaviors for classroom instructors include treating students negatively, failing to plan a course or failing to communicate class requirements to students, and grading exams or papers unfairly (Braxton and Bayer, 1999). A professor who makes jokes based on negative stereotypes may be tolerated (but not appreciated) by students, while one who never hands out a course syllabus may be reported to the dean.

Though norms are subjective human creations, we experience them as objective and independent features of our social environment

This child, who has been living in the context of one set of norms in the family, is about to confront another set of norms—those of the school.

(Reno, Cialdini, and Kallgren, 1993). People attach a good deal of importance to some norms, called **mores** (singular mos), and they mete out harsh punishment to violators. Other norms, called **folkways,** people deem to be of less importance, and they exact less stringent conformity to them (Sumner, 1906). Some norms are formalized and are enforced by special political organizations. These we refer to as **laws.** Folkways, mores, and laws are discussed below.

▲ Folkways

Folkways have to do with the customary ways and ordinary conventions by which we carry out our daily activities. We bathe, brush our teeth, groom our hair, wear shoes or sandals, wave greetings to friends, mow our lawns, and sleep in beds. We view people who violate folkways, especially those who violate a good number of them, as somehow "different" and even "strange." However, ordinarily we do not attach moral significance to folkways. For example, we may regard people who wear soiled clothing as crude but not as sinful, and people who are late for appointments as thoughtless but not evil. Gossip and ridicule are important mechanisms for enforcing folkways.

▲ Mores

Members of a culture or society are more concerned about violations of mores. Murder, theft, rape, treason, and child molestation bring strong disapproval and severe punishment in the United States. Mores are seen as vital to a society's well-being and survival. People usually attach moral significance to mores, and they define people who violate them as sinful and evil. Consequently, the punishment for violators of a society's mores is severe; they may be put to death, imprisoned, cast out, mutilated, or tortured.

Folkways and mores are distinguished from laws by the fact that they are usually enforced by people acting in a spontaneous and often collective manner. On contemporary Pitcairn Island, for example, islanders are afraid that if they do or say something against someone, that person will get back at them at some later date (Birkett, 1997). When one Pitcairner cut down another's banana tree, he was greeted the next morning with 3-inch nails planted in the mud path outside his house. Social censure also is achieved through the ancient but formidable weapon of gossip. Sometimes rumors will reach the culprit within hours, and once accused, a person is as good as guilty (Birkett, 1997).

These efforts at social control involve not only individual interests but also group interests. Because you are a member of numerous groups, other people—your family members, friends, neighbors, and coworkers—may also benefit or suffer from your conduct. If you are arrested or fired, others may experience spillover effects. Indeed, group members are often held accountable for one another's actions. Some U.S. corporations link their employees through group incentive plans, and military boot camps punish everyone in the barracks for one recruit's misconduct. Such spillover effects give group members a stake in regulating one another's behavior. However, in the case of some groups (e.g., criminal and revolutionary organizations) a person's peers often have a stake in helping the violator avoid detection and punishment (Heckathorn, 1990).

▲ Laws

Some norms are formalized into laws, rules that are enforced by a special political organization composed of individuals who have the right to use force (see Vago, 2003). As anthropologist E. A. Hoebel (1958: 470–471) observed: "The essentials of legal coercion are general acceptance of the application of physical power, in threat or in fact, by a privileged party, for a legitimate cause, in a legitimate way, and at a legitimate time." The people who administer laws may make use of physical force with a low probability of retaliation by a third party (Collins, 1975). Laws tend to be the result of conscious thought, deliberate planning, and formal declaration. They can be changed more readily than folkways and mores.

Values

Norms are rules for behavior; **values** are broad ideas regarding what is desirable, correct, and good that most members of a society share. Values are so general and abstract that they do not explicitly specify which behaviors are acceptable and which are not (Rohan, 2000; Hitlin and Piliavin, 2004). Instead, values provide us with criteria and conceptions by which we evaluate people, objects, and events as to their relative worth, merit, beauty, or morality. Th[e] major value configurations within the domina[nt] American culture include the assignment of hig[h] importance to achievement and success, work and activity, efficiency and practicality, material comfort, individuality, progress, rationality, patriotism, and democracy (Williams, 1970). People tend to appeal to values as the ultimate rationales for the choices they make in life.

At times different norms are based on the same values. For instance, two Americans may both place a premium on the same value—social equality. However, one may express this sentiment by supporting affirmative action programs and the other by opposing such legislation as "reverse discrimination," favoring instead "color-blind" civil rights laws. Values also can change over time (Rokeach and Ball-Rokeach, 1989). For example, in many societies around the world, values placing women in a subservient position to men are slowly giving way to egalitarian gender values. The increased presence of women in the workforce, greater educational opportunities for women, and declining fertility have all contributed to this change.

Symbols and Language

Norms and values are intangible aspects of social life, what sociologists term "nonmaterial culture." But if they lack a physical existence, how can we get a handle on them? How in the course of our daily lives can we talk to one another about rules and standards, mull them over in our minds, and appraise people's behavior in terms of them? The answer has to do with symbols. **Symbols** are acts or objects that have come to be socially accepted as standing for something else. They come to represent other things through the shared understandings people have. Consider the word "computer," a symbol that

when spoken or wr[itten] [...] physical ob[ject] [...] mes [...] ation be[...] s) agree [...] linked. [...] hand for [...] ts of the [...] erent forms. [...] ting and leave-taking [...] e different in different cu[ltures] [...] tures used to communicate nu[mbers] [...] niversal. Malawians use their thumb[s to indic]ate one, four fingers paired to indicate f[our, a fi]st to indicate five, and two shakes of a fist to indicate one hundred, a system very different from that used by most Americans (Selin, 2002). Though gestures are easily understood within a society of persons who share their meaning, they are often the basis for misunderstandings between cultures.

Many of the ordinary features of our everyday lives have important symbolic content. Objects, events, and d[...] h as flags, musical performanc[es] [...] eligious icons, ba[d]ges, way[...] [...]rades, a[...] [...] pres[...] soci[...] s and [...] ols of all [...] structured sy[...] sentences) with sp[...] [...]gs. Language is the corne[r...] . It is the chief vehicle by which [...] [comm]unicate ideas, information, attitudes, [emot]ions to one another, and it is the prin[cipal] means by which human beings create culture and transmit it from generation to generation.

▲ The Significance of Symbols

We can gain an appreciation for the part that symbols, particularly words, play in our daily lives by recalling the experiences of Helen Keller, who was stricken with a severe illness at the age of

Is Culture Unique to Humans?

In 1960 Jane Goodall sent a message from Zaire to her mentor, anthropologist Louis Leakey, to let him know that she had observed chimpanzees making tools to "fish" for termites. He telegraphed back, "Now we must redefine *tool,* redefine *Man,* or accept chimpanzees as humans" (Goodall, 1990:19).

At that time scientists believed, and teachers taught, that one of the characteristics dividing humans from all other species was the ability to make and use tools. The sight of a chimpanzee trimming a wide blade of grass and using it to extract termites from a termite mound knocked toolmaking off the list of exclusively human behaviors, and since then many more examples of making and using tools have been found in chimpanzees and other species.

Nearly 50 years later, culture may be suffering the same fate. What makes scientists think animals have culture? Researcher Christophe Boesch claims there are three components of culture common to humans and chimpanzees: Culture is learned from group members; culture is a distinctive collective practice; and culture is based on shared meanings between members of the same group (Boesch, 2003:83).

Chimpanzees use tools—evidence of at least 19 different

Chimpanzee tool-using behaviors appear to be specific to specific groups of chimpanzees, learned from individuals, and passed down to the next generation.

21 months that left her deaf and blind. In her autobiography *The Story of My Life* (1904), Keller recounted that in her early years she remained imprisoned in her body, having only nebulous and uncertain links to the outside world. Later, she learned the American Sign Language for the deaf, and as she grasped the significance of symbols, particularly words, she acquired an intelligent understanding of her environment. The association between a word and an experience allowed her to use the symbol in the absence of the experience. By virtue of symbolic expression, "reality" becomes internally coded in a condensed and more easily manipulated mental form. Helen Keller was reluctant to apply the term "idea" or "thought" to her mental processes before she learned how to employ words. Of equal significance, she could share her experiences with other people and they could share their experiences with her. The ability to use symbols, especially language, was the ticket that admitted Helen Keller to social life and hence to full humanness. With language, she was able to enter the world of shared understandings provided by culture.

Human beings live their lives primarily within symbolic environments. Other organisms kinds of tool use has been published—and they have complex grooming and courtship behaviors. These behaviors are specific to specific groups of chimpanzees, and they seem to be learned from individuals and passed down to the next generation. In one of the groups he studied, Boesch observed young chimpanzees learning to crack nuts using hammers (rocks or branches) and anvils (surface roots) (Boesch, 2003). He found that mother chimps stimulate their offspring's attempts by leaving the supplies needed for nut cracking behind while they search for more nuts. They also help their offspring solve technical problems and facilitate their offspring's attempts by providing better hammers and intact nuts.

What about the "shared meanings" component of culture? Some chimpanzees engage in a behavior called "leaf clipping," in which they bite a leaf into pieces without eating any of it. Leaf clipping, it turns out, has a specific meaning—and the meaning is different in different groups of chimps (Boesch, 2003:86):

All males in the Tai forest regularly leaf-clip before drumming. Among Bossou chimpanzees, leaf clipping is performed in the context of playing, as a means to enlist a playmate, while Mahale chimpanzees leaf-clip as a way to court estrous females. Tai chimpanzees have never been observed to leaf-clip in the context of playing nor in courtship. Similarly, Mahale chimpanzees have never been seen to leaf-clip in the context of playing nor when drumming.

Primate researchers are careful to define exactly what they mean by *culture*. Recent work with orangutans specified that a behavioral variant be considered cultural only if "it is customary (shown by most or all relevant individuals) or habitual (shown by at least several relevant individuals) in at least one site but is absent in at least one other ecologically similar site" (van Schaik et al., 2003:102). The researchers found many such behaviors and concluded that great ape cultures probably have existed for at least 14 milli[...]

Studies of primate culture indicate that it is much more complex than the cultures of other species. Likewise, primatologists agree that human cultures are much more complex than those of primates. The use of symbols—language—plays a major role in making human culture more complex, as it introduces a new method for the social transmission of traditions (Boesch, 2003).

Culture has been studied by sociologists and anthropologists for years; now it is of interest to animal behaviorists and evolutionary biologists as well (Perry and Manson, 2003; Krützen et al., 2005). How genes and culture coevolved, and to what extent our common ancestors had culture, will be topics of research for years to come.

Questions for Discussion

1. What do chimpanzee and orangutan cultures have in common with human culture? Give examples of specific behaviors.

2. How do h[...] th[...]

communicate in a variety of generally programmed ways, including the use of gestures, touch, chemical signals, and sounds, but humans stand apart from other species in their use of language. Although great apes can learn sign language, their facility with it is not equivalent to human language use. In fact, the average human fairly effortlessly learns 60,000 words by the time he or she graduates from high school, whereas chimpanzees, given persistent training, can learn only several hundred hand signs (Hauser, Chomsky, and Fitch, 2002). Research on culture in orangutans has shown that, while human[...] culture, o[...] ously symb[...] k et al., 2003). Box 2.[...] e findings on culture in non[...]

▲ **The Linguistic [...] y Hypothesis**

The languages found am[...] the world's people are quite diverse. Arabs have some 6,000 words that are connected in some way with the camel, involving camels' colors, camels' breeds, camels for different purposes, states of camel pregnancy, and camel behavior. Inuits (Eskimos) make

[handwritten note]: only humans have unambiguously symbolic elements (van schaik et al)

49

minute distinctions among different kinds of snow. And Americans have a vast number of words pertaining to automobiles and accessories.

According to the *linguistic relativity hypothesis* (also known as the *Whorfian hypothesis*), proposed by Edward Sapir (1949) and his student Benjamin L. Whorf (1956), people conceptualize the world differently depending on the nature of the concepts available in their language. Language serves as a screen, admitting some things while filtering out others. For example, people living in the Florida Keys, with only a single word for snow, actually fail to distinguish the many types of snow identified by the many Inuit words. Experience as it is perceived through one set of linguistically patterned sensory screens is quite different from experience perceived through another set (Hall, 1966).

The linguistic relativity hypothesis has been somewhat controversial in social science, and some of its major claims have been challenged (Martin, 1983). Most sociologists would not agree that language determines thought. Regardless of their culture, people can make the same distinctions made by Arabs with regard to camels, Inuits with regard to snow, and Americans with regard to automobiles. Clearly, however, language has a powerful influence on thought by helping or hindering certain kinds of thought. For example, the use of terms such as "broad," "babe," and "chick" to refer to women can promote stereotypical thinking.

▲ Expressive Symbolism and the Production of Culture

Expressive symbolism is an important vehicle for communicating the norms, values, and beliefs of a society. Both elite culture and popular culture, including art, music, and literature, are carriers of expressive symbolism. So are public events, displays, fashion, advertisements, and the public presentations produced by the mass media, religion, sports, science, and other institutions. As sociologist Richard Peterson (1979) has pointed out, expressive symbolism is intimately connected to society in several important ways.

First, expressive symbolism is a reflection of society. We can understand much about how a society is organized by examining its culture. The alienated and powerless position of urban youth, for example, is evident in the antiestablishment graffiti they produce (Lachman, 1988). Likewise, patterns of change in country music lyrics from the 1930s to the 1990s—from expressing the problems of the rural lower class to bewailing the angst of the suburban middle class—mirrored the change in the situation of southerners in the United States (McLaurin, 1992).

Second, expressive symbolism carries a code that enables people to recreate society from one day—and from one generation—to the next. Through experiencing the expressive symbolism of television, literature, popular and classical music, fashion, parades, religious services, demonstrations, and so on, people internalize the values, norms, and beliefs that establish basic goals and guide action. By choosing to consume certain cultural products and not others, people publicly signal their social status (Erickson, 1996; Bryson, 1996). In addition, as some critical and feminist theorists argue, expressive symbolism can be designed to enhance the power positions of certain groups and categories of people at the expense of others. This can be seen in the overt propaganda and patriotic films produced during wartime and the advertising, films, music videos, and pornographic materials that encourage the sexual exploitation of women.

Finally, the form and content of culture is heavily affected by economic, organizational, legal, and technological factors involved with its production; in short, social structure affects culture (Peterson and Anand, 2004). Prior to 1940, for example, very little in American popular music was a direct reflection of either

African-American culture or the culture of rural southerners. After the early 1940s, when the monopoly in music licensing was broken and a second major organization began to license music for radio airplay, there was a major explosion in jazz, rhythm and blues, and what we now know as country music (Ryan, 1985). American culture had not changed so much as there had been a change in the constraints affecting what kinds of culture were produced for mass sale (Peterson, 1982).

Cultural Unity and Diversity

The great merit of culture is that it permits us to circumvent the slow pace of genetic evolution. Behavior patterns that are wired into organisms by their genes do not allow rapid adaptation to changing conditions. In contrast, cultural change can be rapid. Early human cultural evolution probably affected the evolution of the human brain, creating a greater capacity in humans for culture, leading to more cultural evolution, and so on. Indeed, some social scientists contend that cultural evolution is a far more important source of behavioral change for human beings than is biological evolution (Lewontin, Rose, and Kamin, 1984; Wilson, 1988). When cultures change and evolve, cultural unity and cultural diversity are affected, a matter to which we now turn our attention. In this section we will define and discuss cultural universals, cultural integration, ethnocentrism, cultural relativism, and subcultures and countercultures.

Cultural Universals

Although culture provides guideposts for daily living—a blueprint or map for life's activities—these guideposts often differ from one society to another. The "oughts" and "musts" of some societies are the "ought nots" and "must nots" of

How does this funeral scene differ from a typical funeral in the United States? The funeral rite is a cultural universal, but its specific form is dictated by the culture in which it occurs.

other societies; the "good" and "desirable" among this people are the "bad" and "undesirable" among that people. Should this fact of cultural variation lead to the conclusion that cultures are different in all respects and hence not comparable? Or to put the question another way, can we realistically speak of **cultural universals,** the patterned and recurrent aspects of life that appear in all known societies?

There are indeed such common denominators or cultural constants, because all people confront many of the same problems. They must secure a livelihood, socialize children, handle grief, and deal with deviants. Culture represents an accumulation of solutions to the problems posed by human biology and the generalities of the human situation.

George Peter Murdock and his a⸻tes at Yale University (1950) develop⸻ tion of cultur⸻nents t⸻ applicatio⸻ gories o⸻ tures,⸻ ments,⸻ social ⸻ death, re⸻ hood. The⸻ additional topi⸻ to always include expr⸻s for disposing of the corpse,⸻ine the relations of the dead with⸻niversal components do not include th⸻ic details of actual behavior. The univer⸻ relate to broad, overall categories and not to the content of culture. For example, although marriage is found in all cultures, some societies favor monogamy (one spouse), others polyandry (plural husbands), and still others polygyny (plural wives).

[handwritten note: Broad categories → universal. Do not include specific details of actual behavior]

Cultural Integration

The items that form a culture tend to constitute a consistent and integrated whole. For example, societies that value universal education also usually have norms and laws prescribing that children should go to school, organize education into a collective activity, and create expressive symbolism that communicates the values of education, such as degrees, diplomas, graduation ceremonies, and class rings. However, perfect integration is never achieved. The various elements of culture and society are always changing, usually at different rates. This means that there are always inconsistencies, but, as William Graham Sumner (1906:56) observed, the parts are "subject to a strain of consistency with each other." Though human equality and

dignity were important values in American culture from the beginning, for the first 86 years of U.S. history slavery was a legal institution and for another 100 years there were no effective legal guarantees of civil rights for African Americans. This was, as Gunnar Myrdal (1944) pointed out in the title of his landmark study *An American Dilemma,* a contradiction in American culture. The strain of this contradiction was, and is, pushing American society toward a resolution, one that took the form of Supreme Court decisions and civil rights laws in the 1950s and 1960s and continues today in debates about racial equality and affirmative action.

This strain toward consistency means that there are powerful forces linking the various elements of culture. The parts of a culture comprise a closely interwoven fabric, so that the meaning of one part depends on its connections to other parts.

Ethnocentrism

Once we acquire the cultural ways peculiar to our own society, they become so deeply ingrained that they seem second nature to us. Additionally, we have difficulty conceiving of alternative ways of life. Just as a fish never "notices" water unless it is out of it, so we tend never to notice our own culture until we are in someone else's. We judge the behavior of other groups by the standards of our own culture, a phenomenon sociologists call **ethnocentrism.** Sumner (1906:13) described this point of view as one "in which one's own group is the center of everything, and all others are scaled and rated with reference to it." A Peace Corps volunteer living in Blantyre, Malawi, several decades ago found a perfect example: The post office had two letter slots, one labeled "Blantyre" and the other labeled "Elsewhere" (Selin, 2002).

All groups are ethnocentric: families, tribes, nations, cliques, colleges, fraternities, businesses, churches, and political parties. The notion that one belongs to the "best people" can be functional for groups because it provides a kind of social glue cementing people together. But it can also be dysfunctional when it generates intergroup conflict. Combined with competition for scarce resources and a power imbalance between groups, ethnocentrism is particularly destructive (Noel, 1968). It plays a part in group conflicts ranging from small skirmishes to world wars. It can also be of more immediate and practical significance. Some analysts blame our surprise at the September 11 attacks partly on ethnocentrism. Although the threat to civilians was not secret, it seemed "too outlandish to be taken seriously. . . . In the world of intelligence, this is known as mirror-imaging: the projection of American values and behavior onto America's enemies and rivals" (Goldberg, 2003).

Cultural Relativism

Ethnocentrism can get in the way of the scientific study of culture. We cannot grasp the behavior of other peoples if we interpret it in the context of our values, beliefs, and motives. Rather, we must examine their behavior in the light of their values, beliefs, and motives. This approach, termed **cultural relativism,** views the behavior of a people from the perspective of their own culture. In Box 2.2 we see how the calendar systems of various cultures can be understood only in the context of each culture. In sharp contrast to ethnocentrism, cultural relativism employs the kind of value-free or neutral approach advocated by Max Weber (see Chapter 1). p. 14

A perspective characterized by cultural relativism does not ask whether a particular trait is moral or immoral, but what part it plays in the life of a people. For example, early anthropological research found that among some Inuit peoples, the elderly infirm are left behind to perish in the cold. Instead of condemning the practice, social scientists examined the behavior in the context of Inuit culture, where it was defined as

a humane measure (Murdock, 1934). The Inuits believe that individuals experience in the next world a standard of health similar to that which they enjoyed in the period preceding death. Consequently, the Inuits see the practice as minimizing the disabilities and infirmities their loved ones would encounter in the hereafter. Social scientists have pointed out that the practice can be adaptive for a people whose subsistence is precarious and who must strictly limit their dependent population. For Americans who are appalled at the traditional Inuit custom, it is worth noting that many Japanese find quite abhorrent our practice of placing our elderly infirm in nursing homes rather than caring for them at home.

Subcultures and Countercultures

Cultural diversity may also be found within a society. In many modern nations, the members of some groups participate in the main culture of the society while simultaneously sharing with one another a number of unique values, norms, traditions, and lifestyles. These distinctive cultural patterns are termed a **subculture.** Subcultures abound in American life and find expression in various religious, racial, ethnic, occupational, and age groups.

The Old Order Amish are a case in point. The Amish are a religious sect that originated in Germany and Switzerland during the 16th-century conflicts of the Reformation. Because of religious persecution, many Amish migrated to Pennsylvania in the early 1700s. Most Amish families live on farms, although a minority work in skilled crafts like carpentry, furniture making, and blacksmithing. They believe in a literal interpretation of the Bible and turn their backs on modern standards of dress, "progressive" morality, "worldly" amusement, automobiles, and higher education. Above all, the Amish value hard physical work and believe that those who

Is Today Tuesday? That Depends on Culture

Tuesday is Tuesday is Tuesday, right? Or, in some countries, Mardi, or Dienstag, or Martes? Actually, no. In some parts of our world, Tuesday is not Tuesday. In fact, in some parts of our world, people do not use a seven-day week, or a 12-month year, or anything even close to our naming system for markers of time.

As mathematician Marcia Ascher explains in her book *Mathematics Elsewhere,* "[Calendars] are cultural products often involving religion and/or politics combined with observations of the physical universe" (Ascher, 2002:39). Calendars are very diverse, primarily because "one of the main functions [of calendars] is to set the schedule of the culture and, thereby, coordinate the activities of individuals in the culture" (Ascher, 2002:39). Cultural differences, then, are linked to diversity in ways of marking time. Let's look at just one example.

In the Trobriand Islands, where gardening is a major focus of people's lives, the calendar is based on lunar cycles. The important days, when the moon provides enough light for outdoor activities to take place at night, have specific names, while the days with dark nights are unnamed. Each lunar cycle has 29 or 30 days, and each Trobriand year has 12 or 13 months, but the names and number of months vary within a year—and even in different locations within the Trobriands. How can that be? The Trobriands have four different districts, in each of which a different major crop is grown, and each crop has its own particular harvest time. Ascher explains how this affects the Trobriand calendar (2002:43):

The month of Kuluwasasa . . . is *always* the harvest time, and so it occurs first on the outlying island of Kitava, next on the southern end of the main island of Kiriwina, then on the northern end of Kiriwina, and finally on the island of Vakuta.

In other words, wherever and whenever a major crop is being harvested, it is Kuluwasasa.

Because the people of the Trobriands are gardeners, the sun-related seasons are extremely important. During the earth's trip around the sun, there are 12.368 lunar cycles, meaning that the number of lunar cycles in a year has to shift from 12 to 13 every few years to resynchronize the calendar. Rather than rely on record keeping, mathematical calculations, or astronomical knowledge, Ascher explains, the Trobrianders use the internal clock of a marine worm. This worm spawns only once a year, at the time of the full moon. If the worm does not appear in the sea at the expected time in the Trobriand calendar, they repeat the month they are in to recalibrate the calendar, and that Trobriand year will have 13 months.

The Trobriand Islanders' calendar system highlights the importance of the principle of *cultural relativism:* From a sociological point of view, we should evaluate a cultural trait from the perspective of the culture in which it occurs. With regards to organizing time, we should consider two points. First, the way calendars are constructed allows people to function efficiently in their own societies. We would be lost if we had to get to a job interview during the "unripe moon" in the month of Milamala, which would occur at different times on different islands. Similarly, a Trobriand Islander would find it meaningless to be instructed to begin planting on the first Tuesday of October. Second, the methods for constructing calendars are linked to other elements of culture, an example of *cultural integration.* In the Trobriand Islands, getting soil prepared, seeds planted, fencing constructed, and harvesting done are key to the calendar, as are religious rites and festivals that must be accounted for in the organization of time.

Ascher found that in some cultures, calendars focus on organizing ritual and agricultural activities, such as that used in the Trobriands, while others are more concerned with "structuring the flow of historical events" (2002:52) or with incorporating environmental, social structure, or psychological components. Each focus is connected with specific elements of culture.

Because of our *ethnocentrism,* much of what we do every day we assume to be universal human activity. In fact, most of what we do each day is culturally determined—including how we think about what day, what month, and what time of the year it is.

Questions for Discussion

1. How does the culture of the Trobiand Islanders affect their way of creating a calendar?

2. What is another example of a calendar system that is not the same as that used by the majority of people in the United States? With what culture is it associated?

Through clever use of media, advertisers draw upon youth subcultural processes, including identity formation, in order to sell products. This affects youth behavior, but it also affects the content of youth subculture itself.

do not find joy in work are somehow abnormal. Far from being ashamed of their nonconformity to "worldly standards," the Amish pride themselves on being a "peculiar people" who separate themselves from the world (Hostetler, 1980).

Youth culture is another example of a subculture. Western nations have postponed the entrance of their adolescents into adulthood for economic and educational reasons, segregating them in schools and colleges and effectively relieving them from competing with adults for wealth, power, and status in society's mainstream until they are 21 or older. This has created conditions favorable to the development of a unique culture among youth. Instead of competing with adults along the value dimensions of mainstream culture, adolescents compete with each other along dimensions of youth culture.

Youth culture patterns find expression in fads having to do with popular music, entertainment idols, dance steps, personal adornment and hairstyles, and distinctive jargons. Such patterns change over time, keeping youth always distinctive from generations that have come before. FBI agents posing online as teenage girls to catch pedophiles have discovered that to be effective, they need knowledge of youth culture. Suspects question chatters about trends and pop culture to determine whether they're talking to a teenage girl or a law enforcement officer. For help, the agency turned to eighth-grade girls, three of whom taught a series of classes for the FBI. The classes included tips on instant messaging, celebrity gossip, clothing trends, and popular magazines. Among the lessons: "Never begin a chat with 'hello'; never use proper grammar in instant messages; and 'pos' stands for 'parent over shoulder' " (Ly, 2003). Distinctive language patterns exist in many subcultures. Table 2.1 provides examples of some of the different patterns of slang used in different activity subcultures.

Large organizations and corporations such as Microsoft, General Motors, and Exxon also have distinctive subcultures that make working in one organization a very different experience from working in another, even when both are involved in the same activities. If you have transferred from one university to another, you have probably experienced this; the subculture

Table 2.1	Subcultural Behavior: A Sampler of Slang from Work and Sports
To the kitchen staff in a restaurant, the following terms have very specific meanings:	To kayakers, the following terms have very specific meanings:
Pants are down: Oven door is open.	**Racerhead:** What a nonracing boater calls a slalom racer.
Behind!: I'm behind you (with something hot, sharp, or precarious)—don't move!	**Touron:** What a racer might call a nonracing boater.
Plate carrier: Waiter or waitress.	**Stuffed:** To get hammered by a rapid.
Family meal: Meal for all restaurant employees, before or after serving hours.	**Boof:** A jump from the lip of a waterfall so that the boat lands flat, making a "boof!" sound.
Two-top: A party of two persons (also three-top, four-top, etc.).	**Stick:** Paddle.
Big-top: Large party.	**Quiver:** Bunch of paddles.
Work pantry (a verb)**:** Work to prepare salads and cold appetizers.	**Skirt:** The neoprene rubber or coated nylon that seals the cockpit and keeps water out of the boat.
In the weeds: Behind schedule.	**Eddy hop:** A way to attain or to descend a river using eddies as refuges.
Misfire (a noun)**:** An extra order prepared in error.	**Hair boating:** Running really hard, maybe dangerous, water.
Waiter bait: Misfires or other extra food placed in the order window for the plate carriers to snack on.	**Wavewheel:** Like a cartwheel on water.

Source: Interviews conducted in 2001 by the authors with U.S. Olympic kayak team member Lecky Haller and Syracuse, New York, restaurant worker Dave Hughes.

of one college is not the same as that of another. Working at Apple is not the same as working at IBM.

At times the norms, values, and lifestyles of a subculture are substantially at odds with those of the larger society and constitute a **counterculture.** A counterculture rejects many of the behavioral standards and guideposts that hold in the dominant culture. Delinquent gangs, Satanic cults, and the militia movement are illustrations of counterculture groups.

In many societies, countercultures involve primarily adolescents and young adults (Spates, 1983). In the late 1960s and early 1970s, the dominant youth subculture in the United States included the hippie movement and the anti–Vietnam War movement. It was a counterculture that emphasized political beliefs, sexual standards, and attitudes about drug use that challenged mainstream U.S. culture. In recent years, the Internet has helped to facilitate smaller pockets of countercultural activity within different segments of the population, including right-wing survivalists, skinheads, militia activists, radical environmentalists, and opponents of free trade and globalization. The Internet makes it easier for people with specific grievances to communicate better, organize more effectively, and recruit others to their causes (*The Economist,* 2000a).

their exits. Yet even though the actual people that comprise a college change over time, the college endures.

Sociologists view social structure as a social fact of the sort described by Émile Durkheim (see Chapter 1). We experience a social ← p. 13 fact as external to ourselves—as an independent reality that forms a part of our objective environment. Consequently, social structures constrain our behavior and channel our actions in certain directions. When you entered college for the first time, you felt somewhat awkward because you did not yet fit into your college's way of doing things. The college's way is social structure, the shape or form that a particular organization has taken through the years as students, professors, and administrators have interacted on a regular basis.

As sociologist William H. Sewell, Jr. (1992:27), observed: "Structure is dynamic, not static; it is the continually evolving outcome and matrix of a process of social interaction." Thus, a college is not a fixed entity that, once created, continues to operate perpetually in the same manner. All social ordering must be continually created and re-created through the interweaving and stabilizing of social relationships. For this reason, organized social life is always undergoing modification and change. In the next sections, we will discuss the concepts that help us to understand social structure and to describe our social environment: statuses, roles, groups, institutions, and societies.

Statuses

In our daily conversations, we use the word *status* to refer to a person's ranking as determined by wealth, influence, and prestige. However, sociologists employ status somewhat differently: **Status** means a position within a group or society. By means of statuses we locate one another in various social structures. Mother, mayor, management trainer, friend, supervisor, female, elementary school principal, child, Cuban

lture has ... d society ... e customs. Culture ... allows people to interp... heir actions; society consists o... of relationships that people enter ... hey go about their daily activities. For the ... st part, people do not interact in a haphazard or random manner. Rather, their relationships are characterized by social ordering. Sociologists apply the term **social structure** to this social ordering—the interweaving of people's interactions and relationships in more or less recurrent and stable patterns. It finds expression in a matrix of social positions and the distribution of people in them.

Social structure provides an organized and focused quality to our group experiences, and it allows us to achieve our collective purposes. By virtue of social structure, we link certain experiences, terming them, for example, "the family," "the church," "the neighborhood," and "General Motors." A clique, a family, a rock band, an army, a business organization, a religious group, and a nation are social structures. Social structure consists of the recurrent and orderly relationships that prevail among the members of a group or society. It gives us the feeling that life is characterized by organization and stability.

Consider the social structure of your college. Each term you enter new classes, yet you have little difficulty attuning yourself to unfamiliar classmates and professors. Courses in sociology, calculus, American history, English composition, and physical education are offered year after year. A new class enters college each fall, and another class graduates each spring. Football games are scheduled for Saturday afternoons in the autumn, and basketball games for evenings during the winter months. New students, professors, coaches, players, and deans pass through the system and in due course make

American, shopper, professor, convict, and fortune teller are all statuses.

As Theodore Newcomb observed in his classic social psychology textbook (1950), a status is like a ready-made suit of clothes. Within certain limits, the prospective buyer can choose regarding matters of style and fabric. Our choice is limited to a size that will fit, as well as by our pocketbooks. Having made our choice within these limits, we can have certain alterations made. But apart from minor modifications, we tend to be limited to what retailers already have on their racks. Statuses, too, come ready-made, and the range of choice among them is limited. Societies commonly limit competition for statuses with reference to gender, age, and social affiliations. For instance, realistically, not every American can be elected president. Women, African Americans, and members of the lower class suffer severe handicaps from the outset. This observation brings us to a consideration of ascribed and achieved statuses.

▲ Ascribed and Achieved Statuses

Some statuses are assigned to us by our group or society and termed **ascribed statuses.** Age and gender are common ascribed statuses. For example, age is assigned to us according to the passage of time. Besides staying alive, there is nothing one can do to change one's age. Race, ethnicity, and family background are also common bases for assigning statuses to individuals.

We secure other statuses on the basis of individual choice and competition. We call these **achieved statuses.** All societies recognize some kinds of individual accomplishment and failure, which results in the allocation of some statuses on the basis of individual achievement. Quarterback, choir director, physician, ballet dancer, college student, pastor, nurse practitioner, pickpocket, prostitute, president of Exxon, hair stylist, and teacher are illustrations of achieved statuses.

▲ Master Statuses

Some of our statuses overshadow our other statuses both in our own minds and in those of other people. A **master status** is a key or core status that carries primary weight in a person's interactions and relationships with others. For children, age is a master status; similarly, gender is a master status in most societies. Additionally, race and occupation are particularly critical statuses in American life. Master statuses tend to lay the framework within which our goals are formulated and our training is carried out (Adler and Adler, 1989).

▲ Race, Class, and Gender

For many sociologists, categories of race, class, and gender are more than master statuses; they are basic categories for social analysis (Andersen and Collins, 2004; Richardson, Taylor, and Whittier, 1997). From this perspective, race, class, and gender are forms of inequality that profoundly affect human experience and operate as interlocking systems of privilege and oppression (Collins, 2000; Browne and Misra, 2003). One's gender combines with one's class position and one's race to produce a life experience that is substantively different from the life experienced at a different combination of these statuses. Gender inequality may disadvantage women, but the experience of this depends on whether one is, for example, Asian, black, or white; and wealthy, middle class, or poor (e.g., Beisel and Kay, 2004).

Roles

A status carries with it a set of culturally defined rights and duties, what sociologists term a **role.** These expectations define the behavior people view as appropriate and inappropriate for the occupant of a status. Quite simply, the difference between a status and a role is that we occupy a status and play a role.

Sociologists have taken the notion of role from the theater. Actors perform their roles in accordance with a script (analogous to culture), what the other actors say and do, and the

"O.K., you be the doctor, and I'll be the Secretary of Health and Human Services."

© The New Yorker Collection, 1993. Bernard Schoenbaum from cartoonbank .com. All rights reserved.

reactions of the audience. But the theater analogy has its weaknesses. Unlike actors, we are seldom conscious of "acting" according to a script as we go about our daily activities. And in life we must do a good deal of improvising, continually testing and changing our actions in accordance with the behavior of other people.

Roles allow us to formulate our behavior mentally so that we can shape our actions in appropriate ways. They permit us to assume that in some respects we can ignore personal differences and say that people are interchangeable. For example, every American knows the difference between a physician and a carpenter. Hospitalized for emergency surgery, we probably won't ask many questions about who is handling the emergency, as long as it is a physician and not a carpenter.

▲ Role Performance

In real life a gap often exists between what people should do and what they actually do. A role is the *expected* behavior we associate with a status. **Role performance** is the *actual* behavior of the person who occupies a status. People vary in how they implement the rights and duties associated with their roles. You frequently take differences in role performance into account when you select one professor over another for a given course. One professor may have a reputation for coming late to class, lecturing in an informal manner, and assigning difficult term papers. Another professor may be a distinguished authority in the field, monitor class attendance, and assign take-home examinations. Regardless of which professor you select, you will still occupy the status of student and play its associated role. However, you will have to modify your behavior somewhat depending upon your selection.

▲ Role Set

A single status may have multiple roles attached to it, constituting a **role set.** The status of student may involve one role as pupil, one role as peer of other students, one role as loyal supporter of your school's teams, one role as user of the library, and one role as "good citizen" of the college community.

A role does not exist in isolation. Instead, it is a bundle of activities that are meshed with the activities of other people. Indeed, the definition of one role depends upon the existence of another: There can be no professors without students, no wives without husbands, no police officers without criminals, and no psychiatrists without the mentally ill. Every role has at least one reciprocal role attached to it.

Role relationships tie us to one another because the rights of one end of the relationship are the duties of the other. **Duties** are the actions others can legitimately insist that we perform, and **rights** are the actions we can legitimately insist that others perform (Goffman, 1961a). The rights of one role are the duties of the other role. For example, your rights as a student—to receive authoritative material in lectures, to be administered fair exams, and to be graded objectively—are the duties of your professor.

Individuals are linked together in groups through networks of reciprocal roles. Groups consist of intricate complexes of interlocking roles, which their members sustain in the course of interacting with one another. People experience these stable relationships as social structure—a school, a hospital, a family, a gang, an army, and so on.

▲ Role Conflict

Role conflict results when individuals are confronted with conflicting expectations stemming from their simultaneous occupancy of two or more statuses. A football coach whose son is a member of the team may experience role conflict when deciding whether to make his own son or another more talented player the starting quarterback. One way to handle role conflict is to subdivide or compartmentalize one's life and assume only one of the incompatible roles at a time. For example, college students may attempt to segregate their school and home experiences so they do not have to appear before their parents and peers simultaneously.

▲ Role Strain

Role strain occurs when individuals find the expectations of a single role incompatible, so that they have difficulty performing the role. The relationship physicians have with their patients provides an example (Klass, 1987). Doctors are expected to be gentle healers, humanitarians, and self-sacrificing saviors of the sick. They also are expected to be small-business retailers of knowledge that they have obtained at considerable cost and sacrifice. While aggressive bill collecting is consistent with the small-business-retailer aspects of the role, it is inconsistent with that of the gentle healer. Supervisors often confront similar difficulties. They are asked to be both commanding parent figures and reassuring, comforting big brothers or sisters. For the most part there are few well-defined or accepted answers to the dilemmas posed by these contradictory expectations.

Groups

Statuses and roles are building blocks for more comprehensive social structures, such as groups. Sociologists define a **group** as two or more people who are bound together in relatively stable patterns of social interaction and who share a feeling of unity.

As previously pointed out, roles link us within social relationships. When these relationships are sustained across time, four things can happen: First, we come to think of the relationships as encompassed by boundaries, so that people are either inside or outside a group. Second, we attribute an "objective" existence to groups and treat them as if they are real and exact things. Third, we view a group as having a distinct subculture or counterculture—a set of unique norms and values. Fourth, we develop a sense of allegiance to a group that leads us to feel we are a unit with a distinct identity.

Sociologists mean something quite specific when they use the word *group*, and we will discuss this in Chapter 4. Here it is important to distinguish a group from two related entities: *aggregate* and *category*. An **aggregate** is simply a collection of anonymous individuals who are in one place at the same time such as shoppers in a mall or individuals waiting in line for football tickets. Individuals shift in and out of an aggregate rather easily and frequently. Because the people in aggregates interact with one another only transiently and temporarily, patterns of social ordering in them are short-lived. However, this quality should not lead us to dismiss aggregates as inconsequential. They provide the foundation for many forms of collective behavior (see Chapter 13).   ◀— pp. 442–447

A **category** is a collection of people who share a characteristic—such as a status, a physical characteristic, or a behavior pattern—that is deemed to be of social significance. Common categories include the subdivisions of age, gender, race, occupation, and educational attainment, but being tall, living alone, and having indoor plumbing also qualify one for being in a particular category. Categories differ from groups because they are so broad that social relations and group dynamics linking all members may not occur. However, common experiences of persons in categories, particularly those who share a status, may be the basis for social movements or political activity. For example, some women have banded together in the League of Women Voters and the National Organization for Women (NOW) by virtue of an awareness that they are a social category that shares certain problems.

Information regarding categories can have important uses. For example, if we know the proportions of people in each age category in a population, we can make projections that anticipate the demand for various social services, including Social Security and Medicare benefits.

Institutions

Sociologists use the term **institution** for the principal social structures that organize, direct, and execute the essential tasks of living. Each institution is built about a standardized solution to a set of problems. For example, all human societies face the problem of how to protect and nurture children in their early years. This is one of many problems that the institution of the family deals with. All societies face the problem of how to transfer raw materials into products and how to distribute those products to people. This problem is dealt with by the institution called the economy. All societies face the problem of helping people to understand the inexplicable events in their lives; religion is the institution that deals with the death of loved ones, fatal events, and the like.

Admittedly this classification oversimplifies matters. An institution may perform more than one function, and several institutions may contribute to the performance of the same function. Further, there is a wide variety of interconnected institutions that serve diverse human needs and desires, including the institutions of sports, entertainment, organized crime, prostitution, medicine, and journalism.

As sociologists typically define an institution, it encompasses both cultural patterns and social structure. For example, the polity includes political values (such as equality), norms (such as the idea that everyone should vote), and social structural features such as the Supreme Court, Congress, all state and local governments, police departments, and others. Institutions constitute (1) the more or less standardized solutions (cultural patterns) that serve to direct people in meeting the problems of social living, and (2) the relatively stable relationships that characterize people in actually implementing these solutions. Conceived in this way, a cluster of cultural patterns (a set of norms, values, and symbols) establishes the behavior that is expected of us as a certain kind of person (e.g., a student) in relation to certain other kinds of people (e.g., a professor, dean, teaching assistant, departmental secretary, registrar, or bursar). This set of cultural patterns locates us within a network of relationships. The concept of institution, then, implies that we are bound within networks of relationships (groups) in which we interact with one another (play our roles) in terms of certain shared understandings (cultural patterns) that define the behavior expected of us as given kinds of people (statuses).

Societies

Societies represent the most comprehensive and complex type of social structure in today's world. As we noted earlier in the chapter, society refers to a group of people who live within the same territory and share a common culture. By virtue of this common culture, the members of a society typically possess similar values and norms and a common language. Its members perpetuate themselves primarily through reproduction and comprise a more or less self-sufficient social unit. A society can be as small as a tribal community of several dozen people or as large as modern nations with hundreds of millions of people.

Although we often use the term *nation-state* interchangeably with *society,* the two are not necessarily the same. A state is a political entity centering on a government. Among many peoples of the world, the state binds together nationality and tribal groups that in their own right constitute societies. For example, Great Britain is made up of Scots, Welsh, and English. Belgium is composed of Flemings and Walloons. Similarly, many African nation-states contain multiple tribal groups: 250 in Nigeria, 200 in Zaire, and 130 in Tanzania.

Sociologists have classified societies in many ways. One popular approach is based on the principal way in which the members of a society derive their livelihood (Nolan and Lenski, 2005). All peoples must provide for such vital needs as food, clothing, and shelter; the manner in which they do so has vast consequences for other aspects of their lives. Each of these types of societies has different institutions and different numbers of institutions, depending on the complexity of the societies and of the problems to be solved in each.

Hunting and gathering societies represent the earliest form of organized social life. Individuals in groups of about 50 survive by hunting animals and gathering edible foods. Kinship—ties by blood and marriage—is the foundation for most relationships and is the principal institution for hunting and gathering societies. There are no specialized and enduring work groups, governments, or standing armies.

Some 10,000 years ago, human beings learned how to cultivate a number of plants on which they depended for food. The more efficient economies of these *horticultural societies* allow for the production of a social surplus—goods and services over and above those necessary for human survival. This surplus becomes the foundation for social stratification; the specialization of some economic, political, and religious roles; a growth in the importance of warfare; and more complex forms of culture and social structure (Lenski, 1966; Kerbo, 2006). Even so, the upper limit for most horticultural communities is about 3,000 persons.

Five to six thousand years ago the plow heralded an agricultural revolution and the emergence of *agrarian societies* (Childe, 1941), with larger crops, more food, expanding populations, and even more complex forms of social organization. Continuing advances in productive and military technologies contributed to a substantial growth in the power of the state, the size of the territory it controlled, and the emergence of large capital cities. The massive pyramids of

Egypt, the roads and aqueducts of Rome, the great cathedrals of medieval Europe, and the far-flung irrigation systems of the Middle East and China are products of agrarian societies.

About 250 years ago the Industrial Revolution gave birth to *industrial societies* whose productive and economic systems are based on machine technologies. Economic self-sufficiency and local market systems were displaced by complex divisions of labor, exchange relationships, and national and international market systems. The ability to read and write became essential in advanced industrial societies and led to the growth of educational institutions. Many activities that were once the responsibility of families were relinquished to other institutions. Populations grew and people increasingly congregated in cities. Large-scale bureaucracies and formal organizations came to predominate in both the private and public spheres, finding expression in big business, big unions, big universities, big hospitals, and big government.

As we discuss in more detail in Chapter 13, some social analysts contend that pp. 436–440

the United States is currently moving in the direction of a *postindustrial society*. This is presumably a new historical period, often referred to by journalists as the "information age" or "service society." In a postindustrial society increasing numbers of workers find employment in the provision of services rather than the extraction of raw materials and the manufacture of goods. Simultaneously, new techniques permit the automation of many processes in the workplace with the use of computers and complex feedback regulation devices. All these changes are accompanied by the knowledge explosion based on the creating, processing, and distribution of information (Lyman and Varian, 2000), and where they will lead us is hard to predict because the changes are so rapid. For example, in 1990 less than half a million computers in the United States had access to the Internet. This number grew to 30 million by 1998 (Brown and Flavin, 1999), and by 2003, 70 million U.S. households had computers with Internet connections (Day, Janus, and Davis, 2005).

The Chapter in Brief: *Culture and Social Structure*

Components of Culture

Culture provides individuals with a set of common understandings that they employ in fashioning their actions, and makes society possible by providing a common framework of meaning.

❚ *Norms* **Norms** are social rules that specify appropriate and inappropriate behavior in given situations. They afford a

means by which we orient ourselves to other people. **Folkways, mores,** and **laws** are types of norms.

❚ *Values* **Values** are broad ideas regarding what is desirable, correct, and good that most members of a society share. Values are so general and abstract that they do not explicitly specify which behaviors are acceptable and which are not.

■ *Symbols and Language*   **Symbols** are acts or objects that have come to be socially accepted as standing for something else. Symbols assume many different forms, but **language** is the most important of these. Language is the chief vehicle by which people communicate ideas, information, attitudes, and emotions, and it serves as the principal means by which human beings create culture and transmit it from generation to generation.

Cultural Unity and Diversity

■ *Cultural Universals*   **Cultural universals** are patterned and recurrent aspects of life that appear in all known societies. All people confront many of the same problems; culture represents an accumulation of solutions to the problems posed by human biology and the human situation.

■ *Cultural Integration*   The items that form a culture tend to constitute a consistent and integrated whole. For example, societies that value universal education also usually have norms and laws about schools, organize education into a collective activity, and create symbols and share meanings about the value of education and educational organizations.

■ *Ethnocentrism*   The cultural ways of our own society become so deeply ingrained that we have difficulty conceiving of alternative ways of life. We judge the behavior of other groups by the standards of our own culture, a phenomenon sociologists term **ethnocentrism.**

■ *Cultural Relativism*   In studying other cultures, we must examine behavior in the light of the values, beliefs, and motives of each culture, an approach termed **cultural relativism.**

■ *Subcultures and Countercultures*   Cultural diversity can be found within a society in the form of **subcultures.** When the norms, values, and lifestyles of a subculture are at odds with those of the larger society, it is a **counterculture.**

Social Structure

People's relationships are characterized by social ordering. Sociologists apply the term *social structure* to this social ordering—the interweaving of people's interactions and relationships in recurrent and stable patterns.

■ *Statuses*   **Status** represents a position within a group or society. It is by means of statuses that we locate one another in various social structures. Some are assigned to us—**ascribed statuses;** others we secure on the basis of individual choice and competition—**achieved statuses.**

■ *Roles*   A status carries with it a set of culturally defined **rights** and **duties,** what sociologists term a **role.** A role is the expected behavior we associate with a status. **Role performance** is the actual behavior of the person who occupies a status. **Role conflict** arises when individuals are confronted with conflicting expectations stemming from their occupancy of two or more statuses. **Role strain** arises when individuals find the expectations of a single role incompatible.

■ *Groups*   Statuses and roles are building blocks for more comprehensive social structures, including **groups** of two or more people. Roles link us within social relationships. When these relationships are sustained across time, we frequently attribute group properties to them. Sociologists distinguish groups from **aggregates** and **categories.**

■ *Institutions*   **Institutions** are the principal social structures used to organize, direct, and execute the essential tasks of social living. Each institution is built around a standardized solution to a set of problems and encompasses the notions of both cultural patterns and social structure.

Societies   **Societies** represent the most comprehensive and complex type of social structure in today's world. By virtue of their common culture, the members of a society typically possess similar values and norms and a common language. One particular approach for classifying societies is based on the way people derive their livelihood: hunting and gathering societies, horticultural societies, agrarian societies, industrial societies, and postindustrial societies. Another approach rests on the distinction between traditional and modern types.

Glossary

achieved status   A status that individuals secure on the basis of choice and competition.

aggregate   A collection of anonymous individuals who are in one place at the same time.

ascribed status   A status assigned to an individual by a group or society.

category   A collection of people who share a characteristic that is deemed to be of social significance.

counterculture   A subculture whose norms and values are substantially at odds with those of the larger society.

cultural relativism   A value-free or neutral approach that views the behavior of a people from the perspective of their own culture.

cultural universals Patterned and recurrent aspects of life that appear in all known societies.

culture   The social heritage of a people; those learned patterns for thinking, feeling, and acting that are transmitted from one generation to the next, including the embodiment of these patterns in material items.

duties   The actions that others can legitimately insist that we perform.

ethnocentrism   The tendency to judge the behavior of other groups by the standards of one's own culture.

folkways   Norms people do not deem to be of great importance and to which they exact less stringent conformity.

group   Two or more people who share a feeling of unity and who are bound together in relatively stable patterns of social interaction.

institutions   The principal instruments whereby the essential tasks of living are organized, directed, and executed.

language   A socially structured system of sound patterns (words and sentences) with specific and arbitrary meanings.

laws   Rules that are enforced by a special political organization composed of individuals who enjoy the right to use force.

master status   A key or core status that carries primary weight in a person's interactions and relationships with others.

mores   Norms to which people attach a good deal of

importance and exact strict conformity.

norms   Social rules that specify appropriate and inappropriate behavior in given situations.

rights   Actions that we can legitimately insist that others perform.

role   A set of expectations (rights and duties) that define the behavior people view as appropriate and inappropriate for the occupant of a status.

role conflict   The situation in which individuals are confronted with conflicting expectations stemming from their simultaneous occupancy of two or more statuses.

role performance   The actual behavior of the person who occupies a status.

role set   The multiple roles associated with a single status.

role strain   The situation in which individuals find the expectations of a single role incompatible, so that they have difficulty performing the role.

social structure   The interweaving of people's interactions and relationships in more or less recurrent and stable patterns.

society   A group of people who live within the same territory and share a common culture.

status   A position within a group or society; a location in a social structure.

subculture   A group whose members participate in the main culture of a society while simultaneously sharing a number of unique values, norms, traditions, and lifestyles.

symbols   Acts or objects that have come to be socially accepted as standing for something else.

values   Broad ideas regarding what is desirable, correct, and good that most members of a society share.

Review Questions

1. What is the difference between norms and values, and what part does each play in society?

2. How do symbols, and, more particularly, language, shape the way we see our world?

3. Name six cultural universals.

4. What is cultural integration?

5. Define ethnocentrism and describe at least one phenomenon in which it plays a part.

6. What is a subculture? Describe the characteristics of a specific subculture.

7. How do sociologists define status? What is the difference between ascribed and achieved statuses?

8. Give one example of role conflict.

9. Define group, institution, and society.

Internet Connection

 www.mhhe.com/hughes8

Use an Internet search engine such as Yahoo or Google. In the search window, type the word *slang* and then click on the search button. When the next screen appears, explore two or more of the slang sites that appear and write a short report on subcultural slang. What subcultural groups use the slang vocabularies you have uncovered? What are some examples of slang terms? Speculate on some of the reasons that these groups use special vocabularies to communicate among themselves.

Chapter 3

SOCIALIZATION

Foundations for Socialization

Nature and Nurture
Theories of Socialization
Agents of Socialization
Social Communication
Definition of the Situation

The Self and Socialization

Charles Horton Cooley: The Looking-Glass Self
George Herbert Mead: The Generalized Other
Erving Goffman: Impression Management

Socialization across the Life Course

Childhood
Adolescence
Young Adulthood
Middle Adulthood
Later Adulthood
Death

Box 3.1 *Doing Social Research: Does High School Identity Affect Your Adult Life?*
Box 3.2 *Sociology Around the World: What Makes You an Adult?*

She came from a low, sand-coloured house on Golden West Avenue, Temple City. . . . *The house was just like every other on that street—a strip of lawn, the suburban trees—but she had been left in there, day after day, year after year, for nearly twelve years, . . . tied to a potty chair, sewn into a harness to attach her to the seat, only able to move her hands and feet, naked. All day, every day, she was left like that (Newton, 2002:209).*

At age 13, this abused and socially isolated child was discovered by workers in a family aid center. She was the size of an 8-year-old, malnourished, and incontinent. The years spent tied in a sitting position left her physically deformed: "Stooped and frail, her gait pigeon-toed, her body was bent at the waist, her shoulders hunched forward, her hands held up before her like a rabbit" (Newton, 2002:214). Her behavior was equally shocking: "She spat continually, wiping the spit and mucus on to herself. . . . Her eating habits were revolting. . . . She took people's things willfully, pulling on their clothes, invading their space. She would go up to them, getting very close, making eye contact and pointing at the thing of theirs that she wanted, demanding possession. . . . Most difficult of all, she masturbated continually" (Newton, 2002:215).

This child, named Genie by those who worked to rehabilitate her, had essentially no language. On attainment and maturity tests she scored in the range of a 1-year-old. She could understand no more than a few words. Specialists designed a program to rehabilitate and educate her, and her vocabulary increased dramatically, but her ability to form sentences and communicate normally never caught up to her age. Her speech remained slow, awkward, and unclear. Born in 1957, Genie is still alive today, living in an adult care home.

Genie's case is not unique. In the 1940s two girls named Anna and Isabelle were born to single mothers who kept them hidden in secluded rooms, giving them just enough care to be kept alive. When local authorities discovered them, they were about 6 years old. They were extremely retarded and displayed few human capabilities or responses. Sociologist Kingsley Davis reported on these two cases in a classic 1949 study.

How much of your behavior can you trace to your upbringing? How different do you think you would be if you had had minimum contact with other human beings during your childhood? The cases of Genie, Anna, and Isabelle testify that much of the behavior we regard as somehow given in the human species does not occur unless it is put there through communicative and social contact with others. For example, one hypothesis psychologists have advanced to explain Genie's language deficiencies is that childhood is the critical period in the development of language ability and that problems like Genie's cannot be overcome once a child enters puberty.

In comparison with other species we enter the world as amazingly "unfinished" creatures. We are not born as social beings, able to participate in society, but become so only in the course of **socialization**—a process of social interaction by which people acquire the knowledge, attitudes, values, and behaviors essential for effective participation in society. In short, socialization is the process of becoming a social being, a process that continues throughout one's life. The cases of children reared under conditions of extreme isolation illustrate the importance of socialization.

In Chapter 2 we focused our attention on culture. Were it not for socialization, the renewal of culture could not occur from one generation to the next. We humans are uniquely dependent upon a social heritage—the rich store of adaptations and innovations that countless generations of ancestors have developed over thousands of years. Through culture, each new generation can move on from the achievements of the preceding one. Without socialization, society could not perpetuate itself beyond a single generation. Individuals would lack those common understandings necessary to align their actions and to bind their separated lives into a larger whole. Both the individual and society are mutually dependent on socialization. It blends the sentiments and ideas of culture to the capacities and needs of the organism (Davis, 1949:195).

In this chapter we will examine the process of socialization. We will consider its foundations, its relationship to the development of the self, and its changing nature over the life course.

Foundations for Socialization

As the cases of Genie, Anna, and Isabelle clearly demonstrate, our biological endowments are not sufficient to produce a normal human personality in the absence of social interaction. A normal human, then, is a product of both hereditary and environmental factors. In this section we will look more closely at how those factors interact. We also will discuss theories and agents of socialization, examine social communication, and consider how socialization provides a socially constructed reality, what sociologists refer to as the "definition of the situation."

Nature and Nurture

Children from severely deprived backgrounds offer a moving illustration of the nurturing that human nature needs to develop, but the relative contributions of nature and nurture are difficult to determine. The issue used to be, nature or nurture? Today the question more likely to be asked is "How do nature and nurture interact to produce behavior?"

Scientists have frequently asked which factor, heredity or environment, is more important in fashioning a particular trait, such as obesity, extroversion, or an individual's intelligence. They have attempted to determine which of the differences they find among people can be attributed to heredity and which to environment. As genetic research continues, evidence accrues that anorexia (Fetissov et al., 2002), alcoholism (Beylotte, 2003), and antisocial behavior (Caspi et al., 2002) all have genetic components. Some studies suggest that heredity is the primary factor in personality and development. For example, in her 1998 book *The Nurture Assumption,* Judith Rich Harris argued that biological parents' genetic influence on their children is far more important than their social influence. Other studies indicate that once we account for siblings' genetic similarity, they are no more alike in personality, abilities, and adjustment than are people selected at random from the population (Turkheimer and Waldron, 2000). However, research also shows that, however important heritable traits are, the expression of those traits depends on a broad range of environmental factors (Collins et al., 2000).

Studies of identical twins (who have exactly the same genes) have provided a unique opportunity for drawing out genetic versus environmental effects (Guo, 2005). This research found that twins raised apart are as similar as twins raised together on many measures of personality, temperament, interests, and social and political attitudes (Bouchard et al., 1990; Bouchard, 1994; Pinker, 2002), indicating that those characteristics are influenced by genetic factors. At the same time, such studies also suggest that culture and environment may actually play the larger role, accounting for more than half of the variation in personality and behavioral traits (Feldman, Otto, and Christiansen, 2000).

Sometimes the difference between hereditary and environmental causes is only a matter of shifting one's focus. For example, on the Mediterranean island of Sardinia 35 percent of the inhabitants suffer from a disease associated with the lack of a specific enzyme (Harsanyi and Hutton, 1979). The disease is activated when a person lacking the enzyme eats a particular type of bean. In a group of people who lack the enzyme, the disorder can be viewed as environmental in origin; it shows up in people who eat the bean. In a group of people who eat the bean, the disorder would be viewed as genetic in origin; it shows up in people lacking the enzyme.

Given the complexities, it is clearly an oversimplification to think of organisms as passive objects either programmed by internal

"Now I'm going to show you something that's in bad taste, so you'll know what bad taste is."

genetic forces or shaped by the external environment. Substantial evidence indicates that hereditary and environmental factors interact with and affect one another (Feldman, Otto, and Christiansen, 2000; Moffitt, 2005). For example, evidence indicates that the biological influences on behavior may themselves be influenced by the environment. Studies with rats have shown that experiences directly affect neural structure in the brain; environment shapes physiological development (Comery, Shah, and Greenaugh, 1995). Children exposed to toxins in their environment, such as lead, have lower IQs than those not exposed (NIEHS, 2005; Needleman and Bellinger, 1994).

In addition, as children develop, their behavior becomes less directly dependent on nature. Instead, learning becomes more important and the brain itself is affected by interaction with the environment. For example, the physiological development of the brains of small children are affected by early traumatic events (Perry et al., 1995); likewise, the neural connections within the brain are enhanced by a rich, stimulating, and secure early environment. In sum, not only do nature, nurture, and their interaction affect behavior, but behavior and individual experiences affect neurological development that in turn affects subsequent experience and behavior.

We humans, then, are not locked into an unchangeable physical body nor an unchangeable social system; both can change and each exerts an influence on the other. In learning, we modify ourselves by responding; we literally change ourselves by acting. Behavior influences the functions of the brain, and that influences the brain's architecture, so that experience produces lasting effects in the structure and function of the brain (Locke, 1993). We thus are active agents, shaping both ourselves and our environments. As we act on and modify the world in which we live, we in turn are shaped and transformed by our own actions. This dynamic interplay of socialization processes involving the individual and the social and natural environment in which we live is the foundation of human intelligence, knowledge, and culture.

Theories of Socialization

While social scientists acknowledge that we are biological organisms, biological factors have not been fully integrated into social psychological theory, though there is movement in that direction (Gove, 1987; Rossi and Rossi, 1990; Gove, 1994; Udry, 1995; Udry, 2000; Cacioppo et al., 2000; Bergesen, 2004). The theories of socialization emphasized in sociology today continue to emphasize social structure, learning, and social interaction.

The two macrolevel theoretical perspectives in sociology, functionalism and conflict theory,

view socialization as a process that has important consequences for society as a whole (Corsaro and Eder, 1995). For functionalists, society would not be possible if people did not internalize the values, norms, and beliefs that ensure that they can and will occupy the statuses and play the roles that make up social structures (Inkeles, 1968). Conflict theorists also recognize that socialization prepares people to play various roles in society, but they view socialization critically, emphasizing the ways socialization controls people and ensures that social inequities will be reproduced from one generation to the next (Bowles and Gintis, 1976, 2000). Proponents of these macrolevel approaches to socialization view it as a deterministic process, focusing mostly on the outcomes of socialization and tending to ignore both the active individuals and the actual social processes involved.

Three microlevel theories—social learning theory, cognitive developmental theory, and symbolic interactionism—examine how socialization occurs. We will describe each.

▲ Social Learning Theory

One view of how socialization occurs is that we are socialized through positive and negative reinforcement by our parents, friends, and society and that we observe and imitate socialized behavior around us. The two processes emphasized in social learning theory are conditioning and observational learning (Wiggins, Wiggins, and Vander Zanden, 1994). **Conditioning** is a form of learning in which the consequences of behavior determine the probability of its future occurrence (Skinner, 1953). Consequences of behavior that increase the chance that a behavior will occur are *reinforcements;* consequences that reduce that probability are *punishments.* Socialization occurs when a person's behavior is shaped by the reinforcing and punishing activities of other people and groups.

Psychologist Albert Bandura drew attention to the fact that conditioning, which occurs subsequent to behavior, cannot explain the initial learning of a behavior. Through observation, people may learn both a certain mode of behavior and that the behavior may elicit certain rewards or punishments (Bandura, 1965). **Observational learning** (also referred to as modeling or imitation) occurs when people reproduce the responses they observe in other people, either real or fictional.

▲ Cognitive Developmental Theory

Another view emphasizes that a child's socialization occurs in step with his or her cognitive development. Though learning is a fundamental part of socialization, what and how a person learns depends on his or her ability to understand and interpret the world, something that progresses through several stages. The Swiss psychologist Jean Piaget (1926/1955) hypothesized that every normal child goes through four such stages of cognitive development, each of which is dominated by a different scheme for handling information and understanding how the world works.

In the *sensorimotor stage,* from birth to about 18 months, children learn directly through their senses and their movements. Their initial inability to distinguish between themselves and their environment limits the kind of socialization that can occur. Gradually they realize that they exist independently of the people and things around them. The scheme developed in this stage is essential for moving on to more complex understandings of self, others, and the wider world that develop in subsequent stages.

The *preoperational stage* usually lasts from about 18 months to 6 or 7 years old. A major accomplishment of this stage is *representational thought,* made possible by learning symbols and language. However, children at this stage identify symbols very closely with the objects they represent, making thinking rigid and inflexible and making it difficult to distinguish the real from the make-believe. A critical factor inhibiting socialization at this stage is children's extreme egocentricity—their inability to see

things, including themselves, from other people's perspectives. Until this happens, the children's moral sensibility and self-concept remain undeveloped.

From age 6 or 7 until about 11 or 12, children go through the *concrete operational stage* in which they learn to think more abstractly, to do simple arithmetic in their heads, to be able to separate a symbol from the thing it represents, to think less rigidly, and to be able to see things the way others do. Thinking at this stage remains focused on concrete, tangible objects, limiting the abstractions and complexity that can be reached.

Piaget's last stage, from age 11 or 12 to adulthood, is the *formal operations stage,* marked by the further development of abstract and logical abilities, such as the ability to do more complex mathematics and to understand formulas and proofs. Children now begin to be able to develop abstract arguments and to develop a variety of ways of looking at a problem. Identity and moral sensibility become deeper and more complex, influenced by the ability to internalize and critically evaluate the points of view of others.

Psychologist Lawrence Kohlberg (1969; 1981) extended Piaget's framework by arguing that beginning with the preoperational stage, children have a very strong motivation to be competent. Children learn not only through the rather passive conditioning and observational learning processes discussed above, but by actively trying to learn what they need to know about themselves and their environment to be competent, a critical component of socialization.

▲ Symbolic Interactionism

Social learning theory and cognitive developmental theory are rooted in psychology. A third, more sociological view of socialization comes from the symbolic interactionist perspective. Symbolic interactionism is more than just a theory of socialization. As we pointed out in Chapter 1, it is a broad sociological ← pp. 22–24 perspective that helps us understand social processes in many settings. Some symbolic interactionist reasoning is particularly relevant to understanding socialization.

Actions through which people observe, interpret, evaluate, communicate with, and attempt to control themselves—what symbolic interactionists call **reflexive behavior**—are important to socialization (Wiggins, Wiggins, and Vander Zanden, 1994). As we will see, a particularly important kind of reflexive behavior involves people observing their own behavior from the perspective of others. For example, in many cases in which you feel yourself becoming angry, you probably reflect on how your expression of anger will be interpreted by others and then use this reflection to guide your actual expression of anger.

Reflexive behavior is critical in the development of the self—a central part of the socialization process—because it is through reflexive behavior that people learn who they are. And, as with the learning patterns emphasized in cognitive development theory, learning who one is may be influenced by both conditioning and by observational learning. According to the symbolic interactionist view of socialization, however, the individual takes an important and active role in this learning process. Individuals monitor their own behavior, monitor others' responses, make interpretations, try out new ways of behaving, and come to new understandings about themselves.

Agents of Socialization

The family, peers, schools, and the mass media are important agents of socialization. Traditionally the main social environment for young children, the family has provided the earliest and closest models to guide learning. Now that more than 60 percent of mothers with children under school age are in the workforce (NICHD Early Child Care Research Network, 2003), day

care providers and peers also are important early agents of socialization. Sociological research investigates how family structure and parenting styles influence socialization outcomes (Amato and Sobolewski, 2001; Nelson, Clark, and Acs, 2001; Stacey and Biblarz, 2001). With day care the norm for so many infants, toddlers, and preschoolers, researchers also have turned their attention to the effects of nonmaternal care on socialization. Beneficial effects of high-quality day care and preschool programs have been documented (Field, 1991). On the other hand, recent research on kindergarteners found that the more time children had spent in any kind of nonmaternal care before kindergarten, the more likely they were to be assertive, disobedient, aggressive, and in conflict with adults (NICHD Early Child Care Research Network, 2003).

As the child's world expands beyond the family, whether the child is of school age or earlier, the *peer group* becomes an important influence on emotional, cognitive, and social development. An increasingly large part of a child's early social life is spent in the peer group, where the reactions of same-age peers serve as powerful reinforcements and punishments that shape behavior. As a child increasingly identifies with his or her peers and uses them as role models, the child's self-definition becomes strongly influenced by the characteristics and standards of his or her peer group—standards that often vary significantly from those of parents and other adults. The high rates of what parents and others define as "deviant" behavior among youth (see Chapter 5) may stem from this difference in standards of behavior. For youth, such behavior currently includes tattooing, body piercing, underage drinking, experimenting with drugs, and more serious criminal behavior.

Formal socialization occurs in schools through instruction in mathematics, English, and other subjects. But the role of the *school* as agent of socialization goes far beyond teaching

An important role of parents, as agents of socialization, is to control the influence of other agents of socialization such as the Internet.

the standard subjects. Praise and reprimands in schools are structured to teach and enforce school rules, thus socializing children to adapt to impersonal bureaucratic requirements. Emphasis on grades teaches individualistic values of competition and achievement. The gender, racial, and ethnic composition of teaching staffs teaches lessons about what kinds of people are regarded as knowledgeable and competent to wield authority, and may thus reinforce traditional prejudices against minorities and women. Half of all school-age children, kindergarten through eighth grade, are in nonparental care programs after school, with a significant proportion of those participating in school-based care programs or extracurricular activities (Wirt et al., 2003). Extracurricular activities from athletics to helping the teacher are differentially distributed across the student body, leading to differences in socialization experiences and thus outcomes (see Box 3.1).

Although school dominates the lives of most children, television also plays a huge role; the average American child spends between three and six hours with a television every day, watching TV, videotapes, DVDs, and playing video games (American Academy of Pediatrics, 2001). One-third of 2- to 7-year-old American children have a television in their bedrooms; for 8- to 18-year-olds, the number rises to 65 percent. Television and other *media* such as radio, the Internet, popular music, movies, comic books, video games, books, magazines, and newspapers are important in socialization because they provide models for behavior. For example, with 20 to 25 violent acts per hour shown on children's television, media models violent behavior. Laboratory studies, field experiments, survey samples, and longitudinal studies all link television violence to aggression (Anderson and Bushman, 2002), and a long-term study showed that television watching during adolescence and early adulthood was connected to subsequent aggressive acts including assaults, robbery, and criminal weapon use (Johnson et al., 2002). A 15-year longitudinal study showed that exposure to television violence between ages 6 and 9 was significantly correlated with adult aggressive behavior (Huesmann et al., 2003).

Media also provide images that help form our understandings of the world. For example, a portrayal by the mass media of African Americans as poor, involved with drugs, and in trouble with the law creates negative stereotypes, whereas an accurate portrayal of African

Does High School Identity Affect Your Adult Life?

Think back to your high school days. Were you ever the president of Student Council? Did you perform in school plays, play sports, party a lot, regard all organized activities with suspicion, or spend most of your time studying? Which crowd did you hang with?

Adolescents' crowd identities serve not only as labels for others but as public identities for themselves (Barber, Eccles, and Stone, 2001). But do such identities have any impact on our later lives?

In a long-term study of 900 young people who were in high school in the 1980s, researchers Bonnie Barber, Jacquelynne Eccles, and Margaret Stone investigated the impact of social (or "crowd") identity in adolescence on adult outcomes. As an indicator of identity, they used categories borrowed from the well-known and then popular 1985 film about adolescents, *The Breakfast Club*. In 1987, the researchers asked the 10th grade study participants to ignore gender and select which of the five *Breakfast Club* characters was most like them: the Brain, the Princess, the Jock, the Criminal, or the Basket Case. Forty percent selected Princess, 28 percent chose Jock, 12 percent selected Brain, 11 percent picked Basket Case, and 9 percent chose Criminal. Participants also indicated which athletic and other sorts of extracurricular activities they were involved in, which the researchers grouped as follows:

- Team sports.

- Performing arts (school band, drama, or dance).

- School involvement (student government, pep club, cheerleading).

- Prosocial activities (church attendance, community service).

In the first part of their analysis, Barber and her colleagues discovered that the social identity categories were linked to 10th grade activity participation, with Jocks and Criminals most strongly represented in sports, Basket Cases and Princesses in performing arts, and Brains in prosocial activities. Princesses also were well represented in school involvement activities. But did their high school social identities predict what sorts of young adults they would become?

It turns out that for a number of measurements taken in 1996 when the respondents were around 24 years old, the answer was yes. High school identities predicted adult substance use, education, psychological adjustment, and work outcomes. For example, alcohol consumption in early adulthood was significantly correlated with tenth-grade social identity: Jocks and Criminals drank the most, and Basket Cases and Brains the least. Brains were the most likely to have graduated from college by age 24, followed by Princesses, Jocks, Basket Cases, and finally Criminals. The lowest levels of worry were reported by Jocks and Brains, while the highest levels were reported by Criminals and Basket Cases. Similarly, Jocks and Brains had the highest self-esteem, and Criminals and Basket Cases reported the lowest. Jocks were the least likely to report social isolation and Basket Cases the most.

Not many people want to think that their adult lives depend on their identities as high school

sophomores. Why do the crowd identities and activities of 10th graders predict adult outcomes? Barber and her colleagues have some guesses (2001:450–451):

Perhaps adolescents make use of the formal activities and the informal social organizations of the high school to negotiate and formalize their identities. The patterns of behavior expressed, solidified, and formalized first in high school organizations may carry forward, providing continuity in connection to others with similar values and backgrounds as well as ongoing validation of the social identity established in adolescence.

Questions for Discussion

1. Identities of adolescents today may be different from those in 1987. If you were designing a replication of this study and were using contemporary adolescents as subjects, which movie(s) or television program(s) would you use? What characters and what identity models would you pick for your study? What hypotheses would you have? What would you expect to find when you interviewed your subjects again nine years from now?

2. Do the categories brain, princess, and others correctly capture the identities of high school students? If not, what are the relevant categories?

3. Are there alternative explanations of these findings? Were the adult outcomes really caused by adolescent identities, some other psychological dimension(s), or some other factor or set of factors?

Americans in a variety of life pursuits creates positive images and helps dispel negative stereotypes. Media even influence our image of media. Although scientific evidence for the connection between media violence and aggression has increased over time, news media accounts have characterized it as weak, then moderate, and then back to weak, leaving the public with the impression that the data are inconclusive (Bushman and Anderson, 2001).

Which agents of socialization are most important? The direct impact of mass media on the socialization process can be overestimated. The symbolic interactionist perspective suggests that images from television and other media must be defined and interpreted by viewers before they can influence behavior. If the family, peers, and schools create the meanings people use in interpreting media images, then they are the critical agents in socialization. Media-related aggression, for example, can be lessened by reducing exposure to violent media, but it also can be reduced by changing children's attitudes toward the violence they see on television and in video games (Anderson and Bushman, 2002). The effect of television and other media also may be through the displacement of other activities that might socialize children differently; children who watch television are not reading, visiting interesting places, exercising, or playing (American Academy of Pediatrics, 2001).

Social Communication

Communication is a fundamental process in socialization. It is also essential in human adaptation. If we are to adapt to the environment, we must be able to communicate with one another. Indeed, all social interaction involves communication. **Communication** refers to the process by which people transmit information, ideas, attitudes, and mental states to one another and is made possible by the human ability

to create complex symbol systems including language, as discussed in Chapter 2. ◄—[pp. 47–49] It includes all those verbal and nonverbal processes by which we send and receive messages. Without the ability to communicate, each human being would be locked within a private world such as that experienced by Helen Keller before she acquired language. Communication allows us to establish "commonness" with one another; senders and receivers can come together through a given message. It is this commonness that makes socialization possible. Communication is an indispensable mechanism by which human beings attain social goals. It permits them to coordinate complex group activities, and as such it is the foundation for institutional life.

▲ Verbal Communication

For years many social scientists asserted that infants come into the world essentially unprogrammed for language use. Then linguists began noticing similarities in languages throughout the world: all languages have nouns and verbs and allow individuals to ask questions, give commands, and deny statements. Moreover, children acquire language with little difficulty, despite the need to master an incredibly complex, abstract set of rules for transforming strings of sounds into meanings. Even deaf children have a strong bias to communicate in languagelike ways (Goldin-Meadow and Mylander, 1984). And speakers can understand and produce an infinite set of sentences, even sentences they have never before heard or uttered.

In 1957 the eminent linguist Noam Chomsky put these observations together to suggest that human beings possess an inborn language-generating mechanism, which he termed the **language acquisition device.** As viewed by Chomsky (1957, 1980), the basic structure of language is biologically channeled, forming a sort of prefabricated filing system to order the words and phrases that make up human languages. All a child needs to do is

Unanticipated consequences of the use of new communication technologies are common.

DILBERT reprinted by permission of United Feature Syndicate, Inc.

learn the peculiarities of his or her society's language.

Chomsky's hypothesis attracted interest, generated controversy, and remains influential (Jackendoff, 2002). Social scientists have pointed out that because a biological predisposition for the development of language exists does not mean that environmental factors play no part in language development. The example of a boy with normal hearing but with deaf parents highlights this point. His parents communicated by American Sign Language, but the boy was exposed daily to television, with the expectation that he would learn to speak English. His social interactions were limited to people who communicated in sign language. By the time he was 3, he was fluent in sign language, but he neither understood nor spoke English (Moskowitz, 1978). This case suggests that to learn a language, children must be able to interact with people in that language.

In sum, the acquiring of language cannot be understood by examining genetic factors and learning processes in isolation from one another. Instead, complex and dynamic interactions occur among biochemical processes, maturational factors, learning strategies, and the social environment. No one aspect by itself can produce a language-using human being. Although infants possess a genetically guided ground plan that leads them toward language, that ability can be acquired only in a social context.

▲ Nonverbal Communication

Verbal symbols are only the tip of the communication iceberg. Nonverbal messages abound, and we "read" a good deal into them without necessarily being aware of doing so. On the basis of his experiments, psychologist Albert Mehrabian (1968) concluded that the total impact of a message is 7 percent verbal, 38 percent vocal, and 55 percent facial. Another specialist has suggested that "no more than 30 to 35 percent of the social meaning of a conversation or an interaction is carried by its words" (Birdwhistell, 1970:197).

Differences in the environment in which nonverbal communication is used affect its meaning. For example, if a man and woman at a singles bar spot each other and become interested, they signal with eye contact. The man might hold the woman's gaze, look away, and then look back quickly once or twice. If the woman responds in kind, the two may maneuver within speaking distance and strike up a conversation. On the other hand, if you establish and hold eye contact with a stranger on an elevator, it is perceived to be a threatening communication. Similarly, in American culture you generally do not look directly at another person unless you are talking (Mazur, 1985).

Cultural diversity in the workplace has created a need for greater sensitivity among managers and employees regarding people's use of nonverbal communication. For example, white Americans define eye contact in the course of a conversation as showing respect. But many Latinos do not, and many Americans of Asian ancestry deem eye contact with an employer to be an exceedingly disrespectful behavior. Potential conflicts may arise when white supervisors consider Hispanic or Asian employees furtive or rude for casting their eyes about the room. Multicultural training programs seek to teach employers and employees to look beyond their culture-bound notions about what constitutes "proper" and "improper" behavior (Fost, 1992).

There are many nonverbal communication systems, including the following:

- **Body language:** Physical motions and gestures provide signals. The way a person stands or sits, for example, can communicate aggression, receptivity, boredom, or hostility.

- **Paralanguage:** Nonverbal vocal cues surrounding speech—voice pitch, volume, pacing of speech, silent pauses, and sighs—provide a rich source of information. Paralanguage has to do with how something is said rather than with what is said.

- **Proxemics:** The way we employ social and personal space also contains messages. Students who sit in the front rows of a classroom communicate that they are interested, while those in the rear communicate that they are alienated and prone to mischievous activities (Sommer, 1969).

- **Touch:** Through physical contact such as touching, stroking, hitting, holding, and greeting (handshakes), we convey our feelings toward one another. However, touch can also constitute an invasion of privacy, and it can become a symbol of power when people want to make power differences visible.

- **Artifacts:** We commonly employ objects, including certain types of clothing, make-up, hairpieces, eyeglasses, beauty aids, perfume, and jewelry, that tell other people our gender, rank, status, and attitude.

Some aspects of nonverbal communication, such as many gestures, are especially susceptible to cultural influence (Ekman, Friesen, and Bear, 1984; see Figure 3.1). The American "OK" gesture made by joining the thumb and forefinger in a circle has quite different meanings, depending on the culture. An American tourist will find that what is taken to be a friendly sign in the United States has an insulting connotation in France and Belgium: "You're worth zero!" In southern Italy it means "You're a jerk," in Greece and Turkey it conveys an insulting or vulgar sexual invitation, and in Germany it is an obscene anatomical reference. However, some facial expressions seem to have universal meanings. Surprise, disgust, fear, anger, sadness, and happiness were identified from photos by people from five different cultures (Ekman et al., 1988). The ways of displaying and interpreting certain feelings may be universal, but each culture provides its own "display rules" regulating how and when given emotions may be exhibited and with what consequences.

Definition of the Situation

An important part of socialization is learning social definitions of reality—the basic schemes we use to make sense of and to understand the social and physical world. William I. Thomas introduced this through his concept of **definition of the situation:** the interpretation or meaning we give to our immediate circumstances (Thomas and Thomas, 1928; Merton, 1995).

Kiss on the cheek: How many are appropriate? Zero to one in Britain, two on most of the Continent, three in Belgium and French-speaking Switzerland—and in Paris, four.

The V sign: What Churchill meant was "victory"— but the same signal with the knuckles turned out is England's and Australia's equivalent of the American middle finger.

Tapping the nose: In England, Scotland, and strangely, Sardinia, this means, "You and I are in on the secret." But if a Welshperson does it, he means, "You're really nosy."

Twisting the nose: The French gesture of putting one's fist around the top of the nose and twisting it signifies that a person is drunk, but it is not a gesture used in other cultures.

Tapping the temple: Do this almost anywhere in Europe if you want to say someone or something is crazy—except in Holland, where the gesture means, "How clever!"

Thumbs up: This gesture was employed by Roman emperors to spare the lives of gladiators in the Colosseum. It is now favored by American and Western European airline pilots, truck drivers, and others to mean "All right." But in Sardinia and northern Greece, it is an insulting gesture paralleling the middle-finger gesture of American society.

Thumb-and-index circle: America's "OK" sign means just that in much of Europe—though not in Germany, where it is an obscene anatomical reference.

The chin rub: That's what people in France, French-speaking Switzerland, and Belgium do when they're bored. Don't try it elsewhere: no one will get it.

The wave: Careful with this friendly greeting while in Greece. It could be misinterpreted as "Go to hell." When Greeks wave goodbye, they show the backs of their hands.

Figure 3.1   Symbolic Gestures: Barriers to Cross-Cultural Communication
Source: Text from "In Athens, It's Palms In," *Newsweek*, November 12, 1990 © 1990 Newsweek, Inc. All rights reserved. Reprinted by permission.

People vary in their perceptions of and reactions to different situations. For example, a gun means one thing to a soldier and something else to an armed robber; it has still other meanings for a holdup victim, a hunter, or a gun-control advocate. A man mowing the lawn may be seen as beautifying his yard, avoiding his wife, getting exercise, supporting neighborhood property values, annoying a neighbor who is attempting to sleep, or earning a living by mowing lawns.

Our symbolic environment mediates the physical environment so that we do not simply experience stimuli, but a definition of the situation. Although our definitions of the situation may differ, it is only as we arrive at common understandings that we are able to fit our action to the actions of other people. Whatever we do—play football, chat with a friend on the telephone, rob a store, make love, give a lecture, cross a busy intersection, or purchase a book—we must attribute similar meanings to the situation if we are to achieve joint action with others. Moreover, a definition of the situation arrived at on one occasion may not hold for future occasions. Viewed in this manner, culture may be thought of as the agreed-upon meanings—the shared definitions of situations—that individuals acquire as members of a society. Socialization is the process by which these shared definitions are learned and transmitted from one generation to the next.

Sociologists point out that our definitions influence our construction of reality. William I. Thomas and Dorothy S. Thomas (1928:572; Merton, 1995) captured this insight in what has become known as the **Thomas theorem:** "If [people] define situations as real, they are real in their consequences." The Thomas theorem draws our attention to the fact that people respond not only to the objective features of a situation but also to the meaning the situation has for them. Once the meaning has been assigned, it serves to shape not only what people do or fail to do but also some of the consequences of their behavior. In this way, a definition of the situation can become a self-fulfilling prophecy.

For example, one of the reasons that racial prejudices are so damaging is that they are definitions of the situation that can become self-fulfilling prophecies. For many generations whites defined African Americans as racially inferior. Whites controlled the centers of institutional power, and they allocated to African Americans fewer of the privileges and opportunities of society. By acting upon their racial definitions, whites fashioned social structures—institutional arrangements—in which African Americans have enjoyed fewer advantages than whites. And while most African Americans live well above the poverty line (DeNavas-Walt, Proctor, and Lee, 2005), compared to whites, African Americans are less likely to be well educated and have high incomes and more likely to hold menial jobs, live in poor housing, and have poor health than whites. Thus, by creating and applying definitions of the situation, whites have created a social order characterized by institutional discrimination.

The Self and Socialization

The formation of the **self**—the set of concepts we use in defining who we are—is a central part of the socialization process. It is not a biological given but emerges in the course of interaction with other people and is affected by the social structures in which these interactions occur (Burke, 2004; Stets and Harrod, 2004).

The self represents the ideas we have regarding our attributes, capacities, and behavior. In everyday speech, we note the existence of the self in phrases such as proud of myself, talking to myself, losing control of myself, ashamed of myself, testing myself, hating myself, and loving myself. These conceptions represent the heart of our humanness, our awareness that each of us is a unique being apart from other beings and is the same person across time. The image that each of us has that we are a distinct, bounded, coherent being gives us a feeling of psychic wholeness. Individuals who are the victims of some forms of severe mental illness, particularly schizophrenia, lack a stable self-conception and clear self-boundaries—a distinct indication of where they begin and end. Many of them therefore feel at sea in a flood of stimuli (Elliott, Rosenberg, and Wagner, 1984).

The development of the self begins at birth as the process of socialization begins. Sociologist J. Milton Yinger (1965:149) observed:

Retrospectively, one can ask "Who am I?" But in practice, the answer has come before the question. The answer has come from all the definitions of one's roles, values, and goals that others begin to furnish at the moment of birth.

We typically place ourselves at the center of events, a tendency sociologists call an **egocentric bias** (Zuckerman et al., 1983; Schlenker, Weigold, and Hallam, 1990). By virtue of the egocentric bias, we overperceive ourselves as the victim or target of an action or event that in reality is not directed at us. For example, if we are lottery players, we sense that our ticket has a far greater probability of being selected a winner than it has (Greenwald and Pratkanis, 1984). This self-centered view of reality affects the socialization process by shaping our perception of events and later our recall of the events from memory.

Symbolic interactionists point out that we can be objects of our own action. We mentally take a place on the outside and, from this vantage point, become an audience to our own actions and an active agent in our own self-development and change (Kiecolt, 1994). Viewed in this dynamic manner, the self is a process by which we devise our actions in order to fit them to the ongoing actions of other people—a process central to socialization. Sociologists such as Charles Horton Cooley, George Herbert Mead, and Erving Goffman have contributed a

good deal to our understanding of these matters. We will consider their insights, and those of researchers who followed them, in this section.

Charles Horton Cooley: The Looking-Glass Self

At the beginning of the 20th century the notion was prevalent in both scientific and lay circles that human nature is biologically determined. Charles Horton Cooley (1864–1929) vigorously challenged this assertion. He maintained that people transform themselves and their worlds as they engage in social interaction. In particular, Cooley (1902/1964) contended that our consciousness arises in a social context. This notion is best exemplified by his concept of the **looking-glass self**—a process by which we imaginatively assume the stance of other people and view ourselves as we believe they see us. Our ability to take the perspective of another person is a basic requirement of all social behavior. Indeed, research suggests that the looking-glass self functions as a "magnifying glass" during self-perception, so that what people see in themselves while others are present has an extrapowerful impact on their behaviors and self-images (Tice, 1992).

▲ Self-Awareness

Cooley suggested that the looking-glass self is an ongoing mental process characterized by three phases. First, we imagine how we appear to others. For example, we may think of ourselves as putting on weight and becoming "fat." Second, we imagine how others judge our appearance. We are aware, for instance, that people typically think of obese people as unattractive. Third, we have an emotional reaction, such as pride or shame based on what we perceive others' judgments to be. In this case we are likely to experience anxiety or embarrassment regarding our "obese" state. The looking-glass self entails a subjective process and need not accord with objective reality. For example, victims

of anorexia nervosa willfully starve themselves, denying that they are actually thin or ill, in the belief that they are too fat.

The notion of the looking-glass self does not imply that our self-conception changes radically every time we encounter a new person or a new situation. Accordingly, it is useful to distinguish between self-images and self-conceptions (Turner, 1968; Marsh, 1986). A **self-image** is a mental conception or picture that we have of ourselves that is relatively temporary; it changes as we move from one context to another. Our **self-conception** is a more overriding view of ourselves, a sense of self through time—"the real me," or "I myself as I really am." Layers of self-images typically build up over time and contribute to a relatively stable self-conception. For the most part this succession of self-images edits rather than supplants our more crystallized self-conception or identity.

▲ Self-Evaluation

Self-conception is not only a description of who we are. It also includes our evaluation of ourselves. Two important dimensions of this evaluation are self-esteem and personal efficacy (Cast and Burke, 2002).

Self-esteem is the belief that one is a good and valuable person. Why do some people have high self-esteem and others low? Self-esteem is governed by three principles (Rosenberg, 1981). First, as we interact with others, we monitor their behavior for pieces of information about how they are appraising us. These are **reflected appraisals,** appraisals of ourselves that we see reflected in the behavior of others. If we conclude from our observations that others respect and look up to us, we will probably have good self-esteem, but if we think that they look down upon and disparage us, our self-esteem will probably be low. In a complex world we cannot be highly concerned with everyone's views of us, so the most important reflected appraisals tend to be those of people who are most important to us, those we love and care about, and

those we most respect—family, close friends, and those we admire (Murray et al., 2003; Rosenberg, 1973).

People also arrive at evaluations of themselves through **social comparisons,** comparing their performance, ability, or characteristics with those of others and rating themselves as superior, equal, or inferior (Pettigrew, 1967). We cannot compare ourselves with everyone else along all dimensions, so we use dimensions that we learn are important through the various agents of socialization (family, peer group, school, and the mass media), and we compare ourselves with relevant others. That is, instead of comparing themselves with middle-aged people with respect to personal income, adolescents compare themselves with others of their own age and in a similar situation. An adolescent's income may be low in comparison with that of a middle-aged woman at the height of her career, but it may still be a source of high self-esteem if it compares favorably with that of other working adolescents.

Even if we feel that others respect us and we are able to compare ourselves favorably with them, we still may not experience high self-esteem if we do not believe that we can take credit for what produces the respect and the favorable comparisons. By the same token, if we do not blame ourselves for how others are evaluating us or for our negative comparisons, we will probably not suffer low self-esteem. This is because of the principle of *self-attribution:* For a characteristic to affect our self-esteem, we must believe we are responsible for it and therefore deserve the credit or blame that results. For example, a man who gets an "A" in a difficult college course by cheating is not likely to conclude that he is a great scholar, but he may take credit for successful cheating and conclude that he is a very good cheater.

Personal efficacy is another aspect of self-evaluation that is influenced by socialization processes. It is the belief that one can overcome obstacles and achieve goals. The primary determinant of personal efficacy is the nature of personal experience. When we experience ourselves as effective actors and then attribute to ourselves the characteristic of being effective, our personal efficacy is increased (Gecas and Schwalbe, 1983). For example, doing well in school or holding a job that gives one authority and relative autonomy increases personal efficacy (Kohn and Schooler, 1983). However, this means that the development of personal efficacy can be a problem. To develop personal efficacy, one needs to achieve things; lacking personal efficacy, such achievement may be difficult. Structured social inequality is an important factor in personal efficacy (Hughes and Demo, 1989). People with higher education, more autonomous jobs, and higher incomes are all in situations that facilitate experiencing oneself as efficacious. People with little education, routine jobs, and low incomes may be locked into situations in which the sense of efficacy necessary for changing one's situation has little chance of developing.

George Herbert Mead: The Generalized Other

George Herbert Mead (1863–1931), one of the major figures in the symbolic interactionist perspective, elaborated on Cooley's concept of the looking-glass self and contributed many insights of his own to the processes of development of the self and socialization. Mead (1934/1962) contended that we gain a sense of selfhood by acting toward ourselves in much the same fashion that we act toward others. In so doing we "take the role of the other toward ourselves." We mentally assume a dual perspective: We are simultaneously the subject doing the viewing and the object being viewed. In our imagination we take the position of another person and look back on ourselves from this standpoint.

Mead designated the subject aspect of the self-process as "I" and the object aspect as "me." Consider what sometimes happens when you contemplate whether to ask your professor a question. You think, "If I ask a question, he'll consider me stupid. I'd better keep quiet." In this example you imagine the attitude of the professor toward students. In so doing you mentally take the role of the professor and view yourself as an object or "me." It is you as the subject or "I" who decides that it would be unwise to ask the question. The use of personal pronouns in the statement illustrates the object–subject dimensions.

According to Mead, the key to children's development of the self—a central part of the socialization process—resides in their acquisition of language. By virtue of language, we arouse the same tendencies in ourselves that we do in others. We mentally say to ourselves, "If I want to get this person to respond this way, what will it take to do so? What would it take to get me to act in this fashion?" Language allows us to carry on an internal conversation. We talk and reply to ourselves in much the same manner that we carry on a conversation with others. In this fashion, we judge how other people will respond to us.

Sociologist Ralph Turner (1968) clarified and extended Mead's ideas on the self. Turner pointed out that when speaking and acting, we typically adopt a state of preparedness for certain types of responses from the other person. If we wave to a professor, ask a police officer a question, or embrace a friend, we expect that the other person will respond with some action that will appropriately fit our own. As the other person responds, we enter a phase of testing and revision. We mentally appraise the other's behavior, determining whether or not it accords with our expectations. In doing so we assign meaning to that behavior. We then plan our next course of action. For instance, if the person has responded in an unanticipated manner, we might terminate the interaction, begin again with a reassertion of our original intention, disregard the other's response, or abandon our initial course of action and follow the other person's lead. Consequently, symbolic interactionists say that the process of self-communication is essential to social interaction.

According to Mead, children typically pass through three stages in developing a full sense of selfhood: the "play" stage, the "game" stage, and the "generalized other" stage. In play, children take the role of only one other person at a time and "try on" the person's behavior. The model, usually an important person in the life of the child, such as a parent, is called a **significant other.**

Whereas children in the play stage take the role of only one other person at a time, in the game stage they assume many roles. Individuals must take into account the roles of many people, and children must become familiar with the expectations that hold for a variety of roles if they are to play their own roles successfully.

In Mead's third stage, children recognize that they are immersed within a larger community of people and that this community has very definite attitudes regarding what constitutes appropriate and inappropriate behavior. The social unit that gives individuals their unity of self is called the **generalized other.** The attitude of the generalized other is the attitude of the larger community. Although we gain our conceptions of given rules from particular people (our mother, a teacher, or a peer), these notions are generalized or extended to embrace all people within similar situations. To think about our behavior, then, is to interact mentally with ourselves from the perspective of an abstract community of people. According to Mead, the generalized other is the vehicle by which we are linked to society. By means of the generalized other, we incorporate, or internalize, the organized attitudes of our community within our own personalities so that social control becomes self-control. According to Mead, our ability to participate effectively in society is the end result of passing through the play, game, and generalized other stages.

Erving Goffman: Impression Management

Erving Goffman (1922–1982) has provided an additional dimension to our understanding of the self and socialization. Cooley and Mead examined how our self-conceptions arise in the course of social interaction and how we fashion our actions based on the feedback we derive about ourselves and our behavior from other people. Goffman (1959) directed our attention to another matter. He pointed out that only by influencing other people's ideas of us can we hope to predict or control who we become. We have a stake in presenting ourselves to others in ways that will lead them to view us in a favorable light, a process Goffman called **impression management.** In doing so we use both concealment and

Every day we all engage in what Erving Goffman termed "impression management."

strategic revelation. For example, a young professor fresh out of graduate school may spend several hours preparing and rehearsing a lecture in hopes of appearing "knowledgeable" to her students. You are probably aware of engaging in impression management when deciding what to wear for a particular occasion, such as a party, a physician's appointment, a job interview, or a date (Leary and Kowalski, 1990).

Goffman saw the performances staged in a theater as an analytical analogy and tool for depicting and understanding socialization and the shaping of the self, a perspective called the **dramaturgical approach.** He depicted social life as a stage on which people interact; all human beings are both actors and members of the audience, and the parts are the roles people play in the course of their daily activities. According to Goffman, the self is a product of the ongoing performances that characterize a person's everyday interaction with others and of how these performances are interpreted by others. In this view, the self is not so much something that people possess and then carry unchanged from situation to situation, but is a "dramatic effect" (Goffman, 1959: 253) that emerges from social situations in which people attempt to manage others' impressions of them.

Goffman illustrated his approach by describing the changes that occur in waiters' behavior as they move from the kitchen to the dining room. As the nature of the audience changes, so does their behavior. "Frontstage" in the dining room, the waiters display a polite demeanor to the guests. "Backstage" in the kitchen, they openly flaunt and otherwise ridicule the servility they must portray frontstage. Further, they seal off the dirty work of food preparation—the gristle, grease, and foul smells of spoiled food—from the appetizing and enticing frontstage atmosphere. As people move from situation to situation, they drastically alter their self-expression. They undertake to define the situation for others by generating cues that will lead others to act in ways they wish.

Socialization across the Life Course

Socialization is a continuing, lifelong process. The world about us changes and requires that we also change. The self is not carved in granite, somehow finalized for all time during childhood. Life is adaptation—a process of constant renewing and remaking. Three-year-olds are socialized within the patterns of a nursery school, engineering students within their chosen profession, new employees within an office or plant, a husband and wife within a new family, and elderly patients within a nursing home.

In one way or another, all societies have to deal with the **life course** that begins with conception and continues through old age and ultimately death. Societies weave varying social arrangements around chronological age (Nanda and Warms, 2002). A 14-year-old girl may be expected to be a middle school student in one culture and a mother of two in another; a 45-year-old man may be at the peak of a business career, still moving up in a political career, retired from a career as a professional football player, or dead and worshipped as an ancestor in some other society. All cultures divide biological time into socially relevant units. While birth, puberty, maturity, aging, and death are biological facts of life, it is society that gives each its distinctive meaning.

Modern societies are ordered in ways that formally structure people's preparation for new roles through education, rehabilitation, and resocialization. This *role socialization* commonly involves three phases (Mortimer and Simmons, 1978). First, people think about, experiment with, and try on the behaviors associated with a new role, what sociologists term **anticipatory socialization.** Children informally acquaint themselves with such adult roles as spouse and parent by "playing house." Most college-bound high school students go through such a process by learning about and then adopting clothing styles and recreational habits that are common among college students. Second, once individuals assume a new status, they find that they must not only learn the expectations of the associated role, but they may need to shape the role itself in response to new situations and to their individual needs. For example, a couple entering marriage must evolve new interpersonal skills because as children they learned little about the marital role. Third, as individuals move through their lives, they not only enter roles but must disengage or exit from many of them. Such rituals as graduation exercises, marriage, retirement banquets, funerals, and other rites of passage are socially established mechanisms for easing some role transitions. Because socialization across the life course is increasingly important to sociological research, we will take a closer look in this section at some of the transitions that center on life course roles.

Childhood

Our expectation of what childhood is and how long it lasts is an aspect of our culture and affects socialization. Whatever definitions they hold of children, societies begin socializing them as soon as possible. But those definitions affect the socialization that occurs. In the Middle Ages, for example, the concept of childhood as we know it was unheard of. Children were regarded as small adults (Ariès, 1962). No special word existed for a young male between the ages of 7 and 16. The word *child* expressed kinship, not an age period (Plumb, 1972). Not until about the year 1600 did a new concept of childhood begin to emerge.

The notion that children should be attending school rather than working in factories, mines, and fields is also of relatively recent origin. In the 1820s half of the cotton mill workers in New England were children who worked 12- to 15-hour days. Even as late as 1924 the National Child Labor Committee estimated that 2 million American children under 15 were at work, the majority as farm laborers.

What about our view of childhood today? Most infants are fairly malleable in the sense that within broad limits they are capable of becoming adults of quite different sorts. The magnitude of their accomplishments over a relatively short period of time is truly astonishing. For example, by their fourth birthday most American children have mastered the complicated and abstract structure of the English language. And they can carry on complex social interactions in accordance with American cultural patterns.

Children display people-oriented responses at very early ages. Even before their first birthday, children are already contributors to social life (Rheingold, Hay, and West, 1976; Lewis et al., 1989). By 2 years of age, children can make a doll do something as if it were acting on its own. In so doing they reveal an elementary ability for representing other people as independent agents. Most 3-year-olds can make a doll carry out several role-related activities, revealing knowledge of a social role (e.g., pretend to be a doctor and examine a doll). Four-year-olds can typically act out a role, meshing the behavior with that of a reciprocal role (e.g., pretend that a patient doll is sick and a doctor doll examines it, in the course of which both dolls make appropriate responses). During the late preschool years, children become capable of combining roles in more complicated ways (e.g., being a doctor and a father simultaneously). Most 6-year-olds can pretend to carry out several roles at the same time.

The greatest development occurs between 7 and 8 years of age; then the rate of change in conceptualization slows. Indeed, the differences between children who are 7 years old and those who are 8 are frequently greater than the differences between 8-year-olds and 15-year-olds (Barenboim, 1981).

Of course, these patterns are not the same for all children. Not only is there considerable individual variability in child development, but

What Makes You an Adult?

The hard thing is, while the ceremony is going on you're not allowed to move your body an inch. You can't twitch your finger or move your mouth. Even your eyelashes have to stay absolutely still. . . . It's believed that if you survive the first three cuts, it will change your life. And there were my brothers, already circumcised, saying, "Don't blink. Don't move. Don't bring embarrassment to our family." (Lekuton, 2003)

This is how Joseph Lemasolai Lekuton, now a teacher in Virginia, recalls his circumcision at age 13 in a Maasai village in Kenya. "The most important event of my whole life was my circumcision," he says. "In Maa culture, the circumcision ceremony is the initiation that makes a boy a man."

In many cultures *rites of passage and initiation rituals* precisely mark the transition from childhood to adulthood and occur when a child reaches puberty; sexual maturity marks an individual's readiness for marriage and child rearing, both hallmarks of adulthood. While there is great cultural variability, coming-of-age rituals may include tests of strength, endurance of pain, circumcision, scarification, or seclusion. One researcher concluded that "the ordeals, taboos, and solemnity of these rites [was] essential to communicating the seriousness of life and its duties to the initiates" (Nanda and Warms, 2002:132). In other societies the point of transition is less clear. For example, Margaret Mead's classic work *Coming of Age in Samoa* showed that children's participation in society increased gradually, and they reached adulthood with little adolescent trauma (Nanda and Warms, 2002). Similarly, the Inuit people think of maturity as "the exercise of reason, judgment, and emotional control, and it is thought to grow naturally as children grow" (Nanda and Warms, 2002:127).

What determines when one becomes an adult in modern U.S. society? Some see religious and educational milestones as American rites of passage: confirmation, bar and bat mitzvahs, high school and college graduations, and the like. In 1989 anthropologist Michael Moffatt published *Coming of Age in New Jersey,* in which he describes how becoming an adult can take place in college for the American middle class. He saw college as an environment in which students acquire social skills through interacting with other students, take increasing responsibility for their own lives, and learn to survive within a bureaucratic structure.

In 2002 the National Opinion Research Center at the University of Chicago asked U.S. adult survey respondents how important various life transitions and events were as indicators of adulthood. Is it reaching sexual maturity and starting a family, as in some cultures? It turns out that is not important in the United States. A substantial majority of Americans say to be an adult is to be

---

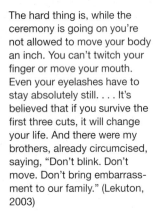

patterns are affected by the social capital of a child's family: their financial resources, cognitive skill of parents, and the connections between family and community (Coleman, 1988, 1990).

Adolescence

During adolescence, individuals undergo revolutionary changes in growth and development. After years of inferiority they suddenly catch up with adults in physical size, strength, and physiological sexual maturation. But in much of the world, adolescence is not a socially distinct period in the human life course (Burbank, 1988).

Although young people everywhere undergo the physiological changes associated with puberty, children in many countries are socialized to assume adult responsibilities by age 13 and even younger.

Many non-Western societies use **puberty rites**—initiation ceremonies—to symbolize the transition from childhood to adulthood. Mild versions of puberty rites in Western societies include the Jewish bar mitzvah and bat mitzvah, confirmation in some Christian denominations, securing a driver's license, and graduation from high school and college. Box 3.2 discusses becoming an adult in America.

financially independent, finished with school, employed full time, and *able* to support a family; in other words, to be fully integrated into the economy. Eighty percent of survey respondents indicated that financial independence was quite or extremely important to being an adult, 90 percent said that formal schooling should be completed, 84 percent said that full-time employment was a marker of adulthood, and 82 percent indicated that one should be able to support a family. Leaving one's family of origin—the family one grows up in—and starting a new family was much less important in people's minds. Just over half of survey respondents thought that it was quite or extremely important to being an adult that one not live with one's parents, a third believed that getting married confers adulthood, and only 28 percent indicated that having children was an important marker of adulthood.

Using this research as a guide, when *do* Americans "come of age"? If we use full-time employment as the indicator of becoming adult, a quarter of 18-year-olds, half of 21-year-olds, and three-quarters of 24-to 49-year-olds qualify for adult status. In other words, the youngest age group for which most people are employed full time is 24. When do Americans finish their formal education? Nearly half of all 20-year-olds are still in school, but by age 22 or 23 about 70 percent are finished with school. Between the ages of 26 and 29 only 13 percent are still in school, and the number keeps dropping. What about moving away from home? More than half of all 18- to 24-year-old males and 46 percent of females live at home (these percentages include unmarried college students living in dorms during the academic year). For 25- to 34-year-olds, those percentages drop to 13.6 (male) and 8.3 (female).

Some cultures mark the transition of their youth from childhood to adulthood at age 12 or 13. In the United States most people make the transition to adulthood by about the age of 26.

Questions for Discussion

1. Why does it take about twice as long to become an adult in the United States as it does in societies based on hunting and gathering or simple agriculture?

2. How and, more importantly, why do the results of this research differ from legal and other institutional criteria for adulthood (e.g., voting, being drafted into the military, standing trial as an adult, buying alcoholic beverages, paying adult ticket prices, and serving in high government positions such as the U.S. Congress and as U.S. President)?

Original data analysis for this box was done by the authors using the General Social Survey data for 2002 (Davis, Smith, and Marsden, 2003). Data on ages by which people have accomplished tasks associated with adulthood comes from Current Population Survey (CPS) data published by the U.S. Census Bureau at http://www.census.gov.

In the United States adolescence appears to be an "invention" of the past 100 years (Kett, 1977; Raphael, 1988). As the nation changed from an agricultural to an industrial society, children no longer had a significant economic function in the family. In time, mandatory school attendance, child labor laws, and special legal procedures for "juveniles" established adolescence as a well-defined social reality.

In the view of neo-Freudians like Erik Erikson (1963, 1968), the main task of adolescents in Western societies is to build and confirm a reasonably stable identity, that development of self so important to socialization. For adolescents, Erikson said, the search for identity is particularly acute.

Erikson's view of adolescence is in keeping with a long Western psychological tradition that has portrayed adolescence as a period of "storm and stress" caused by the difficult transition from childhood to adulthood (Raphael, 1988; Hamburg and Takanishi, 1989). By the mid-1980s, however, research had accumulated challenging the view that adolescence among American youth is inherently a turbulent period (Rosenberg, 1986, 1989; Nottelmann, 1987; Savin-Williams and Demo, 1984). Although the self-images and self-conceptions of young people change, the changes are not invariably "stormy." Rather than experiencing dramatic change and disruption, adolescents gradually fashion their identities based on their sexual circumstances and their evolving competencies and skills (Corsaro and Eder, 1995) resulting in improvement in self-esteem across the adolescent years for most youth.

Although the media make a good deal out of generational differences between adolescents and their parents, the notion of a "generation gap" vastly oversimplifies matters. Research shows that the peer group has the greater influence on musical tastes, personal adornment, and entertainment idols, and in some cases with substance use. But the family has the greater influence on future life goals, fundamental behavior codes, and core values (Gecas and Seff, 1990) and can reduce the risk of substance abuse (Mann, 2003).

Young Adulthood

The socialization process continues as we grow out of adolescence. Recent developments in the Western world—the growth of service industries, the prolongation of education, and the enormously high educational demands of postindustrial society—have lengthened the transition to adulthood (Buchmann, 1989). In some respects our society appears to be evolving a new status between adolescence and adulthood: youth—men and women of college and graduate school age (Neugarten and Neugarten, 1987a, 1987b). In leaving home, youth in their late teens or early twenties may choose a transitional institution, such as the military or college, to start them on their way. Or young people may work (provided they can find a job) while continuing to live at home. During this time a roughly equal balance exists between being in the family and moving out. Individuals become less financially dependent, enter new roles and living arrangements, and achieve greater autonomy and responsibility. With the passage of time the center of gravity in young people's lives

gradually shifts away from the family of origin, and they face two core developmental tasks: learning to build and manage trusting and supporting love relationships (Erikson, 1963) and learning how to adapt to the world of work by managing a career and job changes (Freud, 1938).

In making their way through adulthood, individuals are strongly influenced by **age norms**—rules that define what is appropriate for people to be and to do at various ages. In a sense, people set their personal watches by a **social clock,** and most people can readily report whether they themselves are early, late, or on time with regard to major life events (Neugarten and Neugarten, 1987a, 1987b).

Some psychologists have undertaken the search for what they view as the regular, sequential periods and transitions in the life cycle (e.g., Erikson, 1963). They depict life as a succession of stages. The interaction that occurs between an individual and society—socialization processes—at each stage can change the course of personality, or development of the self, in a positive or a negative direction. Erikson's chief concern was with psychological development, which he divided into the eight major stages of development described in Table 3.1 (p. 91). Each stage poses a unique task that revolves about a crisis—a turning point of increased vulnerability and heightened potential. According to Erikson, the crises posed by each stage must be successfully resolved if healthy development is to take place.

Daniel J. Levinson (1986; Levinson et al., 1978) also approached adulthood from a stage perspective. In Levinson's view, the overriding task confronting individuals throughout adulthood is to create a structure for life through interacting with the environment. But the structure does not become established once and for all time; it must be continually modified and reappraised. Transition periods tend to loom within 2 or 3 years of, and on either side of, the symbolically significant birthdays: 20, 30, 40, 50, and 60.

Table 3.1	Erikson's Eight Stages of Development		
Development Stage	Psychosocial Crisis	Predominant Social Setting	Favorable Outcome
1. Infancy	Basic trust vs. mistrust	Family	The child develops trust in him- or herself, his or her parents, and the world.
2. Early childhood	Autonomy vs. shame, doubt	Family	The child develops a sense of self-control without loss of self-esteem.
3. Fourth to fifth year	Initiative vs. guilt	Family	The child learns to acquire direction and purpose in activities.
4. Sixth year to onset of puberty	Industry vs. inferiority	Neighborhood; school	The child acquires a sense of mastery and competence.
5. Adolescence	Identity vs. role confusion	Peer groups and out-groups	The individual develops an *ego identity*—a coherent sense of self.
6. Young adulthood	Intimacy vs. isolation	Partners in friendship and sex	The individual develops the capacity to work toward a specific career and to involve himself or herself in an extended intimate relationship.
7. Adulthood	Generativity vs. stagnation	New family; work	The individual becomes concerned with others beyond the immediate family, with future generations, and with society.
8. Old age	Integrity vs. despair	Retirement and impending death	The individual acquires a sense of satisfaction in looking back upon his or her life.

Source: From *Childhood and Society*, by Erik H. Erikson. Copyright 1950, © 1963 by W. W. Norton & Company, Inc., renewed © 1978, 1991 by Erik H. Erikson. Reprinted by permission of W. W. Norton & Company, Inc.

People locate themselves during the life course not only in terms of social timetables but also in terms of **life events**—turning points at which people change some direction in the course of their lives. Some of these events are related to social clocks, but many are not, such as suffering severe injury in an accident, being raped, winning a lottery, undergoing a born-again conversion, being in war, living through a disaster, or suffering financial ruin. Not surprisingly, gender affects a person's experience of life events. For example, men are more likely than women to report being distressed by work and financial events; women are more strongly influenced by exposure to negative events within the family (Conger et al., 1993).

Middle Adulthood

Middle adulthood lacks the concrete boundaries of infancy, childhood, and adolescence. It is a catch-all category that includes people from 30 to 65 years according to various definitions. The core tasks of middle adulthood remain much the same as they were for men and women in young adulthood and revolve around love (which we will discuss in Chapter 10) and work.

The central portion of the adult life span of both men and women is spent in work; thus, much of their socialization revolves around work. Levinson (1986; Levinson et al., 1978) found that men in their early thirties tend to establish their niche in the world, dig in, build a nest, and make and pursue long-range plans and goals. In their mid- to late thirties, men seek to break out from under the authority of others and assert their independence. In their early forties, men begin assessing where they stand in relation to the goals they set for themselves earlier. Around 45 some men may experience a "midlife crisis." In contrast to the popular media image of midlife crisis, however, researchers find that middle-aged men and women report less psychological distress than other age groups (Wethington, Cooper, and Holmes, 1997; Kessler et al., 1992).

Evidence suggests that women progress through the same developmental periods as the men in Levinson's study and at roughly the same ages, but there are important differences. Although the timing of the periods and the nature of the developmental tasks are similar, the ways women approach these tasks and the outcomes they achieve are different. To a considerable extent, these differences derive from the greater complexity of women's visions for their future and the difficulties they encounter in living them out. Whereas men see autonomy and competition as central to life, women view life as a means for integrating themselves into human relationships. Psychologist Carol Gilligan (1982; Gilligan, Ward, and Taylor, 1989) argues that the development of women involves the recovery in adulthood of confidence, assertiveness, and a positive sense of self that are lost during adolescence. But studies dealing with phases in adult female development have lagged behind those of men, and there is much to be learned about gender differences in socialization and the effects those differences have.

Later Adulthood

Socialization is as important in old age as in other stages of adult development. Indeed, for many people the last years of one's life may be filled with more dramatic changes than any previous stages. Retiring, losing one's spouse, becoming disabled, moving to a nursing home or other care facility, and preparing for death all require individuals to change and adapt. However, the way "old age" proceeds varies considerably across cultures and for people in different gender, racial, ethnic, and class categories within societies (Calasanti and Slevin, 2001; Newman, 2003).

Like other periods of the life course, the time at which later adulthood begins is a matter of social definition. In preindustrial societies life expectancy is typically short and the onset of old age is early. In U.S. society, race and class affect life expectancy and the onset of old age, with the poor and minorities becoming "old before their time" (Newman, 2003:114).

Societies differ in the prestige and dignity they accord the aged. In many traditional rural societies, elders enjoyed a prominent, esteemed, and honored position (Lang, 1946). In contrast, youth is the favored age in the United States. We have restricted the roles open to the elderly and accord them little prestige.

Despite our unfavorable stereotypes regarding the elderly in the United States, this group is widely varied. Only 11 persons out of 1,000 in the 65 to 74 age group live in nursing homes. The figure rises to 42 for those 75 to 84, and to 182 for those over 85 (U.S. Census Bureau, 2003). Overall, only one American in five who is over age 65 will ever be relegated to a nursing home. Additionally, only 3 percent of the elderly who live at home are bedridden, 5 percent are seriously incapacitated, and another 11 to 16 percent are restricted in mobility. On the other hand, from one-half to three-fifths of the elderly function without any limitation (Goleman, 1994). Recent research indicates that many skills improve with age, especially verbal abilities and social skills (Helmuth, 2003). Adult brains both lose fewer neurons than previously thought and grow new neurons. Further, the elderly have better mental health, fewer negative emotions, and better social relationships than younger people, and they maintain and even improve the skills that are important to them. While openness to new experiences decreases a little in old age, in this time of life, people become more agreeable and conscientious, and, for the most part, they retain their emotional stability as they age further (Roberts, Walton, and Viechtbauer, 2006). Dependency in old age is not inevitable, but a by-product of social definitions and social policies and procedures that vary across cultures, governments, and economic systems (Calasanti and Zajicek, 1997).

Many elderly people continue to lead productive working lives far beyond retirement age.

▲ Role Loss

Old age entails exiting from some social roles. One of the most important of these exits in Western society is retirement from a job. Traditionally, retirement has been portrayed as having negative consequences for the elderly because occupational status is a master status—an anchoring point for adult identity.

In recent years the importance of retirement has been challenged (Calasanti and Slevin, 2001). For one thing, many Americans do not have an uninterrupted work life, and the "unemployment" of retirement may be just one more in a series. Even white men, for whom the idea of a 40-year career may hold true, increasingly report that withdrawal from full-time work is followed by part-time or temporary employment; a clearly defined retirement is less common. Gender plays a role, too; when women "retire," they withdraw only from paid labor. Their roles in cooking, cleaning, shopping, doing laundry, and caring for family members continue. Race also affects the retirement picture. For example, African-American men spend a greater proportion of their lives in the labor market and suffer higher rates of disability than whites (Calasanti and Slevin, 2001). And the effect of class and the economy is obvious: The most wealthy retired are able to pay to make their lives more comfortable, while the elderly poor and middle class are burdened with the daily tasks of living or forced by financial considerations to continue working.

Many elderly individuals also experience another role loss, that of being married. Although 75 percent of American men 65 and over are married and living with their wives, the same holds true for only 44 percent of women; women typically outlive men by 5 to 7 years and usually marry men older than themselves (U.S. Census Bureau, 2003). Research by Helena Znaniecki Lopata (1973, 1981) revealed that the higher a woman's education and socioeconomic class, the more disorganized her self-identity and life become after her husband's death. However, once their "grief work" is accomplished, these women have more resources to form a new lifestyle. Overall, negative long-term consequences of widowhood appear to derive more from socioeconomic deprivation than from widowhood itself (Bound et al., 1991). Lopata found that about half of the widows in her study lived alone, and most of them said they much preferred to do so. Only 10 percent moved in with their married children. Those who lived alone cited the desire to remain independent as their chief reason.

Death

A diagnosis of impending death requires that an individual adjust to a new definition of self. To be defined as dying implies more than the presence of a series of biochemical processes (De Vries, 1981). It entails the assumption of a social status, one in which social structuring not only attends but shapes the dying experience. Consider, for instance, the different social definitions we typically attribute to a 20-year-old who has been given a 5-year life expectancy and those we attribute to a healthy 80-year-old. Likewise, hospital personnel give different care to patients based on their perceived social worth. In a now classic study of a hospital emergency room, sociologist David Sudnow (1967) found that different social evaluations led the staff to work frantically to revive a young child but to acquiesce in the death of an elderly woman.

More recently, in doing cost–benefit analyses of pollution regulations, the Environmental Protection Agency used a figure for the value of a senior citizen's life that was 37.8 percent less than the value for younger people's lives (Hahn and Wallsten, 2003). Finally, although death is a biological event, it is made a social reality through such culturally fashioned events as wakes and funerals.

Changes in medical technology and social conditions have made death a different experience than in earlier times. Dying in the modern world is often drawn out and enmeshed in formal bureaucratic processes (Nuland, 1994). Only a few generations ago most people died at home and the family assumed responsibility for laying out the deceased and preparing for the funeral. Today, only 25 percent of Americans die at home, though most survey respondents say they would prefer to die at home surrounded by the people who love them (Baker, 2003). Nursing homes or hospitals care for the terminally ill and manage the dying experience. A mortuary—euphemistically called a "home"—prepares the body and makes the funeral arrangements or arranges for the cremation of the remains. As a result the average American's exposure to the death of others is minimized. The dying and the dead are segregated from others and placed with specialists for whom contact with death has become a routine and impersonal matter.

Medical advances have done much to change the experience of dying. A century ago, the major causes of death were pneumonia and other acute illnesses. Today 70 percent of U.S. citizens die of long-term illnesses including heart disease, Alzheimer's, and cancer (Baker, 2003). With pain or physical or mental diminishment over a significant period of time part of the picture, Americans are increasingly grappling with the issue of **euthanasia**—the painless putting to death of an individual who suffers from an incurable and painful disease. Debates over whether to legalize euthanasia must distinguish between voluntary and involuntary euthanasia as well as between active and passive euthanasia. Passive euthanasia, the withholding or withdrawing of life supports, requires permission from the dying person in the form of an advance directive that details his or her end-of-life preferences or permission from someone legally authorized by the dying person to make such decisions. In 2001, 65 percent of survey respondents said that they thought doctors should be allowed to "comply with the wishes of a dying patient in severe distress who asks to have his or her life ended" (Pastore and Maguire, 2003).

Another approach that returns death to individuals and families is the hospice movement, which seeks a more humane approach for the care of the terminally ill. A **hospice** is a program or mode of care that attempts to make the dying experience less painful and emotionally traumatic for patients and their families.

Elisabeth Kübler-Ross (1969, 1981) contributed a good deal to the movement to restore dignity and humanity to death. Kübler-Ross argued that it is best if impending death is not hidden and if everyone is allowed to express his or her genuine emotions and to have these feelings be respected. Although there are different styles for dying—just as there are different styles for living—Kübler-Ross (1969) found that dying people typically pass through five stages in accommodating themselves to impending death: denial that they will die, anger that their life will shortly end, bargaining with God or fate to arrange a temporary truce, depression or "preparatory grief," and acceptance. A great many other factors also influence the dying experience, including differences in gender, ethnic membership, personality, the death environment, and the nature of the disease itself. Public and professional awareness of the dying person's experience has given impetus to a more humane approach to death, but increased bureaucratization of the U.S. health care system has not allowed for widespread implementation of that approach. Most physicians still lack training in how to speak about death and dying with patients and their families (Groopman, 2002).

The Chapter in Brief: *Socialization*

Foundations for Socialization

Socialization is the process of social interaction by which people acquire those behaviors essential for effective participation in society, the process of becoming a social being. It is essential for the renewal of culture and the perpetuation of society. The individual and society are mutually dependent on socialization.

■ *Nature and Nurture*   Human socialization presupposes that an adequate genetic endowment and an adequate environment are available. Hereditary and environmental factors interact with and affect each other.

■ *Theories of Socialization*   Theories of socialization include functionalist and conflict theory perspectives as well as three microlevel approaches. Social learning theory emphasizes **conditioning** and **observational learning.** Cognitive developmental theory argues that socialization proceeds differently in the sensorimotor, preoperational, concrete operational, and formal operations stages.

Symbolic interactionists say **reflexive behavior** facilitates the development of the self.

▌ *Agents of Socialization*

One of the most important early agents of socialization is the family. As children grow, peers and schools become important agents of socialization. The mass media, especially television, also serve as agents of socialization.

▌ *Social Communication*

If they are to adapt to their social environment, human beings must be able to communicate.

Communication refers to the process by which people transmit information, ideas, attitudes, and mental states to one another. It includes the verbal and nonverbal processes (**body language, paralanguage, proxemics,** touch, and artifacts) by which we send and receive messages.

▌ *Definition of the Situation*

An important part of socialization is learning what constitutes reality—the basic schemes we use to make sense of and understand the social and physical world. **Definition of the situation** is the interpretation or meaning we give to our immediate circumstances. Our definitions influence our construction of reality, an insight captured by the **Thomas theorem.**

The Self and Socialization

The formation of the **self**—the set of concepts we use in defining who we are—is a central part of the socialization process. The self emerges in the course of interaction with other people and represents the ideas we have regarding our attributes, capacities, and behavior. It typically includes an **egocentric bias.**

▌ *Charles Horton Cooley: The Looking-Glass Self*

Charles Horton Cooley's notion that our consciousness arises in a social context is exemplified by his concept of the **looking-glass self**—a process by which we imaginatively assume the stance of other people and

view ourselves as we believe they see us. **Self-image** is differentiated from **self-conception. Self-esteem** is governed by **reflected appraisals, social comparisons,** and self-attribution. **Personal efficacy** is another aspect of self-evaluation.

▌ *George Herbert Mead: The Generalized Other*

George Herbert Mead contended that we gain a sense of selfhood by acting toward ourselves in much the same fashion that we act toward others. According to Mead, children typically pass through three stages in developing a full sense of selfhood: the play stage, in which the child plays roles modeled on a **significant other;** the game stage; and the **generalized other** stage.

▌ *Erving Goffman: Impression Management*

Erving Goffman pointed out that only by influencing other people's ideas of us can we hope to predict or control what happens to us. Consequently, we have a stake in presenting ourselves to others in ways that will lead them to view us in a favorable light, a process Goffman calls **impression management.** Goffman introduced the **dramaturgical approach.**

Socialization across the Life Course

Socialization is a continuing, lifelong process. All societies have to deal with the **life course** that begins with conception and continues through old age and ultimately death. **Role socialization** involves **anticipatory socialization,** altering roles, and exiting from roles.

▌ *Childhood*

Though societies differ in their definitions of childhood, they all begin the socialization process as soon as possible. Children display people-oriented responses at very early ages and develop very quickly in other ways. The "social capital" contained within a family's environment is of vital consequence in channeling and shaping children's futures.

▌*Adolescence* In much of the world, adolescence is not a socially distinct period in the human life span. Children in many countries are socialized to assume adult responsibilities by age 13 and even younger, sometimes by way of **puberty rites.** Adolescence is not necessarily a turbulent period, nor does a sharp generation gap separate American adolescents from their parents.

▌*Young Adulthood* The developmental and socialization tasks confronting young adults revolve about the core tasks of work and love. Individuals are strongly influenced by age norms and tend to set their personal watches by a **social clock.** Some social scientists have looked for stages through which young adults typically pass. Others believe that unexpected events play a more important role in development. People locate themselves during the life course not only in terms of social timetables but also in terms of **life events.**

▌*Middle Adulthood* Middle adulthood is a somewhat nebulous period. The core tasks remain much the same as they were in young

adulthood. Increasingly, work is coming to be defined for both men and women as a badge of membership in the larger society. Although economic considerations predominate, people also work as a means to structure their time, interact with other people, escape from boredom, and sustain a positive self-image.

▌*Later Adulthood* The last years of one's life may be filled with more dramatic changes than any previous stage. Retiring, losing one's spouse, becoming disabled, moving to a nursing home or other care facility, and preparing for death all require individuals to change and adapt. Societies differ in the prestige and dignity they accord the aged.

▌*Death* A diagnosis of impending death requires that an individual adjust to a new definition of self. Changes in medical technology and social conditions have made death a different experience from that of earlier times. Americans are grappling with the issue of **euthanasia,** and the **hospice** movement has arisen to provide a more humane approach to the dying experience.

Glossary

age norms Rules that define what is appropriate for people to be and to do at various ages.

anticipatory socialization The process in which people think about, experiment with, and try on the behaviors associated with a new role.

body language Physical motions and gestures that provide social signals.

communication The process by which people transmit information, ideas, attitudes, and mental states to one another.

conditioning A form of learning in which the consequences of behavior determine the probability of its future occurrence.

definition of the situation A concept formulated by William I. Thomas, which refers to the interpretation or meaning people give to their immediate circumstances.

dramaturgical approach The sociological perspective associated with Erving Goffman that views the performances staged in a theater as an analytical analogy and tool for depicting social life.

egocentric bias The tendency to place ourselves at the center of events so that we overperceive ourselves as the victim or target of an action or event that in reality is not directed at us.

euthanasia The painless putting to death of an individual who suffers from an incurable and painful disease.

generalized other The term George Herbert Mead applied to the social unit that gives individuals their unity of self. The attitude of the generalized other is the attitude of the larger community.

hospice A program or mode of care that attempts to make the dying experience less painful and emotionally traumatic for patients and their families.

impression management The term Erving Goffman applied to the process whereby we present ourselves to others in ways that will lead them to view us in a favorable light.

language acquisition device The view associated with Noam Chomsky that human beings possess an inborn language-generating mechanism. The basic structure of language is seen as biologically channeled, forming a sort of prefabricated filing system to order the words and phrases that make up human languages.

life course The interweave of age-graded trajectories with the vicissitudes of changing social conditions and future options that characterize the life span from conception through old age and death.

life events Turning points at which people change some direction in the course of their lives.

looking-glass self The term that Charles Horton Cooley applied to the process by which we imaginatively assume the stance of other people and view ourselves as we believe they see us.

observational learning Learning that occurs when people reproduce the responses they observe in other people, either real or fictional; also referred to as modeling or imitation.

paralanguage Nonverbal cues surrounding speech—voice, pitch, volume, pacing of speech, silent pauses, and sighs—that provide a rich

source of communicative information.

personal efficacy The belief that one can overcome obstacles and achieve goals.

proxemics The way we employ social and personal space to transmit messages.

puberty rites Initiation ceremonies that symbolize the transition from childhood to adulthood.

reflected appraisals Appraisals of ourselves that we see reflected in the behavior of others.

reflexive behavior Actions through which people observe, interpret, evaluate, communicate with, and attempt to control themselves.

self The set of concepts we use in defining who we are.

self-conception An overriding view of ourselves; a sense of self through time.

self-esteem The belief that one is a good and valuable person.

self-image A mental conception or picture we have of ourselves that is relatively temporary; it changes as we move from one context to another.

significant other The term George Herbert Mead applied to a social model, usually an important person in an individual's life.

social clock   A cultural timetable based on age norms and used by individuals to pace the major events of their lives.

social comparisons   Comparing one's perfor-mance, ability, or characteris-tics with those of others and rating oneself as positive, neutral, or negative.

socialization   A process of social interaction by which people acquire the knowledge, attitudes, values, and behaviors essential for effective partici-pation in society.

Thomas theorem   The notion that our definitions influence our construction of reality; as stated by William I. Thomas and Dorothy S. Thomas: "If [people] define situations as real, they are real in their consequences."

Review Questions

1. Describe the interplay of nature and nurture as understood today.

2. Name two macrolevel and three microlevel theories of socialization.

3. What are some of the important agents of socialization in today's society? How might they differ from the past?

4. What are some forms of nonverbal com-munication?

5. What is the looking-glass self?

6. What is the generalized other?

7. Describe impression management.

8. What are some of the important characteris-tics of each of the major stages of the life course?

Internet Connection

www.mhhe.com/hughes8

Several agents of socialization were discussed in this chapter, including the family, the school, peers, and the mass media. To what degree does the Internet serve as an agent of socialization? The Internet may socialize people directly, or its im-pact may be that it magnifies or diminishes the ef-fects of other agents of socialization. At the same time, other agents of socialization may buffer or enhance the effects of the Internet. To complete this exercise, use your browser to log into at least three of your favorite websites. (If you have no favorite sites, use any search engine and type your three favorite leisure time activities—one at a time—into the search window, click "search," and follow any links you choose.) Think about how these sites may influence you and others your age. Do the messages you receive from the sites com-plement or conflict with messages you receive from other agents of socialization: parents, peers, school, and other media? Speculate about how and why some agents of socialization are more impor-tant than others.

Chapter 4

SOCIAL GROUPS AND FORMAL ORGANIZATIONS

Group Relationships

Primary Groups and Secondary Groups
In-Groups and Out-Groups
Reference Groups

Group Dynamics

Group Size
Leadership
Social Loafing
Social Dilemmas
Groupthink
Conformity

Formal Organizations

Types of Formal Organization
Bureaucracy: A Functional Approach
  to Organizations

Characteristics of Bureaucracies
Problems of Bureaucracy
Conflict and Interactionist Perspectives
Humanizing Bureaucracies

Anyone who has paid for car insurance as a teenaged driver—or begged their parents to do so for them—knows that the rates are high. And with reason: Insurance companies know that accident rates are high for teen drivers. In fact, the leading cause of death for U.S. teenagers is car crashes; more than a third of all deaths of 15- to 19-year-olds result from motor vehicle crashes (Chen et al., 2000).

This death rate is higher when teens travel in groups. In fact, the more teenage passengers per car, the higher the fatal crash rate for teen drivers. The highest death rate is for drivers with three or more passengers in the car, but simply adding a single male teen passenger nearly doubles the probability that the driver will be killed in a wreck. It is just the opposite for older drivers—for 30- to 59-year-olds, fatal crash rates go *down* significantly for drivers with passengers (Chen et al., 2000).

Groups and group interactions are of great interest to sociologists. What is going on with this driving phenomenon? It turns out that dangerous driving behaviors—driving while drunk or high, speeding, skidding, swerving, running red lights, and the like—are "strongly associated with the presence of peers" (Chen et al., 2000:1581). In other words, teen drivers are much more likely to show off, goof off, and in general take more risks when they are driving around in a group of teenagers who are cheering them on. Older drivers, on the other hand, are probably motivated to be more careful than usual when driving with passengers, especially when those passengers are children.

As we discussed in Chapter 2, a **group** consists of two or more people who are bound together in relatively stable patterns of social interaction and who share a feeling of unity. Groups are not tangible things; rather, they are products of social definitions—sets of shared ideas. As such they constitute constructed realities. In other words, we make groups real by treating them as if they are real, a clear application of the *Thomas theorem* (see Chapter 3). ←p. 81 We fabricate groups in the course of our social interaction as we cluster people together in social units: families, teams, cliques, nationalities, races, labor unions, fraternities, clubs, corporations, and the like. In turn we act on the basis of these shared mental fabrications, creating an existence beyond the individuals who are involved. As we discussed in Chapter 2, groups are social structures that have an existence apart from the particular relationships individual people have with one another. For this reason many groups, like the high school you graduated from, have an existence that extends beyond the life spans of specific people.

With groups, the whole is greater than the sum of its parts. Groups have distinctive properties in their own right apart from the particular individuals who belong to them. In Durkheim's terminology (1895/1938), they are ←p. 13 *social facts* (see Chapter 1). Accordingly, we can speak of families, cliques, clubs, and organizations without having to break them down into the separate interactions that compose them.

Groups provide the structure by which we involve ourselves in the daily affairs of life, yet we may not appreciate the part they play until we are separated from them. How many groups can you think of that form a part of your life? Your answer may include your family; your apartment or dorm mates; your sorority, fraternity, or other more formal organizations; classmates and old friends from high school. If you aren't involved with others at college, you might want to be: Researchers have found that undergraduates are more likely to succeed when they have formed alliances with other students, faculty members, and advisors (DePalma, 1991). Even physical health is associated with relationships with others. Accidents, suicides, alcoholism, tuberculosis, and heart attacks are more common among socially isolated individuals

(Brummett et al., 2001; House, Landis, and Umberson, 1988; Gove and Hughes, 1980), and cancer patients with strong emotional support from others live longer than those who lack such support (Goleman, 1991).

In this chapter we will consider group relationships, group dynamics, and a particular type of group, formal organizations.

Group Relationships

Life places us in a complex web of relationships with other people. As we noted in Chapter 3, our humanness arises out of these relationships in the course of social interaction. Moreover, our humanness must be sustained through social interaction, and fairly constantly so. When an association continues long enough for two people to become linked together by a relatively stable set of expectations, it is called a **relationship.**

People are bound within relationships by two types of bonds: expressive ties and instrumental ties. **Expressive ties** are social links formed when we emotionally invest ourselves in and commit ourselves to other people. Through association with people who are meaningful to us, we achieve a sense of security, love, acceptance, companionship, and personal worth. **Instrumental ties** are social links formed when we cooperate with other people to achieve some goal. Occasionally, this may mean working with our enemies. More often, we simply cooperate with others to reach some end without endowing the relationship with any larger significance.

In this section we will discuss several types of groups: primary groups and secondary groups, in-groups and out-groups, and reference groups.

Primary Groups and Secondary Groups

Sociologists have built on the distinction between expressive and instrumental ties to distinguish between two types of groups: primary and secondary. A **primary group** is a small group characterized by intimate, informal interaction. Expressive ties predominate in primary groups; we view the people—friends, family members, and lovers—as ends in themselves and valuable in their own right. Primary group relationships are more likely to emerge if the number of people is small enough so that each person can establish rapport with each other person, if there is enough face-to-face contact so that people can exchange ideas and feelings in subtle and personal ways, and if people interact frequently and continuously enough to deepen their ties and develop interlocking habits and interests.

A primary group involves two or more people who enjoy a direct, intimate, cohesive relationship with one another.

Primary groups are critical to the socialization process. Within them, infants and children are introduced to the ways of their society. Such groups are the breeding grounds in which we acquire the norms and values that equip us for social life. Sociologists view primary groups as bridges between individuals and the larger society because they transmit, mediate, and interpret a society's cultural patterns and provide the sense of oneness so critical for social solidarity.

Primary groups also are fundamental because they provide the settings in which we meet most of our personal needs. Within them we experience companionship, love, security, and an overall sense of well-being. Not surprisingly, sociologists find that the strength of a group's primary ties has implications for its functioning. For example, the stronger the primary group ties of troops fighting together, the better their combat record (Elder and Clipp, 1988; Copp and McAndrew, 1990). During World War II the success of German military units derived not from Nazi ideology, but from the ability of the German army to reproduce in

the infantry company the intimacy and bonds found in civilian primary groups (Shils and Janowitz, 1948). What made the *Wehrmacht* so formidable was that, unlike the U.S. Army, German soldiers who trained together went into battle together. Additionally, U.S. fighting units were kept up to strength through individual replacement, whereas German units remained on line until there were so many casualties that they had to be pulled back and reconstituted as a new group (Van Creveld, 1982). The Israelis also found that combat units hastily thrown together without time to form close bonds perform more poorly in battle and experience higher rates of psychiatric casualties than units with close bonds (Solomon, Mikulincer, and Hobfoll, 1986).

Primary groups serve as powerful instruments for social control. Their members command and dispense many of the rewards that are so vital to us and that make our lives seem worthwhile. Should the use of rewards fail, members can frequently win compliance by rejecting or threatening to ostracize those who deviate from the group's norms. For instance, some religious cults employ "shunning" (i.e., a person can remain in the community, but others are forbidden to interact with him or her) as a device to bring into line individuals whose behavior goes beyond that allowed by the group's teachings. Even more importantly, primary groups define social reality for us by "structuring" our experiences. By providing us with definitions of situations, they elicit from us behavior that conforms to group-devised meanings. Primary groups, then, serve both as carriers of social norms and as enforcers of them.

A **secondary group** entails two or more people who are involved in an impersonal relationship and have come together for a specific, practical purpose. Instrumental ties predominate in secondary groups; we perceive people as means to ends rather than as ends in their own right. Illustrations include our relationships with a clerk in a clothing store and a cashier at a service station. Sometimes primary group relationships evolve out of secondary group relationships. This happens in many work settings. People on the job often develop close relationships with coworkers as they come to share gripes, jokes, gossip, and satisfactions.

In-Groups and Out-Groups

It is not only the groups to which we immediately belong that have a powerful influence upon us. Often the same holds true for groups to which we do not belong. Accordingly, sociologists find it useful to distinguish between in-groups and out-groups. An **in-group** is a group with which we identify and to which we belong. An **out-group** is a group with which we do not identify and to which we do not belong. In daily conversation we recognize the distinction between in-groups and out-groups in our use of the personal pronouns "we" and "they." We can think of in-groups as "we-groups" and out-groups as "they-groups." In-groups typically provide us with our *social identities*—those aspects of our self-concept that we derive from a sense of belonging to groups and the feelings

and emotional significance we attach to this belonging (Crocker and Luhtanen, 1990).

The concepts of in-group and out-group highlight the importance of *boundaries*—social demarcation lines that tell us where interaction begins and ends. Group boundaries are not physical barriers but discontinuities in the flow of social interaction. Some boundaries are based on territorial location, such as neighborhoods, communities, and nation-states. Others rest on social distinctions, such as ethnic group or religious, political, occupational, language, kin, and socioeconomic class memberships. Whatever their source, social boundaries face in two directions. They prevent outsiders from entering a group's sphere, and they keep insiders within that sphere.

At times we experience feelings of indifference, disgust, competition, and even outright conflict when we think about or have dealings with out-group members. An experiment undertaken by Muzafer Sherif and his associates (1961) showed how our awareness of in-group boundaries is heightened and antagonism toward out-groups is generated by competitive situations. The subjects were 11-and 12-year-old boys, all of whom were healthy, socially well-adjusted youngsters from stable, middle-class homes. The setting was a summer camp where the boys were divided into two groups.

During the first week at the camp the boys in each group got to know one another, evolved group norms, and arrived at an internal division of labor and leadership roles. During the second week the experimenters brought the two groups into competitive contact through a tournament of baseball, touch football, tug-of-war, and treasure hunt games. Although the contest opened in a spirit of good sportsmanship, positive feelings quickly evaporated. During the third week, the "integration phase," Sherif brought the two groups of boys together for various events, including eating in the same mess hall, viewing movies, and shooting off firecrackers. But far from reducing conflict, these settings merely provided new opportunities for the two groups to challenge, berate, and harass one another. The experimenters then created a series of urgent and natural situations in which the two groups would have to work together to achieve their ends, such as the emergency repair of the conduit that delivered the camp's water supply. The pursuit of common goals led to a lessening of out-group hostilities and the lowering of intergroup barriers to cooperation.

This study demonstrates how competition with out-groups can create in-group solidarity and out-group hostility. However, other research shows that feelings of in-group favoritism do not require competition with out-groups, but seem to emerge spontaneously from the belief that one is connected to some category of people (see Box 4.1). In one experiment, subjects were found to be more likely to trust faces resembling their own (DeBruine, 2002), suggesting a biological basis to some in-group behavior.

Reference Groups

More than a century ago American writer Henry Thoreau observed: "If a man does not keep pace with his companions, perhaps it is because he hears a different drummer." Thoreau's observation contains an important sociological insight. We evaluate ourselves and guide our behavior by group standards. But since Americans are dispersed among many different groups—each with a somewhat unique subculture or counterculture—the frames of reference we use in assessing and fashioning our behavior differ. In brief, we have different **reference groups**—social units we use for appraising and shaping attitudes, feelings, and actions (Singer, 1981). Positive reference groups are those having characteristics that we have or wish we had, and negative reference groups are those that represent to us what we are not or do not wish to be. For a high school student who aspires to achieve academically, a positive reference group might be the students who get high grades and belong to the National Honor Society, whereas a negative

reference group could be students who attend erratically and fail their classes.

A reference group may or may not be our membership group. We may think of a reference group as a base we use for viewing the world, a source of psychological identification. It helps account for seemingly contradictory behavior: the upper-class person who supports a revolution, the Catholic who speaks against the Pope, the union member who supports management, and those who collaborate with the enemy in wartime. These individuals have simply taken as their reference group people other than those from their membership group (Hyman and Singer, 1968). The concept thus helps to illuminate such central sociological concerns as social networks, socialization, and social conformity.

Reference groups provide both *normative* and *comparative* functions (Felson and Reed, 1986). Because we would like to view ourselves as members in good standing within a certain group—or we aspire to such membership—we take on the group's norms and values through the process of anticipatory socialization mentioned in Chapter 3. We cultivate its ← p. 86 lifestyles, political attitudes, musical tastes, food preferences, sexual practices, and drug-using behaviors. We also use the standards of our reference group to appraise ourselves—a comparison point against which we judge and evaluate our physical attractiveness, intelligence, health, ranking, and standard of living. When our membership group does not match our reference group, we may experience feelings of **relative deprivation**—discontent associated with the gap between what we have (the circumstances of our membership group) and what we believe we should have (the circumstances of our reference group). Feelings of relative deprivation often contribute to social alienation and provide fertile conditions for collective behavior and revolutionary social movements. The reference group concept, then, contains clues to processes of social change.

4.1 Social Inequalities

What Does Bias Come From? Sometimes, Almost Nothing

When you crack an egg, do you crack it at the small end or at the large end? Who cares, right? Well, if you have a preference, it would place you in one or the other warring nation in Jonathan Swift's *Gulliver's Travels*. Swift was poking fun at the Catholic–Protestant conflict, but social psychologists Myron Rothbart and Oliver P. John (1993:35) saw more: "This example offers a profound insight into the nature of intergroup conflict. . . . In effect, Swift says that differences regarded as profound and intractable may, with a change in perspective, be thought of as trivial." Such an insight applies to conflicts between nations, between groups, and even between individuals today as well

as in Swift's day. But is it well founded?

Rothbart and John described a set of experiments done with English schoolboys that suggest that bias against the out-group can develop among people who have almost no differences at all. Here's the evidence: Social psychologist Henri Tajfel asked schoolboys to estimate the number of dots they saw projected on a screen. Then the boys were told that they would be placed into two categories, underestimators or overestimators of the number of dots. The boys were then told which category they were in, but they were placed into categories randomly—they were not necessarily overestimators if

placed in that category, and vice versa.

Once the boys knew which category they were in, each subject was asked to allocate rewards to two other boys, about whom he knew only their category (over- or underestimator). When both boys receiving rewards were in the same category, the subject divided the rewards for them equally. When one boy was an in-group member (the same category as the subject giving the rewards) and one an out-group member (the other category), the rewards were given preferentially to the in-group member.

Others have replicated this study and affirmed the findings that subjects favor in-group over

Group Dynamics

To understand groups is to understand much about human behavior. Groups are the wellsprings of our humanness. Although we think of groups as things—distinct and bound entities—it is not their static but their dynamic qualities that make them such a significant force. We need to examine what happens within groups. In this section we will consider group size, leadership, social loafing, social dilemmas, groupthink, and conformity.

Group Size

The size of a group is important because it influences the nature of interaction. The smaller the

group, the more opportunities we have to get to know other people well and to establish close ties with them. Two-person groups—**dyads**—are the setting for many of our most intense and influential relationships, including that between parent and child and between husband and wife. Indeed, most of our social interactions take place on a one-to-one basis.

Sociologist John James (1951) and his students observed 7,405 informal interactions of pedestrians, playground users, swimmers, and shoppers and 1,458 people in a variety of work situations. They found that 71 percent of both the informal and work interactions consisted of two people, 21 percent involved three people, 6 percent included four people, and only 2 percent entailed five or more people. Emotions and feelings tend to play a greater part in dyads than out-group members. Rothbart and John commented on the results (1993:36):

> The two groups were not competing for a limited resource. There was no . . . competition or cooperation between the two groups. There was no historical enmity. There was no aroused frustration in the subjects. There was no objectively determined difference between the two groups; the groups did not differ in terms of language, culture, or physiognomy. . . . As a result of . . . categorization, subjects favored ingroup members with greater resources.

The Tajfel experiments are now referred to as the *minimal group paradigm.* This research showed that bias against an out-group does not depend on a history of enmity between the groups, competition, aggression due to frustration, physical differences, religious differences, or any important value differences at all.

How does the minimal group paradigm relate to group conflict in the real world? Some research suggests that simply the act of categorizing people into groups can lead to significant bias against out-groups: "Categorization generated by the minimal group paradigm implicitly activates the expectation of ingroup superiority ("we" are better than "they"), and . . . subjects will then selectively remember ingroup and out-group behaviors in accordance with their perceived superiority" (1993:37).

Other recent research shows that it also activates people's assumption that members of their in-groups are more likely than out-group members to reciprocate favoritism. Gaertner and Insko's 2000 study of the minimal group paradigm found that category members favored the in-group only in situations in which they thought other in-group members could, and would, reciprocate.

So what is bias based on? Well, not much. According to these experiments, merely being told that one belongs to some category is enough to generate group feeling—*for* one's own group and *against* another. "Even in the absence of real differences, competition, and aggression," wrote Rothbart and John, "bias against an outgroup can develop."

Questions for Discussion

1. What was the basis for grouping boys in the Tajfel experiment?

2. Do the results of the minimal group experiments indicate that intergroup conflict is inevitable?

3. In view of minimal groups effects, what should we do in our society to reduce intergroup conflict?

---

they do in larger groups (Hare, 1976). But this factor also contributes to their relatively fragile nature: A delicate balance exists between the parties, so if one of them becomes disenchanted, the relationship collapses. Contrary to what you might expect, two-person relationships tend to be more emotionally strained and less overtly aggressive than other relationships (Bales and Borgatta, 1955; O'Dell, 1968).

The popular adage "two's company, three's a crowd" captures an important difference between two-person and three-person groups. As the German sociologist Georg Simmel (1950) pointed out, forming a **triad** by adding one person to a dyad is far more consequential than adding one person to any other size group. This change fundamentally alters the social situation. Coalitions become possible, with two members joining forces against a third member. With this arrangement, one person may be placed in the role of an "intruder" or "outsider." Under some circumstances, however, the third person may assume the role of a "mediator" and function as a peacemaker.

One recurring question that has attracted the interest of sociologists is, What is the optimum group size for problem solving? For instance, if you want to appoint a committee to make a recommendation, what would be the ideal size for the group? Small-group research suggests that five is usually the best size (Hare, 1976). A strict deadlock is not possible because there is an odd number of members. Further, because groups tend to split into a majority of three and a minority of two, being a minority does not result in the isolation of one person, as it does in the

One reason five-person groups are particularly effective for problem solving is that they are settings in which people can take risks and express themselves freely.

triad. The group is sufficiently large for the members to shift roles easily and for a person to withdraw from an awkward position without necessarily having to resolve the issue formally. Finally, five-person groups are large enough so that people feel they can express their emotions freely and even risk antagonizing one another, yet they are small enough so that the members show regard for one another's feelings and needs. As groups become larger, they become less manageable. People no longer carry on a "conversation" with the other members, but "address" them with formal vocabulary and grammar. As a result they may come to share progressively less knowledge with one another, undermining group stability (Carley, 1991).

Leadership

Imagine a football team without a quarterback, a class of students without a teacher, or youth gangs without chiefs. Without overall direction, people typically have difficulty coordinating their activities. Consequently, in group settings some members usually exert more influence than others. We call these individuals *leaders*. Small groups may be able to get along without a leader, but in larger groups a lack of leadership leads to chaos.

Two types of leadership roles tend to evolve in small groups (Bales, 1970). One, an **instrumental leader,** is devoted to appraising the problem at hand and organizing people's activity to deal with it. The instrumental leader is sometimes referred to as a *task specialist*. The other, an **expressive leader,** focuses on overcoming interpersonal problems in the group, defusing tensions, and promoting solidarity. The expressive leader is sometimes referred to as a *socio-emotional specialist*. The former type of leadership is *instrumental,* directed toward the achievement of group goals; the latter is *expressive,* oriented toward the creation of harmony and unity. Usually each role is played by a different person, since typically it is the stress created by the task leader that is managed or relieved by the social-emotional leader. Attempting to incorporate both functions in a role played by one person can create role strain (see Chapter 2). ◄— p. 66

Leaders differ in their styles for exercising influence. In classic experiments in leadership by Kurt Lewin and his associates (Lewin, Lippitt, and White, 1939; White and Lippitt, 1960), adult leaders working with groups of 11-year-old boys followed one of three leadership styles. In the *authoritarian style,* the leader made unilateral decisions, gave step-by-step directions, assigned work partners, provided subjective praise and criticism, and remained aloof from group participation. In contrast, in the *democratic style* the leader allowed the boys to help make decisions, outlined only general goals, suggested alternative procedures, permitted the members to work with whomever they wished, evaluated the boys objectively, and participated in group activities. In the *laissez-faire style,* the leader adopted a passive, uninvolved stance; provided materials, suggestions, and help only when requested; and refrained from commenting on the boys' work.

The researchers found that authoritarian leadership produces high levels of frustration and hostile feelings toward the leader. Productivity remains high as long as the leader is present, but it slackens appreciably in the leader's absence. Under democratic leadership, members are as productive as under authoritarian leadership but are happier, feel more group-minded and friendlier, display independence (especially in the leader's absence), and exhibit low levels of interpersonal aggression. Laissez-faire leadership resulted in low group productivity and high levels of interpersonal aggression. While these classic studies suggest that democratic leadership is clearly superior, subsequent research failed to confirm that it always yields better results than authoritarian leadership (Bartol and Martin, 1998; Bass, 1981).

Probably no one leadership style works best in all situations. Different styles may be appropriate in different situations, and elements of both democratic and authoritarian leadership are important factors in effective leadership. Other important contingencies include the leader's personality; the ability, skill, and willingness of followers; and whether the task is clearly defined or involves considerable uncertainty (Fiedler and Garcia, 1987; Vroom and Jago, 1988; Hersey and Blanchard, 1988). Although gender differences in leadership are small, and both women and men can be effective leaders, recent research indicates that female leaders exhibit more characteristics of effective leadership than male leaders (Eagly, Johannesen-Smith, and van Engen, 2003).

Social Loafing

The old saying that "many hands make light the work" turns out to be true: Each "hand" in a group does lighter work than he or she would

alone, and the group as a whole does less work than the sum of each of its members working alone. For example, we might expect that three individuals can pull three times as much as one person can and that eight can pull eight times as much. But research reveals that whereas persons individually average 130 pounds of pressure when tugging on a rope, in groups of three they average 117 pounds each, and in groups of eight only 60 pounds each. One explanation is that faulty coordination produces group inefficiency. However, when subjects are blindfolded and believe they are pulling with others, they also slacken their effort (Ingham, 1974). Apparently when individuals work in groups, they work less hard than they do when working individually—a process called **social loafing** (Williams, Harkins, and Latané, 1981; Karau and Williams, 1993).

Presumably people slack off in groups because they feel they are not receiving their fair share of credit or because they think that in a crowd they can get away with less work. Fortunately, research suggests that the loafing effect can be minimized by providing a standard against which members are asked to evaluate the group's performance (Harkins and Szymanski, 1989).

Social Dilemmas

A **social dilemma** is a situation in which members of a group are faced with a conflict between maximizing their personal interests and maximizing the collective welfare (Yamagishi, 1995). Box 4.2 presents one type of social dilemma: the prisoner's dilemma game. Garrett J. Hardin's (1968) "tragedy of the commons" is the classic illustration of a social dilemma. Hardin explored the situation in which a number of herders share a common pasture. Each person may reason that he or she will benefit by adding another cow to the herd, and then another, and so on. But if each person follows this course, the commons will be destroyed through overgrazing and each will ultimately lose. Hardin was

Compete or Cooperate? The Prisoner's Dilemma

Imagine that you are a criminal and that you and your partner in crime have been taken to the police station on suspicion of having committed a crime. The police believe both of you are guilty, but they lack sufficient evidence to turn the case over to the district attorney for prosecution. The police officers place you and your partner in separate rooms, where each of you may confess or maintain your innocence. The police inform you that if both you and your partner remain silent, each of you will get off with 3-year sentences. If both of you confess, you both will serve 7 years. However, should you confess and implicate your partner while your co-conspirator maintains his innocence, you will be released, but your partner will receive a 15-year prison term. The situation will be reversed should you maintain your innocence and your partner confesses. The figure summarizes your alternatives and their consequences.

What you face is a *social dilemma*. A social dilemma exists when behavior that is

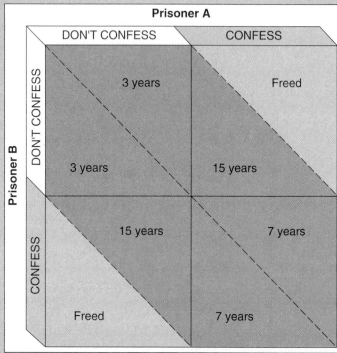

The Prisoner's Dilemma The number in each of the cells shows the number of years each individual would spend in prison.

addressing the problem of population growth, but the notion can be applied to other problems, including pollution.

Social dilemmas are encountered in many other spheres of life as well. Consider the choice confronting a soldier in a foxhole at the outset of a battle. If every soldier remains in the foxhole, the battle will probably be lost and all will be killed (Kerr, 1983).

In many social dilemmas there is a possibility that some other member of the group can and will provide the public good, making one's own contribution unnecessary. This is termed the "free-rider mechanism" (Petersen, 1992;

Yamigishi, 1995). In these situations people can get the benefits of, for example, a social movement with whose goals they agree by contributing nothing and riding free on the efforts of others who are willing to contribute.

Groupthink

In 1961 the Kennedy administration undertook the ill-fated Bay of Pigs invasion of Cuba. Nothing went right for the 1,400 Central Intelligence Agency (CIA)-trained Cuban invaders, most of whom were killed or captured by Fidel Castro's forces. Not only did the advantageous for one party leads to disadvantageous outcomes for others. One way social scientists have examined cooperative and competitive behaviors is by means of the prisoner's dilemma game, described above. As you can gather, the prisoner's dilemma provides a mixed-motive situation in which players must choose between strategies of cooperation and competition.

What would you do under these circumstances? The "don't confess" option is the cooperative one. You show that you trust your partner not to take advantage of the situation by turning state's evidence. But you run the risk that your partner will confess and you will pay a heavy price. The "confess" option is the competitive one. You attempt to improve your situation by betraying your partner. But you also run the risk that your partner will take the same route, ensuring that you both will receive 7-year terms. In brief, the best strategy for you individually results in a particularly punishing outcome if you both select it.

Researchers find that what your opponent consistently does in early games influences how you subsequently respond. When your opponent is consistently (and even foolishly) cooperative, you are more likely to employ a competitive strategy in later games. Should your opponent reciprocate a cooperative move while remaining ready to compete if you do not reciprocate with cooperation, you become more inclined to cooperate. On the other hand, competition begets competition (Dixit and Nalebuff, 1991; Poundstone, 1992).

Robert Axelrod (1984) found that the simplest and most effective strategy for playing the prisoner's dilemma game is one he called "tit for tat." You cooperate on the first move. Thereafter, you respond immediately and in kind to your partner's behavior, following a policy of strict reciprocity: a stringent eye-for-an-eye justice. The strategy seems to work because it combines four properties: It is nice, retaliatory, forgiving, and clear. It is *nice* because it avoids unnecessary conflict as long as the other party reciprocates. Tit for tat is *retaliatory* because it responds to provocation.

The strategy is *forgiving* because it allows the other party to retreat following retaliation. Finally, tit for tat is *clear* and predictable. Clarity is essential so that the other party can grasp the consequences of his or her actions and thereby adapt new strategies that will promote long-term cooperation. Yet tit for tat does not always work. It is particularly vulnerable to cycles of recrimination that end up hurting both parties through relentless feuding (Kollock, 1993).

Questions for Discussion

1. University life is filled with opportunities for competitive or cooperative behaviors. Do you have a generalized strategy of cooperation or competition, or do you use different strategies in different situations?

2. No one gets through life without facing situations that fit the definition of social dilemma. Think of at least two examples from your own life.

invasion solidify Castro's leadership, but it consolidated the Cuban–Soviet alliance and led the Soviet leadership to attempt to place nuclear missiles in Cuba. Later, President John Kennedy was to ask: "How could we have been so stupid?" Not only had the president and his advisers overlooked the size and strength of the Castro army, but in many instances they even had failed to seek relevant information.

Social psychologist Irving Janis (1972, 1982, 1989) suggested that the president and his advisers were victims of **groupthink**—a decision-making process found in highly cohesive groups in which the members become so preoccupied with maintaining consensus that their critical faculties are impaired. In groupthink, members share an illusion of invulnerability that leads to overconfidence, a greater willingness to take risks, and a tendency to ignore contrary evidence. Members of the group demand conformity and apply pressure to those who express doubts about a proposed course of action; they withhold dissent and exercise self-censorship. As a result, decisions are made without the benefit of critical analysis.

Another well-known example of groupthink is the decision process that led to the *Challenger* tragedy in 1986. Engineers who designed and built the solid rocket boosters warned against launching the space shuttle in cold weather. However, NASA decision makers, facing possible budget cuts, experienced considerable pressure from the media and from the intense public interest in the mission that included Christa McCauliffe, the "Teacher in Space." In addition, President Ronald Reagan's State of the Union message was scheduled for the night of the launch date and would have included a mention of the mission had the shuttle been in orbit. Driven partly by these pressures, but isolated from outside influence, NASA decision makers ignored contrary evidence from the engineers and decided to launch in cold weather anyway, a decision that resulted in the loss of the entire crew of seven (Kruglanski, 1986).

Research done since Janis's original formulation (1972) has altered to some degree the thinking of social scientists about groupthink. For example, it is clear that groupthink can occur when decision-making groups are not particularly cohesive; it can result primarily from a strong leader indicating a preference that dominates the thinking of other group members (Bartol and Martin, 1998; Tetlock et al., 1992; see also Granström and Stiwne, 1998; Paulus, 1998). Moreover, though obviously groupthink often leads to poor decisions, there is evidence that it sometimes produces a good outcome, just as high-quality decision-making procedures can occasionally result in a poor outcome (McCauley, 1989).

Conformity

Groupthink research testifies to the powerful social pressures that operate in group settings and produce conformity. Although such pressures influence our behavior, we often are unaware of them. In a pioneering study Muzafer Sherif (1936) demonstrated this point with an optical illusion. If people view a small, fixed spot of light in a darkened room, they perceive it as moving erratically in all directions. However, individuals differ in how far they think the light

"moves." Sherif tested subjects alone and found the reference point for each individual. He then brought together in group settings people with quite different perceptions and asked them again to view the light and report aloud on their observations. Under these circumstances, their perceptions converged toward a group standard. Later, in solitary sessions, they did not return to the standard they had at first evolved but adhered to the standard of the group. Significantly, most subjects reported that they arrived at their assessment independently and that the group had had no influence on them.

Sherif presented subjects with an ambiguous situation; Solomon Asch (1952) asked subjects to match lines of the same length from two sets of cards displayed at the front of the room. He instructed the members of nine-person groups to give their answers aloud. However, only one of the individuals was a subject in the experiment; the others were graduate students working with Asch, and they unanimously provided incorrect answers on certain trials. Despite the obviousness of the correct answer, nearly one-third of all the subjects' judgments contained errors identical with or in the direction of the rigged errors of the majority. Some three-fourths of the subjects conformed on at least one of the trials. Thus, Asch demonstrated that some individuals conform to the false consensus of a group even though the consensus is contradicted by the evidence of their own eyes. Asch's findings have been replicated many times and in many nations and cultures, and although people in some countries conform more than in others, the differences are not very great (Sunstein, 2003).

The Sherif (1936) and Asch (1952) studies illustrate two of the main reasons that people conform: the desire to be correct and the desire to be accepted by the group (Aronson, 1994). It is possible that the conforming subjects in Asch's experiment could see that the task had little significance and thus conformed because it was easy and had no serious consequences. But other experiments have shown that humans are likely to obey orders and to go along with the group even when the stakes are considerably higher (see Box 4.3). The tendency of people to conform and their desire to be accepted by a group is being used by colleges and universities to prevent substance abuse (Sunstein, 2003). The campaigns are based on the idea that most college students overestimate how much drinking and drug use there is on campus and misperceive the tolerance of their peers for substance abuse, leading them to conform with behavior that isn't all that widespread. When students are informed of actual levels of drinking and smoking, they appear to be less likely to become smokers or heavy drinkers.

Formal Organizations

As modern societies have become increasingly complex, so have the requirements of group life. As we noted in Chapter 2 the social organization of traditional societies revolves primarily around kin relations. The division of labor is simple, the people are culturally homogeneous, and there is no formal law. But contemporary societies composed of millions of people can no longer rely entirely on primary group arrangements to accomplish the tasks of social life. Food has to be produced, preserved, and transported over considerable distances to support large urban populations. The residents of large, anonymous communities can no longer count on family members and neighbors to enforce group norms and standards. Children can no longer be educated by the same natural processes by which they learn to walk and talk. For these and many other tasks, people require groups they can deliberately create for the achievement of specific objectives. Such groups are **formal organizations.**

In recent decades the United States has increasingly become a society of large, semiautonomous, and tightly knit formal organizations. Not only is there big government—in municipal organizations as well as the federal government—

but also there are big multinational corporations, big universities, big hospitals, big unions, and big farm organizations. Modern society is emerging as a web of formal organizations that appear, disappear, change, merge, and enter into countless relationships with one another. Although formal organizations have existed for thousands of years, dating back to ancient Mesopotamia, Egypt, and China, only in recent times have their scope and centrality become so pronounced.

In this section we will introduce types of formal organization, define bureaucracy and list its characteristics, discuss problems of bureaucracy, consider various theoretical approaches, and discuss how to humanize bureaucracies.

Types of Formal Organization

People enter formal organizations for a variety of reasons. Sociologist Amitai Etzioni (1975) classified organizations on the basis of these reasons and identified three major types: voluntary, coercive, and utilitarian. **Voluntary organizations** are associations that members enter and leave freely. College campuses abound with examples: hiking and biking groups, service organizations, and intramural sports teams are just a few. Members are not paid for participation; they join voluntary organizations to fill their leisure time, to enjoy the company of like-minded people, to perform some social service, to advance some cause, or to change themselves through self-help organizations (Woodard, 1987).

When voluntary organizations complete their goals, Americans often refashion them, finding new purposes to validate an enterprise. For example, once vaccines eliminated infantile paralysis, the March of Dimes organization reformulated its goals to embrace new health missions (Sills, 1957). In some cases program failure is essential because the effective solution of the problems the organizations address would eliminate the need for their existence. Skid-row rescue missions provide a good illustration of this principle (Rooney, 1980).

Reality TV and Conformity: *The Experiment*

In 2002 the British Broadcasting Corporation (BBC) televised a social science research project. Called *The Experiment,* the show used 15 volunteer subjects who were assigned to be either prisoners or guards in a studio "prison" for 10 days (Haslam and Reicher, 2002; Ritch, 2002). The volunteers for the show/experiment did not know what was going to happen to them, but they were told that "the environment would be challenging, might involve hunger, hardship, and anger, and would resemble a barracks, a prison, or a bootcamp" (Briggs, 2002; Reicher and Haslam, 2003a).

The Experiment was modeled after a 1970s Stanford University study (Haney, Banks, and Zimbardo, 1973; Ritch, 2002). In the original study, conducted by psychologist Philip Zimbardo, 21 male students played the prisoner and guard roles in a mock prison. As the experiment

progressed, the prisoners became more passive and withdrawn and the guards conformed more fully with their guard roles, displaying *institutional aggression.* They forced prisoners to perform useless tasks, sing songs, laugh, or refrain from laughing according to their orders. Although they were instructed not to use physical violence, student guards forced student prisoners to clean toilets with their bare hands, call each other names, and curse at one another (Wiggins, Wiggins, and Vander Zanden, 1994).

Why did the guards' behavior become so nasty? According to Zimbardo and his colleagues, they were simply acting the way they thought prison guards should act. In the 1960s researcher Stanley Milgram discovered that ordinary people readily behave in morally questionable ways in the name of conformity and obedience. In a now-classic experiment, Milgram

used a phony but realistic looking electric chair and instructed a "teacher" to give the "learner" in the electric chair a shock every time the learner made a mistake (Milgram, 1963). Teachers also were told to increase the voltage with each succeeding mistake. The learners were not actually shocked, but the teachers believed that the fake shocks they gave were real. Nevertheless, 65 percent of them obeyed completely and went all the way to the highest voltage. Even when the learners called out for help, asked for the experiment to end, shrieked, and fell silent, the teachers continued to administer "shocks" when instructed to do so by those administering the study.

Milgram then set up an experiment using three teachers—one experimental subject and two "teachers" who were working with him (Milgram, 1964). Each of the three was to recommend a shock

---

People also become members of some organizations—**coercive organizations**—against their will. They may be committed to a mental hospital, sentenced to prison, or drafted into the armed forces. Sociologist Erving Goffman (1961b) studied life in what he called **total institutions**—places of residence where individuals are isolated from the rest of society for an appreciable period of time and where behavior is tightly regimented. In these environments the "inmates" or "recruits" are exposed to **resocialization** experiences that systematically seek to strip away their old roles and identities and fashion new ones. The induction process often includes **mortification.** Individuals are separated from families and friends who provide networks

of support for old ways. They are made vulnerable to institutional control and discipline by being deprived of personal items, clothing, and accessories and are provided haircuts, uniforms, and standardized articles that establish an institutional identity. Often the new members are humiliated by being forced to assume demeaning postures, to engage in self-effacing tasks, and to endure insulting epithets (what sociologists term a *degradation ceremony*). These procedures leave individuals psychologically and emotionally receptive to the roles and identities demanded of them by the total institution.

Individuals also enter formal organizations formed for practical reasons—**utilitarian organizations.** Universities, corporations, farm level, and the lowest recommendation would be administered. In this way, the subject could ensure a low level of shock by recommending a voltage lower that that recommended by the others. But Milgram found that the subjects in these groups of three gave suggested giving learners shocks at *higher* voltages than would a subject acting alone; the subject went along with the higher voltage suggestions of the other two in the group.

Milgram conducted his shock experiment, with slight variations, with nearly 1,000 subjects—all "typical" people. Clearly, the pressure to conform to role expectations and to obey authority caused ordinary people to become nasty "prison guards" and shock-administering "teachers" in these experiments. But the researchers involved in the BBC's *The Experiment* showed that there are important qualifications to these now well-accepted generalizations.

In the BBC study, TV viewers did not get to see the prisoners scrub toilets by hand. In fact, these guards did *not* strongly identify with one another as guards, conform to the stereotypical role of guard, or become abusive to the prisoners. Why were these subjects so different from those in Zimbardo's study? One of the primary differences was that the BBC participants knew their behavior would be observed by millions of viewers. "Practically, [our study] demonstrates how extreme behaviors can be restrained by rendering actors visible and hence accountable to broader or yet-to-be encountered audiences" (Reicher and Haslam, 2003b:31). Although some have drawn upon the Zimbardo study to explain why the powerful often abuse the powerless, the researchers involved in *The Experiment* maintain that Zimbardo's results cannot be seen as a reasonable excuse for such abusive behavior. People

can "resist the roles thrust upon them . . . people *do* have responsibility and choice over the conditions that lead to tyranny" (Reicher and Haslam, 2002).

Questions for Discussion

1. In institutional aggression, people act aggressively or violently because they see it as part of their jobs. Besides guarding prisoners, what examples of work can you think of in which violence is condoned?

2. Think back over the past week. What have you done that you might label *conformity*?

3. What examples of horror and atrocity from history or from recent news events can you think of that may have resulted at least in part from people's desire to conform and to obey instructions?

organizations, labor unions, and government bureaus and agencies are among the organizations people form to accomplish vital everyday tasks. Utilitarian organizations fall between voluntary and coercive organizations: Membership in them is neither entirely voluntary nor entirely compulsory. For example, we may not be compelled to secure employment with a corporation, but if we wish to support ourselves, doing so is an essential element of life.

Bureaucracy: A Functional Approach to Organizations

As we saw in Chapter 1, the pp. 19–20 functionalist perspective attempts to understand the existence and structure of social patterns by examining the contributions those patterns make to the larger system of which they are a part. In modern societies, large complex organizations perform many tasks that are required for those societies to survive and grow. Organizations that manage sewers, the water supply, electricity, phones, public safety, the administration of government, and the manufacturing and distribution of goods are some of the most important examples of these. The functionalist perspective developed the concept *bureaucracy* to explain the existence and structure of this organizational type.

As long as organizations are relatively small, they can often function reasonably well

These students are participating in a utilitarian organization, a university, for a particular reason: to get a degree.

on the basis of informal face-to-face interaction. But if larger organizations are to attain their goals, they must establish formal operating and administrative procedures. Only as they standardize and routinize many of their operations can they function effectively. This requirement is met by a **bureaucracy,** a social structure made up of a hierarchy of statuses and roles that is prescribed by explicit rules and procedures and based on a division of function and authority. Sociologists use the concept in a way that differs sharply from the negative connotation "bureaucracy" has when we use it in everyday conversation to refer to organizational inefficiency.

The bureaucratic form of organization has developed over many centuries in the Western world (Bendix, 1977). It grew slowly and erratically during the Middle Ages and after. Early bureaucracies, like bureaucracies in traditional societies today, were based on patrimonialism, a traditional system of authority in which people are committed to serve traditional leaders, rather than a set of codified rules and procedures.

The result is an organization that is the personal instrument of a master (Ritzer, 2000).

Only in the 20th century did the modern bureaucracy fully flower in response to the dictates of industrial society. As contemporary organizations increased in size and complexity, more structural units and divisions were required. In turn, some mechanism was needed for synchronizing and integrating the various activities. By providing for the performance of tasks on a regular and orderly basis, bureaucracies permit the planning and coordination of these activities in an efficient manner. Additionally, they aim to eliminate all unrelated influences on the behavior of their members so that people act primarily in the organization's interests. Although most complex organizations in the United States are organized as bureaucracies, the degree and forms of bureaucratization vary (Perrow, 1986). In addition, globalization, rapid social change, and the introduction of new technologies are producing much innovation in real-world organizations, and this is changing how social scientists think about organizations (Liker, Haddad, and Karlin, 1999; Jaffee, 2001).

Characteristics of Bureaucracies

The German sociologist Max Weber (1946, 1947) was impressed by the ability of bureaucracies to rationalize and control the process by which people collectively pursue their goals. He developed the concept of bureaucracy as an *ideal type*. By using the term *ideal* in this context, Weber did not mean that the bureaucracy represented a standard of perfection. In fact, Weber was quite critical of bureaucracy as an organizational form. Instead, Weber used the term *ideal type* to ◄— p. 13–14 refer to a concept constructed by sociologists to portray the principal characteristics of a phenomenon. The ideal type of the bureaucracy abstracts common elements from organizations as diverse as a government agency, the Roman Catholic Church, the Teamsters' Union, IBM, and Yale University and arrives at a model for describing and analyzing organizational arrangements. Perhaps no actual organization is exactly like the model in all respects, but the model isolates the important elements of organizational structure in contemporary society, which are presented in Figure 4.1.

At first glance, the abstract description presented in Figure 4.1 seems pretty irrelevant to our daily lives. But it does outline the kind of organizational structure most of us would like to be able to take for granted. Though we dislike bureaucracy and can feel alienated by it, most of us expect that the organizations we encounter will work the way Weber described, and we feel mistreated if they do not.

For example, we wish those holding positions in our schools, government, and corporations to gain these offices and exercise power

---

How Does Weber's Ideal Bureaucracy Work?
1. Each office or position has clearly defined duties and responsibilities. In this manner, the regular activities of the organization are arranged within a clear-cut division of labor.
2. All offices are organized in a hierarchy of authority that takes the shape of a pyramid. Officials are held accountable to their superiors for subordinates' actions and decisions in addition to their own.
3. All activities are governed by a consistent system of abstract rules and regulations that define the responsibilities of the various offices and the relationships among them. They ensure the coordination of essential tasks and uniformity in performance regardless of changes in personnel.
4. All offices carry with them qualifications and are filled on the basis of technical competence, not personal considerations. Presumably, trained individuals do better work than those who gain an office on the basis of family ties, personal friendship, or political favor. Competence is established by certification (e.g., college degrees) or examination (e.g., civil service tests).
5. Incumbents do not "own" their offices and cannot use offices for personal ends. Positions remain the property of the organization, and officeholders are supplied with the items they require to perform their work.
6. Employment by the organization is defined as a career. Promotion is based on seniority or merit, or both. After a probationary period, individuals gain the security of tenure and are protected against arbitrary dismissal. In principle, this feature makes officials less susceptible to outside pressures.
7. Administrative decisions, rules, procedures, and activities are recorded in written documents preserved in permanent files.

Figure 4.1   **Characteristics of Weber's Ideal Bureaucracy**

because of their ability and competence, not because of their race, gender, personal connections, or physical attractiveness (characteristic 4). We would not like courthouse clerks, police officers, or the mayor of our town to sell services to the highest bidder; we define this kind of behavior as the crime of bribery (characteristic 5). We expect that rules will be followed and that exceptions will not be made at the whim of officeholders. For example, we expect that government contracts will be awarded to bidders who follow the correct procedures and submit the lowest bids, not simply to family members of the responsible government official; when we suspect that such a thing has taken place, we complain of nepotism (characteristic 3). When things go wrong with what an organization does, we expect some responsible official to react, track down and correct the problem, and discipline those in the organization who may have fallen short (characteristics 2 and 7). If we are employed in a bureaucracy, we expect there to be clear expectations of what we and others are to do and how we are to coordinate our activities. For example, we expect that other officeholders cannot usurp our authority simply because they want to and can get away with it (characteristic 1). And if we obey the rules and perform competently, we expect that we should be able to make a career within the organization and should not be let go without a very good reason (characteristic 6).

Thus, as much as we sometimes complain about the "red tape" of bureaucracies and although we all might like to be treated as special cases, bureaucracy is with us because we expect it to be there and to function as Weber said that it should. To live otherwise in modern society is almost unthinkable.

Bureaucracy is a fixture of our lives not only because it represents how we expect our public lives to be governed, but because, as Weber argued, it is an inherent feature of modern economic organization, whether capitalist or socialist. While some argue that bureaucracy is a fixture

only of capitalism, Weber argued that under socialism governments and enterprises would be completely dominated by bureaucrats and bureaucracies. Under capitalism, bureaucratic domination is mitigated at least partly; business owners are not bureaucrats and are free to do as they wish, unconstrained by the rules that apply to bureaucrats. For this reason, Weber thought that capitalism would be more likely than socialism to preserve individual freedom and creative leadership in a world dominated by formal organizations (Ritzer, 2000).

But not even Weber was truly optimistic about bureaucracy. He (Weber 1921/1968) and many sociologists who came after him (e.g., Blau and Scott, 1962) have expressed concern that bureaucracies may pose an inherent challenge to human liberty by turning free people into "cogs" in organizational machines. Let us take a closer look at this issue and other problems of bureaucracy as a feature of our social life.

Problems of Bureaucracy

▲ Oligarchy

Organizations, like all other groups, enjoy a formidable capacity for eliciting conformity. As we noted earlier, groups do not simply control and dispense rewards and punishments. They also define social reality by structuring our experiences. Given the predominant role organizations have in contemporary life, some social scientists have expressed concern for the future of democratic institutions. They point out that all too often the needs of organizations take priority over those of individuals (Glassman, Swatos, and Rosen, 1987; Dandeker, 1990). Robert Michels (1911/1966), a sociologist and friend of Weber, argued that bureaucracies contain a fundamental flaw that makes them undemocratic social arrangements: They invariably lead to *oligarchy*—the concentration of power in the hands of a few individuals who use their offices to advance their own fortunes and self-interests. He called this tendency the **iron law**

of oligarchy: "Whoever says organization, says oligarchy" (p. 365).

Michels cited a variety of reasons for the oligarchical tendencies found in formal organizations, even those that are presumably democratic, such as political parties, labor unions, and voluntary associations. First, because they have hierarchical leadership structures involved in everyday administration, most voting by the membership becomes a ritualistic confirmation of leaders' decisions. Second, officials have special advantages: access to information unavailable to others, superior political skills and experience, and control of a variety of administrative resources, including communication networks, offices, and a treasury, that can be used to ward off challengers and co-opt dissidents and rivals. Third, ordinary members tend to be uninterested in assuming leadership responsibilities and are apathetic toward the problems of the organization.

Michels pointed to the history of European socialist parties and labor unions as evidence in support of his thesis. However, not all organizations are oligarchic (Breines, 1980). For example, in their classic study, Lipset, Trow, and Coleman (1956) showed that the International Typographical Union (ITU), composed of typesetters, maintained a democratic tradition by institutionalizing a "two-party system." Union elections were held on a regular basis, with the two parties putting up a complete slate of candidates. Lipset and his colleagues reasoned that where competing groups are active and legitimate, the rank-and-file have the potential for replacing leaders and introducing new policies.

Bureaucracies perform many of the tasks that are required for society to survive and grow. At the same time, as Max Weber and other sociologists have pointed out, they turn people into cogs in organizational machines.

▲ Dysfunctions of Bureaucracy

Bureaucracy may not be as functional as Weber thought. Even when they function as they were designed to, bureaucracies may produce harmful consequences. For example, political scientist Richard Rosecrance (1990) argued that Americans in the post–World War II period came to embrace Weber's bureaucratic society so completely that our corporations became overstaffed, making the nation uncompetitive in world markets. In many organizations, management specialization—not production or meeting consumer needs—became the way to the top. Such outcomes are the typical by-product of a bureaucratic dysfunction that C. Northcote Parkinson (1962) termed **Parkinson's law:** "Work expands so as to fill the time available for its completion." Despite the tongue-in-cheek tone of his writing, Parkinson showed that "the number of the officials and the quantity of the work are not related to each other." He contended that bureaucracy expands not because of an increasing workload but because officials seek to have additional subordinates hired in order to multiply the number of people under them in the hierarchy. These subordinates, in turn, create work for one another, while the coordination of their work requires still more officials.

The relentless growth of bureaucracy is reflected in the federal government. When George Washington was inaugurated as president in 1790, there were nine executive units and 1 in 4,000 Americans was employed by the executive branch. Over the next hundred years, the government bureaucracy grew 10 times as fast as the population, and by 1891, 1 in 463 Americans was a U.S. government employee. This growth continued through most of the 20th century and by 1970, the figure stood at 1 in 69. While the size of government declined under President Clinton and continued to decline under President Bush, it nonetheless employed approximately 1 in 109 Americans in mid-2005 (http://www.opm.gov/feddata/html/2005/july/table1.asp; http://www.census.gov/popest/states/tables/NST-EST2005-01.xls).

The situation has not been better in U.S. business. In the mid-1980s more than half of the typical U.S. corporation consisted of workers uninvolved in operations or production (Rosecrance, 1990). Many U.S. firms undertook massive restructuring and downsizing in the 1990s—in everyday language, many people lost their jobs. Some corporations have attempted to undermine Parkinson's law by developing new structural arrangements made possible by the computer and telecommunications revolution (Wilke, 1993; Huey, 1994). We have yet to see if such attempts to redefine bureaucracies can truly repeal Parkinson's law.

Another dysfunction of bureaucracy was first noted by social critic Thorstein Veblen (1921), who pointed out that bureaucracies encourage their members to rely on established rules and regulations and to apply them in an unimaginative and mechanical fashion, a pattern he called **trained incapacity.** As a result of the socialization provided by organizations, individuals often develop a tunnel vision that limits their ability to respond in new ways when situations change. Government bureaucracies are especially risk-averse because they are caught up in such complex webs of constraint that any change is likely to rouse the ire of important constituencies (Wilson, 1990, 1993). This problem may be particularly significant in very successful organizations that often resist change because of the fear that to do so will prevent repetition of past successes. Such inflexibility can result in self-perpetuating organizational mediocrity.

▲ Bureaucracy Is an Idealized Model

The bureaucratic model is difficult, if not impossible, to realize in practice. A number of forces undermine its operation (Perrow, 1986; Jaffee, 2001). First, human beings do not exist only for organizations. People track all sorts of mud from the rest of their lives, including their prejudicial attitudes, with them into bureaucratic arrangements, and they have numerous interests independent of the organization. Second, bureaucracies are not immune to social change. When such changes are frequent and rapid, the pat answers supplied by bureaucratic regulations and rules interfere with rational operation. Third, bureaucracies are designed for the "average" person. In real life, however, people differ in intelligence, energy, zeal, and dedication, so they are not interchangeable in the day-to-day functioning of organizations. Fourth, forms of informal organization emerge within real bureaucracies in response to the tensions and contradictions of organizational life and thus, as a model of what happens within an organization, the bureaucratic model is incomplete. By competing with the formal organization for members' loyalties and by challenging bureaucratic rules and authority, informal organization is a particularly serious threat to organizational goals. As a result it has been the focus of much attention by sociologists.

"Does this mean I'm out of the loop?"

Informal organization consists of interpersonal networks and ties that arise in a formal organization but are not defined or prescribed by it. Based on their common interests and relationships, individuals form primary groups. These informal structures provide means by which people bend and break rules, share "common knowledge," engage in secret behaviors, handle problems, and "cut corners." Work relationships are much more than the lifeless abstractions contained on an organizational chart that outlines the official lines of communication and authority.

The roots of informal organization are embedded within formal organization and are nurtured by the formality of its arrangements. Official rules and regulations must be sufficiently general to cover a great many situations. In applying general rules to a particular situation, people must use their judgment, so they evolve informal guidelines that provide them with workable solutions. Additionally, to avoid bureaucratic red tape, employees often arrive at informal understandings with one another as a way of keeping the formal organization operating smoothly. Thus, people are tied to the larger group by their membership in primary groups that mediate between them and the formal organization. Further, the impersonality of bureaucratic arrangements distresses many people, and they search for warmth, rapport, and companionship in the work setting through informal relationships.

Factory workers typically evolve their own norms regarding what constitutes a "reasonable" amount of work, and these norms often do not conform with those of management (Roethlisberger and Dickson, 1939; Hamper, 1991). Sociologist Michael Burawoy (1979) studied informal organization among shop workers while working for a year as a machine operator at a large Chicago-area plant. He found that relations on the shop floor were dominated by "making out"—a competitive game the machine operators played by manipulating the rules and regulations governing their work to their benefit.

Conflict and Interactionist Perspectives

Until about 20 years ago, the functionalist approach to bureaucracy identified with Weber dominated American sociology. In large measure sociologists focused their attention on organizations as abstract social structures while often neglecting the behavior of the individuals who comprise them. Indeed, sociologists Peter M. Blau and Richard A. Schoenherr (1971:viii, 357) championed such an approach, observing:

Formal organizations, as well as other social structures, exhibit regularities that can be analyzed in their own right, independent of any knowledge about the individual behavior of their members . . . it is time that we "push men [and women] out" to place proper emphasis on the study of social structure in sociology.

Many sociologists studied formal organizations without noticing the processes by which social structures are produced and reproduced in the course of people's daily interactions. But much has changed in recent years (Scott, 2004) as it has become increasingly clear that organizations in the real world do not operate as the functionalist perspective suggests. Sociologists from differing perspectives have looked beyond the bureaucratic model to understand how organizational reality is generated through the actions of people and groups of people (Benson, 1977; Romanelli, 1991). We will consider two of these approaches: the conflict perspective and the symbolic interactionist perspective.

▲ The Conflict Perspective

Conflict theorists contend that organizational goals reflect the priorities of those who occupy the top positions. Viewed in this manner, organizations are not neutral social structures pursuing clear goals but arenas for conflicting interests in which the social issues and power relations of society are played out (Morrill, Zald, and Rao, 2003; Jaffee, 2001). Marxist social scientists have followed in the tradition of Karl Marx (1970), who saw bureaucracy as a manifestation of the centralizing tendencies of capitalism and an instrument of class domination. They analyze organizations within the context of the broader inequalities that operate within society and find that the distribution of power and the allocation of rewards within them mirror the larger society's class structure (Edwards, 1979; Jaffee, 2001).

In *Capital* (1867/1906) Marx claimed that the modern factory is a despotic regime made necessary by the competitive pressures of the market. These pressures compel technological innovation and work intensification, all of which rest on the availability of workers, who in order to survive must sell their labor power to capitalist employers.

More recent studies by Marxist social scientists suggest that bureaucratic mechanisms arose as much from the desire of capitalists to control workers as from abstract notions of efficiency and rationality (Friedman, 1977; Edwards, 1978). For example, Katherine Stone (1974) found that early 20th-century steel magnates established top-to-bottom chains of command and job ladders to isolate individual workers, break the power of skilled artisans, and combat growing labor militancy.

Marx thought that if a socialist revolution overturned capitalism, the bureaucratic structures inherited from capitalism would have to be altered or eliminated by a revolutionary working class and replaced by a fully democratic structure. However, when a socialist government was finally established following the Russian

Revolution of 1917, the result was not the establishment and perpetuation of democratic organizational forms. The primary elements of their policy in what became the Soviet Union centered on the expansion of bureaucratic offices and the dominance of the state apparatus by a "new class" of Communist party officials (Djilas, 1957), quite the opposite of what Marx had in mind.

A more promising development has been the emergence of the collectivist-democratic organization (Rothschild and Russell, 1986). Such organizations are formed at the grass-roots level in response to the needs of the people who form them, operate on the basis of consensus rather than on bureaucratic authority, and focus on producing products of immediate social value, not products to be sold in the marketplace in pursuit of profit. Examples of collectivist-democratic organizations are food cooperatives, legal collectives, communes, and other low-capitalization enterprises that operate as cooperative businesses (Rothschild and Russell, 1986; Case and Taylor, 1979).

A formidable problem faced by the collectivist-democratic organization is the tendency to degenerate and disappear or to evolve into a standard bureaucracy (Rothschild and Russell, 1986). State sponsorship, creative tax incentive plans, and financing conditional on the maintenance of democratic cooperative structures are among the mechanisms that help perpetuate collectivist-democratic organizations. Only time will tell if these and other means can ensure that this form of organization is a realistic alternative to bureaucracy.

▲ The Symbolic Interactionist Perspective

Symbolic interactionists contend that human beings in organizations are not spongelike, malleable organisms who passively conform to the bureaucratic requirements. Instead, they portray people as active agents who shape and mold their destinies and continually fashion new joint actions based on their definitions of the situation (Blumer, 1969). Organizational constraints only provide the framework with which people appraise and then decide among alternative courses of organizational behavior on the basis of meanings they share with others in the organization. The model of organizations that results is one that emphasizes dynamism and malleability of organizational forms rather than fixed structures and procedures.

A good example of the application of symbolic interactionism to organizations is the classic study by Anselm Strauss and his colleagues (1964) of organizational behavior in two Chicago-area psychiatric hospitals. They treated a formal organization as a **negotiated order**—the fluid, ongoing understandings and agreements people reach as they go about their daily activities. To outsiders the hospitals appeared to be tightly structured organizations that functioned in accordance with strict bureaucratic rules and regulations. However, the researchers found that in practice the hospitals operated quite differently. The organizations were simply too complex for a single set of rules to hold or for any one person to know all the rules, much less in exactly what situations they applied, to whom, in what degree, and for how long. Given these circumstances, most house rules served more as general understandings than as commands, and they were stretched, argued, reinterpreted, ignored, or applied as situations dictated. Individuals reached agreements with one another that provided a consensus for a time, but the understandings were subject to periodic modification and revision.

Chaos did not reign in the hospitals because the negotiations followed patterns that permitted some degree of predictability. Even so, Strauss and his colleagues concluded:

Practically, we maintain, no one knows what the hospital "is" on any given day unless [he or she] has a comprehensive grasp of the combinations of rules, policies, agreements, understandings, pacts, contracts, and other working

arrangements that currently obtain. In a prag-
matic sense, that combination "is" the hospital
at the moment, its social order. (1964:312)

Research on organizations from the perspective of **ethnomethodology** strongly supports the symbolic interactionist view that organizations are shifting, malleable, dynamic entities. *Ethno,* borrowed from the Greek, means "people" or "folk," while *methodology* refers to procedures by which something is done or analyzed. Thus, "ethnomethodology" refers to procedures—the rules and activities—that people employ in making social life and society intelligible (Garfinkle, 1974). While the focus in symbolic interactionism emphasizes a broader range of shared meanings, the two perspectives are very similar. Both view people as agents who do not simply conform to organizational constraints, but actively shape their social lives within organizational contexts.

Ethnomethodologists argue that organizations are not products of their rules, but that people use the rules to explain and justify what they do in organizational contexts.

Sociologist Don H. Zimmerman (1971) applied the ethnomethodological perspective in examining the day-by-day operations of a large-scale organization, a public welfare agency. He studied how the receptionists went about processing applicants for public assistance and apportioning them among caseworkers. The receptionists seemed to follow the "first-come, first-served" rule. But a deeper inspection revealed that receptionists would switch the order of applicants when clients said they had to attend to some urgent matter. Likewise, they would allow some applicants to request a particular social worker. And they routinely assigned "difficult" and "troublesome" applicants to a caseworker known to be good at handling "special problems." In fact, they were skilled at giving the appearance that applicants moved through the system in a sequential and orderly manner, while in fact they followed

their own ad hoc procedures for processing applicants.

Zimmerman concluded that as we go about our activities, we continually develop and interpret what a rule means. Bureaucratic rules and regulations serve as a commonsense method by which we account for our behavior. In deciding how to behave in organizations, people do not ask "What is the rule?" but "What has to be done?" In practice, a rule may be employed or ignored depending on the context. Its main purpose is not to guide action, but to provide an account, explanation, and justification of action.

▲ A Synthesis of Alternative Perspectives

Sociologist Charles Perrow (1982) joined threads from the conflict, symbolic interactionist, and ethnomethodological perspectives to argue that the notion of bureaucratic rationality masks the true nature of organizational life. He claimed that our world is more "loosely coupled"—characterized by a substantial measure of redundancy, slack, and waste—than structural theories admit. Perrow said that organizations do not have goals, only constraints. Take the Sanitation Department of New York City:

To say its goal is to pick up the garbage—even to pick it up frequently, pick it all up, and do it cheaply—does not tell us much. These are not goals of that department but merely loose constraints under which those who use the organization must operate, and these are not really any more important than the following constraints: The cushy top jobs in the department can be used to pay off political debts; some groups can use the Sanitation Department as an assured source of employment and keep others out; upper management can use its positions as political jumping off places or training spots; equipment manufacturers use it as an easy mark for shoddy goods; and, finally, the workers are

Conflict theorists argue that employee-participation programs are designed to function as sophisticated control strategies.

DILBERT reprinted by permission of United Feature Syndicate, Inc.

entitled to use it as a source of job security and pensions and an easy way of making a living. (p. 687)

Perrow contended that private profit-making organizations are not much different. Aerospace companies can be seen as pension plans that make missiles and planes on the side so that their pension plans can be funded. Steel plants are closed even though they make a respectable profit because they are worth more as tax write-offs. Countless other organizations continue to exist even though they fail to provide decent mail service, prepare students for careers, or offer acceptable medical care. But should the organizations fail to satisfy some special-interest group that lives off them, then the consequences are defined as a major social problem. In short, organizations pursue a variety of courses of action, some of them with more enthusiasm than they pursue their publicly stated goals. Perrow concluded, therefore, that organizations do not have goals in the rational sense suggested by organizational theory. Instead, actions are determined by the interests and desires of executives, employees, and other stakeholders, and formally stated

goals are determined after the fact, on the basis of what executives observe themselves doing.

Perrow next linked the conflict perspective to his analysis by arguing that social efforts at stating goals, giving accounts, and attributing rationality to organizations serve elites much more than they serve other people. These efforts create a world in which organizational hierarchy, technological requirements, and profit-making motives become legitimized.

Humanizing Bureaucracies

Since large organizations play such a critical part in our daily lives, it may be well to conclude the chapter by asking, "Can we make bureaucracies more humane instruments for modern living?" If we value freedom and independence— if we are disturbed by the conformity of attitudes, values, and behavior that bureaucracies often induce—then we may wish to set up conditions that foster uniqueness, self-direction, and human dignity. Although affording no panaceas, a number of programs have been proposed that allow individuals greater range for developing their full capacities and potential in the context of organizational life. Let us briefly consider a number of these.

▲ Employee Participation

About the same time that Japanese manufacturers vigorously entered U.S. markets, American business leaders began trying to breathe new life and competitive fire into their companies. Many tried an approach known as "quality circles," "participative management," or "working smarter." A group of up to a dozen workers and one or two managers from the same department meet together on a regular basis to figure out ways of getting along better with each other, making work easier, raising output, and improving the quality of their products. Proponents of the programs say that where management and workers are committed to them, absenteeism, tardiness, grievances, strikes, and labor costs are reduced. Moreover, product quality improves and pilferage lessens.

Although some 6,000 American companies, including General Motors, IBM, and AT&T, adopted employee participation programs, most of these programs failed (Saporito, 1986). A Gallup survey found that only 14 percent of corporate employees who worked for firms with quality-improvement and employee participation programs thought their companies gave them a chance to participate in the important decisions (Bennett, 1990). Conflict theorists argue that because the relationship between management and labor is inherently adversarial, worker participation programs are simply cosmetic efforts that mask corporate attempts to control workers and to avoid collective-bargaining obligations.

Another approach entails "self-managed teams" or "autonomous work groups," an arrangement in which workers largely operate without bosses (Bartol and Martin, 1998). Employees set their own work schedules, prepare their own budgets, and receive group bonuses on the basis of the team's productivity.

Managers, termed "coaches," function as advisers (Selz, 1994). The approach appears highly adaptable within the computer industry, where many tasks are not easily routinized and where small groups, given great freedom, can react quickly to abrupt technological change. Small groups can focus their energies on a single goal, foster creativity, and reward employees commensurate with their contributions (Bartol and Martin, 1998). Beyond the small work groups approach is the "no-collar" approach, in which informally dressed employees manage themselves, use the office as a "funhouse" (because play promotes creativity), and are expected to work 70-hour weeks (Ross, 2003).

Overall, new management strategies over the past 30 years have emphasized a lessening of hierarchy and authoritarianism and an increase in worker participation in workplace decision making. But the changes should not be overestimated. When managers must make a tough decision, they often revert to the direct, authoritarian mode.

▲ Alternative Work Schedules

Some companies have attempted to boost job satisfaction and motivation by allowing some flexibility in how work time is scheduled. Flextime is one example; workers are allowed to decide how to organize their 8-hour workday. Some may wish to come in early and get off early; others may wish to have their early mornings free and work into the evening. These plans can benefit working parents who often need to schedule their work hours so that adequate child care can be arranged. They also benefit companies since they result in lower absentee and turnover rates (Bartol and Martin, 1998).

Another example is the compressed workweek. This plan involves scheduling workers to put in four 10-hour days per week with three days off. Such a plan can work well for construction, for example, where more can be accomplished on-site during each 10-hour day, and workers can enjoy long weekends. For some types of jobs, such as nursing, 12-hour shifts with appropriate time off work well.

▲ Virtual Offices

Some companies find that workers do not need to report to a central office but can work from anywhere and communicate with managers, workers, customers, and others via the Internet (Davidow and Malone, 1993; Jaffee, 2001). These "virtual corporations" with their "virtual offices" provide employees with the ultimate in autonomy and flexibility in organizing their work. Verifone, Inc., a company that designs, manufactures, sells, and services the machines that read credit cards in retail establishments, is a successful example of a virtual corporation (Jaffee, 2001). It has 3,000 employees worldwide, but no corporate office and no identification with a nation-state. Corporate operations never cease, with employees communicating and accessing company information through the Internet.

Though workers may find that working in a virtual office enables them to manage the conflicts between their personal lives and their work lives more effectively, it is unclear what the ultimate impact will be on the structure of organizations. The unintended consequences of such arrangements may include increased alienation, the loss of a sense of community, and a weakening of organizational integration (Snizek, 1995).

▲ Specialized Benefits

In an attempt to reduce employee turnover, some companies offer a variety of new benefits to workers. A number offer child care either on-site or nearby in company-owned buildings, providing parents with opportunities to visit their children during the day and cutting day care costs. Some make contributions to college education funds for employees' offspring. Company-provided transportation to jobs has resulted in reductions in tardiness and absenteeism for some employers. Workers in some states can attend classes on company time to earn their high school graduate equivalency diplomas (GEDs). At least one company offers 24-hour on-call social workers to help employees with their personal problems. These specialized benefits programs reflect both a change in attitudes toward workers and the inability of most companies to offer increased wages (Grimsley, 1997a).

▲ Employee Stock Ownership Plans

By 2002 nearly 10,000 companies in the United States shared some measure of ownership with more than 8 million employees. Workers owned the majority of the stock in some 2,500 companies. Although employee stock ownership plans (ESOPs) grew rapidly from their inception in 1974 until 1990, there has been little overall growth since then. Nonetheless, the number of majority employee- and 100 percent employee-owned companies continues to increase (ESOP Association, 2003).

In many cases large-scale employee ownership has changed the way companies operate, including their labor-management relationships (Klein, 1987; Blasi, 1988). Greater employee initiative in the workplace has been found to cut costs, but much depends on a firm's profitability. When a company becomes profitable, differences tend to get smoothed over quickly, but a firm that continues to lose money will see dissatisfaction rise and difficulties deepen. For instance, in the early 1990s the men and women at Weirton Steel found that ownership did not always translate into power. These employee-owners took pay cuts, accepted layoffs, and acquiesced as management spent $550 million to revamp the company's mill. After years of butting heads with management, the workers launched a battle in 1993 to gain actual control of the firm (Baker, 1993). Thus, employee ownership does not guarantee labor peace.

The Chapter in Brief: *Social Groups and Formal Organizations*

Group Relationships

Groups—two or more people who share a feeling of unity and who are bound together in relatively stable patterns of social interaction—are products of social definitions—sets of shared ideas. As such they constitute constructed realities.

▌*Primary Groups and Secondary Groups.* **Primary groups** involve two or more people who enjoy direct, intimate, cohesive relationships and are fundamental to both us and society. **Expressive ties** predominate in primary groups. **Secondary groups** entail two or more people who are involved in impersonal, touch-and-go relationships. **Instrumental ties** predominate in secondary groups.

▌*In-Groups and Out-Groups.* The concepts of **in-group** and **out-group** highlight the importance of boundaries—social demarcation lines that tell us where interaction begins and ends. Boundaries prevent outsiders from entering a group's sphere, and they keep insiders within the group's sphere.

▌*Reference Groups.* **Reference groups** provide the models we use for appraising and shaping our attitudes, feelings, and actions. A reference group may or may not be our membership group. A reference group provides both normative and comparative functions.

Group Dynamics

The dynamic qualities of groups make them a significant force in human life and important to sociologists.

▌*Group Size.* The size of a group influences the nature of our interaction. Emotions and feelings tend to assume a larger part in

dyads than in larger groups. The addition of a third member to a group—forming a **triad**—fundamentally alters a social situation. In this arrangement one person may be placed in the role of an outsider.

▌*Leadership.* In group settings some members usually exert more influence than others. We call these individuals **leaders.** Two types of leadership roles tend to evolve in small groups: an **instrumental leader** and an **expressive leader.** Leaders may follow an authoritarian style, a democratic style, or a laissez-faire style.

▌*Social Loafing.* When individuals work in groups, they work less hard than they do when working individually, a process termed **social loafing.**

▌*Social Dilemmas.* A **social dilemma** is a situation in which members of a group are faced with a conflict between maximizing their personal interests and maximizing the collective welfare.

▌*Groupthink.* In group settings individuals may become victims of **groupthink.** Group members may share an illusion of invulnerability that leads to overconfidence and a greater willingness to take risks.

▌*Conformity.* Groups bring powerful pressures to bear that produce **conformity** among their members. Although such pressures influence our behavior, we often are unaware of them.

Formal Organizations

For many tasks within modern societies, people require groups they can deliberately create for the achievement of specific goals. These groups are **formal organizations.**

▮ Types of Formal Organization.
Amitai Etzioni classified organizations on the basis of people's reasons for entering them: **voluntary, coercive,** and **utilitarian.**

▮ Bureaucracy: A Functional Approach to Organizations.   Small organizations can often function reasonably well on the basis of face-to-face interaction. Larger organizations must establish formal operating and administrative procedures. This requirement is met by a **bureaucracy.**

▮ Characteristics of Bureaucracies.
Max Weber approached bureaucracy as an ideal type with these characteristics: Each office has clearly defined duties; all offices are organized in a hierarchy of authority; all activities are governed by a system of rules; all offices have qualifications; incumbents do not own their positions; employment by the organization is defined as a career; and administrative decisions are recorded in written documents.

▮ Problems of Bureaucracy.
Bureaucracies have disadvantages and limitations. These include the principle of **trained incapacity, Parkinson's law,** and the **iron law of oligarchy.** If formal organization is to operate smoothly, it requires **informal organization** for interpreting, translating, and supporting its goals and practices.

▮ Conflict and Interactionist Perspectives.   In recent years sociologists from differing perspectives—particularly the conflict, symbolic interactionist, and ethnomethodological approaches—have looked at the ways by which organizational reality is generated through the actions of people and groups of people.

▮ Humanizing Bureaucracies.   Among programs that make large organizations more humane are those that allow employee participation, flextime, small work groups, and employee ownership.

Glossary

bureaucracy   A social structure made up of a hierarchy of statuses and roles that is prescribed by explicit rules and procedures and based on a division of function and authority.

coercive organization   A formal organization that people become members of against their will.

dyad   A two-member group.

ethnomethodology
Procedures—the rules and activities—that people employ in making social life and society intelligible to themselves and others.

expressive leader   A leader that focuses on overcoming interpersonal problems in a group, defusing tension, and promoting solidarity.

expressive ties   Social links formed when we emotionally invest ourselves in and commit ourselves to other people.

formal organization   A group formed deliberately for the achievement of specific objectives.

group   Two or more people who share a feeling of unity and who are bound together in relatively stable patterns of social interaction.

groupthink   A decision-making process found in highly cohesive groups in which the members become so preoccupied with maintaining group consensus that their critical faculties are impaired.

informal organization   Interpersonal networks and ties that arise in a formal organization but that are not defined or prescribed by it.

in-group   A group with which we identify and to which we belong.

instrumental leader   A leader that focuses on appraising the problem at hand and organizing people's activity to deal with it.

instrumental ties   Social links formed when we cooperate with other people to achieve some goal.

iron law of oligarchy   The principle that states that bureaucracies invariably lead to the concentration of power in the hands of a few individuals who use their offices to advance their own fortunes and self-interests.

mortification   A procedure in which rituals employed by coercive organizations render individuals vulnerable to institutional control, discipline, and resocialization.

negotiated order   The fluid, ongoing understanding and agreements people reach as they go about their daily activities.

out-group   A group with which we do not identify and to which we do not belong.

Parkinson's law   The principle that states that work expands so as to fill the time available for its completion.

primary group   Two or more people who enjoy a direct, intimate, cohesive relationship with one another.

reference group   A social unit we use for appraising and shaping our attitudes, feelings, and actions.

relationship   An association that lasts long enough for two people to become linked together by a relatively stable set of expectations.

relative deprivation   Discontent associated with the gap between what we have and what we believe we should have.

resocialization   A process by which a person's old roles and identities are stripped away and new ones are created.

secondary group   Two or more people who are involved in an impersonal relationship and have come together for a specific, practical purpose.

social dilemma   A situation in which members of a group are faced with a conflict between maximizing their personal interests and maximizing the collective welfare.

social loafing   The process in which individuals work less hard when working in groups than they do when working individually.

total institutions   Places of residence where individuals are isolated from the rest of society.

trained incapacity   The term Thorstein Veblen applied to the tendency within bureaucracies for members to rely on established rules and regulations and to apply them in an unimaginative and mechanical fashion.

triad   A three-member group.

utilitarian organization   A formal organization set up to achieve practical ends.

voluntary organization   A formal organization that people enter and leave freely.

Review Questions

1. How do primary groups differ from secondary groups? List three of each from your own life.

2. What are in-groups and out-groups?

3. Define reference group and give at least two examples from your own life.

4. What are two major styles of leadership?

5. Describe a social dilemma from your own life.

6. What is groupthink? Have you ever experienced this phenomenon as a member of a decision-making group?

7. Joining a sorority or fraternity is voluntary. Do such organizations have any characteristics of a coercive organization?

8. Define bureaucracy and list the characteristics of Weber's ideal bureaucracy.

9. What are some of the problems of bureaucracy?

10. What do conflict theorists have to say about bureaucracy? How does it differ from the view of symbolic interactionists?

Internet Connection

www.mhhe.com/hughes8

Open this Web page: **http://lcweb.loc.gov/global/ executive/fed.html.** This site, maintained by the Library of Congress, provides a set of links to the executive branch of the U.S. government. Explore these sites looking for evidence that the executive branch of the U.S. government conforms to Weber's model of bureaucracy. Write a short report on the evidence you have found. Which aspects of Weber's model are revealed here? Which aspects are not? Thinking about the information in these sites and information from other sources, including news reports over the past several years, does the executive branch conform to Weber's ideal type of bureaucracy? Why or why not?

Chapter 5

DEVIANCE AND CRIME

The Nature of Deviance

Social Properties of Deviance
Social Control and Deviance

Theories of Deviance

Anomie Theory
Cultural Transmission Theory
Conflict Theory
Labeling Theory
Control Theory

Crime and the Criminal Justice System

Forms of Crime
Measuring Crime

Drugs and Crime
Race and Crime
Women and Crime
The Criminal Justice System

The term *deviance* suggests unusual and strange behavior of people with twisted minds pursuing twisted things. However, what we think of as deviant is an ordinary part of everyday life. More than a hundred years ago, for example, many students at the best U.S. colleges cheated most of the time. "Whole classes cheated on examinations," says historian Helen Lefkowitz Horowitz (1987:33). "At Yale in the 1860s, perhaps less than half of the compositions were actually written by the supposed author for the occasion."

Today many campuses have honor systems run by the students themselves, yet cheating remains a common form of behavior among college students. In one study, 83 percent of university students admitted to at least one act of academic dishonesty. A quarter said they had lied to an instructor and falsified material on a term paper, a third said they had looked at other students' answers during exams, and nearly a fifth said they had plagiarized a term paper (Cochran et al., 1999; see also Michaels and Miethe, 1989). Other studies suggest that the percentage of students who cheat in college is at least 90 percent and may be as high as 99 percent (Sperber, 2000).

Students aren't alone. In a major 2005 scientific scandal, research by Seoul National University professor Hwang Woo-Suk that had been hailed as a breakthrough in human stem cell production was found to be based on fabricated data, and Professor Woo-Suk was forced to admit to both scientific fraud and lying about his studies (Normile, Vogel, and Couzin, 2006). Nearly 10 percent of a sample of 4,000 U.S. researchers said they had witnessed research misconduct (including such acts as plagiarism and falsifying data) among other faculty, and 13 to 33 percent reported various types of misconduct among graduate students (Decoo, 2002).

Is cheating deviant or is it a normal feature of everyday life? If so many people cheat, why are there still rules against it? These questions introduce two important ideas that form the backdrop for our analysis of deviance. First, whether something is deviant depends on who is evaluating it. In 19th-century colleges, for example, faculty believed that cheating was deviant. Students, on the other hand, believed it was deviant *not* to cheat, and being proud of having achieved good grades through "honest" means was clearly deviant (Horowitz, 1987).

Second, when important *norms,* or rules, are violated, norms and social control function to maintain social organization, social relationships, and the meanings that underlie them. Norms against cheating still exist in spite of widespread cheating because without such norms and mechanisms for their enforcement, the nature of the university and its place in society would be very different. When universities react to cheating, they protect the idea that people earn grades honestly and that grades are at least a rough measure of merit. Norms and defending norms in the face of violation are necessary for social order to exist and to be perpetuated.

In this chapter we will consider the nature and significance of deviance. We will discuss sociological definitions of deviance and see what various sociological perspectives contribute to our understanding of deviance. In addition, we will examine a form of deviance that is particularly prevalent in modern society: crime.

The Nature of Deviance

Deviant behavior is not an anomaly in social life. It is a part of ongoing social processes in all societies and groups and is both cause and consequence of other social processes and outcomes that we discuss in this section.

Social Properties of Deviance

Deviance is behavior that a considerable number of people in a society view as reprehensible and beyond the limits of tolerance. In most cases it is both negatively valued and provokes hostile reactions. Deviance does not exist independently of norms. Without norms, and without the application of norms in interpreting behavior, there is no deviance. That is, deviance is not a property inherent in certain forms of behavior (Erikson, 1962; Becker, 1963; Lemert, 1972); it is a property conferred upon particular behaviors by social definitions. In the course of their daily lives, people use the normative schemes available to them and make judgments regarding the desirability or undesirability of this or that behavior. They then translate their judgments into favorable or unfavorable consequences for those who engage in the behavior. In this sense, then, deviance is what people say it is. You will find this idea clarified in Box 5.1.

▲ The Relativity of Deviance

Which acts are defined as deviant varies greatly from time to time, place to place, and group to group. For example, in many cultures homosexual behavior is considered to be deviant, and any sexual behavior involving juveniles is criminal. For the Etoro of New Guinea, homosexual acts between adult males and young boys are not just a part of everyday life; they are an essential part of the culture.

As reported by anthropologist Raymond Kelly in 1976, the Etoro believe that humans have a special life force they call the *hame.* According to Etoro culture, this vital energy in men can be diminished through witchcraft and also through sexual relations, because it is especially concentrated in semen. Depletion of the life force is accompanied by weakness and illness and is characterized by labored breathing, coughing, short-windedness, and chest pains, all referred to as *hame hah hah.* Each act of sexual intercourse a man engages in depletes his *hame* further, and heterosexual relations among the Etoro are completely prohibited for as many as 260 days per year, or more than 70 percent of the time. The Etoro believe that breaking these prohibitions has serious repercussions, including crop failure. Thus, heterosexual intercourse during the exclusionary period, even between marital partners, is seriously deviant and is severely punished.

Why, then, are homosexual relations essential in this culture? Is not the vital life force lost through loss of semen whether that loss is to a female or a male? Yes, but for the male receiving the semen, it is an essential gain. Boys lack semen—the most critical attribute of manhood to the Etoro—and the Etoro believe that semen must be "planted" in them. Young Etoro males are continually inseminated from age 10 until the early to midtwenties, according to Kelly. All the physical and emotional changes that occur during this time are regarded as the direct results of the oral insemination practiced by the Etoro. Because the *hame* of a youth is strengthened by insemination, there are no prohibitions about when or where such insemination can take place.

As norms vary from one society to the next and from one time to another, so too does deviance. A social audience, through the application of norms, decides whether or not some behavior is deviant. To the Etoro of New Guinea, sexual activity involving children is a normal part of everyday life. In the United States, it can cause an adult to be labeled a criminal.

The concepts that the Etoro use to think about sexuality and the moral system that governs sexual behavior are fundamentally different from the cultural principles that shape sexuality and behavior in our own society—so different, in fact, that some readers may find the example to be difficult to think about. Such reactions illustrate the point of the example: that deviance is relative, and such relativity often involves fundamental, even extreme, differences in how deviance is defined in different cultural systems.

Saying that deviance is relative and is a matter of social definition does not mean that "anything goes" or that morality has no importance. On the contrary, the relativity of deviance means simply that there are many moralities across societies and over time and that we cannot understand deviant behavior and the reactions to it without knowing the normative context in which they occur. As the description of homosexual and heterosexual behavior in Etoro society makes clear, using a traditional Western antihomosexual moral scheme to define deviance among the Etoro would reveal nothing about the processes of deviance and reaction that occur there.

By the same token, because deviance is relative, when sociologists study behavior that they refer to as deviant, they are not implying that the behavior is, in fact, immoral or wrong. The issue of morality is a philosophical, ethical, or religious one. Deviance, however, is a matter of whether shared norms have been violated and/or there has been a social reaction to some presumed violation. For example, white southerners who supported the civil rights movement in the South in the 1960s were clearly deviant in that setting (Durr, 1985), though their behavior was a moral response to an immoral racist social order. And the German police officers who pursued and murdered thousands of Jews during the Holocaust were not deviant in the context of the Nazi regime in Germany (Goldhagen, 1996), though today the term "immoral" hardly describes the severity of the moral reactions that their actions have provoked (e.g., Wiesel, 1961).

▲ The Power to Make Definitions Stick

When people differ regarding their definitions of what is and is not deviant behavior, it becomes a question of which individuals and groups will make their definitions prevail. For example, in 1776 the British labeled George Washington a traitor; 20 years later he was the first president of the United States and beloved as the father of his country.

Spit, Saliva, and the Social Construction of Deviance

To set the stage on the first day of class for their courses in introductory sociology and in the sociology of deviance, Professors John R. Brouillette and Ronny E. Turner of Colorado State University (1992) undertake an exercise that demonstrates the social construction of deviance. After outlining course procedures and content, one of the professors calls on a student to provide a small amount of saliva in a sterilized spoon. Somewhat embarrassed, the student provides the saliva. The professor thanks her and then he gives a brief lecture on the benefits and functions of saliva for the human body; for instance, saliva moistens the linings of the mouth and throat, aids in the prevention of infection, and facilitates digestion.

After discussing the benefits of saliva, the professor offers the student who initially provided the valuable body fluid an opportunity to take the spoon and return the saliva to her mouth. Invariably the student declines. The instructor comments that he has difficulty comprehending why someone would reject such a valued substance in the age of recycling. He then offers the contents of the spoon to a classmate. Some students respond by making gagging sounds. The professor expresses "surprise" and reminds the students that they often share a can of soda, which also involves the sharing of saliva. The instructor then comments:

Not only that, but some students engage in a formerly criminal action, French kissing, which most couples consider intimate, loving, and appropriate. Actually, two people place their lips together, intermingle their tongues, and exchange or mix their saliva. Is this deviant? Certainly not! It's sexy . . . cool . . . and a "turn on." Well, if you believe that's cool, picture this. A couple are parked at the top of Lookout Mountain, passionately embracing each other. The woman pulls a spoon from her purse, which she uses to scrape some saliva from her mouth. To soothe her lover's raging hormones and to show her love for him, she offers him the spoon. Do you think it will turn him on to a point of no return?

This example illustrates the fact that who is defined as deviant and what is defined as deviance depend on who is doing the defining and who has the power to make the definitions stick. Individuals stigmatized and victimized by prevailing social definitions see their circumstances quite differently from those who enjoy power and enforce norms that embody their moral codes. In recent years, some groups, such as gays, lesbians, the disabled, and welfare mothers, have entered the political arena and have had some success in challenging official definitions that portray them as "social problems."

▲ Variability over Time in Definitions of Deviance

Within recent years, many behaviors Americans have traditionally judged to be deviant have undergone redefinition. Not too long ago compulsive gambling, alcoholism, drug addiction, and even many forms of mental illness were defined as evil and sinful. While such notions still persist, the view has increasingly gained currency that these behaviors are medical problems. The disorders are considered illnesses analogous to physical ailments such as ulcers, diabetes, and high blood pressure. Their sufferers are placed in hospitals and given treatment by physicians.

Some people, including the late sociologist and former U.S. Senator Daniel Patrick Moynihan, believed that Americans are "defining deviancy down" so as to explain away and make "normal" what "a more civilized, ordered and healthy society" would and did label "deviant" not too many years ago. The birth rate among unmarried women has increased by nearly 40 percent since 1980, so that now one-third of

The professor next engages class members in a discussion of the difference between "saliva" and "spit." In the course of the discussion he introduces the students to the sociological concept of the social construction of reality:

> There is a difference between spit and saliva. But no chemist will ever find it because the difference is not chemical. It's social. If people believe that spit and saliva are different, they are different. You had better know the difference or suffer the consequences. Spit is saliva in the wrong place or under the wrong circumstances. Nothing inherent in the mouth moisture itself necessitates a particular distinction between spit and saliva; no inherent change occurs. The difference is socially constructed. We social beings have drawn lines around behavior to demarcate deviant from normal, acceptable behavior.

The sociology professor then points out that "spit" and "saliva" are defined differently, depending on who is engaging in a given behavior and on the social context in which the behavior occurs. Mothers are seen wiping dirt from an infant's face with moisture from the mouth. Jesus and other religious leaders reportedly used their "sputum" to cure the blind and the infirm. Moreover, males spit incessantly during athletic contests, a behavior typically deemed "inappropriate" for female athletes. In sum, deviance is socially defined behavior.

Questions for Discussion

1. In 2006, professional football player Sean Taylor of the Washington Redskins was fined $17,000 by the National Football League for spitting in the face of another player during a game. As noted in a *Washington Post* story (Weeks, 2006) about the incident, this reaction would not surprise British sociologist Ross Coomber, who claims that spitting at someone is a form of violence more offensive than hitting them. Do you agree? Why or why not? Explain.

2. Have you ever redefined a behavior in order to label yourself or another deviant or nondeviant? Explain your answer.

Source: Excerpt from "Creating the sociological imagination on the first day of class: The social construction of deviance," by John R. Brouillette and Ronny E. Turner. Teaching Sociology, *vol. 21, 1992. Reprinted by permission of the American Sociological Association.*

all American youngsters are born to unmarried mothers (U.S. Census Bureau, 2003). According to Moynihan and others, fatherlessness and family breakup stand out as key variables associated with poverty, welfare dependency, crime, and other "social pathologies." Yet unmarried parenthood has been systematically redefined as merely another "lifestyle choice."

At the same time, many areas of behavior hitherto deemed benign have had their threshold radically "redefined upward." Old concerns like child abuse and family violence have become amplified in recent years, receiving much media attention. Simultaneously new areas of deviancy, including date rape and politically incorrect speech, have been created. And smoking—once deemed an innocent vice—is coming under progressive regulation and even prohibition.

▲ A Zone of Permissible Variation

In our daily lives we typically find that norms are not so much a point or a line as a zone (Williams, 1970). Even rather specific and strongly supported norms allow a zone of permissible variation. In actual practice, norms permit behavior that may depart from the strict letter of the law. For example, professors are expected to conduct their classes with dignity and decorum. Yet at almost every university some professor develops a reputation for unusual classroom behaviors: standing on the desk, sitting on the lectern, shouting and singing, dramatizing points by imitating voices, all in the course of a single class period. Since such professors often communicate well, are very popular, and are recognized authorities in their fields, the vast majority of students are quickly won over to their antics. Norms usually allow for *variant* behavior, new or at least different behavior that falls within the borders of the acceptable (Merton, 1968).

▲ The Functions and Dysfunctions of Deviance

Not all behavior has a purpose or a use. The same is doubtless true for many instances of deviance. Indeed, most of us think of deviance as "bad"—as behavior that poses a "social problem." Such a view is not surprising given the negative or disruptive consequences of much deviance, or what sociologists call *dysfunctions* (see Chapter 1). But deviance also has ◄ p. 19 positive or integrative consequences for social life, what sociologists call *functions.*

The Dysfunctions of Deviance.   Social organization derives from the coordinated actions of numerous people. Should some individuals fail to perform their actions at the proper time in accordance with accepted expectations, institutional life may be jeopardized. For instance, the desertion of a family by a parent commonly complicates the task of child care and rearing. And when a squad of soldiers fails to obey orders and runs away in the midst of battle, an entire army may be overwhelmed and defeated. Most societies can absorb a good deal of deviance without serious consequences, but persistent and widespread deviance can impair and even undermine organized social life.

Deviance also undermines our willingness to play our roles and contribute to the larger social enterprise. If some individuals get rewards, even disproportionate rewards, without playing by the rules, we develop resentment and bitterness. Morale, self-discipline, and loyalty suffer.

Moreover, our social life requires that we trust social institutions and one another. Trust makes conventional social life, from communities to economic exchange to families, possible. The most mundane, but essential, aspects of life would be impossible without trust. The use of checks and credit cards, for example, requires that we trust our banks to keep our money safe, to honor the checks that we write, and to charge our credit cards only as we have authorized. Normal community life is impossible where people cannot trust that those passing them on the street will not try to harm them. The maintenance of families and family life requires that people can trust others to live up to their obligations. Deviant behavior is dysfunctional because it can undermine this trust, threatening our most important social relationships and institutions.

The Functions of Deviance. Although deviance may undermine social organization, it may also facilitate social functioning in a number of ways. First, as sociologist Edward Sagarin (1975) has pointed out, reacting publicly to deviance can promote conformity. Such reactions create a community of the "good," those who know the cost of deviating and who can now define themselves as an *in-group* in contrast to the *out-group* of deviants.

Smoking, once deemed an innocent vice, is now increasingly regulated.

Second, because norms are not always clear, each time the members of a group censure some act as deviance, they highlight and sharpen the contours of a norm (Stevenson, 1991; Durkheim, 1893/1964). Their negative reactions clarify precisely what behavior is disallowed by the "collective conscience." Sociologist Kai T. Erikson (1962) noted that one of the interesting features of agencies of control is the amount of publicity they usually attract. In earlier times the punishment of offenders took place in the public market in full view of a crowd. Today we achieve much the same result through heavy media coverage of criminal trials and executions.

Third, by directing attention to the deviant, a group may strengthen itself. A shared enemy arouses common sentiments and cements feelings of solidarity. The emotions surrounding "ain't it awful" deeds quicken passions and solidify "our kind of people" ties. As we saw in Chapter 4, frictions and pp. 104–105 antagonisms between in-groups and out-groups highlight group boundaries and memberships. In the same way, campaigns against witches, traitors, perverts, and criminals reinforce social cohesion among "the good people." For instance, Erikson (1966) showed that when the Puritan colonists thought their way of life was threatened, they created "crime waves" and "witchcraft hysterias" to define and redefine the boundaries of their community.

Fourth, deviance is a catalyst for change. Every time a rule is violated, it is being contested. Such challenges serve as a warning that the social system is not functioning properly. For instance, high robbery rates clearly indicate that there are large numbers of disaffected people, that institutions for socializing youth are faltering, that power relations are being questioned, and that the moral structures of the society require reexamination. Thus, deviance is often a vehicle for placing on a society's agenda the need for social repair and remedies. By the same token, deviant activity can simultaneously be a call for an examination of old norms and a new model (Sagarin, 1975). For example, the Reverend Martin Luther King, Jr., and his supporters called the nation's attention to the inhumanity of southern segregation laws through civil disobedience. In due course the civil rights movement led to these laws being changed.

Social Control and Deviance

If the work of the world is to get done, people must follow rules. Social order dictates that people have to be kept in line, at least most people, and that the line must be adhered to within allowable limits (Sagarin, 1975; Gibbs, 1989; Tyler, 1990; Liska, 1986). Without social order, interaction would be a real problem and expectations would be meaningless. Societies seek to ensure that their members conform with basic norms by means of **social control,** the methods and strategies that regulate behavior within society.

Functionalist and conflict theorists differ in how they view social control. As we will see in Chapter 9, functionalists see social p. 286 control, particularly as it finds expression in the activities of the state, as an indispensable requirement for survival. If large numbers of people were to defy their society's standards for behavior, massive institutional breakdown, malfunctioning of society, and chaos would result. In contrast, as we will discuss at greater length in the chapter, conflict theorists contend that social control operates to favor powerful groups and to disadvantage others. No social arrangements are neutral, they argue. Existing institutional structures distribute the benefits and burdens of social life unevenly while maintaining these structures through the techniques and instruments of social control.

There are three main types of social control processes operating in social life: (1) those that lead us to internalize our society's normative expectations, (2) those that structure our world of social experience, and (3) those that employ various formal and informal social sanctions. Let us briefly consider each of these processes.

▲ Internalization of Norms

As we saw in Chapter 3, the members of a society undergo continuous *socialization,* a process by which individuals acquire those ways of thinking, feeling, and acting characteristic of their society's culture. For infants and young children, conformity to the expectations of others is primarily a product of external controls. As they grow older, an increasing proportion of their behavior becomes governed by internal monitors. These internal monitors carry on many of the functions earlier performed by external controls. **Internalization** is the process by which individuals incorporate within their personalities the standards of behavior prevalent within the larger society.

A good example is the set of norms in U.S. society regarding ownership of property. As all parents eventually learn, young children will pick up, play with, and sometimes destroy any item they find attractive. Only through interaction over a long period with parents, caregivers, and peers do children finally learn to "respect other people's property," even when they are not being watched by others.

Critical steps to social control through internalization are (1) learning what the norms are and (2) learning to believe that the norms are legitimate. In addition, through the process of internalization, norms become part of people's personalities, as discussed in Chapter 3 pp. 84–85 with the internalization of the "generalized

Our adherence to norms often depends on what we perceive the rewards or penalties to be.

By permission of Dave Coverly and Creators Syndicate, Inc.

other." Such standards are often accepted without thought or questioning—indeed, we commonly experience them as "second nature." The group is our group, and its norms are our norms. Social control thus becomes self-control.

▲ The Structure of Social Experience

Our society's institutions also shape our experiences. In large part, we unconsciously build up our sense of reality by the way our society orders its social agendas and structures social alternatives. If we are locked within the social environment provided by our culture, we inhabit a somewhat restricted world and it may not occur to us that alternative standards exist. A song popular during World War I questioned what might happen if this form of social control failed: "How ya gonna keep 'em down on the farm after they've seen Paree?" That is, how would the American soldiers be able to resume their conformist rural life after experiencing the wild city life available in Paris, France, in 1917 and 1918, with nightclubs, dancing girls, and prostitutes? Without experiences that take us out of the patterned routines dictated by the institutions that make up our society, we are *culture-bound.* Many nonconformist patterns do not occur to us because they are not known to our society.

▲ Formal and Informal Sanctions

Finally, we conform to the norms of our society because we realize that to do otherwise is to incur punishment. Those who break rules are met with dislike, hostility, gossip, ridicule, and ostracism—even imprisonment and death— while the conformist wins praise, popularity, prestige, and other socially defined good things. Clearly there are disadvantages to nonconformity and advantages to conformity.

Formal sanctions are reactions of official agents of social control, such as the courts, the honor systems that control cheating, and the principal's office in the high school. Students who are caught cheating, for example, may be formally sanctioned by being expelled from school. *Informal sanctions* are reactions to

deviance that occur in small communities, in groups of friends, and in the family. Students who report cheating by their friends may be deviant from the point of view of their friendship group, and may be informally sanctioned by being ostracized. Informal sanctions generally are more effective than formal sanctions, particularly if they are part of the interaction in the primary groups to which people are strongly committed.

Theories of Deviance

Deviance may have both positive and negative consequences for the functioning and survival of groups and societies. But why, we may ask, do people violate social rules? Why are some acts defined as deviance? Why are some individuals labeled deviants when they engage in essentially the same behaviors as other individuals who escape retribution? And why does the incidence of deviance vary from group to group and society to society? It is these types of questions that interest sociologists.

We should keep in mind that a complete understanding of human behavior, including deviant behavior, requires the inclusion of biological and psychological factors along with social factors (Gove, 1994). For example, both biology and psychology have contributed a good deal to our understanding of *schizophrenia*—a severely debilitating form of mental illness that affects about 1 percent of the population. Biologists and psychologists have shown that hereditary factors predispose individuals to some forms of schizophrenia (e.g., Sawa and Snyder, 2005). Studies show that among identical twins (who share 100 percent of their genes), if one twin is schizophrenic, the other has a 50 percent chance of being schizophrenic (Cockerham, 2006).

Yet an understanding of the biological and psychological factors involved in schizophrenia does not provide us with the full story. We also need to take into account sociological factors.

Consider the following example. A man living in the Ozark Mountains has a vision in which God speaks to him, and he begins preaching to his relatives and neighbors. People say he has a "calling." His reputation as a prophet and healer spreads, but when he ventures into St. Louis and attempts to hold a prayer meeting—blocking traffic at a downtown thoroughfare during rush hour—he is arrested. When the man tells the police officers about his conversations with God, they take him to a mental hospital where attending psychiatrists say he is "schizophrenic" and hospitalize him (Slotkin, 1955). Thus, we return full circle to sociological concerns. Again we are reminded that deviance is not a property inherent in behavior but a property conferred upon it by social definitions.

In this section, we depart from our usual consideration of the functionalist, interactionist, and conflict perspectives to discuss five specific theories of deviance that have emerged from these perspectives: the anomie, cultural transmission, conflict, labeling, and control theories. As you will see, each theory of deviance has a connection to the basic reasoning in the three theoretical perspectives we use in this book. Anomie and control grew out of *functionalism,* cultural transmission and labeling emerged from *symbolic interactionism,* and conflict theory is the application of the *conflict perspective* to deviance.

Anomie Theory

As we noted earlier in the chapter, Émile Durkheim (1893/1964, 1897/1951) contended that deviance can be functional for a society. But he also realized that deviance is simultaneously dysfunctional and made another contribution to our understanding of deviance with his idea of **anomie**—a social condition in which people find it difficult to guide their behavior by norms that they experience as weak, unclear, or conflicting. As Durkheim pointed out, anomie is a common occurrence when people's expectations about rewards and gratifications are not closely matched by what they actually receive. In a gold rush, many people believe that they can become wealthy overnight. As a result, some people abandon their families and jobs, travel long distances in search of riches, and set up nontraditional communities that promote crime, violence, prostitution, and general disorder. When an economy collapses and few jobs are available, the rewards that people are used to receiving are no longer available, and deviance, including crime and delinquency, increases. In both of these examples, norms that previously governed work and family life become weak and ineffectual because conformity to these norms no longer allows people to realize their expectations.

▲ Merton's Theory of Structural Strain

Robert K. Merton's theory of structural strain is an adaptation of Durkheim's anomie theory that emerged from the *functionalist* perspective (Liska and Messner, 1999). Merton (1968) built on Durkheim's ideas and linked them to American life. He said that for large numbers of Americans, worldly success—especially as it finds expression in material *wealth*—has become a cultural goal. However, only certain *means*—most commonly securing a good education and acquiring high-paying jobs—are the institutionalized and approved ways to achieve success. There might not be a problem if all Americans had equal access to these institutionalized means for realizing monetary success, but this is not the case. The poor and minorities often find themselves handicapped by little formal education and few economic resources.

Americans who internalize the goal of material success but who do not have access to the institutionalized means are pushed by strong social structural strains toward the use of unconventional means. They cannot achieve the culturally approved goals by using the institutionalized means for attaining them. One solution to this dilemma is to obtain the prestige-laden ends by any means whatsoever, including vice and crime.

Modes of Adaptation	Cultural Goals	Institutionalized Means
I Conformity	+	+
II Innovation	+	−
III Ritualism	−	+
IV Retreatism	−	−
V Rebellion	±	±

+ = Acceptance

− = Rejection

± = Rejection of prevailing values and substitution of new values

Figure 5.1   Merton's Typology of Modes of Individual Adaptation to Anomie

Source: Adapted with the permission of The Free Press, a Division of Simon & Schuster from *Social Theory and Social Structure* by Robert K. Merton. Copyright © 1949, 1957 by The Free Press; copyright renewed 1977, 1985 by Robert K. Merton.

Merton emphasized that a "lack of opportunity" and an exaggerated material emphasis are not enough to produce strains toward deviance. A society with a comparatively rigid class or caste structure may lack opportunity and simultaneously extol wealth—the medieval feudal system serves as a case in point. Only when a society extols common symbols of success for the entire population, while structurally restricting the access of large numbers of people to the approved means for acquiring these symbols, is antisocial behavior generated.

Merton identifies five responses to the ends-means dilemma, four of them deviant adaptations to conditions of anomie (see Figure 5.1).

Conformity.   Conformity will be common in a society in which people accept the cultural goal of material success and the institutionalized means to achieve this goal are available. Such behavior is the bedrock of a stable and properly functioning society.

Innovation.   In innovation, individuals hold fast to the culturally emphasized goals of success, but because the institutionalized means to achieve the goals are not available, they pursue their goals in innovative ways. Such people may engage in prostitution, peddle drugs, forge checks, swindle, embezzle, steal, burglarize, rob, or extort to secure money and purchase the symbols of success.

Ritualism.   Ritualism involves losing touch with success goals while abiding compulsively by the institutionalized means. For instance, the ends of the organization become irrelevant for many zealous bureaucrats. Instead, they cultivate the means for their own sake, making a fetish of regulations and red tape (see Chapter 4). pp. 118–122

Retreatism.   In retreatism individuals reject both the cultural goals and the institutionalized means without substituting new norms. For example, skid row alcoholics, drug addicts, vagabonds, and derelicts have dropped out of society; they "are in society but not of it."

Rebellion.   Rebels reject both the cultural goals and the institutionalized means and substitute new norms for them. Such individuals withdraw their allegiance from existing social arrangements and transfer their loyalties to new groups with new ideologies. Radical social movements on the right and left, such as the militia movement and radical socialism, are good illustrations of this type of adaptation.

▲ Applying Structural Strain Theory

Sociologists have applied structural strain theory to a variety of problems. In a classic study, Albert Cohen (1955) found that lower-class boys often find themselves failing in middle-class school environments that reward verbal skills, neatness, and an ability to defer gratification. The boys respond by banding together in juvenile gangs where they evolve "macho" standards that reward "toughness," "street smarts," and "troublemaking"—standards that allow them to succeed. Sociologists Steven Messner and Richard Rosenfeld (1997a, 1997b) extended Merton's structural strain theory. They argue that the strain toward deviance, particularly crime, is stronger when the economy is the dominant institution in society and when social status is primarily dependent on performance in economic roles. Crime rates are particularly high in societies where people are completely dependent on the labor market for resources necessary for survival; on the other hand, societies that guarantee an acceptable level of income regardless of participation in the labor market have less crime.

▲ Evaluating Structural Strain Theory

Merton's theory of structural strain tells us a good deal about monetary crime (Sagarin, 1975) and particularly about how individual adaptations to variation and change in the structure of opportunities (i.e., means) in society can influence rates of deviance and crime (Shoemaker, 2005). However, critics have pointed out that not all deviance stems from gaps between goals and means (Cohen, 1965). As we will see, people sometimes learn to deviate. If subcultural values and norms are different from those in the mainstream, when people conform to their subculture, they may be in violation of some important societal norms. Violations of fish and game laws among Native Americans, common-law marriage among some ethnic minorities, cockfighting among some groups with southern rural backgrounds, and the production of moonshine liquor among some Appalachian groups are all examples of such subcultural deviance. In sum, the problem may not be anomie or structural strain but a conflict of values.

Cultural Transmission Theory

Structural strain theory provides us with insight into how society may unwittingly contribute to deviance by the way it structures its goals and opportunities. A number of other sociologists have emphasized the similarities between the way deviant behavior is acquired and the way in which other behavior is acquired. One of the first was French sociologist Gabriel Tarde (1843–1904), who argued that criminals, like "good" people, imitate the ways of individuals they have met, known, or heard about. In contrast to law-abiding people, however, they imitate other criminals.

During the 1920s and 1930s, sociologists at the University of Chicago were struck by the concentration of high delinquency rates in some areas of Chicago (Thrasher, 1927; Shaw, 1930; Shaw and McKay, 1942; Sampson and Groves, 1989). In a series of investigations, they found that neighborhood delinquency rates remained much the same over time despite the changing composition of the neighborhoods (Shoemaker, 2005). They concluded that delinquent and criminal behaviors are in part a product of economic conditions, but are also culturally transmitted from one generation of juveniles to the next. As new ethnic groups enter a neighborhood, their children learn the delinquent patterns from the youth already there. Hence, the Chicago sociologists contended that youths become delinquent because they associate and make friends with other juveniles who are already delinquent.

▲ Sutherland's Theory of Differential Association

A classic statement of the cultural transmission of deviance is Edwin H. Sutherland's **differential association** theory. Sutherland (1939) was a sociologist associated with the Chicago tradition of sociology. His theory builds on the *interactionist perspective* and emphasizes the part social interaction plays in molding people's attitudes and behavior. Sutherland said that individuals learn deviance primarily in intimate groups of deviant others, such as small groups of friends (Shoemaker, 2005). People learn not only how to be deviant—for example, how to mug people, how to smoke marijuana, and how to apply graffiti—but also they learn attitudes favorable to deviance. Of course, people who are involved in deviant groups are also usually involved in more conventional relationships in their families, at school, at work, in church, and in other settings. Sutherland argued that if the definitions favorable to deviance outweigh the definitions unfavorable to deviance learned in other situations, deviance is likely to occur.

When parents move to a new neighborhood to get their children away from gang influences, they are applying the principle of differential association. So are parole officers who try to restrict the associations of the paroled prisoners they supervise. By the same token, the theory suggests that imprisonment may be counterproductive when juveniles are incarcerated with experienced criminals.

▲ Applying Cultural Transmission Theory

Recent studies of differential association have provided strong support for the theory (Matsueda, 1988; Shoemaker, 2005). Sociologist James Orcutt (1987), for example, found that having marijuana-smoking friends and favorable attitudes about marijuana are strong predictors of marijuana smoking. However, just as Sutherland's theory suggests, favorable attitudes lead to marijuana smoking only when they are stronger than unfavorable attitudes. Haynie's (2001) study showed that the impact of friends' delinquency on one's own delinquency is much greater when one is popular and central to the group and where the density of ties among friends is high. Box 5.2 shows how differential association helps explain college binge drinking.

▲ Evaluating Cultural Transmission Theory

Cultural transmission theory shows that socially disapproved behaviors can arise through the same processes of socialization as socially approved ones (Kaplan, Johnson, and Bailey, 1987). It is a particularly useful tool for understanding why deviance varies from group to group and from society to society (Matsueda and Heimer, 1987; Crane, 1991). However, the theory is not applicable to some forms of deviance, particularly those in which neither the techniques nor the appropriate definitions and

According to differential association theory, deviant behavior occurs because the definitions favorable to deviance outweigh unfavorable definitions. Those who want marijuana legalized clearly do not share the definitions of marijuana smoking common in mainstream society.

Drink 'Til You're Sick: What Explains College Binge Drinking?

Binge drinking—five drinks at a sitting for males, four for females—is on the rise in the United States (Naimi et al., 2003; Substance Abuse and Mental Health Services Administration, 2005). Although 69 percent of binge-drinking episodes occur among adults ages 26 and older, binge-drinking rates—the number of binges in a given time period—are highest for 18- to 25-year-olds. Indeed, close to half of the college students who drink say that they usually binge when they drink and that getting drunk is a good reason for drinking (Wechsler, Lee et al., 2000). Why is binge drinking so common among college students? No carefully designed studies have been done to answer this question, but available evidence supports both control theory and differential association theory.

Let's look at differential association first. In spite of some recent attempts at change, many campus fraternal organizations seem to encourage excessive drinking (Sperber, 2000). As we can see from the figure, students who are members of fraternities and sororities are much more likely to binge drink than are students in general. And for those who live in fraternity or sorority houses, the percentage of binge drinking is even higher (Wechsler, Lee et al., 2000). Differential association is even more important for underage drinkers, who are six times more likely to binge drink if they live in a fraternity or sorority house than if they live in a traditional single-sex dormitory (Wechsler, Kuo et al., 2000). Fraternal organizations are not the only social contexts that facilitate excessive drinking in college. Despite being exposed to more alcohol education programs than other students are, student athletes—both male and female—are significantly more likely to binge drink than are nonathletes (Nelson and Wechsler, 2001). A primary reason for this, consistent with differential association theory, is that college athletes are more likely than other students to have friends who are binge drinkers, who value partying and sports, and who spend a great deal of time socializing.

What about control theory? Students who are married are far less likely to binge drink, and control theory explains this by pointing to the process of commitment. People who are married have strongly invested in social relationships that could be threatened, damaged, or destroyed by deviant behavior such as binge drinking.

No one theory provides a complete explanation for deviance, and survey data such as that presented here leave us with many unanswered questions. Do students drink excessively because they live in fraternities and sororities, or do they choose to live in fraternities and sororities because they like to drink? Do married students drink less because they are married, or are those who drink little or no alcohol more likely to marry? Carefully designed experiments or surveys that collect data from high school and

attitudes are acquired from other deviants. Illustrations include naive check forgers; occasional, incidental, and situational offenders; nonprofessional shoplifters; non-career-type criminals; and people who commit "crimes of passion." Further, not everyone who has deviant associates is deviant. Different individuals may interpret the same social relationships differently, producing different outcomes.

Although most of the emphasis in cultural transmission theory has been on how criminal behavior is learned from friends, relatives are probably also important. Most incarcerated juvenile delinquents, and about a third of such adult offenders, have immediate family members who also have been in jail or prison. The more severe and chronic the criminal behavior, the more likely that an offender has relatives who have been imprisoned (Butterfield, 1992). More research is needed to determine if this association is due to learning (as cultural transmission theory suggests), to shared environment, to shared genetic inheritance, or to some combination of these factors.

college students at several points in time might help us sort out these questions with more certainty.

Questions for Discussion

1. Do these studies support your experiences or the experiences of other students on your campus?

2. How could labeling theory be used to challenge the implicit claim made in this box that binge drinking is deviant?

3. Which theory or theories of deviant behavior offer an understanding of binge drinking that could be used to develop strategies to control it? How and why?

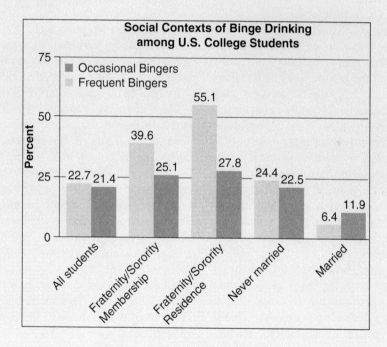

Social Contexts of Binge Drinking among U.S. College Students

Conflict Theory

Cultural transmission theorists emphasize that individuals who are immersed in different subcultures will exhibit somewhat different behaviors because they are socialized in different traditions. Conflict theorists argue that the most important question is, "Which group will be able to translate its values into the rules of a society and make these rules stick?"

Although in recent decades the conflict approach has taken many new directions (Hagan, 1989; Messner and Krohn, 1990; Grant and Martinez, 1997), its early roots can be traced to the Marxist tradition and the conflict perspective that grew out of it (see Chapter 1). pp. 20–22 According to orthodox Marxism, a capitalist ruling class exploits and robs the masses, yet avoids punishment for its crimes. Individuals victimized by capitalist oppression are driven by their struggle to survive to commit acts that the ruling class brands as criminal (Bonger, 1936; Liska and Messner, 1999). Marxists regard other types of deviance—alcoholism, drug abuse,

147

mental illness, family violence, sexual immorality, and prostitution—as products of the moral degeneration and estrangement fostered by the oppression and exploitation of the poor, women, and African Americans or other minorities.

▲ Quinney's Theory of Class, State, and Crime

Because Marx wrote little about crime, it fell to a 20th-century U.S. sociologist, Richard Quinney (1974, 1980), to write a now-classic statement of the conflict theory of crime. Quinney said that the U.S. legal system reflects the interests and ideologies of the ruling capitalist class. Law makes illegal certain behavior that is offensive to the morality of the powerful and that threatens their privileges and property.

Quinney (1980:39) contended that if we are "to understand crime we have to understand the development of the political economy of capitalist society." Since the state serves the interests of the capitalist class, crime is ultimately a class-based political act embedded in capitalist social arrangements.

In striving to maintain itself against the internal contradictions eating away at its foundations, capitalism commits *crimes of domination* (Quinney, 1980:57). Indeed, "one of the contradictions of capitalism is that some of its laws must be violated in order to secure the existing system." These crimes include those committed by corporations and range from price fixing to pollution of the environment. But there are also *crimes of government* committed by the officials of the capitalist state, Watergate being a well-publicized instance. In contrast, much of the criminal behavior of ordinary people, or *predatory crime*—burglary, robbery, drug dealing, and hustling of various sorts—is "pursued out of the need to survive" in a capitalist social order. *Personal crime*—murder, assault, and rape—is "pursued by those who are already brutalized by the conditions of capitalism." And then there are *crimes of resistance* in which workers engage in sloppy work and clandestine acts of sabotage against employers.

▲ Applying Conflict Theory

Conflict theory has led social scientists to investigate the ways in which the making and administration of law are biased by powerful interests (Jacobs and Helms, 1996, 1997). Numerous sociologists have noted that crime is defined primarily in terms of offenses against property (burglary, robbery, auto theft, and vandalism), whereas corporate crime is deemphasized (Sutherland, 1949; Coleman, 1987). Moreover, the penalty for crimes against property is imprisonment, whereas the most common form of penalty for business-related offenses is a monetary fine. In the most comprehensive study of its kind, Clinard and Yeager (1980) found that over a 2-year period, the federal government charged nearly two-thirds of the Fortune 500 corporations (the 500 largest U.S. corporations) with violations of the law. Estimates of the yearly cost of such crimes run as high as $200 billion, compared with $3 to $4 billion a year for conventional street crimes (Clinard and Meier, 2003). This basic problem appears not to have improved over time (Clinard, 1990). In 1994, for example, at the end of a 7-year investigation the 10 largest defense contractors serving the U.S. government were fined more than $250 million for engaging in fraud, and 54 corporate employees involved were convicted of crimes (Clinard and Meier, 2003). And while the Federal Bureau of Investigation (FBI) keeps track of every murder, rape, assault, and auto theft reported in the United States, no agency keeps a record of crimes committed by corporations themselves.

▲ Evaluating Conflict Theory

Though there may be much in conflict theory that is true (Liska and Messner, 1999), statements of the theory are not always clear (Hawkins, 1987). In addition, it is sometimes hard to tell which specific individuals or groups are covered by such terms as "ruling elites," "governing classes," and "powerful interests." In addition, research results are not always consistent with the theory. For example, the theory predicts that "When sanctions are imposed, the most severe sanctions will be imposed on persons in the lowest social class" (Chamblis and Seidman, 1971:475). Some studies have found few (Bernstein, Kelly, and Doyle, 1977) or no (Chiricos and Waldo, 1975) links between the class level of criminal offenders and the sentences received or between unemployment and incarceration (D'Alessio and Stolzenberg, 1995); other studies have found the relationship to be substantial (Lizotte, 1978; Bridges, Crutchfield, and Simpson, 1987); and still others have found that the relationship depends on specific circumstances (Hagan, Bernstein, and Albonetti, 1980; Humphrey and Fogarty, 1987). Although corporations often seek to influence legislation and public policy about deviance, they do not necessarily predominate over other interest groups (Hagan, 1980, 1989). Clearly, additional research is needed. Conflict propositions cannot be accepted as articles of faith but should be more clearly articulated and more carefully investigated.

Labeling Theory

Conflict theorists contend that people often find themselves at odds with one another because their interests diverge and their values clash. Some people gain the power and ascendancy to translate their values and normative preferences into the rules governing institutional life. They then successfully place negative labels on violators of these rules. A number of sociologists took this core notion, expanded on it using ideas from the *interactionist perspective,* and developed labeling theory. Labeling theorists are interested in the process by which some individuals come to be tagged as "deviants," begin to think of themselves as deviants, and enter deviant careers.

▲ Edwin Lemert, Howard S. Becker, and Kai T. Erikson: The Social Reaction to Deviance Approach

The three sociologists responsible for making the classic statements of labeling theory—Edwin M. Lemert (1951, 1972), Howard S. Becker (1963), and Kai T. Erikson (1962, 1966)—make a number of points. First, they contend that no act by itself is inherently deviant or not deviant. The "badness" of an act does not stem from its intrinsic content but from the way other people define and react to it. Deviance is always a matter of social definition. Similarly, according to labeling theory, a person who engages in deviant behavior is deviant only if he or she has been so labeled.

Second, labeling theorists point out that we all engage in deviant behavior by violating some norms. They reject the popular idea that human beings can be divided into those who are normal and those who are pathological. For example, some of us exceed the speed limit, experiment with cocaine, shoplift, cheat on a homework assignment, sample homosexual publications, underreport our income to income tax authorities, swim in the nude, become intoxicated, commit vandalism in celebration of a football victory, or trespass on private property. These actions often are what labeling theorists call **primary deviance**—behavior that violates social norms but usually goes unnoticed by the agents of social control.

Third, labeling theorists say that whether people's acts will be seen as deviant depends on which rules society chooses to enforce, in which situations, and with respect to which people. Not all individuals are arrested for speeding, shoplifting, underreporting income on their tax returns, trespassing, or the like. African Americans may be censured for doing what whites are "allowed" to do, women censured for doing what men are "allowed" to do, certain individuals censured for doing what their friends are also doing, and some may be labeled as deviants even though they have not violated a norm but simply because they are so accused (e.g., they appear "effeminate" and are tagged as "gay"). Of critical importance is the social audience and whether or not it labels the person a deviant.

Fourth, labeling people as deviants has consequences for them. It tends to set up conditions conducive to **secondary deviance**—deviance individuals adopt in response to the reactions of other individuals. In brief, labeling theorists contend that new deviance is manufactured by the hostile reactions of rule makers and rule abiders. An individual is publicly identified, stereotyped, and denounced as a "delinquent," "mental fruitcake," "forger," "rapist," "drug addict," "bum," "pervert," or "criminal." The label serves to lock the individual into an outsider status. Such a master status overrides other statuses in shaping a person's social experiences and results in a self-fulfilling prophecy. Rule breakers come to accept their status as a particular kind of deviant and organize their lives around this master status.

Fifth, people labeled "deviant" typically find themselves rejected and isolated by "law-abiding" people. Friends and relatives may withdraw from them. In some cases they may even be institutionalized in prisons or mental hospitals. Rejection and isolation push stigmatized individuals toward a deviant group with other individuals who share a common fate. Participation in a deviant subculture becomes a way of coping with frustrating situations and for finding emotional support and personal acceptance. In turn, joining a deviant group solidifies a deviant self-image, fosters a deviant lifestyle, and weakens ties to the law-abiding community.

In sum, labeling theorists say that the societal response to an act, not the behavior itself, determines deviance. When the behavior of people is seen as departing from prevailing norms, it sets off a chain of social reactions. Other individuals define, evaluate, and label the behavior. Norm violators then take these labels into account as they shape their actions. In many cases they evolve an identity consistent with a label and embark upon a career of deviance.

▲ Applying Labeling Theory

Unlike structural strain and cultural transmission theory, labeling theory does not focus on why some individuals engage in deviant behavior. Rather, labeling theory helps us to understand why the same act may or may not be considered deviant, depending on the situation and the characteristics of the individuals who are involved.

Sociologist William J. Chambliss (1973) employed labeling theory to explain the differing perceptions and definitions that community members had of the behavior of two teenage gangs. At Hanibal High School, Chambliss observed the activities of the Saints, a gang of eight white upper-class boys, and the Roughnecks, a gang of six lower-class white boys. Although the Saints engaged in as many delinquent acts as the Roughnecks, it was the Roughnecks who were in "constant trouble" and universally considered to be "delinquent." The community, the school, and the police related to the Saints as though they were good, upstanding youths with bright futures, but they treated the Roughnecks as young punks headed for trouble.

A number of factors contributed to the differential treatment given the two groups. For one thing, the Saints had access to automobiles and engaged in out-of-town escapades that were less visible to Hanibal citizens than those undertaken by the Roughnecks in the center of town. For another, when the Saints were confronted with an accusing police officer, they were apologetic and penitent, whereas the Roughnecks were hostile and belligerent. Finally, police officers knew that irate and influential upper-middle-class parents would come to the aid of their youngsters, whereas powerless lower-class parents would have to acquiesce in the law's definition of their son's behavior.

Chambliss (1973) concluded that when the community responded to the Roughnecks as boys in trouble, the boys' pattern of deviancy was reinforced. As their self-conception as deviants became more firmly entrenched, they began to try new and more extreme acts of deviance. Their growing alienation led to greater disrespect and hostility, which increased the community's negative attitude toward them.

▲ Evaluating Labeling Theory

Evidence on the operations of social control organizations often supports labeling theory. From 1880 to 1920, unprecedented numbers of Americans were confined to mental hospitals. But the labeling perspective showed that this was not due to Americans becoming suddenly mad, but rather was caused by a boom in state mental hospital construction and increased funding of state departments of mental hygiene (Grob, 1983; Sutton, 1991). The capacity to confine people had increased.

Research also shows that once people are hospitalized for mental illness, some feel stigmatized by the label "mental patient," and this may make reintegration into the world outside the hospital more difficult (Link et al., 1989, 1991).

Labeling theory also has its critics. While it may help us understand how individuals are labeled as deviants and how labels can promote secondary deviance, labeling theory tells us nothing about causes of primary deviance. Indeed, in many forms of deviance it is the behavior or condition of the people themselves that is primarily responsible for their being labeled deviant. For example, a vast majority of people who are hospitalized for mental illness suffer acute disturbance associated with internal psychological or neurological malfunctioning (Gove, 1970) that cannot be explained solely in terms of the reactions of other people.

Another criticism of labeling theory is its almost exclusive focus on societal reactions in the definition of deviant behavior. If behavior is not deviance unless it is labeled, we cannot classify secret and undetected deviance, such as the embezzlement of funds, the failure to pay income taxes, and the clandestine sexual molestation of children. Clearly, deviance cannot be understood without reference to norms.

Control Theory

The theories discussed above are all attempts to explain why people deviate. Control theory turns the question around and asks why people *do not* deviate (Reckless, 1961, 1967; Hirschi, 1969; Shoemaker, 2005). Though we are frequently concerned that there is too much deviance in our society, what is truly remarkable is how much conformity there is. As you walk to and attend class each day, your behavior and that of others around you almost always fits within a narrow and predictable pattern. Most of us conform most of the time; even "deviants" conform most of the time. Such rigid control is particularly remarkable given that the possibilities for human behavior are virtually infinite, limited only by physical laws and people's imaginations.

Control theory's answer to why people conform is an outgrowth of *functionalist* ideas. People conform because they are integrated into mainstream institutions. Societies that have properly functioning institutions will have low deviance.

▲ Travis Hirschi and the Elements of the Social Bond

Travis Hirschi's study (1969) of juvenile delinquency in Richmond, California, provided a classic statement of control theory. Hirschi's argument is that young people are more likely to conform if their bond to society is strong. This bond has four parts: attachment, involvement, commitment, and belief.

Attachment is the process of being involved in social relationships with others. All social relationships entail some degree of control for all participants. Control is more likely where the psychological and emotional connections among group members are high and members care about one another's opinions (Shoemaker, 2005). Being involved in a family, having friends in the community, and being a member of a club are all examples of attachments that reduce the chance that deviance will occur.

By *involvement*, Hirschi meant involvement in conventional activities. One way to keep people from being deviant is to get them to spend their time conforming. Boy Scouts, Girl Scouts, youth fellowship, band, and athletics are only a few of the myriad activities that parents, schools, religious organizations, and neighborhood associations create to take up the leisure time of children and adolescents. A main purpose of these activities is to provide an alternative to drug and alcohol use, sexual activity, vandalism, and crime.

Commitment refers to the strength of the investment people have made in conventional social ties and relationships. People who have strong commitments in their social lives are not likely to deviate because of the losses they may incur if they are identified as deviant. A student who aspires to become a police officer and who has earned the trust and respect of teachers, school administrators, and local law enforcement officials is unlikely to become a drug dealer; she would risk losing the benefits of the investments she has made in pursuit of her career.

Finally, the bond to society is cemented by *belief* in conventional values and ideas about morality. The less people believe in the conventional values of society, the more likely it is that deviance will occur. If young people do not believe in the conventional idea that having a job or running a legitimate business is the acceptable way to make money, they are more likely to attempt to get money in criminal ways.

▲ Applying Control Theory

Because the essence of control theory is that people will be less likely to deviate if they are integrated into mainstream institutions, much research on control theory has focused on the controlling power of three primary social institutions: religion, the family, and education (Shoemaker, 2005).

Somewhat surprisingly, a number of studies have found that religion seems to have little or no impact on deviant behavior (Jensen and Rojek, 1992; Hirschi and Stark, 1969). The reason is not that religion is ineffective in social control, but that religion is only one of a number of social institutions involved in controlling behavior and therefore it is hard to see its impact. It is easier to see the controlling effect of religion where there is low consensus about the deviant nature of acts; nearly everyone agrees that murder is wrong, but fewer people strongly agree that smoking marijuana is wrong. Religion does control deviant behavior, and its effect is clearly seen where competing secular controls are weak (Tittle and Welch, 1983; Burkett and White, 1974).

Most studies of the family and deviant behavior have been concerned with young people. These studies have shown that intact families and good family relations decrease the chances of delinquent behavior among youths (Shoemaker, 2005). However, the effect of intact families is relatively weak and has not been found in all studies. The more important factor is not family structure (broken versus intact), but the way parents communicate and get along with their children (Yablonsky and Haskell, 1988; Cernkovich and Giordano, 1987).

Involvement in schooling controls deviant behavior not only because it takes up people's time in conventional pursuits, but also because it promotes conventional attachments, commitment, and beliefs. Hirschi (1969) found that attachment to school and having positive relationships with teachers reduced the chance of delinquency. More recent studies continue to find a positive influence in schools. Cernkovich and Giordano (1992) found that attachment and commitment to school reduced delinquency, although this effect was somewhat less among black males. Zingraff's 1994 study showed that schooling is an important deterrent to delinquency even when family relations are poor or abusive. And Crutchfield and Pitchford (1997) showed that among people 18 years and over, being a student reduces the likelihood of criminal involvement.

▲ Evaluating Control Theory

Though much of the research on deviance and delinquency is in accord with control theory

(Shoemaker, 2005), some problems remain. First, the social bond does not control deviance equally well across social groups (Cernkovich and Giordano, 1992; Gardner and Shoemaker, 1989) or as well in other societies as in the United States (Rahav, 1976; Tanioka and Glaser, 1991; Hartjen and Kethineini, 1993). Second, factors other than the bond to society are clearly important; even the best studies show that no more than 50 percent of delinquent behavior is explained by factors emphasized in control theory (Shoemaker, 2005). Third, in some circumstances elements of the social bond are not associated with reduced deviance. For example, as differential association theory indicates, when attachment is to delinquent peers, we observe more deviance. Involvement in conventional activities likewise is not related to less deviance if it allows unstructured time with no authority present (Osgood et al., 1996), as members of traveling high school marching bands and athletic teams often attest. Indeed, the National Longitudinal Study of Adolescent Health, the largest-ever national study of adolescents, showed that spending unsupervised time with friends is much more closely linked to drinking, smoking, using weapons, attempting suicide, and having sex than are race, income, or family structure (Stepp, 2000; see also Blum et al., 2000). Finally, control theory cannot explain deviance that occurs among those who are fully integrated into mainstream society. Those implicated in the deviant acts of white-collar, corporate, and government crime are often the employed, married, churchgoing, respectable middle class.

None of the theories of deviance we have examined provides a complete explanation of deviant behavior. Each one highlights for us an important source of deviance (for example, see Hoffmann, 2003). Deviant behavior takes many forms, so we must approach each form in its own right to determine the specific factors involved. We turn next to a consideration of crime, a form of deviance that is particularly prevalent in modern societies.

Crime and the Criminal Justice System

Within modern societies, law is a crucial element in social control. Unlike informal norms such as folkways and mores, laws are rules enforced by the state. As we defined it at the beginning of the chapter, *deviance* is behavior that a considerable number of people view as reprehensible and beyond the limits of tolerance. **Crime** is an act of deviance that is prohibited by law. As we have seen, not all deviant acts are crimes; they may break rules defined only by folkways and mores. As with other forms of deviance, there is nothing inherent in an act that makes it criminal. For an act to be considered criminal, the state must undertake a political process of illegalizing—or *criminalizing*—it (Jenness, 2004). Because anything can be a crime if a law is established making it illegal, an infinite variety of acts can be crimes.

What crimes have in common is not that they are necessarily acts we regard as immoral or wicked. For example, many Americans consider it no more "evil" to cheat on their income taxes than did their parents or grandparents to purchase and consume illegal alcoholic beverages during Prohibition. Rather, the distinguishing property of crime is that people who violate the law are liable to be arrested, tried, pronounced guilty, and deprived of their lives, liberty, or property. In brief, they are likely to become caught up in the elaborate social machinery of the **criminal justice system**—the reactive agencies of the state that include the police, the courts, and prisons. So common are "scrapes with the law" that U.S. men have nearly a 50 percent chance of being arrested at least once in their lives (Uggen, 2000).

In this section we will describe various forms of crime and discuss the measurement of crime. We will examine the relationship between drugs and crime and consider the criminal behavior of women. Finally, we will describe the components of the criminal justice system and take a look at the purposes of imprisonment.

Forms of Crime

In this section we consider a number of forms of crime within the United States: violent crime, juvenile crime, organized crime, white-collar and corporate crime, crime committed by government, and victimless crime.

▲ Violent and Property Crime

The Federal Bureau of Investigation annually reports on eight types of crime in its Uniform Crime Reports. These offenses are called **index crimes** and consist of four categories of violent crime against people—murder, rape, robbery, and assault—and four categories of crimes against property—burglary, theft, motor vehicle theft, and arson. Index crimes are declining in the United States, with property crimes dropping since 1974 and violent crime since 1994 (Catalano, 2005; Rennison, 2002a). In 2004, the rates of overall violent crime, simple assault, overall property crime, burglary, and theft were the lowest ever recorded by the National Crime Victimization Survey (NCVS), which was initiated in 1973 (see Figure 5.2). Rape, sexual assault, robbery, aggravated assault, and motor vehicle theft rates also were at their lowest points in 2004. Between 1993 and 2004, property crime dropped by 50 percent and violent crimes by 57 percent (Catalano, 2005). Survey respondents' attitudes reflect this drop: In 1994, 37 percent of a random sample named crime and violence as the most important problem facing the country, compared to only 2 percent in 2001 (Pastore and Maguire, 2005).

In spite of this reduction, there is still a large amount of crime in the United States. In 2004

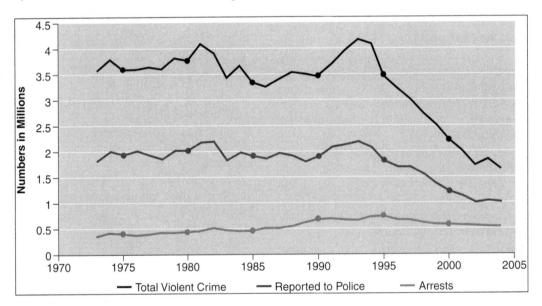

Figure 5.2 **Numbers of Violent Crimes, Violent Crimes Reported to Police, and Arrests for Violent Crimes in the U.S., 1973–2004**

The amount of violent crime in the United States has been declining since the early 1990s, and in 2004 it was the lowest recorded since 1973.

Source: Bureau of Justice Statistics, U.S. Department of Justice (http://www.ojp.usdoj.gov/bjs/glance/tables/4meastab.htm).

there were 16,137 murders in the United States (Federal Bureau of Investigation, 2005). Not including murder, the total number of criminal victimizations—both property and violent crimes—in 2004 was 24.0 million. Violent crimes in the United States decreased to 21 per 1,000 people, and property crimes dropped to 161 per 1,000 households; 0.8 rape or sexual assault per 1,000 people was recorded, along with 9 motor vehicle thefts per 1,000 households and 4 aggravated and 14 simple assaults per 1,000 people (Catalano, 2005).

These decreases in violent crime during the 1990s represent a greater decline than at any time since World War II and resulted in many headlines and discussions on television talk shows. While significant, the rates of decline during the 1990s were not as great as the rates of increase experienced during the 1960s and early 1970s (LaFree, 1999). What accounts for the drop in violent and property crime over recent decades? Pinpointing the causes of crime trends ("booms" and "busts") is difficult because the kinds of data necessary to draw such conclusions have not been collected over a long enough time period. But various explanations have been suggested. Some authors believe that changes in drug subcultures are linked to changes in violent crime rates, with the cocaine/crack subculture of the 1980s responsible for more crime than the marijuana subculture of the 1990s. Other important factors include higher rates of incarceration, more effective gun policies, and increases in the number of police (Levitt, 2004; Bartollas, 2003), a stronger economy, and growing family stability (LaFree, 1999).

Crime data provide information about how crimes occur. For example, 77 percent of murder victims in 2004 knew their assailants, and more than three-quarters of all murder victims were male (Federal Bureau of Investigation, 2005). Forty-four percent of all murders were precipitated by arguments, and firearms were the weapons used in 66 percent of all murders in 2004. In rapes and sexual assaults, 67 percent of victims know their assailant (Catalano, 2005). Sixty-one percent of female aggravated assault

victims know their assailant, 18 percent of them intimately; in other words, women's assailants are likely to be husbands, boyfriends, and acquaintances. Among male aggravated assault victims, 44 percent know their assailants, but only 3 percent are intimately involved with their assailants. Crime victimization rates also show that victims of violent crime are likely to be male, poor, urban, young, and black (see Table 5.1).

Despite its declining crime rate, the United States has a reputation for violent crime. Although its property crime rate is similar to or lower than the rate of property crime in other industrialized nations, the U.S. violent crime rate is higher than that of Western Europe or Australia. Why? Social scientists Franklin Zimring and Gordon Hawkins explored the question in their 1997 book *Crime Is Not the Problem: Lethal Violence in America*. One answer they suggested is that Americans are more heavily armed than citizens of other nations so that property crimes are more likely to lead to death. Guns do not answer the question entirely, however. Even in robberies in which no guns are used, the death rate is three times higher in New York City than in London. Further, 30 percent of U.S. homicides do not involve a gun. Another explanation for the higher violent crime rate in the United States, then, is that people are more likely to have more frequent and more violent personal conflicts than in other countries.

The influence of American television and other media is often invoked as a possible explanation for high rates of violent crime. But James Q. Wilson cites historical evidence that shows that "the homicide rate in New York City has exceeded that of London by a factor of at least five *for the last two hundred years*" (Wilson, 1997:41)—during which, of course, America's youth were not watching crime shows on TV. The assessment by Zimring and Hawkins that lots of conflict and lots of guns are responsible for a high U.S. violent crime rate fits with those of analysts who see a stable economy, family stability, and effective gun control as accounting for the recent drop in the crime rate.

Table 5.1	Rates of Violent Crime in the United States, 2004

	Victims per 1,000 Persons*
Gender	
Male	25
Female	18
Age	
12–15	50
16–19	46
20–24	43
25–34	24
35–49	18
50–64	11
65+	2
Race	
White	21
Black	26
Other	13
Ethnicity	
Hispanic	18
Non-Hispanic	22
Family income	
Less than $7,500	38
$7,500–$14,999	39
$15,000–$24,999	24
$25,000–$34,999	22
$35,000–$49,999	22
$50,000–$74,999	22
$75,000+	17
Residence	
Urban	29
Suburban	18
Rural	20

These crime victimization rates for rape, sexual assault, robbery, aggravated assault, and simple assault (taken as a whole) show that victims of violent crime are more likely to be male, young, black, poor, and urban.

Source: Catalano, Shannan. 2005. *Criminal Victimization 2004*. Washington, DC: U.S. Department of Justice (NCJ 210674; http://www.ojp.usdoj.gov/bjs/pubalp2.htm#cv).

Rates are calculated per 1,000 population ages 12 and older.

▲ Juvenile Crime

We have seen that young people are more likely to be victims of crime. They also are more likely than older people to commit crime. Though persons 15 to 19 years of age represent only 7.1 percent of the population, they constitute 21.3 percent of those arrested for committing crimes (Pastore and Maguire, 2005). The peak age for property crime is 16 to 18 and for violent crime it is 18 to 19 (Pastore and Maguire, 2005). Juvenile involvement in violent crime has increased over the past several decades (Bartollas, 2003). The percentage of people arrested for committing crimes drops steadily with increasing age. If we could prevent all crimes committed by persons under 25 years of age, much of conventional crime would be eliminated from society, though we would still have many white-collar, corporate, and government crimes and about half the homicides. With an ever-increasing number of young people in the country, however, many of whom are at high risk for delinquent behavior, some analysts predict a violent juvenile crime wave (Bartollas, 2003; Siegel and Welch, 2005).

Although school crime and school violence grab big headlines, school crime has declined just as societywide levels of crime have (DeVoe et al., 2003). In the mid-1990s, 1 in 10 students reported having been a victim of crime at school. By 2001, this number had dropped from 10 percent to 6 percent. Children of school age are more than twice as likely to be crime victims outside of school (DeVoe et al., 2003). For example, only 1 percent of all homicides of youth and two-tenths of a percent of youth suicides are associated with school. Rates of nonfatal serious violent crime victimizations are 14 per 1,000 students away from school and 5 per 1,000 at school.

On the other hand, the proportion of high school students who have been threatened or injured with a weapon at school has remained steady at 7 to 9 percent since the early 1990s, despite the fact that over the same period of time the percentage of students who reported carrying a weapon dropped by half (DeVoe et al., 2003). Other sorts of problem behaviors, however, such as bullying, have increased. In 2001, 12 percent of students of middle and high school age reported that hate-related words had been used against them, 20 percent of students reported that their school has street gangs, 5 percent of high school students reported having drunk alcohol on school grounds, and nearly 30 percent said someone had "offered, sold, or given them an illegal drug on school property"(DeVoe et al., 2003).

It is clear that the present system of juvenile justice has encountered substantial failures either in deterring violent crime by the young or in rehabilitating young criminals. Critics point to estimates by some researchers indicating that about 7 percent of young offenders are responsible for up to three-quarters of the violent crimes committed by juveniles (Tracy, Wolfgang, and Figlio, 1990).

How are young people who commit crimes treated? In 1972, half of all juveniles taken into police custody were referred to juvenile court, and nearly half were handled within the arresting police department and released. Only 1.3 percent were referred to criminal or adult court (Pastore and Maguire, 2005). In 2002, the proportion handled within a police department and released had dropped to 18 percent, and nearly three-quarters were referred to juvenile court. Referrals to criminal or adult court rose to 7 percent. Although juveniles may end up in juvenile detention centers, they are not exempt from more serious punishment, including the death sentence. In 2001, the minimum age authorized for capital punishment was 14 for 3 states, 16 for 7 states, 17 for 5 states, and 18 for 16 states and the federal system. Only 2.1 percent of those on death row in 2003 were 17 or younger at the time of their arrest; 10.9 percent were 18 to 19, and 27.0 percent were 20 to 24 (Bonczar and Snell, 2004). Nearly three-fifths of U.S. survey respondents say that juveniles should be treated the same as adults (Pastore and Maguire, 2005).

▲ Organized Crime

Organized crime refers to large-scale bureaucratic organizations that provide illegal goods and services in public demand. Such crime is likely to arise where the state criminalizes certain activities—prostitution, drugs, pornography, gambling, and loan-sharking—that large numbers of citizens desire and for which they are willing to pay. Drug and arms trafficking by major crime organizations is the largest business in the world, bringing in between $700 billion and $1 trillion a year (Adler, Mueller, and Laufer, 2004).

The most publicized crime organization has been an Italian-American syndicate, variously termed the Mafia or Cosa Nostra, which gained a substantial impetus from Prohibition. The Mafia seems to be a loose network or confederation of regional syndicates coordinated by a "commission" composed of the heads of the most powerful crime "families" (Adler, Mueller, and Laufer, 2004; Tittle and Paternoster, 2000). Organized crime is hardly an Italian monopoly, however. Chinese gangs, Colombian and Cuban drug rings, and groups of southern white moonshiners also fall under the category of organized crime. Although we may associate organized crime with various immigrant groups, it is not the case that immigration is tied to higher crime. For example, Hispanic immigrants are less involved in crime than are U.S. citizens (Hagan and Palloni, 1999).

▲ White-Collar and Corporate Crime

One type of crime that has been of particular interest to sociologists is **white-collar crime**—crime most commonly committed by relatively affluent persons, often in the course of business activities (Sutherland, 1949). Martha Stewart and the Enron scandal are well-known examples of white-collar crime in the news. Included in white-collar crime are corporate crime, fraud, embezzlement, corruption, bribery, tax fraud or evasion, stock manipulation, insider trading, misrepresentation of advertising, restraint of trade, and infringement of patents. More recent research has focused on workplace misconduct at a different level, including such things as drinking or doing drugs on the job, short-changing customers, damaging or stealing employers' property, and falsifying time records (Wright and Cullen, 2000).

White-collar crime costs society just as other crimes do, and we are more likely to be victims of corporate crime than of street crime (Simon and Eitzen, 1993). Tax evasion is the most costly white-collar crime in the United States. Fraud, the second-most costly white-collar crime, costs citizens $300 per household in higher insurance premiums (Soupiset, 2003). And *shrinkage,* a term used by retailers to encompass theft by employees, shoplifting, and clerical errors, cost $33.2 billion in 2001 (Pressler, 2003).

Bank and insurance frauds are commonplace; taxpayers are still paying off the cost of the savings and loan industry collapse of the 1980s—$500 billion according to the U.S. General Accounting Office (Calavita, Tillman, and Pontell, 1997), or nearly $2,000 for every adult and child in the United States.

Corporations have been implicated in a variety of crimes, including overcharging the government on contracts, polluting the environment, shortchanging consumers, violating employee privacy, price-rigging school milk contracts, disposing of hazardous waste in violation of the law, adulterating fruit juice, and engaging in accounting irregularities (Clinard, 1990; Rothchild, 1993).

The small number of white-collar criminals who are prosecuted and convicted are rarely given sentences comparable to those of other criminals. Street criminals who steal $100 may find their way to prison, while an executive who embezzles $1 million may receive a suspended sentence and a relatively small fine.

▲ Crime Committed by Government

Conflict theorists have drawn our attention to crime committed by governments (Barak, 1991).

Nazi Germany provides an extreme example: More than 6 million Jews were murdered during the Holocaust of the Hitler years (Dawidowicz, 1975). More recently, other governments have participated in "ethnic cleansing" and murdered citizens who were the "wrong" religion or ethnic background. The U.S. government massacred countless Native Americans during the colonization of the country; even as late as 1890, U.S. Army forces armed with machine guns mowed down nearly 300 Sioux at Wounded Knee, South Dakota (Brown, 1971).

But there are other sorts of government crimes. At the federal level, the Iran-contra scandal during President Reagan's term showed that operatives of the nation's security organizations engaged in secret arms shipments to the Nicaraguan contra rebels during the years that Congress barred aid to them. The Oval Office tapes of the Richard Nixon White House revealed a president bent on victimizing his enemies by using his presidential powers illegally. The accusations of perjury against President Clinton with regard to his testimony about a relationship with White House intern Monica Lewinski consumed much of his second term in office. Today's students have grown up with at least one well-publicized scandal for every presidential administration.

Bribery and corruption have been documented at all levels of government. The illegal dumping of toxic materials, prostitution, gambling, drug running, smuggling of valuable goods from other countries, and a variety of other crimes often occur because officials at various levels find it worth their while to "look the other way." While fraud and embezzlement are significant costs to society, when they occur in government bureaucracies the money comes directly out of taxpayers' pockets. As with white-collar and corporate crime, those involved in government crime are less likely than "street criminals" to be caught and punished despite the fact that their crimes may cost us more.

▲ Victimless Crime

Usually a crime has an identifiable victim who suffers as a result of another person's criminal behavior. A **victimless crime** is an offense in which no one involved is considered a victim (Schur, 1965). These crimes include gambling, the sale and use of illicit drugs, and prohibited sexual activities between consenting adults (e.g., prostitution and, in some states, fornication and homosexuality). In victimless crime, if there is any suffering, it is by the offenders themselves, by "innocent bystanders" (as in the case of experiencing the odors associated with public urination), or by the tax-paying public at large.

The behaviors in question in victimless crime are criminalized because society, or powerful groups within a society, defines them as immoral or in some other way a threat to society.

As we have pointed out, crime is an act of deviance that is prohibited by law. Laws prohibiting victimless offenses thereby create crime and cost society money by way of the efforts to arrest and process suspects. When such laws are struck down, the act is decriminalized, as in the 2003 Supreme Court decision overturning Texas's ban on private consensual sex between same-sex adults (Lane, 2003a).

▲ Technology and Crime

The information revolution has generated new crimes and made old crimes easier to commit. These **high-technology crimes** are defined as attempts to commit crime through the use of advanced electronic media (Adler, Mueller, and Laufer, 2004). High-tech crimes include child pornography, credit card fraud, mail bombings, software piracy, industrial espionage, and computer network break-ins.

Identity theft may be the most dramatic and widespread of the new high-tech crimes. In identity theft, the offender obtains enough information to impersonate someone else and uses this identity to access bank and financial accounts and to apply for credit to obtain goods and funds

fraudulently. Estimates of victimization range from 750,000 to 7 million people a year (O'Harrow, 2003). Identity theft has cost $24 billion over the past decade. And it is not just money that is at stake: Terrorists increasingly use the Internet to obtain identities for themselves as well as information critical to their planning.

Some of the "new technology" crime isn't considered to be crime by the generation that has grown up with the Internet, but the crime victims are fighting back. The provision of super-fast Internet connections to college students has made the downloading of music fast and easy, but this "file swapping" reportedly cost the record industry 10 percent of their profits annually for several years (Dana, 2003). Although pressure from the industry resulted in legislation making such downloads illegal, the practice continued and prompted the Recording Industry Association of America to serve subpoenas in 2003 to frequent file swappers. College students in New York, New Jersey, and Michigan paid between $12,000 and $17,500 in settlements (Dana, 2003). In spite of the criminalization of downloading and file swapping, these activities continue to be widespread, suggesting that consensus on their moral status in the United States has yet to develop.

Measuring Crime

How do we know how many crimes are committed in the United States? Statistics on crime are among the most unsatisfactory of all social data (Biderman and Lynch, 1991). Official crime records suffer from numerous limitations (Tittle and Paternoster, 2000). First, a large proportion of the crimes that are committed go undetected; others are detected but not reported; and still others are reported but not officially recorded when police officers and politicians manipulate their reports to show low crime rates for political purposes. Second, perceptions of crime vary from community to community; what is viewed as a serious crime by a citizen of a small town may be shrugged off by a big-city resident as an unpleasant bit of everyday life.

Two main data sources are used by researchers who study violent crime trends: the Uniform Crime Reports (UCR), collated by the FBI, and the National Crime Victimization Survey (NCVS), collected by the Bureau of Justice Statistics (LaFree, 1999; Klaus, 2002). The rates of various crimes in the United States are substantially higher according to the NCVS than the UCR, which are based on reports to police. Justice Department studies reveal that less than half of all crimes are reported to the police.

What accounts for the public's apparent reluctance to report crime? With property crimes, the most common response (26 percent) is that the crime was not reported because the offender was unsuccessful. People also say they don't report crimes to the police because they reported to another official (17 percent), because the matter wasn't important enough (5 percent), or because they thought the police would not want to be bothered (5 percent) (Pastore and Maguire, 2005). In 2004, 39 percent of property crimes and 50 percent of violent crimes were reported to the police (Catalano, 2005). Only about a third of rapes and attempted rapes are reported, while 85 percent of motor vehicle thefts were reported in 2004. Other research shows that whether citizens report crimes depends primarily on how serious they perceive the crime to be, and there is considerable evidence that the Uniform Crime Reports are valid indicators of serious crimes as defined by the citizenry (Gove, Hughes, and Geerken, 1985).

Self-report-based measures of crime, involving anonymous questionnaires that ask people which offenses they have committed, also reveal much higher rates of crime than those found in official crime statistics. For instance, studies of juvenile crimes show that many youngsters of all social classes break some criminal laws, and that the amount of unreported crime is enormous (Regoli and Hewitt, 2000; Tittle and Paternoster, 2000).

The Uniform Crime Reports focus on crimes that are most likely to be committed by young people and individuals from lower socioeconomic backgrounds. Statistics on many categories of crime, such as white-collar, government, and organized crime, are not routinely compiled. Additionally, some cases of criminal offenses, such as income tax evasion and fraud, are unlikely to be reported in victimization studies.

Drugs and Crime

Drugs have been part of American life since the Jamestown colonists first harvested tobacco in 1611; cocaine and heroin use took root as long ago as the 1890s (Musto, 1987). There's an obvious connection between drugs and crime: Selling, using, and possessing illegal drugs are crimes, and drug involvement often leads to other sorts of crime. A significant proportion of violent offenders are either drug suppliers fighting over territorial rights or drug abusers seeking the means to feed their habit. About a quarter of convicted property and drug offenders say they committed their crime to raise money for drugs (Dorsey, Zawitz, and Middleton, 2003). For older adolescents, drug dealing is one of two primary determinants of illegal gun carrying (Lizotte et al., 2000). Overall, illegal drugs account for approximately $50 billion in criminal income (MacCoun and Reuter, 1997).

The link between drugs and crime is complicated by the fact that society defines which drugs are legal and normative and which are illegal and deviant. Nearly half the adults in the United States have used illegal drugs and a fifth have used prescription drugs for nonmedical purposes (Pastore and Maguire, 2005). But significantly less than half the population is involved in serious drug-related crime. On the other hand, many of us use legal drugs, such as alcohol, caffeine, and nicotine, in ways that endanger our lives and the lives of others. And 3 to 4 million American children take prescription psychiatric drugs, despite the fact that most of these drugs have never been tested for use in children (Brown, 2003).

Despite our ambivalence about drug use, the relationship between drugs and crime is of interest to criminal justice officials, criminologists, and sociologists. In 2001, the largest category of all arrests was drug abuse violations, and the number of arrests involving marijuana rose dramatically in the 1990s. Since 1996, the number of arrests involving marijuana has been greater than for any other type of drug (Dorsey, Zawitz, and Middleton, 2003).

America's "War on Drugs" seems to focus primarily on arrests rather than treatment or prevention. But many argue that continuing to arrest people for drug violations is not the answer. One problem is that the country lacks the facilities to imprison violators. Perhaps more importantly, drug abuse causes long-lasting changes in the abuser's brain (Nestler, 2001), and there is strong evidence that drug addiction is a brain disease, not something that can be cured by a term of imprisonment. Further, the demand for drugs is at the base of the country's drug problem. When an accused "drug lord" was arrested, he stated that violent drug-trafficking gangs would thrive "as long as Americans keep buying marijuana, cocaine and heroin" (Sullivan and Jordan, 2002).

There are many proposals for dealing with drug abuse, including continued prohibition, removing penalties for possession of drugs (depenalization), and legalizing distribution of drugs (legalization). Some argue that depenalization and legalization would decrease crime rates. Marijuana has been depenalized in Italy, Spain, and the Netherlands, and the Dutch have adopted a formal policy of nonenforcement for sales of limited amounts of cannabis (MacCoun and Reuter, 1997). Increasing numbers of U.S. citizens support legalizing marijuana, with the proportion of survey respondents indicating it should be legal rising from 12 percent to 34 percent between 1969 and 2003, but 64 percent are still against it (Pastore and Maguire, 2005). Among college freshmen, the percent supporting legalization rose from 17 in 1989 to 38 in 2003.

Little consensus exists among either the lay public or professionals on the most effective strategies to fight crime through fighting drug use (MacCoun, 1993). Many countries have laws similar to those of the United States, yet the United States has higher rates of drug abuse than other countries (Wilson, 1997); clearly more than government policy plays a part in drug abuse. The connection between drugs and crime also varies among countries; although Australia and the United States have similar drug laws, there are 60 times as many drug-connected deaths in Los Angeles as in Sydney (Zimring and Hawkins, 1997).

While government officials struggle with approaches to slowing crime through fighting drug abuse, statistics show that drug use is on the rise among Americans of college age. One report showed that use of illegal drugs by college students increased during the 1990s (Gledhill-Hoyt et al., 2000), and marijuana use increased at all types of colleges except for those with low binge-drinking rates. Among high school seniors, 70 percent reported having drunk alcohol during 2003 and 35 percent reported having used marijuana; they also report having used amphetamines (10 percent), hallucinogens (6 percent), and cocaine (5 percent). More than half of high school seniors report having never used any illicit drug (Pastore and Maguire, 2005). When survey respondents were asked why teenagers try illegal drugs, 82 percent said peer pressure was a major factor, 79 percent that lack of parental supervision played a major role, and 74 percent that the ease with which teenagers can get drugs was a major factor (The Pew Research Center for the People and the Press, 2001). Box 5.2 (p. 146) presents some of the factors that affect alcohol abuse among college students.

Race and Crime

In 2004, African Americans accounted for 12 percent of the U.S. population, 27 percent of all those arrested for index crimes, and 45 percent of the prison population nationwide (Adler, Mueller, and Laufer, 2004; Pastore and Maguire, 2005). During their lifetimes, 28.5 percent of African-American men will spend time in prison, which makes them 6.5 times more likely to "do time" than white men (Bonczar and Beck, 1997). Race also plays a part in capital punishment, with offenders being more likely to be sentenced to death when the victim is white, and some research shows that the race of the offender also affects outcomes (Radelet and Borg, 2000).

Why are African Americans disproportionately involved in crime and in the criminal justice system? Part of the reason, particularly in regard to violent crime, is that African Americans experience more of what sociologists call "structural disadvantage" (Peterson and Krivo, 2005), the concentration of poverty, low income, family disruption, joblessness, and unemployment at the neighborhood level. When blacks and whites experience the same degree of structural disadvantage, their rates of violent crime are similar (Krivo and Peterson, 1996; 2000). In general, whites are very unlikely to live in structurally disadvantaged neighborhoods. "In fact," as Peterson and Krivo (2005:335) report, "the most disadvantaged white neighborhoods have less deprivation than the typical black community."

How much of the disproportionate representation of African Americans in the criminal justice system is due to racial discrimination? Research is divided. Studies of traffic stops show that black men are a third more likely than white men to be stopped by the police and twice as likely to have their cars searched once they are stopped (Lundman and Kaufman, 2003). Whites who favor the death penalty are more likely to be racially prejudiced and to prefer convicting the innocent over letting a murderer go free (Young, 2004); since potential jurors who oppose the death penalty are typically dismissed from jury duty on capital cases, death penalty juries are thus more likely to be both racially prejudiced and in favor of conviction.

But other studies on arrests, processing, and sentencing do not provide consistent evidence of racial bias. Some studies show that black offenders receive harsher sentences, some find that there are no significant racial differences, and some find that race influences sentencing in certain circumstances (Spohn, 2000). A review by the National Institute of Justice of 40 recent studies of race and sentencing severity showed that race plays a role in sentencing but that the primary determinants of sentencing decisions are the seriousness of the offence and the offender's prior criminal record (Spohn, 2000).

Regardless of the causes of the disproportionate representation of African Americans in the criminal justice system, it has serious consequences. The losses to African Americans are not limited to disproportionate imprisonment and execution. Those imprisoned—approximately 12 percent of all young black men—are unable to support their families or contribute to their communities, and the economic cost of serving time continues beyond one's sentence. Once out of prison, a criminal record is a major barrier to employment, and this problem is substantially greater for blacks than for whites (Pager, 2003; see Box 5.3). Ex-inmates who find employment earn an average of 10 to 20 percent less than those who have not been in prison, and incarceration reduces the rate of wage growth for workers by 30 percent (Western, 2002). Participation in our political system also is taken away, and this appears to have affected election outcomes; 48 of 50 states bar felons, including those on probation or parole, from voting and 10 states bar ex-felons (Uggen and Manza, 2002). As the prison population has grown, the percentage of the population that is disenfranchised also has grown, and that disenfranchised population is made up primarily of young, poor, black males. The imprisonment of so many young black men reduces their life chances, damages the economic life of the black community, dampens civic involvement, and promotes alienation.

5.3 Social Inequalities

Being Black Brings Extra Punishment for Crime

The basic design of this study involves the use of four male auditors (also called testers), two blacks and two whites. The testers were paired by race . . . The testers were 23-year-old college students from Milwaukee who were matched on the basis of physical appearance and general style of self-presentation . . . Within each team, one auditor was randomly assigned a "criminal record" for the first week; the pair then rotated which member presented himself as the ex-offender for each successive week . . . these testers were bright articulate college students with effective styles of self-presentation (Pager, 2003:946–47, 959).

Randomly assigned a "criminal record"? What were these "testers" testing? They were part of sociologist Devah Pager's study of the consequences of a criminal record (Pager, 2003). The pairs of young men applied for a total of 350 jobs during the study, with both members of each same-race team applying for the same jobs. What Pager wanted to know was whether reporting a criminal record on job applications affects the probability of being called back for a job interview. The

criminal record the testers reported was having served 18 months in prison for possession of, with intent to distribute, cocaine.

What did Pager find? The "employment penalty" for a criminal record is severe—and it is much worse for blacks than for whites. The white "clean" tester applications (those with no criminal record indicated) resulted in a 34 percent callback rate, while applications made by a white ex-offender tester generated only half as many callbacks. The black ex-offender tester applications, however, resulted in only a *third* as many callbacks as the black "clean" applications.

Pager's study revealed another significant and surprising finding: The black "clean" testers got fewer callbacks than the white "criminal" testers—14 percent for the clean-record blacks compared to 17 percent for the white ex-offenders. In other words, the callback rate for African-American applicants with no criminal record is *less than half* that for the white "clean" applicants, *and* the effect of having been incarcerated is greater for blacks than for whites.

Each year more than half a million prisoners are released from incarceration back into society, where they need to find employment if they are to support

themselves honestly. Pager's research shows that finding that employment may be quite challenging, especially for African Americans:

> Employers, already reluctant to hire blacks, appear even more wary of blacks with proven criminal involvement . . . the employment barriers of minority status and criminal record are compounded, intensifying the stigma toward this group (Pager, 2003:959).

Questions for Discussion

1. Pager's study focused on entry-level (high school diploma) jobs. Would you expect to find more or less discrimination against applicants with criminal records for jobs requiring more than a high school education? Explain your answer.

2. The state in which Pager conducted her research has laws aimed at protecting "ex-cons" from discrimination by employers. How would the results of her study have differed had she conducted it in a state without such laws? Do you think other states should pass such legislation? Why or why not?

Women and Crime

Women accounted for 24 percent of all arrests in 2004 (Federal Bureau of Investigation, 2005), a proportion that reflects the 1990s trend of an

increasing percentage of females in the criminal population (Steffensmeier and Allan, 1996). In the 2000 arrest rate data, women accounted for 18 percent of violent crime arrests and 32 percent of property crime arrests (Federal Bureau of Investigation, 2005). In some crimes, women outnumber men as perpetrators; 59 percent of those arrested as runaways are female, and 69 percent of prostitution arrests are women. Arrest rates are about equal for women and men in embezzlement; other crimes in which women are arrested at high rates are fraud (45 percent), forgery and counterfeiting (40 percent), and larceny and theft (38 percent) (Federal Bureau of Investigation, 2005). Women's participation in violent crime is much lower than men's, and in 2001 only 51 of the 3,581 prisoners on death row were female (Bonczar and Snell, 2004).

With the increased participation of women in crime has come an increase in research on women's criminal behavior. Recent studies have included investigations on women in prison (Kruttschnitt, Gartner, and Miller, 2000), prostitutes and drug selling and use (Maxwell and Maxwell, 2000), and juvenile offending (Haynie, 2003; Uggen, 2000).

The participation of females in juvenile delinquency is higher than the proportion of adult female criminals; one-quarter of the youths arrested in the United States are females. Girls are typically arrested for less serious offenses than boys; half of all girls arrested are charged with either larceny-theft (often shoplifting) or with running away from home (Chesney-Lind and Shelden, 1998). Studies show that females seem to perceive legal sanctions as more threatening than do males (Blackwell, 2000).

Theories of female delinquency are just emerging (Chesney-Lind and Shelden, 1998). Contemporary research suggests that girls' delinquency is related to many of the same factors as that of boys, but there also are factors unique to females. For example, two-thirds to three-quarters of the girls in runaway shelters and juvenile detention facilities have been sexually abused; such abuse can be the primary motivator for their running away from home, a significant contributor to their total number of arrests. However, self-report studies of crime show that the patterns and causes of male and female delinquency are becoming more alike, and the structural sources of high levels of offending are very similar for men and women (Steffensmeier and Allan, 1996; Steffensmeier and Haynie, 2000).

Gender also plays a part in crime victimization. Whereas males are more likely to be victims of robbery, total assault, and aggravated assault, females are more likely to be victims of rape and sexual assault (Rennison, 2002a). Female victims account for 89 percent of sexual assaults, 76 percent of attempted rapes, and 96 percent of completed rapes (Pastore and Maguire, 2005).

The Criminal Justice System

On television, the evildoer nearly always gets caught and punished. In real life, however, the picture is quite different. According to statistics from the Justice Department, of every 100 criminal victimizations committed in the United States, only 36 are reported to the police. Of these 36, only 7 or 8 are cleared by arrest, meaning that someone is arrested for the crime. Of these 7 persons arrested, only 5 are prosecuted and convicted. Of these, only 1 is sent to prison; the other cases are rejected or dismissed because of problems with the evidence or witnesses, or the perpetrators are diverted into treatment programs. Of those convicted in state courts, more than half receive a sentence of at least 3.5 years, but the average inmate is released in about 1.5 years (see Figure 5.3a for data on the processing of serious criminals). Perhaps not surprisingly, in 2004 only 34 percent of survey respondents said they had much confidence in the criminal justice system (Pastore and Maguire, 2005).

In this section we will briefly consider the components of the criminal justice system: the police, the courts, and the prisons. Each of these components operates at local, state, and federal levels.

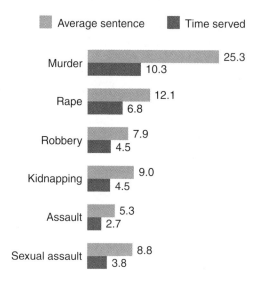

(a) Sentences versus Time Served, 2002

Average years *sentenced* to prison and average years *actually served* by state prison inmates for various convictions

■ Average sentence   ■ Time served

Murder
25.3
10.3

Rape
12.1
6.8

Robbery
7.9
4.5

Kidnapping
9.0
4.5

Assault
5.3
2.7

Sexual assault
8.8
3.8

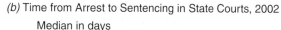
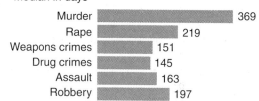

(b) Time from Arrest to Sentencing in State Courts, 2002
   Median in days

Murder   369
Rape   219
Weapons crimes   151
Drug crimes   145
Assault   163
Robbery   197

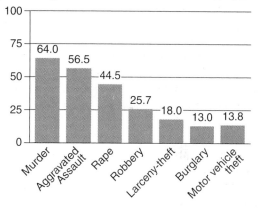

(c) Percentage of Crimes That Result in Arrests, 2002

100
75
50
25
0

Murder 64.0
Aggravated Assault 56.5
Rape 44.5
Robbery 25.7
Larceny-theft 18.0
Burglary 13.0
Motor vehicle theft 13.8

Figure 5.3 The Operation of the Criminal Justice System in the United States

Sources: (a) Bureau of Justice Statistics (http://www.ojp.usdoj.gov/bjs/dtdata.htm#ncrp); (b) and (c) Pastore and McGuire, 2005.

▲ The Police

The police are a citizen's first link with the criminal justice system, and in many ways the most important one. When a crime occurs, the police are usually the first agents of the state to become involved. Yet police officers spend only about 15 percent of their time dealing with crime. Competing demands on their time vary from filling out reports and directing traffic to handling complaints about uncollected trash and responding to medical emergency calls.

Many U.S. communities have implemented "community-based policing" or "problem-oriented policing," in which officers establish positive relationships with residents of specific areas and focus on crime prevention as well as

reacting to crime. In 2002, between 61 percent and 73 percent of respondents said police are excellent or pretty good at solving crime, preventing crime, treating people fairly, not using excessive force, responding quickly, and being helpful (Pastore and Maguire, 2005).

▲ The Courts

In the United States the criminal justice system is an adversary system. The person accused of a crime—the *defendant*—is presumed to be innocent until proved guilty in a court of law by the representative of the state—the *prosecutor*. In many nations the questioning of witnesses is handled by judges, and guilt and innocence are decided by a judge or panel of judges. But the U.S. system assumes that justice is best served

A growing percentage of youth and adults in the criminal population is female.

by pitting opposing lawyers against each other before a neutral judge and jury.

In practice, the fate of most of those accused of crime is determined by prosecutors. Prosecutors typically reject or reduce the severity of 50 to 80 percent of the criminal charges filed by police. The reasons prosecutors cite range from case overload to police inefficiency in producing evidence. Of some 2 million serious criminal cases filed each year in the United States, fewer than one in five goes to trial. The others end in dismissals or guilty pleas.

▲ Prisons

We have said that the crime rate has been declining over the past decades. The prison population, on the other hand, has been steadily increasing. According to Bureau of Justice statistics, in 2004, 7 million people in the United States were in jail, in prison, on probation, or on parole, comprising a total of 3.1 percent of the adult population (http://www.ojp.usdoj.gov/bjs/prisons.htm). There were nearly 1.5 million

inmates in state and federal prisons and more than 0.5 million in local jails, more than four times as many as 30 years ago. The United States has the highest incarceration rate in the world (see Figure 5.4).

Why do we incarcerate more prisoners during a period of declining crime? Some analysts point to a "culture of control," with crime management resources devoted to protecting potential victims by locking away offenders rather than working to eradicate any of the causes of criminal behavior (Garland, 2003). In *The Challenge of Crime,* authors Henry Ruth and Kevin Reitz explain the expanding prison population this way:

From the early 1970s to the mid-1980s, the U.S. prisons expanded because the courts were sending more "marginal" felons to prison than they had in the past. Many burglars or auto thieves who might have been put on probation in the 1950s or 1960s were instead sentenced to incarceration. . . . Then, from the mid-1980s to the early 1990s, prison growth was driven most

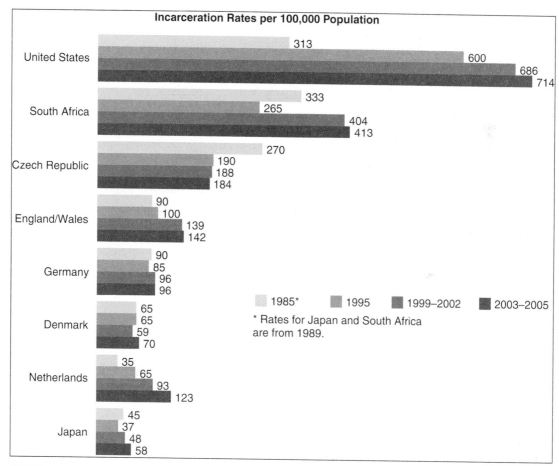

Incarceration Rates per 100,000 Population

Legend:
- 1985*
- 1995
- 1999–2002
- 2003–2005

* Rates for Japan and South Africa are from 1989.

United States: 313, 600, 686, 714
South Africa: 333, 265, 404, 413
Czech Republic: 270, 190, 188, 184
England/Wales: 90, 100, 139, 142
Germany: 90, 85, 96, 96
Denmark: 65, 65, 59, 70
Netherlands: 35, 65, 93, 123
Japan: 45, 37, 48, 58

Figure 5.4   The United States Imprisons a Larger Share of Its Population Than Does Any Other Nation

According to the most recent World Prison Population List issued by the International Centre for Prison Studies at Kings College, London, the United States has the highest incarceration rate among 211 independent countries and dependent territories around the world. As this figure shows, it also has increasingly high incarceration rates compared to other countries. High incarceration rates in the United States are the result of the high crime rate and increasingly harsh criminal justice policies.

Sources: Walmsley, 2005 (available at http://www.prisonstudies.org); www.sentencingproject.org.

forcefully by the war on drugs. . . . In the 1990s, the primary cause of prison growth changed again. For the first time in the expansionist era, the chief engine of the prison build-up became longer sentences rather than more prison admissions. (2003: 95–96)

Other researchers suggest different causes of prison growth. Sociologist John Sutton (2000) has documented connections between the labor market and prison populations and concluded that when opportunities for employment increase, prison growth decreases.

Further, he found that declines in welfare spending result in increases in incarceration rates.

What purpose is served by locking offenders away? Let's take a look at traditional purposes of imprisonment.

Punishment.   Prior to 1800 it was widely assumed that the punishment of deviants was required if the injured community was to feel morally satisfied. In recent years there has been a renewed interest in punishment. The "moral order" argument runs like this: Certain acts are basically antisocial and heinous (e.g., murder, rape, genocide, and the sexual abuse of children). When grossly immoral behavior goes unpunished, people's commitment to social order and to basic values and norms is weakened; punishment is essential to maintain moral order. This approach draws on the functionalist perspective for support.

Rehabilitation.   Toward the latter part of the 18th and the early part of the 19th centuries, the idea that prisons might rehabilitate criminals came to the forefront. The word *penitentiary* was coined to describe a place where a criminal might repent and then resolve to follow a law-abiding life. Rehabilitation may include educational, vocational, or psychological programs geared at helping inmates overcome drug and alcohol addiction, earn their general equivalency diplomas, and gain job skills.

Critics of rehabilitation cite statistics on the high rate of **recidivism** (relapse into criminal behavior). In a recent study, it was found that 67.5 percent of those released from prisons were rearrested within 3 years. The prisoners had been charged with an average of 5 offenses each before their release, and another 2.7 in the 3 years after their release (Langan and Levin, 2002). Recidivism is particularly high for those charged with robbery and property crimes. Complicating matters is the fact that the likelihood of rehabilitation is affected not only by

what happens during imprisonment, but whether released prisoners are able to reintegrate into the community. This process is strongly influenced by the individual's social circumstances both prior to incarceration and after release, including the social environment of peers, family and community, and state-level policies, particularly those related to post-release supervision (Visher and Travis, 2003). In any case, rehabilitation programs have not been popular since the 1970s (Paley, 2006).

Deterrence.   The notion of deterrence rests on assumptions about human nature that are difficult to prove. Even so, a significant body of research indicates that crime is the result of active decision making by perpetrators (McCarthy, 2002), and that the certainty of apprehension and punishment does tend to lower crime rates (Waldo and Chiricos, 1972; Wolfgang, Figlio, and Sellin, 1972; Paternoster, 1989). But allegiance to a group and its norms typically operates as an even stronger force than the threat of societal punishment in bringing about conformity (Heckathorn, 1988, 1990). By the same token, informal standards and pressures within delinquent subcultures may counteract the deterrent effects of legal penalties (Tittle and Rowe, 1974; Heckathorn, 1988, 1990). Recent research has shown that longer sentences and harsher prison conditions are associated with more post-release crime, not less (Chen and Shapiro, 2005).

Incapacitation.   There are those who argue that neither rehabilitation nor deterrence really works, but that imprisonment can be used to reduce crime rates because it keeps criminals off the streets. Peter W. Greenwood (1982) asserts that incarcerating one robber who is among the top 10 percent in offense rates prevents more robberies than incarcerating 18 offenders who are at or below the median. On the other hand, long prison sentences may represent a waste of prison capacity; most crimes are committed by young people, and most "career criminals" retire fairly early from these careers.

▲ Capital Punishment

Capital punishment is the imposition of the death sentence for a capital offense. Since 1622, 18,000 to 20,000 people have lost their lives in America through capital punishment (Adler, Mueller, and Laufer, 2004). Capital offenses vary by state and have included murder, kidnapping, rape, drug trafficking, and treason (Bonczar and Snell, 2004). Legal execution methods also vary by state and include lethal injection, electrocution, lethal gas, hanging, or firing squad. In 2004, 58 executions were carried out by lethal injection and one by electrocution (Bonczar and Snell, 2004).

Is capital punishment widely used in the United States? In 2002, 68 inmates were executed in 13 states, with three states (Texas, Missouri, and Oklahoma) accounting for two-thirds of the executions (Snell and Maruschak, 2002). One inmate was electrocuted; the others were executed by lethal injection. In 2001, 66 prisoners were executed; in 2000, the number was 85. The number of executions is dwarfed by the list of those waiting for execution; in 2001, 3,581 inmates were on death row.

What purpose does capital punishment serve? One argument in favor of applying the death penalty is *deterrence,* the idea that punishing offenders deters others from committing similar crimes. Research has shown, however, that capital punishment is not superior to long prison sentences in deterring crime (Radelet and Borg, 2000). Another use of capital punishment is *incapacitation;* an executed offender cannot be a repeat offender. Supporters of capital punishment also have argued that it is less costly than long-term imprisonment, although recent analyses show that the cost of trials and lengthy appeals far outruns the cost of imprisonment, changing cost to an argument against

capital punishment in contemporary times. Nevertheless, the death penalty has gained in popularity over the years, and the majority of U.S. adults currently support capital punishment (Pastore and Maguire, 2005). Forty years ago, only 38 percent said they believed in the death penalty, but in 2001 that proportion had risen to 67 percent. When asked why they favor the death penalty for murderers, nearly two-fifths of those favoring the death penalty in 2003 responded with retribution—supporters of capital punishment say the punishment fits the crime; 13 percent say that murderers "deserve" the death penalty (Pastore and Maguire, 2005).

In 2003, Republican Governor of Illinois George Ryan made headlines by commuting the death sentences of 167 people to life imprisonment (Pierre and Lydersen, 2003). Calling his state's death penalty system "arbitrary and capricious," Ryan made his decision after a study that found 13 wrongly convicted inmates and four that had been tortured into false confessions. In the past 35 years, 80 people have been released from their death sentences when it was discovered that they were in fact innocent of the crime of which they had been convicted (Radelet and Borg, 2000). Americans know there are problems with the system; although 66 percent of respondents support capital punishment, only 55 percent say they think the death penalty is applied fairly, and that number drops to 32 percent for black respondents (Pastore and Maguire, 2005).

▲ Other Penalties and Approaches

For all of those who are incarcerated, many more criminal offenders do not serve time in jails and prisons. Probably the most widely used response to criminal behavior is *probation,* the integration of offenders into law-abiding society under the supervision of a trustworthy person (Adler, Mueller, and Laufer, 2004). Probationers are bound by specific conditions but are able to work, care for their families, and pay taxes. Currently, nearly 4 million people are on probation in the United States. *Parole* is somewhat similar to probation, but it involves releasing a prisoner, again under supervision, before the end of his or her sentence. In *home confinement programs,* offenders serve time at home, usually monitored by electronic devices. Offenders may also pay fines, be required to perform community service, or pay restitution to victims. About 40 percent of convicted felons are required to serve time in prison or jail or on probation *and* comply with other penalties, including paying fines, paying victim restitution, receiving treatment, or performing community service (Bureau of Justice Statistics, 2003).

The Chapter in Brief: *Deviance and Crime*

The Nature of Deviance

In all societies the behavior of some people at times goes beyond that permitted by the norms. Social life is characterized not only by conformity but by **deviance,** behavior that a considerable number of people view as reprehensible and beyond the limits of tolerance.

▎ *Social Properties of Deviance*

Deviance is not a property inherent in certain forms of behavior; it is a property conferred upon particular behaviors by social definitions. Definitions as to which acts are deviant vary greatly from time to time, place to place, and group to group. We typically find that norms are not so much a point or a line but a zone. Deviant acts also can be redefined, as has happened in recent years in the United States. Most societies can absorb a good deal of deviance without serious consequences, but persistent and widespread deviance can be dysfunctional. But deviance may also be functional by promoting social solidarity, clarifying norms, strengthening group allegiances, and providing a catalyst for change.

▎ *Social Control and Deviance*

Societies seek to ensure that their members conform with basic norms by means of **social control.** Three main types of social control processes operate within social life: (1) those that lead us to internalize our society's normative expectations **(internalization),** (2) those that structure our world of social experience, and (3) those that employ various formal and informal social sanctions.

Theories of Deviance

Other disciplines are concerned with deviance, particularly biology and psychology. Sociologists focus on five main theories.

▎ *Anomie Theory*

Émile Durkheim contributed to our understanding of deviance with his idea of **anomie.** Robert K. Merton built on Durkheim's ideas of anomie and social cohesion. According to his theory of structural strain, deviance derives from societal stresses.

▎ *Cultural Transmission Theory*

A number of sociologists have emphasized the similarities between the way deviant behavior is acquired and the way in which other behavior is acquired—the cultural transmission theory. Edwin H. Sutherland elaborated on this notion in his theory of **differential association.**

He said that individuals become deviant to the extent to which they participate in settings where deviant ideas, motivations, and techniques are viewed favorably.

■ *Conflict Theory*   Conflict theorists ask, "Which group will be able to translate its values into the rules of a society and make these rules stick?" and "Who reaps the lion's share of benefits from particular social arrangements?" Marxist sociologists see crime as a product of capitalist laws.

■ *Labeling Theory*   Labeling theorists study the processes whereby some individuals come to be tagged as deviants, begin to think of themselves as deviants, and enter deviant careers. Labeling theorists differentiate between **primary deviance** and **secondary deviance.**

■ *Control Theory*   Control theory attempts to explain not why people deviate but why people do *not* deviate. Travis Hirschi argued that young people are more likely to conform if their bond to society is strong. This bond has four parts: attachment, involvement, commitment, and belief.

Crime and the Criminal Justice System

Crime is an act of deviance that is prohibited by law. The distinguishing property of crime is that people who violate the law are liable to be arrested, tried, pronounced guilty, and deprived of their lives, liberty, or property. It is the state that defines crime by the laws it promulgates, administers, and enforces.

■ *Forms of Crime*   An infinite variety of acts can be crimes. Federal agencies keep records on **index crimes**—violent crimes against people and crimes against property. Juvenile crime is crime committed by youth under the age of 18. **Organized crime** is carried out by large-scale bureaucratic

organizations that provide illegal goods and services in public demand. **White-collar crime** is crime committed by relatively affluent persons, often in the course of business activities. Crime can be committed by corporations and by governments. In **victimless crime** no one involved is considered a victim.

■ *Measuring Crime*   Statistics on crime are among the most unsatisfactory of all social data. A large proportion of the crimes that are committed go undetected; others are detected but not reported; and still others are reported but not officially recorded.

■ *Drugs and Crime*   Drugs and crime are related both directly—selling, using, and possessing illegal drugs all are crimes—and indirectly—drug involvement often leads to other sorts of crimes. Drug problems can be dealt with by recognizing that addiction is a brain disease. Other approaches include continued prohibition, depenalization, or legalization.

■ *Race and Crime*   African Americans make up 12 percent of the U.S. population, 27 percent of all those arrested for index crimes, and 45 percent of the U.S. prison population. Their disproportionate representation in the criminal justice system has serious social consequences, with imprisonment preventing young black males from supporting their families, criminal records decreasing employment opportunities, and voting rights being withheld from felons in most states and from ex-felons in some.

■ *Women and Crime*   A growing percentage of youths and adults in the criminal population is female. One-quarter of the youths arrested in the United States are girls; overall, one in five arrests are female. Girls are more likely than boys to be arrested for such offenses as running away from home.

The Criminal Justice System   The **criminal justice system** is made up of the reactive agencies of the state that include the police, the courts, and prisons. Despite the declining crime rate in the United States, the prison population has been steadily climbing.

There have been four traditional purposes of imprisonment: punishment, rehabilitation, deterrence, and selective confinement. **Capital punishment** is the application of the death penalty for a capital offense. Criminal offenders also may be subjected to probation, parole, fines, victim restitution, community service, or in-house arrest.

Glossary

anomie   A social condition in which people find it difficult to guide their behavior by norms they experience as weak, unclear, or conflicting.

capital punishment   The application of the death penalty for a capital crime.

crime   An act prohibited by law.

criminal justice system   The reactive agencies of the state that include the police, courts, and prisons.

deviance   Behavior that a considerable number of people in a society view as reprehensible and beyond the limits of tolerance.

differential association   The notion that the earlier, the more frequent, the more intense, and the longer the duration of the contacts people have in deviant settings, the greater the probability that they, too, will become deviant.

high-technology crime   crime committed through the use of advanced electronic media.

index crimes   Crimes reported by the Federal Bureau of Investigation in its Uniform Crime Reports. These offenses consist of four categories of violent crime against people—murder, rape, robbery, and assault—and four categories of crime against property—burglary, theft, motor vehicle theft, and arson.

internalization   The process by which individuals incorporate within their personalities the standards of behavior prevalent within the larger society.

organized crime   Large-scale bureaucratic organizations that provide illegal goods and services in public demand.

primary deviance   Behavior that violates social norms but usually goes unnoticed by the agents of social control.

recidivism   Relapse into criminal behavior.

secondary deviance   Deviance that individuals adopt in response to the reactions of other individuals.

social control   Methods and strategies that regulate behavior within society.

victimless crime   An offense in which no one involved is considered a victim.

white-collar crime   Crime committed by relatively affluent persons, often in the course of business activities.

Review Questions

1. Define deviant behavior and give two examples.

2. What functions does deviant behavior have?

3. What are the three main types of social control?

4. List and briefly describe the five main theories of deviance.

5. Define crime and list at least six types of crime.

6. Why are so many crimes not reported to the police?

7. Why is the prison population increasing in the United States?

8. Do you think capital punishment should be legal in the United States? Support your answer.

Internet Connection

 www.mhhe.com/hughes8

Use your browser to open the website for the Federal Bureau of Investigation (FBI), **http://www.fbi.gov/.** Explore this site, particularly through the "press room" button and the "Uniform Crime Reports" button, and look for information on how much crime was committed in the United States in the most recent time period and how crime has changed over the recent past. Write a short report on what you find.

Chapter 6

SOCIAL STRATIFICATION

Patterns of Social Stratification

Open and Closed Systems
Dimensions of Stratification

The American Class System

Is There Inequality in American Society?
Identifying Social Classes
The Significance of Social Classes
Poverty in the United States

Social Mobility

Forms of Social Mobility
Social Mobility and Status Attainment
What Is Happening to the American Dream?

Explanations of Social Stratification

The Functionalist Theory of Stratification
The Conflict Theory of Stratification
A Synthesis of Perspectives

A s part of an introductory sociology course, students were asked to record their observations of inequality on campus. One student contributed the following:

Our math classroom is on the third floor of a building that overlooks the top floor of a parking ramp. At most three or four cars are parked up there, although it contains enough space for at least fifty cars. The lower levels of the ramp are also fairly empty. The ramp is only for the use of faculty. We students have to park some distance from campus and even then we have to get to school by 7:30 in the morning if we are to find a parking space. . . . The faculty enjoy many privileges. They have special offices; departmental chairpersons have more spacious offices; and deans and the university president have even more magnificent offices. The faculty have "faculty restrooms" which are distinct from those simply labeled "restroom." Each dean has his own private restroom.

This student observed something that pervades all aspects of social life: social stratification. **Social stratification,** the term sociologists apply to the ranking or grading of individuals and groups into hierarchical layers, represents structured inequality in the allocation of rewards, privileges, and resources. Some individuals, by virtue of their roles or group memberships, are advantaged, while others are disadvantaged.

College life is not exempt from these patterns, despite the fact that college communities might seem to be places in which administrators, faculty, and students work together in the pursuit of knowledge and human betterment. In fact, wherever one turns, social inequality confronts the members of the college community.

The student quoted above was complaining about disparities among students, faculty, and administrators, but it is possible to observe social stratification without leaving the ranks of students. Your status as a university student may differ depending on whether you're an athlete (and within the world of athletics, on whether you're an especially valuable player), an exceptional student, a commuter, a senior, or a fellowship student. Status also may be based on physical attractiveness, accomplishments in intramural sports or other extracurricular activities, or involvement in counterculture movements. The position of your family outside the campus may influence your position on campus: Race, ethnicity, wealth, and prestige all play important roles, often determining group memberships and social connections. In student clubs and organizations, there are presidents, vice presidents, secretaries, and treasurers, all of whom are ranked with respect to one another and have more power and prestige than the other members. Student government has offices of power and prestige, often controlled by members of fraternities and sororities. Greek organizations also typically hold the key to election of the Homecoming Queen and King.

If social stratification affected only such matters as who gets elected Homecoming Queen, we might not devote an entire chapter to its discussion. But social stratification does much more: It results in some members of society benefitting greatly and others suffering. Most societies of the world are organized so that their institutions systematically distribute benefits and burdens unequally among different categories of people. Social arrangements are not neutral, but serve and promote the goals and interests of some people more than those of other people.

In this chapter we will examine patterns of social stratification. We will attempt to answer the questions of who gets what and why. We will use a country with which we are familiar, the United States, to discuss class systems. We will see how social inequality has serious consequences for individuals' lives: It affects income, lifestyle, health, and even the number of years one can be expected to live. We will define and discuss social mobility, and we will see what the conflict and functionalist perspectives have to offer to our understanding of social stratification.

Patterns of Social Stratification

Social stratification depends upon but is not the same thing as **social differentiation**—the process by which a society becomes increasingly specialized over time. Very early in their history, human beings discovered that a division of functions and labor contributed to greater social efficiency. Consequently, in all societies we find that different people typically perform different tasks and as a result they occupy different statuses.

Although the statuses that make up a social structure may be *differentiated,* they need not be *ranked* with respect to one another. For instance, the statuses of farmer and shop owner in a rural community are differentiated, but one is not obviously of higher rank than the other. They are merely different. Social differentiation creates a necessary condition for social ranking, but it does not create the ranking itself. Whenever we find social stratification we find social differentiation, but not the other way around.

We begin our consideration of social stratification by examining open and closed stratification systems and some of the important dimensions of stratification: economic standing, prestige, and power.

Open and Closed Systems

Stratification systems differ in the ease with which they permit people to move in or out of particular strata (Kerbo, 2006). As we will see later in the discussion of social mobility, people often move vertically up or down in rank or horizontally to another status of roughly similar rank. Where people can change their status with relative ease, we refer to the arrangement as an **open system.** In contrast, where people have great difficulty in changing their status, we call the arrangement a **closed system.** A somewhat similar distinction is conveyed by the concepts *achieved status* and *ascribed status* that ← p. 58 we considered in Chapter 2. Achieved statuses are open to people on the basis of individual choice and competition and are common in open stratification systems. Ascribed statuses are assigned to people by their group or society and are typical of closed systems.

Although no societies are entirely open or entirely closed, the United States provides a good example of a relatively open system. The American folk hero is Abe Lincoln, the poor boy who made good, the rail-splitter who through hard work managed to move from log cabin to the White House. The American dream portrays a society in which all people can alter and improve their lot.

The United States is founded neither on the idea that all people should enjoy equal status nor on the notion of a classless society. Rather, the democratic creed holds that all people should have an equal *opportunity* to ascend to the heights of the class system. According to U.S. cultural beliefs, the rewards of social life flow to people in accordance with their merit and competence and in proportion to the contribution they make to their community and society. These beliefs generate much optimism about people's chances of enjoying society's rewards. Most Americans believe that they have a good chance of getting ahead, that they have a better standard of living than their parents, and that their children will have a better chance of succeeding than they had (Scott and Leonhardt, 2005; Davis, Smith, and Marsden, 2005; Newport, 1997). In practice, however, the ideal is not fully realized, and the optimism is not fully justified. Though the American system was founded on the ideal of achievement, ascribed statuses based on race, gender, age, and other social dimensions still have an important influence on people's chances of success.

The Hindu caste arrangement, particularly as it operated in India prior to 1900, serves as an example of a closed system. Under the traditional Hindu system, life was ordered in terms of castes in which people inherited their social status at birth from their parents and could not change it in the course of their lives. Members of the lower castes in India were considered inferior and were scorned, snubbed, and oppressed by higher-caste members regardless of personal merit and behavior. Even today, caste still shapes behavior in some localities, especially in rural areas, setting the rules of courtship, diet, housing, and employment (Nanda and Warms, 2002).

Although the distinction between open and closed systems of stratification is clear in theory, in practice systems of one type typically have some of the characteristics of the other type. In Box 6.1 (p. 178) you will see that the U.S. system of racial inequality has many characteristics of a caste system.

Dimensions of Stratification

Karl Marx and Max Weber have helped us to unravel the nature of social stratification. Marx believed that the key to social stratification in capitalist societies is the division between those who own and control the crucial means of production—the oppressing capitalist class or bourgeoisie—and those who have only their labor to sell—the oppressed working class or proletariat. In Marx's view, these two groups and their conflicting interests provide the foundation for stratification in capitalist nations. For Marx, social stratification consists of a single economic dimension.

Weber (1946) felt that Marx provided an overly simplistic image of stratification. He contended that other divisions exist within society that are at times independent of class. Consequently, he took a multidimensional view of stratification and identified three components: *class* (economic standing), *status* (prestige), and *party* (power). Each of these dimensions constitutes a distinct aspect of social ranking. Some statuses rank high in wealth, prestige, and power,

Is Race the Basis for an American Caste System?

Americans often are fascinated by India's traditional caste system. The idea of groups of people having special status and performing only certain jobs seems very undemocratic. The Brahmins, the most pure caste, serve as priests and have special privileges. The Kshatriyas protect society, holding top military and political positions. The Vaisyas fill farming, livestock production, and commerce jobs, and the last caste, the Sudras, serves those above it. The untouchables, not strictly a part of the caste system, do those jobs Hindus consider to be the most polluting: working with body parts, excrement, and dead bodies.

Does the United States have a caste system? We have said that in some ways the United States provides a good example of an open system of stratification. But we will see in Chapter 7 that the United States also has an entrenched system of racial inequality. Is it a racial caste system?

Let's see if the basic characteristics of a caste system apply to American society. In a caste system, caste membership is hereditary, marriage within one's caste is mandatory, moving out of one's caste is nearly impossible, and occupation is strongly related to caste (Hurst, 1998).

Hereditary caste membership obviously applies to race. In India, people are sometimes able to move up in the caste system by "marrying up." In the United States, in contrast, the racial status of biracial children born of black and white parents has traditionally been governed by what is often referred to as the "one drop rule" (Davis, 1991): In the South during the eras of slavery and Jim Crow laws, a

person with "one drop of black blood" was black. This idea translated into the practice of classifying a person as black if he or she had any known black ancestors (Davis, 1991).

Does the "one drop" rule still hold today? Professional U.S. golfer Tiger Woods has a mother from Thailand and a father with African, European, and Native American ancestors (Page, 1997), and he has described himself as "Cablinasian" (for Caucasian, black, Indian, and Asian), yet he is widely regarded as African American in the United States (Nolan, 1997; Foster, 1997; Brand-Williams, 1997).

The second basic characteristic, that marriage within one's caste is mandatory, is not true in the legal sense; there are no longer any laws in the United States that forbid interracial marriages. But in the United States in the 1990s, fewer than .68 percent of all marriages involving whites and blacks were marriages between a white and a black person (U.S. Census Bureau, 2003).

The third characteristic of caste, that mobility is virtually impossible, is clearly true of the black–white distinction. There is essentially no mobility from black to white or from white to black for typical white and black people in the United States. Of course, the phenomenon of "passing" can occur; persons with a small amount of African background and substantial, obvious "white" characteristics have been known to "pass for white" (Johnson, 1927/1989; Scales-Trent, 1995). But passing is something that occurs only in a closed system; were there no racial caste system, passing would have no meaning.

The fourth characteristic, that occupation is strongly related to caste, also describes American society to a substantial degree. Occupations that can be held by blacks or whites are not dictated by law. But in the 19th and 20th centuries, African-American physicians, dentists, engineers, and corporate executives were nearly nonexistent, and nearly all agricultural field workers in the South were black. By now, there has been substantial occupational mobility for African Americans, just as there has been for lower-caste persons in India in the late 20th century. But the occupational distribution in the United States retains significant castelike properties. African Americans are substantially overrepresented in low-status service and manufacturing jobs and underrepresented in highly paid, high-status professional jobs—just as the caste model predicts.

The southern United States before the civil rights movement clearly operated under a castelike system based on race. African Americans rode in the back of the bus, drank from "colored" water fountains, and used "colored" restrooms. The racial caste system in the United States today may be less rigid than this, but nonetheless it has yet to completely disappear.

Questions for Discussion

1. We have argued that the four characteristics of a caste system apply to American society with regard to race. Do you agree? Support your position.

2. Is being gay another factor on which an American caste system is based? Why or why not?

such as that of most physicians. Yet the rankings of some statuses may be dissimilar. Some prostitutes and professional criminals enjoy economic privilege, although they possess little prestige or power. Members of university faculties and the clergy, while enjoying a good deal of prestige, typically rank comparatively low in wealth and power. And some public officials may wield considerable power but receive low salaries and little prestige. For the most part, however, these three dimensions hang together, feeding into and supporting one another (Kerbo, 2006). Let us examine each of them in turn.

▲ Economic Standing

The economic dimension of stratification consists of wealth and income. **Wealth** has to do with what people own at a particular point in time. **Income** refers to the amount of new money people receive within a given time interval. Thus, wealth is based on what people have, whereas income consists of what people get. For example, one individual may have a good deal of property—wealth—in the form of rare coins, precious gems, or works of art, but receive little income from it because it does not grow in value or generate any regular income. Another individual may receive a high salary—income—but have little wealth. A salary of $2 million a year does not generate much wealth if the person receiving it spends $2 million a year on travel, food, entertainment, and personal services.

▲ Prestige

Prestige involves the social respect, admiration, and recognition associated with a particular social status. It entails a feeling that we are admired and well thought of by others. Prestige is intangible, something that we carry about in our heads. However, in our daily lives we commonly seek to give prestige a tangible existence through titles, special seats of honor, deference rituals, honorary degrees, emblems, and conspicuous displays of leisure and consumption. These activities and objects serve as symbols of

prestige to which we attribute social significance and meaning. Much of our interaction with others consists of subtle negotiation over just how much deference, honor, respect, and awe we are to extend and receive.

We show deference—behavior dramatizing and confirming a person's superior ranking—in many ways. In *presentation rituals* we engage in symbolic acts, such as revealing regard and awe by bowing, scraping, and displaying a humble demeanor. In *avoidance rituals* we achieve the same end by maintaining a "proper distance" from prestigious figures.

More than a century ago, Thorstein Veblen (1899) highlighted the part that *conspicuous leisure* and *conspicuous consumption* play in revealing social ranking. He noted that it is not enough merely to possess wealth and power to gain and hold prestige. The wealth and power must be put on public view, for prestige is awarded only on evidence. One way we undertake to advertise high status is to lavish expenditure on clothing, because we can size up one another's apparel at a glance. The automobile serves a similar purpose, particularly a very expensive one. Veblen documented how relative success, tested by comparing one's own economic situation with that of others, becomes an established end. Thus, comparisons find symbolic expression, since displaying one's bankbook or stock certificates would be impractical and considered in poor taste.

As our social positions change throughout the life cycle, the sorts of things that serve as symbols of status change. For young people, having the right clothes is often very important. Tattoos and piercing various parts of the body with jewelry can serve as status symbols for youth. Knowing a great deal about sports, movies, or popular music all serve as status symbols, as does being on the cutting edge of any kind of fashion, be it in clothes, music, cars, computers, literature, or another cultural product. These also may be important to adult status, but the core of adult status has to do with

"Actually, son whether the glass is half full or empty isn't important—it's who owns the glass!"

From *The Wall Street Journal* (4/5/94). Reprinted by permission of Cartoon Features Syndicate.

income, occupation, and lifestyle (Coleman and Rainwater, 1978) and with the status of the people in one's social networks. Adult status is symbolized primarily by where one lives, the nature of one's occupation, and the roles one plays as well as by the status of those with whom one associates in the community, in voluntary organizations, and in informal social relations.

Family background and wealth count for less than they did early in the 20th century. Simultaneously, an individual's "personality" and "gregariousness" have taken on greater importance. Although people still think that money is the most important thing, the lifestyle individuals project and the values they reflect are a critical part in determining their prestige (Jackman and Jackman, 1983).

▲ Power

Prestige typically leads others to conform to our wishes through voluntary compliance, deference, and acceptance; power, in contrast, entails conduct by which we compel others to do what they do not wish to do. As we will see in Chapter 9, power determines which individuals and groups will be able to translate their preferences into the reality of social life. **Power** refers to the ability of individuals and groups to realize their will in human affairs even if it involves the resistance of others. It provides answers to the question of whose interests will be served and whose values will reign. Wherever we look, from families to juvenile gangs to nation-states, we find that some parties disproportionately achieve their way. Even in such a simple matter as eye contact, we find the operation of power. Low-power people typically look less at an individual when they are speaking to a high-power person than when they are listening. In contrast, high-power people display nearly equivalent rates of looking while speaking and listening (Ellyson et al., 1980).

Power affects the ability of people to make the world work on their behalf. To gain mastery of critical resources creates dependency and thus allows one to gain mastery of people. To control key resources is to interpose oneself (or one's group) between people and the means whereby people meet their biological, psychological, and social needs. To the extent that some groups command rewards, punishments, and persuasive communications, they are able to dictate the terms by which the game of life is played, making its outcome a foregone conclusion.

The American Class System

We have discussed open and closed systems of stratification and economic standing, prestige, and power. How is stratification actually manifested in society? In this section we will look first at the question of how much inequality there is in the United States. We will then describe how social classes are identified, discuss the significance of social class, and look at poverty in the United States.

Is There Inequality in American Society?

Traditionally, Americans have thought of theirs as an egalitarian society. As the Declaration of Independence puts it, the United States is a country in which all persons are "created equal." If so, there would be little for a student of stratification to study in the United States. What does the data show on this issue? It is sometimes difficult to reliably measure inequality in power and prestige, so let's look at inequality in terms of something we can easily measure: economic standing in terms of income and wealth.

Figure 6.1 shows the percent of aggregate income received by each fifth (or 20 percent) of households in the United States. In a highly egalitarian society, where we still might expect

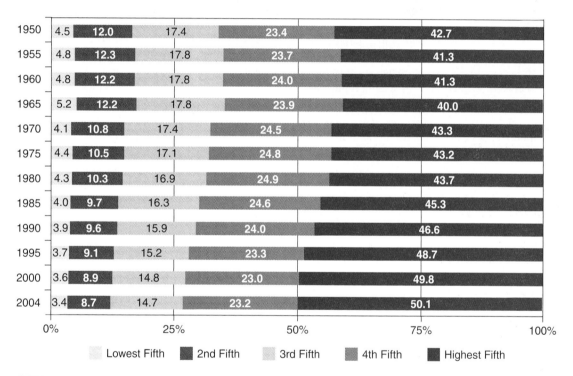

Lowest Fifth   2nd Fifth   3rd Fifth   4th Fifth   Highest Fifth

Figure 6.1   **The Rich Get Richer and the Poor Get Poorer: Share of Income Received by Households in the United States, 1950–2004**

Income data show that the United States is moving away from income equality, not toward it. Within each bar, the percentages represent the percentage of the total income in the United States that is received by each fifth of households, from the lowest (i.e., poorest) fifth to the highest (i.e., wealthiest) fifth. Looking at 1950, for example, we see that the poorest fifth of households received only 4.5 percent of the income for the whole country, while the wealthiest fifth received 42.7 percent. Since 1950, percentages have fluctuated a bit, but, in general, the percentages received by each of the poorer three-fifths of U.S. households have decreased and the percentage received by the wealthiest fifth has increased.

Source: Figure generated by the authors using data from the U.S. Census Bureau, *Current Population Survey,* Annual Demographic Supplements. (http://www.census.gov/hhes/www/income/histinc/h02ar.html)

some inequality, the percentages within each year should be fairly close to each other. Where substantial inequality is present, we expect large differences across the categories, with very small shares going to the poorest fifth and large shares going to the highest fifth. Over the past 45 years, the lowest 20 percent of households in income in the United States never received more than 5.2 percent of aggregate income, while the highest 20 percent has always received 40 percent or more. Since the mid-1960s, income inequality in the United States has been increasing, most rapidly between 1980 and 1992 (Jones and Weinberg, 2000), and is now at its highest level in over 50 years. In 2004, the top 5 percent of families received 21.8 percent of the income, more than four times what it would receive if incomes were equal across families. (http://www.census.gov/hhes/www/income/histinc/h02ar.html)

Inequality in wealth is even greater. We define income as money people receive within a given time interval, such as wages and salaries, while wealth is what they own at a particular time. Figure 6.2 presents an analysis of data from the Federal Reserve Board's 2004 Survey of Consumer Finances (see Bucks, Kennickell, and Moore [2006] for a description of the data). Wealth can be measured by the net worth of a household, the value of all assets minus debts. The top 20 percent of households in wealth own more than 80 percent of all wealth. If we combine this highest fifth with the next highest category (the "fourth fifth"), we find that nearly 95 percent of wealth is owned by the top 40 percent of households, leaving just over 5 percent of all wealth distributed among the remaining 60 percent of households.

White households are far wealthier than African-American and Hispanic households. For every dollar in wealth owned by a white household, the average African-American household owns 15 cents and the average Hispanic household owns 11 cents.

The very rich in the United States increased their share of the nation's total pool of privately held wealth during the economic boom of the 1980s and 1990s, and this trend continued into the early 2000s (Keister and Moller, 2000; Kennickell, 2003; Johnston, 2003). The latter half of the 1990s was a time of sharp acceleration in the growth of wealth for the 400 richest people in the United States. Between 1995 and 1999, the number of U.S. billionaires doubled, and the total amount of wealth owned by the richest 400 people grew by more than 95 percent (Kennickell, 2000). According to the Federal Reserve Board Survey of Consumer Finances, wealth is distributed so unequally in the United States that in 2004 the wealthiest 1 percent of U.S. households owned 33.3 percent of all private wealth, more than the bottom 90 percent of households combined (30.5 percent of total wealth).

Clearly, there is much inequality in the United States to explain. Sociologists agree that social inequality is a structured aspect of contemporary life. In saying this, they mean more than that individuals and groups differ in the privileges they enjoy, the prestige they receive, and the power they wield. Structuring means that inequality is hardened or institutionalized, so that there is a system for determining who gets what. Inequality does not occur in a random fashion but follows relatively consistent and stable patterns that persist. One reason for this persistence is that inequalities are typically passed on from one generation to the next. Individuals and groups that are advantaged commonly find ways to ensure that their offspring will also be advantaged; for those that are disadvantaged, the disadvantage may persist for generations.

Identifying Social Classes

Sociologists have borrowed the term *stratification* from geology. Geologists usually find it rather easy to determine where one stratum of rock ends and another begins. But social strata often shade off into one another so that their boundaries are dim and indistinct. How do we go about identifying social strata, or classes, in the United States?

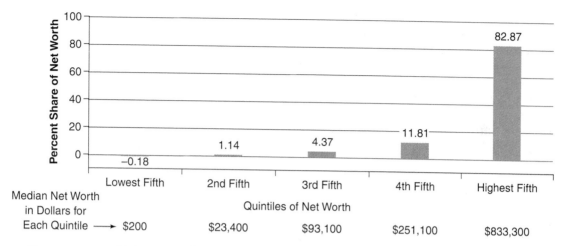

a. If we measure wealth by net worth (assets minus debts), inequality in wealth is extremely high in the United States. More than 80 percent of the wealth is owned by the wealthiest 20 percent of families. The poorest 20 percent of families owe more than they own. The bottom three-fifths of families (6o percent) own less than 6 percent of all wealth.

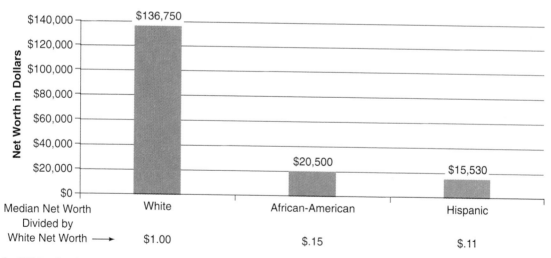

b. White families are, on average, much wealthier than African-American and Hispanic families. Differences in median net worth across the three categories show that for every dollar of net worth owned by a typical white family, the typical African-American family owns 15 cents, and the typical Hispanic family owns 11 cents.

Figure 6.2   **The Concentration of Wealth in the United States, 2004**

Source: Analysis by the authors of data from the 2004 Survey of Consumer Finances, Board of Governors of the Federal Reserve System.

Income Inequality within Societies:
A Look around the World

We have shown that wealth and income are distributed unevenly in U.S. society. How do we compare with other countries? How much does income inequality within countries vary around the world and over time? Is income inequality a persistent feature of societies throughout the world? And finally—but perhaps most importantly—how would we answer such questions?

Until the 1990s, it wasn't possible to answer the questions we have posed. A set of data put together by World Bank economists Klaus Deininger and Lyn Squire (1996) allows us to make at least some tentative answers to these questions. Deininger and Squire calculated the percent of aggregate income received by each fifth (or 20 percent) of the population from low income to high for 108 countries from the late 1940s to the 1990s. They set quality standards for the data they would accept so that they could make cross-country comparisons.

What does the data show? As the accompanying figure for the 1990s shows, there is substantial inequality in every region of the world, with the income share of the poorest fifth never rising to 10 percent, and that of the wealthiest fifth of the population never falling below 37 percent. Deininger and Squire's (1996) analysis of inequality over time showed no change in the basic overall structure of income inequality. Inequality is highest in sub-Saharan Africa and in Latin America and the Caribbean. Inequality is lowest in the formerly socialist countries of Eastern Europe.

What about the United States? It clearly is *not* one of the most egalitarian societies in the world. While it used to have relatively moderate inequality compared to other countries, Deininger and Squire's analysis showed that inequality in the United States has been increasing since the early 1980s even while it was decreasing in other parts of the world (Deininger and Squire, 1996), and it is now moderately high, as shown earlier in this chapter. Studies of wealth inequality show similar findings. Since the early 1990s, wealth inequality in the United States has exceeded that of all industrialized countries (Keister and Moller, 2000; Wolff, 1995, 1996).

A primary goal of studying social stratification is to understand the powerful social and economic forces at work that create and perpetuate income inequality. If such inequality varied

In the course of our everyday conversations, we talk about the "upper class," "middle class," and "lower class," referring to these social classes as distinct groups. Do such groups actually exist? Two views are found among sociologists concerning the accuracy of this popular conception (Lucal, 1994; see also Sørensen, 2000). The first view holds that classes are real, bounded strata that exist in conflicting relations with one another (the *relational model*). Although this position has been a central element in Marxist formulations (Marx and Engels, 1848/1955; Wright, 1985), it also emerges in the work of other sociologists who have identified a blue-collar/white-collar division in American life (Blau and Duncan, 1972; Sobel, 1989). The second view portrays U.S. society as essentially classless, one in which class divisions are blurred by virtue of their continuous and uninterrupted nature (the *distributional model*). Seen in this manner, social classes are culturally quite alike and simply reflect gradations in rank rather than hard-and-fast social groups (Hodge and Treiman, 1968; Eichar, 1989).

The differing conceptions derive in large measure from different approaches to identifying social classes: (1) the objective method, (2) the self-placement method, and (3) the reputational method. Although all the approaches produce some overlap in classes, there are appreciable differences in the results afforded by each (Kerbo, 2006). Moreover, each approach has certain advantages and disadvantages. Let's consider each method more carefully.

randomly or could be easily changed, we would expect much more variation than these worldwide data show. Deininger and Squire's study illustrates the fact that income inequality is a persistent feature of life in every region of the world.

Questions for Discussion

1. Equality was one of the principles upon which the United States was founded, yet the United States now has increasingly high inequality in income. Is this a contradiction? How would you explain the coexistence of the value of equality and increasing income inequality in the United States?

2. Some of the poorest regions of the world have the highest income inequality. What social, political, and economic factors do you think are behind this pattern?

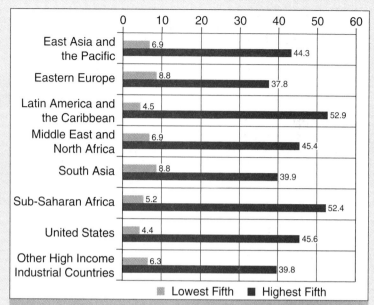

Percent of Total Income Received by Those in the Lowest and Highest Fifths of the Population in Income in the 1990s

Source: Figure generated by the authors using data from Deininger and Squire (1996) and U.S. Census Bureau (1997).

▲ The Objective Method

The **objective method** views social class as a statistical category. The categories are formed by sociologists and/or statisticians. Most commonly, people are assigned to social classes on the basis of income, occupation, or education (or some combination of these characteristics). The label *objective* can be misleading, for it is not meant to imply that the approach is more "specific" or "unbiased" than either of the others. Rather, it is objective in that it uses numerically measurable criteria to categorize individuals. Figure 6.3 shows one way of depicting the distribution of Americans by family income.

The objective method provides a statistical measure for investigating various correlates of class, such as life expectancy, mental illness, divorce, political attitudes, crime rates, and leisure activities. It is usually the simplest and least expensive approach to research social classes because statistical data can be obtained from government agencies and the Census Bureau. However, there is more to class than simply raw statistical data. In the course of their daily lives, people size up one another on many standards of excellence. It is not only the actual income, education, or occupational categories that matter, but also the meanings and definitions others assign to these qualities.

For example, one part of the cultural definition of an occupation is its prestige, the respect and admiration people accord it. Sociologists wishing to assign an "objective" ranking to occupations that reflects the subjective meanings

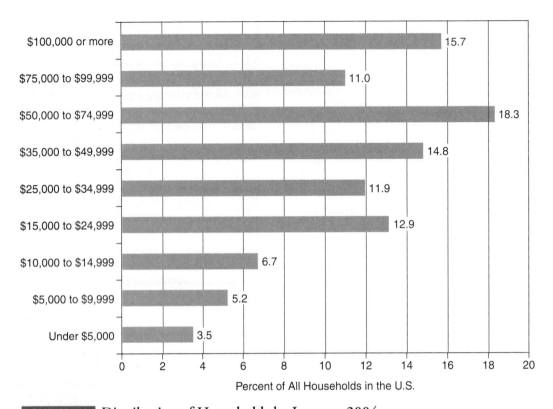

Figure 6.3   **Distribution of Households by Income, 2004**

Source: Figure generated by the authors using data from the U.S. Census Bureau, 2005.
(http://pubdb3.census.gov/macro/032005/hhinc/new01_001.htm)

people attach to occupations use occupational prestige scores. To determine the prestige of occupations, researchers do large surveys and ask respondents to estimate the social standing of each of a large number of occupations. The results can be used to assign prestige scores to the occupations of respondents in other studies (see Table 6.1). Many electricians, funeral directors, and farm owners run very successful businesses and have high incomes. But because of the meanings people attach to these occupations, their prestige rankings fall in the middle of the range, as can be seen in Table 6.1.

Prestige, however, is not the only dimension underlying differences among occupations. According to Weeden and Grusky (2005), if we wish to have more complete accounts of how

class is associated with various outcomes, such as those discussed in the next section on the significance of social classes, we should measure class by using detailed occupational categories. As noted above, if we use occupational prestige to measure class, we would constrain funeral directors and mail carriers, which actually differ on a variety of underlying dimensions, to be the same. Using detailed occupational categories allows us to explore whether outcomes of being in those different categories may be different.

▲ The Self-Placement Method

The **self-placement method** (also known as the subjective method) has people identify the social class to which they think they belong. Class is viewed as a social category, one in which

Table 6.1	Prestige Rankings of Occupations	

Occupation	Score
Physician	86
Lawyer	75
College teacher	74
Chemical engineer	73
Dentist	72
Clergy	69
Pharmacist	68
Secondary school teacher	66
Registered nurse	66
Accountant	65
Athlete	65
Elementary school teacher	64
Police officer, detective	60
Editor, reporter	60
Financial manager	59
Actor	58
Librarian	54
Social worker	52
Electrician	51
Funeral director	49
Mail carrier	47
Secretary	46
Insurance agent	45
Bank teller	43
Farm owner	40
Automobile mechanic	40
Restaurant manager	39
Sales counter clerk	34
Cook	31
Waiter and waitress	28
Garbage collector	28
Janitor	22
Parking lot attendant	21
Vehicle washer	19
News vendor	19

Sources: Keiko Nakao, Robert W. Hodge, and Judith Treas, 1990. "On revising prestige scores for all occupations," GSS Methodological Report No. 69, Chicago: National Opinion Research Center; General Social Surveys, Davis, Smith, and Marsden, 2005.

Note: Americans ranked a number of occupations in terms of prestige in national surveys. The highest possible score an occupation could receive was 90 and the lowest 10. The table shows the ranking of a number of the occupations.

people group themselves with others they perceive as sharing certain attributes in common. The class lines may or may not conform to what social scientists think are logical lines of cleavage in the objective sense. Researchers typically ask respondents to identify their social class.

Within American life a family's class position historically derived from the husband's position in the labor market. But long-term social and economic changes, particularly the movement of many women into the workplace and declining family size, have altered the way many women assess their class identity (Baxter, 1994). Most employed women used to appraise their class position primarily in terms of the class position of their husbands. Now both men and women look at husband's and wife's combined income in identifying class but only at the husband's occupational prestige (Yamaguchi and Wang, 2002).

The major advantage of the self-placement approach is that it can be applied to a large population. However, the approach has its limitations. The class with which people identify may represent their aspirations rather than their current associations or the appraisals of other people. Nearly all the respondents to a 2005 *New York Times* poll identified themselves as working, middle, or upper middle class. Although five class categories were offered, very few wealthy respondents labeled themselves upper class, and the poorest poll respondents did not identify themselves as lower class (Scott and Leonhardt, 2005).

▲ The Reputational Method

In the *self-placement* method, people are asked to rank themselves. In the **reputational method,** they are asked how they classify other individuals. This approach views class as a social group, one in which people share a feeling of oneness and are bound together in relatively stable patterns of interaction. Therefore, class rests on the knowledge of who associates with whom. The approach gained prominence in the 1930s when W. Lloyd Warner and his associates studied the class structure of three communities: "Yankee

City" (Newburyport, Massachusetts), a New England town of some 17,000 people (Warner and Lunt, 1941, 1942); "Old City" (Natchez, Mississippi), a southern community of about 10,000 (Davis, Gardner, and Gardner, 1941); and "Jonesville" (Morris, Illinois), a midwestern town of about 6,000 (Warner, 1949). In Yankee City and Old City, Warner identified six classes: the upper upper, the lower upper, the upper middle, the lower middle, the upper lower, and the lower lower. Warner's sociological conception of the U.S. class system was popularized by the media and gained considerable public appeal. Even today his formulations carry considerable weight in how the American public has come to view and think about social class in American life.

The reputational method is a valuable tool for investigating social distinctions in small groups and small communities. It is particularly useful in predicting associational patterns among people, but it is difficult to use in large samples where people have little or no knowledge of one another.

▲ Combining Approaches

Warner and his associates did most of their research before World War II, and most of it was done in small-town America. In 1978, sociologists Richard D. Coleman and Lee Rainwater updated and expanded our understanding of class structure to include urban America. They combined the self-placement and reputational methods, interviewing residents of Kansas City and Boston and asking them about their perceptions of the levels of contemporary living. The resulting categories that these urban residents used to rank one another and themselves are still relevant as a general description of class stratification in the United States:

- People who have really made it. At the very top of the U.S. class structure is an elite class of wealthy individuals.

- People who are doing very well. Corporate executives and professional people make up this class.

- People who have achieved the middle-class dream. These individuals enjoy the "good life" as defined in material terms, but they lack the luxuries of those in the higher classes.

- People who have a comfortable life. While enjoying a "comfortable" life, the members of this class have less money at their disposal than the people above them and they live in less fashionable suburbs.

- People who are just getting by. Some Americans enjoy "respectable" jobs, but "getting by" puts a strain on their resources.

- People who are having a difficult time. Members of this group find "the going tough." Both the husband and the wife work, but their income is low.

- People who are poor. These are "people who are down and out." Many of them receive government assistance and benefits.

These divisions, though descriptive, are somewhat unwieldy. Sociologists as well as laypeople usually find it easier to employ the labels "upper class," "middle class," "working class," and "lower class" (poor people) when considering class distinctions. Research suggests that these terms correspond reasonably well with objective class indicators such as income, education, occupational skill level, and manual versus nonmanual jobs (Kerbo, 2006). However, the terms mask important divisions and interests among groups in U.S. society. Moreover, they do not necessarily correspond with self-placement identifications. Even so, these class terms remain useful both because they have the most meaning for the most people and because they are significantly related to major occupational and property divisions.

▲ One Dimension or Many?

Sociologist Talcott Parsons (1940, 1953) pointed out some 60 years ago that social position is determined by one's location on some dimension or dimensions of value. As subcultures based on ethnicity, lifestyle, religious commitment, patterns of consumption, occupation, age, and other dimensions become increasingly important in American cultural life, they have formed the basis of what we might call "status spheres" (Berger and Berger, 1972; Wolfe, 1968). People are increasingly likely to compete with one another within these spheres rather than along a single dimension of status. High status in one sphere may count for little in another; a high-ranking member of the outlaw motorcycle subculture (bikers) may appear to be "just another bum" to someone whose life is dominated by miniature furniture collecting. Likewise, the best fiddle player in Nashville may find it impossible to distinguish between a principal investigator (high status) and a research associate (middle status) on a research team in a large university. As a consequence, class distinctions in the United States that were once clear have become harder to discern, and a good many Americans seem to be confused about where they stand in the class hierarchy (Labich, 1994).

The Significance of Social Classes

Few aspects of social life affect so strongly the way people behave and think as does social class. For one thing, it largely determines their **life chances**—the likelihood that individuals and groups will enjoy desired goods and services, fulfilling experiences, and opportunities for living healthy and long lives. Broadly considered, life chances have to do with people's level of living and their options for choice. For example, social class affects education. The higher the social class of parents, the further

their children go in school and the better they perform (Mickelson, 1990). Long-term poverty experienced during childhood affects cognitive ability, and poverty experienced during adolescence affects cognitive achievement (Guo, 1998). By 5 years of age, youngsters who have always lived in poverty have IQs on average 9 points lower than those who were never poor; this gap cannot be explained by differences in mothers' education, divorce rates, or race (Elias, 1994).

Class also affects health and life expectancy (Scott, 2005). As a physician expressed in the *Journal of the American Medical Association,* "Lower socioeconomic status (SES) is probably the most powerful single contributor to premature morbidity and mortality, not only in the United States but worldwide" (Williams, 1998:1745). Health is affected by income, education, and social class in all industrialized societies (Dunn and Hayes, 2000). As with education, childhood poverty continues to affect health into adulthood (Reynolds and Ross, 1998). Although health risk factors including obesity, smoking, and lack of exercise are more common among people of low socioeconomic classes, researchers also point to differences in exposure to occupational and environmental health hazards in explaining class differences in morbidity and mortality (Lantz et al., 1998).

Research shows, however, that more than lifestyle and exposure to health hazards is responsible for the correlation of social class and health. While sociologists Mirowsky and Ross (2003) argue that the primary factor is education, the effect of social class may be through a variety of pathways (Link and Phelan, 1995). Whatever the specific causes, the importance of social class is clearly illustrated by research showing that social class is associated with mortality due to preventable causes (e.g., appendicitis), but not with mortality due to nonpreventable causes (e.g., gallbladder cancer) (Phelan et al., 2004).

Social class affects life chances in other ways. During the Vietnam War, some 80 percent of the 2.5 million men who served in Southeast Asia—of 27 million men who reached draft age during the war—came from working-class and impoverished backgrounds (Appy, 1993). When the *Titanic* sank in 1912, passengers traveling in first class were more than twice as likely to survive than those traveling third class (Dawson, 1995).

Social class also affects people's **style of life**—the magnitude and manner of their consumption of goods and services. Convenience foods—TV dinners, potato chips, frozen pizza, and Hamburger Helper—are more frequently on the menus of lower-income than higher-income households. Lower-class families drink less vodka, scotch, bourbon, and imported wine but consume more beer and blended whiskey. Social class even affects such things as the styles of furniture people buy and the programs they watch on television.

Social class is associated with various patterns of behavior. For instance, voting increases with socioeconomic status in most Western nations (Gaither and Newberger, 2000). And people in the lower classes begin sexual activities at a younger age, but people in the upper classes are more tolerant of sexual variations and engage in a wider variety of sexual activities (Laumann et al., 1994). In sum, one's social class leaves few areas of life untouched.

Poverty in the United States

More than 30 years after President Lyndon Johnson announced that his Great Society program would end poverty in the United States, poverty remains a significant feature of American life. Census Bureau statistics reveal that the percentage of Americans below the poverty line dropped from 22.4 percent in 1959 to a low of 11.1 percent in 1973. The poverty rate has fluctuated since then, with a recent upturn (see Figure 6.4). In 2004, the official poverty rate was 12.7 percent, with 37 million people living in poverty (DeNavas-Walt, Proctor, and Lee, 2005).

What exactly is poverty? Who are the poor in the United States? Does the United States have an "underclass"? What causes poverty? And how does the United States approach the problems of poverty? We will discuss these issues in this section.

▲ Defining Poverty

The definition of poverty is a matter of debate. In 1795, a group of English magistrates decided that a minimum income should be "the cost of a gallon loaf of bread, multiplied by three, plus an allowance for each dependent" (Schorr, 1984). Today the Census Bureau defines the threshold of poverty in the United States as the minimum amount of money families need to purchase a nutritionally adequate diet, assuming they use one-third of their income for food. Traditionally, liberals have contended the line is too low because it fails to take into account changes in the standard of living (Ruggles, 1992). Conservatives have said it is too high because the poor receive in-kind income in the form of public assistance, including food stamps, public housing subsidies, and health care (Rector, 1990). In 2004, the poverty threshold for a family of four (including two children) was $19,157 (DeNavas-Walt, Proctor, and Lee, 2005). For a single person under 65 to be defined as poor, he or she must earn less than $9,827 per year.

▲ Who Are the Poor?

About 62 percent of the nation's poor live in large cities, but between 2001 and 2002 the poverty rate increased not among city dwellers but among those who live in suburbs (Proctor and Dalaker, 2003). High poverty counties are found in Appalachia, the Mississippi delta, and Texas along the Mexican border. The poverty rate is highest in the South, with Mississippi, Louisiana, and New Mexico leading the states with the highest poverty rates. Overall, poverty has become increasingly the lot of single and divorced parents and their children. For example, in 2004 the poverty rate for married-couple

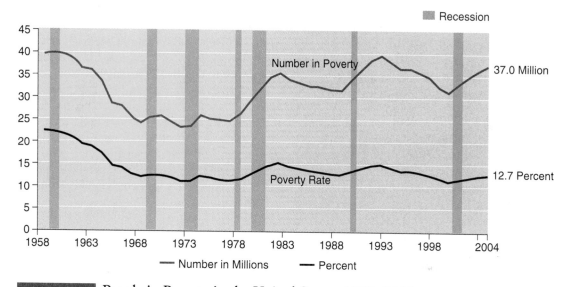

Figure 6.4   **People in Poverty in the United States, 1959–2004**

In 2004 the government classified a family of four as poor if it had cash income of less than $19,157.

Source: DeNavas-Walt, Carmen, Bernadette D. Proctor, and Cheryl Hill Lee, 2005. *Income, poverty, and health insurance coverage in the United States: 2004.* U.S. Census Bureau, Current Population Reports, P60–229. Washington DC: U.S. Government Printing Office (available online at http://www.census.gov/prod/2005pubs/p60-229.pdf).

families was 5.5 percent, while that for families headed by a female with no spouse present was five times higher (DeNavas-Walt, Proctor, and Lee, 2005). This feminization and juvenilization of poverty has changed course as women have made gains in both employment and wage equality (Bianchi, 1999). Nevertheless, women still have a significantly higher risk of poverty than men (Haynie and Gorman, 1999). In 2004, fatherless families represented 17.4 percent of the nation's families, but 48.3 percent of the households living in poverty. In the same year, 17.8 percent of all American children— 13 million children—were living in poverty (DeNavas-Walt, Proctor, and Lee, 2005). Poverty rates vary greatly by race, with non-Hispanic whites (8.6 percent) and Asians (10.0 percent) having the lowest rates and Hispanics (21.9 percent) and African Americans

(24.7 percent) the highest rates of poverty (DeNavas-Walt, Proctor, and Lee, 2005).

The poverty rate for the elderly dropped from 35.2 percent in 1959 to 10.4 percent in 2002. Even so, 20 percent of widowed and 24 percent of divorced older women remain impoverished. Farmers are more likely to be poor than their city cousins, and there are thousands of American farmworkers who are poor, many of whom lack access to toilets and clean water at their work sites. Handicapped individuals are more than twice as likely as other workers to be poor. About 23 percent of working-age people who receive food stamps and 37 percent of Medicaid recipients are disabled.

Not everyone who is poor receives welfare. And contrary to popular stereotype, whites use government safety-net programs more than African Americans and Hispanics. Although the

More than 25 million white people were living in poverty in 2004. Although African Americans are more likely than whites to be poor, 68 percent of the poor in the United States in 2004 were white (DeNavas-Walt, Proctor, and Lee, 2005).

poverty *rate* is lower for whites, there were 16.8 million non-Hispanic whites living in poverty in 2004, compared to 9 million African Americans and the same number of Hispanics (DeNavas-Walt, Proctor, and Lee, 2005).

▲ An "Underclass"?

The term *underclass* has been applied by some social scientists to a population of people, concentrated in an inner city, who are *persistently* poor, unemployed, and dependent on welfare (Coughlin, 1988). Initially, sociologist William Julius Wilson (1987) championed the concept to describe the plight of "the truly disadvantaged." Some argue that the term *underclass* has come to reflect the stereotype that the poor have created their own plight and that the inhabitants of inner-city neighborhoods are both fundamentally different from other Americans and violently dangerous. In fact, as sociologist Christopher Jencks (1992) has pointed out, people described as in the underclass vary considerably from one another on a variety of dimensions. The term "underclass" is used by sociologists not as a stereotype, but to describe the phenomenon of persistent poverty. As historian Jacqueline Jones (1992) showed, the kind of poverty associated with contemporary urban ghettos has a long history dating back at least to the Civil War and has included white sharecroppers, Appalachian white migrants, and marginal white factory workers of the North.

Simply being poor does not make a person a part of the underclass. Indeed, the underclass constitutes a minority of the poor. Research indicates that over a four-year period in the 1990s, about 34 percent of the population lived in poverty for at least two months, but only 2 percent were continuously in poverty over the entire period (Iceland, 2003). The underclass is a core of inner-city poor, those individuals and families who are trapped in an unending cycle of joblessness and dependence on welfare or criminal earnings. Their communities are often plagued by drug abuse, lawlessness, crime, violence, and poor schools (Wilson, 1996). Many women in the underclass were teenage mothers and high school dropouts who subsequently found themselves sidetracked without the resources or skills to escape a life of poverty. The rise of female-headed families is associated with the inability of men in the underclass to find steady jobs (Wilson, 1987, 1991; Massey, 1990; Jencks, 1992).

In the next section we consider the three major theories of poverty.

▲ Theories of Poverty

Various theories have been advanced through the years to explain poverty.

One approach looks to the characteristics of the poor to explain their difficulties. According to the **culture of poverty** thesis, the poor in class-stratified capitalist societies lack effective participation and integration within the larger society (Lewis, 1966). Clustered in large ghettos in cities such as New York, Mexico City, and San Juan, the poor develop feelings of marginality, helplessness, dependence, and inferiority, which allegedly breed weak ego structures, lack of impulse control, a present-time orientation characterized by little ability to defer gratification, and a sense of resignation and fatalism. The resulting lifeways are both an adaptation and a reaction of the poor to their disadvantaged positions. They become self-perpetuating patterns as the ethos associated with the culture of poverty is transmitted to successive generations (Murray, 1994). Political scientist Lawrence M. Mead (1992) offered a modified version of the theory, arguing that the sources of contemporary poverty are essentially psychological and not cultural. He argued that the dependent poor share the values of the larger society but lack the confidence to try to live by them.

Many sociologists argue that the culture of poverty thesis has serious shortcomings (Valentine, 1968; Duncan, Hill, and Hoffman, 1988; Jaynes and Williams, 1989; Demos, 1990). For instance, as we pointed out in Chapter 1, Elliot Liebow depicted the economically poor streetcorner men of Washington, D.C., as very much immersed in American life and not as carriers of an independent culture of poverty. They, too, want what other American men want, but they are blocked from achieving their goals by a racist social order.

Another view sees poverty as largely *situational*. This view is supported by a study that showed that a majority of the U.S. population uses the welfare system at some point (Rank, 2004; Rank, 2003; Rank and Hirschl, 2001).

Two-thirds of Americans between the ages of 20 and 65 will use a welfare program, and 90 percent of those who do will use it more than once. Similarly, a long-term study done in the 1970s, 1980s, and 1990s found that between 2 and 3 percent of U.S. families could be classed as persistently poor over multiple years, and about 25 percent of families received welfare at some time, averaging about 8 months' duration (Iceland, 2003; U.S. Bureau of the Census, 1995; Duncan, Hill, and Hoffman, 1988). Many people who slip into poverty do so for a limited time after major adverse events, such as divorce or illness. For many families, welfare serves as a type of insurance protection, something they use for a brief period but dispose of as quickly as they can. The study, undertaken by the University of Michigan's Institute for Social Research (Duncan, 1984, 1987; Duncan, Hill, and Hoffman, 1988), casts doubt on the culture of poverty thesis. Instead it portrays the poverty population as a pool, with people flowing in and out. The researchers found "little evidence that individual attitudes and behavior patterns affect individual economic progress." To a far greater extent, individuals "are the victims of their past, their environment, luck, and chance."

Still another view portrays poverty as a *structural feature* of capitalist societies. The cyclical movements between economic expansion and contraction—boom and bust—contribute to sharp fluctuations in employment. More than a century ago Marx contended that an industrial reserve army is essential for capitalist economies. The industrial reserve army consists of individuals at the bottom of the class structure who are laid off in the interests of corporate profits during times of economic stagnation and then rehired when needed for producing profits during times of economic prosperity. It is disproportionately composed of minorities, who traditionally have been the last hired and the first fired. Contemporary structuralists say that a "new industrial order," characterized by a significant shift from manufacturing to service-sector employment, has produced massive vulnerability among all blue-collar workers. This structuralist view sees poverty as deriving from a lack of income-producing employment (Moller et al., 2003). Problems in the economic organization of society also result in high inner-city rates of family disintegration, welfare dependency, drug abuse, and crime (Marks, 1991; Jones, 1992).

▲ Poverty Programs

For much of Western history, assistance to the poor has taken the form of private charity sometimes augmented with public relief. But government intervention has not always been truly charitable. For instance, in 18th-century England, poor laws provided workhouses for the able-bodied indigent to discourage people from adding themselves to the ranks of paupers. Much of the 18th- and 19th-century debate surrounding definitions of poverty and its remedies is similar to that of today.

The first large national poverty programs in the United States were established as part of President Franklin D. Roosevelt's New Deal in the 1930s. Two of these programs had a significant impact on poverty: Social Security and Aid to Families With Dependent Children (AFDC). The Social Security program, designed to aid the disabled and prevent poverty in old age, has sharply reduced poverty among the elderly so that by 2004, persons over age 65 were less likely than persons aged 18 to 64 to be in poverty (DeNavas-Walt, Proctor, and Lee, 2005). The AFDC program provided aid to poor families with children. Though it did not end poverty, it did provide humanitarian relief, and the increased aid provided as part of President Lyndon Johnson's Great Society program of the 1960s reduced the percent of persons in poverty (Kerbo, 2006), the results of which can be seen in Figure 6.4 (p. 191).

How does the United States compare with other countries? Despite a persistent perception that the U.S. government spends enormous amounts of money to support the poor, in fact the United States is the only industrialized nation that has no guaranteed income program for families in poverty and no national health program to meet the medical needs of its citizens (Kerbo, 2006).

The AFDC program survived until 1996, when it was replaced by the Temporary Assistance for Needy Families (TANF) program as part of former President Bill Clinton's welfare reform. The welfare reform program focuses primarily on encouraging work, eliminating long-term use of welfare, and handing welfare over to the states. Its key elements are:

1. Welfare recipients must work after two years of assistance.

2. Recipients are limited to five years' total assistance, including cycling on and off.

3. The guarantee of assistance that was built into AFDC has been replaced with a system of block grants to the states, money that can be used largely as each state wishes. Under this new system, states may limit assistance to less than five years and may use the money from the federal government for things other than welfare assistance (Bane, 1997; Super et al., 1996).

The promotion of marriage also is a key element of TANF, with "encouraging the formation and maintenance of two-parent families" a stated means to ending dependence on government benefits (Lichter, Graefe, and Brown, 2003). The welfare reform program was reauthorized under President George Bush's administration in 2003.

What are the consequences of welfare reform? Judging its success is a matter of perspective. The number of people receiving government assistance definitely decreased. Between 1996 and 2004, the number of people receiving government handouts dropped by 7.5 million, and by 2001 the welfare caseload was lower than it had been since 1969 (Lichter and Jayakody, 2002). The proportion of people on welfare—less than 3 percent—was the lowest on record. Further, welfare reform seems to have been accompanied by a slowdown in out-of-wedlock childbearing and a rise in family stability (DeParle, 2004). The majority of people leaving the welfare rolls found employment, most full time (Corcoran et al., 2000).

The decline in welfare recipients, however, did not translate into a decrease in the poverty rate (Lichter and Jayakody, 2002). Although poverty rates did fall in the first years after welfare reform, the size of the decline did not match the numbers of people off welfare. And each year since 2000, poverty rates have increased (DeNavas-Walt, Proctor, and Lee, 2005). According to some analysts, welfare reform served primarily to transform welfare recipients into the working poor (O'Connor, 2000). Although people found jobs, they were not earning enough money to rise above the official poverty line—and that line does not take into account the work-related expenditures welfare leavers incur, such as child care and transportation. One result of this is that the number of children living without their parents has increased; for black children living in cities, the percentage of children left with friends, relatives, or foster families has doubled (Bernstein, 2002).

Why are people who work full time unable to rise above the poverty line? One reason is that the cost of living—and especially the cost of housing—has increased much more quickly than the level of wages. A report released in 2002 by the National Low Income Housing Coalition indicated that the average household needs an income of $14.66 per hour in a full-time job to be able to afford a two-bedroom rental, close to three times the federal minimum wage of $5.15 (Kennedy, 2002). That number was based on a national average; in some areas, the income required is much higher. Despite the variability in housing costs, there is no state in which an extremely low-income family can afford to rent a decent two-bedroom house at

market value (MCCD, 2003). And surveys show that one clear result of pushing people off welfare has been to *decrease* wages for low-skilled workers (Kerbo, 2006).

How might poverty be handled differently? Based on the assumption that poverty is caused by low income and a lack of well-paying jobs (Jencks, 1992), Bane and Ellwood (1994) suggested replacing welfare with a system of income-support policies designed to reinforce principles of family, work, and independence. First, people who work should not be poor; minimum wages should be set high enough to keep people in low-paying jobs out of poverty. Eleven states have set minimum wages higher than the federal level (Armas, 2003), and more than 50 cities have livable wage ordinances that require government-hired contractors to pay wages in line with local costs of living (Krasikov, 2001). Second, families should not be forced to rely on the income of only one parent. The government needs to better enforce laws requiring absent parents to pay child support and should provide child-support payments when support from parents is not forthcoming. Third, jobs must be made available to those who are willing to work. The government should be the employer of last resort to provide jobs when the economy falters and in areas where jobs are scarce.

Social Mobility

In many societies individuals or groups can move from one level (stratum) to another in the stratification system, a process called *social mobility*. Social inequality has to do with differences in the distribution of benefits and burdens; social stratification is a structured system of inequality; and **social mobility** refers to the shift of individuals or groups from one social status to another.

Social mobility can occur in at least two ways. First, societies change, altering the division of labor, introducing new positions, undermining old ones, and shifting the allocation of resources. Sometimes such social change occurs because members of the lower strata resent their exclusion from higher ranks and work to change the established social order. Second, social mobility can take place when shifts occur in the availability of different types of talent. Although those in the higher strata may monopolize the opportunities for training and education, they do not control the natural distribution of talent and ability. People often must be recruited from the lower ranks to perform roles in society that increase their status.

In this section we will describe the forms social mobility can take, discuss social mobility and status attainment processes, and take a look at the "American Dream."

Forms of Social Mobility

Social mobility can take a number of forms. For example, mobility may be vertical or horizontal. **Vertical mobility** involves movement from one social status to another of higher or lower rank. As we saw in Table 6.1, Americans differ in the prestige ratings they give to various occupations. If an auto mechanic (prestige score 40) became a lawyer (score 75), this shift constitutes upward mobility. On the other hand, if the auto mechanic became a garbage collector (score 28), this change involves downward mobility. If the auto mechanic took a job as a restaurant manager (score 39), this shift represents horizontal mobility. **Horizontal mobility** entails movement from one social status to another of approximately equivalent rank.

Mobility also may be intergenerational or intragenerational. **Intergenerational mobility** involves a comparison of the social status of parents and their children at some point in their respective careers (e.g., as assessed by the rankings of their occupations at roughly the same age). Research shows that a large minority, perhaps even a majority, of the U.S. population

U.S. Secretary of State Condaleeza Rice was born into a middle-class family. Her success illustrates both inter- and intra-generational mobility.

moves up or down at least a little in the class hierarchy in every generation. **Intragenerational mobility** entails a comparison of the social status of a person over an extended time period. There are limits to the variety of most people's mobility experience. Small moves tend to be the rule, and large moves the exception.

Social Mobility and Status Attainment

When sociologists talk about social mobility, they usually have intergenerational occupational mobility in mind. Over the history of the United States, social mobility has occurred as a result of changes in occupational structure and the economy (Beeghley, 2000). Many Americans assume that the chances of moving up the social ladder are greater in the United States than in other countries. In fact, chances for upward mobility in the United States are no better, and in some cases worse, than they are in other industrialized countries (Scott and Leonhardt, 2005; Breen and Jonsson, 2004). In general, more Americans are upwardly mobile than downwardly mobile across generations.

What accounts for the higher rate of upward than downward intergenerational mobility in the United States? First, changes in occupational structure over time: With technological advances, more jobs are created toward the top of the occupational structure than toward the bottom. Second, fertility differences associated with social class: White-collar fathers generate fewer children than blue-collar fathers, making more room toward the top of the class hierarchy. Over time, more than twice as many men have moved into white-collar jobs as have moved out of them (Davis, 1982).

▲ The Classic Studies

We can learn more about social mobility by looking at status attainment studies, which identify the processes by which individuals enter occupations and attain status in society. Two classic sociological studies of status transmission and attainment have pinpointed some key factors. The first involved the development of a technique for studying the course of an individual's occupational status over the life cycle (Blau and Duncan, 1972). Called the **socioeconomic life cycle,** it involves a sequence of stages that begins with birth into a family with a specific social status and proceeds through childhood, socialization, schooling, job seeking, occupational achievement, marriage, and the formation and functioning of a new family unit. The second study, conducted by William Sewell and his associates (Sewell et al., 1970; Sewell and Hauser, 1975), was based on a survey of high school seniors and follow-up work over the decade following their graduation from high school.

Both these studies found that education—the years of schooling completed—has the greatest influence on occupational attainment. Blau and Duncan concluded that the social status of one's parents has little *direct* impact on occupational attainment; rather, it plays an *indirect* role on status attainment through its affect on schooling. Sewell and his associates found that another important factor linking family background to adult status was the level of achievement aspirations one learned in the family. A study that followed the participants of

Sewell and colleagues' original study from the 1950s to the 1990s found that the impact of family background on occupational attainment operates entirely through educational achievement and cognitive ability (Warren, Hauser, and Sheridan, 2002). In another recent study, Elman and O'Rand (2004) showed that advantaged social origins lead to completion of college before one's first job, and this combination produces a sharp boost to adult wages.

▲ The Critics

Critics of status attainment research contend that it has a functionalist bias (Knottnerus, 1991). They argue that it is not the case that the job market is fully open to individuals who acquire positions based on education and ability. Although some of the most important factors affecting status attainment among white males have been identified, it turns out that for women and African Americans the processes of status attainment are different.

▲ Race

Let's look first at African Americans. A nationwide sample of boys revealed a number of differences between blacks and whites in terms of educational attainment (Portes and Wilson, 1976). Using a model similar to that developed by Sewell and others, based on parents' education, offspring's education and aspirations, and other factors, these researchers found that the model predicted attainment for whites better than it did for blacks. This suggested that the factors that are most important for educational attainment among blacks were not included in the model. Socioeconomic background, mental ability, and academic performance were found to be more important for white attainment, while self-esteem and educational aspirations were significant variables for blacks. Similarly, while Elman and O'Rand (2004) found that education increased adult wages for both whites and blacks, the effects of education on wages are greater for whites.

▲ Gender

Research in Great Britain has shown that social mobility findings for white men cannot also be generalized to women (Abbott and Wallace, 1997). While the proportion of jobs done by women and the proportion of women working for pay both have increased, women typically come in as routine workers and at the bottom of job categories. Similarly, in the United States, women are more likely than men to be and remain at the bottom of any scale of salaries and wages and less likely than men to be or remain at the top (Gittleman and Joyce, 1995). Daughters are less likely than sons to "inherit" their fathers' occupations and are more likely to be influenced by their mothers' occupations (Hurst, 1998). For males, education is one of a number of variables affecting status attainment; for females, education is clearly *the most significant* factor related to status attainment (Hurst, 1998; see also Elman and O'Rand [2004]). Women also are more likely than men to be affected by family and home-life factors; Waddoups and Assane (1993) found that having a child dampens the upward mobility of women but not of men.

▲ Race and Gender

Race also interacts with gender in status attainment. In a study of women in Memphis, researchers found that white women raised in working-class families received less support and encouragement for educational and career attainment than did white women raised in middle-class families and black women raised in either working- or middle-class families (Higginbotham and Weber, 1992). For example, 86 percent of the black middle-class women said their families supported their going to college, compared to 70 percent of the white middle-class women, 64 percent of the black working-class women, and only 56 percent of the white women raised in working-class homes.

"Actually, Lou, I think it was more than just my being in the right place at the right time. I think it was my being the right race, the right religion, the right sex, the right socioeconomic group, having the right accent, the right clothes, going to the right schools. . . ."

▲ Dual Labor Market

Higginbotham and Weber's study looked at only one aspect of educational and occupational attainment in the United States, but it makes clear the point that the structural model of Blau and Duncan and the social/psychological model of Sewell and his colleagues do not explain all that we need to know about status attainment for a diverse population in the United States. Another factor operating to channel individuals into various occupations is the **dual labor market,** with the primary, or *core,* sector of the economy offering "good jobs" and the secondary, or *periphery,* sector offering "bad jobs" that provide poor pay, poor working conditions, and little room for advancement. Recruitment to these two sectors varies, with African Americans, Hispanics, Native Americans, and women found more often in the periphery sector (Beck, Horan, and Tolbert, 1980; Sakamoto and Chen, 1991). If we want to gain a better understanding of how status attainment functions not just for white men but for both women and men of a variety of races and ethnicities, we need to look beyond education and fathers' occupations and look instead at how race, class, and gender affect the status attainment process.

What Is Happening to the American Dream?

America has long been viewed as the land of opportunity, and Americans increasingly think that it is possible to move into a higher social class (Scott and Leonhardt, 2005). The American Dream is the belief that an average person, through hard work and perseverance, can achieve as much as he or she wishes. A central part of this belief is that even people born in poverty can live a decent life; that is, have a nice home, own a car, and send their children to college. In short, if they work hard and play by the rules, they can join the middle class.

Is it true? The data on income and wealth inequality we have presented in this chapter would seem to indicate that a significant number of Americans are losing the race for prosperity; the rich get richer while the poor stay poor—or get poorer. Status attainment studies demonstrate that the American Dream is a different reality depending on one's gender, race, and ethnicity. Some social scientists see the United States as becoming a nation of "haves" and "have nots," with fewer people in between.

An analysis of incomes showed that between the ages of 25 and 75, half of Americans will spend at least a year in poverty, half will spend a year in affluence (10 times the poverty level), and only 2 percent will spend that entire 50-year period somewhere between poverty and affluence (Rank and Hirschl, 2001). Yet moving out of poverty is getting more difficult for Americans. In a review of studies of social mobility, Aaron Bernstein (2003) found that 53 percent of the families that were poor at the beginning of the 1990s were still poor at the end of the decade, a higher percentage than in previous decades. The percentage of poor young people—5 percent—earning college degrees has not changed in 30 years. And the ability of young men to achieve a higher socioeconomic status than their fathers has declined significantly since just a few decades ago. Bernstein also found that immigrants are less likely today than in the past to achieve economic stability and success.

Part of the reason for these changes is transformation that has occurred in the occupational structure. Industrial change is eliminating high-paying jobs and replacing them with low-paying ones. Smokestack industries, such as machine tools, autos, and steel, provide many middle-income jobs; when deindustrialization causes their share of total employment to fall sharply, the middle class shrinks. As jobs in manufacturing decline, most new jobs are created in the service and trade sectors of the economy. But service industries display a two-hump distribution in income—highly paid administrative and professional workers, such as physicians and professional workers, at the top, and low-paid workers, such as hamburger flippers and telephone sales people, at the bottom.

Despite the fact that inequality has increased, that "equal opportunity" may not be so equal, and that median household income declined each year from 1999 to 2004, in real dollars most Americans are well off compared to household incomes from the 1970s and early 1980s (see Figure 6.5). That may account for the optimism noted earlier in this chapter: Most Americans believe that they have a good chance of getting ahead, that they have done better than their parents, and that their children will have more opportunities than they had (Davis, Smith, and Marsden, 2005; Newport, 1997; Kraar, 1990).

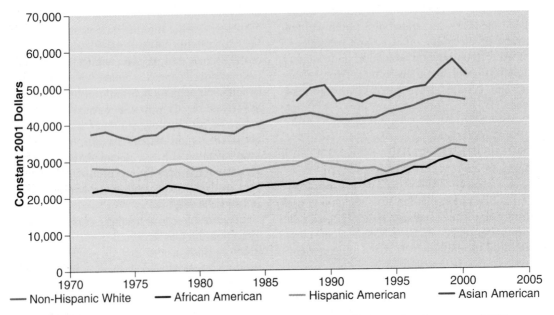

Figure 6.5 **Median Income of Households by Race/Ethnicity, in Constant 2001 Dollars, 1972–2001**

The American Dream: Coming True, but Not for Everyone. The median income figures used to make this graph have been adjusted for inflation (i.e., they are in "real" or "constant" dollars) so that we can compare them over time to see if incomes have been rising or falling. These data show that real household income fluctuates over time with the economy. While it has been on a generally upward trend since the early 1970s, it has declined recently. Regardless of fluctuations, the higher incomes that people expect as part of the American Dream do not flow equally to all groups.

Source: Figure generated by the authors using data from the U.S. Census Bureau, 2003.

Explanations of Social Stratification

As sociology developed, the question of why social inequality and division should characterize the human condition provided a central focus of the new science. Through the years, two strikingly divergent answers have emerged. The first—the *conservative* thesis that is rooted in functionalism—has supported existing social arrangements, contending that an unequal distribution of social rewards is a necessary instrument for getting the essential tasks of society performed. In sharp contrast, the second view—the *radical* thesis that is rooted in conflict theory—has been highly critical of existing social arrangements, viewing social inequality as an exploitative mechanism arising out of a struggle for valued goods and services in short supply.

The Functionalist Theory of Stratification

The functionalist theory of social inequality holds that stratification exists because it is beneficial for society. All societies require a system of stratification if they are to fill all the statuses comprising the social structure and to motivate individuals to perform the duties associated with these positions. Consequently, society must motivate people at two different levels: (1) It must instill in certain individuals the desire to fill various positions, and (2) once the individuals are in these positions, it must instill in them the desire to carry out the appropriate roles. This theory was most clearly set forth in 1945 by Kingsley Davis and Wilbert Moore, although it has been subsequently modified and refined by other sociologists. Davis and Moore argued that social stratification is both universal and necessary, and hence no society is ever totally unstratified or classless.

Society must concern itself with human motivation because the duties associated with the various statuses are not all equally pleasant to the human organism, are not all equally important to social survival, and are not all equally in need of the same abilities and talents. Moreover, the duties associated with a good many positions are viewed by their occupants as onerous. Hence, in the absence of motivation, many individuals would fail to act out their roles. For example, imagine being a dentist. How likely is it that talented and intelligent people would train to become dentists—pulling teeth, working to correct extensive (and bad-smelling) decay, bending near to people's faces even when they have runny noses, coughs, and bad breath, causing people pain, anxiety, and distress—if the pay and status were not fairly high? Maintaining the dental health of our population is important to society, and so we need to motivate people to become dentists.

On the basis of these social realities, functionalists contend that a society must have (1) some kind of rewards that it can use as inducements for its members, and (2) some way of distributing these rewards among the various statuses. Inequality is the motivational incentive that society has evolved to meet the problems of filling all the statuses and getting the occupants to enact the associated roles to the best of their abilities. Since these rewards are built into the social system, social stratification is a structural feature of all societies.

Employing the economists' model of supply and demand, functionalists say that the positions most highly rewarded are those (1) that are occupied by the most talented or qualified incumbents (supply) and (2) that are functionally most important (demand). For example, to ensure sufficient physicians, a society needs to offer them high salaries and great prestige. If it did not offer these rewards, functionalists suggest that we could not expect people to undertake the "burdensome" and "expensive" process of medical education. People at the top must receive the rewards they do; if they do not, the positions would remain unfilled and society would disintegrate.

▲ Evaluation of the Functionalist Perspective

This structure-function approach to stratification has been the subject of much criticism. For one thing, the labor market does not operate freely, rewarding only those of high ability. Often jobs and positions are allocated on the basis of social connections and power (see Box 6.3). In addition, many people are born into family positions of privilege or lack of privilege, and as we saw in our discussion of social mobility, this may have a strong influence on where people end up in the stratification system (Kim, 1987).

A 1980s study showed that nearly two-thirds of the chief executives in 243 large U.S. corporations grew up in upper-middle or upper-class families. Such findings lead conflict theorists to contend that society is structured so that individuals *maintain* a ranking that is determined by birth and that is *irrespective* of their abilities, and thus that stratification is *dysfunctional* rather than functional. Melvin Tumin (1953), in his classic critique of the functional theory of stratification, argued that because access to important, highly paid occupations is

6.3 Social Inequalities

Why Do Doctors Deliver Babies?

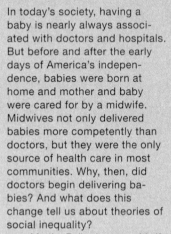

In today's society, having a baby is nearly always associated with doctors and hospitals. But before and after the early days of America's independence, babies were born at home and mother and baby were cared for by a midwife. Midwives not only delivered babies more competently than doctors, but they were the only source of health care in most communities. Why, then, did doctors begin delivering babies? And what does this change tell us about theories of social inequality?

Martha Ballard was a midwife from 1785 to 1812, a time when women, serving as midwives, provided most of the health care for most of the people in the United States. As Ballard's 27 years of record keeping show, she delivered 816 babies, treated a wide variety of illnesses, manufactured her own medicinal syrups and ointments, and prepared bodies for burial. According to historian Laurel Thatcher Ulrich, who used

Ballard's diary to write her Pulitzer prize–winning *A Midwife's Tale,* the midwife's extensive knowledge was gained not through attendance at a medical school but on the job, working with other women and by herself to care for others in her community.

Ballard observed and participated in a major change in health care in the United States—a change from reliance on midwives to employment of professionally trained—but not necessarily more competent—physicians. Her personal competitor was a young physician named Benjamin Page, who charged $6 to deliver a baby while she charged $2. Page was clearly less experienced and less capable than Ballard at delivering babies. For example, he misused the newly popular drug laudanum, a form of opium, putting one laboring woman into a stupor that stopped her labor completely. In Ballard's opinion, Page was the cause of more than one infant's death. She wrote in her diary, "Mrs Kimball . . . was delivered of a

dead daughter on the morning of the 9th instant, the operation performed by Ben Page. The infant's limbs were much dislocated as I am informed" (Ulrich, 1990:178). And again, "The wife of James Bridg was delivered this morn at 1 hour of a son. It was Born dead and is to be interd this Evening. Doctor Page was operator. Poor unfortunate man in the practice" (Ulrich, 1990:178). Yet Page persisted in offering his services.

Ulrich's description of the involvement of physicians in childbirth suggests that Martha Ballard's experience was the rule and not the exception. Records show that deaths of mothers and babies *increased* rather than decreased when physicians began routinely attending births in the 19th century. Ulrich noted that births attended by physicians also involved a much higher rate of complications than those attended by midwives and suggested that birth was being *made* more complicated by physicians' use of forceps and

not entirely determined by ability, many talented people are discouraged from moving into such positions and as a result our society functions less effectively and is less productive than it could be. Recent research by Kim A. Weeden (2002) shows that social and legal barriers around occupations such as licensing restrictions, educational requirements, associational representation, and unionization restrict the labor supply, increase demand, and thus increase salaries and wages in higher status occupations. These income-enhancing processes are

independent of functional occupational characteristics such as the complexity of an occupation's knowledge base.

Critics also point out that many of the positions of highest responsibility in the United States—in government, science, technology, and education—are not financially well rewarded (Bok, 1993). The officers of the largest U.S. corporations, for example, earn about 100 times more than the president of the United States and about 200 times more than Supreme Court justices. Critics also ask whether garbage drugs such as ergot and opiates in deliveries that a midwife would have considered routine.

Why would people employ a young, inexperienced physician? Ulrich explains his appeal: "Ben Page had certain advantages: a gentlemanly bearing, a successfully completed apprenticeship, and credit with certain younger members of the Kennebec elite" (Ulrich, 1990: 178–79). His list of patients included a judge's daughter and the wives of an attorney, a merchant, and a printer, all of whom were new to the town and, like Page, educated and ambitious. Medical sociologist Paul Starr pointed out in his history of U.S. medicine (1982) that the more educated people were, the more likely they were to accept physicians' claims of superior skill; physicians were similar to the elite in education, often shared a similar position of respect in the community, and were involved in the same social networks.

At this critical time, from the late 1700s to the 1840s, women like Martha Ballard and young women who wished to start a career in midwifery did not have the option of going to medical school and making the kind of social connections with the elite that male physicians could. In spite of women's extensive experience in medical matters during this period, male physicians were adamantly opposed to the admission of women into medical school, into the profession (Starr, 1982; Ulrich, 1990), or even into medical training specifically for midwives. The first women's medical school in the United States was not founded until 1848 (Starr, 1982). By that time men were firmly in control of the medical practice of obstetrics and the up-and-coming ambitious American citizenry had developed a strong preference for them.

The case of Martha Ballard and Benjamin Page provides a clear example of the constraints that operate in the labor market. The change from a reliance on midwifery to employment of physicians occurred not because physicians were better than midwives at what they did, but because they were men and as such were already connected to other powerful institutions, including law, education, business, and politics. Young physicians such as Benjamin Page were employed—and paid higher rates—to do something they weren't very good at. Though midwives were as competent or more competent than any physician at prenatal care and delivering babies, men had more power and better social connections and were able to drive the women out of their traditional role.

Questions for Discussion

1. Are the positions people hold and the rewards they enjoy a consequence of their abilities and contributions to society?

2. What were the primary determinants of the change from midwifery to physician-provided health care in the United States?

3. Midwife-attended births today have a 19 percent lower infant mortality rate, 33 percent lower rate of infant deaths during the first four weeks of life, and 31 percent lower risk of low-birthweight babies than physician-attended births (MacDorman and Singh, 1998). What accounts for the high rate of participation of physicians in delivering babies?

collectors, with their lower pay and prestige, are more important to the survival of the United States than top athletes who receive incomes in seven and even eight figures. Entertainers also receive disproportionately high incomes. In 2002, Ozzy Osbourne, the heavy metal rock star who stars in a reality TV program in which he uses bad language and seems seriously befuddled, earned $30 million (Brenner, 2003). "Judge Judy," a TV judge, earns $25 million a year, while Supreme Court Justice Ruth Bader Ginsburg earns $190,100 annually (Brenner, 2004). In sum, the notion that many low-paying positions are functionally less important to society than high-paying positions is often difficult to support.

The Conflict Theory of Stratification

The conflict theory of social equality holds that stratification exists because it benefits individuals and groups who have the power to dominate and exploit others. Whereas functionalists stress the common interests that members of society share, conflict theorists focus on the interests that divide people. Viewed from the conflict perspective, society is an arena in which people struggle for privilege, prestige, and power, and advantaged groups enforce their advantage through coercion (Grimes, 1991).

The conflict theory draws heavily on the ideas of Karl Marx. As discussed in Chapter 1, Marx believed that a historical perspective is essential for understanding any society. To grasp how a particular economic system works, he said that we must keep in mind the predecessor from which it evolved and the process by which it grows. For instance, under feudalism, the medieval lords were in control of the economy and dominated the serfs. Under the capitalist system, the manor lord has been replaced by the modern capitalist and the serf by the "free" laborer—in reality a propertyless worker who "has nothing to sell but his hands."

Marx contended that the capitalist drive to realize surplus value is the foundation of modern class struggle—an irreconcilable clash of interests between workers and capitalists. *Surplus value* is the difference between the value that workers create (as determined by the labortime embodied in a commodity that they produce) and the value that they receive (as determined by the subsistence level of their wages). Capitalists do not create surplus value; they appropriate it through their exploitation of workers. Consequently, as portrayed by Marx, capitalists are thieves who steal the fruits of the laborer's toil. The capitalist accumulation of capital (wealth) derives from surplus value and is the key to—indeed, the incentive for—the development of contemporary capitalism. Marx believed that the class struggle will eventually be resolved when the working class overthrows the capitalist class and establishes a new and equitable social order.

Workers may remain exploited and oppressed for a protracted period, blinded by a *false consciousness*—an incorrect assessment of how the system works and of their subjugation

For her work as a "desperate housewife" on TV, Teri Hatcher earns approximately $1.25 million a year. A real house wife engages in a significant amount of household labor and earns nothing for these efforts.

and exploitation by capitalists. But through a struggle with capitalists, the workers' "objective" class interests become translated into a subjective recognition of their "true" circumstances and they formulate goals for organized action—in brief, they acquire *class consciousness*. Hence, according to Marxists, if the working class is to take on its historical role of overturning capitalism, "it must become a class not only 'as against capital' but also 'for itself'; that is to say, the class struggle must be raised from the level of economic necessity to the level of conscious aim and effective class consciousness" (Lukacs, 1922/1968:76). It is not enough for the working class to be a "class in itself"; it must become a "class for itself."

Marxists have long argued that investigating stratification that uses dimensions such as income, education, and occupational prestige overlooks the key underlying issue in stratification: one's relations to the means of production. In an influential series of studies designed to rectify this problem, Erik Olin Wright (1985, 1993; Steinmetz and Wright, 1989) investigated class relations in the United States, using Marx's idea that class must be defined in terms of people's relation to the means of production. He identified four classes: capitalists (people who own large businesses), managers (those who manage large businesses), workers (nonmanagers employed by others), and the petite bourgeoisie (small entrepreneurs such as shop owners, restaurateurs, and real estate and insurance agents). Using samples of people in the labor force, Wright found that these categories are about as good in explaining differences in income among people as occupation and education. Even allowing for the effects on income of occupation, education, age, and job tenure, capitalists have higher incomes than the other classes. Thus, Wright concluded that being a capitalist makes a difference (Kamolnick, 1988).

▲ Evaluation of the Conflict Perspective

The emphasis on economic relations in Marx's conflict theory results in a limited view of both conflict and power. Conflict is a pervasive feature of human life and is not restricted to economic relations. Ralf Dahrendorf (1959) held that group conflict is an inevitable aspect of society that would not be eliminated by revolution as Marx had argued. The Marxist dichotomy between the capitalist class and the working class directs our attention away from other important conflicts that animate social life in modern societies. Debtor and creditor have stood against

each other throughout history, as have consumers and sellers. And divisions between racial and ethnic groups, skilled workers and unskilled laborers, and union organizations have been recurrent features of the American landscape.

Ownership of the means of production constitutes only one source of power. Control over human beings—the possession of the means of administration—provides another (Giddens, 1985), as illustrated by the communist regimes in the former Soviet Union and the nations of Eastern Europe prior to 1991. Power also flows from knowledge. More than 50 years ago, the Austrian economist Joseph A. Schumpeter (1883–1950) emphasized that knowledge, technology, and innovation are the cornerstones (more than price competition) for energizing economic life (Swedberg, 1991). For example, within contemporary American life, engineers, systems analysts, and software design specialists derive organizational and social power by virtue of their expertise. In large corporations, a good deal of power derives from office rather than ownership. But in all these examples, influence lasts only as long as officeholders stay in their positions. Their hold on power is often tenuous and they are easily replaceable. Much the same picture emerges from government. The people who actually hold and exercise power are not the owners of the means of production, and they are powerful only as long as they hold office. Marx's response to this point would be his contention that in a capitalist society the government is an administrative unit that runs the society in the service of those who own the means of production. As we will see in Chapter 9, there are a variety of positions in social science about this issue.

A Synthesis of Perspectives

Many sociologists have noted that both the functionalist and conflict theories have merit, but that each is better than the other in answering different questions (Sorokin, 1959; van den

Berghe, 1963; Milner, 1987). For example, as the functionalists have proposed, some of the distribution of rewards within the occupational structure is explained by the supply and demand factors in the labor and job markets (Kerbo, 2006). But, as conflict theorists have pointed out, the markets for labor and jobs are not free and unrestricted, and some of the inequality in outcomes can be explained by differences in power and influence across social classes.

Some sociologists have tried to synthesize the functionalist and conflict perspectives. Harold R. Kerbo (2006), for example, has argued that stratification systems are institutions that have evolved in order to reduce conflict. Without systems of stratification, there would be continuing conflict and aggression over the distribution of scarce resources. Institutionalized inequality provides at least a temporary answer to the question "who gets what and why." Kerbo bases much of his reasoning on the work of sociologist Gerhard Lenski (1966), who tried to formally integrate the functionalist and conflict perspectives. Lenski agreed with functionalists that the chief resources of society are allocated as rewards to people who occupy vital positions and that stratification fosters a rough match between scarce talents and rewards. But as a society advances in technology, it becomes capable of producing a considerable surplus of goods and services. This surplus gives rise to conflicts over who should control it. Power provides the answer to the question of control and determines the distribution of the surplus. Consequently, with technological advance an increasing proportion of the goods and services available to a society are distributed on the basis of power. In short, Lenski held that the functionalist and conflict positions provide part of the answer, but that neither contains the whole truth.

The Chapter in Brief: *Social Stratification*

Most societies are organized so that their institutions systematically distribute benefits and burdens unequally among different categories of people. Sociologists call the structured ranking of individuals and groups—their grading into horizontal layers or strata—**social stratification.**

Patterns of Social Stratification
Social stratification depends upon, but is not the same thing as, **social differentiation**—the process by which a society becomes increasingly specialized over time.

■ *Open and Closed Systems* Where people can change their status with relative ease, sociologists refer to the arrangement as an **open system.** A **closed system** is one in which people have great difficulty in changing their status.

■ *Dimensions of Stratification*
Sociologists typically take a multidimensional view of stratification, identifying three components: economic standing (**wealth and income**), **prestige,** and **power.**

The American Class System
Inequality follows relatively consistent and stable patterns that persist through time. We often refer to advantaged and disadvantaged groups in the United States as the upper class, middle class, and lower class.

■ *Is There Inequality in American Society?* Since the early 1970s income inequality in the United States has been increasing and is now at its highest level in 50 years. In 2001, the top 20 percent of the population received half of the income. Inequality in wealth is even greater.

■ *Identifying Social Classes*   Three primary methods are employed by sociologists for identifying social classes: the **objective method,** the **self-placement method,** and the **reputational method.**

■ *The Significance of Social Classes*   Social class largely determines people's **life chances** and **style of life** and influences patterns of behavior, including voting and sexual behavior.

■ *Poverty in the United States*   Children and the elderly account for nearly half of all Americans living in poverty. Three theories predominate regarding poverty: the **culture of poverty** theory, poverty as *situational,* and poverty as a *structural* feature of capitalist societies.

Social Mobility
In many societies individuals or groups can move from one level (stratum) to another in the stratification system, a process called **social mobility.**

■ *Forms of Social Mobility*   Social mobility takes a number of forms. It may be **vertical** or **horizontal** and **intergenerational** or **intragenerational.** When sociologists talk about social mobility, they usually mean intergenerational occupational mobility.

■ *Social Mobility and Status Attainment*   More Americans are upwardly mobile than downwardly mobile across generations. Sociologists study the course of an individual's occupational status over the life cycle by looking at the **socioeconomic life cycle.** Education has the greatest influence on

occupational attainment for white men. The processes of status attainment are different for women and blacks than for white males. Critics of status attainment research contend that it has a functionalist bias and that the **dual labor market** operates to sort people into **core** or **periphery** sector jobs.

■ *What Is Happening to the American Dream?*   Controversy surrounds the issue of whether the American middle class is an endangered species. Although "equal opportunity" does not apply to all Americans, depending on race, gender, and ethnicity, in real dollars most Americans are better off than their parents.

Explanations of Social Stratification
The question of why social inequality and division should characterize the human condition has provided a central focus of sociology.

■ *The Functionalist Theory of Stratification*   The functionalist theory of social inequality holds that stratification exists because it is beneficial for society. Society must concern itself with human motivation because the duties associated with the various statuses are not all equally pleasant to the human organism, important to social survival, and in need of the same abilities and talents.

■ *The Conflict Theory of Stratification* The conflict theory of social inequality holds that stratification exists because it benefits individuals and groups who have the power to dominate and exploit others. Marx contended that the capitalist drive to realize surplus value is the foundation of modern class struggle.

■ *A Synthesis of Perspectives*   Both functionalist and conflict theories have merit, but each is better than the other in answering different questions. A number of sociologists, including Gerhard E. Lenski, have looked for ways of integrating the two perspectives.

Glossary

closed system A stratification system in which people have great difficulty changing their status.

culture of poverty The view that the poor possess self-perpetuating lifeways characterized by weak ego structures, lack of impulse control, a present-time orientation, and a sense of resignation and fatalism.

dual labor market An economy characterized by two sectors. The primary, or core, sector offers "good jobs," and the secondary, or periphery, sector offers "bad jobs."

horizontal mobility Movement from one social status to another that is approximately equivalent in rank.

income The amount of money people receive.

intergenerational mobility A comparison of the social status of parents and their children at some point in their respective careers.

intragenerational mobility A comparison of the social status of a person over an extended period of time.

life chances The likelihood that individuals and groups will enjoy desired goods and services, fulfilling experiences, and opportunities for living healthy and long lives.

objective method An approach to the identification of social classes that employs such yardsticks as income, occupation, and education.

open system A stratification system in which people can change their status with relative ease.

power The ability of individuals and groups to realize their will in human affairs even if it involves the resistance of others.

prestige The social respect, admiration, and recognition associated with a particular social status.

reputational method An approach to identifying social classes that involves asking people how they classify others.

self-placement method An approach to identifying social classes that involves self-classification.

social differentiation The process by which a society becomes increasingly specialized over time.

social mobility The process in which individuals or groups move from one level (stratum) to another in the stratification system.

social stratification The structured ranking of individuals and groups; their grading into hierarchical layers or strata.

socioeconomic life cycle A sequence of stages that begins with birth into a family with a specific social status and proceeds through childhood, socialization, schooling, job seeking, occupational achievement, marriage, and the formation and functioning of a new family unit.

style of life The magnitude and manner of people's consumption of goods and services.

vertical mobility Movement of individuals from one social status to another of higher or lower rank.

wealth What people own.

Review Questions

1. What is social stratification? What are three components of it?

2. Describe the differences between open and closed systems.

3. Discuss inequality in U.S. society with regard to wealth and income.

4. How do sociologists identify social classes?

5. How many people in the United States are living in poverty? How do sociologists account for the existence of poverty?

6. What is social mobility and how does it occur?

7. How do the processes of status attainment differ for different groups of people?

8. How do the functionalist and conflict theories of stratification differ?

Internet Connection

 www.mhhe.com/hughes8

Income inequality is a persistent feature of American life. Go to the area of the U.S. Census Bureau's website that presents historical data on income inequality in U.S. society, **http://www.census.gov//hhes/income/histinc/histinctb.html.** Explore this area for information on how income inequality has changed over time in the United States. Some of this information will be more detailed than you need. Check through the tables until you come to something that clearly presents some aspect of income inequality over time. Using the data presented to inform your argument, write a short report about income inequality in the United States. Does inequality exist? How do you know? How has it changed over time?

Chapter 7

INEQUALITIES OF RACE AND ETHNICITY

Racial and Ethnic Stratification

Races
Ethnic Groups
Minority Groups

Prejudice and Discrimination

Prejudice
Discrimination
Institutional Discrimination

Patterns of Intergroup Relations: Assimilation and Pluralism

Assimilation
Pluralism

Racial and Ethnic Groups in the United States

Hispanics/Latinos
African Americans
American Indians and Alaskan Natives
Asian Americans
White Ethnics

Sociological Perspectives on Inequalities of Race and Ethnicity

The Functionalist Perspective
The Conflict Perspective
The Interactionist Perspective

The Future of Ethnic and Minority Group Relations

Intergroup Relations
Ethnicity

Box 7.1   *Doing Social Research: Teasing Out Prejudiced Beliefs*

Box 7.2   *Social Inequalities: Affirmative Action Affirmed by High Court*

Box 7.3   *Sociology Around the World: Model Minorities—Does Class or Do Values Spell Success?*

Most college students learn how to organize and present information about themselves in a résumé to show off their education, skills, and experience in the best possible light. Unfortunately, there's an essential ingredient to a cover letter and résumé that you cannot control but that can hurt your chances of getting an interview. That ingredient? Your name.

That's right, your name—and the race it suggests. Researchers (Bertrand and Mullainathan, 2003) sent 5,000 fake résumés to 1,300 employers. Half of the résumés contained names selected from a list of 20 "stereotypically black names" (Tanisha, Jamal, Lakisa), and the other half had names from a list of "stereotypically white names" (Emily, Brad, Kristen). The results? Applicants with white names averaged 1 callback for every 10 résumés, while African-American names on résumés resulted in 1 callback for every 15 resumes sent out. A white name, the researchers found, was the equivalent of an additional eight years of job experience in terms of producing callbacks. As you might expect, a "glittering" résumé (one showing that the applicant had lots of job experience and excellent qualifications) generated many more calls—but only for white names. Identical résumés with African-American names were hardly more likely to get callbacks than the average résumés. The researchers concluded that "racial discrimination is still a prominent feature of the labor market." Obviously this pattern of discrimination contributes to racial differentials in unemployment and earnings.

Didn't the U.S. Congress pass civil rights laws in the 1960s that outlawed discrimination? It did, but passing laws does not immediately translate into equal treatment for all. The U.S. Justice Department can use the 1964 Civil Rights Act to obtain injunctions that order restaurants, gas stations, theaters, hotels, and other establishments to stop discriminatory practices. Nevertheless, race and ethnicity are significant factors of life in the United States—factors that affect health, employment, income, residence, and happiness.

Sociologists are interested in race and ethnicity and the stratification that results from them. Where do race and ethnicity come from? Why and how are they associated with the distribution of society's rewards? How and why do racial and ethnic stratification change? This chapter tries to answer these questions by examining the process of racial and ethnic stratification. We will discuss prejudice and discrimination and various patterns of relationships among groups. We will describe a number of the racial and ethnic groups in the United States. Last, we will take a look at the insights the functionalist, conflict, and interactionist perspectives provide into matters of racial and ethnic inequality.

Racial and Ethnic Stratification

Societies throughout the world contain peoples with different skin colors, languages, religions, and customs. These physical and cultural traits, by providing high social visibility, serve as identifying symbols of group membership. In turn,

individuals are assigned statuses in the social structure—through a process of ascription—based on the group to which they belong (see Chapter 2). Many of the same pp. 57–58 principles we will consider in this chapter also apply to other *socially marginalized groups*—vulnerable and frequently victimized populations who typically have little economic, political, and social power, including cancer and acquired immunodeficiency syndrome (AIDS) patients, the elderly, children, and lower-level employees. In this section we will discuss races, ethnic groups, and minority groups, and the potential these groupings create for conflict and separation.

Races

Do you belong in a racial category? When the U.S. Census Bureau collected data in 2000, every U.S. resident was asked to indicate his or her race. Choices were as follows:

- White.
- Black, African American, or Negro.
- American Indian or Alaska Native.
- Asian Indian.
- Chinese.
- Filipino.
- Japanese.
- Korean.
- Vietnamese.
- Other Asian.
- Native Hawaiian.
- Guamanian or Chamorro.
- Samoan.
- Other Pacific Islander.
- Some other race (Ogunwole, 2002).

Respondents could choose as many races as were appropriate—both "Black" and "White," for example, for a respondent with parents of different races, or "Chinese," "Black," and "American Indian," if that fit the respondent.

The many different racial classification schemes employed by the U.S. Census over the past 200 years were shaped by a variety of social, political, and cultural factors (Snipp, 2003). The Census 2000 questions on racial identity reflect an increasingly diverse U.S. population and an increase in the number of multiracial citizens. But what is race? How do sociologists define it?

The concept of race frequently is used to refer to differences among groups in their physical characteristics. For example, we readily recognize that groups of Norwegians, Chinese, and Ugandans look different; people in various parts of the world differ in certain hereditary features, including the color of their skin, the texture of their hair, their facial features, their stature, and the shape of their heads.

Scientists, however, have considerable difficulty identifying races and categorizing people in terms of them (Molnar, 1997; Begley, 2003). For the most part, races are not characterized by fixed, clear-cut differences, but by fluid, continuous differences, and these differences also change considerably with time (Lee and Bean, 2004; American Anthropological Association, 1997).

Everyday racial categories used in the United States today came originally from popular ways of classifying people that emerged in Europe in the 15th and 16th centuries (Jordan, 1969) following Columbus's voyages to the New World. However, it has never been fully established that these categories have any scientific utility. Indeed, scientists are far from agreement in dividing human populations into "races" (Cooper, Kaufman, and Ward, 2003; Burchard et al., 2003). The problem is that human beings cannot easily be classified into cut-and-dried "racial" categories, and the number of features that humans everywhere share are substantially larger and of considerably greater importance than their differences.

Recent research shows that the characteristics typically used to classify people into racial categories (skin color, hair texture, and facial features) vary more across races than do genes in general (Feldman, Lewontin, and King, 2003). When researchers examine the full range of genetic data, there are fewer differences, overall, between races than within races; about 94 percent of genetic variation is within races, and less than 5 percent is between them (Rosenberg et al., 2002).

How, then, is the concept "race" useful? For sociologists race is a social construct (Davis, 1991). A **race** is a group of people who see themselves, and are seen by others, as having hereditary traits that set them apart. What interests sociologists is the social significance people attach to various traits. By virtue of individuals' social definitions, skin color or some other racialized trait becomes a sign or mark of a social status (Denton and Massey, 1989).

How do symbols of race become markers of social status that define some people as deserving and privileged and others as undeserving outsiders? According to sociologists Michael Omi and Howard Winant (1994), this happens through *racial formation,* a process by which social, economic, and political forces create and perpetuate racial categories and meanings; and racial categories, in turn, affect social, political, and economic processes and structures.

Racial formation is a process that occurs at both the micro and macro levels. At the micro level, people internalize racial identities in accord with how their society defines them. In the United States, white people develop a white identity, African Americans have a black or African-American identity, and so on. These identities are a major factor in structuring people's everyday lives in their communities, at work, in school, in church, in the family, in encounters with strangers, and in other social situations. At the macro level, race is an organizing principle that affects the nature and content of political, economic, and cultural activities, organizations, and institutions. This occurs in part because of the internalized racial identies of the people who make up these institutions, identities that affect the processes and outcomes of these institutions and are reinforced by such processes and outcomes.

In Omi and Winant's theory, race is socially and culturally defined and is thus not a significant biological reality. But that does not mean that race is a mere illusion. Consistent with the Thomas Theorem (Chapter 3), because race is defined as real, it is real in its consequences. These consequences significantly affect how people define themselves, how they interact with others, how they form political and economic alliances, and how they organize their everyday lives and communities. And because racialized social statuses are typically unequal, people experience unequal outcomes in society because of their race.

▲ Race, Ability, and Culture

It has been common throughout history for people to believe that race is associated with personality, moral character, competency, intelligence, and other characteristics. Prominent among recent claims of this kind is the widely publicized study *The Bell Curve* (Herrnstein and Murray, 1994) that included the argument that racial groups differ in intelligence. The consensus in the scientific community today, however, is that the biological factors that presumably underlie race do not cause race differences in intelligence (Fischer et al., 1996; Jencks and Phillips, 1998; Arrow, Bowles, and Durlauf, 2000), and that claims such as those of Herrnstein and Murray ignore the important impact that environmental conditions have on the measurement of intelligence.

For example, research shows that among African Americans, European ancestry, as measured by skin color or by blood type, has no association with measures of intelligence. This is not the finding we would expect if biological factors linked to race were causally linked to

intelligence (Nisbett, 1998). In addition, research in Western societies over the past 50 years shows substantial increases in scores on intelligence tests that are much larger than can be explained by genetic change. This finding indicates that environmental factors, particularly culture, can exercise a strong influence on group differences in measured intelligence (Flynn, 2000).

▲ Racism

An important concept based on race is **racism.** Racism exists at two levels, individual and institutional. At the *individual level,* racism is the belief that some racial groups are naturally superior and others are inferior. Individual racism depends on two ideas that have been discredited in contemporary scholarship: (1) that people may be reliably classified into biologically meaningful racial groups (Rosenberg et al., 2002; Feldman, Lewontin, and King, 2003) and (2) that these groups are inherently different in regard to ability, character, intelligence, social behavior, and culture (Block and Dworkin, 1976; Fischer et al., 1996; Nisbett, 1998). Generally, this form of racism gives rise to attitudes of aversion and hostility toward others based on their race. We discuss this below in the section on prejudice.

At the *institutional level,* racism involves discriminatory policies and practices that result in unequal outcomes for members of different racial groups. We discuss this below in the section on discrimination. While individual racism exists in people's beliefs and attitudes, institutional racism is imbedded in the social structure and may operate independently of individual racism.

Ethnic Groups

Groups that we identify chiefly on cultural grounds—language, folk practices, dress, gestures, mannerisms, or religion—are called **ethnic groups.** Within the United States, Jewish Americans, Italian Americans, and Hispanics are examples of ethnic groups. The ethnicity choices for the Census 2000 were "Hispanic or Latino" and "Not Hispanic or Latino," along with Mexican, Chicano, Puerto Rican, Cuban, and others, which respondents were to select in addition to their race(s) selections.

Ethnic groups often have a sense of peoplehood, and to some degree many of them deem themselves to be a nation (Marger, 2006; Stack, 1986). In addition, ethnic groups have a sense of shared history and shared fate that can draw people together into a powerful social unit.

Ethnic identities often are "constructed" by their bearers. For instance, an Asian-American consciousness has arisen among many disparate Asian nationality groups in the United States (Espiritu, 1992). The new identity arose in part as a response to political expediency. Political mobilization also has contributed to a supratribal identity among many Native Americans (Nagel, 1994).

Minority Groups

Within the United States, African Americans, Hispanics, American Indians and Native Alaskans, Asian Americans, and Jews have been the victims of prejudice and discrimination. They are said to be members of minority groups.

Sociologists commonly distinguish five properties as characteristic of minority groups (Wagley and Harris, 1964; Vander Zanden, 1983):

1. A minority is a social group whose members experience discrimination, segregation, oppression, or persecution at the hands of another social group, the *dominant group,* and lack access to the power necessary to change their situation.

2. A minority is characterized by physical or cultural traits that distinguish it from the dominant group.

3. A minority is a self-conscious social group characterized by a consciousness of oneness.

For sociologists, race is a social construct, not a set of biological traits. Gregory Howard Williams, whose father was half black, grew up thinking he was white and being treated by others as if he were white. In his book Life on the Color Line *(1995), he describes what happened when he, his schoolmates, and others in the community learned of his father's background: overnight, he became black.*

Its members possess a social and psychological affinity with others like themselves, providing a sense of *identity.*

4. Membership in a minority group is generally not voluntary. It is often an ascribed position because an individual is commonly born into the status.

5. The members of a minority, by choice or necessity, often marry within their own group (endogamy).

We may define a **minority group** as a racially or culturally self-conscious population, with hereditary membership and a high degree of in-group marriage, that suffers oppression at the hands of a dominant group (Williams, 1964). The critical characteristic that distinguishes minority groups from other groups is that they lack power.

Although some sociologists have limited the concept minority group to groups that have hereditary membership, such as ethnic groups, the concept has wide applicability to the situation of any social category that is singled out by a dominant group for unequal treatment by virtue of presumed physical or cultural differences. In a now classic article, Helen Mayer Hacker (1951, 1974) argued that women were a minority group and had many of the same minority characteristics as African ← p. 251 Americans (see Chapter 8). Gay men and lesbians similarly share a minority status in contemporary society, as do others whose sexual orientations differ from what is conventional and traditional in American society.

Prejudice and Discrimination

Prejudice and discrimination are so prevalent in contemporary life, so much a part of the racial and ethnic stratification that exists in the United States, that we often assume they are merely part of human nature. Yet this view ignores the enormous variation among individuals and societies in levels of prejudice and discrimination. Even in Hitler's Germany, where large numbers of Germans supported and participated in the Nazi Holocaust (Goldhagen, 1996), some "Aryans" opposed anti-Semitism and helped Jews escape. And whereas Asians have found acceptance in Hawaii and have prospered there, on the West Coast and in British Columbia they have had a long history of persecution (Glick, 1980). Similarly, whites held a positive image of blacks in the ancient world, a situation very different from recent history (Snowden, 1983). Even during the civil rights movement in the United States, individuals varied in levels of prejudice.

Some southern whites had progressive racial attitudes and supported the African-American struggle for equality (e.g., Durr, 1985).

In this section we will define and discuss prejudice and discrimination and consider institutional discrimination.

Prejudice

Prejudice refers to attitudes of aversion and hostility toward the members of a group simply because they belong to it and hence are presumed to have the objectionable qualities ascribed to it (Allport, 1954; Devine, 1989). As such, prejudice is a subjective phenomenon—a state of mind. Racial prejudices generally have three components: (1) a cognitive component that provides a description of members of the target group, often including negative stereotypes such as "lazy," "thoughtless," "criminal," or "unfeeling"; (2) an affective component that involves negative reactions and emotional feelings about the group; and (3) a behavioral component that may include the tendency to discriminate or behave negatively toward members of the group.

Why are people prejudiced toward members of other groups? Social scientists in the United States have been studying this issue for more than 75 years and have come up with two kinds of explanations, one emphasizing social psychological processes and the other emphasizing social structure.

▲ Social Psychology

Social psychological theories argue that social interaction can produce prejudices in individuals. In frustration-aggression theory, prejudice is a form of scapegoating that results from displaced aggression. For example, members of the dominant group may blame immigrants or minority groups when the economy is in decline. Authoritarian personality theory argues that the tendency to be prejudiced emerges out of overly strict child-rearing practices that result in people valuing obedience to authority and desiring to dominate others. There is some value in these theories, but neither provides a satisfactory explanation of the prejudice we observe in society. Frustration-aggression theory cannot explain why ethnic minority groups are chosen as targets of prejudice (Marger, 2006). And prejudice is often so widespread and pervasive that it could not be entirely due to the existence of persons who have authoritarian personalities.

Socialization theories of prejudice argue that prejudiced attitudes are part of the culture people internalize during socialization by parents, friends, and associates in the community, whose messages are reinforced by educational experiences and stereotypes presented in media. Socialization theory can explain widespread prejudice that is learned and supported by the cultural environment. But it cannot fully explain how and why prejudice can change form and continue to exist when important agents of socialization such as major media outlets and the education system produce messages that oppose prejudice and bigotry.

▲ Social Structure

Social structural theories, in contrast, argue that prejudice is a cultural mechanism emerging out of competition and conflict between groups, and that it can be an important factor enabling a single group to achieve and maintain dominance. In the view of realistic group-conflict theory (Campbell, 1965; Bobo, 1983; Sears et al., 2000), when the interests of groups coincide, intergroup attitudes will be relatively positive. However, if the interests of groups diverge, as is the case when groups compete for scarce resources such as land, jobs, or power, negative prejudicial attitudes will result.

In his now classic "sense of group position" theory, Blumer (1958) argued the prejudice flows from people's perceptions of the position of their group relative to other groups. Actual competition for scarce resources is not essential. Prejudice by a dominant group is the result of (1) a sense that they are superior to members of the minority group; (2) a feeling that minority members are different and alien;

(3) a sense that dominant group members have a proprietary claim to privilege, power, and prestige; and (4) a fear and suspicion that members of the minority have designs on dominant group benefits.

Social structural theories of prejudice predict that as the positions of groups change in society, the content of prejudices will change also, reflecting the new structural reality. Prejudice researchers have observed such a pattern in recent years. Though white prejudice against African Americans was strong throughout most of U.S. history, rooted in the structures of slavery and Jim Crow racism (Jordan, 1968), traditional forms of prejudice declined dramatically following the social changes brought about by the 1960s civil rights movement. Whites now are much less likely to believe that blacks are biologically inferior (but see Box 7.1), are less likely to support racial segregation, and are more likely to support the principle of racial equality than in the past (Schuman et al., 1997; Firebaugh and Davis, 1988).

▲ Symbolic Racism

As traditional racial prejudice declined, new forms of prejudice emerged. This new complex of attitudes is termed **symbolic racism** (Kinder and Sears, 1981), modern racism (McConahay, 1986), or racial resentment (Kinder and Sanders, 1996) by various researchers, and it has been increasing in recent years (Valentino and Sears, 2005). It stereotypes African Americans as people who do not share the American work ethic, who would rather be on welfare than work, who would be as well off as whites if they would "try harder," and who have recently been "getting more than they deserve." According to group conflict and group position theories, symbolic racism is a reflection of whites' concern that further reductions in racial inequality will result in loss of the special status that whites in the United States have enjoyed over the years (Bobo, 1983; Bobo and Kluegel, 1993; Hughes, 1997). Evidence in support of this comes from research showing that even as

7.1 Doing Social Research

Teasing Out Prejudiced Beliefs

In 1957, white people in Little Rock, Arkansas, had to be restrained by soldiers to keep them from attacking the first nine black children to attend a white high school in accordance with the Supreme Court's desegregation ruling. Two years before that, Emmett Till, a 14-year-old African-American boy, was murdered—beaten, shot, and thrown into a river in Mississippi—by white men who were angry that he had whistled at a white woman.

We have come a long way in only 50 years. African-American students are as likely as white students to finish high school and go on to college—often at integrated schools—and close to a fifth of all blacks over the age of 25 have a college degree. Most whites now agree with the principles of racial equality, and only 1 in 10 whites admit to disapproving of interracial marriage (Davis, Smith, and Marsden, 2003).

Yet prejudice and discrimination continue; African Americans are still underrepresented in the professional workforce and as graduates of colleges and universities. And some of what we might call "old-fashioned racism" still exists. Over the years survey researchers have asked respondents if they thought blacks were as intelligent as white people, or whether the black–white gap in income and high-status jobs was due to a lack of in-born learning ability among blacks. Since the

1940s the percent of whites reporting a belief in black intellectual deficiency has dropped from more than half (and more than 70 percent in the South) to 13 percent in 1994 (17 percent in the South) (Schuman et al., 1997). But when whites were given a chance to separately *rate* the intelligence of blacks and of whites, an interesting finding emerges: 46.6 percent of whites rate their own group as more intelligent than blacks (analysis by authors using data in Davis, Smith, and Marsden, 2003).

What accounts for these findings? First, it is possible that when whites respond to surveys they engage in what Erving Goffman called "impression management" (see pp. 85–86 in Chapter 3)—when asked whether whites are more intelligent than blacks, they respond no because they think it is the socially acceptable answer. A more accurate reflection of their beliefs—that whites are more intelligent—emerges when they are asked the two questions separately. This interpretation of the findings indicates whites are more prejudiced than many thought, but it also indicates significant cultural change; nearly 50 years ago the whites jeering at the nine young blacks entering Central High School didn't care whether the whole world knew that they believed in black inferiority. We now live in a culture in which it is socially unacceptable to voice

such opinions (Schuman et al., 1997).

Second, whites may not realize that they are prejudiced. They may actually believe, when asked specifically, that whites are not more intelligent than blacks. Asking the two questions separately may bring unconsciously held prejudices to light.

Third, whites may rate groups differently on the two intelligence questions because they interpret the questions as meaning intelligence-as-related-to-education; that is, they may be considering that most minority groups have much more limited educational opportunities than whites. When they rate African Americans as less intelligent than whites, they may actually be rating abilities developed through education rather than native intelligence.

Whatever the explanation, it is important to remember that a simple shift in questioning procedure and wording can result in a very different pattern of response.

Questions for Discussion

1. Do you think people who respond to surveys on racial attitudes tell the truth? What motivates people to respond the way they do?

2. Do people in minority groups have prejudices about whites? If so, what are they? How would you structure survey items to answer this question?

whites' support for the *principle* of racial equality has increased, support for policies that would effectively reduce racial inequality has not changed appreciably (Schuman et al., 1997).

Symbolic racism and similar attitudes are now the prime determinants of whites' racial policy attitudes (Kinder and Sanders, 1996; Tuch and Hughes, 1996; Hughes, 1997).

Discrimination

We have said that prejudice is an attitude or a state of mind. **Discrimination** is action. Discrimination is a process in which members of one or more groups or categories in society are denied the privileges, prestige, power, legal rights, equal protection of the law, and other societal benefits that are available to members of other groups. Discrimination is a form of racism when those discriminated against are a racial minority. As traditional prejudice toward blacks has shifted to symbolic racism, so has discrimination changed in its nature. Since the end of World War II in 1945, whites have shifted from more blatant forms of discrimination to more subtle forms (Bobo, Kluegel, and Smith, 1997; Kinder and Sanders, 1996; Lipset, 1987; Sears, Sidanius, and Bobo, 2000).

Prejudice does not necessarily coincide with discrimination—a one-to-one relationship does not inevitably hold between attitudes and overt actions. While we expect prejudiced people to discriminate, and unprejudiced persons not to, sociologist Robert K. Merton (1968) pointed out that two other outcomes are possible and exist because of different social pressures: unprejudiced people who discriminate and prejudiced people who do not.

Merton points out that organizational policy and climate and the law strongly influence people to behave in ways that are inconsistent with their attitudes. Discrimination, therefore, is not entirely dependent on individual attitudes. In the United States individual attitudes have been liberalized over the past few decades, but social pressures remain that perpetuate discrimination. One way this can happen is through institutional discrimination.

Institutional Discrimination

The institutions of society may function in such a way that they produce unequal outcomes for different groups. This is called **institutional discrimination,** or *institutional racism* if the disadvantaged group is a racial minority. Businesses, schools, hospitals, and other key institutions need not be staffed by prejudiced individuals in order for discrimination to occur (Carmichael and Hamilton, 1967). For example, employers often specify the qualifications candidates must have to be considered for particular jobs. Usually the qualifications have to do with prior job-related experience and some measure of formal education. The standards

"Well, it all depends. Where are these huddled masses coming from?"

7.2 Social Inequalities

Affirmative Action Affirmed by High Court

Davin Fischer sensed he had been given a special break when Georgetown University admitted him two years ago. His high school record was strong but perhaps not as stellar as those of some of his future classmates, a fact that sat uneasily with him in the months before he came to campus. *(Argetsinger, 2003:A6)*

Why was Fischer admitted if his grades weren't as good as some of the other applicants? Because colleges and universities do not consider only grades and test scores in making admissions decisions. Fischer's admission could have been affected by any of a number of factors colleges and universities review—his athletic skills, his musical ability, his hometown, his admissions essay, or his parents' race, ethnicity, or income. The factor that gave Davin Fischer an edge over students with better high school grades and standardized test scores was that his father had graduated from Georgetown.

"Legacy" applicants, as they are called, have a significantly higher probability of gaining admission at many schools. Children of graduates are about twice as likely as the average applicant to be admitted at Georgetown and at the University of Virginia and three times more likely to get into Harvard (Argetsinger, 2003). If you had better grades than Davin Fischer and didn't get into Georgetown, would you feel cheated?

Although it receives less weight than legacy in the admissions procedures at many schools, the factor that gets most press attention and is most controversial is race. Should colleges and universities be allowed to consider the race of applicants in making admissions decisions? If schools give preference to African American or other minority students simply because they are not white, are white students being discriminated against? Those are the affirmative action questions U.S. Supreme Court justices were asked to consider in 2003, when suits against the

University of Michigan law school and its undergraduate program were brought to the country's highest court.

Before we discuss the case, let's review the basics. What is "affirmative action"? Affirmative action is not a term for one specific action or policy; rather, it is a family of policies aimed at resolving racial, ethnic, and gender inequalities in the United States. The term stems from a speech made by President Lyndon Johnson in the 1960s in which he declared that it was not enough to remove barriers from minority groups; the nation also needed to take *affirmative action* to promote the inclusion of all races and ethnicities in society (Harper and Peskin, 2005).

The original affirmative actions planned by federal and state governments included four general categories. The first of these was opportunity enhancement, which included programs aimed at encouraging people of a diversity of backgrounds to apply for jobs or admission to schools. The second category included

appear nondiscriminatory because they apply to all individuals regardless of race, creed, or color. But the result of applying such "color-blind" employment standards often is to bar entry into the work world for particular racial or ethnic groups whose members have lacked opportunities for education and work experience.

African Americans have been particularly victimized by institutional racism. Research on resumes and callbacks (discussed at the beginning of this chapter), on job applications (presented in

Box 5.3), and on other steps to employment provide evidence: At each point along the road toward building a satisfying career African Americans must overcome greater obstacles than those encountered by whites (Pager, 2005; Bertrand and Mullainathan, 2003; Braddock and McPartland, 1987). Moreover, the handicaps associated with poverty—an absence of skills, inadequate education, and low job seniority—tend to perpetuate the very low status position that produces them (Wilson, 1987, 1996).

goals and timetables; federal contractors and recipients of federal aid were required to lay out their plans for including people from underrepresented categories, such as minorities and women. Third were plans for giving preferences to minorities in licenses and contracts, and lastly were quota and preferences programs for admissions and employment.

Do we need affirmative action? Why not just ban practices and policies that discriminate against job and school applicants on the basis of race, ethnicity, or gender? Physician Jordan Cohen sums it up well in a discussion about the importance of affirmative action for medical school admissions:

> Although the civil rights movement of the late 1960s and early 1970s succeeded in outlawing the overt barriers that restricted minority enrollment in medical schools, the legacy of centuries of racial discrimination persisted. High rates of poverty, lack of access to educational opportunities, lower educational achievement among family members, as well as other factors conspired to limit significantly the number of underrepresented minority students who chose to apply to medical school. (2003:1145)

Until students from all racial and ethnic backgrounds have an "equivalent range" of academic credentials, he says, it will not be possible to create medical school classes that reflect society's diversity without considering race and ethnicity in admissions decisions.

Let's get back to the Supreme Court case. Although the justices voted against the use of a racial point system by the University of Michigan's undergraduate program and thus confirmed the illegality of quota programs, they preserved the concept of affirmative action and upheld the consideration of race in admissions. Justice Sandra Day O'Connor wrote the majority opinion, stating, "In order to cultivate a set of leaders with legitimacy in the eyes of the citizenry, it is necessary that the path to leadership be visibly open to talented and qualified individuals of every race and ethnicity" (Greenhouse, 2003). As in the last affirmative action case heard by the Supreme Court, in 1978, it was ruled that race can be one of a number of important factors—but not the only determining factor—in admissions policies.

Despite affirmative action's reputation for controversy, the Michigan case generated lots of support from leaders across the country. On the side of the university's use of race as an admissions factor were Harvard, Stanford, and Columbia Universities; General Motors and several dozen Fortune 500 companies; the American Bar Association; labor unions; and high-ranking military officers (Lane, 2003b). And by the way—remember Davin Fischer, whose chances of being admitted were doubled by virtue of being the offspring of a Georgetown alum? Being black would have improved his chances only by seven percentage points.

Questions for Discussion

1. Visit the admissions office of your college or university and ask for information on the factors that are used to make admission decisions. What are the factors? How important is each factor in admissions decisions? What goals do these policies serve at your institution? Are the policies fair and effective? Explain.

2. Why might a medical school want its student body to "reflect society's diversity"?

In brief, equality of opportunity, even if realized in American life, does not necessarily produce equality of outcome. Consequently, African Americans and many other minorities have concerned themselves not merely with removing the barriers to full opportunity but with achieving the fact of *equality of outcome*—parity in family income, housing, and the other necessities for keeping families strong and healthy. It has been this sentiment that has propelled proponents of affirmative action, still a controversial issue (see Box 7.2).

One mechanism by which institutional discrimination is maintained is **gatekeeping**—the decision-making process whereby people are admitted to offices and positions of privilege, prestige, and power within a society. Generally gatekeepers are professionals with experience and credentials in the fields they monitor—for example, individuals in personnel, school admission, and counseling offices. Although in theory gatekeepers assess candidates on the basis of merit, skills, and talents—and not in terms of race, ethnicity, class, family, or religion—their decisions have been biased (Pettigrew and Martin, 1987; Chase and Bell, 1990; Farkas et al., 1990; Karen, 1990). As we noted at the beginning of the chapter, just having a "black" name is a disadvantage in applying for a job (Bertrand and Mullainathan, 2003).

Another aspect of institutional discrimination is that merit, skills, and talent are relative matters. Which group's *values* will be used for judging who is "capable," "bright," "conscientious," and "resourceful"? Historically, gatekeepers have been white and male, and they have selected candidates who have resembled themselves in family patterns, dress, hairstyle, personal behavior, and the ownership and use of property.

Another mechanism of institutional discrimination is called **environmental racism**— the practice of locating incinerators and other types of hazardous waste facilities in or next to minority communities. One researcher found that 21 of Houston's 25 legally operating incinerators, mini-incinerators, and landfills were in predominantly African-American neighborhoods (Horowitz, 1994).

Patterns of Intergroup Relations: Assimilation and Pluralism

In multiethnic societies, ethnic groups may either lose their distinctiveness through a process of *assimilation* or retain their identity and integrity through *pluralism*. In this section we will examine these two patterns of intergroup relations.

Assimilation

In the early 1800s two major ethnic groups in the United States were the Germans and the Dutch. Today neither group is important in ethnic group dynamics in this country. Why? These groups and others from northwestern Europe assimilated, along with the British, into what we now think of as the white population. **Assimilation** refers to those processes whereby groups with distinctive identities become culturally and socially fused. Within the United States two views toward assimilation have dominated. One—the "melting pot" tradition—has seen assimilation as a process whereby peoples and cultures would produce a new people and a new civilization. The other—the Anglo-conformity view—has viewed American culture as an essentially finished product on the Anglo-Saxon pattern, and has insisted that immigrants promptly give up their cultural traits for those of the dominant American group. Governments in the United States have often favored the latter view through policies that provide English-only government services and education that promotes dominant group values and language (Marger, 2006).

Assimilation is a complex process in which cultural changes precede widespread structural change. Members of different groups within a single society must share some cultural elements in order to communicate and carry on ordinary interaction. When cultural elements of one group change in the direction of another group, we call this cultural assimilation, or *acculturation*.

Most cultural assimilation involves cultural traits of the dominant group being taken on by less powerful groups. For example, Africans brought to the American South to be slaves learned the language and religion of the slave masters. But acculturation is to some degree always a two-way street. American popular music forms such as blues, jazz, gospel, and rock have strong roots in African music. American English reflects a German influence through words such as "gesundheit" and "kindergarten" and a Dutch influence through sailing terms such as "skipper" and in the use of "cookie" instead of the English "biscuit."

Cultural assimilation makes more extensive social relations among groups possible. When members of different ethnic groups participate with one another in the major institutional structures of society, this is structural assimilation, commonly referred to as *integration*. Typically, structural assimilation occurs first in secondary groups—at work and at school, for example. Only after there has been a considerable breakdown of ethnic group barriers does structural assimilation routinely occur at the primary group level—clubs, cliques, neighborhood relations, and close friendships. According to Milton Gordon's (1964) theory, once structural assimilation occurs, routine marriage across ethnic group boundaries (marital assimilation) and the sharing of a single ethnic identity (identificational assimilation) are natural consequences. Eventually social participation, cultural sharing, and intermarriage may occur to such an extent that it is impossible to distinguish the ethnic groups that were formerly distinct within a society. This is the final stage of assimilation, *amalgamation*.

Pluralism

Recent immigrants to the United States appear to be largely assimilating into American society in terms of socioeconomic status, residence, language, and intermarriage (Waters and Jimenez, 2005). However, ethnic groups do not always completely assimilate into a dominant society or into one another. In fact, racial and ethnic groups have the *potential* for carving out their own independent nation from the existing state. Political separatism may offer racial and ethnic groups a solution that is not available to other disadvantaged categories. Examples abound in the contemporary world of separatist movements, including the French Canadians in Canada, the Palestinians in Israel, the Irish Catholics of Northern Ireland, the various Muslim and Christian factions in Lebanon, and the Sikhs in India's Punjab.

However, this is not the path taken by mainstream ethnic movements in the United States. American Jews, African Americans, Chinese Americans, and numerous other groups have assimilated in some important ways but also have retained their identities and significant degrees of distinctiveness for many years. This is an example of **pluralism,** a situation in which diverse groups coexist and boundaries between them are maintained.

Pluralism may be perpetuated because minority groups do not wish to be assimilated, valuing their separate identities and customs. Such groups generally favor what Marger (2006) called *equalitarian pluralism;* cultural identity and group boundaries are maintained, but ethnic group members participate freely and equally in political and economic institutions. Equalitarian pluralism is the goal of many American minority groups that are now culturally distinctive but economically and politically disadvantaged. Switzerland provides a good example of cultural pluralism. It comprises several ethnic groups, including French, Germans, and Italians, each maintaining its own language, and the government operates with several "official" languages.

Pluralism also may be promoted by dominant groups who wish to maintain their power and privilege by controlling the participation of minority groups in society. This is *inequalitarian pluralism;* ethnic group distinctiveness is maintained but economic and political participation of minority groups is severely limited by the dominant group. The caste system of racial segregation in the southern United States before the 1960s is a good example of inequalitarian pluralism.

Government policy may heavily influence the course that pluralism takes. Equalitarian pluralism is fostered and encouraged through the legal protection of minorities. For example, Canada's bilingual policies, in allowing the Province of Quebec to declare French the official language in government, commerce, and education, help to prevent total assimilation of French Canadians into a Canada that is dominated by the English-speaking population.

Because minority groups invariably disfavor inequalitarian pluralism, government policy is generally required to maintain it. This may be done by preventing minority populations from contact with the majority. The U.S. government's Indian Removal Act of 1830, which resulted in the forcible removal of virtually all Native Americans from the southeastern states to

Multicultural programs, which promote pluralism, have proliferated on campuses across the United States in response to the increasing diversity of the college student population.

land west of the Mississippi in the 1830s and 1840s, serves as an example. Governments also may promote the continued subjugation of minority groups through "internal colonialism." For example, before the fall of white power in South Africa, whites maintained *apartheid* arrangements that allowed for the political and economic subjugation of blacks and other non-Europeans. Inequalitarian policies are at their most extreme when they entail the expulsion or extermination of minorities. History abounds with examples of **genocide**—the deliberate and systematic extermination of a racial or ethnic group.

Racial and Ethnic Groups in the United States

We have defined races and ethnic groups and considered the nature of minority groups and the potential for conflict and separation. We have discussed prejudice, discrimination, and institutional discrimination. Here we will take a closer look at the circumstances of a number of groups within the United States to see the effects of racial and ethnic stratification.

The United States is in transition from a predominately white society rooted in Western European culture to a global society composed of diverse racial and ethnic groups. While 69 percent of the U.S. population was non-Hispanic white in 2002 (McKinnon, 2003), by the year 2050, according to Census Bureau projections, today's minorities will comprise nearly 50 percent of the U.S. population (U.S. Census Bureau, 2004a; Figure 7.1). In some regions of the country the nonwhite population exceeds the white population today. Los Angeles, for example, is 42 percent white, and El Paso and San Antonio are 74 and 53 percent Hispanic (U.S. Census Bureau, 1999). Hispanic Americans are expected to grow to 24 percent of the population in 2050 (U.S.

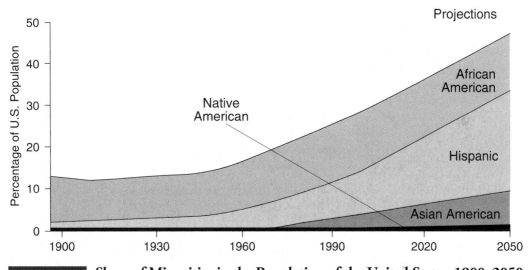

Projections

Figure 7.1 Share of Minorities in the Population of the United States, 1900–2050

The figures for future years represent population projections by the U.S. Census Bureau.

Source: Adapted from William P. O'Hare, "America's Minorities—The Demographics of Diversity," *Population Bulletin,* Vol. 47, No. 4, 1992, figure 1, p. 9. Reprinted by permission of Population Reference Bureau, Inc. Data added from U.S. Census Bureau, 2004.

Census Bureau, 2004). The Asian-American population is expected to grow to 8 percent of the total population by midcentury. The African-American population is projected to grow to nearly 15 percent in 2050. Native Americans will remain below 1 percent but are expected to increase from 0.7 to 0.9 percent (U.S. Census Bureau, 1999).

In this section we will look more closely at the circumstances of Hispanics/Latinos, African Americans, Native Americans, Asian Americans, and white ethnics.

Hispanics/Latinos

In 2002, those who were born in or whose ancestors were born in Latin American nations or in Spain became the largest ethnic minority group in the United States; more than one-eighth of the U.S. population is now Hispanic, or as some prefer, Latino (Ramirez and de la Cruz, 2002).

How to refer to this group is controversial. Some claim that the term *Hispanic,* adopted by

the Census Bureau years ago for the purpose of collecting data, is offensive because it was applied by a dominant group to a minority group, and its use is forbidden by some television stations (Granados, 2000). People descended from Spanish-speaking ancestors may prefer to identify themselves as "Latino" (or "Latina," for females), by their own specific ethnic group, or as just plain American. But a poll of 1,200 Hispanic/Latino registered voters showed that 65 percent preferred the term *Hispanic;* similar results were found in disparate regions of the country (Granados, 2000). Which term is more inclusive also is contested: Some claim that "Latino" excludes some of the people who can be called "Hispanic" and others maintain the opposite. The Census Bureau is now using the terms *Hispanic* and *Latino* interchangeably (Ramirez and de la Cruz, 2002), as we will in this section.

While there has been some blurring of differences among some Hispanic origin groups,

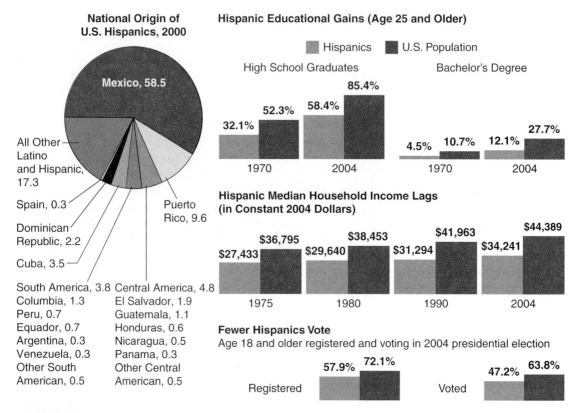

National Origin of U.S. Hispanics, 2000

Mexico, 58.5

All Other Latino and Hispanic, 17.3

Spain, 0.3

Dominican Republic, 2.2

Cuba, 3.5

Puerto Rico, 9.6

South America, 3.8
Columbia, 1.3
Peru, 0.7
Equador, 0.7
Argentina, 0.3
Venezuela, 0.3
Other South American, 0.5

Central America, 4.8
El Salvador, 1.9
Guatemala, 1.1
Honduras, 0.6
Nicaragua, 0.5
Panama, 0.3
Other Central American, 0.5

Hispanic Educational Gains (Age 25 and Older)

■ Hispanics   ■ U.S. Population

High School Graduates

32.1%   52.3%   58.4%   85.4%
1970   2004

Bachelor's Degree

4.5%   10.7%   12.1%   27.7%
1970   2004

Hispanic Median Household Income Lags (in Constant 2004 Dollars)

$27,433 $36,795
1975

$29,640 $38,453
1980

$31,294 $41,963
1990

$34,241 $44,389
2004

Fewer Hispanics Vote
Age 18 and older registered and voting in 2004 presidential election

57.9%   72.1%
Registered

47.2%   63.8%
Voted

Figure 7.2 Hispanics/Latinos in the United States

Mexican Americans constitute by far the largest Hispanic group in the United States. Hispanics lag behind the general population in education, income, and voting behavior.

Source: Data on national origin from Gurman (2001), available at http://www.census.gov/prod/2001pubs/c2kbr01-3.pdf. Data on education from the U.S. Census Bureau, March Current Population Surveys, available at http://www.census.gov/population/socdemo/education/tabA-2.pdf. Income data from DeNavas-Walt, Proctor, and Lee, 2005. Voting data from Holder, 2006, available at http://www.census.gov/prod/2006pubs/p20-556.pdf.

making many Hispanic Americans more conscious of themselves as a homogeneous group, the Census Bureau provides data on four distinct categories: Mexicans, Puerto Ricans, Cubans, and Central and South Americans (see Figure 7.2).

The 40.4 million Hispanics living in the United States in 2004 represents a substantial increase from the 14.6 million recorded in 1980 and 22.4 million in 1990 (U.S. Census Bureau, 1996, 1999, http://www.census.gov/population/www/socdemo/hispanic/cps2004.html). Between 2000

and 2002, Latinos accounted for half of the population increase for the entire country, with more than 50 percent of the Latino increase attributed to international migration (Ramirez and de la Cruz, 2002). Just over 40 percent of the Hispanic population in 2004 was foreign born (http://www.census.gov/population/ www/socdemo/hispanic/cps2004.html).

Latinos now account for nearly half of the foreign-born population in the United States, up from only 9 percent in 1960; Mexico alone accounts for nearly one-third of the foreign-born population (http://www.census.gov/population/www/socdemo/hispanic/cps2004.html). Although foreign-born Hispanics may be found anywhere, their populations are concentrated in just a few areas. For example, half of the Mexico-born population lives in Los Angeles, Chicago, and Texas, and 75 percent of the Caribbean-born population lives in New York and Miami (U.S. Census Bureau, 2000b). In some cities, particularly in California, New Mexico, Florida, and Texas, the population is between 37 percent and 74 percent Hispanic. Similarly, foreign-born and native Latinos in the United States are concentrated in specific areas of the country, with 54.6 percent of Mexican Americans living in the West, 75 percent of Cubans living in the South, and 58 percent of Puerto Ricans living in the Northeast (Ramirez and de la Cruz, 2002). About a quarter of the Latino foreign-born population have become naturalized citizens, although the proportion is different for different groups; 41 percent of the Caribbean-born and 15 percent of the Mexico-born population are naturalized citizens (U.S. Census Bureau, 2000b).

The tenuous status of many Hispanic immigrants in the United States has given rise to an immigrant' rights movement and contributed to this massive 2006 demonstration.

▲ Education and Employment

As might be expected for recent immigrants in any country, Latinos lag behind the rest of the country in terms of education, employment, and income. Among Hispanics age 25 and older, only 12.1 percent had completed college in 2004, compared with 30.6 percent of non-Hispanic whites and 17.6 percent of African Americans (http://www.census.gov/population/socdemo/education/tabA-2.pdf). Fewer than half of foreign-born Latinos in the United States have a high school education or higher (U.S. Census Bureau, 2000b), compared with 57 percent of the combined native and foreign-born population (Ramirez and de la Cruz, 2002). Educational credentials vary greatly among ethnic groups, with 76.1 percent of the South America–born population and only 45.8 percent of the Mexico-born population having at least a high school education (Ramirez, 2004).

The education disadvantage extends to employment and income, as well. For the foreign-born Hispanic population, more than half of every ethnic group—and as many as 83 percent, for Mexico-born—are employed as service and skilled workers and farm and other manual laborers (U.S. Census Bureau, 2000b). Even with the native Latino population added in, only 14.2 percent of Hispanics are employed in managerial or professional occupations, compared to 35.1 percent of non-Hispanic whites (Ramirez and de la Cruz, 2002). In 2001, 21.4 percent of Hispanic families were living in poverty, compared with a 7.8 percent rate of poverty for non-Hispanic whites (Ramirez and de la Cruz, 2002).

▲ Mexicans

With a population of 25 million (Ramirez and de la Cruz, 2002), Mexican Americans make up nearly two-thirds of the Hispanic population in the United States. Many of them trace their ancestry to the merging of the Native American population with Spanish settlers. Like African Americans and Native Americans, people of Mexican ancestry did not originally become a part of American society through voluntary immigration. With the exception of the American Indians, they are the only American minority to enter the society through the conquest of their homeland. Though Mexican Americans have been longer in the United States than other Hispanic origin groups, their median income ranks below and their unemployment rate above that of Cubans and Central and South Americans. Though they are now primarily an urban-based group, they also still are disproportionately found in agricultural occupations as seasonal or permanent workers. Almost a quarter of the country's Mexican Americans live below the poverty line (Ramirez, 2004).

▲ Puerto Ricans

Although Puerto Ricans have lived in the continental United States for more than 100 years, the major emergence of Puerto Rican communities in the United States began after World War II when large numbers of people began migrating to escape unemployment in Puerto Rico. Puerto Rico is a Commonwealth of the United States (it was designated a U.S. territory in 1898), and its citizens migrate from the island to the "mainland" and back again fairly easily and inexpensively, a flow that probably contributes to the strong ethnic communities and low inter-marriage rates among Puerto Ricans. Among Hispanic groups, Puerto Ricans have a high poverty rate; 25.8 percent of Puerto Ricans live below the poverty level (Ramirez, 2004). They have been victims of intense prejudice and discrimination and extreme occupational segregation (Bean and Tienda, 1987).

▲ Cubans

In 1950 the Census Bureau counted only 34,000 Cubans; during the late 1950s and throughout the 1960s, the United States welcomed Cubans seeking asylum from the Castro regime, and the population now stands at 1.2 million (Ramirez, 2004). Cuban Americans have been the most socioeconomically successful of the Hispanic origin groups. Early immigrants were political rather than economic refugees. Many professional, highly educated, and urban people were among the first immigrants who laid the foundation for a vibrant ethnic enclave economy, primarily in Miami (Portes, 1987; Portes and Jensen, 1989). The poverty rate for Cuban Americans is 14.6 percent, the second lowest rate of all the Latino groups (Ramirez, 2004). More than 60 percent of the Cuban American population age 25 or over has at least a high school education, a higher proportion than is true for Mexican, Puerto Rican, and Central American Latinos (Ramirez, 2004). Three-quarters of Cuban Americans live in the South, with a very large population in the Miami area (Ramirez and de la Cruz, 2002).

▲ Central and South Americans

As recently as 1970 there were only a few hundred thousand people from Central and South America living in the United States (Bean and Tienda, 1987). In 2002 that number had risen to 3.2 million (Ramirez, 2004). The greatly increased immigration from Latin America in recent decades is one of the major factors contributing to the overall dramatic increase in the U.S. Hispanic population. The major increases have come primarily from Colombia, Ecuador, El Salvador, and the Dominican Republic. Other countries fairly well represented in the United States include Guatemala, Nicaragua, Peru, and Argentina (Bean and Tienda, 1987). Approximately 19.9 percent of Central and 15.0 percent of South Americans in the United States live below the poverty line (Ramirez, 2004).

African Americans

In spite of serious obstacles caused by past and present racism and discrimination, the African-American population in the United States has been remarkably successful. In 2002, African Americans comprised 13 percent of the U.S. population (McKinnon, 2003). The South was home to 55 percent of the nation's blacks, and more than half of all African Americans were living in central cities.

Until 2001, poverty rates had been declining for African Americans. More than half of all black married-couple families were earning $50,000 or more per year in 2002, with 27 percent earning incomes greater than $75,000. Similar proportions of white and black men are employed in technical, sales, and administrative support jobs, but black men and women are disproportionately represented in service jobs and as operators, fabricators, and laborers. The unemployment rate was twice as high for blacks as for whites in 2002, and although blacks accounted for only about a fourth of the country's citizens living in poverty, the African-American poverty rate (23 percent) was almost three times higher than that of non-Hispanic whites (McKinnon, 2003).

▲ Background

The subjugation of African Americans as slaves began in the 17th century and was well rooted in the British colonies by the time of the American Revolution. Slavery was carried on by the new American nation when it achieved independence, and democracy was extended only to the male, white population. The Thirteenth Amendment to the Constitution, which outlawed slavery, was ratified following the end of the Civil War in 1865. But 1865 and 1866 also saw the passage of "black codes" discriminating against African Americans in every southern state, as well as outbreaks of violence against blacks and the formation of the Ku Klux Klan. The 1866 Civil Rights Act was passed by Congress to nullify the black codes, and during Reconstruction, African-American males were granted the right to vote. Many freed slaves learned to read and write, and the first black senators and state legislators were elected. But by the 1890s, the situation for African Americans in the United States had deteriorated again. In most southern states blacks were barred from voting, and during the 1890s and early 1900s lynching attained its most staggering proportions. Jim Crow laws mandating segregation were passed throughout the South. As recently as the early 1960s, blacks and whites used separate drinking fountains and restrooms, and children attended segregated schools.

▲ The Civil Rights Movement

The stage was set for drastic change in the South when the Supreme Court ruled on May 17, 1954, that mandatory school segregation was unconstitutional. In the years that followed, the Supreme Court moved toward outlawing legalized segregation in all areas of American life. Simultaneously, the civil rights movement of the 1960s galvanized popular support for the enactment of new civil rights legislation, particularly the Civil Rights Acts of 1964, 1965, and 1968. As the United States entered the 1970s, resistance mounted among segments of the white community, particularly against affirmative action measures and against busing children to promote school integration, and many public schools today are "segregated" by virtue of the races and ethnicities of neighborhood residents. But the Supreme Court decision in 2003 to preserve the use of affirmative action programs at universities endorsed "the role of racial diversity on campus in achieving a more equal society" (Greenhouse, 2003) (see Box 7.2).

▲ Race or Class?

Are opportunities for African-American economic advancement affected more by race or by class position? Sociologist William Julius Wilson (1978, 1987; Wilson and Aponte, 1985) argued that race had become less important than social class because civil rights legislation and affirmative action programs have resulted in greater educational, income, and occupational differentiation. African Americans with good educations and job skills rapidly moved into the American middle class, while African Americans with limited educations and job skills became the victims of soaring joblessness and welfare dependency. Structural factors—the disappearance of hundreds of thousands of low-skill jobs, mainly involving physical labor—contributed to inner-city African Americans becoming a severely disadvantaged class. Now poor urban African Americans find themselves relegated to all-black neighborhoods where they are socially isolated from mainstream American life (Charles, 2000; Massey and Denton, 1993; Massey and Eggers, 1990). But supporting the increasing importance of class is research showing that blacks of high socioeconomic status are more likely to have interactions in their own neighborhoods with whites of high socioeconomic status than are blacks of low socioeconomic status to interact with whites in their neighborhoods (St. John and Clymer, 2000).

Wilson said that racism created a large African-American lower class that was then perpetuated by changes in the economy and job trends (Wilson, 1996, 1987, 1991). Data from the census also suggest that the gap between poor and affluent African Americans has grown over time, reflecting not only the economic success of a rising African-American middle class but the increasing isolation and despair among African Americans who have fallen further out of the economic mainstream (http://www.census.gov/hhes/www/income/histinc/h04.html).

▲ The Other Side

Not all sociologists agree with Wilson's argument about the declining significance of race (Collins, 1983; Pomer, 1986; Hughes and Hertel, 1990), and there is now widespread agreement that race is still an important factor in American society. Sociologist Charles V. Willie (1979, 1991) argued that discrimination and racist practices still persist in American life and confront all African Americans regardless of their social class. He interpreted income, education, and housing data as revealing that blacks and whites with similar qualifications are treated unequally in the marketplace—evidence of a "racial tax" levied on African Americans for not being white. Considerable differences are also found in measures of psychological well-being between blacks and whites regardless of social class, suggesting that there also are psychological costs to being an African American in the United States (Hughes and Thomas, 1998).

An education reformer with the National Urban League agrees that racism continues to affect African-American progress, blaming it on the differences in achievement between black and white students in public schools (Raspberry, 2002). A physician commenting about the importance of affirmative action in medical school admissions said "powerful social, economic, cultural, and educational forces still operate along racial and ethnic lines in this country" (Cohen, 2003:1148). In direct contradiction to Wilson's class argument, the medical school admission test scores of minority students with a family income greater than $80,000 are *lower* than the test scores of nonminorities with family incomes of less than $30,000 (Cohen, 2003).

The persistence of disadvantages makes it difficult to disentangle the effects of class and race today. Although 77 percent of African-American families do not live in poverty, the percentage that does still far exceeds the percentage of poor white families. The poverty associated with female-headed households also takes its toll: 43 percent of black families are headed by females, with no spouse present, and

Education
Persons 25 years and older, with 4 years of college or more, by percentage of their racial group

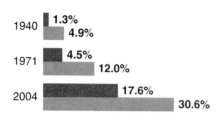

1940 1.3%
      4.9%

1971 4.5%
      12.0%

2004 17.6%
      30.6%

Family Income
Percentage of racial group by total income; 2004 dollars

$50,000 to $74,999

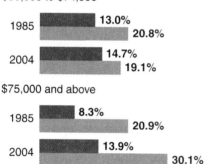

1985 13.0%
      20.8%

2004 14.7%
      19.1%

$75,000 and above

1985 8.3%
      20.9%

2004 13.9%
      30.1%

Occupation
Employed civilians, 2004, by percentage of their racial group in specific jobs

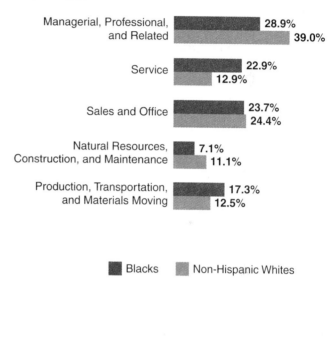

Managerial, Professional, and Related 28.9%   39.0%

Service 22.9%   12.9%

Sales and Office 23.7%   24.4%

Natural Resources, Construction, and Maintenance 7.1%   11.1%

Production, Transportation, and Materials Moving 17.3%   12.5%

■ Blacks   ■ Non-Hispanic Whites

Figure 7.3   **African-American Progress in the United States: A Mixed Message**
Although African Americans have made gains in American life, race problems endure. The United States has not become an integrated society despite the expansion of the African-American middle class.

Sources: Education data from the U.S. Census Bureau, March Current Population Surveys 1971 and 2002, and 1940 Census of Population, available at http://www.census.gov/population/socdemo/education/tabA-2.pdf. Income data from DeNavas-Walt, Proctor, and Lee, 2005. Occupation data tabulated by the authors from the Statistical Abstract of the United States, 2004 (U.S. Census Bureau, 2004) Table 590.

35 percent of those families live in poverty (McKinnon, 2003). Female-headed white families account for only 13 percent of all white families. African-American students, then, are more likely than white students to suffer from the range of problems associated with poverty.

African Americans have made significant advances in education in recent years. Similar percentages of blacks and whites finish high school and go on to college (McKinnon, 2003). But fewer blacks (16.6 percent of males, 18.5 percent of females) than whites (32.9 percent of males, 28.4 percent of females) finish college (http://www.census.gov/population/socdemo/education/tabA-2.pdf). Blacks remain less likely to be employed in managerial and professional specialty jobs and more likely to be employed in service and labor occupations.

Even when blacks are highly educated, they receive less reward in terms of authority than do whites (Smith, 1999). Figure 7.3 provides data on the persistence of the gap between African Americans and whites.

Young African Americans face particularly difficult problems. They confront grim job prospects. The leading cause of death among African-American males is homicide (accidents are second, and suicide is third [Anderson and Smith, 2005]). Although black suicide rates have been historically low compared to those for whites, the suicide rate for young black men has increased dramatically over the past 20 years, due in part to the concentrated disadvantage experienced by young black men in urban areas (Kubrin, 2006). Overall, young black men with little education are facing particularly serious problems (Mincy, 2006). More than half of all black men living in inner cities do not finish college (Eckholm, 2006; Orfield, 2004). In 2004, among black men in their 20s, half of high school graduates and 72 percent of high school dropouts were jobless (that is, unemployed or incarcerated); 21 percent of those who were not in college were in jail or prison (Eckholm, 2006). By their mid-30s, about 60 percent of black male high school dropouts had been in prison or jail. Recent research indicates that more black high school dropouts in their late 20s are in prison on any given day than are employed (Eckholm, 2006).

Sociologist Elijah Anderson (1978, 1990, 1994) has devoted much of his career to the study of inner-city problems. His work takes us inside the world of inner-city African-American young men and portrays the havoc that interpersonal violence and aggression brings to their lives. He found that violent inclinations spring from the frustrations and alienation associated with the lack of good jobs, the stigma of race, and the fallout from drug use and trafficking. Anderson contended that a paucity of good jobs plays a large role in urban ills, a conclusion supported by William J. Wilson's (1996) study on the impact of unemployment.

In sum, the gap between many African Americans and whites remains substantial; class interacts with race and gender to produce the social cleavages that remain a continuing feature of American life (Colasanto and Williams, 1987; Massey and Denton, 1993; Clayton, 1996).

American Indians and Alaskan Natives

In 2000, 4.3 million persons who reported that they were American Indian or Alaskan Native lived within the United States (Ogunwole, 2006). Although there are some 500 tribes, ranging in size from under 100 to more than 250,000 tribal members, American Indians and Alaskan Natives make up less than 2 percent of the total U.S. population (Ogunwole, 2006). If these figures reflected a natural increase, they would represent a population increase of 26 to 110 percent over 10 years, compared to a 13 percent increase for the United States as a whole, but it is more likely that they also reflect changes in the way American Indians are counted (Paisano, 2003).

American Indians and Alaskan Natives vary substantially in their history, lifestyles, kin systems, language, political arrangements, religion, economy, current circumstances, and identities. They are perhaps the most unusual American ethnic group, in that each tribe is a nation with special political rights dealing with another nation, the United States. In addition, for many tribes, their ethnicity is "rooted in particular plots of ground" (Page, 2003:2). As with Hispanics/Latinos, this group has many names, including Indian, indigenous peoples, First People, and Native American. American Indians and Alaskan Natives are the most severely disadvantaged of any population within the United States (Snipp, 1989; Visgaitis, 1994).

▲ Background

Estimates of how many American Indians and Alaskan Natives were living in what is now the United States before the arrival of Europeans vary widely, ranging from about 1 million to 18 million and more (Page, 2003). Most nations were farming and fishing peoples with relatively stable communities. Initially, the European powers treated the native groups with respect, as nations that could be either enemies or allies. But as whites increasingly wanted land, tribal territories were appropriated and their inhabitants killed or driven inland. By the beginning of the 20th century, the U.S. population of Indians had dropped to 250,000—a 75 percent to 95 percent population reduction, depending on what estimate of pre-European-contact population

Although Native Americans have survived, increased in population, and maintained a cultural presence, they remain the most severely disadvantaged of any population within the United States on a number of dimensions.

is used (Page, 2003). Widespread and fast-moving epidemics of diseases brought by white immigrants killed many American Indians before they even saw a European. Entire tribes have vanished through massacres by whites, disease, destruction of their economic base, or absorption by other groups, and some linguists predict that as few as 30 American Indian languages will be spoken by 2050.

The Removal Act of 1830 provided for the relocation of all eastern tribes to lands west of the Mississippi River. This "Trail of Tears" is widely regarded as one of the most dishonorable chapters in U.S. history. At least 70,000 people were removed; more than 20,000 died en route. West of the Mississippi, the tragedies of defeat and expropriation were repeated. When native groups resisted, they were systematically slaughtered (Josephy, 1991).

Inconsistencies and vacillations in U.S. government policy are to blame for the plight of American Indians and Alaskan Natives. Today about one-third live on reservations (Ogunwole,

2006), which cover 52.4 million acres in 27 states. Forty-one percent of those on reservations live below the poverty level; almost 70 percent of Navajos, the largest nation, are still without electricity. Overall, unemployment among males 20 to 64 years old is about 60 percent (Valente, 1991; Kilborn, 1992). Life expectancy in some tribes is 45 years. Other problems include alcoholism, suicide, obesity, adult-onset diabetes, and other health problems. Tribes across the United States also are grappling with some of the nation's worst pollution problems—uranium tailings, land and water contamination, chemical lagoons, and illegal dumps (Satchell, 1993).

Despite the myriad problems faced by Native Americans, they have both survived and increased in population since the low of 100 years ago. The two-thirds of Indian people who live off reservations live primarily in cities; the largest Indian populations are in Los Angeles, Tulsa, New York, Oklahoma City, San Francisco, and Phoenix (Page, 2003). Native American crafts are much sought after, and American

Indian religious practices have been adopted by whites as part of "New Age" spiritualism. Pow wows are a popular form of entertainment for Indians and non-Indians alike, Native American cultural artifacts and sacred lands have won federal protection, and Indian novelists are nationally recognized. As Page puts it, "An Indian presence, and one that is set forth by the Indians themselves, is now to be felt in the overall culture of America to an extent unseen before" (2003:406).

Asian Americans

There is a great diversity of Asian Americans in the United States. According to the 2000 census, the ancestry of this group breaks down into 2.4 million Chinese, 1.9 million Filipinos, 1.6 million Asian Indians, 1.1 million Koreans, 1.1 million Vietnamese, and 795,000 Japanese (Reeves and Bennett, 2004). In addition, there are smaller numbers of Laotians, Cambodians, Thais, Hmong, and Pakistanis. All told, 10.1 million persons of Asian origins live in the United States, according to the 2000 Census (Reeves and Bennett, 2004). More than half of all Asian Americans live in California, New York, and Hawaii (Barnes and Bennett, 2002). Asian Americans are twice as likely as non-Hispanic whites to live in central cities, and the populations of some cities in California are now between a quarter and a half Asian American (Barnes and Bennett, 2002).

Asian Americans now enjoy the highest median family income of the nation's ethnic groups: $57,518 in 2004 (DeNavas-Walt, Proctor, and Lee, 2005). They are known for their educational and occupational successes; of those 25 years or older, half the men and 44 percent of the women have finished at least four years of college, compared to 32 percent (males) and 27 percent (females) of non-Hispanic whites (Reeves and Bennett, 2003). See Box 7.3 for more on the "model minority." But Asian-American leaders also point out that Asian-American groups have

problems such as crime, high suicide rates, mental disorders, and disintegrating families, especially among poor refugees and immigrants who have difficulty coping with a strange, new society (Lee, 1990). And although their median income is higher than that of whites, their income per member of the household is lower— $19,833 compared to $20,155 for non-Hispanic whites (DeNavas-Walt, Proctor, and Lee, 2005; http://www.census.gov/population/socdemo/ hh-fam/cps2004/ tabAVG1.csv).

Although many Asian-American youths enjoy remarkable academic success, on the job, Asian-American workers face discrimination and are often the victims of racially motivated harassment and violence (Dugger, 1992; Mura, 1992). By the same token, Asian Americans find that they soon "top out," reaching positions beyond which their employers fail to promote them. The Census Bureau's March 2005 Current Population Survey found that the median income for Asian-American males aged 25 or over with a bachelor's degree was $52,184, about 85 percent of the median income of non-Hispanic white males with the same education, $60,710.

▲ Chinese

During the early days of the gold rush, the Chinese were welcomed as a source of cheap labor, but when the speculative gold bubble burst, whites faced competition with Chinese workers and attitudes changed. California led the nation in the passage of anti-Chinese laws, many of which remained in effect until the 1950s; for instance, the California state constitution provided that corporations could neither directly nor indirectly employ Chinese, and it empowered cities and towns to remove Chinese from within city limits.

The Chinatowns of New York City, San Francisco, and a few other large cities expanded as a result of sharp increases in immigration from Hong Kong and Taiwan made possible by the passage of immigration legislation in 1965 that did away with the old quota system, under

The internment of 120,000 Japanese during World War II was based more on racism than on national security; none of the nation's other "enemies in residence" (German and Italian Americans) were subjected to internment and not one Japanese American was ever convicted of spying.

which only 105 Chinese were allowed entry each year. Above the gaudy storefronts of the nation's Chinatowns, Chinese families are jammed into tiny apartments. More than 71 percent of Chinese in the United States were born overseas (Reeves and Bennett, 2004).

▲ Japanese

The Japanese also have been victims of prejudice and discrimination. On two occasions the government launched an effort to exclude them from American life. In 1907 President Theodore Roosevelt reached an agreement with Japan to limit the immigration of Japanese to the United States. Later, during World War II, the government placed some 120,000 Japanese (two-thirds

of whom were U.S. citizens) in 10 internment camps.

A large number of the original immigrants made a place for themselves in California's economy through farming. Wives and families were allowed to join the Japanese men already in the United States; by 1940 nearly two-thirds of Japanese Americans were native born (Marger, 2006). As with Chinese Americans, the average family income of Japanese Americans in the second and subsequent generations is significantly higher than that of non-Hispanic whites (U.S. Commission on Civil Rights, 1988); the income of Japanese Americans is higher than that of any other Asian-American group (Reeves and Bennett, 2004). Box 7.3

Model Minorities—Does Class or Do Values Spell Success?

Why do some minorities suffer from poverty, unemployment, and discrimination while others do not? The nation's media have heralded Asian Americans as "the model minority" and "a superminority." Among white ethnic groups, Jewish immigrants and American-born Jews have long been recognized for their quick rise in U.S. society. And while Hispanic Americans as a whole are socioeconomically disadvantaged, Cubans in particular have had quite rapid economic success. What accounts for the successes of these model minorities? Is it their values or is it their class background?

One explanation for successful ethnic groups is that their values contribute to their upward mobility. This argument contends that thrift, strong family ties, and hard work are the keys to Asian-American success and that their emphasis on education and excellence places them at an advantage in U.S. society. For example, a much higher proportion of Asian-American adults than of whites have completed college. Asian-American students are more likely than other students to enroll in college preparatory programs; they take more math and science courses and also spend more time on homework than other students (Zigli, 1984; Butterfield, 1986; O'Hare and Felt, 1991).

The "values" explanation for Jewish success is similar. Jews have encouraged independence and achievement more than other white ethnic groups, and their emphasis on education extends back for centuries (Marger, 2006). More than half of all Jewish adults have a college degree, compared with 21 percent of U.S. adults in general (Goldstein, 1992). As a result Jewish males are concentrated far more in the professional occupations (39 percent of Jewish males versus 16 percent of all white males) and far less in the working class (20 percent versus 52 percent of all U.S. white males).

But there's another explanation for the success of ethnic groups in the United States, and this explanation takes us back to the immigrants' roots, to their countries of origin. Sociologist Stephen Steinberg (1989) argued that Jewish immigrants had a significant advantage over other immigrants when they first came to the United States. Italians and other groups of European immigrants were primarily of peasant stock; Jews were frequently urban merchants or manufacturers, and they arrived in the United States at a time when its industrial economy was expanding rapidly and their skills could be put to immediate

discusses some of the reasons for the economic success of this and other ethnic groups.

▲ Other Asian Groups

Asian Americans are a varied group, with considerable contrasts and diversity. In 1970 the largest proportion of Asian Americans was comprised of Chinese and Japanese, but they now represent about a third of the total Asian-American population. While the Chinese are still the largest component, there are nearly as many Filipinos. Koreans and Asian Indians in the United States are increasing steadily. The Japanese component of America's Asian population is becoming smaller because of low immigration and birth rates (Marger, 2006).

Some of these many groups have achieved reasonable success in U.S. society; Chinese, Filipino, Japanese, and Asian Indian Americans all have median family incomes higher than the median for the United States as a whole. However, Korean, Vietnamese, Cambodian, Hmong, and Laotian Americans have family incomes lower than the U.S. median (Marger, 2006). The earnings of Laotians, Cambodians, and Vietnamese who have come from rural areas and who possess few marketable skills are particularly low (Dunn, 1994).

(and remunerative) use. In other words, class, not values, was the determining factor.

Likewise, some Asian immigrant groups have included a high proportion of doctors and engineers and others with advanced education, and their success in the United States reflects their upper-class, professional backgrounds in their home countries. Much of the potential for success was brought with these immigrants when they entered the United States. The income of lower-class Asian immigrants who come from rural areas and who possess few marketable skills is quite low (Dunn, 1994; Marger, 2006). Much of the success of Asians also may be due to other structural factors, such as the development of ethnic enclave economies that formed as a result of discrimination (Hirschman and Wong, 1986; Bonacich and Modell, 1980).

The experiences of Cuban immigrants also supports the class explanation for the success of ethnic groups in the United States. While other Hispanic groups came to the United States in hopes of economic betterment, many Cuban immigrants in the early 1960s were middle-, upper-middle-, and upper-class citizens. These advantaged immigrants used their material, educational, and social resources (networks and relationships from pre-Castro Cuba) to create an ethnic enclave economy that benefited them and subsequent Cuban immigrants (Portes and Bach, 1985; Marger, 2006). Without a doubt strong family values and a willingness to sacrifice and work hard were critical factors in the success of Cuban Americans. However, the material and social advantages they brought with them assured success for a substantial number of Cuban Americans in considerably less than one generation.

Jewish, Asian, and Cuban Americans are good models of how some ethnic groups in the United States have achieved success. What their stories tell us, however, may be less about the importance of values, beliefs, and good habits, and more about the strong influence of material and social advantages in the success of immigrants in a new land.

Questions for Discussion

1. Pundits, radio talk show hosts, and other social commentators sometimes argue that disadvantaged minority groups in the United States such as Hispanics and African Americans would not be disadvantaged if they followed the examples set by "model minorities." How reasonable is this advice?

2. In your experience as a student, have you observed variability in academic success across various ethnic categories either in high school or college? If so, what factors do you think account for these differences? If not, do you think minority status or ethnicity is in any way responsible for students' academic performances in the schools you have attended? Why or why not?

White Ethnics

▲ Historical Immigration

Most of the original white settlers of what became the United States were British. Although there were large numbers of people of other nationalities, particularly Germans and Dutch, the British dominated the society with their language, their Protestant religion, and their legal system. Immigration, mostly from northwestern European countries, continued throughout the 19th century, bringing considerable numbers of Irish, Scandinavians, and Germans. But the largest influx came between 1885 and 1920 when about 25 million immigrants entered the United States. Many of these largely Catholic and Jewish immigrants, who are the ancestors of those we now speak of as "white ethnics," came not from northwestern Europe as earlier immigrants had but from eastern and southern European countries such as Italy, Greece, Poland, Russia, and Serbia. Differing from the English-speaking Protestant population in culture, language, and religion, these immigrants appeared alien to most Americans. Their apparent challenge to the cultural dominance of the old Protestant middle class stimulated the growth of prejudicial nativist sentiments that fueled a social and political backlash, resulting in significant discrimination, particularly against the Irish and Italians.

In spite of these problems and the associated prejudice and discrimination, the ethnic groups established in the United States as a result of immigration from the 1880s to the 1920s are now largely integrated into U.S. society and have generally prospered. The typical pattern for these groups was that the first generation would gain a solid foothold in the working class, the second generation would go to work early in life to help support their families, and the third and subsequent generations would take advantage of educational opportunities to move into higher-status occupations (Marger, 2006; Greeley, 1977; Yans-McLaughlin, 1982). Jewish mobility was an exception to this pattern, with very large numbers entering the middle class in the second generation (see Box 7.3). Success of these groups has been a consequence of much structural assimilation; some marital assimilation also has occurred (Lieberson and Waters, 1988), as Gordon (1964) predicted it would.

▲ The Situation Today

The success of these immigrant groups, great as it has been, is not complete. Though they have achieved much in state and local politics, U.S. national political leadership, including the Congress and the executive branch, is heavily dominated by white Protestant males of northwestern European heritage (Marger, 2006). The same is true of the largest corporations.

Some sociologists, such as Greeley (1974), argue that the degree of overall assimilation of white ethnic groups has been overestimated and that many Americans still identify themselves as Jews, Poles, Irish, and Italians and have distinctive attitudes, behaviors, and political interests. Research by Alba (1990) and Lieberson and Waters (1993) confirmed that most white Americans know their ethnic ancestry, but also showed that white ethnicity is neither deep nor stable. It tends to be what Gans (1979) called "symbolic ethnicity." This is an ethnicity that contributes to individual identity and family relationships, but does not create or sustain strong ethnic group ties. Alba (1990) found that among whites, the most common ethnic experiences are private and innocuous: eating ethnic foods, discussing one's ethnic background with others, feeling curious about others' ethnic experiences, and attending ethnic festivals.

Why has white ethnicity become symbolic? As Mary Waters (1990) pointed out, ethnicity does not have much effect on the everyday life of white Americans. It does not affect where they can live, what jobs they can get, who their friends are, whether they will be discriminated against, or, for the most part, whom they will marry. For these reasons, individual white ethnicities are increasingly a matter of choice that some Americans make, Waters maintained, because symbolic ethnicity provides individual identity and communalistic feelings with none of the costs that real ethnic affiliations require.

Sociological Perspectives on Inequalities of Race and Ethnicity

Functionalist, conflict, and interactionist theorists have different explanations for racial and ethnic stratification. In this section we will consider the contributions of each of these three major sociological perspectives to our understanding of the inequalities of race and ethnicity.

The Functionalist Perspective

Because functionalists conceive of society as resembling a living organism in which the various parts of a system contribute to its survival, they are interested in how these divisions affect the function of the whole social system when they consider race and ethnicity.

▲ Dysfunctions

Functionalists argue that social consensus on core values and beliefs is an important foundation of social integration and stability and thus helps a society maintain its equilibrium. Ethnic differentiation may be dysfunctional because it reduces consensus, increases the chances of conflict, and thereby threatens the equilibrium of a society, as occurred in Iraq in 2005–2006. Ethnic stratification may be particularly disruptive because it combines two societal cleavages, one based on culture and the other based on economic rewards and political power. Conflicts attributable to problems of ethnic stratification may reach a frequency and intensity that imperil the whole social system, as occurred in Lebanon in the 1970s and 1980s and in the former Yugoslavia in the 1990s.

But functionalists do not predict that ethnically differentiated societies will necessarily disintegrate or be perpetually unproductive and unjust. Instead, they suggest that because the tendency toward equilibrium and stability is very strong, ethnic stratification will gradually decline.

▲ Functions

According to the functionalist perspective, ethnic conflict may also serve some important functions in a society. First, conflict promotes group formation, and groups are the building blocks of a society. It facilitates a consciousness of kind—an awareness of shared or similar values. The distinction between "we," the in-group, and "they," the out-group, is established in and through conflict. Groups in turn ◀ pp. 104–105 bind people together within a set of social relationships. And they define the statuses people occupy in the social structure, particularly positions that are ascribed.

Second, not only is a group defined and its boundaries established through conflict, but conflict also promotes group cohesion. It makes group members more conscious of their group bonds and may increase their social participation, providing them with a means of identification in an uncertain, alienated world.

Third, ethnic and racial conflict may function as a safety valve for the society as a whole (Hepworth and West, 1988; Berkowitz, 1989). Prejudice provides for the release of hostile and aggressive impulses that are culturally taboo within other social contexts. By channeling hostilities from within family, occupational, and other crucial settings onto permissible targets, the stability of existing social structures may be promoted. This is known as the *scapegoating* mechanism.

Fourth, functionalists point out that a multiplicity of conflicts between large numbers of differing groups within a society may be conducive to a democratic as opposed to a totalitarian order. The multiple group affiliations of individuals contribute to a variety of conflicts crisscrossing society. As noted in Chapter 2, if people are opponents in one conflict but allies in another, deep cleavages along one axis can be prevented. The different groups thus created operate as a check against one another and ensure input to the government from a variety of diverse points of view. In contrast, totalitarian societies have a maximum concentration of power in one institution—the monolithic state.

The Conflict Perspective

Conflict theorists contend that prejudice and discrimination can best be understood in terms of tension or conflict among competing groups. They point out that three ingredients commonly come into play in the emergence and initial stabilization of racism (Noel, 1972; Vander Zanden, 1983): ethnocentrism, competition, and unequal power.

As we noted in Chapter 2, ◀ pp. 52–53 *ethnocentrism* involves the tendency to judge the behavior of other groups by the standards of one's own. When individuals are strongly ethnocentric, they find it easy to perceive the out-group as an object of loathing. Competition intensifies ethnocentric sentiments and may lead to intergroup strife (Olzak, 1992). When people perceive that their own group can realize its goals only at the expense of another group, intergroup tensions are likely to mount, each group will see the other as a threat, and prejudicial attitudes will be generated toward the out-group (Beck and Tolnay, 1990; Olzak, 1990; Fossett and Kiecolt, 1989; Quillian, 1995, 1996). The boys' camp experiment undertaken by Muzafer Sherif and his associates (1961) and described in Chapter 4 documents this process. ←── pp. 104–105

Competition provides the motivation for systems of social inequality, and ethnocentrism channels competition along racial and ethnic lines, but power determines which group will subordinate the other (Noel, 1972). Without power, prejudices cannot be translated into discrimination, and groups cannot turn their claims on scarce resources into institutional discrimination. In brief, power is the mechanism by which domination and subjugation are achieved.

Marxist-oriented theorists take the conflict thesis even further. They say that racial prejudice and exploitation arose in the Western world with the rise of capitalism (Cox, 1948; Szymanski, 1976; Geschwender, 1978) and benefit capitalists in four ways. First, ideologies of racial superiority make colonialism and racist practices palatable and acceptable to the white masses. Second, racism is profitable because capitalists can pay minority workers less. Third, racist ideologies divide the working class by pitting white workers and minority workers against one another. Fourth, capitalists require minority workers as an industrial reserve army that can be fired during times of economic stagnation and rehired during times of prosperity (see Chapter 6).

Marxists blame capitalists for generating racism, but sociologist Edna Bonacich (1972, 1975; Cheng and Bonacich, 1984) said that economic competition within a split labor market underlies the development of tensions among ethnic groups. A **split labor market** is an economic arena in which large differences exist in the price of labor at the same occupational level.

Bonacich noted that when a group sells its labor at rates substantially lower than the prevailing ones, higher-paid labor faces severe competition to maintain its advantage. When the cheaper labor is of a differing racial or ethnic group, the resulting class antagonism takes the form of racism.

Regardless of the precise form that conflict theories take, they nonetheless contrast sharply with functionalist theories that normal social processes contribute to stability rather than to division and social strife.

The Interactionist Perspective

Interactionists argue that the way we act is dependent on the meanings we attach to people, objects, and events. Because these meanings are produced in social interaction, interactionists say that the world we experience is *socially constructed*. In this view ethnic groups are rooted in neither physical characteristics of people nor their primordial attachments. According to Shibutani and Kwan (1965), "Ethnic groups . . . generally do not share a common genetic strain; they are products of social interaction."

Communication was the key variable in ethnicity to Shibutani and Kwan (1965). Ethnicity arises when communication channels between groups are limited and different groups develop different systems of meanings. Ethnic distinctions tend to diminish when people in different groups experience the world in similar ways, are treated alike by others, and are able to communicate freely and easily with members of other groups. The more a group uses a single communication channel, the more isolated it is and the more it tends to view the other groups from the perspective of its own system of meaning. This ethnocentrism is what produces prejudice.

When ethnic groups are stratified and the advantages enjoyed by the dominant group are fixed by custom and law, the prejudices of dominant group members, developed in cultural isolation from minority groups, will reflect a "sense of group position" (Blumer, 1958)—that is, a belief that the dominant group is superior and has a proprietary claim to privileges and resources and that the minority groups are not only alien, but are a threat to the dominant group's advantageous position.

Although interactionists such as Shibutani and Kwan see ethnic stratification and the discrimination that accompanies it as the end result of competition and conflict among groups over scarce resources (as do the proponents of the conflict perspective), it is important to remember that groups can be conflictual only if they see themselves as distinct and different; otherwise people cooperate as part of the same group or society. Ultimately, the causes of ethnic conflict and ethnic stratification are to be found in the social definitions groups have of each other and in the norms and patterns of interaction that perpetuate these definitions. As Shibutani and Kwan put it, "ethnic stratification persists as long as people on both sides of the color line approach one another with common expectations of how each is to act in the presence of the other."

The Future of Ethnic and Minority Group Relations

Intergroup Relations

In the late 1800s and early 1900s the United States was a truly diverse multicultural society. Germans, French, Scandinavians, Bohemians, Russians, Italians, Greeks, Armenians, Irish, Scots, Poles, and many other groups—each speaking its own language—populated the nation's cities and farms. The children and grandchildren of these people grew up living in houses next to each other, went to school together, spoke English with one another, married people from each other's families, went into business with one another, and thought of themselves and one another primarily as Americans.

This idyllic outcome is by no means the assured or even the desired outcome for the many minority groups that increasingly populated the United States as we moved into the 21st century. The Americans with African, Hispanic, Asian, and Native American roots are not only culturally and linguistically distinct but also have racial characteristics that distinguish them. Because of the meanings attached to race, language, and culture in contemporary U.S. society, ethnic status for these groups is not "symbolic," is not a matter of choice, but remains heavily ascriptive. This has two implications. First, ethnicity is not the same experience in the United States for white ethnics as it is for other minority groups (Waters, 1990), a problem that is likely to make communication about ethnic matters difficult and to perpetuate misunderstanding. Second, the ethnic and minority distinctions that define the structure of contemporary America are not likely to diminish as quickly or in quite the same way as those of the white ethnics.

What is likely to happen? Of course no one knows, but let us ask ourselves what the major perspectives, the functionalist, conflict, and interactionist, predict will happen.

The functionalist and conflict perspectives both suggest that if ethnic stratification continues in a society, then conflict and strife are likely outcomes. Both would predict that conflicts will be particularly likely and severe if class and ethnic cleavages coincide.

Where the two perspectives differ is that the functionalists believe that there are long-run social trends that are eliminating ascription and other irrational features from modern, industrial, socially differentiated societies. Basically, the problem we face is to manage the change from ascriptive to achievement-based stratification systems. From this view the civil rights movement (and other equality-oriented movements such as the women's movement) are as much a consequence as they are a cause of these changes.

The conflict perspective, on the other hand, predicts that ethnic stratification will remain as long as it is in the interests of powerful dominant groups to keep it in place. If we want to reduce ethnic stratification, we will have to directly intervene through government policies that will increase the chances that minority groups increase their share of power and resources. According to this view, the civil rights activism that promotes affirmative action and civil rights legislation is an important causal agent in such change.

For interactionists, ethnic stratification cannot exist unless people define each other as different. Interactionists would predict that as long as segregation and isolation of minority groups persist, particularly that of the poorest groups, ethnocentrism will continue and probably worsen. Racism will not disappear, but will only change; the emergence of symbolic racism and new, subtle forms of discrimination that we noted earlier in the chapter may be examples of such a change. Only if we break down barriers to interaction and communication will people begin to experience their common humanity, see one another as part of the same world, and work together to solve common problems.

Ethnicity

What is likely to happen to ethnicity? Most observers suggest that if ethnic stratification persists, then ethnicity will persist as well.

Minority group members will turn to their ethnic group for support, strength, and political mobilization. We should observe the emergence of new ethnicities as various groups of immigrants, minority, and even majority group members having a coincidence of interests define themselves as members of the same group. Some have suggested this is happening now in the emergence of "Hispanic Americans" and "Asian Americans," groups that, as we have seen, contain many nationalities. Alba (1990) argued that white ethnics were evolving into a group of "European Americans." Lieberson and Waters (1988) pointed to the increasing number of Americans who, when asked for their heritage, say that they are just "Americans," and suggested that this may indicate the emergence of a new ethnic group of "unhyphenated whites."

If ethnic stratification diminishes significantly, it is possible that ethnicity for all groups will become increasingly "symbolic." If ethnic status does not dictate one's chances to be successful in life or is not needed to provide one with the hope that unjust conditions will be changed, then it is possible that its significance will reduce to being a source of individual identity and familial communion. In this situation ethnic groups will remain a rich source of personal meaning, but they will no longer enter into political and societal dynamics as they have in the past.

The Chapter in Brief: *Inequalities of Race and Ethnicity*

Some U.S. racial and ethnic groups continue to be the victims of prejudice and discrimination. Sociologists address these questions: Where do race and ethnicity come from? Why and how

are they associated with the distribution of society's rewards? How and why do racial and ethnic stratification change?

Racial and Ethnic Stratification

Stratification represents institutionalized inequality in the distribution of social rewards and burdens.

■ *Race*   The use of the concept of race for sociologists is as a social construct; a **race** is a group of people who see themselves—and are seen by others—as having hereditary traits that set them apart. An important concept based on race is **racism,** the belief that some racial groups are naturally superior and others are inferior.

■ *Ethnic Groups*   Groups that we identify chiefly on cultural grounds—language, folk practices, dress, gestures, mannerisms, or religion—are called **ethnic groups.** Ethnic groups often have a sense of peoplehood and may deem themselves to be a nation.

■ *Minority Groups*   Racial and ethnic groups are often minority groups. Five properties characterize a minority; most critical is that they lack power.

Prejudice and Discrimination

■ *Prejudice*   **Prejudice** refers to attitudes of aversion and hostility toward the members of a group simply because they belong to it and hence are presumed to have the objectionable qualities ascribed to it. A new form of prejudice against African Americans has been labeled **symbolic racism** by sociologists.

■ *Discrimination*   **Discrimination** is action, what people actually do in their daily activities, and involves the arbitrary denial of privilege, prestige, and power to members of a minority group. Since World War II whites have shifted from more blatant forms of discrimination to more subtle forms.

■ *Institutional Discrimination*   The institutions of society may function in such a way that they produce unequal outcomes for different groups. This is called **institutional discrimination. Gatekeeping** and **environmental racism** are mechanisms by which institutional discrimination occurs.

Patterns of Intergroup Relations: Assimilation and Pluralism

In multiethnic societies, ethnic groups may either lose their distinctiveness through a process of assimilation or retain their identity and integrity through pluralism.

■ *Assimilation*   **Assimilation** refers to those processes whereby groups with distinctive identities become culturally and socially fused. Two views toward assimilation have dominated within the United States, the "melting pot" view and the Anglo-conformity view.

■ *Pluralism*   In U.S. society, many groups have retained their identities and distinctiveness for many years, an example of **pluralism,** a situation in which diverse groups coexist and boundaries between them are maintained. In *equalitarian pluralism,* ethnic group members participate freely and equally in political and economic institutions. In *inequalitarian pluralism,* economic and political participation of minority groups is severely limited by the dominant group and may even entail **genocide.**

Racial and Ethnic Groups in the United States

The United States is undergoing a transition from a predominately white society rooted in Western European culture to a global society composed of diverse racial and ethnic groups. By the year 2050 today's minorities will comprise nearly half of the U.S. population.

■ *Hispanics/Latinos*   The nation's Hispanic population is not a consolidated minority. Latino groups have different histories, distinct concentrations in different areas of the United States, and substantially different demographic and socioeconomic characteristics. Hispanics typically earn less than non-Hispanics.

◼ *African Americans* African Americans have made tremendous progress but remain disadvantaged. The expected lifetime earnings of African-American men are significantly lower than those of white men, and housing segregation remains substantial. The full integration of African Americans is unlikely in the foreseeable future, primarily because of continuing social and economic barriers and low rates of interracial marriage.

◼ *American Indians and Alaskan Natives* Native American peoples vary substantially in their history, lifestyles, kin systems, language, political arrangements, religion, economy, current circumstances, and identities. They are the most severely disadvantaged of any population within the United States. Poverty and unemployment rates are high.

◼ *Asian Americans* The average family income of Chinese, Japanese, and Korean Americans in the second and subsequent generations is almost one-and-a-half times higher than that of non-Hispanic whites. But Asian Americans are a varied group, with considerable contrasts and diversity. The earnings of Laotians, Cambodians, and Vietnamese are generally low.

◼ *White Ethnics* Most white Americans, including those of northwestern European background, know and identify with their ethnic ancestry, but white ethnicity is neither deep nor stable. "Symbolic ethnicity" is an ethnicity that contributes to individual identity and perhaps to family communion, but does not create or sustain strong ethnic group ties.

Sociological Perspectives on Inequalities of Race and Ethnicity

◼ *The Functionalist Perspective*
Functionalists say that ethnic differentiation reduces consensus, increases the chances of

conflict, and threatens the equilibrium of a society, but it also promotes group formation and cohesion, functions as a safety valve through *scapegoating,* and helps maintain a democratic order.

◼ *The Conflict Perspective* Conflict theorists contend that prejudice and discrimination can best be understood in terms of tension or conflict among competing groups. At least three different conflict theories exist, and they are related to ethnocentrism, Marxism, and the **split labor market.**

◼ *The Interactionist Perspective*
Interactionists say that the world we experience is **socially constructed.** In this view, ethnic groups are seen as products of social interaction. Ethnicity arises when communication channels between groups are limited and the different groups develop different systems of meanings.

The Future of Ethnic and Minority Group Relations
Ethnic status for Americans with African-, Hispanic-, Asian-, and Native American roots is not "symbolic," is not a matter of choice, and remains heavily ascriptive.

◼ *Intergroup Relations* Functionalists believe there are long-run social trends that are eliminating ascription and other irrational features from modern, industrial, socially differentiated societies. The conflict perspective predicts that ethnic stratification will remain as long as it is in the interests of powerful dominant groups to keep it in place. Interactionists say that as long as segregation and isolation of minority groups persist, ethnocentrism will continue and probably worsen.

◼ *Ethnicity* If ethnic stratification persists, then ethnicity will persist as well; if it diminishes significantly, perhaps ethnicity for all groups will become increasingly "symbolic."

Glossary

assimilation Those processes whereby groups with distinctive identities become culturally and socially fused.

discrimination The arbitrary denial of privilege, prestige, and power to members of a minority group whose qualifications are equal to those of members of the dominant group.

environmental racism The practice of deliberately locating incinerators and other types of hazardous waste facilities in or next to minority communities.

ethnic groups Groups identified chiefly on cultural grounds—language, religion, folk practices, dress, gestures, mannerisms.

gatekeeping The decision-making process whereby people are admitted to offices and positions of privilege, prestige, and power within a society.

genocide The deliberate and systematic extermination of a racial or ethnic group.

institutional discrimination The functioning of the institutions of society in a way that produces unequal outcomes for different groups.

minority group A racially or culturally self-conscious population, with hereditary membership and a high degree of in-group marriage, which suffers oppression at the hands of a dominant segment of a nation-state.

pluralism A situation where diverse groups coexist side by side and mutually accommodate themselves to their differences.

prejudice Attitudes of aversion and hostility toward the members of a group simply because they belong to it and hence are presumed to have the objectionable qualities ascribed to it.

race A population that differs from other populations in the incidence of various hereditary traits.

racism The belief that some racial groups are naturally superior and others are inferior.

split labor market An economic arena in which large differences exist in the price of labor at the same occupational level.

symbolic racism A form of racism in which whites feel that blacks are too aggressive, do not play by the rules, and have negative characteristics.

Review Questions

1. What is race? How do sociologists define it?
2. What is an ethnic group?
3. List the five characteristics of minority groups.
4. What is the difference between prejudice and discrimination?
5. How does institutional discrimination work?

6. Define and contrast assimilation and pluralism.

7. Briefly describe the major racial and ethnic groups in the United States.

8. How do the functionalist, conflict, and interactionist perspectives explain racial and ethnic stratification?

Internet Connection

www.mhhe.com/hughes8

Research discussed in this chapter indicates that subjective racism and prejudiced attitudes have moderated considerably in the United States over the past 50 years. However, extreme prejudice still exists in the United States. Go to the website of the Southern Poverty Law Center, **http://www.splcenter.org/**. Explore this website for evidence of the existence of ethnocentrism and prejudice in the United States today. On the basis of these investigations and your reading of the current chapter, write a short report on (1) the nature and extent of extreme prejudice in the United States, (2) the causes of such prejudice, and (3) what can be done to eliminate it or reduce its negative effects.

Chapter 8

GENDER INEQUALITY

Gender Stratification

Sexism and Patriarchy
Gender Inequality Around the World
Gender Inequality in the United States

Sources of Gender Differences

Gender and Biology
Gender and Culture
Gender Identities

Sociological Perspectives on Gender Stratification

The Functionalist Perspective
The Conflict Perspective

The Interactionist Perspective
The Feminist Perspective

What do *Black Beauty, Finding Nemo, Chicken Run, Babe, Toy Story, The Lion King, The Princess Diaries,* and *Monsters, Inc.* have in common?

(a) They are top box-office grossing films.

(b) They are rated G.

(c) They have mostly male characters.

(d) They are watched by kids, in theatres and on video, over and over and over.

(e) All of the above.

Did you guess "e"? You're right. These and 94 other top box-office grossing G-rated live-action and animated films—all released between 1990 and 2005—were analyzed by University of Southern California researchers for gender balance (Kelly and Smith, 2006). Of a total of 4,249 speaking characters in the 101 films, 28 percent are female. Only a quarter of all the characters (speaking and nonspeaking) are

female, and only 17 percent of the characters in crowd scenes are female. Even the narration is male dominated, with 83 percent of narrators being male.

Does it matter? Clearly, women have come a long way since the beginning of the 20th century, when many of them were farm wives slaving over hot stoves or were urban workers confined to low-paying occupations such as seamstress, laundry worker, or maid. Today, women in the United States can vote, run for office, control their own finances, and work outside the home in professional occupations, and they are increasingly likely to do work previously thought of as "men's work."

At the same time, women still make up only a small proportion of our elected leaders, for the most part are passed over when top executives are being selected, are mostly excluded from a wide variety of male-dominated occupations and careers, are portrayed and treated as sex objects in many ways, and, when they work, often carry the burden of two full-time jobs, one in the paid workforce and one as an unpaid housekeeper and child care worker in the family.

Patterns of gender representation in G-rated movies both reflect and help to perpetuate such gender disparities. These movies teach and reinforce the belief that activities of men are at the center of what is important, that men have the initiative and presence of mind to solve problems, and that men are the ones who have the authority, intelligence, and background to tell us what is worth knowing about the unfolding of events.

Of course, many factors go into producing gender inequality, and imagery that reinforces inequality in the media, including movies, is only one piece of the puzzle.

Just as our society structures inequalities based on race and ethnic membership, so it institutionalizes inequalities based on gender (Martin, 2004). Men and women differ in their access to privilege, prestige, and power. Despite advances in the United States and elsewhere, the distribution problem of who gets what, when, and how has nearly always been answered in favor of males.

In Chapter 6 we examined stratification by class, and in Chapter 7 we looked at the role race and ethnicity play in stratification. In this chapter we examine inequalities based on gender. We begin by considering sex, gender, sexism, and patriarchy. We then take a closer look at the status of women in society, both in the United States and around the world. We will discuss the acquisition of gender identities, looking at the parts played by biology, culture, and socialization. Finally, we will see what the functionalist, conflict, interactionist, and feminist perspectives have to offer to our understanding of gender stratification.

Gender Stratification

Throughout the world, human activities, practices, and institutional structures are organized with respect to the social distinction people make between men and women—in brief, by gender.

For the most part the state, the law, politics, religion, higher education, and the economy are institutions that have been historically developed by men, are currently dominated by men, and are symbolically interpreted from the standpoint of men. As such they are "gendered institutions." The only major institution in which women have had a central, defining role, although a subordinate one, has been the family (Acker, 1992).

Before we continue our discussion of gender stratification, we need to define some basic terms. **Sex** refers to whether one is genetically male or female and determines the biological role that one will play in reproduction. **Gender,** on the other hand, is a form of social differentiation; it refers to the sociocultural distinction between males and females. While sex is given in nature, gender is a socially constructed framework human beings have created to make sense of and deal with the sex difference.

Gender identities are the conceptions we have of ourselves as being male or female. One's gender identity is part of one's self-concept and consequently is a product of social interaction (see Chapter 3). Our gender identity p. 83 emerges as we enact gender roles and are reacted to by others as being either male or female.

Gender roles are sets of cultural expectations that define the ways in which the members of each sex should behave. Gender roles influence a wide range of human behaviors, including how people speak, dress, walk, engage in courtship, get angry, play sports, deal with distress, and choose a career.

The gender roles defined by a society have profound consequences for the lives of its men and women. They constitute master statuses that carry primary weight in people's interactions and relationships with others (see Chapter 2). pp. 57–58 In doing so they place men and women in the social structure, establishing where and what they are in social terms. Thus, gender roles establish the framework within which men and women gain their identities, formulate their goals, and carry out their training. Gender roles are a major source of social inequality.

In this section we will consider sexism and patriarchy. We will then take a closer look at women's roles and gender inequality in society both around the world and in the United States.

Sexism and Patriarchy

Gender inequality is perpetuated by a set of complex processes referred to as **sexism.** Like racism, sexism operates at two levels. At the *individual level* sexism is the belief that one sex is superior to the other. This form of sexism involves two basic ideas: (1) that because of inherent biological differences, men and women are naturally suited to different roles and (2) that this is the primary cause of the differential distribution of status, power, and income by gender. At the *institutional level* sexism involves policies, procedures, and practices that produce unequal outcomes for men and women. In principle, sexism refers to disadvantages that may be experienced by either sex. In reality, the patterns of gender inequality in history and throughout the world today generally involve disadvantages for women and advantages for men. What we usually mean by sexism, then, is a set of cultural and social processes that justify and promote disadvantage for women.

▲ Do Women Constitute a Minority Group?

Sexism operates against women the way racism operates against persons of minority racial backgrounds. However, although they are similar to a minority group, women are clearly not in the minority in most societies. Given higher mortality rates for men, as men and women age, there are increasingly more women than there are men. But as we noted in the previous chapter, being a minority group does not require relatively low numbers. The key characteristic of a minority group is that it *lacks power* relative to a dominant group. And this is true of the situation of women in virtually every society.

Let's look again at the five properties of a *minority group* we considered in ◄━ pp. 215–216 Chapter 7, this time with women in mind.

1. Historically, women have encountered *prejudice and discrimination* and have not had access to the institutionalized power needed to readily change this situation.

2. Women possess *physical and cultural traits* that distinguish them from men, the dominant group.

3. Through the efforts of the women's liberation movement and consciousness-raising groups, women have increasingly become a *self-conscious social group* characterized by an awareness of oneness.

4. *Membership is involuntary* since gender is an ascribed status that is assigned to a person at birth.

5. Only the fifth characteristic, endogamy, does not apply to women, because, of course, women are not required to marry women.

The existence of sexism not only disadvantages women, but also has a wide-ranging impact on how we think about our lives and the places of women and men in them. As sociologist Jessie Bernard put it in a discussion of the impact of sexism on women:

[Sexism is] the unconscious, taken-for-granted, assumed, unquestioned, unexamined, unchallenged acceptance of the belief that the world as it looks to men is the only world, that the way of dealing with it which men have created is the only way, that the values which men have evolved are the only ones, that the way sex looks to men is the only way it can look to anyone, that what men think about what women are like is the only way to think about what women are like. (Quoted in Gornick and Moran, 1971:xxv.)

▲ Patriarchy

The most pervasive form of institutional sexism is **patriarchy,** a system of social organization in which men have a disproportionate share of power. Patriarchy is rooted in cultural and legal systems that historically gave fathers authority in family and clan matters, made wives and children dependent on husbands and fathers, and organized descent and inheritance through the male line. Sociologist Judith Lorber (1994) believes that early societies may have been egalitarian for thousands of years, and Jeannine Davis-Kimball (1997) cites archaeological evidence of female military and social power. One possibility is that patriarchy emerged gradually as economic arrangements of societies became more complicated (Barber, 1994; Ortner, 1996). Most sociologists believe that patriarchal systems serve the interests of men at the expense of women, and nearly all societies around the world today are patriarchal.

Gender inequality exists in every society around the world, but recent changes have moved many women who traditionally did only unpaid domestic labor into the paid labor force.

Although in some societies political change has undermined the legal basis of patriarchy, and attitudinal change has undermined its cultural power, modern societies include many patriarchal elements. An obvious one is the practice of women and children taking the last name of the husband and father; in the United States, only about 10 percent of all married women have not adopted their husbands' names (Span, 1998). More importantly, men have more social, economic, and political power than women in societies around the world, the topic of our next section.

Gender Inequality around the World

The U.S. State Department's 2006 human rights report, which included reports from 196 nations, portrayed a grim picture of day-to-day discrimination against and abuse of women around the world. "Violence and societal discrimination against women" were cited as serious problems in many countries. In Ghana, Bangladesh, and many other countries the trafficking of women and children for the sex trade and for forced labor remains a significant problem. Underage prostitution, sex tourism, and the sexual abuse of children also are listed in the human rights reports of many countries. Overall, one in three women has experienced violent victimization (Garcia-Moreno et al., 2005). The governments of many countries turn a blind eye to the abuse of women, and in many nations the state is a major institutional source of discrimination. In the Middle East and Northern Africa, for example, the legal system often excuses a man for killing his wife for alleged immoral acts—an "honor killing."

Worldwide half a million women annually die from pregnancy-related problems, including botched abortions (Ashford, 2002). One-sixth of all women who give birth in the less-developed countries of the world develop long-term disabilities as a result of complications experienced during pregnancy and childbirth. Around the world, more than a quarter of the babies born are unwanted or unplanned, but women's ability to control their fertility has improved significantly. In less-developed countries, the percent of women using contraception has increased from 9 percent in 1960 to 58 percent in the late 1990s (Population Reference Bureau, 2005). In some countries, a strong traditional preference for sons results in a higher proportion of boys' surviving to age one, with causes of death for the girls including sex-selective abortion, infanticide, discrimination, and neglect (Population Reference Bureau, 2002b).

Women are sexually victimized throughout the world. One form of victimization is the traditional ethnic practice of female genital mutilation, listed in many countries' human rights reports (U.S. State Department, 2006; Hayford, 2005; Yount, 2002). Another form of sexual victimization is the transmission of HIV to young women and girls by older men. Half of the world's HIV-infected population is now female, and in sub-Saharan Africa, 15- to 24-year-old women are three times more likely to be HIV-positive than men of the same age (Lamptey, Johnson, and Khan, 2006; Quinn and Overbaugh, 2005). Mass rape and sexual sadism in war are still common around the world, often accompanying the collapse of social order that occurs during war. International criminal charges against Serbians included the rapes of as many as 20,000 Bosnian Muslim women during the civil war that erupted in 1992 after Yugoslavia broke apart (Adler, Mueller, and Laufer, 2004).

Two-thirds of the world's illiterates are female. In Middle Eastern and North African countries, the illiteracy rate is approximately twice as high for females as for males (UNESCO, 2006). The education gender gap is closing, however, with primary school enrollments high in most countries and increasing numbers of women participating in secondary and higher education. Worldwide, women are making significant gains in higher education (United Nations, 2003). Women make up an increasing share of the labor force, although they still are concentrated in just a few occupations, have little or no authority on the job, and receive less pay than men.

Women around the world do considerably better than U.S. women in some areas. More than 160 countries around the world provide paid maternity leave by law; the United States does not (Heymann et al., 2002). A number of nations have had a woman prime minister or president, including Great Britain, Canada, Ireland, Norway, Germany, Finland, Portugal, Iceland, the Philippines, Argentina, Bolivia, Nicaragua, Poland, Israel, Turkey, India, Pakistan, Bangladesh, Sri Lanka, Haiti, Netherlands Antilles, and Dominica (Lewis, 2006). For the first time, a country has achieved nearly equal representation of men and women in its legislature, and the world average for the percentage of women in the national parliaments has risen to 16.4. Many countries now have 30 and 40 percent of their legislatures composed of women, far ahead of the United States (see Figure 8.1).

Changes for women also can be seen in other aspects of their lives. In 2002, Japan convened a meeting of 30 of its national academic societies to plan strategies for increasing the proportions of women in scientific and engineering fields (Normile, 2002). In Europe, an action plan for promoting women's participation in science was adopted in 1999 (Dewandre, 2002). The percentage of women in the industrial research workforce is higher in Ireland, Greece, Portugal, France, Denmark, and Spain than it is in the United States, although it does not exceed 30 percent in any industrialized nation and stands at under 10 percent in some (Holden, 2003).

In general, worldwide social attitudes, norms, and institutions deem women to be inferior—and discrimination tends to start at birth. An International Labor Organization report, based on a survey of 41 nations, concluded

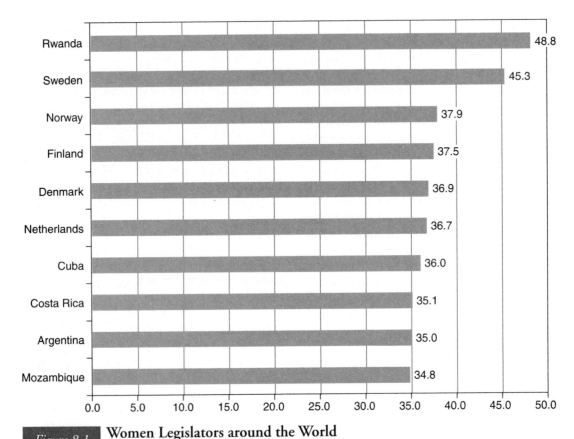

Figure 8.1 Women Legislators around the World

Nearly 50 percent of Rwanda's legislators are women, the highest proportion in the world. Sixty-nine other countries are ahead of the United States, where 15.2 percent of legislators are female. A number of countries have no women legislators whatsoever, including Bahrain, Nepal, Micronesia, Saudi Arabia, and the United Arab Emirates.

Source: Figure generated by the authors using data for the lower, or single, House of each country; data from the Inter-Parliamentary Union's website, www.ipu.org.

that women will need another 1,000 years to match the political and economic clout of men (Sanchez, 1993).

Gender Inequality in the United States

Social scientists have long noted many similarities between the status of African Americans and that of women within the United States

(Myrdal, 1944; Hacker, 1951, 1974; Smith and Steward, 1983). Look, for example, at racist and sexist stereotypes. Both African Americans and women have been portrayed as intellectually inferior, emotional, irresponsible, dependent, and childlike. Both groups lack power, and the rationalization for their subordination has been similar—the myth of "contented African Americans who know their place" and the notion that "women's place is in the home." Recent generations of both African Americans and women have challenged those stereotypes by participating in social movements for equal rights.

How disadvantaged are women in U.S. society? That varies from state to state (see Box 8.1). In this section we look at the division of labor in the family, gender stratification in the workplace, the "glass ceiling," disparities in pay, career patterns, sexual harassment and rape, politics and government, and the women's movement.

▲ Dividing Labor in the Family

Sexual inequality has historically been sustained by assigning the economic-provider role to men and the child-rearing role to women. Labor in the public sphere has been rewarded by money, prestige, and power, whereas labor in the domestic sphere typically has been isolated and undervalued (Crittenden, 2001; Daniels, 1987; Ferree, 1990; Kessler-Harris, 1990). Gender stereotypes arise in response to a gender division of labor and then serve to rationalize it by attributing to the sexes substantially different personality characteristics and traits (Hoffman and Hurst, 1990).

Across the years the gender division of labor has operated to bind women to their reproductive function. Women were viewed as providing a man with sexual and domestic services in exchange for his financial support. Within this arrangement a sexual double standard prevailed that permitted men, but not women, considerable sexual freedom. Until the 20th century, English and American common law viewed women as undergoing "civil death" upon marriage. Women lost their legal identity when they married and, in the eyes of the law, became "incorporated and consolidated" with their husbands. A wife could not own property in her own right or sign a contract. And a husband could require his wife to live wherever he chose and to submit to sexual intercourse against her will—a practice we now call rape.

Today marriage and family have become less of an organizing force in the lives of

Since 1950 the number of American mothers who work outside the home has tripled, but most of them still do most of the household and childcare work as well.

contemporary American women. Over the last four decades, younger-generation women have come to experience and lead dramatically different lives than their older counterparts. Work outside the home is no longer limited by obligations that traditionally bound women to husbands and children. Although they still place a high value on marriage and the family, younger women are now more likely to delay marriage and childbearing (see Chapter 10). pp. 327–328 Since the 1980s, women in the younger generation have been taking greater control of their lives and are integrating labor-force participation and family responsibilities more independently than their older counterparts (McLaughlin et al., 1988).

For Gender Equality, It Matters Where You Live

The quality of people's lives has much to do with individual choices, abilities, and aspirations. But social institutions also affect quality of life. Women's vastly different experiences in different societies illustrate the importance of social institutions for gender equality and women's quality of life.

Women's experiences differ within the United States, too. In fact, women's political participation, employment and earnings, social and economic autonomy, reproductive rights, and health and well-being vary substantially from state to state. These factors have been assessed in an ongoing research project, *The Status of Women in the States,* conducted by the Institute for Women's Policy Research (Werschkul and Williams, 2004).

So—if you're a woman or a man interested in gender equality and better outcomes for women— where should you live? In 2004, the best states for women to live in were Vermont, Connecticut, Minnesota, and Washington. The worst state was Mississippi, followed by South Carolina, Kentucky, Arkansas and Oklahoma (tied), Tennessee, and Texas. How does the IWPR decide? The top states must rank in the top 10 of all the states in at least one of the factors listed above and must *not* appear in the bottom half of all states in any of the factors. In contrast, the worst states are identified as those that rank in the bottom 10 for at least

one factor and in the bottom half for all factors.

How different are the differences? Let's look at political participation and representation as an example. In Hawaii only 51 percent of the state's women are registered to vote, while in North Dakota the comparable figure is 91 percent. In state legislatures, the proportion of women ranges from 9.4 percent (South Carolina) to 36.7 percent (Washington). Four states have had two female U.S. Senators at the same time; five states have never had a woman elected to either the Senate or the House.

While some of the states are "all good" or "all bad," others are strange mixes of benefits and problems for women. Women in the District of Columbia, for example, had the highest earnings in the nation in 2004, the least difference in pay between men and women, and the highest proportion of women in management and professional occupations. On the other hand, District women have the worst overall health status, high rates of poverty, and low rates of health insurance coverage.

Some general findings have emerged from the research. Racial and ethnic disparities in women's health status are wide in every state. The significantly higher probability that African-American women will die of heart disease or breast cancer or will have

AIDS is among the specific findings on health status. Another general finding is that a small wage gap, high earnings, and high representation in professional and managerial occupations co-occur in many states.

The IWPR research also identifies general patterns of progress and lack thereof for American women. Among the disappointing findings they list are an increase in women's poverty in eight states and only a very small decrease in nine others, a decrease in reproductive health services in a number of states, and only a very small increase in the proportion of women state legislators.

Questions for Discussion

1. How do you think your home state measures up in terms of women's rights? Go to www.iwpr.org/states and find data for your state. What institutional factors (e.g., law, economy, politics, education, health care, religion) do you think determine the position of your state in the ranking?

2. One route to gender equality is to promote policies that lead to changes in social structure. How might the factors assessed by IWPR be linked through this idea?

▲ Gender Stratification
in the Workplace

In 2004, the labor-force participation rate for U.S. women 16 and older was 59.2 percent. In other words, nearly 60 percent of women age 16 or over were working or looking for work (U.S. Department of Labor, 2006). Almost half—46 percent—of all U.S. workers are women. Have American women always worked outside the home? The labor-force participation of married women in the United States over the past 200 years is represented by a U-shaped curve, with relatively high participation rates in the 1790s, declining rates accompanying industrialization during the 19th century, and rising rates after the beginning of the 20th century—and mounting substantially after 1960. Although the participation of married women in the labor force fell during the 19th century, single women entered the labor force in increasing numbers throughout that period. In recent decades lower fertility and changing social attitudes contributed to the jump in the labor-force participation of women, while higher rates of divorce impelled more women to join the workforce. African-American women have always worked for pay in larger proportions than white women (Herring and Wilson-Sadberry, 1993). In 2004, 75.1 percent of black women with children under age six were working, while 58.4 percent of white women with young children worked (U.S. Census Bureau, 2006).

In the United States 66 percent of single and 60 percent of married women 16 and older are now in the paid labor force, compared with 70 percent of single and 77 percent of married men (U.S. Census Bureau, 2006); see Figure 8.2 for a comparison with other countries. Since 1950 the number of American mothers employed outside the home has tripled. In 68.2 percent of the families with children under age 18, the mother is employed. Among mothers of teenagers, 78.8 percent are in the labor force (U.S. Census Bureau, 2006). Even women with very young children are increasingly part of the labor force; 59.3 percent of women with children under age six and 55.1 percent with children under age three are employed.

Women have gained ground by entering college in higher numbers than men (U.S. Census Bureau, 2006). In 2002, women caught up with and passed men in one educational arena: The number of women aged 25 and over with a high school diploma exceeded that of men (Bergman, 2003). Women also have been moving into higher-paying fields traditionally dominated by men. For example, between 1980 and 2004 the percentage of women lawyers rose from 14 percent to 29 percent (U.S. Census Bureau, 2006). In the same time period, the proportion of female doctors increased from 13 percent to 27 percent and half the entering medical students for the 2003–2004 school year were women (Association of American Medical Colleges, 2003). Additionally, the Department of Education reports that more than 4 in 10 Ph.D. degrees are now earned by women (Gerald and Hussar, 2002).

Despite these changes many of the current figures on the employment of women bear a striking resemblance to those of previous decades. There was little substantial change in the gender segregation of occupations between 1900 and 1970. Levels of segregation did decline in the 1980s and 1990s, but the decline slowed between 1990 and 1997 (Wells, 1999). The stereotypes many of us hold are based on fact: In 2004, it was still true that 96.9 percent of all secretaries and administrative assistants were female, 92.2 percent of registered nurses were female, 91.5 percent of all hairdressers and cosmetologists were women, and 81.3 percent of elementary and middle-school teachers were female (U.S. Census Bureau, 2006). On the other hand, only about 30 percent of lawyers, physicians, and surgeons were women in 2004; 20 percent of detectives, criminal investigators, and farm and ranch managers were women,

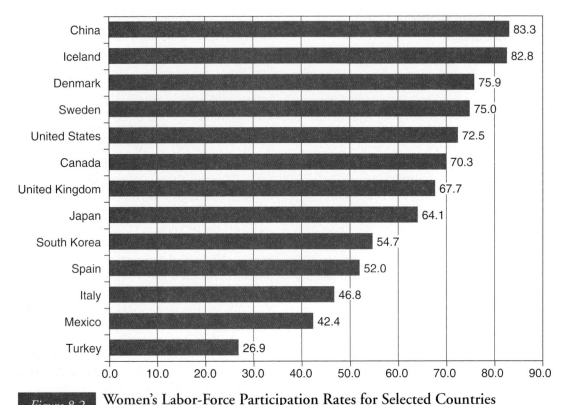

China	83.3
Iceland	82.8
Denmark	75.9
Sweden	75.0
United States	72.5
Canada	70.3
United Kingdom	67.7
Japan	64.1
South Korea	54.7
Spain	52.0
Italy	46.8
Mexico	42.4
Turkey	26.9

Figure 8.2   **Women's Labor-Force Participation Rates for Selected Countries**
The participation of women in the paid labor force in the United States is not the highest in the world, but neither is it the lowest.

Source: Figure generated by the authors using 2000 data from the following sources: Organization for Economic Cooperation and Development (OECD) for all countries except China, http://www1.oecd.org/scripts/cde/members/ifsindicatorsauthenticate.asp; for China, World Bank, http://devdata.worldbank.org/genderstats/home.asp. Women's labor force participation rate presented in this chart is the number of women in the labor force divided by the number of women in the population aged 15 to 64 and multiplied by 100.

about 5 percent of pilots and firefighters were female, and there is a sizable list of occupations with no women employees whatsoever.

Men and women sort into occupational categories in some general ways: 59 percent of men work in precision production, craft, and repair jobs; executive, administrative, and managerial positions; professional specialty; and sales, while 73 percent of women work in administrative support; professional specialty; service work; and hold executive, administrative, and

managerial positions (Spraggins, 2003). The increase in female employment has come largely through the displacement of men by women in some low-paying categories and through the rapid expansion of "pink-collar" occupations such as secretary, bookkeeper, and receptionist.

The "sticky floor" is an apt metaphor for the occupational frustrations experienced by most U.S. working women in low-paying dead-end jobs.

Although some women face a "glass ceiling" in their careers, most women are limited by a "sticky floor"—women are concentrated in low-paying service, support, and nurturance occupations.

SIX CHIX by Margaret Shulock. Reprinted with permission of King Features Syndicate.

▲ The Glass Ceiling

The number of women top executives and board directors has increased over the years, but positions at the top still elude women executives. Women in business crash into what has been labeled the "glass ceiling," a set of invisible barriers that prevent women from advancing. When glass ceilings do not stop women, glass walls do; these are barriers that prevent women from moving laterally in corporations and thereby gaining the experience they need to advance vertically (Lopez, 1992). A 2003 survey showed that both male CEOs and executive women say a major obstacle for women is insufficient work experience (Catalyst, 2003).

In 2001, 45 percent of the jobs classified as executive, administrative, and managerial were held by women (U.S. Census Bureau, 2003). But by 2005 only a very few of these women were at the very top: Only 1.4 percent of Fortune 500 companies have female CEOs or presidents (Catalyst, 2006). Yet change has occurred; in 2003, 50 of the Fortune 500 companies had women filling at least a quarter of their corporate officer positions, up from only 25 in 1995 (Catalyst, 2003). A closer look at specific companies shows that women corporate officers are doing best in traditionally "feminine" work, such as apparel, publishing, and soaps and cosmetics. Avon, for example, has more women in management positions than any other company, with a female CEO and half its board positions filled by women (Catalyst, 2003).

Women who make it to the top get there differently. One analysis of women CEOs showed that at least half were "imported" from outside the company, while male CEOs almost always come from the inside (Reed, 2005).

Getting more women into top executive positions will require active steps to eradicate stereotypes about women, according to a 2005 study (Catalyst, 2006). This survey of both male and female corporate leaders showed that perceptions of men and women leaders are based on gender stereotypes, not on fact-based information. A major finding was that men consider women to be less skilled at problem solving than men are. With men far outnumbering women in top management positions, this idea "dominates current corporate thinking" and prevents women from advancing. The report recommends that companies educate managers and executives about stereotyping and ways to overcome it and that the achievements of women leaders be showcased.

In another Catalyst study comparing women's business advancement in Canada, the United Kingdom, and the United States, the top career advancement strategies used by women in all three countries was "consistently exceeding performance expectations and developing a style with which male managers are comfortable" (Catalyst, 2003).

▲ Disparities in Pay

Women earn less than men. On average, women employed full-time in 2004 earn only 77 cents for each dollar earned by males, up from 60.7 cents per dollar in 1960 (U. S. Census Bureau, 2006).

More women than men have low incomes, with 4.4 percent of women but only 2.8 percent of men reporting incomes of less than $10,000 and 12.9 percent of females but only 10.4 percent of males living below the poverty level. At the other end of the income level, 15.8 percent of men but only 5.5 percent of women reported annual earnings of $75,000 and over in 2001 (Spraggins, 2003). Although the wage gap has closed over the past several decades, the rate of decrease has slowed (Hartmann and Lovell, 2003) and significant disparities remain overall (see Figure 8.3a) as well as within occupational categories (see Figure 8.3b). Though the education gap between men and

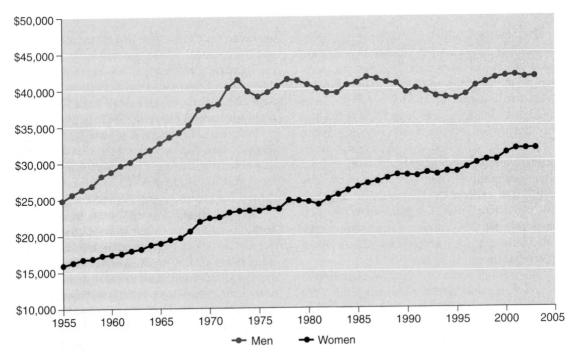

Figure 8.3a **Disparities in Earnings Remain Significant**
a. Median yearly earnings of full-time, year-round workers in the United States by gender, in constant 2003 dollars, 1955–2003. Recent gains by women in terms of the ratio of their earnings to those of men is due both to a decrease in earnings of men and to an increase in earnings of women.

Source: U.S. Census Bureau, March Current Population Surveys, available at: http://www.census.gov/hhes/income/histinc/p36ar.html.

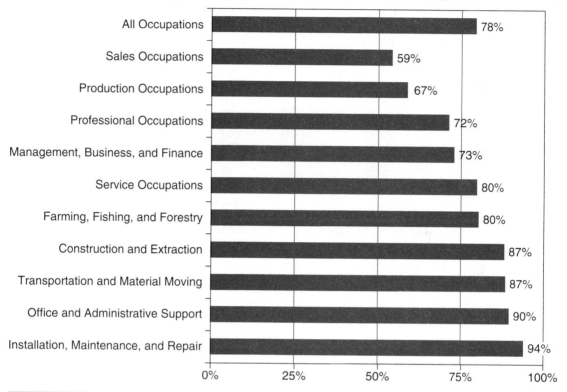

Women's Weekly Earnings as a Percentage of Men's Weekly Earnings for Full-Time Wage and Salary Workers by Occupation in the U.S., 2003

Occupation	Percentage
All Occupations	78%
Sales Occupations	59%
Production Occupations	67%
Professional Occupations	72%
Management, Business, and Finance	73%
Service Occupations	80%
Farming, Fishing, and Forestry	80%
Construction and Extraction	87%
Transportation and Material Moving	87%
Office and Administrative Support	90%
Installation, Maintenance, and Repair	94%

Figure 8.3b   **Disparities in Earnings Remain Significant (*continued*)**

b. In all occupations, women earn an average of 78 cents for every dollar earned by men. The ratio of female-to-male median weekly earnings for full-time wage and salary workers in the United States is especially low in sales occupations and especially high in installation, maintenance, and repair.

Source: Calculated by the authors from data in Bureau of Labor Statistics news release, "Usual Weekly Earnings of Wage and Salary Workers: Third Quarter 2003," available at: http://www.bls.gov/news.release/archives/wkyeng_10172003.pdf.

women has closed, there is a sharp disparity in earnings between men and women at all levels of education (see Figure 8.3c).

Paying a woman less to do the same job a man does is illegal. What, then, explains the pay gap? It is affected by many factors. Sociologist Paula England (1993) suggested three major explanations. First, discrimination in hiring and placement reduces women's chances for high-paying jobs in occupations dominated by men,

such as management, craft occupations, and some professions. Second, jobs that are occupied mostly by women provide lower wages than jobs that are dominated by men. In one analysis, it was found that nurses were paid less than fire truck mechanics, and librarians were paid less than custodians. Pay differentials for gendered occupations account for much, but not all, of the earnings gap (Boraas and Rodgers, 2003). Third, women often have less job experience than men

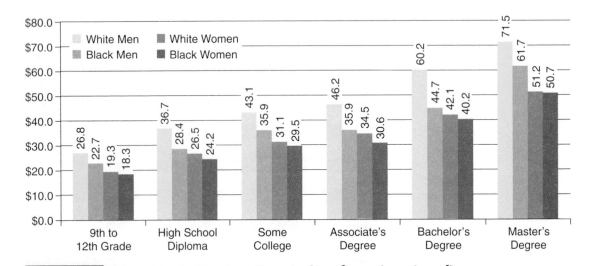

Figure 8.3c   **Disparities in Earnings Remain Significant (*continued*)**

c. Yearly earnings in thousands of dollars of full-time, year-round workers 25 years and older, by gender, race, and education, 2004. Black and white women earn less in every educational category than black and white men.

Source: U.S. Census Bureau, Current Population Survey, 2005 Annual Social and Economic Supplement, available at: http://pubdb3.census.gov/macro/032005/perinc/new03_000.htm.

because they interrupt their careers to care for children. This "motherhood penalty" has been found to be 5 percent per child even after the cost of lost experience is accounted for, a penalty the researchers attributed to discrimination by employers against mothers and/or the effect of motherhood on productivity at work (Budig and England, 2001).

Other related factors also contribute to the pay gap. For example, on average, women work fewer hours than men and are less likely to work full-time, but this fact and other factors do not completely explain the gender gap in pay. A recent study of graduates of the University of Michigan law school found that men's salaries were 52 percent higher than women's salaries. The researchers looked at hours worked, law school grades, marital status, number of children, number of years practicing law, and type of legal practice and found that 23 percent of women's salary disadvantage remained unexplained by these factors (Noonan, Corcoran, and

Courant, 2005). The wage ratio also is affected by age, with the youngest female employees earning wages the most similar to young men and the oldest women having the greatest disparity in pay (Hartmann and Lovell, 2003). These differences reflect differences in education and experience. Wage gaps also vary across the country. In the District of Columbia, women earn 92.4 percent of men's earnings, while women in Wyoming earn 66.3 percent of men's income (Werschkul and Williams, 2004).

Differences in earnings vary by race and ethnicity. In 2001, Hispanic women earned 54 cents to every dollar earned by white men, while the wage ratio for Asian and Pacific Islander women was 77 cents compared to a dollar for white men (Hartmann and Lovell, 2003). White women, the majority of female employees, earned 75.1 cents to the dollar earned by white men, and African-American women earned 66.8 cents per dollar earned by white men. According to an analysis by the Institute for

Women's Policy Research, if the wage gap continues to close at the rate that it did between 1989 and 2002, women will not reach wage parity for another 50 years (Werschkul and Williams, 2004).

▲ The Second Shift

Although American men, particularly younger men, are contributing more effort to doing housework, it is for the most part attitudes rather than behaviors that are changing. Whether or not they work outside the home, the burden of housework still falls disproportionately upon women (Bittman et al., 2003). This unequal involvement of working mothers and wives in household work was labeled "the second shift" more than a decade ago, reflecting the idea that working women start a second shift of work when they get home from their paid work (Hochschild, 1990). Time-diary studies of housework in Australia showed that women averaged 23 hours of housework per week (excluding child care), while husbands averaged 11 hours per week (Bittman et al., 2003). In the United States, comparable numbers were 18 hours for wives and 13 hours for husbands.

In another study of housework in the United States, between 50 and 75 percent of the respondents agreed that wives do more laundry, cleaning, cooking, grocery shopping, and bill paying (Deane, 1998). Respondents also agreed that husbands are more likely to mow the lawn, shovel snow, make minor repairs, and take out the trash. Women most often arranged for child care (in 68 percent of the couples surveyed), called baby-sitters (66 percent of couples), stayed home from work when a child was sick (58 percent), and arranged children's transportation (57 percent) (Deane, 1998).

Despite their greater household responsibilities, women allocate just as much effort on paid jobs as men—indeed, some research suggests they work harder in the workplace (Bielby and Bielby, 1988). Not surprisingly, when women assume overwhelming responsibility for household duties, they suffer stress and overload (Moen and Yu, 2000). Their dissatisfaction with the division of household work also can affect their marital happiness. One researcher found that women who expect to do all the housework (and do) have relatively happy marriages, while women who think that men should contribute to the maintenance of a home (and they don't) have more unhappy marriages (Greenstein, 1996). Men's attitudes play a part. Another study found that women perceive their situations as less unfair when husbands believe that housework should be shared—even if the husbands are not really doing much of the work (DeMaris and Longmore, 1996).

Sociologists find that women who work outside the home decrease their housework as their earnings increase (Bittman et al., 2003). Likewise, as men's contributions to family income decrease from all to half the total family earnings, their time spent on housework increases (Greenstein, 2000).

▲ Career Patterns: Out of Sync with Family Life

Overall, the career patterns of women can be quite different from those of men. The economic advancement of women is complicated by the social organization of child care. Economist Sylvia Ann Hewlett observed (quoted in Castro, 1991:10):

we have confused equal rights with identical treatment, ignoring the realities of family life. After all, only women can bear children. And in this country, women must still carry most of the burden of raising them. We think that we are being fair to everyone by stressing identical opportunities, but in fact we are punishing women and children.

Women who have children encounter substantial career disadvantages (Crittenden, 2001; Desai and Waite, 1991; Glass and Camarigg, 1992; Tilghman, 1993). The years between ages 25 and 35 are critical in the development of a career. Yet these are the years when women are most likely to have children. If they leave the labor force to do so, they suffer in their ability to acquire critical skills and to achieve promotions. Very often they also suffer a complete loss of income for the time they are away from work, and they may also leave with no guarantee that they can return; the United States is one of only three industrialized nations that do not provide paid maternity leave by law (see Table 8.1). New mothers who return to work within a few months may find themselves shunted from a career track to a "mommy track"; male managers conclude that the women are no longer free to take on time-consuming tasks or as motivated to get ahead and fail to consider them for promotion (Wadman, 1992).

Equal opportunity for women in public spheres remains substantially frustrated by gender-role differentiation within the family. Sociologist Mirra Komarovsky (1991:23) observed:

[I]n order to provide real options for men and women we shall have to reorganize economic and other institutions in a profound way, more profound in my opinion, than would be necessary, for example, to solve the problems of the black minority in the United States. . . . Social investments in child care, maternity and paternity leaves, flexible work hours, job sharing, and other changes will be required to balance the private and public worlds for both men and women.

Although many companies are now attempting to appear "family-friendly," family issues continue to impede women's careers (Shellenbarger, 1992). Sociologist Arlie Russell Hochschild (1997) spent three years doing research on family and work at a midwestern Fortune 500 company that promoted family-friendly policies. She found that executives demanded increasingly longer hours of work from employees without regard to the impact on families. In one family Hochschild followed, the husband took a short paternity leave, but both he

Table 8.1	**Other Countries Provide Greater Maternity Benefits**	
Country	Weeks of Leave Provided	Percent of Pay
France	26	100
Hungary	24	100
Belarus	18	100
Denmark	18	100
Austria	16	100
Netherlands	16	100
Poland	16	100
Spain	16	100
Gabon	14	100
Germany	14	100
Mexico	12	100
Zambia	12	100
Portugal	6	100
Sweden	72	80
Iceland*	36	80
Italy	20	80
Ireland	18	70
Czech Republic	28	69
Japan	14	60
Canada	17	55
Australia	52	0
Swaziland	12	0
United States	12	0

Iceland provides 3 months paid leave for the mother, 3 months paid leave for the father, and an additional 3 months paid leave for the father or mother.

Source: Clearinghouse on International Developments in Child, *Youth and Family Policies,* 2003; United Nations, 2003 (*The World's Women 2000: Trends and Statistics,* Table 5.C).

and his wife felt that the company was not ready to have employees who wanted to spend time with their families.

As we might expect, given women's reproductive responsibilities, the factors that affect a woman's labor-force participation are different at different times in her life (Lehrer, 1999). For example, how much a woman and her husband earn affects the woman's employment decisions, but the strength of this effect varies a great deal across time. Mothers of preschoolers, for instance, are more likely to seek part-time employment rather than full-time or no employment in response to increases in wage rates. Lehrer (1999) concluded that factors not typically considered are important in determining women's involvement in the labor market. We will further address child care and other problems related to women in the paid labor force in Chapter 10. ◀── pp. 341–343

▲ Sexual Harassment and Rape

The 2005 movie *North Country,* which portrays a sexual harassment case from the 1970s, drew national attention to a common workplace hazard for women (Graff, 2005).

The Equal Employment Opportunity Commission defines sexual harassment as "unwelcome" sexual attention, whether verbal or physical, that affects an employee's job conditions or creates a "hostile" working environment (Adler, 1991). Examples of sexual harassment include unsolicited and unwelcome flirtations, advances, or propositions; graphic or degrading comments about an employee's appearance, dress, or anatomy; the display of sexually suggestive objects or pictures; ill-received sexual jokes and offensive gestures; sexual or intrusive questions about an employee's personal life; explicit descriptions of a male's own sexual experiences; abuse of familiarities such as "honey," "baby," and "dear"; unnecessary, unwanted physical contact such as touching, hugging, pinching, patting, or kissing; whistling and catcalls; and leering. In 2004, violations of sexual harassment law resulted in awards and settlements of $35.5 million (Graff, 2005).

Explanations of sexual harassment include societal-, organizational-, and individual-level approaches (Welsh, 1999). Researchers who have studied sexual harassment on the job find that women are much more likely to be harassed than men, and that important factors affecting sexual harassment in the workplace are power differences (financially vulnerable people are more likely to be harassed) and masculinity (Uggen and Blackstone, 2004).

Sexual harassment is not limited to the workplace. Half of all female college students who participated in a nationwide survey reported having been subjected to sexist remarks, catcalls, and whistles. In addition, 15.5 percent reported sexual victimizations other than rape, 13.1 reported having been stalked, 20 percent reported getting obscene phone calls, and 10 percent had had false rumors spread about their sex lives (Fisher, Cullen, and Turner, 2000).

Rape is the most violent form of sexual victimization, and it is a form of sexual violence that victimizes women much more than it does men (Kessler et al., 1995). The legal definition of forcible rape varies across states in the United States, but it is generally defined as forcing persons to engage in sexual intercourse against their will. It can also include forcing a person to engage in oral sex and other sex acts. Defined in this way, rape of men by women is extremely rare (Thio, 1998). But rape of women by men is anything but rare: Reasonable estimates of the percentage of women in the United States who have been raped by men sometime in their lifetimes range from 10 to 25 percent (see Box 8.2).

Why do men rape women? Most rapists are *not* psychologically disturbed, sexually inadequate, or unable to relate to women in a normal way. Because psychological explanations at the individual level leave so much unexplained, sociologists have turned to explanations that emphasize culture, socialization, and social structure.

Culture can create a context in which rapes are more likely to occur. It does this through the creation and dissemination of norms, values,

How Many People Get Raped?

Researcher Mary Koss made headlines—and drew heavy criticism—when she published her findings that more than a quarter of all college women have experienced an act that met the legal definition of rape (Koss, Gidycz, and Wisniewski, 1987). Her estimate was 10 to 15 times higher than comparable rates reported by the Bureau of Justice in statistics from their National Crime Victimization Survey (NCVS). Why are the numbers so different?

Rape may be the crime for which it is most difficult to get reliable numbers, and it seems that how the data are gathered is critical. The Uniform Crime Reports (UCR) data, measured by the FBI Index of Crime, are based on police reports of crime. Before a rape appears in the UCR, it must be reported to the police, and the police must be satisfied that "a man must have had (1) carnal knowledge of a woman, (2) forcibly, and (3) against her will" (Gove, Hughes, and Geerken, 1985).

While the NCVS typically uncovers higher rates of rape than appear in the UCR, the questions used to determine these rates do not actually ask a woman if she has ever been raped. A woman must tell the interviewer that she has been raped in response to general questions about whether she has ever been attacked or threatened. Rape itself is never mentioned; it is up to the person being questioned to volunteer the information (Gove, Hughes, and Geerken, 1985).

An obvious way to get more information is to ask people directly whether they have been raped. A national survey that asked this question of both men and women found that 9.2 percent of women and less than 1.0 percent of men had ever been raped in their lifetimes (Kessler et al., 1995). Both numbers are significantly higher than those that appear in either the National Crime Survey or the UCR.

Even higher rates are obtained when the question is asked in a different way. When respondents were asked if anyone had ever forced them to do something sexual, 22 percent of women and 4 percent of men responded yes (Laumann et al., 1994; Michael et al., 1994). A study of nearly 5,000 women attending U.S. colleges and universities also found that what is asked makes a big difference (Fisher, Cullen, and Turner, 2000). This study included a comparison component that used methods similar to those used in the NCVS. The main study, which used extremely detailed questions about "unwanted sexual experiences," found rates of rape and attempted rape that were 11 and 6 times higher than the rates found by the comparison study.

The rates reported by Bonnie Fisher and her colleagues (2000) are in line with those reported by Mary Koss (1987) for college women and by others for the general population. Fisher's survey responses showed that 1.7 percent of the college women had experienced a rape and 1.1 percent an attempted rape during an average period of about seven months. What does such a rate mean? For a school with 10,000 female students, more than 350 of them experience rape or attempted rape in a single academic year. Projected over the five years

and ways of thinking that encourage and justify rape. Examples are music videos, movies, television shows, magazine displays, and pornography that portray women as sex objects, always being ready for sex, and being coerced or forced into sexual activity, perhaps even "enjoying it." Masculine culture among young men often involves patterns of discussion, joking, and banter that treat women primarily as objects of sexual desire and as legitimate targets in sexual pursuits (Fields, 1993; Thio, 1998). This may not directly cause rape, but it creates a normative environment that makes the world safer for rape and rapists (Martin and Hummer, 1995). Studies show that campus athletes, perhaps the most heavily influenced by the culture of masculinity, are more likely to exhibit sexual aggression than other college men (Koss and Gaines, 1993; Nelson, 1994; Crosset et al., 1996).

Cultural factors might not be such important factors in rape and sexual harassment if it were not for gender inequality. Because of gender inequality, women lack the power to respond forcefully and effectively to prevent harassment and rape and to deal with situations leading to them. In addition, some social scientists argue that sexual harassment, sexual aggression, and rape are methods men use to intimidate women,

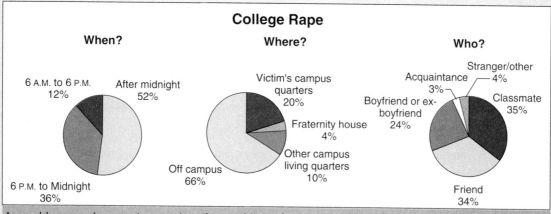

College Rape

When?

- 6 A.M. to 6 P.M. 12%
- After midnight 52%
- 6 P.M. to Midnight 36%

Where?

- Victim's campus quarters 20%
- Fraternity house 4%
- Other campus living quarters 10%
- Off campus 66%

Who?

- Acquaintance 3%
- Stranger/other 4%
- Boyfriend or ex-boyfriend 24%
- Classmate 35%
- Friend 34%

It would appear that rape is not primarily a problem of public life. These data for college women apply to the general population. Rapists are not likely to be lurking in dark alleys; they are likely to be sitting in your living room or next to you in a car. Rape is primarily a problem of private life, and rapists are most likely to be people with whom the rape victim has a close personal relationship.

Source: Figure generated by the authors using data from Fisher, Cullen, and Turner, 2000.

that most students now spend getting an undergraduate degree, one-fifth to one-quarter of all college women would experience a rape or attempted rape.

How many rapes we believe occur seems to depend primarily on how victims are asked about their experiences. Fisher and her colleagues concluded, "The use of graphically worded screen questions . . . likely prompted more women who had experienced a sexual victimization to report this fact to the interviewer" (Fisher, Cullen, and Turner, 2000:14).

Questions for Discussion

1. If you were researching rape, what problems would you face in determining the number of rapes that occur in a given time period?

2. The data on college rape show that rapists are most likely to be someone the victim knows, perhaps intimately. Why do rapes occur in such situations? What strategies would help prevent such rapes?

keeping them dependent, powerless, and out of male-dominated jobs (Graff, 2005; Peterson, 1992).

Culture and gender inequality combine to powerfully influence the prevalence of rape and sexual aggression. Sanday's (1981) study of small societies showed that societies with high rates of rape were those where males were heavily dominant and in which sexual aggression was a symbol of masculinity and of men's control and mastery of women, while those with little rape were those that discouraged sexual aggression. Sanday (1996) and other researchers (Schwartz and DeKeseredy, 1997; Martin and Hummer, 1995; Schwartz, 1995) have found that college campuses with low rates of rape are those in which the culture of masculinity is not strong and where sexual assault and rape are taken seriously and severely punished. Those with high rates of rape are those where the student culture values heavy drinking, male dominance, and traditional masculine values.

▲ Politics and Government

The number of women in politics in the United States has increased in recent years. In the eight years preceding 2004, the number of women serving as state governors jumped from one to nine, women in the House of Representatives went from 49 to 60, and female senators increased from 9 to 14 (Werschkul and Williams, 2004). Thousands of women have entered politics at the local and state levels over the last several decades, enlarging the pool of candidates for higher office. By the early 1990s, nearly a third of local officials were women (U.S. Census Bureau, 1999). Between 1980 and 1995 the number of women state supreme court judges went from 14 to 51 (Songer and Crews-Meyer, 2000). Women also were more likely than men to register to vote in nearly every state in 2004 and more likely than men to vote in all but seven states (Werschkul and Williams, 2004).

But political success has not come easily to American women (Witt, Paget, and Matthews, 1993), and it is not proceeding at a steady pace. Although the number of women in the U.S. House and Senate has increased, the proportion—15 percent—has grown only slightly in recent years (Werschkul and Williams, 2004), and the proportion of women legislators is much smaller in the United States than in many other countries (see Figure 8.1). If the United States adds women to Congress at the rate it did during the past decade, we will have equal numbers of male and female Senators and representatives in about 100 years (Wershkul and Williams, 2004).

Three sets of factors play a part in women's representation in politics (Paxton and Kunovich, 2003). Structural factors include the low "supply" of women candidates, as political candidates tend to come from law and other professions in which women have been underrepresented. Political factors include the low "demand" for women candidates. Ideological beliefs were assessed in a cross-national study to determine a national "climate" measure, based on responses to questions about women's place in politics, education, and the labor force. The researchers found that ideology played a more important role than politics in predicting women's political representation in a country, affecting both supply and demand (Paxton and Kunovich, 2003).

Does having women in positions of leadership make a difference? A study of state supreme court judges found that female judges voted more liberally than males in the cases studied, death penalty and obscenity cases (Songer and Crews-Meyer, 2000). The researchers also found that male judges were more likely to support liberal positions when there was a woman among their ranks. Voters apparently also perceive differences between female and male candidates for office, some based on gender stereotypes but some not (Koch, 1999). Koch's study of citizens' evaluations of Senate candidates found that female candidates were more likely to be judged favorably with regard to their ability to handle social issues and leadership but unfavorably with regard to competence. And Gallup poll results show that 57 percent of U.S. citizens believe that government would be better if more women held political office (Smith, 2001).

Perhaps more important is the potential for women in positions of power to make real social structural changes. For example, it is unlikely to be mere coincidence that in Sweden, with one of the highest proportions of women legislators in the world, maternity benefits also are among the best in the world (see Table 8.1).

▲ The Women's Movement

Over the past 40 years, no social movement has had a more substantial impact on the way Americans think and act than the women's movement. In the 1960s the women's movement built upon earlier movements while gaining new impetus from the involvement of women in the civil rights movement (Taylor, 1989; Buechler, 1990; Simon and Danziger, 1991). Cross-national research suggests that the "first wave" (1800–1950) of women's movements focused primarily on legal equality, including the pursuit of suffrage, or the right to vote; the "second wave" (since the 1960s) has centered primarily on social equality, particularly in jobs and education (Chafetz and Dworkin, 1986; Schnittker, Freese, and Powell, 2003).

American society and other societies around the world are changing, and we see this in the increasing numbers of women who are achieving positions of leadership and authority. Seen here is Ruth J. Simmons, president of Brown University and former president of Smith College.

The revival of feminist activity in the 1960s was spearheaded by a variety of groups. Some, such as the National Organization for Women (NOW), were organized at the national level by well-known women. Others were grassroots groups that engaged in campaigns for abortion reform or welfare rights, consciousness-raising discussion sessions, or promotion of the interests of professional or lesbian women.

▲ Persistence and Change

We have discussed disparities in pay, promotion discrimination, sexual violence against women, and many other matters. Traditional family roles are in a state of flux, a state of affairs that we will discuss much more in Chapter 10. In many ways, opportunities for women have changed dramatically over the past several decades. In

many other ways, women are still significantly disadvantaged.

Just one example of a disadvantage faced by women serves to illustrate how deeply embedded in social structure such disadvantages are. In 2001, men receiving Social Security benefits were getting an average of $905 per month, while women were getting an average of $697 per month (Hinden, 2001). What accounts for this disparity? Benefits are based primarily on years worked and wages earned. Because women still earn, on average, 77 cents for each dollar a man earns, and because women's reproductive responsibilities result in their working fewer years than men, women get smaller retirement benefits (Hinden, 2001). What is required to make Social Security benefits equal for men and women? Either major changes in the way Social Security benefit levels are determined, or major changes in the way men and women are compensated for all the kinds of work they do.

Some feminists also contend that progress in some arenas has been counterbalanced by other problems faced by women. In her book *The Beauty Myth* (1991), Naomi Wolf argued that in terms of how women feel about themselves physically they are "worse off than our unliberated grandmothers." She cited the rise in cosmetic surgery, the obsession with weight loss, and pornography's hold on media sales in the United States as elements of a "violent backlash" against feminism. Susan Faludi (1991:xviii) similarly described "a powerful counterassault on women's rights" that attempts to "retract the handful of small and hard-won victories that the feminist movement did manage to win for women."

The Institute for Women's Policy Research has been tracking changes in gender inequalities for a number of years. In its 2004 report it concludes (Werschkul and Williams, 2004),

During the 20th century, women made significant economic, political, and social advances, but they are still far from enjoying gender equality.

Throughout the United States, women earn less than men, are seriously underrepresented in political office, and make up a disproportionate share of people in poverty. Even in areas where there have been significant advances in women's status, rates of progress are slow.

As more women reach positions of economic, political, and social power, it is possible that changes will occur at a more rapid pace.

Sources of Gender Differences

We have been focusing on gender inequality with respect to the macro-structural features of society. What about more micro- or individual-level explanations for gender differences? In this section we will look at gender differences and biology, culture, and identity.

Gender and Biology

The biological aspects of gender consist of the physical differences between men and women: Women have the capacity to ovulate, carry a fetus until delivery, and provide it with milk after birth; men have the ability to produce and transmit sperm. Women and men differ in their responses to drugs and other medical interventions as well as in their susceptibilities to many illnesses (Simon, 2005).

The role biology plays in producing behavioral differences between men and women is far less clear than the role it plays in physical differences. In the 1970s, psychologist Eleanor E. Maccoby and Carol N. Jacklin (1974) surveyed over 2,000 books and articles on sex differences and concluded that there are four fairly "well-established" differences between boys and girls:

1. Beginning about age 11, girls show greater verbal ability than boys.
2. Boys are superior to girls on visual-spatial tasks in adolescence and adulthood, although not during childhood.

3. At about 12 or 13 years of age, boys move ahead of girls in mathematical ability.
4. Males are more aggressive than females.

More recently, Janet Shibley Hyde (2005) reviewed 46 *meta-analyses,* in which researchers combine and summarize research findings from many studies of the same question. The 46 papers Hyde reviewed all were meta-analyses of gender difference studies, and they included a wide variety of specific topics: verbal skills, mathematical skills, physical strength, reading comprehension, spatial visualization, aggression, helping behaviors, sexuality, leadership abilities, self-esteem, depression, cheating, moral reasoning, and many more.

Hyde found that 78 percent of the gender differences in these meta-analyses were small or close to zero—in other words, hardly differences at all. Gender differences in most aspects of communication are small, as are gender differences in moral reasoning and moral orientation. Males and females differ very little in life satisfaction, happiness, self-esteem, their attitudes about work, their approaches to leadership, their reading and mathematics abilities, and many other variables.

Do men and women differ at all? Some gender differences were found to be large and reasonably stable, showing up in a variety of studies. Hyde's review of gender difference studies showed that the largest differences are in motor performance, especially after puberty when male bone size and muscle mass begin to exceed that of females. Specifically, males are, on average, able to throw faster and further than females. There also are moderate differences for other measures of motor performance, with men having a stronger grip and being able to sprint faster.

Some of the measures of sexuality also showed large gender differences; males are more likely than females to masturbate frequently and to have a positive attitude about sex in casual and uncommitted relationships. A moderate gender difference was found for aggression, with men and boys more likely than women and girls to engage in physical aggression.

What about Maccoby and Jacklin's (1974) findings on verbal, mathematical, and visual-spatial abilities? Hyde's (2005) review found gender differences ranging in size from very small to moderate for cognitive variables. Two exceptions were moderate to large differences favoring males in mechanical reasoning and mental rotation. Only very small or small differences were noted in mathematics, with females ahead in concepts, computation, and mathematics anxiety but boys ahead in problem solving and mathematics self-confidence. Similarly, very small differences were found in language skills, and studies contradicted one another, with girls ahead of boys in vocabulary in one study but behind in another.

Hyde's (2005) review of the information gathered in many studies also showed that some gender differences change with growth and development. Others depend on social context, with differences in aggression, smiling, interrupting, mathematical performance, and helping behaviors changing and even reversing under different circumstances.

In spite of arguments that deemphasize biology in gendered behavior, this issue is far from settled. Recently some sociologists have proposed formally integrating social and biological factors in a single framework, and have argued that the effect of gender socialization depends on biological factors and vice versa. For example, Udry (2000) showed that prenatal exposure to testosterone (a male hormone that is found in both sexes) in females reduces the effects of gender socialization on adult gendered behavior. Udry concluded that biological and socialization factors work together in generating gendered behavior, but that biology also sets individual limits on gender socialization and additional limits to the macro-construction of gender. Udry's findings and conclusions are controversial and generated debate, making it clear that more research will be needed before

"Are you the opposite sex or is it ME?"

Used by permission of Hank Ketcham and © by United Media.

we can arrive at firm conclusions in this area (Kennelly, Merz, and Lorber, 2001; Miller and Costello, 2001; Risman, 2001; Udry, 2001).

Gender and Culture

Despite the very few gender differences identified by researchers, all societies assign gender roles, the sets of cultural expectations that define the ways in which the members of each sex should behave. Anthropological evidence suggests that gender roles probably represent the earliest division of labor among human beings. Consequently, we are all born into societies with well-established cultural guidelines for the behavior of men and women (see Box 8.3).

That these cultural expectations are based on any "real" gender differences is cast into doubt by the results of a survey of 224 societies (Murdock, 1935). Anthropologist George P. Murdock found in his cross-cultural survey that vast differences exist in the social definitions of what constitutes appropriate masculine and feminine behavior.

"There's a Totally Cute Girl Smoking a ——————ing Cigar!"

Many—perhaps most—college students today believe that gender inequality is pretty much a thing of the past. Because they grew up in a time when women could vote, work outside the home, run for office, go to college, and the like, some students find feminist ideology—well, extreme. So complacent are many students that they are quick to reject arguments of feminist sociologists that our culture promotes gender inequality through its "compulsory heterosexuality." But the results of more than 650 field observations recorded by sociology students over a 15-year period offer substantial evidence that compulsory heterosexuality is deeply embedded in American culture (Nielsen, Walden, and Kunkel, 2000).

Students were assigned to think up some way to violate a gender norm and to record what happened as a result of their violation. They were to choose and perform in public some act typically associated with the opposite sex and record both the reactions of others and their own feelings. Over the years, students came up with more than one hundred different "gender transgressions." Male students

crocheted in public, bought sanitary napkins, wore women's clothes or shoes, cried, carried purses, tried out "women's occupations," painted their fingernails, and read romance novels. One even threw a Tupperware party. Female students opened doors for men, smoked cigars and pipes, chewed tobacco, sent men flowers, went shirtless while doing sports activities, bought condoms, and read *Playgirl*. Some displayed knowledge about "guy stuff," such as cars and sports.

And what were the reactions to these norm violations? Surprisingly, especially given the wide variety of projects, the reactions were easily categorized—and completely different depending on whether the norm violator was a woman or a man. Men were labeled homosexual or potentially homosexual, and women were considered either to be sexually aggressive and promiscuous or of dubious attractiveness to men. Comments heard by the male gender norm violators included, "We gotta sweet fella here," "What a fag!" and "Fairies aren't allowed in here." Comments recorded by female gender norm violators included, "It's a good thing she's

married because she probably wouldn't get any dates," "Is this any way for two pretty young girls to behave?" and "There's a totally cute girl smoking a ——————ing cigar!"

The experiences of the hundreds of students involved in this study clearly demonstrate the power of gender expectations. Gender-role norms function as a signal of the willingness of those adhering to them to be part of the heterosexual world, and they provide sanctions for those who would violate them. Feminist sociologists argue that compulsory heterosexuality is deeply embedded in our culture and in the demands it makes on us in our everyday lives. This study supports that argument.

Questions for Discussion

1. Have you ever knowingly or unknowingly violated a gender norm? What did you do? What was the reaction of those around you?

2. How do you feel when you see men dressed as women? Or women with men's haircuts, no makeup, and men's clothes? Explain your reaction.

Indeed, as shown in Table 8.2, the allocation of duties often differs sharply from that of our own society. For example, for generations U.S. communities have had laws restricting the weights that a working woman is permitted to lift. Yet the Arapesh of New Guinea assigned women the task of carrying heavy loads because their heads were believed to be harder and stronger than those of men. Among the Tasmanians of the South Pacific, the most dangerous type of hunting—swimming out to remote rocks in the sea to stalk and club sea otters—was assigned to women. Moreover, women formed the bodyguard of Dahomeyan kings because they were deemed to be particularly fierce fighters. And although most peoples believe that men should take the initiative in sexual matters, the Maori of New Zealand and the Trobriand Islanders (near New Guinea) give this prerogative to women (Ford and Beach, 1951).

Table 8.2	The Division of Labor by Sex in 224 Societies				
	Number of Societies and Sex of Person by Whom the Activity Is Performed				
Activity	Men Always	Men Usually	Either Sex	Women Usually	Women Always
Hunting	166	13	0	0	0
Trapping small animals	128	13	4	1	2
Herding	38	8	4	0	5
Fishing	98	34	19	3	4
Clearing agricultural land	73	22	17	5	13
Dairy operations	17	4	3	1	13
Preparing and planting soil	31	23	33	20	37
Erecting and dismantling shelter	14	2	5	6	22
Tending and harvesting crops	10	15	35	39	44
Bearing burdens	12	6	35	20	57
Cooking	5	1	9	28	158
Metalworking	78	0	0	0	0
Boat building	91	4	4	0	1
Working in stone	68	3	2	0	2
Basket making	25	3	10	6	82
Weaving	19	2	2	6	67
Manufacturing and repairing of clothing	12	3	8	9	95

Source: Reprinted by permission from *Social Forces,* May 15, 1937. "Comparative Data on the Division of Labor by Sex," by George P. Murdock. Copyright © The University of North Carolina Press.

The great variation in the gender roles of men and women from one society to another points to a social foundation for most of these differences (Bernard, 1987; South and Trent, 1988; Intons-Peterson, 1988). So do the changes observed from one time to another in sex-linked behavior patterns within the same society, such as hair length and style and clothing fashions. All this suggests that gender roles are largely a matter of social definition and socially constructed meanings.

An example of the importance of the part social definitions play in gender roles is found in studies of **hermaphrodites,** individuals whose reproductive structures are sufficiently ambiguous that it is difficult to define them exclusively as male or female. Social definitions play a crucial role in influencing the gender identities of hermaphrodites. At birth the child is classed as a boy or a girl, and a whole series of environmental forces then come into play (Money and Tucker, 1975:8689).

Gender Identities

Gender identities are the conceptions we have of ourselves as being male or female. Most people have a good fit between their anatomy and their gender identity. Boys generally come to behave in ways their culture labels "masculine," and girls learn to be "feminine."

But there are some individuals for whom this is not the case. The most striking examples are *transsexuals*—individuals who have normal sexual organs but who psychologically feel like members of the opposite sex. Transsexuality should not be confused with homosexuality. Homosexuality is a sexual orientation, not a confused gender identity; lesbians have a strong sense of themselves as females, and they are sexually attracted to other females. In some cases of transsexuality, medical science has found a way to modify the person's anatomy to conform with the person's gender identity.

How do individuals develop gender identities? In this section we examine four explanations.

▲ Freudian Explanations

Throughout much of the 20th century, social scientists were strongly influenced by the work of Sigmund Freud. Freud and his followers claimed that gender identity and the adoption of sex-typed behaviors are the result of an *Oedipal conflict* that emerges between the ages of three and six. During this period children discover the genital differences between the sexes. According to Freudians, this discovery prompts children to see themselves as rivals of their same-sex parent for the affection of the parent of the other sex. Such desires and feelings give rise to anxiety, which Freud said is resolved by children coming to identify with the parent of the same sex. Boys thus acquire masculine self-conceptions and girls learn feminine self-conceptions. Freud's work is now primarily of historical importance; empirical research testing Freud's theory has largely discredited it.

▲ Cultural Transmission Theory

Unlike Freud and his followers, *cultural transmission* theorists contend that the acquisition of gender identities and behaviors is not the product of an Oedipal conflict but a gradual process of learning that begins in infancy (Bandura, 1971, 1973; Fagot, Leinbach, and O'Boyle, 1992). They suggest that parents, teachers, and other adults shape a child's behavior by reinforcing responses that are deemed appropriate to the child's gender role and discouraging inappropriate ones. Moreover, children are motivated to attend to, learn from, and imitate same-sex models because they think of same-sex models as more like themselves (Mischel, 1970). Children are given cues to their gender roles in a great variety of ways, from the way their rooms are decorated to the toys they are given to play with and the clothes they are given to wear.

▲ Cognitive-Development Theory

Cultural transmission theory portrays children as passive individuals who are programmed for behavior by adults. *Cognitive-development theory* calls our attention to the fact that children actively seek to acquire gender identities and roles.

According to cognitive-development theory as discussed in Chapter 3 (Kohlberg, p. 73 1966, 1969; Kohlberg and Ullian, 1974), children come to label themselves as "boys" or "girls" when they are between 18 months and three years of age. Once they have identified themselves as males or females, they want to adopt behaviors consistent with their newly discovered status. This process is called *self-socialization*. According to Kohlberg, children form a stereotyped conception of maleness and femaleness—an oversimplified, exaggerated, cartoonlike image. Then they use this stereotyped image to organize behavior and cultivate the attitudes and actions associated with being a boy or a girl.

Both the cultural transmission and cognitive-development theories of gender-role learning have received research support (Maccoby and

Jacklin, 1974; Bem, 1981; Serbin and Sprafkin, 1986; Martin and Little, 1990). Social and behavioral scientists increasingly see gender-role acquisition to be explained by elements from both theoretical approaches.

▲ Self-Construals and Gender

In Chapter 3 we discussed self- p. 83 conception and identity. Psychologists Susan Cross and Laura Madson used differences in self-construal, which is essentially synonymous to our term self-conception, to explain gender differences in the United States (Cross and Madson, 1997). Individuals in some societies develop a sense of self that is very interdependent; in East Asian cultures, for example, self-definition is based primarily on relationships and group memberships. Maintaining harmonious relationships with others is extremely important. Such a definition of self is referred to by psychologists as an *interdependent self-construal.* In contrast, many Western societies are individualistic, and self-definition is based on individualism: One's unique attributes and the importance of an individual distinguishing him- or herself from others are key to developing a sense of self. This definition of self has been called an *independent self-construal.*

Cross and Madson, with other researchers, pointed out that the independent self-construal model describes men better than it does women in the United States and that most U.S. women can probably be best described by the interdependent self-construal model. Many social influences in the United States promote independent ways of behaving, feeling, and thinking for men; for women, relational ways of behaving, feeling, and thinking are more likely to be promoted. This major difference in self-construal between men and women in the United States, Cross and Madson argued, has important consequences in terms of gender differences, including those in cognition, motivation, emotion, and social behavior. For example, they found that women are more willing to express most emotions, while men are more willing to express anger. Women are also more likely to be sensitive to the emotions of others and base their own emotions on those.

Sociological Perspectives on Gender Stratification

As noted in Chapter 1 the roles, p. 17 contributions, and experiences of women were not a major part of theory and social research for most of the history of sociology. Well into the 20th century, female social scientists, who were most likely to make contributions in this area, were marginalized and never able to establish themselves in academic sociology. As a result, traditional theories included little that was relevant to the issue of gender inequality. Perhaps the first work to attempt a systematic understanding of the differentiation of gender roles was Parsons and Bales' (1955) study of the family from the functionalist perspective. But as we will see below, many sociologists view this work as both an attempt to explain gender roles *and* as a justification of prevailing gender inequalities.

Since the 1960s, however, sociologists have been heavily influenced by feminist thinking (see Chapter 1). And while neither pp. 16–17 the conflict nor the interactionist perspective includes an organized theory of gender inequality, feminists and contemporary sociologists have drawn upon the insights of the conflict and interactionist perspectives to develop an understanding of the nature of gender inequality and the sociocultural forces that perpetuate it.

As you will see, the functionalist, conflict, and interactionist perspectives offer interpretations of gender stratification that resemble and parallel their positions on class and racial or ethnic stratification. We will look more closely at each in this section, along with a discussion of the feminist perspective on gender inequality.

The Functionalist Perspective

Functionalists suggest that a division of labor originally arose between men and women because of the woman's role in reproduction. Because women were often pregnant or nursing, preindustrial societies assigned domestic and child-rearing tasks to them. In contrast, men were assigned hunting and defense tasks because of their larger size and greater muscular strength. Functionalists contend that a gender division of labor promoted the survival of the species and therefore was retained.

Sociologists Talcott Parsons and Robert Bales (1955) built upon principles derived from the study of the dynamics of small groups in refining their functionalist position. They argued that two types of leaders are essential if a small group is to function effectively (see Chapter 4). *Instrumental leaders* ◄─ pp. 108–109 (task specialists) devote their attention to appraising the problem at hand and organizing people's activity to deal with it. *Expressive leaders* (social-emotional specialists) focus on overcoming interpersonal problems in the group, defusing tensions, and promoting solidarity. Parsons and Bales suggested that families are also organized along instrumental-expressive lines. Men specialize in instrumental tasks, particularly roles associated with having a job and making money, and women in expressive tasks, supporting their husbands, doing household labor, and caring for children.

Essentially, Parsons and Bales were arguing that it was functional and beneficial for the society, for families, and for individuals if males play instrumental, goal-oriented roles and females play expressive roles, supporting husbands and nurturing children. Through the 1960s, 1970s, and 1980s many sociologists attacked this position as taking an idealized family form from the United States in the 1950s and claiming that it was the uniquely superior model for gender and family relations in industrial societies. Other patterns exist and meet the needs of individuals, families, and the society: for example, the household where both wife and husband work and the household headed by a single parent with resources that allow access to high-quality child care. Critics of the functionalist approach also pointed out that this idealized structure makes men the more powerful actors and women relatively powerless and dependent on men. By arguing that this arrangement is necessary, functionalism becomes a powerful justification for the existence of gender inequality.

The Conflict Perspective

Much of the critique of functionalism from the 1950s to the 1980s came from conflict theorists who rejected functionalist arguments as simply offering a rationale for male dominance. They contended that a sexual division of labor is a social vehicle devised by men to ensure for themselves privilege, prestige, and power in their relationships with women. Gender inequality exists because it benefits men, who use the power it gives them to ensure its perpetuation. By relegating women to the home, men have been able to deny women those resources they need to succeed in the larger world. More particularly, conflict theorists have advanced a number of explanations for gender stratification (Collins, 1975; Vogel, 1983; Collier, 1988; Bradley, 1989; Chafetz, 1990). Some argue that the motivation for gender stratification derives from the economic exploitation of women's labor. Others say that the fundamental motive is men's desire to have women readily available for sexual gratification. Still others emphasize that the appropriation of women is not for copulation but for procreation, especially to produce male heirs and daughters who can be used as exchanges in cementing political and economic alliances with other families.

Sociologist Joan Acker (1992) suggested that in industrial capitalist societies, production is privileged over reproduction. Whereas business, commerce, and industry are viewed as an essential source of well-being and wealth, child-rearing, child care, and elder care are seen as secondary and wealth-consuming. Although "the family" is enshrined and idealized, reproduction (the domain of women) is shrouded in societal shadows and devalued.

The Interactionist Perspective

Interactionism has had a very important impact on the thinking of sociologists about gender inequality. If meanings form the basis of social life, then as meanings change, patterns of social interaction can change, thus changing the nature of social structure. Sociologists also have made use of the interactionist idea that we experience the world as a constructed reality. They developed the idea that while sex is given in nature, gender is socially constructed; it is a product of sociocultural processes involving symbols and meanings. Interactionists argue that cultural meanings, including those that give rise to gender inequality, are continuously emerging and changing through social interaction. If so, then people can intentionally change the structure of gender differentiation and inequality by changing the meanings that underlie them. For example, when men define themselves in traditional masculinist terms, value male dominance, and view women primarily as objects of sexual pleasure, rape and sexual harassment are more likely to occur. When we replace these meanings with those that value gender equality and view women as complete human beings, the rates of rape and sexual harassment decline.

Another example of how interactionism has influenced specific ideas about gender inequality can be seen in the study of gender stereotyping in everyday language. Our use of language can imply that women are secondary to men, in less powerful positions than men, or less competent than men, all of which thus encourages us to think about women in ways that perpetuate inequality. This happens when we use words like "men" and "he" to refer to both men and women, when we refer to presidents and doctors as "he," but secretaries and teachers as "she," and when we refer to adult women as "girls" but refrain from calling adult men "boys." Use of such a symbolic framework encourages people to think of women stereotypically as less suited for powerful instrumental roles, to behave toward them accordingly, and to limit the options available for women's self-definition (Richardson, 1987). Interactionist theorists argue that by influencing people's identities in this way, everyday sexist language helps to perpetuate gender inequality, and that changing our language patterns can help to eliminate it.

The Feminist Perspective

As we pointed out in Chapter 1, pp. 16–17 feminism is not a single theory but an evolving set of theoretical perspectives. Just as conditions for women may not change rapidly until some critical number of women attain positions of economic, social, and political power, so sociological research focused on women's experiences and activities has increased as a function of women becoming research sociologists. Feminist critique of or addition to other perspectives on gender inequality has emerged in recent decades. For example, Miriam Johnson (1993) argued that serving the expressive function in family and society need not lead to disadvantage for women, but that it has led to disadvantage because it exists in the context of a patriarchal culture that values men's instrumentality over women's expressiveness. Changing the patriarchal normative order instead of changing patterns of role differentiation, then, is a more effective way to reduce gender inequality. However, this cultural change has so far eluded us, and we are left with the question of how patriarchal structures can be functional (Lengermann and Niebrugge Brantley, 2000b). If they are, it would appear that they are primarily functional for men.

Myra Marx Ferree and Elaine J. Hall (2000) provide another critique of functionalism.

While functionalists see group differences as beneficial, they explain, feminists "see this grouping process as a socially costly repression of individual variation and potential." Ferree and Hall argue that inequality does not arise from individual differences between people. Rather, their gender-relations model of inequality posits that social structures produce inequality and gender differences follow from them:

Gender is organized through micro-, meso-, and macro-level processes that apply gender labels to jobs, skills, institutions, and organizations as well as to people and that use these labels to produce, express, and legitimate inequality. . . . When gender itself operates in and through macro-social institutions, what it produces is not just differences. . . , but inequality (2000:476).

Sociologists Cecilia Ridgeway and Lynn Smith-Lovin (1999) point out that gender is significantly different from other forms of social inequality. Unlike racial and ethnic inequality or class stratification, the key players in gender inequality—men and women—interact extensively at home, at work, at church, and in a variety of role relationships. These everyday interactions, they contend, recreate the gender system. Such interactions would act to undermine the gender system only in two cases: (1) if the interactions feature women with status or power advantages over men or (2) if they are peer interactions not driven by cultural beliefs about the competence of males and females.

Feminist research has added substantially to our knowledge of women's experiential, subjective, and emotional lives. Though a variety of perspectives make up the "feminist perspective," they are unified in the effort to develop understandings of gender inequality that can be used to transform society and women's lives.

The Chapter in Brief: *Gender Inequality*

Gender Stratification

Men and women differ in their access to privilege, prestige, and power. The distribution problem of who gets what, when, and how has traditionally been answered in favor of males. **Sex** is a biologically determined characteristic; **gender** is a socially constructed characteristic. All societies use anatomical differences to assign **gender roles. Gender identities** are the conceptions we have of ourselves as being male or female.

▌ *Sexism and Patriarchy* Sexism operates at both an individual level and an institutional level. The most pervasive form of institutional sexism is **patriarchy.** Women exhibit four of the five properties associated with a *minority group.*

▌ *Gender Inequality around the World* No nation treats its women as well as its men. Women in many countries suffer discrimination and abuse, yet women around the world do considerably better than U.S. women in some areas.

▌ *Gender Inequality in the United States* U.S. women have made substantial gains over the past decades but continue to do most of the household work and child rearing. Despite increasing involvement in the paid workforce, women continue to be excluded from top jobs and to earn less than men. Sexual harassment remains a common workplace hazard for women, and somewhere between 10 and 25 percent of women have been raped. Men still dominate U.S. political life.

Sources of Gender Differences

Gender roles can be seen as arising from biological development or cultural contributions.

■ *Gender and Biology*   The biological aspects of gender consist of the physical differences between men and women, but the role biology plays in producing behavioral differences between men and women is shrouded in controversy.

■ *Gender and Culture*   Gender roles probably represent the earliest division of labor among humans. Various societies have specific social definitions of appropriate behavior for males and females.

■ *Gender Identities*   Gender identities are the concepts we have of ourselves as being male or female. Theories of the acquisition of gender identities include Freudian, cultural transmission, and cognitive-development. Differences in self-construal may explain gender differences in the United States.

Sociological Perspectives on Gender Stratification

The major sociological perspectives offer interpretations of gender stratification that resemble and parallel their positions on class and racial or ethnic stratification.

■ *The Functionalist Perspective*
Functionalists suggest that families are organized along instrumental-expressive lines, with men specializing in instrumental tasks and women in expressive tasks.

■ *The Conflict Perspective*   Conflict theorists contend that a sexual division of labor is a social vehicle devised by men to ensure themselves of privilege, prestige, and power in their relationships with women.

■ *The Interactionist Perspective*
Interactionists argue that gender inequality persists because of the way we define men and women and their appropriate roles in society. Language helps perpetuate inequality.

■ *The Feminist Perspective*   Feminism is not a single theory but an evolving set of theoretical perspectives. Feminists argue that women are disadvantaged because society is patriarchal; the assignment of group differences is socially costly and repressive. Everyday interactions between men and women recreate and support the gender system.

Glossary

gender   The sociocultural distinction between males and females.

gender identities   The conceptions we have of ourselves as being male or female.

gender roles   Sets of cultural expectations that define the ways in which the members of each sex should behave.

hermaphrodites   Individuals whose reproductive structures are sufficiently ambiguous that it is difficult to define them exclusively as male or female.

patriarchy   A system of social organization in which men have a disproportionate share of power.

sex   A reference to whether one is genetically male or female; determines the

biological role that one will play in reproduction.

sexism   The set of cultural and social processes that justify and promote disadvantage for women.

Review Questions

1. Define sex and gender.
2. How do the terms *gender role* and *gender identity* differ?
3. What is patriarchy?
4. Briefly summarize the variability in quality of life experienced by women around the world.
5. How do U.S. women compare with U.S. men in terms of occupations, employment, earnings, and representation in politics?
6. Compare and contrast biological and cultural bases for gender differences.
7. Briefly describe the theories of gender identity acquisition.
8. How do the functionalist, conflict, interactionist, and feminist perspectives explain gender inequalities?

Internet Connection   www.mhhe.com/hughes8

The most powerful political positions in most societies have almost always been held by men. Until recent years, women's involvement in the formal operations of political institutions has been minimal. Go to the website of the Inter-Parliamentary Union, **http://www.ipu.org/**. Explore this site for information about women's involvement in

political institutions in societies around the world. Using this information, and other information in the current chapter, write a short report about the nature of gender inequality in politics and the efforts of governments and political organizations and associations to promote change.

Chapter 9

POLITICAL AND ECONOMIC POWER

Power, Authority, and the State

The State
Sociological Perspectives on the State
Legitimacy and Authority

Political Power

Types of Government
Political Power in the United States
Models of Power in the United States

Economic Power

Comparative Economic Systems

The Power of Corporations

The Power of National Corporations

The Power of Multinational Corporations in the
Global Economy
The Control of Corporations

The Sociology of Work

Changes in the Work Experience
The Significance of Work
Satisfaction and Alienation in Work

In North Korea's capital city, strict rationing of electricity results in total darkness by 10 P.M. Factories and hotels stand empty and idle. Parts of the city are without water for days on end. When Keith Richburg, a foreign correspondent for the *Washington Post,* visited North Korea in the late 1990s, he found people starving in the countryside. He visited a hospital that had no lights, heat, stretchers, food, antibiotics, or intravenous drips, and a shortage of anesthesia. He went to an orphanage where 20 percent of the children were expected to die because they were beyond help and where 70 percent of the children were there because their parents had died from malnutrition or disease (Richburg, 1997). Recent reports indicate that these problems continue, with public executions of starving people caught stealing food (Amnesty International, 2004). According to refugees and aid groups, government assistance was going to the politically loyal and economically active.

North Korea is a vivid illustration of the intimate connections among power, politics, and economics and of the enormous impact political and economic processes have on the lives of ordinary people. When the Soviet Union collapsed in 1991, North Korea found itself in trouble. As one of the world's last Marxist states, North Korea had imported fuel from the Soviet Union, its major petroleum supplier. The Soviet Union also had provided subsidies to North Korea, and it had been the major market for North Korean exports. A change in political power in one part of the world—the end of the Soviet Union—hurt North Korea's economy very badly. Economic problems were exacerbated by major flooding and a severe drought. The changes in economic and political power in this country, inextricably connected to the collapse of the Soviet Union, have transformed the lives of the people of North Korea.

Individuals and groups who control critical resources—rewards, punishments, and persuasive communications—are able to dictate the way social life is ordered. To command key organizations is to command people and to influence the direction and the outcomes in their lives. Thus, power is the bedrock of social organization (Bierstedt, 1950). Changes in how power is organized and distributed in a society lead to changes in how institutions and groups are created and perpetuated, and thus to fundamental changes in a society's way of life.

As we noted in Chapter 6, *power* is the ability of individuals and groups to realize their will in human affairs even if it involves the resistance of others. But when we say that some people have more power and other people have less, we are doing more than describing people's characteristics. We are describing their social relations with others.

As sociologist Richard Emerson (1962) argued, power is an attribute of a social relationship. If we have two people, A and B, the power of person A over B is determined by B's dependence on A. Thus, if A is in control of resources needed or desired by B, A will have some degree of power over B. A's power will be at its maximum when B has no alternative sources of the resource outside the A-B relationship. A and B need not be people. They can be groups, organizations, ethnic groups, or nations—any person or social unit that can be in a social relationship with another.

Viewed from this power-dependence framework, power is closely linked to economics. An *economy* is a social institution that organizes the production, distribution, and consumption of goods and services. Goods and services are the resources that individuals, groups, organizations, and nations need to survive. Control of resources, particularly control of production and distribution, leads directly to power. Alexander Hamilton expressed this nicely in *The Federalist* in 1788: "In the general course of human nature, a power over a man's subsistence amounts to a power over his will."

Power is not distributed randomly or arbitrarily; it is institutionalized in a patterned, recurrent manner and hence is embedded in stable social arrangements. It gives direction to human affairs, channeling people's actions along one course rather than another. The power that makes a real difference in the way social life works is the power that flows from the dominant organizations and institutions. In this chapter we examine power that makes a real difference—that which is vested in economic and political institutions.

Power, Authority, and the State

The State

The **state**—the political institution—is an arrangement that consists of people who exercise an effective monopoly in the use of physical coercion within a given territory. The state rests on **force**—power whose basis is the threat or application of punishment. Clearly the ability to take life and inflict suffering affords a critical advantage in human affairs. In effect, force constitutes a final court of appeals; there is usually no appeal to force except the exercise of superior force. Sovereign nations restrict, and even prohibit, the independent exercise of force by their subjects; otherwise, governments could not suppress forceful challenges to their authority (Lenski, 1966; Lehman, 1988). But even though force is ultimately the basis of the state, it is only in unusual situations that societal power actually takes this form.

The state is a relatively recent institution in human history. The existence of a state, which requires that some people be able to devote time and energy to organizing power resources, was not possible as long as people could only produce enough to keep everybody alive. Changes in subsistence patterns that permitted

Police officers help citizens with many everyday problems, but the firearms they carry are a constant reminder that they are agents of the state, which has a monopoly on the legitimate use of deadly force.

the 1960s, the United States also followed the conventional welfare-state path with the state directly financing and providing a variety of social services. Beginning in the 1970s, however, the nation shifted the focus of its public activity increasingly toward the managing and financing of various medical and elderly benefits through the private market. As the state has taken on more activities, it has become increasingly bureaucratic, guiding itself by explicit rules and procedures based on a division of function and authority as described by Max Weber's model of *bureaucracy* (Bourdieu, 1994), as discussed in Chapter 4. pp. 117–118

the production of a *social surplus*—goods and services over and above those necessary for survival—provided the foundations for the state (see Chapter 2). External factors such p. 62 as threats and trading partners also played a part. A state typically arose as part of a larger social arrangement or system of states called nation-states. The nation-state arrangement legitimates sovereignty, state purposes, a military, and territorial jurisdiction (Giddens, 1985).

The domain of the state in Western nations has expanded over time. A growing number of activities in education, medicine, the family, religion, working conditions, and technology have become incorporated within its general welfare function (Skocpol and Amenta, 1986). The public welfare expenditures of Western capitalist democracies rapidly increased after World War II, but the pace has slackened since the late 1970s. In some nations, especially those like Sweden with social democratic governments, social programs were transformed into comprehensive systems of universal benefits that guaranteed the citizenry a basic standard of living—what has been called the *welfare state*. During the New Deal years and through

Sociological Perspectives on the State

Functionalists depict the state as an essential social institution that evolved as societies moved from traditional to modern ways. This image of the state predates contemporary sociological theory; it was articulated by 17th- and 18th-century social philosophers such as Thomas Hobbes (1588–1679), who said human beings were "naturally" a perverse and destructive lot. He conjectured that early in history human beings had voluntarily entered into a social agreement providing for central authority and collective defense as a measure to rid themselves of rampant brutality, violence, and chaos. But other philosophers such as Jean Jacques Rousseau (1712–1778) disagreed. According to Rousseau, private property was the root of human social evils. Once private property was established, the state followed as an institution to define and defend property rights. In their original "state of nature," Rousseau said, human beings were "noble savages"—spontaneous, outgoing, loving, kind, and peaceful. The advent of private property ended this idyllic existence, bringing with it corruption, oppression, and obedience to a privileged class. Rousseau's approach foreshadowed the modern conflict perspective on the state. Let us examine the functionalist and conflict views more carefully.

▲ The Functionalist Perspective on the State

Functionalists contend that there is a good reason the state arose and has assumed a dominant position in contemporary life: Society must maintain order and provide for the common good. More particularly, they point to four primary functions performed by the state.

Planning and Direction.
The complexity and scope of many activities in contemporary society require overall coordination and integration; personal and informal arrangements no longer suffice, and new norms are needed. Such norms—*laws*—result from conscious thought, deliberate planning, and formal declaration. In addition, in times of war, financial panic, or natural disaster, "central direction" is required, performed by only one or at most a few individuals who have the power and authority to implement their plans (Davis, 1949).

Enforcement of Norms.
In modern, complex societies characterized by a preponderance of secondary relationships, informal means of social control such as ridicule and shaming are relatively ineffective. Once laws are created, a special body or organization—the state—is required to ensure law and order by enforcing legal norms.

Arbitration of Conflicting Interests.
Because many resources are scarce and divisible—particularly privilege, prestige, and power—people find themselves in conflict as they pursue their goals. If no bonds other than the pursuit of immediate self-interest were to unite people, society would quickly degenerate into a Hobbesian nightmare in which "war against all" prevails. Some agency is required that is sufficiently strong to contain conflict within tolerable limits—and that agency is the state (Goode, 1972).

Protection against Other Societies.
Both war and diplomacy call for centralized control and mobilization if a people are to maximize their position relative to their adversaries. The state meets this requirement. Indeed, sociologist Charles Tilly (1990) surveyed European history and concluded that states are shaped primarily by the need to prepare for and wage war.

▲ The Conflict Perspective on the State

Functionalists see the state as a rather benign institution. Not so conflict theorists! They contend that the state is a vehicle by which one or more groups impose their values and stratification system upon other groups. As they view the matter, the state has its origin in the desire of ruling elites to give permanence to social arrangements that benefit themselves. More fundamentally, they depict the state as an instrument of violence and oppression.

Conflict theorists see the state arising in history along with the production of a social surplus, which we defined earlier as the goods and services over and above what is necessary for survival. In hunting and gathering societies, land is communally owned, and the members of the community share the food derived from it. The intensive agriculture technologies in agricultural societies produce food surpluses, so it is no longer essential that every human be employed in subsistence activities. Some members of society, those who can engineer more power for themselves, can live off the surplus produced by others. A new institution, the state with its police power, is required to enforce the unequal distribution of social and material rewards in order to preserve the position of this privileged elite.

In time, a powerful state can reach outside itself and dominate people in other regions and societies. The empires of Britain, Spain,

Austro-Hungary, Russia, and its successor, the Soviet Union, are historical examples of ruling elites who mobilized the power of the state in pursuit of resources that would result in even more power. This process creates subject peoples and establishes dominant-majority relationships. In the 20th century we have seen the dismantling of these empires and the emergence of a host of formerly subjugated peoples pursuing long-repressed yearnings of nationhood. Many, including Indians, Pakistanis, South Africans, Czechs, Hungarians, and Ukrainians, have succeeded, while others such as the Kosovars and Chechens, whose struggles have been reported frequently in the news early in the 21st century, are still working on it.

Conflict among Conflict Theorists.

There is a difference of opinion among conflict theorists regarding the nature of the state. Marxist controversies have given impetus to the debate and have prompted sociological researchers to pursue their own explorations. Some theorists *(instrumental theorists)* have taken literally the *Communist Manifesto*'s dictum that "the executive of the modern state is but a committee for managing the common affairs of the whole bourgeoisie." Seen in this manner, the state is an instrument that is manipulated, virtually at will, by the capitalist class (Beirne, 1979).

Other conflict theorists *(structural theorists)* contend that the state apparatus exercises "relative autonomy" in its relationship with the capitalist class. They say that the state is not simply the instrument of the capitalist class, but is an entity with its own interests and capacities that affect society (Skocpol, 1980; Quadagno, 1984). The state's actions, therefore, are not always in the interests of any particular class or of the society at large (Barkey and Parikh, 1991). According to this view, relentless *class conflict* between capitalists and workers, boom and bust economic cycles, and intercorporate conflict place limits on the ability of the capital-

ist class to manipulate political institutions at will. Although the state may promote a climate favorable to capitalism, it must also legitimate the sanctity of the social order and maintain internal peace (O'Connor, 1973).

The collapse of communism in much of the world has diminished the appeal of Marxist explanations of the state (van den Berg, 1988). But current research on social policy and the welfare state and comparative-historical studies of state formation owe much to sociological interest generated by Marxist debates (Tilly, 1990; Gilbert and Howe, 1991; Carruthers, 1994).

Legitimacy and Authority

Force may be an effective means for seizing power, and it remains the ultimate foundation for the state, but it is not the most effective means for political rule (Lenski, 1966). As officials of the Soviet and Eastern European communist regimes discovered, force is both inefficient and costly. Moreover, honor is denied to those who rule by force alone. And finally, if an elite is inspired by revolutionary visions for building a new social order, the ideals remain unfulfilled unless the masses come to embrace the new order as their own. The English leader and orator Edmund Burke (1729–1797) captured the essence of these matters when he noted that power that is based on the use of force alone is temporary. A person who hijacks an airliner by threatening to shoot passengers has considerable power, but it is extremely unstable and is not likely to last long.

All this highlights the importance of the distinction that sociologists make between power that is legitimate and power that is illegitimate. Legitimate power is **authority.** When individuals possess authority, they have a recognized and established right to give orders, determine policies, pronounce judgments, settle controversies, and, more broadly, act as leaders. Legitimacy— the social justification of power—takes a number of forms. Sociologist Max Weber (1921/1968) suggested a threefold classification of authority based on the manner in which the power is socially legitimated: legal-rational, traditional, and charismatic.

▲ Traditional Authority

In **traditional authority,** power is legitimated by the sanctity of age-old customs. Often the claim to such authority rests on birthright, and it is perceived as eternal, inviolable, and sacred. For example, medieval kings and queens in Europe ruled in the name of "a divine right" ordained by God. A good deal of moral force stands behind traditional authority.

▲ Legal-Rational Authority

In **legal-rational authority,** power is legitimated by explicit rules and rational procedures that define the rights and duties of the occupants of given positions. Weber depicted this type of authority as prevailing in his ideal-type bureaucracy (see Chapter 4). Under this ◄ pp. 117–118 arrangement, officials claim obedience on the grounds that their commands fall within the impersonal, formally defined scope of their office. Obedience is owed not to the person but to a set of impersonal principles that have been devised in a rational manner. Presumably, these principles are derived from a set of abstract goals that people agree with. For example, we obey the police officer directing traffic because we agree that traffic must flow smoothly and that for this to occur, people must conform to a set of rational principles and rules devised to ensure this.

The authority of government leaders is accepted in the United States because Americans accept the premise that the law is supreme. Americans accept the exercise of power because they have come to believe that policies and orders are formulated in accordance with rules to which they subscribe. The system would crumble were a large number of Americans to reject these "rules of the game." Ideally, legal-rational authority is a government of laws, not of people.

▲ Charismatic Authority

In **charismatic authority,** power is legitimated by the extraordinary superhuman or supernatural attributes people attribute to a leader. Founders of world religions, prophets, military victors, and political heroes commonly derive their authority from charisma (meaning "gift of grace"). Followers are devoted to the person of the leader, not to tradition or to abstract rational rules and principles. Jesus, Napoléon Bonaparte, Fidel Castro, Julius Caesar, Adolf Hitler, Joan of Arc, and Ayatollah Ruhollah Khomeini all are examples.

The term *charisma* has passed from Weber's writings into our everyday language, and we often speak of "charismatic" leaders such as John F. Kennedy or "charismatic" pop stars such as Elvis Presley. But Weber did not have such examples in mind when he developed the concept of charisma. To Weber a charismatic leader makes an impact on history, transforming social structure by mobilizing followers to pursue the leader's goals.

Weber viewed each of these three bases of authority as *ideal types,* concepts sociologists construct to portray the principal characteristics of a phenomenon. Hence, in practice any specific form of authority may involve various combinations and aspects of all three. For example, Franklin Delano Roosevelt gained the presidency through legal-rational principles. By the time he was elected president for the fourth time, his leadership had a good many traditional elements to it, while his great popularity meant that his leadership had some charismatic properties.

Political Power

Politics refers to the processes by which people and groups acquire and exercise power. We commonly think of politics as a feature of governments. But there is also politics in religious groups, educational groups, and scientific groups—even in friendship groups and families.

When power is organized and wielded by the state, we speak of it as **political power.** In the modern state, power is wielded through democratic, authoritarian, or totalitarian means, depending on how much participation states allow from citizens and how much control is exercised over the everyday lives of citizens. Though democratic governments appear to be organized in the interests of average citizens, social scientists are not in agreement about how "democratic" such states are. In this section we discuss forms of government, political power in the United States, and models of political power.

Types of Government

Government entails those political processes that have to do with the authoritative formulating of rules and policies that are binding and pervasive throughout a society. Three quite different types of government have competed in recent generations for people's allegiance: totalitarianism, authoritarianism, and democracy. Each can be considered an ideal type because in practice many nations have regimes with mixtures of totalitarian, authoritarian, and democratic elements.

▲ Totalitarianism
Totalitarianism is a "total state," one in which the government undertakes to control all parts of the society and all aspects of social life such as occurs in contemporary North Korea. Those individuals and groups (elites) who dominate the state apparatus seek to control all subordinate governmental units, all institutions, and even individual families and cliques. The two major historical prototypes of totalitarianism—Nazi Germany under Hitler and communist Russia under Stalin—remind us that this form of government can incorporate either a capitalistic or a socialistic economy.

A totalitarian society typically has three characteristics: a monolithic political party, a compelling ideology, and pervasive social con-

trol. One political party is permitted, and it brooks no opposition. Only a small proportion of the population are party members, although party membership is a requisite for all important social positions. A totalitarian ideology is utopian in nature. It stipulates grandiose schemes for social reconstruction and societal betterment. To enforce its power and propagate its ideologies, a totalitarian regime employs every available means of social control. It uses educational and communications networks as well as exercising terror by a secret police.

▲ Authoritarianism
Authoritarianism is a political system in which the government tolerates little or no opposition to its rule but permits nongovernmental centers of influence and allows debate on some issues of public policy. Contemporary examples include Cuba under Fidel Castro and Egypt under Hosni Mubarak. Sometimes authoritarian governments evolve out of totalitarian governments, as occurred over the 1970s and 1980s in the People's Republic of China and the Soviet Union. In the ensuing years, the Soviet Union disintegrated and China replaced many of the socialist elements of its economy with capitalist features. However, in neither case did a democratic government emerge. Even though authoritarian and totalitarian governments are often unpopular, when they fail, they are not automatically replaced by democratic regimes.

▲ Democracy
Democracy is a political system in which the powers of government derive from the consent of the governed and in which regular constitutional avenues exist for changing government officials. It is an arrangement that (1) permits the population a significant voice in decision making through the people's right to choose among contenders for political office, (2) allows for a broad, relatively equal citizenship among the populace, and (3) affords the citizenry protection from arbitrary state action. However,

The heavily contested 2000 presidential election was decided by the U.S. Supreme Court's ruling that the re-count of votes should cease. Despite the energy that had been put into pre- and post-election campaigning, both sides accepted the outcome.

democratic governments are not distinguished from totalitarian or authoritarian regimes by the absence of powerful officials, and for the most part democracy is not characterized by the rule of the people themselves. Only in relatively rare instances, such as the New England town meeting, do we encounter *direct democracy*—face-to-face participation and decision making by the citizens. Rather, most democratic nations are characterized by *representative democracy*—officials are held accountable to the public through periodic elections that confirm them in power or replace them with new officials.

What Factors Promote Democracy?

A number of sociologists have undertaken a search for those factors that promote a social climate favorable to a stable democracy (Lindblom, 1990; Patterson, 1991; Lipset, 1994).

One factor they identify is the existence of conflict and cleavage associated with a competitive struggle over positions of power, challenges to incumbents, and shifts in the parties holding office. Many well-organized but countervailing interest groups serve as a check against one another. **Interest groups** are organizations of people who share common concerns or points of view. Each group is limited in influence because, in the process of governing, officials must also take into account the **interests,** or points of view, of other groups.

A strong **civil society**—a social realm of mediating groups, networks, and institutions that sustains the public life outside the worlds of the state and the economy—is conducive to democratic life (Cohen and Arato, 1992). For example, in the United States today we have a broad array of public interest and political organizations across the ideological spectrum that address a variety of issues and concerns of the populace. These include the Christian Coalition, the National Rifle Association, Planned Parenthood, and the American Civil Liberties Union, to name only a very few. Citizens of all political and moral persuasions can link to organizations that are pursuing their goals. Having a large number of such competing groups provides many links to government and ensures that no single group or institution can attain a monopoly of power.

Relatively stable economic and social conditions also seem to favor a democratic order (Neuhouser, 1992). Significant institutional failure confronts people with stressful circumstances that can make them vulnerable to extremist social movements. For example, Germany underwent ruinous inflation and economic dislocation in the 1920s that made the middle classes susceptible to Nazism.

Finally, a stable democracy benefits from an underlying consensus among the populace that a democratic government is desirable and valid. Citizens believe they can realize their goals within the existing organizational framework because they enjoy "fair play" access to the seats of power. As we will see, voting is a key mechanism for achieving consensus. Although Americans wage their election campaigns with great fury and fervor, once the election returns are in, the candidates and parties accede to the results. The contest between Al Gore and George W. Bush for the presidency in 2000 is a good example of this. Once the U.S. Supreme Court decided the legal issue in Bush's favor, Gore's supporters recognized the legitimacy of the legal process and the outcome and did not resort to extralegal and violent remedies.

Political Power in the United States

Both totalitarian and democratic governments are marked by competition for political positions. But what distinguishes democracies and the American system is that the contest for positions of power is legitimized—norms define political competition and opposition as expected and appropriate. Free and competitive elections, the right to form opposition parties, freedom to criticize those in power, freedom to seek public office, and popular participation are among the commonly accepted hallmarks of democratic procedures. Central to the process are political parties, popular electoral participation, interest-group lobbying, and the mass media.

▲ Political Parties

A **political party** is an organization designed to gain control of the government by putting its people in public office. It is not the same as an interest group, which seeks to control government policy decisions without assuming the direct responsibility of running the government. In contrast, political parties pursue the control of government as an end. Thus mass-based political parties tend to abandon or modify policy views that interfere with their gaining or maintaining political office.

Within American life, the major political parties function as brokers or intermediaries between the people and the government (Lipset, 1993). The relatively pragmatic nature of the parties and the structural peculiarities of the two-party system reflect this fact. To win control of the government, each party must shape itself to make the widest possible appeal to the electorate. This requirement tends to pull each party toward a centrist position, leaving the more extreme elements at the fringes. In close elections both the Republican and Democratic parties strive for the support of the same uncommitted, often middle-of-the-road, voters. In many respects, then, the two parties end up resembling one another. Occasionally one of their more extreme factions gains control of the presidential nominating machinery, but then they commonly suffer electoral disaster, such as the fate of the Goldwater Republican right in 1964 and the McGovern Democratic left in 1972. Critics of the U.S. political system say that centrist forces

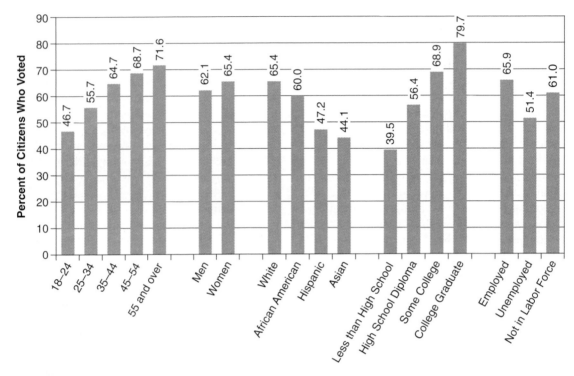

Source: Chart generated by authors from data presented in Holder (2006), available at: http://www.
census.gov/prod/2006pubs/p20-556.pdf

Figure 9.1 Who Votes? Percent of Eligible Citizens Who Voted in the 2004 Presidential Election

and pressures result in the lack of a real choice for voters. Proponents point out that what is really happening is that the parties are performing one of their chief functions: compromising different and conflicting points of view prior to the election (Olson and Meyer, 1975).

▲ Electoral Participation and Voting Patterns

The U.S. political system is rooted in the participation of its citizenry in the governmental process through periodic elections. The principle that each person has one vote is seen as a basic mechanism for offsetting the inequalities that otherwise abound in the society by virtue of

class, gender, and racial inequalities. Still, many Americans do not vote. In 2000, only 60 percent of eligible voters voted in the presidential election; in contrast, in 1876, when memories of the Civil War were still fresh, 82 percent of eligible voters—mostly limited to white males—cast ballots. As indicated in Figure 9.1, nonvoters are more likely to be young, less educated, and of minority status than those who do vote. Voting is associated with participation in groups, both religious and nonreligious (Cassel, 1999) and, in young adults, with having been active in instrumental extracurricular activities (Glanville, 1999). Generally speaking, higher-status people see a relationship between politics and their own

9.1 Social Inequalities

What Oppression Teaches—The Long Reach of Disenfranchisement

Why don't people long oppressed by authoritarian regimes create effective democracies as soon as authoritarianism is lifted? Why, for example, has it not been easy to establish democracy in Afghanistan and Iraq after the demise of authoritarian regimes in the two countries in 2002 and 2003? Social structures teach people patterns of behavior that are not quickly and easily changed when the rules and laws governing political participation are changed. Though not as drastic as a change in regime, American women gaining the right to vote provides a focused example of this effect in action.

In 1920, the Nineteenth Amendment to the Constitution extended to women the right to vote: "The right of citizens of the United States to vote shall not be denied or abridged by the United States or by any State on account of sex." Women had worked long and hard to gain this right. Yet not nearly as many women as men voted in the first elections after the passage of the voting rights amendment. In fact, it was not until many years afterward that men and women voted at equal rates. Women born after 1925, who grew up after the Nineteenth Amendment was passed and voting for women had become an "inalienable right," were the first group to go out and vote in equal numbers.

Sociologists Glenn Firebaugh and Kevin Chen (1995) showed that the oppression people experience during their early years can continue to affect their behavior long after the oppression itself is lifted. Using postelection survey data gathered from 1952 to 1988, Firebaugh and Chen found that the odds of women born in 1896 voting in any election were less than half as great as the odds of men voting. This disenfranchisement effect—women failing to vote despite having gained the right to do so—was only slightly less in a second group of women, those born between 1896 and 1905. The effect was again smaller for women born between 1906 and 1915, although women in this cohort still did not vote at the same rates as men, and women born between 1916 and 1925 also were somewhat less likely to vote than men.

This study illustrates the long-lasting effects of historical conditions experienced during one's formative years. The data these researchers used were based on elections beginning *30 years* after women gained the right to vote in the United States, yet women born and socialized during and immediately after the period when women could *not* vote continued to vote at lower rates than men. Voting rates for men and women have now converged; women socialized in an era during which women have the right to vote are just as likely to vote as men are. As Firebaugh and Chen put it (1995:978): "After passage of the Nineteenth Amendment, historical conditions no longer 'taught' young women the impropriety of voting."

Questions for Discussion

1. Does the research presented here explain any of the voter data shown in Figure 9.1 on page 292?

2. This box suggests people learn not to be involved in voting if they are denied the right to vote. Can you think of other features of democracies in civil society that may be slow to develop after the demise of authoritarian regimes?

lives, but many lower-status people do not see the political system as offering them anything, or at least anything they can relate to effectively. Although in recent years women have been slightly more likely to vote than men (Jamieson, Shin, and Day, 2002), it has not always been so. Prior to 1920 women were not allowed to vote in most elections, and even after 1920 the voting rates of women were depressed (see Box 9.1).

Low voting rates may indicate that many Americans believe they cannot affect the political process on the national level. Indeed, politicians spend considerable time building up a vast array of incumbent protections designed to

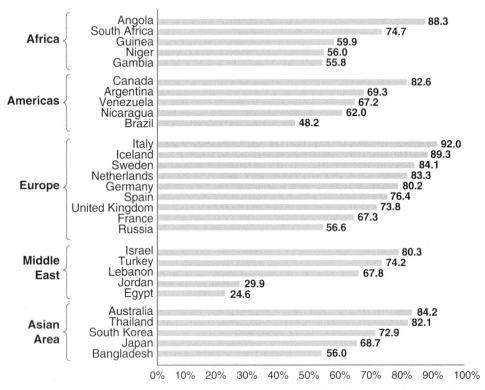

Africa
- Angola — 88.3
- South Africa — 74.7
- Guinea — 59.9
- Niger — 56.0
- Gambia — 55.8

Americas
- Canada — 82.6
- Argentina — 69.3
- Venezuela — 67.2
- Nicaragua — 62.0
- Brazil — 48.2

Europe
- Italy — 92.0
- Iceland — 89.3
- Sweden — 84.1
- Netherlands — 83.3
- Germany — 80.2
- Spain — 76.4
- United Kingdom — 73.8
- France — 67.3
- Russia — 56.6

Middle East
- Israel — 80.3
- Turkey — 74.2
- Lebanon — 67.8
- Jordan — 29.9
- Egypt — 24.6

Asian Area
- Australia — 84.2
- Thailand — 82.1
- South Korea — 72.9
- Japan — 68.7
- Bangladesh — 56.0

0% 10% 20% 30% 40% 50% 60% 70% 80% 90% 100%

Percent of the voting age population who voted in parliamentary elections, 1945–2001

Figure 9.2   **Going to the Polls: A Global View**

Voter participation in U.S. national elections is traditionally low: 54.7 percent of those old enough to vote voted in the 2000 presidential election and 41.9 percent in the 1998 Congressional elections (U.S. Census Bureau, 2003). How many voters in other countries took advantage of their right to vote in their countries' elections?

Source: Figure generated by the authors using data from Lopez Pintor and Gratschew, 2002.

squeeze out their political competition (Ginsberg and Shefter, 1990), resulting in incumbent senators and representatives winning more than 90 percent of the time in most elections since 1964. The turnout rate in presidential elections is typically much lower in the United States than in other nations (see Figure 9.2). In western Europe, Canada, Australia, and New Zealand, the state is responsible for compiling and maintaining electoral registers. The United States is the only nation where the entire burden of registration falls on the individual rather than the government.

There are important differences in how various segments of the population vote. Generally, voters who are better off tend to support Republican candidates and those who are less well off tend to support Democratic candidates. Even so, Democrats still receive a significant proportion of their votes from higher-status people, and the Republican George W. Bush did well among blue-collar workers. Prior to the 1930s African-American voters tended to support the Republican Party, the party of Abraham Lincoln and African-American emancipation, but since Franklin D. Roosevelt and the New Deal they have voted overwhelmingly Democratic. Religion is often a good predictor of voting, but patterns can change. For many years Catholics were more likely to vote for Democratic than Republican candidates (Hamilton, 1972), but with the movement of many Catholics out of the working class, this is no longer true. However, the tendency of Jews to vote Democratic remains stable, and since the 1970s Christians have been solid and consistent supporters of Republicans. Americans with disabilities are more likely to vote Democratic (Gastil, 2000). Although the voting patterns of men and women have not traditionally differed, in recent years women have been more likely than men to support the Democratic party. Overall, there is a persistence of voter identifications with particular parties. Changes do occur, although not as precipitously as is commonly imagined (Alwin and Krosnick, 1991; Connelly, 2000). The rate of ticket splitting (casting votes for different party candidates) is between 20 and 28 percent (Forgette and Platt, 1999).

▲ Interest-Group Lobbying

As we noted in the discussion of democracy, people who share common concerns or points of view are called *interests,* and the groups that organize them are called *interest groups.* A distinction is often made between special-interest groups and public-interest groups. **Special-interest groups** primarily seek benefits from which their members would derive more gains than the society as a whole. Examples include chambers of commerce, trade associations, labor unions, and farm organizations. **Public-interest groups** pursue policies that presumably would be of no greater benefit to their members than to the larger society. Consumer protection organizations are good illustrations of public-interest groups.

Among special-interest groups that have attracted considerable controversy are **political action committees (PACs)** that are set up to elect or defeat candidates, but not through the organization of a political party. PACs were specifically authorized by the Federal Election Campaign Act of 1971, but they had existed before then. Political action committees typically exert their influence by contributing money to candidates who will support their interests. They base their contributions less on ideological or geographical factors than on whether the recipient sits on a congressional committee that can help them (Berke, 1990). Many PACs hedge their bets by contributing to both candidates in a campaign, ensuring that they later will have access to the winner. Although members of Congress are presumably elected to represent the people in their states, more than half the

CALVIN and HOBBES © 1992 Watterson. Reprinted with permission of UNIVERSAL PRESS SYNDICATE. All rights reserved.

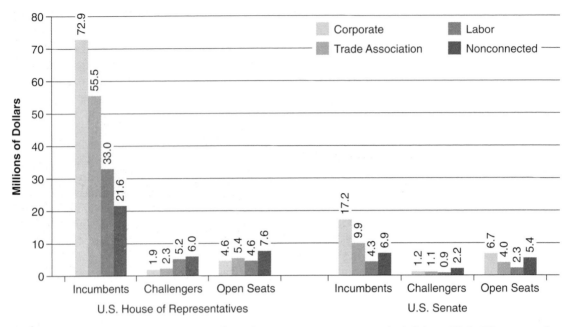

Figure 9.3 **Contributions by Political Action Committees (PACs) to U.S. House and Senate Candidates, in Millions of Dollars, 2003–2004, by Type of PAC**

Source: Figure generated by the authors using data from the U.S. Census Bureau, 2006.

senators seeking reelection to the Senate finance their campaigns primarily from contributions acquired outside their home states instead of from contributions made chiefly by their constituents (Berke, 1990). As Figure 9.3 shows, PACs run by business corporations contribute more money than other types of PACs, and they give much more of it to incumbents than to challengers. Contributions are the way interest groups gain access to legislators to plead their cases and obtain special favors for given pieces of legislation (Clawson, Neustadtl, and Scott, 1992). Labor unions, for example, were found to distribute contributions to both Democrats and Republicans who had previously supported prolabor legislation (Burns, Francia, and Herrnson, 2000).

▲ The Mass Media

The **mass media** consists of organizations—newspapers, magazines, television, radio, motion pictures, and the Internet—that undertake to convey information to a large segment of the public. Studies show that more than two-thirds of Americans get most of their news from television (Pew Research Center for the People and the Press, 2005). The public secures information about candidates from television through news broadcasts and paid advertising.

Often the media's main role is that of "agenda setting": Media coverage places an issue or problem foremost on the public's agenda, where it can become a central factor influencing the public's perception of the performance of an incumbent or challenger (Iyengar, 1991). Although there is little credible evidence that the television networks knowingly favor particular presidential candidates, they do influence public attitudes by their selection of news events. Recent research findings contradicted the commonly held idea that the media is biased against

Republicans: Democratic and Republican gubernatorial candidates were not treated any differently over 20 years of newspaper coverage (Niven, 1999).

Increasingly, campaigns are being turned over to high-powered professionals who advise candidates on every detail, ranging from which issues they should tackle to the images they should project in their media appearances. Physical appearance and "good looks" have surfaced as paramount matters in an era when packaging candidates for the media is so critical. Moreover, TV advertising, for which candidates spend nearly half their campaign funds, gives greater emphasis to style and personality than substance. Computer technology is employed to target specific voter groups and then bombard them with TV advertising and direct-mail appeals specifically tailored to their interests. Campaign managers use public opinion polls not only to find out how voters perceive their candidates but to determine what voters want to hear their candidates say (Altschiller, 1988; Oreskes, 1990).

According to the elitist perspective, it is the "power elite" that make fateful decisions such as the 2003 invasion of Iraq by the United States.

Models of Power in the United States

One of the longest-running debates in social sciences in the United States has to do with the nature of *power* in the United States. Is power concentrated in the hands of the few or distributed widely among various groups within American life? What is the basis of power? Is the exercise of power in the United States unrestricted or is it limited by the competing interests of numerous groups? Social scientists have supplied quite different answers to these questions, represented by three theoretical perspectives: the Marxist (or ruling class), the elitist, and the pluralist.

▲ The Marxist Perspective

Marxist theory has had a profound impact on sociological thinking about power and social organization. Sociologists following in the Marxist tradition, such as J. Allen Whitt (1979, 1982), hold that political processes must be understood in terms of the ways in which the major social institutions (especially the economic institution) are organized. Rather than focusing primarily upon the individuals who control the seats of power (as do power elite theorists), Whitt looked to the biases inherent in social institutions as shaping political outcomes. He portrayed society as structured in ways that place constraints on decision makers and render their formulation of policy largely a foregone conclusion. Given the capitalist logic of institutions in Western nations, the ruling class usually need not take direct action to fashion outcomes favorable to its interests. The political outcomes are built within the capitalist ordering of affairs by the way agendas are set and alternatives are defined.

▲ The Elitist Perspective

The elitist perspective found early expression in the ideas of several European sociologists of the late 19th and early 20th centuries, including Vilfredo Pareto, Gaetano Mosca, and Robert Michels. They undertook to show that the concentration of power in a small group of elites is inevitable within modern societies (Olsen, 1970). These theorists rejected Marx's idealistic vision of social change that would bring about a classless and stateless society. Instead, they depicted all societies past the bare subsistence level—be they totalitarian, monarchical, or democratic—as dominated by the few over the many. They held that the masses cannot and do not govern themselves. Even so, change occurs across time through the gradual replacement of one group of elites by another.

Within the United States, elitist theory has taken a somewhat different course, particularly as it was formulated in the work of sociologist C. Wright Mills (1956). Mills contended that the major decisions affecting Americans and others—especially those having to do with issues of war and peace—are made by a small number of individuals and groups whom he terms the "power elite." The real rulers of the United States, said Mills, come from three groups: corporation executives, the military, and high-ranking politicians. According to this view, it is these groups that formulate important policies such as the procurement of major weapons systems and make fateful decisions such as the 2003 invasion of Iraq by the United States.

The elitist model depicts elites as unified in purpose and outlook because of their similar social backgrounds, their dominant and overlapping positions in key social institutions, and the convergence of their economic interests (Domhoff, 1983, 1990; Akard, 1992). For instance, sociologist Michael Useem (1983) contended that an "inner circle" of interconnected corporate officers and directors assumes the stewardship of U.S. political and social affairs. He found that inner-group members are more likely to belong to exclusive social clubs, have upper-class parents, participate in major business associations, serve on government advisory boards, belong to the upper levels of nonprofit and charitable organizations, gain media coverage for themselves, maintain informal contacts with government leaders, and prefer one another's company. According to elitist theorists, elites invariably get their way whenever important public decisions are at stake. Their power is pervasive; it leaves few areas of social life untouched and results in a relatively stable distribution of power.

▲ The Pluralist Perspective

The pluralist perspective sharply contrasts with both the power elite and Marxist models. Pluralist theorists start with interest groups as the basic feature of organized political life. They say that no one group really runs the government, although many groups have the power to veto policies that run counter to their interests (Riesman, 1953; Dahl, 1961). Important decisions are made by different groups, depending on the institutional arena—business organizations, labor unions, farm blocs, racial and ethnic associations, and religious groups. When their interests diverge, the various interest groups compete for allies among the unorganized public. But the same group or coalition of groups does not set broad policies. Instead, group power varies with the issue. A mounting body of sociological research reveals that politics in the United States typically proceeds within many relatively self-contained policy domains, each operating more or less independently with its own issues, actors, and processes (Burstein, 1991a).

Most groups remain inactive on most issues and mobilize their resources only when their interests are immediately at stake. The resulting distribution of power tends to be unstable because interests and alliances are typically short-lived and new groups and coalitions are always being organized as old ones disintegrate. Government may achieve substantial autonomy by operating as a broker or balancing agent among competing interest groups, but the result is not necessarily effectiveness in administration. Some pluralists say that so many interest groups have sprung up in the United States, each demanding special attention to its own concerns, that government has become paralyzed (Shea, 1984).

▲ Conclusions

What conclusions can we draw from the contending models of power? Each model has something of value to tell us, and a reasonable perspective on power would combine elements from each perspective (Burris, 1988). For example, elitist theorists such as Mills and even Marxian-oriented theorists do not argue that a power elite or governing class completely dominates U.S. society. When important decisions are made—especially on the critical issues of war and peace and on matters concerning the economy—many interest groups compete for influence, but some corporate, military, and political power centers clearly have greater input than other groups. Yet given the divisions within the highest echelons of the U.S. government on welfare and defense spending and tax policies, it is exceedingly difficult to make a convincing case for a unified power elite.

And as structural Marxists remind us, political and economic institutions seem to gain an existence separate from the specific individuals who have ownership or positions of authority within them. Thus the question is not only, Who runs America? but also, What runs America? See Box 9.2 for another perspective.

Economic Power

Politics and economics are intimately related. Political systems not only create laws and exercise police power, they also facilitate the operation of the economy. In a **socialist economy** the government directly controls the economy, in many cases setting prices and wages and deciding what will be produced. In a **capitalist economy** the government oversees and sets parameters for the economy, but in many ways leaves the economy alone, allowing the market to decide what the economy will do. In all cases economic organizations, whether they are government bureaucracies or large corporations, wield considerable power. One way we experience this power is as employees, doing the bidding of a company in order to get a paycheck and move up the ladder of success. But economic organizations also wield power in other ways, working to create a favorable environment for themselves by controlling the markets and political systems in which they operate. In this section, we will discuss the different kinds of economic systems and how they fit into the global economy. In addition, we will focus on the power of corporations and the nature of work in modern society.

Comparative Economic Systems

All societies confront three basic economic problems. *What* goods and services should they produce and in what quantities? *How* should they employ their limited resources—land, water, minerals, fuel, and labor—to produce the desired goods and services? And for *whom* should they produce the goods and services? The manner in which they answer these questions has profound consequences for the nature and the structure of the societies. For instance, if they decide to produce guns and weaponry in large quantities, the standard of living of their citizens will be lower than if they emphasize the satisfaction of consumer needs. How they go about producing the desired goods and services shapes the world of work, how it is organized, the satisfactions it provides, and the status it accords. And decisions regarding the "for whom" question influence the distribution of wealth, income, and prestige. The answers to these questions derive from the structuring of power within societies.

Stealth Democracy

Are you registered to vote? Do you think your vote makes a difference in election outcomes? In large national elections, the probability that any one voter will cast the vote that decides the election is essentially zero (Kanazawa, 2000). Yet millions of Americans vote in every election. Why do they bother?

Sociologist Satoshi Kanazawa (2000) was intrigued by this question. Not only do individual votes not make a difference, but there also is no penalty for not voting. The outcomes of elections are enjoyed or suffered by everyone, whether you vote or not. "Why then," Kanazawa asks, "would rational actors invest their personal time and energy into going to the polls to cast their ballots?"

Kanazawa (2000) adapted a theory that proposes that people change their behaviors according to their experiences. Using election data from six different presidential elections to test this model, he found that it helps explain voting behavior. Voters whose candidate is elected feel as if their vote has made a difference and are more likely to vote again, while those whose candidate loses feel as if their efforts were wasted and are less likely to vote in the next election. Similarly, nonvoters seem to be motivated to vote in the next election if the candidate they support loses—"If only I had voted for her, she might have won!"—while nonvoters whose favorite candidate gets elected apparently assume that their support wasn't needed and are less likely to vote in the future.

Voting behavior, then, seems to be influenced by whether election outcomes reward or punish voters and nonvoters according to their preferences. But what are their preferences? What are voters really looking for in candidates?

Campaign rhetoric seems to assume that Americans care about the issues, want to be informed about policies and decisions, and want to vote for a candidate to whom they can feel connected. But John R. Hibbing and Elizabeth Theiss-Morse (2002), who have been using survey data to study Americans' attitudes toward their government for a decade, disagree:

[People] do not want to make political decisions themselves; they do not want to provide much input to those who are assigned to make these decisions; and they would rather not know all the details of the decision-making process. Most people have strong feelings on few if any of the issues the government needs to address and would much prefer to spend their time in nonpolitical pursuits.

In fact, Hibbing and Theiss-Morse conclude that Americans prefer something they term *stealth democracy*:

[They] want democratic procedures to exist but not to be visible on a routine basis. . . They want to know that the opportunity will be there for them even though they probably have no current

intention of getting involved in government or even of paying attention to it.

What sorts of issues get citizens riled up and ready to be more involved in politics? If you guess war, tax cuts, or gay marriage, you're wrong. What really gets Americans is thinking that government officials might be benefiting personally from their positions. "Citizens are usually less concerned with obtaining a policy outcome," the Hibbing and Theiss-Morse report found, "than with preventing others from using the process to feather their own nests."

Irritation with political leaders' self-interested behavior, then, might motivate citizens to vote in large numbers. The impact of each vote on the outcome, of course, decreases as the size of the turnout increases. But Kanazawa's findings suggest that the process of voting should lead to more political engagement in the future.

Questions for Discussion

1. Young people who are 18 to 25 have very low rates of voting. Is this fact explained by Kanazawa's theory? Why or why not?

2. What do you think explains the lack of interest in politics and government decision making that Hibbing and Theiss-Morse found among Americans? Do you think that the tendency they described varies in the population? If so, how?

As we pointed out in Chapter 2, ◄—[pp. 62–63] people have responded differently over the course of human history to the dictates posed by economic survival. Hunting and gathering economies were the earliest form of organized social life. Horticultural, agrarian, and industrial modes of production followed. Postindustrial social organization, focusing more on services than on manufacturing and integrating new information and communication technologies, will include profound changes in patterns of economic behavior and in market structure (International Labor Organization, 2001). Changes in the way people produce, distribute, and consume goods and services result in strong pressures for change in other institutional arrangements as well.

Over the 20th century two fundamentally different types of economic systems competed for people's allegiance, the capitalist market economy and the socialist command economy. Each took a quite different approach to economic organization. And each has substantially different social and political implications.

▲ The Big Differences

Modern economic systems differ from one another in two important aspects. First, they provide different answers to the question, How is economic activity organized—by the market or by the plan? Second, they provide different answers to the question, Who owns the means of production—individuals or the state? However, these questions do not demand an "either-or" answer. No contemporary nation falls totally at one or the other pole, although the United States and the pre-1991 Soviet Union typically supplied opposite answers to both questions.

▲ Market and Command Economies

A *market economy* is one in which decisions about what will be produced, how much will be produced, and what products cost are made in economic transactions between consumers and producers. Products that consumers do not want,

or that are overproduced, fall in price. Items that are in short supply and that people want rise in price. Price movements act as signals to profit-making individuals and firms. They cut back on goods with falling prices and increase the production of goods with rising prices. Economists call this mechanism *consumer sovereignty.*

Underlying this approach is the belief that if each economic unit is allowed to make free choices in pursuit of its own best interests, the interests of all will be best served. However, markets have little in the way of traditional morality built into them. A truly free market can supply products many people would rather not exist, including prostitution, child pornography, drugs of all kinds, and the services of hired killers, to name only a few.

A *command economy* is one in which the state or central planning authority determines the items that will be produced and their quantities. A command economy is often very good in moving a peasant society toward industrialization by mobilizing the masses to build miles of railroad and large dams. But a command economy finds it difficult to produce a complex array of consumer goods in the absence of market signals.

Free-market and command economies also differ in how they go about allocating resources to various productive activities. In free-market economies, competition among suppliers of goods and labor services is thought to ensure the most efficient and productive use of resources. Command economies, in contrast, are based on the assumption that rational decision making affords better results than the haphazard operation of market forces.

▲ An Economy for Whom?

Market and command economies differ in how they handle the issue of how income is distributed. Historically, one of the major criticisms of the market system has been that it fails to distribute income equitably. Market economies rely on the same price system that determines wages, interest rates, and profits for the distribution of income among people in the society. Income payments go in substantial amounts to private owners of physical capital—capitalists—or those who manage capitalist enterprises. Critics contend that some problems like the environmental crisis (see Chapter 12) and the absence of jobs for young inner-city African Americans are not easily solved through the free market (see Chapter 6) because such solutions do not produce a profit for capitalists. Accordingly, they say that different standards are called for in mature industrial societies like the United States where free markets and social welfare must be balanced (Heilbroner, 1993).

▲ Mixed Economies

When we look at the contemporary world, we are hard-pressed to find a pure form of a capitalist market economy. Even the United States in the early 19th century, which many economic historians deem to be as close to an example of pure capitalism as one can find, had government subsidies for railroads and canals. And socialist countries had black markets and other "underground" market mechanisms. Most nations today are characterized by mixed economies that include elements of both command and market economies.

Liberal market economies, such as the United States and Great Britain, are closer to the capitalist ideal and allocate and coordinate resources primarily through markets, while *coordinated market economies,* such as Germany, Japan, and Sweden, use a variety of non-market mechanisms such as negotiation and traditional relationships to solve allocation and coordination problems (Berger, 2005).

In societies with coordinated market economies, most production is privately owned, but there may be a large public sector with publicly owned enterprises involved in public transportation, health care, air travel, mining, oil production, education, utilities, and more. Some of these societies, such as Sweden, Finland, and Denmark, have high taxes, particularly on the wealthy, and use the money to redistribute some

of the wealth and to fund extensive social welfare and family support programs. In addition to having much lower economic inequality than the United States, societies with mixed economies usually score better than the United States on some important quality-of-life indicators such as rates of crime, divorce, infant mortality, and life expectancy—though the United States does have lower rates of both suicide and births to unmarried women than Sweden, Denmark, or Finland (U.S. Census Bureau, 2006; World Health Organization, 2003).

The Power of Corporations

The government is an important participant in the U.S. economy, but the primary productive role is played by private business. Although most of the more than 20 million businesses in the United States are small, large corporations have a substantial impact on the economy. In this section we will discuss national corporations, multinational corporations, and various ways in which corporations are controlled.

The Power of National Corporations

When you drive a car, operate a computer, replace a lightbulb, purchase gasoline, or eat a breakfast cereal, you are using products manufactured by an oligopoly. An **oligopoly** is a market dominated by a few firms, the giants of U.S. business such as General Motors, IBM, and General Electric.

These firms exercise enormous power in American life. The decisions made by their executives have implications and ramifications that reach throughout the nation, including effects on transportation, the environment, what we eat and drink, and the other products we use. They also affect the lives of millions of U.S. workers.

DILBERT (11/18/91) reprinted by permission of United Feature Syndicate, Inc.

▲ Corporate Downsizing and Its Effects on Workers

Today's corporation is no longer a secure or stable workplace. For example, restructuring and downsizing of large U.S. corporations meant the loss of 4 million jobs in America's 500 largest companies during the 1980s (Melloan, 1993), and these trends continue into the present (Russakoff, 2006). Corporate executives contend that large-scale staff reductions are essential if their companies are to maintain competitiveness in a fast-changing global marketplace. Yet considerable evidence suggests that companies slashing jobs often end up with more problems than profits. A 1991 survey examined more than 850 downsized corporations and found that only 41 percent met the profitability goals they had set for themselves.

Sagging employee morale is a major roadblock that stands in the way of profit growth from downsizing. Workers begin to ask, "Am I going to have a job?" rather than, "This is a great place to work; how can I make it better?" (Snizek, 1994). Many companies offer their older employees early retirement, but most such companies find they lose people they consider necessary and good performers. Firms also commonly make the mistake of eliminating workers but not the work, so that the surviving employees have to labor faster or more hours. The con-sequences are employee burnout and work left undone (Snizek, 1994) or the ratcheting up again of costs by rehiring (Boroughs, 1992).

▲ Economic Transitions and the Internet Revolution

The U.S. economy has long been in flux. Every year thousands of manufacturing jobs are created and thousands more are destroyed as firms go out of business or change operations and other firms start new production lines. The source of much of this change is the rise of the service sector of the economy—comprising industries such as insurance, Internet service, accounting, information processing, and financial services—that provide services rather than manufactured products. As some manufacturing jobs are exported to countries with cheaper labor costs, new jobs are created in this country in service industries. As people lose high-paying manufacturing jobs, they are forced to retrain to make themselves valuable on the job market.

The information and communications technology revolution of the last decade of the century has the potential to cause yet more dramatic changes. Despite the huge increase in numbers of people using the Internet and companies operating over the Internet, the annual volume of "e-commerce" at the end of the 1990s was too small a percentage of the total U.S. economy to have affected productivity growth (Litan and Rivlin, 2000). In the early 2000s, only about 1 percent of retail trade sales was in e-commerce. But in the early 2000s, half of all investments in plants and equipment were in computer and telecommunications technology (Litan and Rivlin, 2001), and by late 2005, 2.5 percent of all retail trade in the United States was in e-commerce (U.S. Census Bureau, 2006).

A conference held in 2000 to discuss the impact of the Internet on various sectors of the U.S. economy concluded that it could increase productivity growth in the following ways (Litan and Rivlin, 2000):

- Significantly reduce the cost of producing and distributing goods and services.

- Increase management efficiency.

- Increase competition.

- Increase the effectiveness of marketing and pricing.

- Increase consumer choice, convenience, and satisfaction.

Changes are inevitable, but analysts disagree about which direction they will take. Skeptics say that large gains in productivity or consumer welfare should not be expected anytime soon. But others expect that use of the Internet will spread from large- and medium-sized companies to small companies rapidly and that its use creates a significant potential for creating a large number of jobs for technically sophisticated workers and raising the standard of living (Litan and Rivlin, 2000).

The Power of Multinational Corporations in the Global Economy

The rise of multinational corporations and the growing internationalization of the world economy have given a new dimension to economic power (Szymanski, 1981; Fennema, 1982;

Biersteker, 1987; Barnet and Cavanagh, 1994). **Multinational corporations** are firms that have their central office in one country and subsidiaries in other countries. With the use of computer communications technology, companies no longer even need a geographical center. Managers and members of work teams can communicate as easily from country to country as they can from office to office. Today the annual income from sales of the largest multinational corporations exceeds the gross national product of most countries in which they do business. About half of the largest economic units in the world are not nations at all but multinational corporations.

▲ Division of Labor

Multinational corporations are playing a growing role in the structuring of the division of labor within the world economy. The economic integration of less developed nations into the structures of a world economy can be traced to European exploration and colonization beginning in the 15th century. The arrangement has been characterized by the differentiation of core and periphery regions (Wallerstein, 1974, 1980, 1989). **Core regions** consist of geographical areas that dominate the world economy and exploit the rest of the system; **periphery regions** consist of areas that provide raw materials to the core and are exploited by it. At first the peripheral areas exported spices, coffee, tea, and tobacco to Europe. Later, they became suppliers of agricultural and mineral raw materials, while their advantaged classes provided markets for industrial goods from Europe (Boswell, 1989; Chase-Dunn, 1989). Today companies go abroad to develop a source of cheap raw materials and in search of lower wages. This caused huge losses in textile, clothing, and shoe manufacturing jobs in industrialized countries and huge gains in developing countries in recent years.

▲ Made in America?

U.S. multinationals now have a major stake in keeping much of their production overseas. They manufacture and sell nearly three times as much

Losses of U.S. jobs in the early 2000s reflect the exportation of jobs to countries, such as India, where labor costs are lower.

abroad as they make in and export from the United States. Likewise, multinational firms import to the United States parts they use in manufacturing that can be made more cheaply by foreign suppliers. Multinationals are not only the biggest exporters in the United States, but also the nation's biggest importers, often bringing more into the United States than they ship out. The globalization of economic activity has fostered a trend toward a form of "stateless" corporation (Sklair, 1991). In the emerging global economy, it is becoming increasingly difficult to say what is an "American," "Japanese," or "Swedish" product. In some cases, for instance, vehicles sold in the United States are built in 12 countries, with parts coming from all over the

world. Indeed, it is now impossible to purchase a completely American-made vehicle.

▲ Impact on Third World Nations

There is considerable controversy about what impact multinational corporations in general have had on less-developed or peripheral nations. One view, associated with mainstream Marxism, claims that international capitalism has made capitalist countries from precapitalist ones and established the foundation for worker-led socialist revolutions. The contrasting view argues that foreign investments in a country creates dependencies that have less positive impact than domestic investment does (Dixon and Boswell, 1996; Firebaugh, 1996). The economies of developing nations have often become tied to a single industry, increasing dependence on foreign investors, distorting patterns of national economic development, and rendering the nations especially vulnerable to bust-and-boom economic cycles (Noble, 1989; Stokes and Anderson, 1990).

▲ What About the Internet?

The Internet has dramatically changed the way companies, including multinational corporations, do business. There are literally millions of websites (Wiseman, 2000).

Although some see the Internet as likely to increase productivity and benefit consumers, the International Competition Policy Advisory Committee issued a report warning that expansion of e-commerce could result in threats to open competition, primarily through price signaling and cartel creation.

Work is becoming increasingly independent of location, and analysts predict that this will change the quality of work, management practices, and the way work is contracted out (International Labor Organization, 2001). While use of the new information and communication technologies results in job loss, new employment opportunities also are created: "The highest rates of job creation, job destruction, and job switching occur among the most technologically innovative firms in sectors where overall employment is growing" (International Labor Organization, 2001:6). The use of new information and communication technologies has the potential for increasing employment in developing countries (International Labor Organization, 2001). Some analysts estimate that up to 5 percent of the service-sector jobs in industrialized nations—approximately 12 million jobs—could be relocated to developing nations. But the "digital divide" is a significant barrier. Despite the Internet's phenomenal growth and increasing availability in nearly every country in the world (United Nations Conference on Trade and Development, 2005), the fact remains that the highest rates of Internet use are in wealthier countries, where Internet costs are only half of what they are in poor countries. The highest reported rate is in Sweden, where 75.5 percent of the population uses the Internet (United Nations Conference on Trade and Development, 2005). Politics also plays a part. In Cuba, where what citizens hear and read is tightly controlled by the government, Internet technology also is under government control (Wilson, 2000). In 2004, only 1.3 percent of the Cuban population were Internet users, compared to nearly 6 percent in nearby Haiti and 9 percent in the Dominican Republic (United Nations Conference on Trade and Development, 2005).

The Control of Corporations

We have seen that the decisions made by corporations have vast consequences not only for the citizens of one country but also for the global community. They have a substantial impact upon employment opportunities, economic conditions (depression and inflation), consumer choices, and political authority.

Who controls corporations—who are their decision makers? In 1932 Adolph Berle, Jr., and Gardiner C. Means published *The Modern Corporation and Private Property,* a book that

has had a profound impact on scholarly thought on the matter. They wrote that corporate power resides with chief executives who themselves have little financial stake in the firms they manage. The logic of their argument rested on the assertion that the stock of most large corporations is widely dispersed. Consequently, no shareholders possess a sufficient block of stock to impose corporate policy on the managers who make the day-to-day decisions for their firms. This state of affairs has been labeled "the managerial revolution" (Burnham, 1941).

▲ Emphasizing Short-Term Profits

Some critics see the managerial revolution as the source of many of America's current economic problems, with corporations rewarding executives who display impressive short-term results. U.S. executives keep research and technology on short rations and skimp on the investment needed to ensure competitiveness in the future; they are slow to innovate and avoid risk. Critics also charge that U.S. industries are managed by persons increasingly oriented toward realizing profits by financial stratagems, commodity speculation, and fast-return investments. Large investors and speculators—called corporate raiders—have found that they can make a good deal of money by buying and selling companies.

Critics also say that executives adopt strategies that allow substantial expense accounts and high salaries for themselves. In 2001, for instance, the typical chief executive officer (CEO) in a modest-sized U.S. firm received nearly $2 million in total compensation—41 times the average U.S. worker's pay. In contrast, the average Japanese CEO makes only 12 times the earnings of the average Japanese worker, and the average CEO in Germany makes 13 times the pay of the average worker there (see Figure 9.4).

Economists Marianne Bertrand and Sendhil Mullainathan studied determinants of CEO pay from 1977 to 1994 and found that increases in the value of a company's stock led to increases

	CEO Compensation	Average Worker's Compensation	Ratio of CEO Pay to the Average Worker's Pay by Country
South Africa	$394,672	$ 7,145	55
Mexico	866,831	16,141	54
Brazil	530,220	10,304	51
Venezuela	635,045	12,572	51
Malaysia	300,414	6,043	50
Argentina	879,068	17,882	49
United States	1,932,580	46,813	41
Hong Kong	736,599	18,766	39
Singapore	645,740	17,230	37
China (Shanghai)	89,498	2,950	30
United Kingdom	668,526	26,325	25
Canada	787,060	33,914	23
Australia	546,914	24,311	22
Netherlands	604,854	27,271	22
Italy	600,319	28,006	21
New Zealand	287,345	14,502	20
Spain	429,725	22,880	19
France	519,060	32,499	16
Taiwan	229,212	15,565	15
Sweden	413,860	28,175	15
Germany	454,974	34,583	13
South Korea	214,836	17,164	13
Japan	508,106	43,663	12
Switzerland	404,580	42,384	10

Figure 9.4 **Ratio of CEO Pay to the Average Worker's Pay by Country**
Chief executive officers in large U.S. companies earn more than their counterparts in most other industrialized and emerging nations, but the gap between a CEO and a skilled industrial worker is greater in some other countries (2001 data).

Source: Towers Perrin report: "Worldwide Total Remuneration 2001–2002," available at towersperrin.com

in CEO pay, whether the increasing stock value was due to executive performance or fluctuations in economic conditions that were beyond the executive's control. In other words, increases in CEO pay are affected as much by luck as by doing a good job (Bertrand and Mullainathan, 2001). In 2002, the third year of a sharp decline both in corporate performance and in stock prices in the United States, CEO pay nonetheless increased by 6 percent (McGeehan, 2003),

which was significantly greater than the increase in the average worker's pay.

The disparity between workers' pay and CEOs' pay is much greater in very large corporations. Research on the total compensation (salary, bonuses, stock options, and other stock distributions) of CEOs in America's 800 largest corporations shows that the average compensation for the 100 highest paid CEOs was $37.5 million in 1999 (Piketty and Saez,

2001). This was about $1,046 for every $1 made by the average worker in the United States in that year ($35,864). In 1970, the ratio of top CEO pay to the average worker's pay was only $39 to $1. This increase from $39 to $1,046 is much greater than the increase in the performance of these large corporations or of the economy over this period, suggesting that top CEOs' pay is not tightly connected to either CEO job performance or to economic growth in general.

The managerial perspective, with its emphasis on leadership discretion, has largely dominated the thinking of American sociologists and economists since the 1930s. However, in recent years a growing chorus of social scientists have advanced the view that important constraints operate on managers in discharging their responsibilities (Fligstein, 1990; Fligstein and Brantley, 1992). For one thing, because corporations are dependent on suppliers of raw materials, customers, employees, investors, and lenders, usually referred to as *stakeholders*, executives must act in ways that do not threaten these important relationships (Mintz and Schwartz, 1985; Loomis, 1988). **Corporate interlocks**—networks of individuals who serve on the boards of directors of multiple corporations—are another set of constraints.

Because members of the corporate board of one corporation may be board members or executives in other corporations, these corporate interlocks are mechanisms whereby corporate managers are constrained to some degree by interests of those outside the corporation (Kerbo, 2006). Interlocks also serve firms with the means to gather the strategic information their officials need to make corporate decisions and build favorable relationships with other firms (Bartol and Martin, 1994; Kerbo, 2006).

Professional managers exercise considerable authority in corporate decision making. But executive officers continue to be governed by the requirement that they optimize profits. The ascendance of corporate managers has not freed corporations to pursue goals and policies that consistently run counter to profit

maximization. Changes in management may be considerable over the coming decades; the use of new information and communication technologies is greatest in companies that have most thoroughly changed the way decisions are made and work is organized (International Labor Organization, 2001).

The Sociology of Work

Power extends into the workplace. Among other things, it determines whether or not work will be available, how work will be organized, and the manner in which work will be remunerated. In a capitalist market economy, such as that found in the United States, the problem of organizing economic activity begins with a system of property rights involving the uses of resources and a structure of authority for mobilizing these resources. Property rights consist of the claims individuals or groups have on objects; conversely, they define the conditions under which some individuals or groups are excluded from the use or enjoyment of these objects. As we noted earlier in the chapter, the means by which people secure their livelihoods in a capitalist market economy—the factories, mines, offices, and farms—are privately owned and oriented to the production of profits.

Changes in the Work Experience

The work experience of Americans has undergone significant change over the past 160 years and continues to undergo change (see Figure 9.5). Although more than 70 percent of the labor force worked on farms in 1820, by 1910 only 31 percent of Americans were engaged in agriculture. Today the number of individuals employed in professional, management, technology, administrative, and service jobs has exceeded the 70 percent of people who were involved in farming a century and a half ago, with only 2 percent of the labor force today in agriculture and about 25 percent in blue-collar jobs and manufacturing.

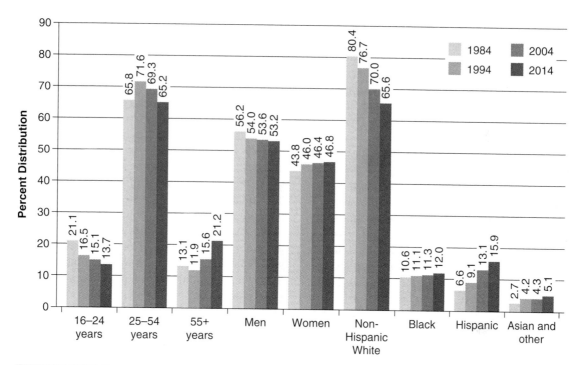

Figure 9.5 **Percent Distribution of the Labor Force by Age, Gender, and Race/Ethnicity by Decade, 1984–2014**

These analyses by analysts at the Bureau of Labor Statistics use data from the U.S. Census Department Current Population Surveys from 1984, 1994, and 2004 and projections to the year 2014. Percentages for each category are within year. For example, in 1984, men were 56.2 percent of the labor force and women were 43.8 percent. These analyses show that the labor force is becoming older, is increasingly diverse racially and ethnically, and is nearly evenly divided by gender. Nonetheless, in the foreseeable future, the labor force will remain dominated by persons of middle age and by non-Hispanic whites. [Percentages do not always add up to 100 within year due to rounding, because Hispanics may be of any race, and because those of "other" race/ethnicity are not included.]

Source: Data are adapted from Toossi (2005).

These changes have been accompanied by a shift from a nonindustrial to an industrial society and now to a service and information society. In nonindustrial societies the family overshadows and dominates other institutional spheres. Working (earning a living) is not readily distinguishable from other social activities. The situation is quite different in industrial societies (Dubin, 1976). First, the workplace is physically segregated from the home. Second, working time is temporally separated in the daily cycle from leisure time. Third, specialized organizational structures—complex authority hierarchies—take over the management of work activities (Stinchcombe, 1983). Finally, the economic institution increasingly becomes the focus of other institutions, with the family, government, religion, and education accommodating to its requirements.

Life and work in an economy dominated by information and communication technologies will be affected by values, agreements, and institutions different from those of an industrial era (International Labor Organization, 2001). An "Internet economy" offers the potential for a better balance between work and leisure or work and family life. It can also pressure employees to work all the time, wherever they are, and working more hours is a problem Americans already have (Schor, 1993).

The Significance of Work

People work for many reasons. "Self-interest" in its broadest sense, including the interests of family and friends, is a basic motivation for working in all societies. But self-interest need not involve only providing for subsistence or accumulating wealth. Among the Maori, a Polynesian people of the South Pacific, a desire for approval, a sense of duty, a wish to conform to custom and tradition, a feeling of emulation, and a pleasure in craftsmanship are additional reasons for working (Hsu, 1943). Within the United States, too, work is not simply a response to economic necessity. Surveys over the past 30 years reveal that between 65 and 77 percent of Americans say they would continue to work even if they could get enough money to live comfortably for the rest of their lives (Davis, Smith, and Marsden, 2003). In 1997, a Gallup Poll found that nearly 60 percent would continue working even if they won $10 million in the lottery (Moore, 1997).

Work has many social meanings (Levinson, 1964). When individuals work, they gain a contributing place in society. That they receive pay for their work indicates that what they do is needed by other people and that they are a necessary part of the social fabric. Work is also a major social mechanism for placing people in the larger social structure and affording them identities. Much of who individuals are, to themselves and others, is interwoven with how they earn their livelihood.

▲ The Importance of Control

Work affects an individual's personal and family life in many ways (Small and Riley, 1990).

Jobs that permit occupational self-direction—initiative, thought, and independent judgment in work—foster people's intellectual flexibility. Individuals with such jobs become more open in approaching and weighing evidence on current social and economic issues. The effects of occupational self-direction also generalize to other nonwork settings. Individuals who enjoy opportunities for self-direction in their work are more likely to become more self-confident, less authoritarian, less conformist in their ideas, and less fatalistic in their nonwork lives than other individuals. In turn, these traits lead in time to more responsible jobs that allow even greater latitude for occupational self-direction (Kohn and Schooler, 1983). Such work autonomy may increase with the Internet revolution, as most enterprises using new technologies also move to decentralized decision making and task oriented teamwork (International Labor Organization, 2001).

A variety of workplace conditions—the restriction of opportunity to exercise self-direction, work overload, poor quality of interpersonal relations on the job, few opportunities for cooperative problem solving, job insecurities, job loss, and low earnings—have emotional repercussions that can lead to negative family interactions (Menaghan, 1991). So the job affects the person and the person affects the job in a reciprocal relationship across the life course (Kohn and Schooler, 1983; Kohn et al., 1990). Our work is an important socializing experience that influences who and what we are.

Satisfaction and Alienation in Work

Sociologists find that individuals in occupations that combine high economic, occupational, and educational prestige typically show the greatest satisfaction with their work and the strongest job attachment (Kohn and Schooler, 1973, 1982; Hartman and Pearlstein, 1987). However, the prestige factor partly subsumes a number of other elements, including the amount of control and responsibility that goes with an occupation. The opportunity to exercise discretion, accept challenges, and make decisions has an important bearing on how people feel about their work (Keita and Sauter, 1992; Lawler, 1992) for both males and females (Neil and Snizek, 1988). The most potent factors in job satisfaction are those that relate to workers' self-respect, their chance to perform well, their opportunities for achievement and growth, and the chance to contribute something personal and quite unique. Surveys show that the vast majority of Americans, 85 percent, are very or moderately satisfied with the work they are doing (Davis, Smith, and Marsden, 2003). Even so, only about 40 percent would keep their present jobs if they had the opportunity to choose some other job, perhaps indicating that changing responsibilities is an important factor in job satisfaction.

▲ Alienation and a Lack of Power

When individuals fail to find their work fulfilling and satisfying, they may experience **alienation**—a pervasive sense of powerlessness, meaninglessness, normlessness, isolation, and self-estrangement (Seeman, 1959). Alienation may be structured into the nature of the work itself. For example, in a classic study, Robert Blauner (1964) showed that when work is simple, repetitive, and engages workers in only a small part of the overall work process, workers feel disconnected and alienated from it. One expression of alienation is *job burnout*—a sense of boredom, apathy, reduced efficiency, fatigue, frustration, and despondency. A recent study by the Gallup Organization found that only 26 percent of employed adults in the United States are engaged in their work, 55 percent are not engaged, and 19 percent are "fully disengaged." Not surprisingly, the study found that worker disengagement is associated with higher absenteeism

from work and leads to a reduction of about $300 billion in annual economic performance. The study also showed that disengaged workers are more likely to report that stress at work caused them to behave poorly with their families and are less likely to report that they "have the important things they want" in their lives (*The Washington Post,* 2001). While the independence of work location associated with the "information economy" has the potential to benefit workers, it can also result in isolation and dead-end careers in data processing (International Labor Organization, 2001). Employee contracts and benefits in the digital age may leave workers powerless and unprotected. Any benefits it confers may be unequally distributed; fewer women than men have used the Internet, and the gap is larger in areas of more intensive Internet use (Bimber, 2000).

▲ Marx and Durkheim

Two somewhat different perspectives on alienation are provided by Karl Marx and Émile Durkheim (Lukes, 1977). Marx saw alienation as rooted in capitalist social arrangements. For Marx, work is our most important activity as human beings. Through work we create our world and ourselves. The products of our labor reflect our nature and form the basis for our self-evaluations. Further, through work we experience ourselves as active beings who shape the world about us. But according to Marx (1844/1960), individuals in capitalist societies lose control of their labor and become commodities, objects used by capitalists to make a profit. They are alienated from productive activity, the products of their labor, their coworkers, and their own human potential. Rather than being a process that is inherently satisfying, work becomes an unfulfilling activity that simply produces a subsistence wage.

In Marx's view, alienation is a structural condition. Regardless of how they feel about it, workers are alienated; having no control over the conditions of their work, they can control neither their well-being nor their survival. If workers say they are satisfied, Marx would say they experience false consciousness .

In contrast to Marx, Durkheim depicted alienation as arising from the breakdown of the cohesive ties that bind individuals to society. For Durkheim the central question was whether people are immersed in a structure of group experiences and memberships that provide a meaningful and valued context for their behavior. A group either coheres and makes life comprehensible and viable for individuals or it fails to do so, engendering pathology (akin to what we called *anomie* in Chapter 5). ◄── pp. 142–144 Whereas Marx emphasized freedom from social constraint as the source of human happiness, Durkheim stressed that human happiness depends on a society that provides people with rules. Rules, said Durkheim, integrate individuals into cohesive social groups and give direction and meaning to their activity.

Both Marx and Durkheim identified forces that can result in alienation. Clearly, since so much of life is spent at work, both the nature of work and the quality of group bonds at work can profoundly affect human happiness, satisfaction, and how people come to think about themselves.

The Chapter in Brief: *Political and Economic Power*

Power, Authority, and the State
Power determines which individuals and groups will be able to translate their preferences into the reality of day-to-day social organization.

▮ *The State*   The **state** rests on **force** and consists of people who exercise an effective monopoly in the use of physical coercion within a given territory.

▮ *Sociological Perspectives on the State*
Functionalists say the state performs four functions: enforcement of norms, overall social

planning and direction, arbitration of conflicting interests, and protection of a society's members and interests against outside groups. Conflict theorists say the state is a vehicle by which one or more groups impose their values and stratification system upon other groups and depict it as an instrument of violence and oppression.

▮ *Legitimacy and Authority*
Sociologists distinguish between power that is legitimate and power that is illegitimate. Legitimate power is **authority.** Sociologist Max Weber suggested that power may be

legitimated by **traditional, legal-rational,** and/or **charismatic** means.

Political Power

Politics refers to the processes by which people and groups acquire and exercise power. **Political power** is power that is organized and wielded by the state.

▌ *Types of Government*
Government can take the form of **totalitarianism, authoritarianism,** or **democracy,** which is promoted by a strong **civil society.**

▌ *Political Power in the United States*
A constitutional system of government defines and prescribes the boundaries within which political power is pursued in the United States. Central to American political processes are **political parties,** popular electoral participation, **interest-group** lobbying (including **political action committees**), and the **mass media.**

▌ *Models of Power in the United States*
Marxist theory holds that political processes are affected by class interests and conflict. The elitist model depicts major decisions as being made by a power elite. The pluralist perspective says that no one group really runs the government.

Economic Power

Modern economic systems provide a different answer to the question of how economic activity is organized—by the market or by the plan—and to the question of who owns the means of production—individuals or the state.

▌ *Comparative Economic Systems*
Capitalist economies rely heavily on free markets and privately held property, and **socialist economies** rely primarily on state planning and publicly held property. Most nations are characterized by mixed economies that include elements of both.

The Power of Corporations

The government is an important participant in the U.S. economy, but the primary productive role is played by private business.

▌ *The Power of National Corporations*
Large corporations exercise enormous power in American life and constitute **oligopolies.** The decisions made by their executives have implications and ramifications that reach throughout the nation.

▌ *The Power of Multinational Corporations in the Global Economy*
The rise of **multinational corporations** and the growing internationalization of the world economy, including **core regions** and **periphery regions,** have given economic power a new dimension. Such firms rival nations in wealth and frequently operate as private governments pursuing their worldwide interests by well-developed foreign policies.

▌ *The Control of Corporations*
Some social scientists say that a managerial revolution has separated ownership and effective control in corporate life, but others point to the institutional constraints, such as **corporate interlocks,** that operate on corporate decision makers.

The Sociology of Work

Power extends into the workplace, determining whether work will be available, how work will be organized, and the manner in which work will be remunerated.

▌ *Changes in the Work Experience*
The work experience of Americans has undergone significant change over the past 160 years; the proportion working on farms has declined, while the proportion employed in service industries has risen. Work in nonindustrialized societies is very different from work in industrialized societies.

▌ *The Significance of Work*
People work for many reasons in addition to "self-interest," and work has many social meanings, especially those that define a person's position in the social structure.

▌ *Satisfaction and Alienation in Work*
Individuals in occupations that combine high

economic, occupational, and educational prestige typically show the greatest satisfaction with their work and the strongest job attachment. When individuals fail to find their work satisfying and fulfilling, they may experience **alienation.** Marx and Durkheim had differing conceptions of alienation.

Glossary

alienation   A pervasive sense of powerlessness, meaninglessness, normlessness, isolation, and self-estrangement.

authoritarianism   A political system in which the government tolerates little or no opposition to its rules but permits nongovernmental centers of influence and allows debate on issues of public policy.

authority   Legitimate power.

capitalist economy   An economic system relying primarily on free markets and privately held property.

charismatic authority Power that is legitimated by the extraordinary superhuman or supernatural attributes people attribute to a leader.

civil society   A social realm of mediating groups, networks, and institutions that sustains public life outside the worlds of the state and the economy.

core regions   Geographical areas that dominate the world economy and exploit the rest of the system.

corporate interlocks Networks of individuals who serve on the boards of directors of multiple corporations.

democracy   A political system in which the powers of government derive from the consent of the governed and in which regular constitutional avenues exist for changing government officials.

force   Power whose basis is the threat or application of punishment.

government   Those political processes that have to do with the authoritative formulating of rules and policies that are binding and pervasive throughout a society.

interest groups Organizations of people who share common concerns or points of view.

interests   People who share common concerns or points of view.

legal-rational authority Power that is legitimated by explicit rules and rational procedures that define the

rights and duties of the occupants of given positions.

mass media   Those organizations—newspapers, magazines, television, radio, and motion pictures—that undertake to convey information to a large segment of the public.

multinational corporations Firms that have their central office in one country and subsidiaries in other countries.

oligopoly   A market dominated by a few firms.

periphery regions Geographical areas that provide raw materials to the core and are exploited by it.

political action committees (PACs)   Interest groups set up to elect or defeat candidates, but not through the organization of a political party.

political party   An organization designed to gain control of the government by putting its people in public office.

political power   Power that is organized and wielded by the state.

politics   The processes by which people and groups acquire and exercise power.

public-interest groups Interest groups that pursue policies that presumably would be of no greater benefit to their members than to the larger society.

socialist economy   An economic system relying primarily on state planning and publicly held property.

special-interest groups Interest groups that primarily seek benefits from which their members would derive more gains than the society as a whole.

state   An arrangement that consists of people who exercise an effective monopoly in the use of physical coercion within a given territory.

totalitarianism   A "total state" in which the government undertakes to control all parts of the society and all aspects of social life.

traditional authority Power that is legitimated by the sanctity of age-old customs.

Review Questions

1. Define *the state* as sociologists use the term.
2. How do the functionalist and conflict perspectives on the state differ?
3. What do sociologists mean by legitimacy and authority? What are the three types of authority and how do they differ?
4. Define politics and political power.
5. How do totalitarianism, authoritarianism, and democracy differ?
6. What are the major elements of American political processes?
7. What is an oligopoly? What part do oligopolies play in the United States?
8. How do multinational corporations function?
9. Who controls corporations?
10. How has work changed in the United States in the last 100 years? What is alienation? What is the significance of work to most people?

Internet Connection

 www.mhhe.com/hughes8

Are you registered to vote? Have you voted in a local, state, or national election? Use an Internet search engine such as yahoo.com or Google to find out what sorts of people are most likely to vote in national elections. Try using "voter characteristics" for searching. Are the percentages you find different from those presented in Figure 9.1? Are the data for a presidential election different from a midterm (Senate and House) election?

Chapter 10

THE FAMILY

Structure of the Family: A Global View

Forms of the Family
Forms of Marriage
Patterns of Courtship

Marriage and the Family in the United States

Life within Marriage
Parenthood
Two-Income Families
Beyond the Traditional Nuclear Family

Challenges for American Families and American Society

Family Violence, Child Abuse, and Incest
Child Care

Divorce
Care for the Elderly

Sociological Perspectives on the Family

The Functionalist Perspective
The Conflict Perspective
The Interactionist Perspective

Box 10.1   *Sociology Around the World: A Wide Variety in Family Values*

Box 10.2   *Social Inequalities: Family Backgrounds and Unequal Childhoods*

Box 10.3   *Doing Social Research: Racial Diversity within Families*

Some believe that the family has undergone a grave loss over the past 40 years. They cite gay marriage, easy divorce, the postponement of marriage, a rise in the proportion of the never-married, and the ready availability of contraception as forces that have eroded the family and compromised its "ultimate function"—the licensing of reproduction.

Others believe the family is not disintegrating but merely changing, revealing its flexibility and resilience. They say that traditional family forms are no longer appropriate for contemporary times, adding that the structures were flawed as conformity-ridden, male-dominated, and oppressive. They admit that the meaning of marriage has been changing and with it the family institution but claim that pronouncements concerning the death of the family are greatly exaggerated. No matter what we think family is,

most of us think it's tremendously important. "Protecting family" was ranked at the top of 57 personal values by a majority of survey respondents in the United States, Canada, and many other countries (Roper Starch Worldwide, 2000).

Whether the American family has been disintegrating or merely changing over the last half of the 20th century, widespread behavioral changes have occurred in the United States and throughout Western societies. Table 10.1 compares the circumstances of American children in the late 1990s with those in 1960; Figure 10.1 reveals substantial shifts in American family arrangements. The "family question," despite its many guises, is not new. Concerns about the family have a long history (Coontz, 1992), and it is safe to assume that debate will continue. In this chapter we will look first at the structure of the family from a global perspective, including forms of

317

Table 10.1	**A Comparison of the State of U.S. Children, 1960 and 2003–4**	
	1960	2003–4
Children born to unmarried mothers	5%	34.6%
Mothers returning to work within 1 year of a child's birth	17%	54.2%
Children under 18 living in a one-parent family (approx.)	10%	32.2%
Infant mortality (deaths before first birthday)	28/1,000	7.0/1,000
Children under 18 living below the poverty line	27%	17%
Married women with children under 6 years old in labor force	18.6%	59.3%

Source: U.S. Census Bureau, 2006.

marriage and family and patterns of courtship around the world. We will then focus on marriage and family in the United States, both the traditional nuclear family and other forms of family life. We will look at special challenges American families and American society face, including divorce, family violence and abuse, child care, and care for the elderly. Finally, we will see what the three major sociological perspectives have to offer to our understanding of the family.

Structure of the Family: A Global View

What is the family? Even experts on the family have trouble defining it; textbooks for courses on the family offer multiple definitions (e.g., Cherlin, 2002; Hutter, 1998; Olson and DeFrain, 1997). Many of us think of the family as a social unit consisting of Mom, Pop, and the kids, living alone in a comfortable home of their own—the image conveyed by a "Kodak family" about to open gifts under a Christmas tree. But as we will see in the course of the chapter, this definition is too restrictive. Even in the United States, this model of the family—a married couple, breadwinner husband and homemaker wife, raising children—now comprises only one in five families. Moreover, in many societies it is the kin group, and not a married couple and their children, that is the basic family unit. With so many Americans living in single-parent households, stepparent households, childless households, gay and lesbian households, and unmarried cohabiting male and female households, a number of sociologists suggest that it would be better to dispense with the concept of "family" altogether and focus instead upon "sexually bonded primary relationships" (Scanzoni et al., 1989).

Sociologists have traditionally viewed the **family** as a social group whose members are related by ancestry, marriage, or adoption and live together, cooperate economically, and care for the young (Murdock, 1949). However, some are unhappy with this definition, arguing that psychological bonds and intimacy are what families are all about; they see the family as a close-knit group of people who care about and respect each other (e.g., Lauer and Lauer, 2000). Many Americans are now willing to accept alternatives to traditional notions of the family. The family, then, is a matter of social definition. Because the family is a social construct, family ties are often independent of legal or kin status (Gubrium and Holstein, 1990).

Defining the family is not simply an academic exercise. How we define it determines the kinds of families we will consider normal or deviant, and what rights and obligations we will recognize as legally and socially binding.

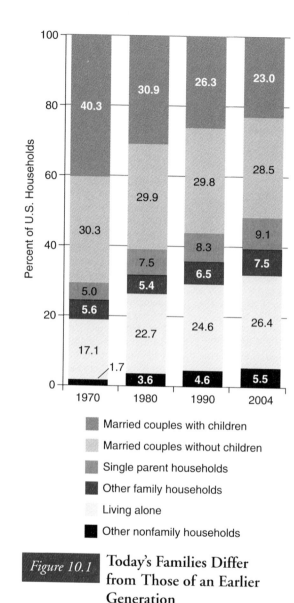

Figure 10.1   **Today's Families Differ from Those of an Earlier Generation**

Source: Figure generated by the authors using data from the U.S. Census Bureau (2006).

A growing number of judges and legislators are now extending to qualifying domestic partners some of the benefits traditionally accorded married heterosexuals, including health benefits,

property and life insurance, bereavement leave, and annuity and pension rights.

In this section we will look at forms of the family, forms of marriage, and patterns of courtship in the United States and around the world.

Forms of the Family

Families are organized in many ways. Individuals differ in their thoughts about whether parents should be married, how many children make a perfect family, whether male or female offspring are preferable, and even whether having children at all is important (see Box 10.1). More fundamentally, families vary in their composition and in their descent, residence, and authority patterns—characteristics we examine here.

▲ Composition

Social relationships between adult males and females can be organized within families by emphasizing either spouse or kin relationships. In the **nuclear family** arrangement, spouses and their offspring constitute the core relationship; blood relatives are functionally marginal and peripheral. In contrast, in the **extended family** arrangement, kin—individuals related by common ancestry—provide the core relationship; spouses are functionally marginal and peripheral. Americans typically find themselves members of two nuclear families. First an individual belongs to a nuclear family that consists of oneself and one's father, mother, and siblings, what sociologists call the **family of orientation.** Second, since over 90 percent of Americans marry at least once, most are members of a nuclear family that consists of oneself and one's spouse and children, the **family of procreation.**

Extended families are found in numerous forms throughout the world. In the Nayara soldiering caste of southwestern India during the

A Wide Variety in Family Values

The family is among the most important institutions in every society, but exactly how people value the family varies from one society to the next. A Gallup survey in 16 countries on four continents found a wide variety in attitudes about the importance of parents being married, the ideal number of children to have, whether a boy or a girl was preferable, and even in the degree to which people desire to have children at all (Gallup, 1997).

The ideal number of children for a family varies among countries, from India, where 87 percent of the survey respondents indicated that up to two children was the perfect number, to Iceland, where 69 percent indicated that three or more was the perfect number. Other countries favoring small families (with up to two children as ideal) included Spain, Germany, Colombia, Hungary, Thailand, and Great Britain. Countries favoring three or more children included Guatemala and Taiwan. The United States is divided on the issue of the perfect number of children, with 50 percent favoring up to two children and 41 percent favoring three or more children.

Survey respondents also were asked whether, if they could have only one child, they would prefer to have a girl or a boy. Although more than half the respondents replied "no opinion" in many countries (e.g., Tawian, Hungary, Guatemala, Canada, Singapore, Germany, Iceland, and Spain), when respondents did have an opinion they tended to prefer boys. In only a few countries did a preference for girls beat a preference for boys, and only by a slim margin.

Finally, whether children are important to one's sense of fulfillment also varied by country, but in almost every country surveyed most respondents agreed that they were. In Hungary 94 percent of the respondents said it was necessary to have a child to feel fulfilled. The United States was at the opposite extreme, with only 46 percent of respondents indicating that having a child was important and 51 percent indicating that it was not. In 2000, 19 percent of 40- to 44-year-old U.S. women had not had children, a rate double that from 1980 (U.S. Census Bureau, 2003). Other countries whose respondents felt having a child was important were India, Taiwan, Iceland, Thailand, Lithuania, and Singapore.

Men and women within each country generally agreed on the questions discussed above. The only question on which men and women had clear differences of opinion was gender preference. Women had either no gender preference or a slight preference for boys; men had a strong preference for boys, around the world but especially in the United States and in several less industrialized countries.

Valuing the family may be universal, but family values are not. These findings strongly suggest that, like other cultural traits, family values vary because of differing social, economic, and other factors, such as religion. They also suggest that as our society, economy, and culture change, we are likely to observe more changes in our American family values.

Questions for Discussion

1. How do you account for the small proportion of Americans who believe having a child is important?

2. Why do you think people who express a gender preference for their offspring primarily prefer boys?

pre-British period, spouse ties were virtually absent (Fuller, 1976). When a woman was about to enter puberty, she was ritually married to a man chosen for her by a neighborhood assembly. After three ceremonial days, she was ritually separated from him and was then free to take on a series of visiting husbands or lovers. Although a woman's lovers gave her regular gifts on prescribed occasions, they did not provide support. When a woman had a child, one of the men—not necessarily the biological father—paid a fee to the midwife and thus established the child's legitimacy. However, the man assumed no economic, social, legal, or ritual rights or obligations toward the child. It was the mother's kin who took responsibility.

For some time sociologists assumed that industrialization undercut extended family patterns while fostering nuclear family arrangements. A closer look shows a different pattern. By virtue of high mortality rates, the nuclear family had come to prevail in England before the Industrial Revolution got under way (Laslett, 1974, 1976; Stearns, 1977; Quadagno, 1982). When Tamara K. Hareven (1982) examined family life in a textile community in 19th-century New Hampshire, she discovered that industrialism promoted kin ties. Not only did different generations often reside together in the same household, but they provided a good deal of assistance to one another. Indeed, economic dislocations and the increased availability of nonnuclear kin may actually have encouraged the formation of extended family households in the early industrialization of England and the United States (Ruggles, 1987). Overall, a growing body of research suggests that a large number of factors—in addition to the nature of the political economy—interact with one another to produce a diversity of family life patterns (Hutter, 1998; Cherlin, 2002; Kertzer, 1991).

▲ Descent

Societies trace descent and pass on property from one generation to the next in one of three ways. Under a **patrilineal** arrangement, a people reckon descent and transmit property through the line of the father. Under a **matrilineal** arrangement, descent and inheritance take place through the mother's side of the family. Under the **bilineal** arrangement, both sides of an individual's family are equally important. Americans are typically bilineal, reckoning descent through both the father and the mother; however, the surname is transmitted in a patrilineal manner.

▲ Residence

Societies also differ in where a couple take up residence after marriage. In the case of **patrilocal residence,** the bride and groom live in the household or community of the husband's family. The opposite pattern prevails in **matrilocal residence.** For example, among the Hopi of the Southwest, the husband moves upon marriage into the dwelling of his wife's family, where he eats and sleeps. In the United States newlyweds tend to follow **neolocal residence** patterns, in which they set up a new place of residence independent of either of their parents or other relatives.

▲ Authority

Although the authority a man or woman enjoys in family decision making is influenced by their personalities, societies nonetheless dictate who is expected to be the dominant figure. Under **patriarchal authority,** the eldest male or the husband fills this role. The ancient Hebrews, Greeks, and Romans and the 19th-century Chinese and Japanese provide a few examples. Logically, the construction of a **matriarchal authority** family type is very simple and would involve the vesting of power in women. Yet true matriarchies are rare (Hutter, 1998), and considerable controversy exists about whether the balance of power actually rests with the wife in any known society (Stephens, 1963). Matriarchies can arise through default upon the death of or desertion by the husband. In a third type of family, the **egalitarian authority** arrangement, power and authority are equally distributed between husband and wife. This pattern has been on the increase in the United States.

Forms of Marriage

Marriage refers to a socially approved sexual union between two or more individuals that is undertaken with some idea of permanence. The parties to a marriage must be members of two different kin groups, which has crucial implications for the structuring of the family. Indeed, the continuity and therefore the long-term welfare of any kin group depends on obtaining spouses for the unmarried members of the group from other groups. A kin group has a stake in retaining some measure of control over at least a portion of its members after they marry (Lee, 1977). In this section we will define and discuss exogamy, endogamy, incest taboos, monogamy, polygyny, polyandry, and group marriage.

▲ Exogamy and Endogamy

All societies regulate the pool of eligibles from which individuals are expected to select a mate. A child's kin generally have more in mind than simply getting a child married. They want the child married to the right spouse, especially where marriage has consequences for the larger kin group. Two types of marital regulations define the "right" spouse: endogamy and exogamy. **Endogamy** is the requirement that marriage occur within a group. Under these circumstances people must marry within their class, race, ethnic group, or religion. **Exogamy** is the requirement that marriage occur outside a group. Under these circumstances people must marry outside their kin group, be it their immediate nuclear family, clan, or tribe.

Regulations relating to exogamy are based primarily on kinship and usually entail **incest taboos,** rules that prohibit sexual intercourse with close blood relatives and exist today in virtually every society (Olson and DeFrain, 1997). Such relationships are not only prohibited but also bring reactions of aversion and disgust. At one time social scientists singled out incest taboos as the only universal norm in a world of diverse moral codes. But sociologist Russell Middleton (1962) found that brother–sister marriage was not only permitted but frequently practiced by the ancient Egyptians. He speculated that brother–sister marriage served to maintain the power and property of a family and prevented the splintering of an estate through inheritance. A similar arrangement apparently occurred among the royal families of Hawaii, the Inca of Peru, and the Dahomey of West Africa.

Norms that govern marriage in many ethnic groups, including those among Orthodox Jews, specify endogamy, *the requirement that marriage occur within the group.*

There have been numerous attempts to account for both the existence and the prevalence of incest taboos. Some have argued that incest taboos came about because of real or imagined negative effects of "inbreeding." However, the incest taboo has been found even in cultures where people were unaware of the father's role in reproduction (Hutter, 1998). Anthropologist Claude Lévi-Strauss (1956) suggested that incest taboos promote alliances between families and reinforce their social interdependence; the Zulu have a saying: "They are our enemies, and so we marry them."

▲ Types of Marriage

The relationships between a husband and wife may be structured in one of four ways: **monogamy,** one husband and one wife; **polygyny,** one husband and two or more wives; **polyandry,** two or more husbands and one wife; and **group marriage,** two or more husbands and two or more wives. Monogamy appears in all societies, although other forms may not only be permitted but preferred. Monogamy was the preferred or ideal type of marriage in fewer than 20 percent of 862 societies included in one cross-cultural sample (Murdock, 1967).

Polygyny has enjoyed a wide distribution throughout the world. The Old Testament, for example, records polygynous practices among the Hebrews. In China, India, and the Islamic countries, polygyny has usually been the privilege of the wealthy few. In the United States, it is not legal, but it does exist. A man in Utah with five wives and 29 children was charged with bigamy and rape in 2000. An additional 30,000 polygynists are thought to be practicing "underground" (Arrillaga, 2000). The arrangement tends to be favored where large families are advantageous and women make substantial contributions to subsistence.

Although polygyny has a wide distribution, polyandry is exceedingly rare. Polyandry usually does not represent freedom of sexual choice for women; often, it involves the right or the opportunity of younger brothers to have sexual access to the wife of an older brother. If a family cannot afford wives or marriages for each of its sons, it may find a wife for the eldest son only.

Social scientists are far from agreement on whether group marriage has ever existed as a cultural norm. There is some evidence that it did occur among the Kaingang of the jungles of Brazil, the Marquesans of the South Pacific, the Chukchee of Siberia, and the Todas of India. At times, polyandry appears to slip into group marriage, where a number of brothers share more than one wife (Stephens, 1963).

Patterns of Courtship

Marriage brings a new member into the inner circle of a family, and relatives have a stake in who is to be the spouse. Random mating might jeopardize these interests: If sons and daughters were permitted to "fall in love" with anybody, they might choose the wrong mate. Instead, courtship in many societies follows specific and traditional patterns, the topic of discussion of this section. We will consider the nature of love, look at how societies regulate courtship, and examine some of the factors important to mate selection.

▲ The Social Regulation of Love

Although love has many meanings, we usually think of the strong physical and emotional attraction between a man and a woman as **romantic love.** The ancient Greeks saw such love as a "diseased hysteria," an overwhelming force that irresistibly draws two people together and leads them to become passionately preoccupied with one another.

Sociologist William J. Goode (1959) found that some societies give romantic love more emphasis than others. At one extreme, societies view marriage without love as mildly shameful; at the other, they define strong romantic attachment as a laughable or tragic aberration. The American middle class falls toward the pole of positive approval; the 19th-century Japanese and Chinese fell toward the pole of disapproval; and the Greeks after Alexander and the Romans of the empire took a middle course.

▲ How Do Societies Control Love?

Societies undertake to control love in a variety of ways. One approach is *child marriage,* which was employed at one time in India. A child bride went to live with her husband in a marriage that was not physically consummated until much later. Similarly, in an *arranged marriage* the parents of the bride and groom make the arrangements for the marriage, sometimes when both are too young to marry but also when both are of marriageable ages. The parents of the bride may know of the groom through friends or relatives or may simply answer a newspaper advertisement.

Another approach involves the *social isolation* of young people from potential mates. For instance, the Manus of the Admiralty Islands secluded their young women in a lodge built on stilts over a lagoon. The *close supervision* of couples by chaperones was an arrangement found among 17th-century New England Puritans. Finally, *peer and parental pressures* may be brought to bear. For example, in the United States parents often threaten, cajole, wheedle, and bribe their children to limit their social contacts to youths with "suitable" ethnic, religious, and educational backgrounds. The net result of these approaches is the same—a person's range of choice is narrowed by social barriers.

▲ Factors in Mate Selection

Given a field of eligible mates, why do we fall in love with and marry one person and not another? A variety of factors are at work. One is **homogamy,** the tendency of like to marry like. People of similar age, race, religion, nationality, education, intelligence, health, stature, attitudes, and countless other traits tend to marry one another to a degree greater than would be found by chance. Although homogamy seems to operate with respect to social characteristics, the evidence is less clear for psychological factors such as personality and temperament.

Physical attractiveness also plays a part in mate selection. We prefer the companionship and friendship of attractive people to that of unattractive people (Feingold, 1990). However, since the supply of unusually beautiful or handsome partners is limited, we tend in real life to select partners who have a degree of physical attractiveness similar to our own (Murstein, 1972, 1976; Feingold, 1988). According to the **matching hypothesis,** we typically experience the greatest payoff and the least cost when we follow this course; individuals of equal attractiveness are those most likely to reciprocate our advances.

The **complementary needs** theory (Winch, 1958) refers to two different personality traits that are the counterparts of each other and that provide a sense of completeness when they are joined. Dominant people find a complementary relationship with passive people, and talkative people find themselves attracted to good listeners. Interpersonal attraction depends on how well each partner fulfills the role expectations of the other and how mutually gratifying they find their "role fit" (Bluhm, Widiger, and Miele, 1990; Collins and Read, 1990).

Exchange theory links these three factors. It is based on the notion that we like those who reward us and dislike those who punish us (Molm, 1991; Lawler and Yoon, 1993). Many of our acts derive from our confidence that from them will flow some benefit—perhaps a desired expression of love, gratitude, recognition, security, or material reward. In the course of interacting, we reinforce the relationship by rewarding each other. Thus, people with similar social traits, attitudes, and values mutually reward one another. In selecting partners of comparable physical attractiveness, we minimize the risk of rejection while maximizing the profit from such a conquest. And the parties in complementary relationships offer each other high rewards at low cost to themselves. In sum, exchange theory proposes that people involved in a mutually satisfying relationship will exchange behaviors that have low cost and high reward.

Marriage and the Family in the United States

The American family has become such a debated subject that sociologists sometimes appear to be at war with one another. Some argue that marriage and family have positive effects on children and marriage partners (Glenn, 1997; Popenoe, 1993). Others—perhaps the majority—say that there are both negative and positive effects and that those who extol the virtues of "family" are traditionalists and conservatives (Scanzoni, 1997; Skolnick, 1997; Cherlin, 1997). This section focuses on the issues that underlie this debate.

We will examine life within marriage, parenthood, and two-income families. Then we will discuss some of the many types of lifestyles in the United States beyond the traditional nuclear family: singlehood, single parenthood, stepfamilies, cohabitation, and gay and lesbian couples.

Life within Marriage

Most adult Americans hope to establish an intimate relationship with another person and make the relationship work. This finding underlies a study of American couples undertaken by sociologists Philip Blumstein and Pepper Schwartz (1983). Though the study is more than 20 years old, it is still the best study of its kind and has much to tell us about American marriages.

▲ More Conventional than Expected

American couples are more conventional than Blumstein and Schwartz expected them to be. For example, although 60 percent of the wives were employed outside the home, only 30 percent of the men and 39 percent of the women believed that both spouses should work. As we discussed in Chapter 8, when the wives ◄— p. 263 had full-time jobs, they still did the greater part of the housework. Men do more housework than they used to, but women still do most of the housework and child care, even when both husband and wife have full-time jobs (Bittman et al., 2003).

Blumstein and Schwartz found that American men could take pleasure in their partner's success only if it were not superior to their own. In contrast, women were found to be happier and relationships were more stable when the male partners were ambitious and successful. Most married couples pooled their money. However, regardless of how much the wife

earned, they measured their financial success only by the husband's income.

▲ Emotional and Sexual Relations

Most of the married couples had sexual relations at least once a week. People who had sex infrequently were just as likely to have a long-lasting relationship as those who had sex often. While couples were happier when the opportunity to initiate and refuse sex was shared equally by the partners, in more than half of the cases the husbands were still the primary initiators. Women tended to link sex and love; men often did not. Less than a third of the couples engaged in extramarital activities. Husbands were more often repeatedly unfaithful than wives, but their transgressions did not necessarily represent dissatisfaction with either their partner or the relationship as a whole. Women, in contrast, often strayed just once, mostly out of curiosity; but for them, infidelity was more likely to blossom into a full-fledged love affair.

Blumstein and Schwartz also found that early in the marriage men were more likely than women to feel encroached upon by the relationship and to complain that they needed more "private time." But in long-standing marriages, the wives complained more often that they did not have enough time by themselves. Further, women were more likely than men to say they were the emotional caretakers of the family, although 39 percent of the men indicated that they focused more on their marriage than they did on their work. In about a quarter of the marriages, both partners claimed they were relationship-centered.

▲ Marriage in Middletown

Like Blumstein and Schwartz, Theodore Caplow and his colleagues (1982) expected to find the American nuclear family in trouble when they undertook a restudy of Robert S. and Helen Merrill Lynd's sociological classic of the 1920s, "Middletown" (1929, 1937). The Lynds had made Middletown, a pseudonym for Muncie, Indiana, into a leading sociological laboratory. Caplow and his associates concluded that the doomsayers were wrong and that the family had not lost its attractiveness. Comparing Middletown in the 1970s to Middletown in the 1920s, they found "increased family solidarity, a smaller generation gap, closer marital communication, more religion, and less mobility" (1982:323). They say their findings were as surprising to them "as they may be to our readers." Other researchers have come to essentially the same conclusions (Whyte, 1990).

▲ Are We Giving Up on Marriage?

That depends on who answers the question. Sociologist Judith Stacey would be likely to answer that we ought to give up on marriage. "The Family," she says, "is a concept derived from faulty theoretical premises and an imperialist logic, which even at its height never served the best interests of women, their children, or even of many men" (Stacey, 1996:50). Linda Waite and Maggie Gallagher (2000), on the other hand, recently published *The Case for Marriage,* a book aimed at demonstrating that married people and their children are better off financially, emotionally, and physically. One of the most consistent findings in health research, for example, is that married people typically have better mental and physical health than the nonmarried (Gove, Style, and Hughes, 1990; Gove, Hughes, and Style, 1983).

There also is a racial divide in the answer to this question. In 2000, 81 percent of white families were married couples, while about 14 percent were headed by a woman only and another 5 percent headed by a man only. In contrast, 47 percent of black families were married couples, with nearly as many families (45 percent) headed by a woman alone and 8 percent by a man (U.S. Census Bureau, 2003). The numbers for Asian and Pacific Islander families are similar to those for whites (79.6 percent married couples, 13.2 percent female-headed, 7.1 percent male-headed), and those for Hispanic families are somewhere in between (67.9 percent married couples, 23.4 percent female-headed, 8.7 percent male-headed). In 2000, nearly 40 percent of African Americans age 18 and over had never been married, compared with 28 percent of Hispanics and 21 percent of whites.

What if you probe the general public—or people who are married? Public opinion surveys indicate that Americans depend very heavily on marriage for their psychological well-being (Waite and Gallagher, 2000; Gove, Style, and

In 2002, 53 percent of African-American children were living with a single parent. Two thirds of all U.S. children living with a single mother have family incomes of less than $30,000 a year.

Hughes 1990; Glenn and Weaver, 1981). Although divorce rates increased dramatically earlier in the century, they have declined gradually since the early 1980s. And almost everyone tries marriage; only about 5 percent of Americans never marry. Most people who get divorced also get remarried.

However, American men and women are marrying at a later age than they have in recent history (U.S. Census Bureau, 2003; see Figure 10.2). The median age at first marriage for U.S. men rose to 27.4 in 2004 from a low of 22.6 in the mid-1950s. For U.S. women the figure rose to 25.8 years, up from a low of 20.2 years, also in the mid-1950s. In 1890 half of all women were married by the age of 22. Although people are postponing marriage, by their early 40s, 84 percent of men and 88 percent of women have been married at least once. Marriage is no longer seen as a prerequisite for childbearing; 31 percent of U.S. children are born to unmarried parents (U.S. Census Bureau, 2003).

Increasing numbers of Americans no longer view marriage as a permanent institution but as something that can be ended and reentered. The goal of "having a happy marriage" currently ranks well above "being married to the same person for life" and even farther above merely "being married" (Glenn, 1992). And people seem to be reaching that goal: Almost two-thirds of married Americans rate their own marriages as "very happy."

Parenthood

Married couples who decide to have children find their lives transformed by parenthood. Among other changes, costs go up when children are added to a family: Total annual expenditures per child are approximately $6,750 for a low-income family and $13,500 for a high-income family (U.S. Census Bureau, 2003). In this section we will discuss the family life course, the adjustments husbands and wives make to their new roles as parents, and the "empty-nest syndrome."

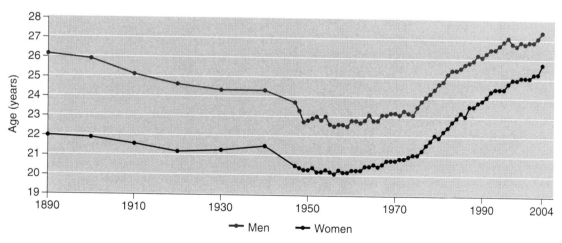

Figure 10.2 **Median Age at First Marriage in the United States, 1890–2004**

Source: U.S. Census Bureau, Annual Demographic Supplement to the March 2004 Current Population Survey, Current Population Reports, available at http://www.census.gov/population/socdemo/hh-fam/ms2.pdf.

▲ The Family Life Course

Nuclear families that are not disrupted by divorce, desertion, or death typically pass through a series of changes and realignments across time, what sociologists call the **family life course.** These changes and realignments are related to the altered expectations and requirements imposed on a husband and wife as children are born and grow up.

The family begins with the husband–wife pair and becomes increasingly complex as members are added, creating new roles and multiplying the number of relationships. The family then stabilizes for a time, after which it begins shrinking as each of the adult children is launched. Finally, it returns once more to the husband–wife pair, and eventually terminates with the death of a spouse. Of course, many individual and family behaviors do not occur at the usual ages or in the typical sequence assumed by the family life course model. At times decisive economic, social, political, or military events intervene to alter the normal course of events (Elder, 1983.)

▲ Adjusting to New Roles

Each change in the role of one family member can affect all the other members. The arrival of the first child compels the reorganization of a couple's life. Parents have to juggle their work roles, alter their time schedules, change their communication patterns, and relinquish some privacy. Parenthood competes with the husband or wife role. After the birth of a first child, husbands and wives who could once focus unlimited attention on their spouses now have to split their attention between spouse and child. The result is that young parents may feel that their spouses are not paying enough attention to them. Not surprisingly, marital adjustment ratings, an indicator of marital satisfaction, typically fall after the birth of a first child (Belsky and Rovine, 1990). The addition of a second child changes the family again, reducing the mother's participation in the paid labor force, increasing her responsibilities

in housework, and making fathers feel more a part of the family (Boodman, 2000). A consistent finding is that the psychological well-being of parents is a little worse than that of childless couples, and it remains lower until children grow up and move out of the household (Evenson and Simon, 2005). And despite the changes a child brings to their lives, most couples report enormous satisfaction with parenthood, ranking their families as more important than work, recreation, friendships, or status.

▲ The Empty Nest

Clinical psychologists and psychiatrists have stressed the problem parents face when their children leave home. But most couples do not experience difficulty with the "empty-nest" period; the majority view this stage as a time of "new freedoms." Indeed, national surveys show that middle-aged women whose children have left home experience greater general happiness and enjoyment of life, in addition to greater marital happiness, than middle-aged women with children still living at home (White and Edwards, 1990; Vander Zanden, 1993). With changes in the family life course, the "empty nest" has become an ill-defined stage; young adults are establishing their own households later and often return to reside for varying lengths of time in their parents' home (Hill and Young, 1999).

Two-Income Families

Nearly 60 percent of all mothers with children under six years of age are now in the workforce (see Figure 10.3). In 1950 only one in eight were working. And while three-quarters of survey respondents think it would be best for children if only one parent worked outside the home, two-thirds say that is not a realistic option (Public Agenda, 2001). In 1998 a record 59 percent of women with infants were employed, a proportion that had dropped to 54.2 percent by 2004 (U.S. Census Bureau, 2006).

Dual-income couples evolve new patterns and traditions for family living and face

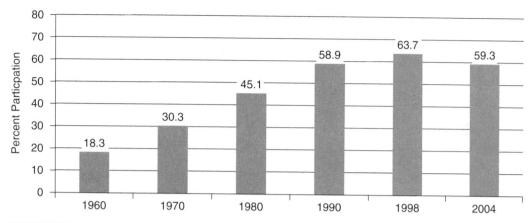

Figure 10.3 Labor-Force Participation Rates for Married Women in the U.S. with Children under Six Years Old, 1960–2004

Source: Figure generated by the authors using data from the U.S. Census Bureau, 2006.

challenges and opportunities not experienced by families with only one breadwinner (Guelzow, Bird, and Koball, 1991; Vannoy and Philliber, 1992). In this section we will consider some of the dynamics of such families: the effects of employment on women and children, who cares for the children, and who makes the decisions.

▲ Effects on Women

Women who work outside the home still spend significantly more time on housework than do men (Bittman et al., 2003; Crittenden, 2001; Shelton, 2000), working the "second shift" we discussed in Chapter 8. When children ◄ p. 263 enter the equation, the workload increases, and women are penalized in the labor force for their reproductive responsibilities (Budig and England, 2001; England, 2000). There's an emotional toll as well as an economic one; most women say that mothers in the paid labor force experience more stress than mothers who stay home (Public Agenda, 2001).

Nevertheless, paid employment is typically beneficial to women's mental health and self-esteem. Studies show that both married women working at a paid job who want to work and married women who are not in the paid labor force and do not want to be have good mental health (Ross, Mirowsky, and Huber, 1983). The problems arise for women who are either working or staying home when they don't want to. Husbands helping with housework and husbands having a positive attitude about their spouse's employment both reduce the psychological distress of working women (Ross, Mirowsky, and Huber, 1983). Sociologist Arlie Russell Hochschild (1997) has argued that unpaid household labor is more demanding than any work anyone does in the paid workplace. Although she also argued that the workplace has traditionally been a refuge for men and was increasingly so for women, recent research (Kiecolt, 2003) indicates that this is not the case. Over the past 30 years, home has been more likely to be a haven from work than vice versa for both men and women, and the trend for home to be a haven has increased for women and remained stable for men.

▲ Effects on Children

Many people fear that when both parents work, children lose out in terms of supervision, love, and cognitive enrichment. What do sociological studies show?

Research findings are contradictory regarding the effects of maternal employment during a child's first year, with some studies reporting negative cognitive and social outcomes (Baydar and Brooks-Gunn, 1991; Nash, 1997) and others finding only minimal negative outcomes (Parcel and Menaghan, 1994). But in general maternal employment does not appear to harm children, as long as the hours worked are not excessive (Amato and Booth, 1997). High-quality day care and preschool programs have been shown to be beneficial to children (Field, 1991); the problem is that only 40 percent of the nation's children have access to such high-quality care (Public Agenda, 2001).

On the plus side, working mothers provide a different role model for their children, one associated with less traditional gender role concepts and a higher evaluation of female competence (Hoffman, 1989; Debold, Wilson, and Malave, 1993). Perhaps as a result, their children tend to be more unconventional (Amato and Booth, 1997). In addition, because socioeconomic status affects the ways that families link to the wider society, the benefits of growing up in a two-income family can be considerable (see Box 10.2).

▲ Who Cares for the Children?

With the entry of women into the labor force, arrangements for child care are shifting from care in the home to care outside the home. Preschoolers with employed mothers are cared for by fathers, grandparents, siblings, babysitters, or nannies and in day care centers, preschools, and family day care programs (U.S. Census Bureau, 2003). Half of all three- and four-year-olds are now enrolled in school programs. Many public schools now provide before- and after-school programs and breakfasts and dinners in addition to the school lunch (Epstein, 2005). Families in which the employed mother lives in poverty spend about a quarter of their income for child care services; better-off families

pay about 6 percent of their family income on child care. Despite the prevalence of day care and the increasing role public schools play in child care, a fair number of children under the age of six are still being cared for primarily or entirely by their parents, even if both parents work. A quarter of the mothers who work up to 35 hours per week manage to do so with no nonparental child care arrangements, and 12 percent of those who work 35 hours or more use no child care (U.S. Census Bureau, 1999).

▲ Who Makes the Decisions?

In two-income families the man typically has a larger voice in major household decisions than the woman. Although having an income increases the wife's authority to make some decisions, evidence suggests that it does not provide her with power sufficient to win disputes with the husband (Cherlin, 1999; Blumstein and Schwartz, 1991). For example, when a husband is offered a better position in another area of the country, the wife typically makes the move regardless of the effect the transfer will have on her career (Bielby and Bielby, 1992). As women's earnings gain on men's, however, their new economic power can shift relationships. Nearly 34 million working wives in the United States bring home 31 percent of the family income (Krafft, 1994), and this contribution makes a difference. In nearly one-fifth of dual-career couples, the wife earns more than the husband. Although this is becoming more common, men often feel their self-esteem threatened in this situation, and such couples run a high risk of psychological and physical abuse, marital conflict, and sexual problems (Kessler and McRae, 1981; Rubenstein, 1982; Hays, 1987).

Family researchers Linda Waite and Maggie Gallagher (2000) say that marriage works best when wives and husbands need each other, but that these dependencies should be freely chosen. Whether both partners are paid for their work or not, marriage should be viewed as a "true partnership," not a shifting balance of domination and subordination.

10.2 Social Inequalities

Family Backgrounds and Unequal Childhoods

Sociologists have long known that social class has a powerful impact on children's life chances. In a classic study, sociologist James Coleman and his colleagues (Coleman et al., 1966) found that family background was the most important determinant of educational inequality. But what specific family processes are responsible for the link between parents' social class and children's outcomes? This question was addressed in a recent study by Annette Lareau (2002). Lareau systematically observed the daily lives of poor, working-class, middle-class, and upper-middle-class families with 9- and 10-year-old children, spending hours at a time with each family. She found that organized activities dominate the lives of middle-class children; their parents engage in what she calls "concerted cultivation"—they manage their children's lives to optimize the cultivation of their talents and abilities. In poor and working-class families, leisure activities are left to the children themselves; their parents facilitate "the accomplishment of natural growth," and the provision of organized leisure activities is not seen as an essential part of good parenting.

Middle- and upper-middle-class children benefit directly from their parents' attempts to cultivate their talents; further, they gain a sense of entitlement and the skills for getting what they want or need from others, Lareau says. The poorer children she followed, on the other hand, learned to "keep their distance from people in positions of authority, to be distrustful of institutions, and . . . to resist officials' authority" (2002:773).

Data from the Census 2000's "A Child's Day" report (Lugaila, 2003) confirm Lareau's observations and bring into sharp focus the disadvantages faced by many American children. Five percent of all kids under 12, for example, had not been taken on an "outing" during the month before parents filled out their census surveys; an outing includes a trip to a park, a church, a playground, a grocery store, or a visit with friends or relatives. That's 2.4 *million* children who apparently did nothing but go to school and come back home, for an entire month. Eight percent of the nation's 1- to 5-year-olds— 1.6 million kids—had not been read to at all in the week before the survey, and only half were read to every day. As Lareau found in her observational study, many children engage in a variety of organized activities such as soccer, baseball, gymnastics, dance, Girl Scouts, Boy Scouts, violin lessons, choir, and the like, but many children do not.

For many of the factors in the "Child's Day" report, family background, especially the income and education of the parents, is the critical element. For example, family characteristics that are associated with lower levels of reading to children include living in poverty, having parents with a high school education or less, and having never-married parents. Children who live in poverty do not "go on outings," as the Census Bureau puts it, and they are much less likely to be involved in organized sports, clubs, or lessons. The level of education of the parents plays a major role in a child's participation in extracurricular activities, with about half of the children of parents with advanced degrees participating in sports, clubs, and lessons, compared to 20 to 30 percent of the children whose parents have a high school education or less. School opportunities are sorted by social class, too; half of the children whose parents have advanced degrees are enrolled in "gifted classes," compared to only 14 percent of the children whose parents have a high school education or less.

In other words, the children who might benefit greatly from extra attention, special activities, and more caring from adults in their lives—children from low-income families, children whose parents have little education, children from broken homes—are the least likely to get it. As Lareau (2003) says in the book that elaborates her research, America is a land both of opportunity and of inequality.

Questions for Discussion

1. Based on the findings presented here, what sorts of enrichment programs would you recommend for children living in poverty?

2. Are there benefits to a childhood that is not dominated by organized activities?

Beyond the Traditional Nuclear Family

Much of the public debate over the family in the United States may be misguided because it uses the stereotypical white, middle-class family of the 1950s as a point of departure for either praise or criticism of subsequent changes. Further, the image most of us hold of the 1950s family is less informed by reality than by old television series like *Leave It to Beaver, Ozzie and Harriet,* and *The Donna Reed Show* (Kain, 1990; Skolnick, 1991).

In fact, family relationships are becoming more varied. Transracial adoption results in families whose diversity reflects that of U.S. society (see Box 10.3). Increasing numbers of children grow up with several sets of parents and an assortment of half brothers and half sisters and stepbrothers and stepsisters. Americans now may have any of a number of **lifestyles,** the overall patterns of living people evolve to meet their biological, social, and emotional needs. In this section we examine a number of lifestyle options: stepfamilies, singlehood, single parenthood, unmarried cohabitation, and gay and lesbian couples.

▲ Stepfamilies

Remarriage frequently results in stepfamilies, also termed "reconstituted" and "blended" families. Because more than half of remarried persons are parents, their new partners become stepparents. One in six American families are stepfamilies; 35 million Americans live in a stepfamily, including 20 percent of the nation's children under age 18. About 40 percent of remarriages unite two divorced persons; half of them are a first marriage for one member of the couple.

Andrew Cherlin (1978, 2002) has called remarriage an "incomplete institution." Because the situation created by such marriages is ambiguous, most stepparents attempt to recreate a traditional family, which is the only model they have. But a stepfamily functions differently than the traditional nuclear family (Pill, 1990;

Larson, 1992). For one thing, the stepparent role does not necessarily approximate that of a biological parent, particularly in authority, legitimacy, and respect. For another, the family tree of a stepfamily can be very complex and convoluted, populated not only by children of both spouses but by six sets of grandparents, relatives of former spouses, relatives of new spouses, and the people former spouses marry. Matters are further complicated because stepparents and stepchildren have no mutual history and often have had no previous opportunity to bond.

Nine out of 10 stepchildren live with their biological mother and a stepfather. Stepfathers usually underrate their parenting skills and their contributions to the lives of their stepchildren. Indeed, their stepchildren and spouses give them higher marks than they give themselves (Bohannan and Erickson, 1978). Children living with stepfathers apparently do just as well, or just as poorly, in school and in their social lives as children living with natural fathers. And children with stepfathers on the whole do better than children from homes where the father is absent (Beer, 1988; Fine and Kurdek, 1992).

▲ Singlehood

The number of Americans living alone more than doubled (increased 100 percent) between 1970 and 2000, a much greater increase than the 16 percent growth in married couples. By 2000 26.7 million Americans were living alone; more than one of every four occupied dwelling units had only one person in it. Figure 10.4 shows the percent living alone by age category. Divorced (8.8 million), widowed (8.6 million), and never-married (12.9 million) persons constitute distinct groups of those aged 15 and older who head nonfamily households, including those who live alone (U.S. Census Bureau, 2003). The high incidence of divorce, the ability of the elderly to maintain their own homes alone, and the deferral of marriage among young adults have contributed to the high rate of increase in the number of nonfamily households.

10.3 Doing Social Research

Racial Diversity within Families

Some Americans strongly oppose transracial adoption, claiming that children need to be raised by parents of their own race. What does the research show? Social scientist Rita J. Simon (1996) began studying transracial adoptees and their families in 1971 and followed the families until their children reached adulthood. Simon used the research method of intensive interviewing to conduct her study. Each family was visited by a team of one male and one female graduate student in 1971; often one interviewer was white and the other black. Simon and her associates interviewed 204 parents and 366 children during this first stage of her research. In 1979, 1983, and 1991, Simon was able to reinterview a sizable proportion of the parents and children.

What did Simon discover about the children's racial attitudes and racial identity? During 1971 and 1972 she and her associates found a complete absence of a racial preference for whites on the part of all the children. The children correctly identified themselves as black or white, and they showed no preference for white or negative reactions to black. In 1983, self-esteem scores were essentially the same for black adoptees, other transracial adoptees, white adoptees, and white birth children. A family integration scale similarly revealed no significant differences among the four groups of children; adopted children apparently felt as integrated into family life as birth children.

Perhaps the most compelling information about transracial adoption comes from the children themselves when they had reached adulthood. In 1991 Simon told the now-adult transracial adoptees and birth children that the National Association of Black Social Workers and several councils of Native Americans strongly opposed transracial adoption and asked them how they felt about that. Eighty percent of the transracial adoptees and 70 percent of the birth children said that they disagreed; 5 percent of the transracially adopted children said they agreed, and the others said they were not sure.

When asked directly what effect being adopted and raised by white parents had on their self-image, a third said it had a positive effect, a third said it had no effect, and a third said they did not know. None of the transracially adopted children responded that it had a negative effect.

It would appear that in most racially diverse families, parents and children, both adopted and birth, do very well.

Questions for Discussion

1. Our society is increasingly characterized by racial diversity. What are some ways families can be racially diverse? Do you expect a decrease or increase in family racial diversity?

2. U.S. society has increased its acceptance of white parents adopting children of other races. What do you think societal reaction would be to parents of other races adopting white children?

Research strongly suggests that people live alone because they choose to (Michael, Fuchs, and Scott, 1980). People who live alone can avoid unwanted intrusions of others and have more latitude to construct their lives the way they wish to. This is probably why the mental health of persons who live alone is as good as or better than that of unmarried persons living with others (Hughes and Gove, 1981).

In 2000, 52 percent of men and nearly 40 percent of women age 25 to 29 had never been married. This is more than double the 1970 rate. More liberal sex standards, the high divorce rate, money woes, and the pursuit of education and careers have spurred young adults to marry later than at any time since the Census Bureau started keeping track in 1890. Even so, the population remaining single today is smaller than it was in 1900, when fully 42 percent of all American adult men and 33 percent of adult women never married (Kain, 1984).

Changes in patterns of reported happiness by marital status were uncovered in the 1980s. For many years research had shown that married

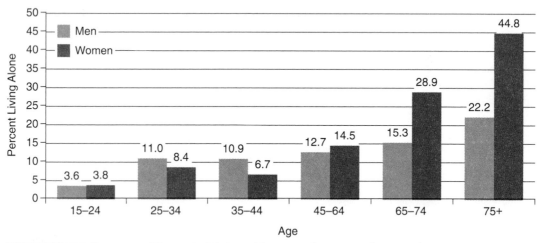

Figure 10.4 Percent of Persons Living Alone in the United States by Age and Gender, 2004

Source: Figure generated by the authors using data from the U.S. Census Bureau, 2006.

people reported greater happiness than unmarried, including the never-married. However, in the late 1970s the difference in happiness reported between the never-married and the married began to shift. By the mid-1980s the differences between the never-married and the married had almost disappeared for men and had narrowed considerably for women (Glenn and Weaver, 1988). This pattern remains essentially the same today (Adams, 1998).

▲ Single Parenthood

More than one American youngster in four lives with just one parent. Of all such children, 82 percent live with their mothers. However, the number of men raising children on their own has risen; in 2002, 5 percent of the nation's children were living with their fathers only, or 18 percent of the children living in single-parent households (Fields, 2003). About two-thirds of single fathers are divorced; roughly 25 percent are among the never-married; and only 7.5 percent are widowers. The largest share of youngsters in single-parent homes—38.6 percent—are living with a divorced parent, and 30.6 percent are living with a parent who has never married; others reside

with a parent who is married but separated or are offspring of a widowed parent (U.S. Census Bureau, 2003). In 2002, 53 percent of African-American children under the age of 18 were living with a single parent. A quarter of Hispanic children, 20 percent of white children, and 15 percent of Asian-American children also were in single-parent families (Fields, 2003).

As we pointed out in Chapter 6 ◄— p. 191 female-headed households are likely to be low-income households. In 2002, 30 percent of all children lived in families with incomes less than $30,000, compared with 65 percent of children living only with their mothers and 45 percent of children living only with their fathers (Fields, 2003). In the case of divorce, marital separation frequently produces a precipitous and sustained decline in household income for the mother and child. The overall financial situation of female-headed households in terms of their net worth can be seen in Figure 10.5.

Unwed motherhood is also on the increase. According to the Census Bureau, one in five of the nation's never-married women 15 to 44 years old have become mothers (Bachu, 1997). Thirty-one percent of all births in the United

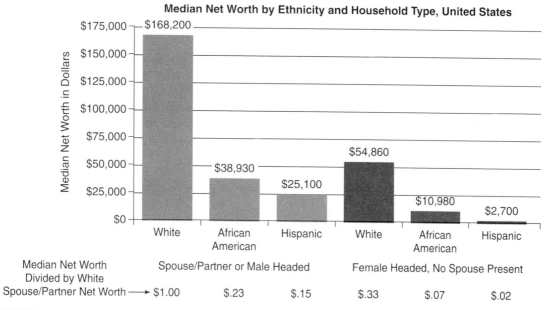

Median Net Worth by Ethnicity and Household Type, United States

	Spouse/Partner or Male Headed			Female Headed, No Spouse Present		
	White	African American	Hispanic	White	African American	Hispanic
Median Net Worth Divided by White Spouse/Partner Net Worth →	$1.00	$.23	$.15	$.33	$.07	$.02

Figure 10.5   **The Financial Status of Female-Headed Households**

Net worth, or wealth, of a household is all the assets of that household minus all debts. Female-headed households have far less net worth than other households. The situation of African-American and Hispanic female-headed households is particularly grave; they have on average 7 and 2 cents, respectively, for every dollar of net worth owned by a white male-headed or spouse/partner household.

Source: Figure generated by the authors using data from the 2004 Survey of Consumer Finances, Board of Governors of the Federal Reserve System.

States were to unwed mothers in 2001 (U.S. Census Bureau, 2003). Though unwed motherhood is more likely to occur among women in the lower class and those in disadvantaged racial minority groups, recent increases in unwed motherhood have been much greater among whites, and rates for teenagers actually fell 11 percent between 1994 and 1998 and has continued dropping. Such births do not necessarily result in single-parent families; two-fifths of recent nonmarital births were to cohabiting couples (Ventura and Bachrach, 2000).

Women heading a single-parent family typically experience greater stress than women in two-parent families (Fassinger, 1989; Simons et al., 1993). For one thing, lack of job training,

loss of skills during the childbearing years, and discriminatory hiring and promotion patterns often mean that single mothers work for low wages. Female family heads report much lower self-esteem, a lower sense of effectiveness, and less optimism about the future than their counterparts in two-parent settings. But research shows that women who head households on their own may choose not to marry depending on a variety of factors, including mistrust of men, fear of domestic violence, household decision making, respectability, and whether the potential marriage partner has a stable job with decent earnings (Edin, 2000).

Single fathers encounter many of the same problems as single mothers. Indeed, research shows that being single and having children to raise is worse on the mental health of men than on that of women (Simon, 1998; Hughes, 1989). Juggling work and child care poses considerable difficulties, especially for fathers with preschool youngsters. Because men are not much involved in child care when they are married, they have little to fall back on when they become single fathers.

Many families headed by single parents survive their hardships with few ill effects; some even blossom as a result of the spirit of cooperation brought out by their difficulties. However, a disturbing number of children and their parents are saddled with problems. Some studies show that juvenile delinquency is twice as likely to occur in a single-parent home as in a two-parent home. Children of single parents are more likely to drop out of school, be unemployed when they reach adulthood, have out-of-wedlock children, become sexually active at an earlier age, and cohabit (Musick and Bumpass, 1999). Lack of parental supervision and persistent social and psychological strains are usually complicated by the problems of poverty (Mann, 1983; Bank et al., 1993).

▲ Cohabitation

Marriage is differentiated from other types of intimate relationships by its institutionalized status. The number of unmarried adults who share living quarters with an unrelated adult of the opposite sex—a type of intimate relationship termed *cohabitation*—has increased in recent decades; 5.6 million American households were made up of unmarried couples in 2003 (U.S. Census Bureau, 2006). A little over 10 percent of all unmarried persons, and 15 percent of the unmarried under 25 years old, currently cohabit. In 2002, 11 percent of the children living with a single mother were living in a household that included the mother's unmarried partner, and 33 percent of the children that lived with a single father were living with his unmarried partner (Fields, 2003). Forty percent of all out-of-

wedlock births were to cohabiting parents (Bumpass and Lu, 2000), and cohabitation was the subject of much sociological research (Smock, 2000). For white and Hispanic teens, living in cohabiting families is worse than living with single mothers; those living with cohabitors are more likely to have school troubles and emotional and behavioral problems (Nelson, Clark, and Acs, 2001). Cohabiting also seems to be less effective than remarriage at providing economic stability for the children of divorce (Morrison and Ritualo, 2000).

Only 2 percent of American women born between 1928 and 1932 cohabited before marrying or attaining age 30; 40 percent of those born between 1958 and 1962 did so (Schoen and Weinick, 1993). Cohabiting before marriage has become quite prevalent, with a majority of first marriages preceded by cohabitation (Cherlin, 2002). It is even more common before remarriage. Changes in the economy, including the increase in the labor-force participation of women and the decline in the relative importance of the family in the transmission of power and wealth, have contributed to the growing social acceptance of cohabitation (Parker, 1990).

The high proportion of married couples who live together prior to marriage suggests that premarital cohabitation may become institutionalized as a new step between dating and marriage. Half of cohabiting survey respondents said they had definite plans to marry their partners and 31 percent said they thought they would (Bumpass et al., 1991). Cohabitation also may serve as a substitute for marriage (Cherlin, 2002). The proportion of couples who marry after cohabiting has decreased and the percentage of cohabiting couples who have children and do not marry has increased. Young people who cohabit become less eager to have children and more tolerant of divorce than those who do not cohabit (Axinn and Barber, 1997). Persons who cohabit prior to marriage are more likely to eventually divorce (DeMaris and Rao, 1992), but this tendency is limited to serial cohabiters (those who cohabit at different times with different partners) and to those with multiple premarital sexual partners. Teachman (2003) finds that persons whose premarital sex and/or cohabitation is limited to the person they eventually marry do not have an elevated risk of marital disruption. Teachman concludes that "premarital sex and cohabitation limited to one's future spouse has become part of the normal courtship process for marriage" (Teachman, 2003:444). Young women with high earnings now are more likely to cohabit than marry, while the opposite is true for young men with high earnings (Cherlin, 2002).

Couples living together but not married are far less liberated about money, sex, and housework than their nontraditional living arrangement might suggest. Like married men, cohabiting men are more likely to initiate sexual activity, make most of the spending decisions, and do far less of the housework than their working women partners (Blumstein and Schwartz, 1983; South and Spitze, 1994). Unmarried couples see themselves as less securely anchored than married couples and accordingly feel more tentative about their ability to endure difficult periods. Half of cohabiting relationships last a year or less and only 10 percent last five years (Bumpass and Lu, 2000).

▲ Gay and Lesbian Couples

Homosexuality also serves as the basis for family life, though with some differences from heterosexual couples. In terms of love and relationship satisfaction, heterosexual couples, gay couples, and lesbian couples do not differ (Savin-Williams and Esterberg, 2000). Gay and lesbian couples are more likely than heterosexual couples to be well-educated. Their average incomes are similar, but homosexual couples are less likely to own their own homes (Associated Press, 2003a). Compared with married couples, gay and lesbian couples are more likely to split up household tasks so that each partner performs an equal number of different tasks. However, lesbian couples tend to share more tasks, whereas gay couples are more likely to have one or the other partner perform the tasks (Kurdek, 1993).

Until recently, cohabitation was the only option for homosexual "family life" in the United States. Unlike Belgium, Denmark, and the Netherlands, where same-sex marriage is legal, the United States has provided little legal protection for homosexual couples. Vermont and Connecticut have civil union laws, giving gay and lesbian couples the same rights as heterosexual married couples, and Massachusetts has granted full marriage rights to homosexual couples. In 2005, the California Senate also passed a gay marrriage bill (Dignan and Argetsinger, 2005). Some cities and counties also have provisions for unmarried couples to register as domestic partners, with rights conferred ranging from being allowed to visit hospitalized partners to sharing health insurance benefits (Cherlin, 2002).

Population Size of Homosexuals. Most estimates of the homosexual population range from 1 to 3 percent (Barringer, 1993; Crispell, 1993). One study found that 1.4 percent of women and 2.8 percent of men identified themselves as gay, lesbian, or bisexual (Laumann et al., 1994). The percent of persons who have engaged at some time in homosexual activity may be substantially higher: at least 20 percent of males, according to a Kinsey Institute study (Fay et al., 1989). However, another study puts the figure lower, at 7 percent for men and nearly 4 percent for women (Laumann et al., 1994). The major problem with all these estimates is that they rely on self-reports and therefore almost certainly underestimate rates of homosexual involvement. Many people may be afraid to admit to homosexual activity out of fear of discrimination or ostracism.

What Is Homosexuality? Is homosexuality a condition or characteristic of people, or is it simply a way we have of describing an activity that some people engage in? Kinsey's study

(Kinsey, Pomeroy, and Martin, 1948) revealed the interesting fact that homosexuality/heterosexuality was not a simple dichotomy. Kinsey found people all along the continuum from exclusively homosexual to exclusively heterosexual, combining homosexuality and heterosexuality in a variety of ways. Though he did find the majority to be exclusively heterosexual, he also found people who engaged in homosexual activity in certain periods in the life course and not in others. On the basis of findings like these, many sociologists and psychologists have concluded that it is more reasonable to think about heterosexual and homosexual *practices,* not homosexual *individuals* (Bell, Weinberg, and Hammersmith, 1981; Kirkpatrick, 2000). In this "constructionist" view, homosexuality and heterosexuality are social constructions that describe behaviors, roles that people may play, and identities, not inherent characteristics of persons.

The alternative "essentialist" view argues that homosexual orientation is either inborn or is fixed very early in one's development and thus is an inherent part of what an individual is (LeVay, 1996, 1991). LeVay's 1991 study presented evidence that there are differences in the brain structures of homosexual and heterosexual men. Other studies show that identical twins, who share 100 percent of their genes, are more likely to have the same sexual orientation than fraternal twins, who are as genetically alike as any siblings (Burr, 1996). However, it is still not clear whether findings such as these reflect the fact that homosexual preferences are caused or sustained by biological factors. In 1975 the American Psychological Association urged medical practitioners to stop thinking of homosexuality as a mental illness, and in 1997 it passed a resolution to limit therapy aimed at converting homosexuals to heterosexuals (Weiss, 1997).

What is not controversial is that, for the most part, gay and lesbian people, except for their sexual orientations and practices, are a cross section of the U.S. population, differing little from their heterosexual counterparts (Bell and Weinberg, 1978; Blumstein and Schwartz, 1983). They are found in all occupational fields, political persuasions, religious faiths, and racial and ethnic groups. Some are married, have children, and lead lives that in most respects are indistinguishable from those of the larger population.

Attitudes toward Gay Marriage. Two years after the Netherlands legalized gay marriage, nearly 8 percent of weddings were same-sex couples and the relationships were increasingly seen as commonplace and even "old-fashioned" (Richburg, 2003). What about in the United States? Jeni Loftus (2001) used national survey data from 1973 to 1998 to look at attitudes toward homosexuality. She found that Americans' attitudes toward the morality of homosexuality have fluctuated over that time period, with increasingly liberal attitudes since 1990, and they have become steadily less willing to restrict the civil liberties of homosexuals over that same period. Most Americans think homosexuals should have equal rights in terms of job opportunities (Saad, 1996), and despite the Catholic church's rejection of homosexual activity, U.S. Catholic bishops have urged parents of homosexuals to accept and love them (Murphy, 1997). The percentage of Americans who think gay sex is wrong has dropped, and gay characters star on both sitcoms and reality TV shows (Bumiller, 2003).

When it comes to marriage and family, Americans are not quite ready to give their full approval to same-sex unions. In 2003, the Supreme Court struck down a Texas law against sodomy, and social conservatives began warning that traditional marriage was endangered (Bumiller, 2003). When the Episcopal church gave its bishops the option to allow priests to bless committed homosexual relationships, polls showed that "a strong majority" of

Except for their sexual preferences and practices, gays and lesbians differ little from their heterosexual counterparts. Some are or have been married, have children, and lead lives that in most respects are indistinguishable from those of the larger population.

the public disapproved, especially frequent churchgoers (Morin and Cooperman, 2003). At the end of 2003, a *New York Times/CBS News* poll found that 55 percent of Americans favored a constitutional amendment that would ban homosexual marriage (Seelye and Elder, 2003). In 2004 four states had constitutional amendments prohibiting same-sex marriage, and 34 had enacted restrictions (*The Washington Post,* 2004).

Challenges for American Families and American Society

Some family problems stay in the family; others spill over into society. For example, family violence, child abuse, and incest produce scarred members of society, many of whom go on to have families of their own in which the same terrible acts are repeated. The challenges posed by abuse and neglect, child care, divorce, and an increasing population of elderly are complicated by the public debate over the family we discussed in the chapter introduction. As sociologist and U.S. Senator Daniel Patrick Moynihan (1985) observed, conservatives—fearing government interference—prefer to talk about family values but not new governmental initiatives. Liberals, fearing a "blaming-the-victim" mentality, like to talk about public policy initiatives but not family values. Taking a more centralist position, Dennis A. Ahlburg and Carol J. De Vita (1992:39) observed:

Valuing the family should not be confused with valuing a particular family form. . . . Social legislation (or "pro-family" policies) narrowly designed to reinforce only one model of the American family is likely to be shortsighted and have the unintended consequence of weakening, rather than strengthening, family ties. Recognizing the diversity of American families and addressing the complexity of their needs must lie at the heart of the policy debates on family issues.

Family Violence, Child Abuse, and Incest

Mounting evidence suggests that family violence, child abuse, and incest are much more common than most Americans had suspected. The expression "coming out of the closet" is an apt one when applied to battered women and victims of child abuse and sexual molestation. They have been as reluctant to reveal their plight as gay persons have been to reveal their sexual orientations. In this section we will present and discuss some of the data available about family violence, child abuse, and incest.

▲ Family Violence

Estimates of family violence vary widely. Nearly a quarter of women report having been physically assaulted by an intimate partner, and 8 percent report rape by an intimate partner (Cherlin, 2002). The World Health Organization (WHO) maintains a database on violence against women. In a study of 10 countries, they found that 35 to 76 percent of women over the age of 15 have been physically or sexually assaulted, most by a partner (Garcia-Moreno et al., 2005). In the United States, 22 percent of women have been assaulted by an intimate partner (WHO, 2000). The Centers for Disease Control and Prevention has estimated that at least 6 percent of pregnant women are battered by their spouses or partners (Hilts, 1994). At least 1 in 10 married women have experienced marital rape (Straus and Gelles, 1986, 1990).

Although both men and women engage in violence, men typically do more damage than their female partners and many more women than men report victimization (Cherlin, 2002). Many of the people who abuse domestic partners also use violence against others (Moffitt et al., 2000). Women put up with battering for a variety of reasons (France, 2006). The fewer the resources a wife has in the way of education or job skills, the more vulnerable she is in the marriage. And violence is not faced only by young women— survey data suggest that 3 to 5 million Americans over 50 are in physically abusive relationships (France, 2006).

▲ Child Abuse

One need spend only an hour or so in a supermarket or a shopping mall to observe instances of children being physically or verbally abused. Such public behavior is but the tip of the iceberg. A 1994 *USA Today*/CNN/Gallup Poll found that 67 percent of American adults agree that "a good, hard spanking" is sometimes necessary in disciplining a child, despite accumulating evidence that children who get spanked regularly are more likely to cheat or lie, to be disobedient at school, to bully others, and to have less remorse for what they do wrong (Straus, Sugarman, and Giles-Sims, 1997). Child abuse goes far beyond unnecessary spanking; abuse cases may involve burning, scalding, beating, and smothering. Neglect of children is a closely related problem. In 2001, there were 903,000 confirmed cases of child maltreatment;

The functionalist perspective on the family stresses that an important function of the family is care and protection of family members, but evidence on child abuse demonstrates that families do not always serve this function.

more than half were neglect victims (U.S. Department of Health and Human Services, 2003). Approximately 1,300 children died in 2001 of abuse or neglect.

Child abuse that results in homicide is unfortunately not rare. In fact, the age at which females are most at risk of homicide is from birth to age one, and the perpetrators are nearly always parents, family friends, or guardians (Tucker, 2000). Although the chances of males being murdered during infancy are even greater than for females, it is not the most dangerous time of life for them; the male homicide rate is more than four times higher at age 21 (Tucker, 2000). Child welfare workers say that risk to infants is related to whether parents and caregivers have any parenting skills and to situational factors including stress and social isolation.

▲ Incest and Sexual Abuse

The status of incest as a taboo has not kept it from taking place but merely from being talked about. Probably the best available figures on sexual abuse come from a national survey of more than 2,000 adults undertaken in 1985 for the *Los Angeles Times* by psychologist David Finkelhor and his colleagues. They found that 27 percent of the women and 16 percent of the men disclosed a history of some sort of sexual abuse during their childhood (Darnton, 1991). A study of first intercourse experiences found that girls who had sex at ages 11 or 12 were much more likely to have partners much older than themselves, and both older partners and early first intercourse were associated with a greater number of problem behaviors (Leitenberg and Saltzman, 2000).

The perpetrator in sexual abuse is commonly the father, uncle, or other male authority figure in the household, "family tyrants" who employ physical force and intimidation to control their families (Finkelhor, 1979; Herman and Hirschman, 1981). The mothers in incestuous families are commonly passive, have a poor self-image, and are overly dependent on their husbands, much the same traits found among battered wives. The victims of molestation are usually shamed or terrified into treating the experience as a dirty secret.

The sexual abuse of children often leads to behavior problems, learning difficulties, sexual promiscuity, runaway behavior, drug and alcohol abuse, gastrointestinal and genitourinary complaints, compulsive rituals, clinical depression, low self-esteem, and suicidal behavior. Victimized women tend to show lifetime patterns of psychological shame and stigmatization (Kendall-Tackett, Williams, and Finkelhor, 1993; Malinosky-Rummell and Hansen, 1993).

▲ Looking to the Future

The problems of family violence, child abuse, and incest have emerged as major public issues. Some, but not all, researchers find that the arrest of offenders is the most effective means for preventing new incidents of wife battery (Berk and Newton, 1985; Sherman et al., 1992). The adoption of no-fault divorce laws is associated with a drop in suicides among women, murder of women by their partners, and domestic violence against both men and women (Wolfers and Stevenson, 2006). A cultural revolution of attitudes and values is required to eradicate the abuse of women and children (Gelles, Straus, and Harrop, 1988; Buzawa and Buzawa, 1990).

Child Care

Fourteen million American preschool-aged children are cared for by someone other than their parents (U.S. Census Bureau, 2003). Parents may use nannies, grandparents and other relatives, home day care providers, or other child care arrangements, but the most commonly used form of child care is the day care center. Half of all kindergarten-age children to eighth-graders also are in nonparental care after school (Wirt et al., 2003). For the many children of single-parent households, nearly half of whom are living in poverty, and for other of our nation's poor children, the way they are raised and the child care resources that are available to them have the potential to help them improve their lives. How all our children are cared for should be a matter of concern even to those Americans who have no children; they are, as politicians love to point out in speeches, "our future."

▲ Some Good News

Most child psychologists agree that high-quality day care and preschools are good for children (Kagan, Kearsley, and Zelazo, 1978; MacKinnon and King, 1988; Field, 1991), and 78 percent of children's advocates say that the care and attention children receive in a top-notch day care center are "just as good" as they receive at home (Public Agenda, 2000). Such programs are characterized by small group size, high staff-child ratios, well-trained staffs, good equipment, and attractive and nurturing environments.

▲ And Lots of Bad News

Much of the day care currently available to U.S. parents is of poor quality. Nearly 90 percent of children's advocates name the lack of affordable, quality day care as a very serious problem, with a shortage of well-trained and experienced professionals a major contributor to the problem (Public Agenda, 2000). Further, the day care that is available to the poorest families in the nation is typically of very low quality. Researchers find that a child's well-being is compromised in centers where group size is large, the ratio of caretakers to children is low, and the staff is untrained or poorly supervised (Belsky, 1990). Others say that even at the best centers, some of the essential building blocks for development are missing because of the very nature of center-based day care (Greenspan, 1997) and that motivated parents can provide a superior social and intellectual environment (Fox and Lobsenz, 1996). Child care workers rank among the lowest 10 percent of wage earners in the United States, and the high turnover rate of such workers creates low continuity of care for children. Approximately two-thirds of a national sample of parents of young children indicated that they were very concerned that children in a day care center might be neglected or unsupervised, fail to get personal attention, pick up bad manners or behaviors, or suffer physical or sexual abuse (Public Agenda, 2000).

▲ No National Policy

Child care advocates warn that failure to develop a national policy toward child care will result in "a generation of neglected children." The United States is one of the few industrialized nations that does not have a comprehensive day care program. Access to early childhood education and care is a statutory right in Denmark, Finland, Sweden, France, Belgium, Italy, Germany, and Britain (Child Policy, 2004), and Japan has a "uniformly excellent" publicly supported day care system (Yamamoto and Struck, 2002). Only 2 percent of U.S. business and government employers sponsor day care centers for their workers' children, and only 4 percent of employees nationwide are eligible for employer-assisted child care benefits (Vobejda, 1997). Further, while the United States provides no paid maternity leave by law, more than 140 countries, including most other industrialized nations, do.

What does good care entail? In 2000 T. Berry Brazelton and Stanley I. Greenspan published *The Irreducible Needs of Children,* in which they describe what they see as essential to the emotional and physical health and development of babies and children:

- An ongoing nurturing relationship.
- Physical protection, safety, and regulation.
- Experiences tailored to individual differences.
- Developmentally appropriate experiences.
- Limit setting, structure, and expectations.

- Stable, supportive communities and cultural continuity.

- A protected future.

National policy decisions about caring for the nation's children would need to incorporate these or other standards to ensure that child care centers are not simply what consumer activist Ralph Nader describes as "children's ware-houses." But most parents think public policy should focus on parental leave instead of on child care. Three-quarters of survey respondents believe it is better for children to be at home with a parent, and 81 percent believe that children are more likely to get the affection and attention they need from a stay-at-home parent (Public Agenda, 2001).

▲ Alternatives to Day Care

As the debate about whether day care is as good as Mother continues, increasing numbers of women are finding alternatives. One alternative is *sequencing*—arranging one's life to provide time to work, time to have children and stay home with them, and time to reenter the outside workforce again (Cardozo, 1996). But as we discussed in Chapter 8, women pay the price of interrupting their careers to care for children in the forms of loss of job experience, reduced wages, and discrimination from employers. While some people insist that two incomes are essential in the United States, a significant number find that it is possible to live—and even save for the future—on one middle-class income. Another alternative to full-time employment and full-time day care for children is part-time work or work from the home. Some child-friendly employers now allow babies and children to "come to the office"; one researcher found that 8.9 percent of employed mothers were caring for their children at work (Trost, 1990).

Clinical psychiatrist and pediatrician Stanley I. Greenspan (1997) recommended a "four-thirds solution": Each parent works two-thirds time and spends one-third of the time raising the children. Greenspan also called for government and industry support, including government incentives for employers to provide part-time work options, more flextime, and guaranteed parental leave.

Divorce

Although divorce rates increased sharply from the 1960s to the early 1980s, they have declined almost as dramatically since then (see Figure 10.6). Yet divorce rates still are high in comparison to historical trends, and divorce is a common part of contemporary society. When today's elderly were establishing families, divorce was relatively infrequent. With the number of divorced people increasing over the past 30 years and young people delaying the formation of new unions, the number of divorced people per 1,000 married people has more than tripled in the past three decades. There are now 165 divorced people for every 1,000 married people (U.S. Census Bureau, 2003). Societal attitudes toward divorce have changed as well. Divorce court television shows provide the public with an intimate look at strained relationships, and Miami has a "Divorce Bus," a portable courtroom in which uncontested divorces are granted in 90 seconds for "$500 a pop" (Roig-Franzia, 2003).

▲ The Effects of Divorce on the Family

More than half of the couples who divorce have children. Researchers find that children of divorced or single parents have higher levels of anxiety, depression, stress, aggression, and school problems and are more likely to drop out of school and become parents themselves at a young age (Lugaila, 2003).

Financial problems complicate the difficulties of both women and men. Only half of divorced mothers receive any money at all from their children's fathers, and this is seldom much.

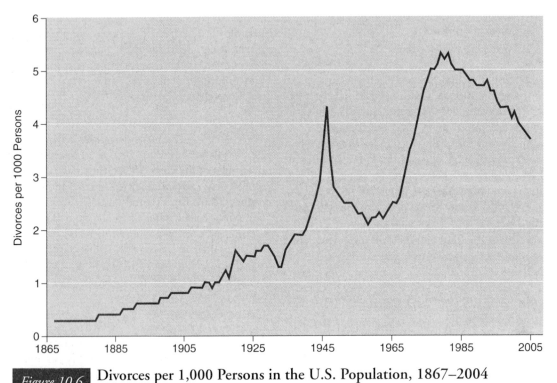

Figure 10.6 **Divorces per 1,000 Persons in the U.S. Population, 1867–2004**
Divorce rates in the U.S. increased dramatically in the 20th century. The social disruptions caused by World War II produced a very sharp spike in the immediate post-war years. Rates have been declining since the early 1980s. Divorce rates in this chart from the 19th century and very early 20th century are based on limited data.

Source: Figure generated by the authors using data from the U.S. Department of Health, Education, and Welfare (1973), U.S. Department of Health and Human Services (1996), U.S. Census Bureau (2006), and the National Vital Statistics Reports (available at http://www.cdc.gov/nchs/data/nvsr/nvsr53/nvsr53_21.pdf).

Most men also experience an economic decline following divorce (McManus and DiPrete, 2001). Moreover, divorce is not the end of family changes but often the beginning. Most divorced parents remarry, and because the rate of divorce among remarriages is greater than among first marriages, many children experience complex family lives (Furstenberg and Cherlin, 1991).

The notion that divorce has adverse consequences for children influences many couples to remain unhappily married until their youngsters reach adulthood. However, some evidence suggests that staying together for the sake of the children is not necessarily helpful if the marriage is marred by conflict, tension, and discord. Many of the emotional, behavioral, and academic problems children exhibit after their parents divorce are apparent before the time of the actual breakup of the family. Marital discord has a negative effect on children's emotional bonds with both parents (Amato and Sobolewski,

2001). On the other hand, clinical psychologist Mary Pipher argues that children may not be affected if their parents are unhappy but that divorce "shatters many children" (Pipher, 1994:133). Family sociologist Linda Waite says research supports that view: "As long as Mom and Dad don't fight too much, [children] thrive under the love, attention, and resources two married parents provide" (Waite and Gallagher, 2000:144).

▲ Long-Term Effects

Although divorce may be more commonplace today, it is no more a routine experience for adults than it is for children. In many cases divorce exacts a greater emotional and physical toll than almost any other type of stress, including death of a spouse (Kitson and Holmes, 1992). Separated and divorced people are over-represented in mental institutions; more likely to die from cardiovascular disease, cancer, pneumonia, and cirrhosis of the liver; and more prone to die from accidents, homicides, and suicides.

Middle-aged and elderly women are especially devastated by divorce. These women—called *displaced homemakers*—often have dedicated themselves to managing a home and raising children and then find themselves jettisoned after years of marriage. Within the United States, some 100,000 people over the age of 55 divorce each year.

Grown children of divorce have lower levels of psychological well-being (Amato and Sobolewski, 2001) and die, on average, four years sooner than adults who were raised by parents who did not divorce (Tucker et al., 1997). Children of divorce are more likely to marry as teens but less likely to marry at all once they get past age 20 (Wolfinger, 2003). On the other hand, adult children of divorced parents are now significantly less likely to divorce than children of a generation or two ago; between 1974 and 1993 the propensity to divorce if one's parents had divorced declined by about 50 percent (Wolfinger, 1999).

▲ After Divorce

Most divorced people remarry. About five of every six divorced men and three of every four divorced women marry again. Divorced men are more likely to remarry than women. Because men usually marry younger women, divorced men have a larger pool of potential partners from which to choose. Divorced men also are more likely to marry someone not previously married. About 61 percent of men and 54 percent of women in their thirties who remarry will undergo a second divorce. It seems that individuals drag into the new marriage many of the insecurities and personality problems that disrupted the previous one. With one divorce under their belt, they are less hesitant about securing a second one should trouble appear.

Care for the Elderly

As life expectancy increases, so does our population of elderly people. Some 52 percent of Americans between the ages of 53 and 61, and 44 percent of those between the ages of 58 and 66, have at least one living parent. Social scientists call middle-aged adults the "sandwich generation" because they find themselves with responsibilities for their own teenage and college-age children and for their elderly parents. In 80 percent of the cases, any care an elderly person requires is provided by his or her family. Family assistance supplements what the elderly receive from savings, pensions, Social Security, Medicare, and Medicaid. One benefit of family connections is economic: Only 5 percent of people 65 and older who live in families live below the poverty level, while 21 percent of individuals that age do (U.S. Census Bureau, 1999).

Care for the elderly falls most often on daughters and daughters-in-law. These women have historically functioned as our society's "kin-keepers" (Brody, 1990; Brody et al., 1994). Although one study found that working men and women spent approximately equal time caring for elderly relatives (Bond, Galinsky, and Swanberg, 1998), over all, women are more involved in elder care than men. Daughters are three times more likely than sons to provide parental care (Dwyer and Coward, 1991), and 61 percent of the women also work.

Although the average caregiver is 45 years old, female, and married, 35 percent of caregivers to the elderly are themselves older than 65 years of age, and 10 percent are older than 75. The motivations, expectations, and aspirations of the middle-aged and the elderly at times differ because of their different positions in the life cycle. Intergenerational strain is usually less where financial independence allows each generation to maintain separate residences. Both the elderly and their adult offspring seem to prefer intimacy "at a distance" and opt for independent households as long as possible. Elderly parents who call upon their children for assistance are more likely to be frail, severely disabled, gravely ill, or failing mentally.

Sociological Perspectives on the Family

We have been following three major sociological perspectives—the functionalist, conflict, and interactionist—as we move through our introduction to sociology. What do these major theoretical frameworks have to tell us about the family?

The Functionalist Perspective

As we have noted in other chapters, functionalist theorists stress that if a society is to survive and operate with some measure of effectiveness, it must guarantee that certain essential tasks are performed. The performance of these tasks—or *functions*—cannot be left to chance (see Chapter 1). To do so would be to run pp. 19–20 the risk that some activities would not be carried out, and the society would disintegrate. Although

acknowledging that families show a good deal of variation throughout the world, functionalists seek to identify a number of recurrent functions families typically perform (Davis, 1949).

▲ Reproduction

If a society is to perpetuate itself, new members have to be created; families perform that function by providing social and cultural supports and motivations for having children.

▲ Socialization

The family functions as an intermediary in the socialization process between the larger community and the individual. At birth, children are uninitiated in the ways of culture, and thus each new generation subjects society to a recurrent "barbarian invasion" (see Chapter 3). Through the process of socialization, children become inducted into their society's ways, and the family usually serves as the chief culture-transmitting agency.

▲ Care, Protection, and Emotional Support

Human children must be fed, clothed, and provided with shelter well into puberty. Throughout the world, the family has been assigned the responsibility for shielding, protecting, sustaining, and otherwise maintaining not just children, but also the infirm and other dependent members of the community (Rossi and Rossi, 1990). The family also provides an important source for entering into intimate, constant, face-to-face contact with other people. Healthy family relationships afford companionship, love, security, a sense of worth, and a general feeling of well-being.

▲ Assignment of Status

Infants must be placed within the social structure. The family confers ascribed statuses (see Chapter 2) that (1) orient a person to pp. 57–58 a variety of interpersonal relationships, including those involving parents, siblings, and other kin, and that (2) orient a person to basic group memberships, including racial, ethnic, religious, class, national, and community relationships.

▲ Regulation of Sexual Behavior

A society's norms regulate sexual behavior by specifying who may engage in sexual behavior with whom and under what circumstances. In no known society are people given total freedom for sexual expression. Although some 70 percent of the world's societies permit some form of sexual license, even those societies typically do not approve of childbirth out of wedlock— this is the **norm of legitimacy;** like other norms, this one is occasionally violated, and those who violate it are usually punished.

Critics of the functionalist perspective point out that these tasks can be performed in other ways. Indeed, by virtue of social change, many of the economic, child care, and educational functions once performed by the family have been taken over by other institutions. Even so, the family tends to be the social unit most commonly responsible for reproduction, socialization, and the other functions we considered.

The Conflict Perspective

Functionalists spotlight the tasks carried out by the family that serve the interests of society as a whole. Many conflict theorists, in contrast, have seen the family as a social arrangement benefiting some people more than others. Friedrich Engels (1884/1902), Karl Marx's close associate, viewed the family as a class society in miniature, with one class (men) oppressing another class (women). He contended that marriage was the first form of class antagonism in which the well-being of one group derived from the misery and repression of another. The motivation for sexual domination was the economic exploitation of a woman's labor.

▲ Women as Sexual Property

Sociologist Randall Collins (1975, 1988a) has said that historically men have been the "sexual aggressors" and women the "sexual prizes for men." Women have been victimized by their smaller size and vulnerability as childbearers. Across an entire spectrum of societies women have been seen as sexual property, taken as booty in war, used by their fathers in economic bargaining, and considered as owned by their husbands.

According to Collins, marriage is a socially enforced contract of sexual property. Within Western tradition, a marriage was not legal until sexually consummated, sexual assault within marriage was not legally rape, and the principal ground for divorce was sexual infidelity. A woman's virginity was seen as the property of her father, and her sexuality as the property of her husband. Thus, rape has often traditionally been seen less as a crime perpetrated by a man against a woman than as a crime perpetrated by one man against another man.

In recent years, however, economic and political changes have improved women's bargaining position. The sexual bargains women strike can focus less on marriage and more on immediate pleasure, companionship, and sexual gratification.

▲ Conflict as Natural and Necessary

Other social scientists have approached the issue of conflict somewhat differently. At the turn of the century psychoanalyst Sigmund Freud (1930/1961) and sociologist Georg Simmel (1908/1955, 1908/1959) also advanced a conflict approach to the family. They contended that intimate relationships inevitably involve antagonism as well as love. Sociologists like Jetse Sprey (1979) developed these ideas and suggested that conflict is a part of all systems and interactions, including the family and marital interactions. Viewed in this fashion, the family is a social arrangement that structures close interpersonal relationships through ongoing processes of negotiation, problem solving, and conflict management. This view is compatible with the interactionist perspective.

The Interactionist Perspective

As we saw in Chapters 2 and 3 symbolic interactionists emphasize that human beings create, use, and communicate with symbols. One way in which families reinforce and rejuvenate their bonds is through the symbolic mechanism of *rituals*. Social scientists find that household rituals such as gathering for meals are a hidden source of family strength. It seems that when families preserve their rituals, their children fare better emotionally, even when the family faces other disruptive problems (e.g., alcoholism). Some therapists help families establish rituals as a means to heal family stresses and tensions (Goleman, 1992; Pipher, 1997).

The symbolic interactionist perspective is a useful tool for examining the complexities of a relationship. When the roles of one family member change, there are consequences for other family members. For example, we have seen that parenthood alters the husband–wife relationship by creating new roles and increasing the complexity of the family unit. Likewise, family life is different in homes where a mother is in the paid labor force or where an economic provider is unemployed. And the loss of critical family roles caused by divorce has vast implications for family functioning (Gubrium and Holstein, 1990).

The Chapter in Brief: *The Family*

Structure of the Family: A Global View

The way in which we define the family determines the kinds of **family** we will consider to be normal or deviant and what rights and obligations we will recognize as legally and socially binding.

▌ *Forms of the Family*   In the **nuclear family** arrangement, spouses and their offspring constitute the core relationship. In the **extended family** arrangement, kin provide the core relationship. Most Americans will belong to a **family of orientation** and a **family of procreation**. Descent and inheritance can be **patrilineal, matrilineal,** or **bilineal,** and couples may take a **patrilocal, matrilocal,** or **neolocal** residence. Most societies are **patriarchal,** with some industrialized nations becoming more **egalitarian;** none are known that are truly **matriarchal.**

▌ *Forms of Marriage*   **Marriage** refers to a socially approved sexual union undertaken with some idea of permanence. Two types of marital regulations define the "right" spouse: **endogamy** and **exogamy. Incest taboos** are rules that prohibit sexual intercourse with close blood relatives. Societies further structure marriage relationships in one of four ways: **monogamy, polygyny, polyandry,** and **group marriage.**

▌ *Patterns of Courtship*   Societies "control" love through child and arranged marriage, social isolation of young people, close supervision of couples, and peer and parental pressures. A variety of factors operate in the selection of a mate: **homogamy,** physical attractiveness (the **matching hypothesis**), and **complementary needs. Exchange theory** provides a unifying link among these factors.

Marriage and the Family in the United States

Some see the nuclear family as the source of many modern woes, others as the last bastion of morality in an increasingly decadent world.

∎ *Life within Marriage*   Most adult Americans hope to establish an intimate relationship with another person and make the relationship work. However, increasing numbers of Americans no longer view marriage as a permanent institution but as something that can be ended and reentered.

∎ *Parenthood*   Nuclear families that are not disrupted by divorce, desertion, or death typically pass through a series of changes and realignments across time, what sociologists call the **family life course.** Altered expectations and requirements are imposed on a husband and wife as children are born and grow up.

∎ *Two-Income Families*   More than 60 percent of all mothers with children under age six are in the paid workforce. Such women also do more of the housework and child care than men. Research findings about the effect of working mothers on children are varied. In one-fifth of such couples the woman is the chief breadwinner.

∎ *Beyond the Traditional Nuclear Family*   Americans have a variety of **lifestyles,** the overall pattern of living that people evolve to meet their biological, social, and emotional needs. Among the lifestyles Americans find themselves adopting are singlehood, single parenthood, cohabitation, and relationships based on **homosexuality.**

Challenges for American Families and American Society

Some family problems stay in the family; others spill over into society.

∎ *Family Violence, Child Abuse, and Incest*   Family violence, child abuse, and incest are more common than most people think. The sexual abuse of children often leads to behavior problems, learning difficulties, sexual promiscuity, runaway behavior, drug and alcohol abuse, and suicidal behavior.

∎ *Child Care*   Most child psychologists agree that high-quality day care and preschools provide acceptable child care arrangements. The United States is one of the few industrialized nations that have no comprehensive day care program and the quality of child care available is often poor.

∎ *Divorce*   Divorce exacts a considerable emotional and physical toll from all family members. Children raised by single parents are more likely to drop out of high school, to use drugs, to have teen births, to have illegitimate children, and to be poorer than children raised in two-parent homes. More than half the adults who remarry undergo a second divorce.

∎ *Care for the Elderly*   Social scientists call middle-aged adults the "sandwich generation" because they find themselves with responsibilities for their own teenage and college-age children and for their elderly parents. Grown children still bear the primary responsibility for their aged parents.

Sociological Perspectives on the Family

∎ *The Functionalist Perspective*
Functionalists identify a number of functions families typically perform: reproduction; socialization; care, protection, and emotional support; assignment of status; and regulation of sexual behavior through the **norm of legitimacy.**

∎ *The Conflict Perspective*   Conflict theorists have seen the family as a social arrangement benefiting men more than women. Some conflict sociologists say that intimate relationships inevitably involve antagonism as well as love.

∎ *The Interactionist Perspective*
Symbolic interactionists emphasize that families reinforce and rejuvenate their bonds through the symbolic mechanism of rituals such as family meals and holidays.

Glossary

bilineal   An arrangement based on reckoning descent and transmitting property through both the father and the mother.

complementary needs   Two different personality traits that are the counterparts of each other and that provide a sense of completeness when they are joined.

egalitarian authority   An arrangement in which power and authority are equally distributed between husband and wife.

endogamy   The requirement that marriage occur within a group.

exchange theory   The view proposing that people involved in a mutually satisfying relationship will exchange behaviors that have low cost and high reward.

exogamy   The requirement that marriage occur outside a group.

extended family   A family arrangement in which kin—individuals related by common ancestry—provide the core relationship; spouses are functionally marginal and peripheral.

family   Traditionally defined as a social group whose members are related by ancestry, marriage, or adoption and who live together, cooperate economically, and care for the young.

family life course   Changes and realignments related to the altered expectations and requirements imposed on a husband and a wife as children are born and grow up.

family of orientation   A nuclear family that consists of oneself and one's father, mother, and siblings.

family of procreation   A nuclear family that consists of oneself and one's spouse and children.

group marriage   The marriage of two or more husbands and two or more wives.

homogamy   The tendency of like to marry like.

homosexuality   A preference for an individual of the same sex as a sexual partner.

incest taboos   Rules that prohibit sexual intercourse with close blood relatives.

lifestyle   The overall pattern of living that people evolve to meet their biological, social, and emotional needs.

marriage   A socially approved sexual union between two or more individuals which is undertaken with some idea of permanence.

matching hypothesis   The notion that we typically experience the greatest payoff and the least cost when we select partners who have a degree of physical attractiveness similar to our own.

matriarchal authority   A family arrangement in which power is vested in women.

matrilineal   An arrangement based on reckoning descent and inheritance through the mother's side of the family.

matrilocal residence   The residence pattern in which a bride and groom live in the household or community of the wife's family.

monogamy   The marriage of one husband and one wife.

neolocal residence   The residence pattern in which newlyweds set up a new place of residence independent of either of their parents or other relatives.

norm of legitimacy   The rule that children not be born out of wedlock.

nuclear family   A family arrangement in which the spouses and their offspring constitute the core relationship; blood relatives are functionally marginal and peripheral.

patriarchal authority   A family arrangement in which power is vested in men.

patrilineal   An arrangement based on reckoning descent and inheritance through the father's side of the family.

patrilocal residence   The residence pattern in which a bride and groom live in the household or community of the husband's family.

polyandry   The marriage of two or more husbands and one wife.

polygyny   The marriage of one husband and two or more wives.

romantic love   The strong physical and emotional attraction between a man and a woman.

Review Questions

1. Differentiate between nuclear and extended families and between family of orientation and family of procreation.

2. Describe the various forms of marriage found around the world.

3. How do courtship patterns control love?

4. What is the family life course?

5. What sorts of lifestyles do Americans adopt besides the traditional nuclear family?

6. Name and describe some of the challenges facing American families today.

7. How do the functionalist, conflict, and interactionist perspectives on the family differ?

Internet Connection

www.mhhe.com/hughes8

Using a search engine such as **google.com,** search on "family values." Choose a number of the sites you find and explore them further. Write a short report about the many ways "family values" are defined in our society. How is this term thought about differently by different interest and cultural groups, including political and religious groups?

RELIGION, EDUCATION, AND MEDICINE

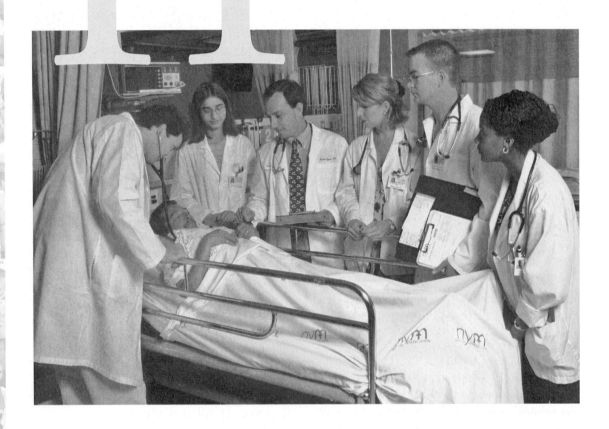

I n this chapter we turn our attention to three interconnected institutions: religion, medicine, and education. Each of these is focused on the solution to a set of problems encountered in social living. Depending on the time of history and culture under study, these institutions have interwoven their solutions to such problems. In the pages that follow we will see how religious, educational, and medical institutions have evolved to meet basic needs for society.

Religion

Sociologists are interested in religious beliefs and commitments and in the effect religion has on health, the family, politics, and other matters (Sherkat and Ellison, 1999). For example, throughout U.S. history the influence of religion on politics and government has been strong. Religion has historically played a major role in American social movements and does so today. Indeed, one of President George W. Bush's first actions after taking office was to outline his "faith-based initiatives," plans for facilitating the work that churches and other religious organizations do to help solve various problems of society. His call for action came at a time when religion was already at work on social issues. Liberal religious groups and the nation's Catholic bishops have pushed for improved social services for the disadvantaged. The Christian right set a different agenda, one based on the Christian roots, heritage, and values of an older America. What role should religion play in public policy? This debate focuses not on the right of religious activists to lobby for laws consistent with their beliefs, but on determining the place a religiously defined morality has in a pluralist society (Olson and Carroll, 1992).

In this section we will review the varieties of religious behavior found among people around the world and take a look at religious organizations. We will consider secular change, religion in contemporary life, fundamentalism and evangelicalism, and issues of church and state. Finally, we will see what the sociological perspectives have to offer to our understanding of religion.

What Is Religion?

Religion has to do with those socially shared and organized ways of thinking, feeling, and acting that concern ultimate meanings about the existence of the supernatural or "beyond" (Stark and Bainbridge, 1987). As Émile Durkheim (1912/1965) pointed out, religion is centered in beliefs and practices that are related to sacred as opposed to profane things. Durkheim described the **sacred** as involving those aspects of social reality that are set apart and forbidden. The **profane** has to do with those aspects of social reality that are everyday and commonplace. The sacred, then, is extraordinary, mysterious, awe-inspiring, and even potentially dangerous—it is distinct from normal, routine life (Berger, 1967). The same object or behavior can be profane or sacred, depending on how people define it. A wafer made of flour when seen as bread is a profane object, but it becomes sacred to Catholics as the body of Christ when it is consecrated during the Mass. Because the sacred is caught up with strong feelings of reverence and awe, it can usually be approached only through **rituals**—social acts prescribed by rules that dictate how human beings should behave in the presence of the sacred. In their religious behavior, human beings fashion a social world of meanings and rules that govern how and what they think, feel, and act.

A Global View: Varieties of Religious Behavior

Research shows that religion plays a role in most people's lives, but its importance varies significantly across the globe. Only 15 percent of the world's population is nonreligious or atheist (having no belief in God) (U.S. Census Bureau, 1999). The rest of the world can be categorized by their adherence to various religions, including Hindus (12.8 percent) and Muslims (19.6 percent), Buddhists (6.0 percent) and Roman Catholics (17.3 percent), Protestants (5.3 percent) and Jews (0.1 percent), Sikhs, Baha'is, and New-Religionists. However, data from the World Values Survey (Inglehart et al., 2000) show that the percentage of people reporting that religion is "very important" in their lives ranges from between 80 and 90 percent in Nigeria, Ghana, Bangladesh, and Pakistan to less than 10 percent in Sweden, the Czech Republic, Japan, and China (see Figure 11.1), with an average of about 33 percent across the 71 surveys conducted worldwide.

Religious behavior is so varied that we have difficulty thinking about it unless we devise some means for sorting it into relevant categories. Although no categories do justice to the diversity and richness of the human religious experience, sociologist Reece McGee (1975) provided us with a scheme that is both insightful and manageable: simple supernaturalism, animism, theism, and a system of abstract ideals.

▲ Simple Supernaturalism

A belief in the supernatural entails the notion of **mana,** a diffuse, impersonal, supernatural force that exists in nature for good or evil. Mana is usually employed to reach "here-and-now" goals—control of the weather, assurance of a good crop, cure of an illness, good performance on a test, success in love, or victory in battle. With mana people do not entreat spirits or gods to intervene on their behalf; they *compel* a superhuman power to behave as they wish. For instance, carrying a rabbit's foot is thought to bring good luck, while the bad luck associated with the number 13 is avoided by not labeling hotel and office building floors as "13."

▲ Animism

Animism is a pattern of religious behavior that involves a belief in spirits or otherworldly beings.

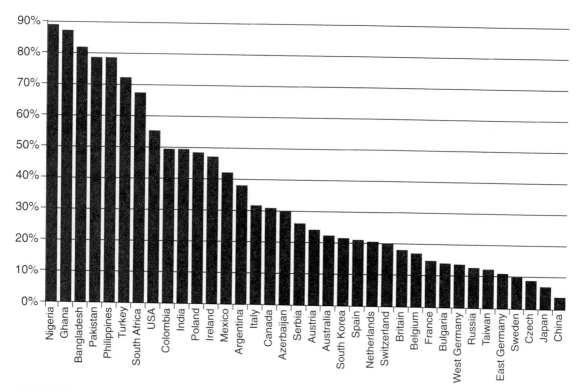

Figure 11.1   **Percent Reporting That Religion Is "Very Important" in Their Lives**
Source: Figure generated by the authors using data from selected countries surveyed in the World Values Survey, 1981–1984, 1990–1993, and 1995–1997 (Inglehart et al., 2000).

People have seen spirits throughout nature—in animals, plants, rocks, stars, rivers, and at times in other individuals. Love, punishment, reverence, and gifts have all been used to deal with superhuman spirits, as have cajolery, bribery, and false pretenses. Additionally, in animism, as with mana, supernatural power is often harnessed through rituals that compel a spirit to act in a desired way.

▲ Theism

In **theism** religion is centered in a belief in gods who are thought to be powerful, to have an interest in human affairs, and to merit worship. Judaism, Christianity, and Islam are forms of **monotheism,** or belief in one god. They have established religious organizations, religious

leaders or priests, traditional rituals, and sacred writings. Ancient Greek religion and Hinduism (practiced primarily in India) are forms of **polytheism,** or belief in many gods with equal or relatively similar power. Hindu gods are often tribal, village, or caste deities associated with a particular place—a building, field, or mountain—or a certain object such as an animal or a tree.

▲ Abstract Ideals

Finally, some religions focus on a set of abstract ideals. Rather than centering on the worship of a god, they are dedicated to achieving moral and spiritual excellence. Many of the religions of Asia are of this type, including Taoism, Confucianism, and Buddhism. Buddhism is directed toward reaching an elevated state of consciousness, a method of purification that provides a release from suffering, ignorance, and selfishness. In the Western world, humanism is based on ethical principles. Its adherents discard all theological beliefs about God, heaven, hell, and immortality, and substitute for God the pursuit of good in the here and now.

Religious Organizations

Norms, beliefs, and rituals provide the cultural fabric of religion, but there is more to the religious institution than its cultural heritage. As with other institutions, there is also the structural mosaic of social organization whereby people are bound together within networks of relatively stable relationships. In this section we will focus on four types of religious organization: churches, denominations, sects, and cults.

▲ Church

Sociologists use the familiar term "church" to refer to a form of religious organization that has never existed in the United States but has been common in history and still exists in parts of the world. **Church** is a religious organization that considers itself uniquely legitimate and typically enjoys a positive relationship with mainstream society. It usually operates with a bureaucratic structure and claims to include most members of a society. Religions organized along church lines are either integrated into a society's government or operate with explicit government sanction and support. Its members are born into the church if their parents are affiliated with it; they do not have to join the church. The aim of the church is professedly universal. Its response to competing groups is to suppress, ignore, or co-opt them (see Table 11.1).

The church attaches considerable importance to the means of grace that it administers, to the system of doctrine that it has formulated, and to the administration of rituals that it controls through an official clergy. It strives to dominate all aspects of social life—to teach and guide the members of society and dispense saving grace. The church type is best exemplified by the Roman Catholic Church of 13th-century Europe and the Church of England.

▲ The Denomination

The **denomination** accepts the legitimacy claims of other religions and enjoys a positive relationship with the dominant society. In many cases it is a sect in an advanced stage of development and adjustment to the secular world. The membership of the denomination comes largely from the middle class. The moral rigor and religious fervor of the sect are relaxed. It usually has an established clergy who have undergone specialized training at a theological seminary to prepare for their positions.

The denomination is content to be one organization among many, all of which are deemed acceptable in the sight of God. Examples of denominations include most of the major religious groups in the United States: Presbyterians, Baptists, Congregationalists, Methodists, Unitarians, Lutherans, Episcopalians, Roman Catholics, and Reform and Conservative Jews.

▲ The Sect

The **sect** is a religious organization that stands apart from mainstream society but is rooted in established religious traditions. The sect considers itself uniquely legitimate but is at odds with the dominant society. It usually consists of a small, voluntary fellowship of converts, most of whom are drawn from disadvantaged groups. The sect does not attempt to win the world over to its doctrines but instead practices exclusiveness. The sect is often founded by individuals who break away from another religious body and claim that they represent the true, cleansed version of the faith from which they split (Stark and Bainbridge, 1979; Wilson, 1990). Members who entertain heretical opinions or engage in immoral behavior are subject to expulsion. The sect thinks of itself as a religious elite. Sect members believe that other religious interpretations are in

Table 11.1 Types of Religious Organization

Characteristic	Church	Denomination	Sect	Cult
Size	Large	Moderate	Small	Small
Relationship with secular world	Affirms prevailing culture and social arrangements	Supports current culture and social arrangements	Renounces or opposes prevailing culture and social arrangements	Although critical of society, focuses on evil within each person
Relationship with other religious groups	Claims lone legitimacy	Accepts pluralistic legitimacy	Claims lone legitimacy	Accepts pluralistic legitimacy
Religious services	Formal services with minimal congregational participation	Formal services with limited congregational participation	Informal services with high degree of congregational participation	Informal meetings that draw upon the participation of adherents
Clergy	Specialized; professional; full-time	Specialized; professional; full-time	Unspecialized; little formal training; part-time	Charismatic; founder or leader has little formal training
Doctrines	Literal interpretations of scriptures	Liberal interpretation of scriptures	Literal interpretation of scriptures	New and independent tradition with a rather secularized view of the divine
Social class of members	All social classes	Middle and upper	Primarily disadvantaged	Chiefly middle and educated
Sources of members	Born into the faith; seeks universal membership	Often requires later validation of membership acquired from parents	Voluntary confessional membership	Often lacks formal membership
Emphasis	Religious education and transmission of religion to the children of members	Religious education and transmission of religious values to youth	Evangelism and adult membership	Living one's life in accordance with basic tenets
Church property	Extensive	Depends on affluence of members	Little	None or limited

Source: Adapted from Glen M. Vernon, *Sociology of Religion*, New York: McGraw-Hill, 1962, p. 174.

357

Active participation in religious organizations continues to be important for many Americans, and the United States remains one of the world's most religious countries.

suspicion, cults have a sense of vulnerability and thus an interest in publicly supporting norms of tolerance.

Cults usually do not require their new members to pass strict doctrinal tests, but instead invite all to join their ranks. However, many cults are authoritarian and attempt to control the entire lives of their members. For example, the members of the Heaven's Gate Cult, who committed mass suicide in San Diego, California in 1997, were rigidly controlled by their leaders in terms of where they lived, what they did each day, whom they visited, what they wore, and even what they ate.

error, and they portray the larger society as decadent and evil (see Table 11.1). It is often a form of social dissent, exemplified by the Anabaptists of the 16th- and 17th-century Reformation and the Mormons, Shakers, and Quakers of the 18th and 19th centuries. Most sects are small, and many of them fail to grow larger. Should they survive, gain adherents, and become dominant, they have a natural tendency to become church-like. If they become widely popular in a religiously diverse and competitive environment like the United States, they become more like denominations.

▲ The Cult

While a sect is formed out of an existing religion, a **cult** is a religious movement that represents a new and independent religious tradition (Stark and Bainbridge, 1979, 1987). The cult is alienated and viewed as deviant by the dominant society, but it tends to accept the legitimacy of other religious groups. Having no religious tradition, it is difficult for a cult to claim sole legitimacy. In addition, knowing that others view them with

▲ Summing Up

Whereas churches and denominations typically exist in accommodation with the larger society, sects and cults often find themselves at odds with established social arrangements and practices. Cults differ from sects in that they are not rooted in existing religious traditions and they tend to be more tolerant of other religious groups. In this respect, cults resemble denominations. In contrast, the sect, like the church, defines itself as being uniquely legitimate and possessing exclusive access to truth or salvation. This model is depicted in Figure 11.2.

Religion and Secular Change: The Protestant Ethic

People's religious beliefs and practices can promote socioeconomic change. Max Weber (1904/1958, 1916/1964, 1917/1958) studied several world religions in order to discern how a religious **ethic**—the perspective and values engendered by a religious way of thinking—can

	Positive Relationship with Society	Negative Relationship with Society
Claims Lone Legitimacy	CHURCH	SECT
Accepts Pluralistic Legitimacy	DENOMI-NATION	CULT

Figure 11.2 Types of Religious Organizations

Source: Adapted from Roy Wallis, *Sectarianism: Analyses of Religious and Non-Religious Sects.* New York: Wiley, 1975, p. 41. Reprinted by permission of Peter Owen Ltd.

affect people's behavior. He suggested that there are periods in historical development when circumstances push a society toward a reaffirmation of old ways or toward new ways. At such critical junctures, religion—by supplying sources of individual motivation and defining the relationship of individuals to their society—can be a source of historical breakthrough. While a religious ethic does not mechanically determine social action, it can give it impetus by shaping people's perceptions and definitions of their material and ideal interests.

▲ Did Protestantism Lead to Capitalism?

In *The Protestant Ethic and the Spirit of Capitalism* (1904/1958), Weber sought a link between the rise of the Protestant view of life and the emergence of capitalist social arrangements in Western society. He maintained that the development of capitalism depended upon the creation of a pool of individuals who had the attitudes and values necessary to function as entrepreneurs. Once capitalism is established, it carries on in a self-perpetuating fashion.

The critical problem, Weber said, is to uncover the origin of the motivating spirit of capitalism in precapitalist society. He believed that Protestantism, particularly in the form of Calvinism, was crucial to, but not the only factor in, the rise of this spirit. Calvinism is based on the teachings of the French Protestant theologian and reformer John Calvin (1509–1564) and found expression in a variety of religious movements including Puritanism, Pietism, and Anabaptism.

Weber noted that Protestantism and modern capitalism appeared on the historical scene at roughly the same time, that capitalism initially attained its highest development in Protestant countries and regions, and that it was mostly Protestants, not Catholics, who became the early capitalist entrepreneurs. Based on these observations, Weber (1904/1958:64) concluded that the **Protestant ethic,** particularly as it was embodied in Calvinist doctrine, instilled an "attitude which seeks profit rationally and systematically."

▲ The Doctrine of Predestination

The Calvinist ethos had other elements that fed capitalist motivation, particularly its *doctrine of predestination.* Calvin rejected the idea that a person's status in the afterlife is determined by the way he or she behaves here on earth. Instead, Calvin taught that at birth every soul is predestined for heaven or hell. This notion was especially disquieting because people did not know whether they were among the saved or the damned. According to Weber, Calvin's followers, in their search for reassurance, came to accept certain earthly signs of **asceticism** as proof of their salvation and genuine faith: hard work, sobriety, thrift, restraint, and the avoidance of fleshly pleasures. The Calvinists, preoccupied with their fate, subtly began to cultivate these very behaviors. Self-discipline and a willingness to delay gratification are qualities that lead people to amass capital and achieve economic success. Capitalist entrepreneurs could pursue profit and fulfill their Christian obligation; the Calvinist ethos took the spirit of capitalism out of the realm of individual ambition and translated it into an ethical duty.

▲ Other Origins of Capitalism

Many scholars since Weber have raised serious questions regarding his hypothesis (Samuelsson, 1961; Cohen, 1980). They have looked to other factors in explaining the origins of capitalism, including a surge in commerce during the 15th and 16th centuries, technological innovations, the influx of capital resources from New World colonies, unrestrained markets, and the availability of a free labor force. Further, sociologist Randall G. Stokes (1975) showed that the beliefs comprising the Protestant ethic do not necessarily lead people to engage in entrepreneurial activities. Even so, Weber's early work, although not necessarily accurate in all its particulars, remains a sociological landmark. It demonstrates the impact religion can have on human affairs in producing outcomes that are not necessarily intended or foreseen by its adherents.

Adapting Tradition: Religion in Contemporary Life

Religion may draw upon people's spiritual yearnings and adapt them to modern life. Many Western intellectuals had anticipated that processes of rationalization would lead to the gradual withering away of religious ideas and institutions. This view found expression in the **secularization thesis,** the notion that profane (nonreligious) considerations gain ascendancy over sacred (religious) considerations in the course of social evolution (Herberg, 1955; Chaves, 1994). In much the manner that industrialization, urbanization, bureaucratization, and rationalization have been equated with modernization, so secularization has been widely assumed to accompany the transformation of human societies from simple to complex forms.

▲ Is Secularization Occurring?

Some evidence seemingly supports the secularization thesis. The Gallup polling organization has been questioning Americans since 1937 on their religious practices. In 2000, 44 percent of the U.S. adult population said they had attended a church or synagogue in the seven-day period preceding the time of the interview, and 68 percent said they were church or synagogue members (U.S. Census Bureau, 2003). However, actual head counts have revealed that only 20 percent of Protestants and 28 percent of Catholics show up for Sunday services (Hadaway, Marler, and Chaves, 1993). In a more recent survey, 53 percent of respondents said that being religious meant "making sure that one's behavior and day-to-day actions match one's faith" (Farkas et al., 2000). Only 5 percent equated it with church attendance.

Nevertheless, despite the apparently low turnouts for worship services, very little sociological evidence supports the notion that secularization is taking place in American life (Hadden, 1987; Greeley, 1989). Indeed, the United States remains one of the world's most religious countries (see Box 11.1). Religion remains a powerful force in the United States, and survey respondents believe it has the potential to do even more. If more Americans were deeply religious, a strong majority of respondents said, crime would decrease, volunteer and charity work would increase, and parents would do a better job of raising children (Farkas et al., 2000). The vast majority of Americans say they believe in the existence of God and life after death; significantly, the proportion of Americans professing belief in God or some higher power has not dipped below 90 percent over the past half-century (Princeton Religion Research Center, 1994; Davis, Smith, and Marsden, 2003).

In the 1990s, a new set of ideas in the sociology of religion, referred to by some as the "New Paradigm" (e.g., Warner, 1993), reformulated the idea of secularization to make sense

Is the Significance of Religion Declining in the United States?

Many of the first European immigrants to the North American continent made their journey to find religious freedom. As schoolchildren, we all are taught the stories of the Pilgrims, the strict Puritans of New England, and the struggles of the pioneers to establish churches on the prairie frontier. The earliest days in the history of the American colonies seem steeped in religiosity.

Is religion still significant in U.S. society? The secularization thesis argues that modern societies will give up on religion and become increasingly secular. Some religious and moral leaders publically worry that this is happening. Yet a look at some empirical data may provide a surprise for those who believe U.S. society has been undergoing secularization over its history.

First, the percent of Americans who believe in God in some form is extremely high: 93 percent, according to recent surveys (e.g., Davis, Smith, and Marsden, 2003). Only about 3 percent are atheists (do not believe in God) and nearly 4 percent are agnostics (do not know if God exists). Second, according to historical and contemporary data (Finke and Starke, 1992; U.S. Census Bureau, 1999; Newport and Saad, 1997), the percentage of Americans who claim membership in a church or synagogue has risen dramatically over the past 200 years. When the Declaration of Independence was signed, only 17 percent of the population belonged to a church or synagogue. By 1860 that number had risen to 37 percent, and in 1926 it had increased again to 58 percent. But these figures pale in comparison to

the 71 percent of Americans who claimed church or synagogue membership in 1975, and in 2000 that number stood at 68 percent, almost the highest it has ever been (U.S. Census Bureau, 2003).

To make the point a little differently, having no religious preference is currently very uncommon in the United States. According to data from the General Social Surveys, 1972 to 2002 (Davis, Smith, and Marsden, 2003), from the early 1970s to 1991 only 6 to 8 percent of Americans on average indicated no religious preference; over 90 percent identified themselves as Catholic, Jewish, members of various Protestant denominations, or another religion. In recent years, the percent of those with no religious preference has increased to about 14 percent (Hout and Fischer, 2002; Davis, Smith, and Marsden, 2003), but this does not mean that people are becoming nonreligious. More than two-thirds of those with no preference have some kind of belief in God or a higher power, with nearly 30 percent believing in God and having no doubts about it (Hout and Fischer, 2002).

The increase in the number of fundamentalists, those who view the Bible as literally the word of God, at least partially accounts for the high rate of church affiliation in the United States. Those denominations that sociologists of religion consider to be fundamentalist include Baptists, along with the Assemblies of God, the Seventh-Day Adventists, the United Pentecostal Church, and the Church of God. Among those identifying their religions in 1996, 22 percent said they were

Baptists, compared with 8 percent Methodist, 7 percent Lutheran, 4 percent Presbyterian, and 3 percent Episcopalian, all more liberal Protestant denominations. Indeed, Baptists are second only to Roman Catholics in total membership in the United States. The increase in membership of these denominations between 1960 and 1990 ranged from 12 to 900 percent, while memberships in more liberal churches declined by 28 to 59 percent (Stark, 1996).

So: Has American society been becoming more secular over its history? Is it in religious decline? Despite some changes, religious involvement and commitment remains strong in the United States. While mainline religious denominations have lost some members, fundamentalist groups have increased their share and are now as strong as they ever have been. Although the 1990s saw a decline in people expressing a religious preference, a 200-year trend in church membership indicates a general increase in religious involvement in the United States, not a decline.

Questions for Discussion

1. The data presented here show that secularization is not increasing in the United States. Look at the data in Figure 11.1. How does the United States compare to other industrialized countries? What do you think explains this?

2. What do you think accounts for the growing membership in fundamentalist churches in the United States? Why do you think Baptist and Roman Catholic churches have the two largest church memberships?

of the continuing significance and vitality of religion in American life. According to the new paradigm, since religion is the only institution that can answer the ultimate questions of the meaning and purpose of life for most people, it is an inevitable feature of human society. Secularization is a process in which religions become increasingly worldly and less focused on the supernatural (Stark, 1996). But instead of resulting in people turning to science for ultimate answers, secularization weakens old religious groups that are becoming less focused on the supernatural and creates opportunities for new ones. Secularization in the United States has followed exactly this pattern, producing a decline in the old mainline Protestant denominations and an increase in strength among evangelical, fundamentalist, and sectlike groups. In this view, secularization is a "process that leads not to irreligion but to a shift in the sources of religion" (Stark, 1996:437). As long as there is a free market in religion (see "The Religious 'Marketplace,' " below) and people can change their religious attachments, secularization initiates a process that revitalizes religion rather than promoting its demise.

Fundamentalism and Evangelicalism

In recent years the nation has undergone a fundamentalist and evangelical revival that has represented an attempt to capture the roots of religious inspiration and shape them to the contemporary world (Hunter, 1983, 1987; Johnson, 1990). *Fundamentalism* is a Protestant movement that opposes "modernist" theology and seeks to conserve the basic principles underlying traditional Christianity; it views the Bible as the literal and unerring word of God and reaffirms traditional authority. *Evangelicalism* is a "glad tidings" movement whose members profess a personal relationship with Jesus Christ; adherents believe that the Bible provides the only authoritative basis for faith, stress the

importance of personal conversion, and emphasize the importance of intense zeal for Christian living. Although the public often lumps fundamentalists and evangelicals together, their differences are every bit as great as those dividing Catholics, Episcopalians, Methodists, and Baptists (Hadden and Shupe, 1988).

▲ Resisting Change

Many religious conservatives have entered the political arena. More than a quarter of Americans are white evangelical Protestants. Although there is not a single Christian Right, the assortment of organizations, constituencies, and leaders who share traditional family values, favor school prayer, and oppose abortion, gay rights, and the teaching of evolution is large and powerful (Luo, 2006). More than half the Americans surveyed in 2000 said it would be wrong to consider a candidate's religious affiliation when voting, although they would like political leaders to be more religious. But evangelicals were more likely than other groups to say that deeply religious politicians would make better leaders and that they should be less willing to compromise on key issues, instead voting as their religious beliefs dictate (Farkas et al., 2000).

▲ The Religious "Marketplace"

According to Finke and Stark (1992), religions that gain members in the religious "marketplace" are the hardline ones. They portrayed religious groups as functioning much in the manner of firms competing for souls. Experiments have shown that "a sanctioning institution is the undisputed winner in a competition with a sanction-free institution" (Gürerk, Irlenbusch, and Rockenback, 2006:108). In religion, the "winners" have historically been "upstart sects," groups that today include Pentecostal, Holiness, and Fundamentalist sects. In colonial times the established denominations went into decline when confronted with competition from Baptist and Methodist sects. In turn Methodism went into decline when its circuit-rider clergy dismounted and became professionalized, its hellfire and brimstone theology cooled, and its rustic camp meetings became "respectable middle-class summer resorts" (Finke and Stark, 1992).

High-cost faiths—those that impose sacrifices and even stigmas on their members— consistently outperform their more mainstream counterparts; hardline religious groups also get rid of "free riders" who dilute the congregation's solidarity by using it for weddings, funerals, and an occasional spiritual boost without affording much in return (Iannaccone, 1994). In addition, denominations and individual churches that can extract more resources from members in terms of time and money grow faster than others (Iannaccone, Olson, and Stark, 1995). There seems to be an indissoluble link between how much a religion demands and how much its members feel it can offer in return. The "losers" are the mainline denominations, especially the Congregationalists, Presbyterians, and Episcopalians, who have evolved a well-educated, seminary-trained clergy.

▲ Islamic Fundamentalism

Fundamentalism is a feature of all religious traditions that change and evolve over time. Islam is no exception. A pivotal event in Islamic fundamentalism in this century was the Iranian Revolution of 1979, in which the Ayatollah Khomeini, an Islamic religious leader, overthrew the Shah Mohammed Riza Pahlavi, replacing his monarchy with a theocratic regime rooted in Islamic traditions and anti-Western fervor.

In creating this revolution, religious leaders drew on the people's intense resentment of persistent Western dominance and the imposition by the shah of Western ways that many Iranians viewed as incompatible with Islam. Through this revolution, Islamic fundamentalism went beyond religion and became a vehicle for political and nationalistic expression. Islamic fundamentalists also challenged several secular-oriented governments in North Africa and the Middle East in a pattern that can be seen as a

defensive measure against the intrusions of Western society (Miller, 1992). Islamic fundamentalism has proven itself to be less reactionary than reactive: Its leaders have typically used traditional Islamic principles and ideas to power their resistance against outside forces, modernity, relativism, pluralism, and compromisers within their tradition (Marty and Appleby, 1992).

However, it is important to stress that Islam and Muslims are not monolithic. Throughout the world, Muslims are religiously, politically, and culturally pluralistic (Esposito, 1992). Episodes of terrorism, such as the September 11, 2001, attacks that were conducted by fundamentalist Islamic political extremists, are representative neither of Islamic fundamentalism nor of Islam in general. In fact, such terrorist acts signal not the growing power of fundamentalist political Islam, but rather its failure to mobilize and retain power in the Muslim world (Kepel, 2002; Roy, 1998).

State-Church Issues

The First Amendment provided the foundation for the principle of the separation of church and state, by which organized religion and government have remained substantially independent of each other in the United States. Compared with many other nations, the United States has maintained a remarkably hands-off attitude toward religion. Some sociologists believe that the absence of a coerced monopoly has compelled American religious institutions to operate in a pluralistic environment comparable to a market economy (Warner, 1993). Even so, in a number of cases laws have been enacted and upheld by the Supreme Court that have impinged upon religious practices, including those against polygamy among Mormons and against snake-handling by charismatic Christians.

▲ Civil Religion

Although most Americans deem an individual's religious beliefs and practices to be a strictly private matter, there are nonetheless certain common elements of religious orientation most Americans share. These religious dimensions are expressed in a set of beliefs, symbols, and rituals that sociologist Robert Bellah (1970; Bellah and Hammond, 1980) called **civil religion.** Its basic tenet is that the American nation is not an ultimate end in itself but a nation under God with a divine mission. Civil religion provides a supernatural legitimacy for nationalism. Although religious pluralism prevents any one denomination from supplying all Americans with a single source of meaning, civil religion compensates by providing an overarching sacred canopy.

According to functionalism, religious rituals create among people a shared consciousness that contributes to a social bonding.

Civil religion finds expression in the statements and documents of the Founding Fathers, presidential inaugural addresses, schoolchildren's Pledge of Allegiance, national holidays, historic shrines, mottos, and patriotic expressions in times of crisis and peril. There are four references to God in the Declaration of Independence. Every president but one has mentioned God in his inaugural address. And the government engages in many religious practices, from the phrase "In God We Trust" on its currency to the prayers said in Congress. Significantly, both sides of U.S. electoral politics (e.g., Reverends Jesse Jackson and Jerry Falwell) employ civil religion to interpret and legitimate their places and agendas within national life (Williams and Demerath, 1991).

▲ Religion and Morality

Determining the place a religiously defined morality should hold in a pluralist society continues to generate controversy in the United States. Abortion provides a good illustration. There are those who insist that abortion is a private moral choice and that the state has no right to make the practice illegal. Others, particularly antiabortion groups, contend that abortion is no more a matter of private moral choice than slavery was and that the state has an obligation to stop it. In a nationwide survey, only 35 percent (or fewer, depending on the issue) of respondents believe that elected officials should base their votes on their religious beliefs, even on such issues as abortion, the death penalty, and gay rights (Farkas et al., 2000). Survey respondents favored a moment of silence over spoken prayers in the public schools and expressed respect for religious diversity. Jewish and nonreligious respondents were particularly wary about mixing politics and religion.

The Functionalist Perspective

Functionalist theorists look to the contributions religion makes to society's survival. They reason that if every known society seems to have something called religion, its presence cannot be dismissed as a social accident (Davis, 1951). Accordingly, they ask what functions are performed by religion in social life.

▲ Durkheim: Religion as a Societal Glue

In *The Elementary Forms of Religious Life* (1912/1965), the last of his major works, Émile Durkheim showed how religion serves the functions of social cohesion and social control in a study of the Arunta, an Australian aboriginal people. The Arunta practice **totemism,** a religious system in which a clan (a kin group) takes the name of, claims descent from, and attributes sacred properties to a plant or animal. Durkheim said that the totem plant or animal is not the source of totemism but a stand-in for the real source, society itself. He contended that religion—the totem ancestor, God, or some other supernatural force—is the symbolization of society. By means of religious rituals, the group in effect worships itself. For functionalists the primary functions of religion are the creation, reinforcement, and maintenance of social solidarity and social control.

Religious rituals operate in two ways: First, they provide vehicles by which we *reveal* to one another that we share a common mental state; second, they *create* among us a shared consciousness that contributes to a social bonding.

Durkheim argued that the religious person is not the victim of an illusion. Behind the symbol—religion—lies a real force and reality: society, which, like religion, provides moral authority and inspires a sense of self-sacrifice, devotion, and even divinity (see "Civil Religion," on pp. 363–364). Durkheim concludes that when religion is imperiled and not replaced by a satisfying substitute, society itself is jeopardized: Individuals pursue their private interests without regard to the dictates of the larger social enterprise.

▲ Meaning and Uncertainty

Although science can tell us much about physical, chemical, and biological processes, it cannot inform us about the purpose of the universe and our place in it. It cannot tell us what the meaning of our lives is. While some people are satisfied with the notion that the universe and

life have no ultimate purpose, and that our existence as beings is ended with death, most people are not. One important function of religion is to provide answers to such questions. The answers that religion provides stress the supernatural and often link the individual to the supernatural through an intense emotional experience.

By focusing on questions of meaning and purpose, religion also helps people in dealing with life's uncertainties and tragedies: sudden deaths, disasters, epidemics, droughts, famines, wars, accidents, sickness, social disorder, guilt, personal defeat, humiliation, and injustice. Religion also often is involved in the transitional stages of life. Most religions celebrate and explain the major events of the life cycle—birth, puberty, marriage, and death—through rites of passage (ceremonies marking the transition from one status to another).

▲ Functionalism and Social Change

Another function religion performs is to serve as an impetus to social change (Warner, 1993). Social changes that are legitimated and justified in shared religious terms may be easier to accept and may proceed with less disruption than those that have a purely secular basis.

For example, African-American churches have historically made a significant contribution to the mobilization of protest, as was evident in the civil rights movements of the 1950s and 1960s. African-American churches provided the civil rights movement of the 1960s with an established mass base, a leadership structure that for the most part was economically independent of the white power structure, meeting places for the organization of protest activities, and a viable financial foundation. Currently, African-American churches are a major force in the economic development and revitalization of inner-city neighborhoods. Similarly, the gay liberation movement has practiced the art of church-based mobilization. The Metropolitan Community Church in New York City was at the organizational center of the movement to legitimate gay culture in the United States.

The Conflict Perspective

From the writings of functionalist theorists we gain a view of religion as a valuable and positive source promoting social integration and solidarity. We derive a quite different image from conflict theorists. Some of them depict religion as a weapon in the service of ruling elites who use it to hold in check the explosive tensions produced by social inequality and injustice. Others see religion as a source of social conflict and point to religious strife in the Middle East, India, and Northern Ireland. Still others, not so different from functionalists, see religion as a source of social change.

▲ Marx: Religion as the Opium of the People

The stimulus for many of the contributions made by conflict theorists comes from the work of Karl Marx. Marx (1844/1960:43–44) portrayed religion as a painkiller for the frustration, deprivation, and subjugation experienced by oppressed peoples: "the opium of the people." He said it soothes their distress but that any relief it may provide is illusory.

Marx saw religion as producing an other-worldly focus that diverts the oppressed from seeking social change in this world. More particularly, religion engenders a false consciousness among the working class that interferes with its attainment of true class consciousness. The focus on the supernatural and the afterlife also alienates people from themselves by directing their attention away from the material conditions of their own existence and their potential for controlling their own lives. This process of alienation is one of the primary mechanisms enabling the ruling class to dominate the working class and to exploit them for their labor power (Marx, 1844/1960:122).

▲ Maintaining the Status Quo

Conflict theorists see an inherently conservative aspect to religion. The sense of the sacred links a person's present experience with meanings derived from the group's traditional past. Religious beliefs and practices provide taken-for-granted truths that are powerful forces militating against new ways of thinking and behaving. Practices handed down from previous generations, including institutional inequalities and inequities, become defined as God-approved ways and highly resistant to change.

For example, American slavery was justified as part of God's "natural order." In 1863 the Presbyterian Church of the South met in General Synod and passed a resolution declaring slavery to be a divine institution ordained by God. In 1954 segregation was justified on similar grounds. Louisiana State Senator W. M. Rainach defended segregation in 1954: "Segregation is a natural order—created by God, in His wisdom, who made black men black and white men white" (*Southern School News,* 1954:3). Likewise, the Hindu religion threatens believers who fail to obey caste rules with reincarnation (rebirth) at a lower caste level or as an animal. Imperialism has often been supported by religious or quasi-religious motivations and beliefs. In the 1890s President William McKinley justified his decision to wage the expansionist war against Spain and seize Cuba and the Philippines as a way of "Christianizing" and civilizing these people (McGuire, 1981:188).

Religious organizations themselves are frequently motivated to legitimate the status quo because they also have vested interests to protect, including power, land, and wealth (Collins, 1981).

▲ Conflict Theory and Social Change

Some conflict theorists see religion as an active force shaping the contours of social life. Thus, it can play a critical part in the birth and consolidation of new social structures and arrangements. While acknowledging that some aspects of religion inhibit change, like the functionalists, they point out that others challenge existing social arrangements and encourage change (Billings, 1990). Under some circumstances religion can be a profoundly revolutionary force that holds out a vision to people of how things might or ought to be. Religion is not invariably a functional or conservative factor in society, but often one of the chief, and at times the only, channel for bringing about social revolution.

Throughout history religion has provided an unusually effective vehicle for change because of its ability to unite people and their social lives. American history has been no exception. The religious movements associated with the Great Awakening in the late 18th and early 19th centuries were an important impetus to the abolitionist movement and later to the temperance and prohibition movements. They also had an impact on the democratization of the U.S. political system, promoting popular participation in what was largely an oligarchy of the economically privileged.

Education

Social scientists view **learning** as a relatively permanent change in behavior or capability that results from experience. Because learning is so vital to social life, societies seldom leave it to chance. Most societies undertake to transmit particular attitudes, knowledge, and skills to their members through formal, systematic training—what sociologists call the institution of **education.**

Education is one aspect of the many-sided process of socialization by which people acquire behaviors essential for effective participation in society (see Chapter 3). It entails an explicit process in which some individuals assume the status of teacher and others the status of student and carry out their associated roles.

Schools initially came into existence several thousand years ago to prepare a select few for a limited number of leadership and professional positions. Only in the past century or so have public schools become the primary vehicles by which the members of a society are taught the three Rs,

affording them the literacy skills required by large-scale industrial and bureaucratic organizations. The curricula of schools—such "core" subjects as mathematics, natural science, and social science—are remarkably similar throughout the world. Exactly how government interacts with education, however, differs cross-culturally.

In this section we will examine the bureaucratic structure of schools, the effectiveness of schools in the United States and elsewhere around the world, alternatives to traditional public education, and the availability of higher education. We will then take a look at the functionalist, conflict, and interactionist perspectives on education.

The Bureaucratic Structure of Schools

Until a few generations ago schooling in the United States usually took place in a one-room schoolhouse. One teacher taught all eight grades, with the more advanced and older students helping the less capable and younger students with their lessons. As long as the schools remained relatively small, they could operate on the basis of face-to-face interaction.

Like hospitals, factories, and businesses, however, schools grew larger and more complex. To attain their goals, they had to standardize and routinize many of their operations and establish formal operating and administrative procedures. In brief, they turned to a bureaucratic arrangement, a social structure made up of a hierarchy of statuses and roles prescribed by explicit rules and procedures and based on a division of function and authority (see Chapter 4). ◄ pp. 115–118

At the very top of this organizational arrangement is the federal government, which through a variety of agencies, including the Department of Education and the federal court system, profoundly influences educational life. State educational authorities set the number of days in a school year and allocate state money for specified programs.

The formal organization of American schools and colleges typically consists of four levels: (1) the board of education or trustees, (2) administrators, (3) teachers or professors, and (4) students. The control of most schools and colleges is vested in an elected or appointed *board* of laypeople. The board generally appoints and assigns administrators and teachers, decides on the nature of educational programs, determines building construction, and approves operational budgets. The *administrators*—superintendents, principals, presidents, chancellors, and deans— are responsible for executing the policies of the board. Although in theory the board determines policy, in practice many policy questions are settled by administrators. *Teachers* are the immediate day-to-day link between the larger system and individual *students,* the latter occupying the lowest position in the school bureaucracy. In sum, the school system is characterized by a chain of command, a network of positions functionally interrelated for the purpose of accomplishing educational objectives.

By virtue of bureaucratic arrangements, most school environments are remarkably standardized in both their physical and social characteristics. These patterns are most apparent at the elementary and secondary school levels. For example, time is usually highly formalized. The Pledge of Allegiance is followed by math at 8:35, which is followed by reading at 9:10, which is followed by recess, and so on over the course of the day.

Individual behavior is governed by sets of rules—no loud talking during desk work, raise your hand to talk during discussions, keep your eyes on your paper during tests, and no running in the halls. The physical layout of the school and the omnipresent symbols of adult authority emphasize and reinforce the subordinate status of the pupils.

The Effectiveness of Schools

In 1983 *A Nation at Risk* warned Americans that the crisis in their public schools posed a threat to national security and economic vitality. Twenty years later, another commission evaluating public education in the United States found that test scores had not changed in 30 years, high school graduation rates had declined, students were doing no more homework, and overall there was little improvement (Chubb et al., 2003). The U.S. economy had done well, they concluded, in spite of public education, not because of it. Further, although the commission found improvements in the distribution of resources to schools, it did not find any decrease in the ethnic and racial achievement gap that haunts the United States. High school graduation rates are currently highest for Asian Americans (85.7 percent), followed closely by whites (84.9 percent) but more distantly by blacks (78.5 percent) and Hispanics (57.0 percent). The disparities are much greater at the college level, with 42.9 percent of Asian Americans finishing college, but only 26.1 percent of whites, 16.5 percent of blacks, and 10.6 percent of Hispanics (U.S. Census Bureau, 2003). Although high schools could use help, the commission concluded that elementary and middle schools, where fundamentals are taught and learning patterns are set for life, are in need of a "thorough reform" (Chubb et al., 2003).

Not all the news is bad, however. Recently, Scholastic Aptitude Test (SAT) scores have been rising (see Figure 11.3). The differences between males and females have been narrowing, starting to close the large gaps that opened in the 1980s.

Of course, the effectiveness of schools and academic achievement of students depends not only on what happens in schools but also on the structural inequities we discussed in Chapters 6, 7, and 8, and on the larger social and cultural environments of the students, including their families and communities, and the environment in which the school is located.

▲ Rating Education Globally

In 2003, a U.S. Department of Education study ranked the fourth and eighth graders of many countries in mathematics and science (TIMSS,

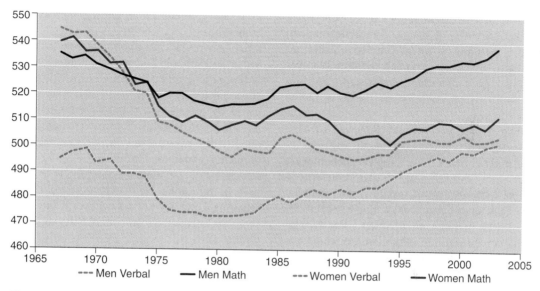

Figure 11.3 **SAT Scores by Gender, 1967–2003**

Source: Figure generated by the authors using data on 2003 college-bound seniors provided by the College Entrance Examination Board, and available at http://www.collegeboard.com/about/news_info/cbsenior/yr2003/html/links.html.

2006). The study was a repeat of two earlier studies, conducted four and eight years previously. Fourth-grade exam results for U.S. students did not change appreciably over the eight-year period, but they did fall in the rankings with other countries. In mathematics, U.S. fourth graders were 8th of 15 ranked countries, behind Singapore, Japan, Hong Kong, England, Latvia, Hungary, and the Netherlands, and in science, they were 5th of 15 countries. While eighth graders' test scores had improved since the 1995 TIMSS exams and their country rankings also had improved, they still placed much lower than fourth graders, behind 14 other countries in mathematics and behind 8 in science. A 2000 study by the Organization for Economic Cooperation and Development ranking 15-year-olds from 28 countries had similar results, with U.S. students just barely average in reading test scores and below average in mathematics and science (U.S. Census Bureau, 2003).

Psychologist Harold W. Stevenson and his colleagues (1992, 1993), who spent more than 15 years in cross-cultural studies of U.S., Chinese, and Japanese educational practices and school experiences, found that American schoolchildren lag behind schoolchildren in Japan and Taiwan from the day they enter school. Stevenson and his colleagues blamed the poorer performance of American youngsters on the shorter school year in the United States—180 days versus 240 in Japan and Taiwan—and the shorter school day (a half hour to two hours shorter). They also cite time spent on academic activities (less in the United States) and on viewing television (more in the United States). In addition, they found that Japanese and Taiwanese parents placed greater emphasis than their American counterparts on the importance of children's working hard at school and on homework.

But a Department of Education study reached different conclusions about why U.S. students lag behind (Sanchez, 1996). Its researchers surveyed teachers, analyzed math and science curricula of each nation, and videotaped classrooms to see how the subjects were being taught. They found that U.S. students spend more class time on science and math and are usually assigned more homework than students in Japan. They also found that heavy television watching was as common in Japan as in the United States.

The researchers did find, however, that the *way* math and science were taught differed. In Japan and Germany, for example, teachers were much more likely to develop math concepts in the classroom instead of simply stating the concept. The study also found that expectations were lower in the United States. The eighth-grade math curriculum in the United States was similar to a seventh-grade curriculum in most of the other countries studied. A 2005 study of science education in the United States graded state standards for science and awarded only 7 A's (Gross et al., 2005). Thirteen states got F's, and the others fell in between.

▲ Characteristics of Effective Schools

Social scientists have examined what makes a school effective. Child psychiatrist Michael Rutter (1979) studied London students and schools. The critical element distinguishing schools was their "ethos" or "climate." Successful schools fostered expectations that order would prevail in the classrooms, and they did not leave matters of student discipline to be worked out by individual teachers. As a result, it was easier to be a good teacher. Additionally, the effective schools emphasized academic concerns—care by teachers in lesson planning, group instruction, high achievement expectations for students, a high proportion of time spent on instruction and learning activities, the assignment and checking of homework, and student use of the library. The researchers also found that schools that fostered respect for students as responsible people and held high expectations for appropriate behavior achieved better academic results. In the more successful schools, many students assumed responsibilities

as group captains or as participants in school assemblies.

Other research supports the conclusion that successful schools foster expectations that order will prevail and that learning is a serious matter (Lee and Bryk, 1989). Much of the success enjoyed by private and Catholic schools has derived from their ability to provide students with an ordered environment and strong academic demands (Coleman, Hoffer, and Kilgore, 1982a; Putka, 1991). Academic achievement is just as high in the public sector when the policies and resulting behavior are like those in the private sector (Coleman, Hoffer, and Kilgore, 1982b; Grann, 1999).

Alternatives to Traditional Public Schools

In a movement some predict will transform education in the United States, parents are increasingly choosing to educate their children in ways other than enrolling them in traditional public schools. The number of students attending charter schools and private schools or being educated at home has increased significantly in the past several years (see Figure 11.4).

The number of charter schools, which receive taxpayer money but make their own decisions about how to teach, grew from none to 2,400 in about a decade (Maranto, 2003). Except for those on Indian reservations, there was only one charter school in the United States in 1992; in 2002, charter schools were serving 2.2 percent of the public school students in California, 4 percent of those in Delaware, Michigan, and Colorado, 7.4 percent in Arizona, and 14.5 percent of the students in Washington, D.C. (Palmer and Gau, 2003). Charter schools vary widely in their instructional approach and in the degree to which they are used in each state; in some states, "cyber" charter schools are being tested, with students "attending school" over the computer (Fletcher, 2002).

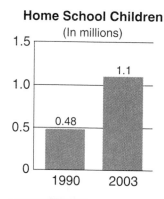

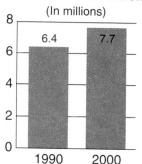

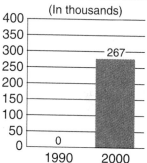

Figure 11.4   **Classroom Alternatives**
Traditional public schools are facing a new level of competition.

Source: U.S. Census Bureau, 2003; Princiotta, Bielick, and Chapman, 2006.

Private schools educate even more students: 14 percent of all kindergarten through 12th graders were enrolled in private schools in 2000 (U.S. Census Bureau, 2003).

Enrollment in private Christian academies doubled in 10 years. Catholic schools, which had had a long period of declining enrollment, now have increasing enrollment and increasing numbers of non-Catholic students (Sanchez, 1997). The provision of vouchers for low-income children to attend private schools has increased private-school enrollments.

While not yet available as an alternative to elementary or secondary school, online learning is providing older Americans with the opportunity to take college classes at home or enabling students to take distance education classes in addition to their on-campus classes. In 2003, 8.4 percent of U.S. college students were taking distance education courses (U.S. Census Bureau, 2003).

The number of students taught at home was approximately 1.1 million in 2003, 2.2 percent of the total U.S. student population (Princiotta, Bielick, and Chapman, 2006). Home schooling is legal in every state. Although it is difficult to compare achievement among home-schooled

and other students, research indicates that home-schooled children do well on standardized tests (Byfield, 2001). Studies also show that home-schooled children do not suffer disadvantages in self-esteem, leadership, or other dimensions of personal development (Medlin, 2000).

The Availability of Higher Education

Despite our cherished picture of the United States as a place where education is available to all, college and university student populations are highly skewed in terms of race, ethnicity, and family income. Although we tend to picture college students as "youngsters" fresh out of high school, only 20 percent of the nation's undergraduates are young people between 18 and 22 years of age who are pursuing a parent-financed education. Two-fifths of all students are part-timers; and more than one-third of all undergraduates are over age 25.

The likelihood that African Americans and Hispanics receive a college education has improved over the past 40 years, but sharp disparities with whites and now Asian Americans remain (U.S. Census Bureau, 2003). Many factors make it difficult for minority youth to gain entrance to and then remain in college. First, many of the students have weaker academic preparation in elementary and secondary schools than white students. Second, most campuses lack a "critical mass" of minority students and faculty who can serve as role models and make new students feel at home. Third, many minority students are first-generation collegians, and they do not secure the emotional or financial support from home that second- and third-generation collegians receive (Johnson, 1988).

The cost of a college education plays an important role in selecting who will receive a degree. In recent years the cost of higher education has outpaced the growth in family income and of available financial aid and is nearly triple the rate of inflation. Families with a child in a private college were found to spend a third of their income on college costs, up from a quarter in the early 1990s, and families with a child attending a public university spend about a fifth of their income on college (Whitson, 2006). Early admissions programs are thought to work to the disadvantage of low-income applicants (Mathews, 2003). And although half of all students receive some kind of financial assistance, one study showed that white students received a larger dollar amount of aid per student (Bruno, 1996).

The Functionalist Perspective

Viewed from the functionalist perspective, schools make a number of vital contributions to the survival and perpetuation of modern societies. Functionalists see schools as serving to complete socialization, socially integrate a diverse population, screen and select individuals, and develop new knowledge. In this section we will look at each of these functions in more detail.

▲ Completing Socialization

Many preliterate and peasant societies lack schools. They socialize their youngsters in the same "natural" way that parents teach their children to walk or talk. According to functionalists, the knowledge and skills required by contemporary living cannot be satisfied in a more or less automatic and "natural" way. Instead, a specialized educational agency is needed to transmit to young people the ways of thinking, feeling, and acting mandated by a rapidly changing urban and technologically based society.

▲ Social Integration

Functionalists say that the education system functions to inculcate the dominant values of a society and shape a common national mind.

Functionalists say that one of the functions of public education is social integration. In performing this function, schools promote dominant values and try to shape a common national consciousness.

Within the United States students learn what it means to be an American, become literate in the English language, gain a common heritage, and acquire mainstream standards and rules. Youngsters from diverse ethnic, religious, and racial backgrounds are immersed within the same Anglo-American culture and prepared for responsible citizenship (see Chapter 7). Historically, the nation's schools have played a prominent part in Americanizing the children of immigrants (Dunn, 1993); now, by including diversity as a part of the curriculum, many schools are also emphasizing the multicultural nature of the United States. Likewise, the schools are geared to integrating the poor and disadvantaged within the fabric of dominant, mainstream institutions. How well the educational institution performs these functions is a debatable matter.

▲ Screening and Selecting

We noted in Chapter 2 that all ◀— p. 58 societies ascribe some statuses to individuals independent of their unique qualities or abilities. Other statuses are achieved through choice and competition. No society entirely ignores individual differences or overlooks individual accomplishment and failure. Modern societies in particular must select certain of their youth for positions that require special talents. The educational institution commonly performs this function, serving as an agency for screening and selecting individuals for different types of jobs. By conferring degrees, diplomas, and credentials that are prerequisites for many technical, managerial, and professional positions, it determines which young people will have access to scarce positions and offices of power, privilege, and status. For many members of modern society, the schools function as "mobility escalators," allowing able, gifted individuals to ascend the social ladder (Krymkowski, 1991).

▲ Research and Development

For the most part, schools are designed to produce people who fit into society, not people who set out to change it. However, schools, particularly universities, may not only transmit culture; they also may add to the cultural heritage. Contemporary U.S. society places a good deal of emphasis on the development of new knowledge, especially in the physical and biological sciences, medicine, and engineering. In recent decades the nation's leading universities have increasingly become research centers. This emphasis on research has led universities to judge professors not primarily in terms of their competence as teachers but as researchers with a primary function of the university being viewed as research.

A survey of tenure-track faculty members at four-year institutions revealed that the more hours an instructor spends in class per week, the lower the pay; faculty who teach only graduate students get paid the most; and the more time faculty members spend on research, the higher the compensation (Jacobson, 1992). Functionalism sees the university combining the functions of research and education. Even when students are not themselves involved in research projects, they benefit from the intellectual stimulation a research orientation brings to university life.

The Conflict Perspective

Conflict theorists see schools as agencies that reproduce and legitimate the current social order through the functions they perform. By reproducing and legitimating the existing social order, the educational institution is seen as benefiting some individuals and groups at the expense of others (Collins, 1977, 1979, 1988b). Let's take a closer look at how conflict theorists think this occurs.

▲ Reproducing the Social Relations of Production

Some conflict theorists depict U.S. schools as reflecting the needs of capitalist production and as social instruments for convincing the population that private ownership and profit are just and in the best interests of the entire society (Apple, 1982). The **correspondence principle** states that the social relations of work find expression in the social relations of the school (Bowles and Gintis, 1976). Schools mirror the workplace and hence on a day-to-day basis prepare children for adult roles in the job market. The authoritarian structure of many schools reproduces the bureaucratic hierarchy of the corporation, rewarding diligence, submissiveness, and compliance. The system of grades employed to motivate students parallels the wage system for motivating workers. In short, the schools are seen as socializing a compliant labor force for the capitalist economy.

▲ Control Devices

Conflict theorists agree with functionalist theorists that schools are agencies for drawing minorities and the disadvantaged into the dominant culture. But they do not see the function in benign terms. Sociologist Randall Collins (1976) contended that the educational system serves the interests of the dominant group by defusing the threat posed by minority ethnic groups. In large, conflict-ridden, multiethnic societies like the United States, the schools become instruments to Americanize minority people. Compulsory education erodes ethnic differences and loyalties and transmits to minorities and those at the bottom of the social hierarchy the values and lifeways of the dominant group. Schools, then, are viewed by conflict theorists as control devices employed by established elites.

▲ Productive Capital

Conflict theorists see the research and development function of the universities quite differently than functionalist theorists do. For example, Michael W. Apple (1982) provided a Marxist twist to the functionalist argument by contending that the educational institution produces the technical and administrative knowledge necessary for running a capitalist order.

Viewed in this manner, education is part of the system of production. It not only reproduces existing social arrangements but also develops the know-how needed by capitalists to fuel the economy and gain competitive advantage in world markets (Barrow, 1990).

▲ Credentialism

Collins (1979) also downplayed the functionalist argument that schools serve as mobility escalators. He cited evidence that students acquire little technical knowledge in school and that most technical skills are learned on the job. Although more education is needed to obtain most jobs, Collins said that this development is not explained by the technical requirements of the job. The level of skills required by typists, receptionists, salesclerks, teachers, assembly-line workers, and many others is not much different than it was a generation or so ago. Collins called these tendencies **credentialism**—the requirement that a worker have a degree for its own sake, not because it certifies skills needed for the performance of a job.

Because education functions as a certification of class membership more than of technical skills, it functions as a means of class inheritance. For example, Scholastic Aptitude Test (SAT) scores play a particularly important role in determining acceptance or rejection by the nation's elite colleges and universities; approximately 84 percent of all U.S. four-year colleges use the SAT for admissions purposes. SAT scores also are highly correlated with family income and parents' education, and vary with race and ethnicity (see Figure 11.5). Asian-American and white students have the highest scores on average, with Asian Americans doing particularly well on the mathematics portion of the test. The SAT scores of Native Americans are lower, those of Hispanics still lower, and those of African Americans the lowest.

At one time a college degree brought an elite occupational status with elite pay; today it brings a middle-class status with middle-class

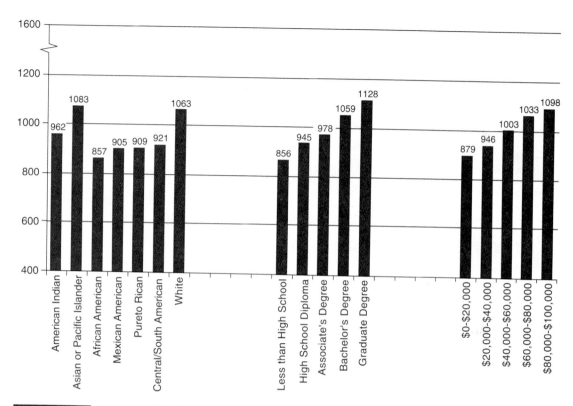

Figure 11.5 Average Total SAT Scores of College Bound Seniors by Race/Ethnicity, Parents' Education, and Family Income

Total SAT scores, the sum of scores for the verbal and the math tests, vary considerably by socioeconomic status and race/ethnicity. Verbal and math scores follow the same patterns across the categories in this figure, except that Asian/Pacific Islanders score higher than whites on the math test, and a little lower than whites on the verbal test.

Source: Figure generated by the authors using data on 2003 college-bound seniors provided by the College Entrance Examination Board and available at: http://www.collegeboard.com/prod_downloads/about/news_info/cbsenior/yr2003/pdf/2003_TOTALGRP_PRD.pdf.

pay. Even so, a degree after high school seemingly affords financial benefits (see Figure 11.6). A study that compared data from identical twins to distinguish the impact of nurture from that of nature estimated that on average each year of education (from grade school through graduate school) adds 16 percent to a person's lifetime earnings (Passell, 1992). Moreover, the gap between those with more and less education appears to be increasing. Some economists say that the United States is moving to a two-tiered society, with education levels explaining much of the division (Freadhoff, 1992).

The Interactionist Perspective

Classrooms can be seen as self-contained little worlds teeming with behavior. Symbolic interactionists undertake to capture these little worlds in their work. These sociologists do not

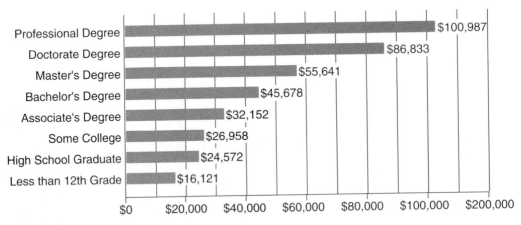

Figure 11.6 The Financial Value of a Postsecondary Education: Mean Earnings by Education

Average income increases with greater education.

Source: Figure generated by the authors with data from the U.S. Census Bureau (2003).

view the school as a "black box" in which something goes in and something comes out. Instead, they are interested in the processes occurring in schools; we will look at some of those processes in this section.

▲ Communication

Communication is the heart of classroom life. Philip W. Jackson (1968) estimated from his observations in several elementary classrooms that teachers average over 200 interpersonal exchanges every hour of the school day. Much of the communication is one-way, with the teacher telling and students listening. Indeed, since the teacher functions as the communication *gatekeeper,* students are often frustrated in taking the initiative in communicative interaction. Additionally, the physical arrangement of the traditional classroom—with students seated in rows facing the teacher—effectively channels most communication flows through the teacher. One consequence of these procedures and arrangements is that they tend to produce individuals who are programmed for input and not communication output.

▲ Social Inequality

Classroom research also sheds provocative insights on social inequality (Mehan, 1992). Many data suggest, for instance, that schools perform relatively well with upper- and middle-class youngsters. We would expect this to be the case, for the schools are staffed by middle-class teachers, the school's structure is modeled after middle-class life, and better school facilities are provided for these youngsters. According to a survey conducted by the College of Education at Ohio State University, more than one-third of its student teachers did not feel they were competent to teach youngsters of different races, cultures or income levels (Hanley, 1988). Big-city schools, which have the poorest youngsters with the most difficult problems, get the least money, while suburban schools, which have the wealthiest youngsters from the best-educated homes, get the most money. Tracking, or ability grouping, tends to be associated with social class, race, and ethnicity, with minority group members and those with low incomes ending up in the non-college-prep tracks (Levine and Havighurst, 1992).

Interactionists and conflict theorists are also interested in what they call the **hidden curriculum,** which consists of a complex of unarticulated values, attitudes, and behaviors that subtly mold children in the image preferred by the dominant institutions. Teachers model and reinforce traits that embody middle-class standards—industry, responsibility, conscientiousness, reliability, thoroughness, self-control, and efficiency. Even when teachers are originally from another social class, they still view their role as one of encouraging the development of a middle-class outlook on such matters as thrift, cleanliness, punctuality, neatness, ambition, sexual morality, and respect for property and established authority. Children learn to be quiet, to be on time, to line up, to wait their turn, to please their teachers, and to conform to group pressures. In some cases middle-class teachers, without necessarily being aware of their bias, find inner-city and minority children unacceptable. Their students tend to respond by taking the attitude, "If you don't like me, I won't cooperate with you." The net result is that the youngsters fail to acquire basic reading, writing, and math skills.

▲ Self-Fulfilling Prophecies

Educational self-fulfilling prophecies, or *teacher-expectation effects,* also victimize inner-city and minority children. The children fail to learn because those who are charged with teaching them do not believe that they will learn, do not expect that they can learn, and do not act toward them in ways that help them to learn (Clark, 1965). Tracking can feed into teacher-expectation effects. If a group is labeled low achieving, teachers are likely to approach it differently. Among inner-city and minority youngsters, negative teacher-expectation effects breed student alienation and school failure, encourage oppositional forms of behavior designed to undermine the school's control strategies, and foster attitudes that lead to the mocking, taunting, and ostracism of children who do their homework and strive toward academic excellence (Solomon, 1992).

Medicine

Like the educational institution, the functions now carried out by the medical institution were once embedded in the activities of the family and religious institutions. Only in relatively recent times has **medicine** emerged as a distinct institution, providing an enduring set of cultural patterns and social relationships responsible for problems of health and disease. The World Health Organization defines **health** as "a state of complete physical, mental, and social well-being and not merely the absence of disease or infirmity." We usually assess people's health by how well they are able to function in their daily lives and adapt to a changing environment. Health, then, has a somewhat different meaning for a soldier, a nursing home resident, an airline pilot, a steelworker, a high school football player, a presidential candidate, and a computer programmer. In contrast to health, most of us think of disease as an undesirable, serious, and limiting circumstance. **Disease** is a condition in which an organism does not function properly because of biological causes. The problems may result from microbial infection, dietary deficiency, heredity, or a harmful environmental agent.

In this section we will look at the American health care delivery system, consider health care costs and managed care, and compare the U.S. system with health care in other countries. Then we will see what the sociological perspectives contribute to our thinking about medicine.

The U.S. Health Care Delivery System

Many societies have evolved one or more "specialist" positions to deal with sickness (Hughes, 1968). Curers, shamans, physicians, nurses, and other practitioners are relied upon to explain illness and to offer means for eliminating or controlling it. Drugs, poultices, surgery, bone-setting, confinement, acupuncture, electric shock, leeching, talking, ritual, magic, and appeal to the supernatural are techniques used by medical practitioners in one or more societies. Additionally, medical practitioners serve as gatekeepers who legitimately channel people into the sick role. And in modern societies physicians certify that people have been born, have died, are fit to work, are eligible for disability benefits, are entitled to accident claims, and are a danger to themselves or society.

How does the United States deal with sickness? In this section we will examine the health care system in the United States, including a discussion of hospitals, physicians, and nurses.

▲ A Disease-Cure System

In some senses the United States does not have a "health care system" but a "disease-cure system" instead (Konner, 1993; Spiegel, 1994). The public believes, and a good many physicians behave as if, most illnesses are curable. Americans typically view the body as if it were a machine with replaceable parts: Defects can be identified, removed, and replaced through medical treatment, be it by means of drugs, surgery, organ transplants, or gene therapy.

The expectation of cure in the U.S. health care system has generated an explosion of invasive, expensive, and often risky medical interventions. The emphasis falls on disease, not on the people who have the diseases. For example, most clinicians and researchers in the field of coronary artery disease concentrate on ways to clear out fatty plaque buildups in arteries or to replace clogged arteries surgically. These techniques do not cure the disease, work less often than we wish, are performed at great risk to patients, and cost a colossal amount of money.

Much evidence suggests that behaviors such as eating a diet low in saturated fat and cholesterol, avoiding smoking, and getting moderate exercise can both prevent and reverse much heart disease. Yet 31 percent of U.S. adults meet the medical definition of obesity, with another 65 percent of the population overweight (National Center for Health Statistics, 2005). Although some have a genetic predisposition for weight gain, our lifestyle choices play a major role. Similarly, a 2005 Harvard study found that more than a third of cancer deaths worldwide could be prevented if people changed their behaviors (Danaei et al., 2005). Smoking, drinking alcohol, not eating enough fruits and vegetables, overweight and obesity, practicing unsafe sex, and lack of exercise all were found to be cancer risk factors that, if avoided, could prevent 2.43 million cancer deaths annually. But rather than focusing on disease prevention and promoting health, most Americans still look to the "disease-cure system" to solve their problems. Social pathologies such as drug and alcohol abuse and poor health practices such as lack of exercise and unhealthy diet show up in medical costs for all of us (Kuttner, 1994; Health and Human Services, 2000).

▲ Hospitals

Separate facilities for the ill came into existence among the ancient Greeks. But not until the Middle Ages in western Europe did the hospital movement begin in earnest. By 1450 there were some 600 hospitals in England alone. Most hospitals were run by Catholic religious orders because healing and health care were deemed to be the province of religion. The hospitals also cared for the poor, the disabled, and the itinerant. The linking of medical and social functions had grave health consequences. Travelers housed with sick people in one hospital would then carry germs to the next hospital, readily infecting people whose resistance to disease was already low. Toward the end of the 17th century and during the 18th century, financial abuses and the mismanagement of funds by some religious orders led local governments to take on greater responsibility for the management of hospitals. About the same time, care of the indigent was physically segregated in facilities separate from the ill (Rosen, 1963).

By the late 19th century, hospital services were improving. Advances in medical research, especially bacteriology, provided a stronger scientific basis for treatment and the control of infection. New diagnostic tools such as X rays and advances in surgical procedures made many diseases, injuries, and deformities more amenable to medical operations. By the turn of the century, the trustees of charity hospitals began to woo doctors who cared for well-to-do patients at home. An increasing number of charity hospitals refurbished their rooms and advertised their amenities. In the process the hospitals ceded considerable control to private physicians, who were more concerned with making the hospital a workshop for the treatment of paying patients than a center for administering charitable care. Hospitals became businesses governed by commercial incentives. As insurance developed first for hospital bills and later for physicians' bills, the hospital industry and the medical profession flourished. By 1965 Congress had established Medicare to pay some of the health care costs of the elderly, and Medicaid for those of the "deserving" poor. By the mid-1960s, then, hospitals, physicians, private insurers, and the government had devised a system for financing health care that was ripe for big business and the emergence of for-profit hospital chains (Gray, 1991; Lindorff, 1992).

▲ Physicians

Sociologist Paul Starr (1982) traced the transformation of health care from a household service to a market commodity and the rise of the private medical practice. He showed that well into the 19th century most U.S. doctors eked out scant incomes. Following the Civil War, however, a contracting household economy, a growing urban population, and more efficient transportation and communication expanded the market for medical services. By the turn of the 20th century doctors were well on the road to endowing their profession with a "cultural authority" sufficient to justify claims to self-regulation, state

protection, client deference, and control of the means of work. In turn, doctors capitalized on these gains to develop medical specialties and mutual networks that decreased competition and increased their economic and political power. By the 1930s private practitioners had acquired sufficient influence and prestige to establish themselves as virtually the sole arbiters of medicine in the United States. They dominated hospitals, medical technology, and other health practitioners, including nurses and pharmacists. Additionally, doctors institutionalized their authority through a system of medical education and standardized educational licensing.

▲ The Doctor-Patient Relationship

Interaction between a physician and patient was traditionally governed by inequality. Like other professionals, doctors derived their power from their command of an esoteric body of knowledge acquired through academic training and leavened by a service orientation toward the client. The "competence gap" justified both the physician's assumption of authority and the client's trust, confidence, and compliance.

A 1991 survey conducted by the American Medical Association found that patients may no longer stand in such awe of physicians. Sixty-three percent of the American public agreed that "doctors are too interested in making money"; only 42 percent agreed that "doctors usually explain things well to their patients"; and only 31 percent agreed that "most doctors spend enough time with their patients" (Nazario, 1992). Consequently, a new type of relationship based on consumerism has emerged between many physicians and their patients. It focuses on the purchaser's (the patient's) rights and the seller's (the physician's) obligations. Nevertheless, a recent study of encounters between patients and doctors found that it is doctors who manage the direction of the discussion, even though it is patients who have questions to be answered (Roberts, 2000). Dissatisfaction with care provided by physicians and other factors have fostered the growth of alternative therapies, including chiropractic, acupuncture, biofeedback, homeopathic medicine, herbalism, and reflexology; a third of the population today consults alternative healers (Eisenberg et al., 1993).

▲ Nurses

The nursing profession grew out of the religious and charitable activities of early hospitals. Religious orders of nuns took on the care of the sick and the poor. By the latter half of the 19th century, however, increasing numbers of nonreligious personnel were employed to perform various custodial functions in hospitals. Since the jobs required no formal training and were deemed to be menial labor, many poor and uneducated women entered the field. This heritage has contributed to the undeservedly low prestige that the profession of nursing has long endured (Baer, 1991). Additionally, wages in nursing, like those in other fields with a large concentration of women, remain low even today, despite the fact that most nurses now earn a bachelor of science degree in nursing in a four-year college degree program, and many go on to secure master's degrees in specialized areas.

Through the years the profession of nursing has remained almost exclusively female—in 2002, 91.9 percent of America's nurses were women. About 60 percent of all registered nurses work in hospitals, where they serve simultaneously as managers of hospital wards and assistants to physicians. These dual functions often place nurses in situations of role conflict because they are responsible to both administrative and medical authorities. Nurses have been steadily acquiring more autonomy in health care. At the same time, their workloads have increased so greatly that many say they cannot give patients the quality of care they need (Gordon, 1997; Trafford, 2001).

Rising Health Care Costs: Is Managed Care the Answer?

From a virtual cottage industry dominated by individual physicians and not-for-profit hospitals, health care is evolving into a network of corporations running everything from hospitals and home health care services to retirement homes and health spas. The United States is the only western industrialized nation that does not guarantee basic health care services to all its citizens (Quadagno, 2005), yet its spending on health care is enormous. In 2004, health care expenditures accounted for 16 percent of the nation's gross domestic product (GDP), a proportion up from about 7 percent in 1970 (Kaufman and Stein, 2006). In contrast, only about 10 percent of the GDP of Canada, and less than 7 percent of that of Japan and the United Kingdom, is expended on

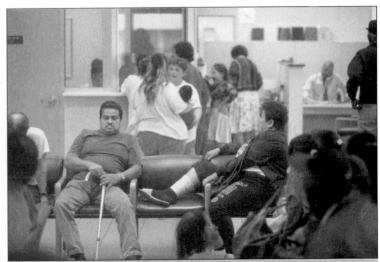

For families with no primary-care physician or clinic, hospital emergency rooms are increasingly used for noncritical care.

health care, although these nations provide universal coverage. So formidable has the medical care industry become that some critics have labeled it "the medical-industrial complex."

▲ What Accounts for the Rise in Costs?

A number of forces have pushed up the costs of medical care in the United States.

1. The classical rules that govern marketplace exchanges have not been applied to the health care industry. The sellers—doctors and hospitals—have traditionally determined the price and product options; and the buyers—patients—have bought what the sellers have ordered instead of shopping around.

2. Labor costs have risen sharply; since 1950 the number of hospital workers per bed has more than tripled. Simultaneously, administrative costs have grown three times faster since 1970 than costs for health care personnel.

3. The continual upgrading in the scope and intensity of medical services is costly. Technological advances include such accepted practices as hip replacement and coronary-bypass surgery, new therapies, and new diagnostic techniques.

4. The U.S. population is getting larger and older, and this fact alone contributes about 1 percentage point a year to the increase in real costs.

5. Modern medicine does not reduce the percentage of sick people. It actually increases it by keeping more people alive, although not cured.

6. Finally, we have expanded our concept of health to encompass mental and psychological difficulties and "conditions" such as infertility.

▲ Competitive Health Services

Soaring health care costs have led to new arrangements for financing health care. Their theme is "competition"—the notion that physicians, hospitals, and other health providers should compete for patients in a price-sensitive market, not unlike the markets for other goods and services. Another approach to holding down costs is to keep people out of the hospital. Increasingly, hospitals and independent medical companies are setting up satellite outpatient surgical centers, mobile diagnostic laboratories, hospices, and walk-in clinics for routine care. At the same time, government, in seeking to cut costs, has become progressively more involved in regulating the activities of both hospitals and physicians. The cost of government health care spending has mounted. In 1960 the federal government paid only 11 percent of the nation's health care costs; today it picks up more than 30 percent of the tab (U.S. Census Bureau, 2003).

▲ Managed Care

Medicine is increasingly becoming a corporate undertaking. Many physicians have set up professional corporations to achieve the benefits of group practice and to take advantage of special tax-sheltering provisions. Walk-in clinics—quick-treatment centers that do not require an appointment—are being established in countless communities. Private corporations such as Humana hire physicians for their health care clinics. And managed care arrangements, such as health maintenance organizations (HMOs) and preferred provider organizations (PPOs), are winning growing numbers of patients.

Managed care arrangements are designed to guide the process of patient care through the incorporation of payment plans, regulations on how and where patients can be treated, and requirements for providers of all aspects of care from prescription drug services to home health and hospice care. In 1984, nearly all insured employees in the United States were covered by conventional insurance without any managed care provisions. By 1990, 57 percent of all employees were covered by conventional insurance that used managed care arrangements (Weiss and

Lonnquist, 1994). Managed care also forms the basis of the new health care delivery systems in the country, such as HMOs and PPOs, and these systems are increasingly responsible for providing health services. HMOs had 79.5 million subscribers by the end of 2001, and in 2003 a third to a half of the populations of 17 states were enrolled in HMOs (U.S. Census Bureau, 2003).

Under health care network arrangements such as HMOs and PPOs, an employer or an insurer typically contracts with a network of physicians to provide its employees or members with health care for a fixed sum of money each year. Although many physicians complain that joining health care networks appreciably lessens their autonomy and incomes, the economic dictates of contemporary private practice often lead them to take this route.

▲ Does It Work?

Every year more than 57,000 people die in the United States because they fail to receive the health care that the medical profession knows they need, according to "The State of Health Care Quality 2003" (McMillen, 2003). The report included assessments of health care across the country and found the performance of the health care system to be "wildly inconsistent." When asked about the report's findings, the president of the American Academy of Family Physicians said, "We have an incredibly dysfunctional health care system." In a 2006 comparison of the United States and England, researchers found that although the United States spends more than twice as much money as England does on health care, U.S. residents are much less healthy than are citizens of England (Banks et al., 2006). Among other problems, many people in the United States do not have any health insurance (see Box 11.2), but well-to-do Americans also are less healthy than British people of the same socioeconomic status.

Critics worry that the financial incentives associated with HMOs and PPOs provide a disincentive to provide patients with quality care. A 2003 study showed that 31 cents of each dollar spent on health care in the United States pays for administrative costs, almost double the rate in Canada (Woolhandler, Campbell, and Himmelstein, 2003). For many health care consumers, the cost is too high. During a two-year period of study, a third of all Americans had no health insurance for part or all of the time, and half of all bankruptcy filings in the United States are due to medical bills (Quadagno, 2005).

One point of view is that HMOs maximize profit by keeping people healthy, focusing on health maintenance and disease prevention; another is that they maximize profit by failing to adequately provide services. The characteristics of managed care that save money—reduced hospital stays, more out-patient services to avoid hospitalization, limited choice of physicians, limited use of specialists, and others—are some of the aspects of managed care most condemned by those who feel it is transforming American health care in the wrong direction.

Alternatives to the U.S. Health Care System: A Global Perspective

Health care is managed differently in different countries. In China health care has been provided at essentially no charge for most citizens, although that is changing along with free-market changes. Health care was paid for with employer contributions for teachers and office and factory workers; with government contributions for students, the military, and government employees; and with contributions from communes for the rural population (Weiss and Lonnquist, 1994). In Great Britain 90 percent of the funding for its National Health Service comes from general taxation; only a minuscule amount comes from patient payments. Except for medications, dental care, and some optical treatments, for which there are minimal charges, health care is provided at no cost (Weiss and Lonnquist, 1994). In Kenya a national health service employs physicians and owns hospitals, but health care is also available from private practitioners, religious mission clinics, and traditional native folk healers (Cockerham, 2006).

Widespread dissatisfaction with the U.S. health care system has led some American leaders to contend that the United States should provide all its citizens with the essentials of adequate health care as an entitlement, regardless of their ability to pay, as is done in some other countries. How does such a system work? Let's take a closer look at Canada.

▲ Canada's Health Care Plan

In 1971, the Canada Health Act mandated that the government pay for all medically necessary physician and hospital services. It allowed the 11 provinces and two territories to administer their own programs, negotiate doctors' fees, and set hospital budgets.

The lower costs of health care in Canada are due to lower physician and hospital costs (physician fees are 2.4 times higher and hospital fees nearly 3 times higher in the United States than in Canada) and a slower rate in the introduction of new, expensive technology. Administration costs are also lower in Canada, where paperwork and administration absorb about 11 percent of the nation's health care spending; in the United States, some 24 percent goes to paperwork and administration.

Infant mortality rates are 20 percent lower in Canada than in the United States and Canadian life expectancy is three years longer. Moreover, death rates in U.S. and Canadian hospitals are similar for a variety of procedures. Significantly, U.S. citizens receive, on a per capita basis, only about three-quarters of the doctors' services that Canadians do. It seems that by capping fees for procedures, Canadians have increased rather than limited access to care because the arrangement has induced doctors to do more procedures to maintain their incomes.

But the Canadian government-sponsored health care system is not without its critics, who point to long waits for some medical procedures and services and limitations in services and hospital beds (Farnsworth, 1991).

In 2003, 8,000 physicians and medical students called for a national health program that would provide health insurance to all Americans, calling our current system profitable but chaotic (Richmond and Fein, 2003). Nearly 60 percent of survey respondents support a government-run health care system along with increased taxes to provide better health care coverage (Quadagno, 2005).

A single-payer system, or Canadian-style solution, for health care reform would decimate the U.S. health insurance industry in one swift stroke. It would require enormous increases in federal spending, and the government would very likely gain vast new powers over what services would be covered and which facilities would be expanded or shut down. But that power now is held by insurance companies. As the physicians calling for universal health insurance put it, "Physicians and patients alike are being held hostage to decisions of for-profit insurers" (Richmond and Fein, 2003).

The Functionalist Perspective

Functionalists note that health is essential to the preservation of the human species and organized social life. If societies are to function smoothly and effectively, there must be a reasonable supply of productive members to carry out vital tasks. Where large numbers of people are ill or physically unfit (as in some developing nations where malaria is widespread), low vitality, low productivity, and poverty abound as major social problems. Moreover, community personnel, resources, facilities, and funds must be withdrawn from other essential activities to care for the nonproducing sick (Hertzler, 1961).

Functionalists say the medical institution evolved across time to deal with problems of health and disease. More specifically, they see the medical institution performing a number of key functions in modern societies. First, it treats and seeks to cure disease. Second, the medical

Who Are the Uninsured?

If you are one of the lucky people in the United States who has health insurance, you probably don't know how much an office visit or a trip to the emergency room costs. Beyond your co-pay, it's likely that you don't know the cost of your antibiotic prescription or your blood test.

The uninsured know. Joshua Eyre, a 31-year-old self-employed teahouse owner, spent two weeks in the hospital having a series of tests aimed at finding the cause of his extraordinarily high blood pressure, but doctors were unable to determine anything conclusive. The tests ruled out some possible problems but came up with nothing definite—and the two weeks cost Eyre more than $27,000 (Ishida, 2003).

Joshua Eyre and 41 million other Americans—15 percent of the population—lack health insurance (Institute of Medicine, 2003). And although Joshua Eyre is white, it is more common that African Americans and Latinos be uninsured. More than 30 percent of Latino Americans are uninsured, and another 22 percent depend on Medicaid (DeNavas-Walt, Proctor, and Lee, 2005). About 20 percent of African Americans are uninsured, with a quarter dependent on Medicaid. About 10 percent of Asian and white Americans depend on Medicaid for health care, and about 15 percent are uninsured.

Quality of care received by patients varies in a similar way, with 85 percent of poor people experiencing worse care than high-income people and 53 percent of Hispanics and 43 percent of blacks experiencing worse care than whites (Kaufman and Stein, 2006).

What explains these differences? Uninsurance is related to the racial and ethnic differences in education, employment, and income that we have discussed in previous chapters. A higher proportion of black and Hispanic workers are unemployed or have jobs without benefits, including health insurance, than whites and Asian Americans. The poor and unemployed also obviously cannot afford to purchase private insurance coverage.

Our immigrant health care also is in crisis, with immigrants receiving about half the health care services that native-born Americans do, regardless of their legal status and insurance coverage (Connolly, 2005). Immigrant children are especially at risk, receiving in care only about a quarter as many of the health care dollars spent annually on native-born children.

Why should those of us who have health insurance and access to high-quality health care concern ourselves with those who do not? Beyond social decency, we should care because the 41 million uninsured people in

our country are associated with social and economic costs. The Institute of Medicine's 2003 report "Hidden Costs, Value Lost" points out that uninsurance causes developmental and educational losses in children, lost workforce productivity, financial risk and uncertainty in families with even a single uninsured person, and financial stresses and instability for health care institutions (Institute of Medicine, 2003). Extending health insurance to all Americans, it concludes, would reflect positively on our democratic commitment to "equal opportunity and mutual concern and respect"; it would also benefit the economy and our health care system and thus the entire society.

Questions for Discussion

1. How would a national plan for health insurance for all Americans change the access to health care for minority and low-income people and, as a consequence, benefit people who already have insurance?

2. Which ethnic/racial group presented in the figure has the highest proportion of job-based insurance? Who has the lowest percentage of privately purchased insurance? Based on what you have learned in previous chapters, why do these disparities persist?

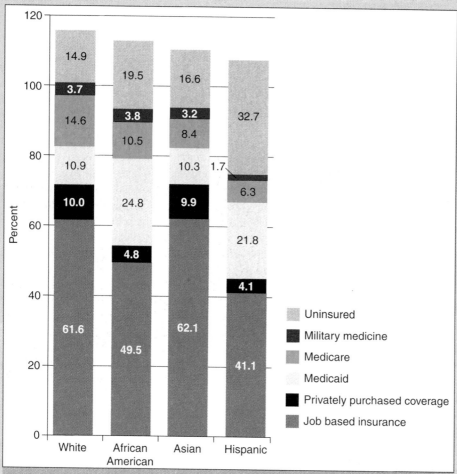

Health Insurance Coverage in the United States: Employment benefits provide health insurance coverage for the greatest percentage of U.S. citizens, but substantial numbers of people are uninsured.

Source: Figure generated by the authors using 2004 data from DeNavas-Walt, Proctor, and Lee (2005).
Note: Percentages do not add to 100 because people may be covered by more than one type of insurance.

institution attempts to prevent disease through health maintenance programs (HMOs), including vaccination, health education, periodic checkups, and public health and safety standards. Third, it undertakes research in the prevention, treatment, and cure of health problems. Fourth, it serves as an agency of social control by defining some behaviors as "normal" and "healthy" and others as "deviant" and "unhealthy."

Sociologist Talcott Parsons (1951) expanded upon the functionalist position in his analysis of the **sick role**—a set of cultural expectations that define what is appropriate and inappropriate behavior for people with a disease or health problem (see also Turner, 1987). He said one way societies contain the negative effects of health problems is through institutionalizing illness in a special role, one having the following characteristics:

- Sick people are exempt from their usual social roles and responsibilities. They need not attend school or go to work, and other people will not censure them for doing so.

- Sick people are not thought to be at fault for their condition. Being sick is a physical matter, not a moral one.

- Sick people have the duty to get well and "not enjoy themselves too much." Because being sick is an undesirable state, sick people are obligated to seek competent help from medical practitioners.

- Sick people should cooperate with medical practitioners and follow their instructions.

Like other functionalists, Parsons assumes illness must be socially controlled lest it impair societal functioning.

The Conflict Perspective

Implicit in the functionalist image of the sick role is the assumption that health care services are impartially and equally available to all members of a society. This image is challenged by conflict theorists (Waitzkin, 1983). They say that people of all societies prefer health to illness. Yet some people achieve better health than others because they have access to those resources that contribute to good health and to recovery should they become ill.

Conflict theorists point out that the higher our social class, the more likely we are to enjoy good health, receive good medical care, and live a long life. Poor people experience more disability and lower levels of health than affluent people. Even though access to health care among the poor has improved in recent years, low socioeconomic status is still the strongest predictor of illness and death in the United States and the world (Williams, 1998). It has been argued that educational differences are most responsible for this disparity, with well-educated people more likely to live a healthy lifestyle and to be able to avoid economic hardship (Mirowsky and Ross, 2003). There is also a racial divide. Much research indicates that racial and ethnic minorities receive lower quality health services than whites, even when their incomes and insurance coverage are the same (Smedley, Stith, and Nelson, 2003).

In practice, U.S. medical care has traditionally operated as a dual system in which the poor have utilized public sources—hospital outpatient departments, emergency rooms, and public clinics—while middle- and upper-income Americans use private sources such as physicians in private or group practice. Patients using public sources must often maneuver between multiple clinics to obtain their services, and the services are usually disease-oriented rather than preventive. In addition, the atmosphere in these institutions is often dehumanizing. Since African Americans, Hispanics, and Native Americans are more likely than whites to be poor, these groups also experience higher rates of disease and shorter life expectancies (National Center for Health Statistics, 1996). For example, Hispanics have a higher rate of young adult mortality than whites (Hummer et al., 2000). Neighborhoods with high concentrations of African-American residents and low income have higher mortality probabilities for all residents (LeClere, Rogers,

"I think the dosage needs adjusting. I'm not nearly as happy as the people in the ads."

Advertising by drug companies increasingly affects doctor-patient relationships and our understanding of health and disease.

and Peters, 1997). Lung cancer rates are higher in Alaska Natives than in other groups, and African Americans have the highest rates of lung, colon, and prostate cancer (Brown, 1999).

The Interactionist Perspective

Symbolic interactionists view "sickness" as a condition to which we attach socially devised meanings. By way of analogy, consider the blight that attacks potatoes and corn. "Blight" is merely a humanly fashioned construct: If we wished to cultivate parasites instead of potatoes or corn, we would not view the condition as blight. In like manner, the invasion of an individual's body by cholera germs no more carries with it the stamp of sickness than the souring of milk by other forms of bacteria. For a condition to be interpreted as a sickness, the members of a society must define it as such.

Some conditions are so prevalent among a population that people typically do not consider them as unusual or symptomatic. Among many Hispanics in the Southwest, diarrhea, sweating, and coughing are taken-for-granted, everyday occurrences. Similarly, lower-back pain is a common condition experienced by many lower-class American women, who often view it not as a product of disease or disorder but as an integral part of their day-to-day lives.

Interactionists also are interested in how the medical profession and others define certain conditions as diseases. In *Selling Sickness,* authors Ray Moynihan and Alan Cassels (2005) explain how pharmaceutical corporations "sell" disease, convincing the public that menopause is an ailment that must be treated, for example, and marketing medical tests and treatments for conditions that a decade or two ago were not considered to be illnesses. Medical remedies also are subject to culturally and societally devised meanings (Goode, 1993).

In some cases a medical treatment is discovered *before* the condition is seen as a medical one. The discovery that the stimulant Ritalin has a calming effect on some youngsters led to the conclusion that their disruptive behavior, short attention span, temper tantrums, fidgeting, and difficulty in learning is a disorder—"attention-deficit hyperactivity disorder" (ADHD), the designation employed by the American Psychiatric Association (Conrad and Schneider, 1980). This new medical category was later expanded to adults (Conrad and Potter, 2000).

Today, an increasing number of behaviors that earlier generations defined as immoral or sinful are coming to be seen as forms of sickness, a process sociologists call the **medicalization of deviance.** Drug abuse, alcoholism, and child abuse are regarded in many quarters as psychological difficulties that are "medical" problems requiring treatment by physicians, especially psychiatrists. Whether incest, murder, and rape should be viewed as "crimes" that are best handled by jailers or as "sicknesses" best treated by medical practitioners is currently controversial.

The Chapter in Brief: *Religion, Education, and Medicine*

Religion

■ *What Is Religion?* **Religion** has to do with those socially shared and organized ways of thinking, feeling, and acting that concern ultimate meanings and assume the existence of the supernatural or "beyond." Religion is centered in beliefs and practices that are related to **sacred** as opposed to **profane** things and often involves **rituals.**

■ *A Global View: Varieties of Religious Behavior* Religious behavior is so varied that sociologists attempt to categorize it. One scheme distinguishes between simple supernaturalism, **animism, theism,** and a system of abstract ideals.

■ *Religious Organizations* Sociologists distinguish between four ideal types of religious organization: **churches, denominations, sects,** and **cults.** Whereas churches and denominations exist in a state of accommodation with the larger society, sects and cults find themselves at odds with established social arrangements and practices.

■ *Religion and Secular Change: The Protestant Ethic* Max Weber studied several world religions to see how a religious **ethic** can affect people's behavior and claimed that religion could be a source of social change. Specifically, he linked the rise of capitalism to the **Protestant ethic,** particularly Calvinism and **asceticism.**

▌ *Adapting Tradition: Religion in Contemporary Life*   The **secularization thesis** states that profane considerations gain ascendancy over sacred considerations in the course of social evolution, but little evidence supports the notion that secularization is occurring in the United States.

▌ *Fundamentalism and Evangelicalism*   Fundamentalist and evangelical groups are on the rise in the United States and elsewhere in the world. Fundamentalism opposes modernity and reaffirms traditional authority, accepting the Bible as the literal word of God. Evangelicals profess a personal relationship with Jesus Christ.

▌ *State-Church Issues*   The First Amendment to the U.S. Constitution has provided the foundation for the principle of the separation of church and state. The basic tenet of **civil religion** is that the United States is a nation under God with a divine mission.

▌ *The Functionalist Perspective*   Functionalist theorists look to the contributions religion makes to societal survival and are interested in **totemism.** According to Émile Durkheim, religion is the symbolization of society.

▌ *The Conflict Perspective*   Some conflict theorists depict religion as a weapon in the service of ruling elites who use it to hold in check the explosive tensions produced by social inequality and injustice. Other conflict theorists see religion as an active force shaping the contours of social life.

Education

Social scientists view **learning** as a relatively permanent change in behavior or capability that results from experience. **Education** is one aspect of the many-sided process of socialization by which people acquire behaviors essential for effective participation in society.

▌ *The Bureaucratic Structure of Schools*   As schools grew larger, they had to standardize and routinize many of their operations and establish formal operating and administrative procedures.

▌ *The Effectiveness of Schools*   Successful schools foster expectations that order will prevail and that learning is a serious matter. Cross-cultural research suggests that teachers in some other countries spend more time developing concepts rather than simply stating them.

▌ *Alternatives to Traditional Public Schools*   Parents are increasingly choosing to educate their children in ways other than in traditional public schools. Alternatives include charter schools, religious schools, nonreligious private schools, and home schooling.

▌ *The Availability of Higher Education*   College and university student populations are highly skewed in terms of race, ethnicity, and family income. Only 20 percent of the nation's undergraduates are young people between 18 and 22 years of age who are pursuing a parent-financed education.

▌ *The Functionalist Perspective*   Viewed from the functionalist perspective, a specialized educational agency is needed to transmit the ways of thinking, feeling, and acting mandated by a rapidly changing urban and technologically based society.

▌ *The Conflict Perspective*   Conflict theorists see schools as agencies that reproduce and legitimate the current social order, citing

credentialism as one factor and the **correspondence principle** as another. By reproducing and legitimating the existing social order, the educational institution benefits some individuals and groups at the expense of others.

▌ *The Interactionist Perspective*
Symbolic interactionists see classrooms as little worlds teeming with behavior. They see U.S. schools primarily benefiting advantaged youngsters and alienating disadvantaged youngsters through the **hidden curriculum** and **educational self-fulfilling prophecies.**

Medicine
The functions now carried out by the institution of **medicine** were once embedded in the activities of the family and religious institutions.

▌ *The U.S. Health Care Delivery System*
In recent decades the medical care industry has grown appreciably larger, consuming about 14 percent of the nation's gross domestic product. Hospitals, physicians, and nurses comprise central roles in the health care delivery system.

▌ *Rising Health Care Costs: Is Managed Care the Answer?*
Soaring health care costs have led to new arrangements for financing it. Managed care arrangements are part of many traditional insurance plans. They also form the basis for health maintenance and preferred provider organizations.

▌ *Alternatives to the U.S. Health Care System: A Global Perspective*
Health care is managed differently in different countries. In China health care is provided at essentially no charge for most citizens. In Great Britain 90 percent of the funding for its National Health Service comes from general taxation. In Kenya a national health service employs physicians and owns hospitals, but health care is also available from other sources. Canada's system provides medically necessary physician and hospital services to all citizens.

▌ *The Functionalist Perspective*
Functionalists note that **health** is essential to the preservation of the human species and organized social life. One way societies contain the negative effects of health problems and **disease** is through institutionalizing illness in a **sick role.**

▌ *The Conflict Perspective*
Conflict theorists note that some people achieve better health than others because they have access to those resources that contribute to good health and recovery should they become ill.

▌ *The Interactionist Perspective*
Interactionist theorists view sickness as a condition to which we attach socially devised meanings. For example, an increasing number of behaviors that earlier generations defined as immoral or sinful are coming to be seen as forms of sickness—the **medicalization of deviance.**

Glossary

animism   A belief in spirits or otherworldly beings.

asceticism   A way of life characterized by hard work, sobriety, thrift, restraint, and the avoidance of earthly pleasures.

church   A religious organization that considers itself uniquely legitimate and enjoys a positive relationship with the dominant society.

civil religion   Elements of nationalism and patriotism that take on the properties of a religion.

correspondence principle The notion set forth by Samuel Bowles and Herbert Gintis that the social relations of work find expression in the social relations of the school.

credentialism   The requirement that a worker have a degree that does not provide skills needed for the performance of a job.

cult   A religious movement that represents a new and independent religious tradition.

denomination   A religious organization that accepts the legitimacy of other religious groups and enjoys a positive relationship with the dominant society.

disease   A condition in which an organism does not function properly because of biological causes.

education   The transmission of particular attitudes, knowledge, and skills to the members of a society through formal, systematic training.

educational self-fulfilling prophecies (also called *teacher-expectation effects*) The fact that many children fail to learn, especially inner-city and minority youngsters, because those who are charged with teaching them do not

believe that they will learn, do not expect that they can learn, and do not act toward them in ways that help them to learn.

ethic   The perspective and values engendered by a religious way of thinking.

health   As defined by the World Health Organization, "a state of complete physical, mental, and social well-being and not merely the absence of disease or infirmity."

hidden curriculum   A complex of unarticulated values, attitudes, and behaviors that subtly fit children in the image of the dominant institutions.

learning   A relatively permanent change in behavior or capability that results from experience.

mana   The notion that there is in nature a diffuse, impersonal, supernatural force operating for good or evil.

medicalization of deviance An increasing number of behaviors that earlier generations defined as being immoral or sinful are coming to be seen as forms of sickness.

medicine   An institution providing an enduring set of cultural patterns and social arrangements responsible for problems of health and disease.

monotheism   The belief in one god.

polytheism   The belief in many gods with equal or relatively similar power.

profane   Those aspects of social reality that are everyday and commonplace.

Protestant ethic   The Calvinist ethos that embodied the spirit of capitalism.

religion   Those socially shared and organized ways of thinking, feeling, and acting that concern ultimate meanings and assume the existence of the supernatural or "beyond" and that are centered in beliefs and practices related to sacred things.

rituals   Social acts prescribed by rules that dictate how human beings should comport themselves in the presence of the sacred.

sacred   Those aspects of social reality that are set apart and forbidden.

sect   A religious organization that stands apart from the dominant society but is rooted in established religious traditions.

secularization thesis The notion that profane (nonreligious) considerations gain ascendancy over sacred (religious) considerations in the course of social evolution.

sick role A set of cultural expectations that define what is appropriate and inappropriate behavior for people with a disease or health problem.

theism A religion centered in a belief in gods who are thought to be powerful, to have an interest in human affairs, and to merit worship.

totemism A religious system in which a clan (a kin group) takes the name of, claims descent from, and attributes sacred properties to a plant or animal.

Review Questions

1. What is religion? Discuss the differences among supernaturalism, animism, theism, and abstract ideals.

2. How do churches, denominations, sects, and cults differ?

3. What is the Protestant ethic?

4. Describe the secularization thesis.

5. How are fundamentalists and evangelicals different?

6. How do the church and the state interact in the United States?

7. Compare the functionalist and conflict perspectives on religion.

8. How does learning differ from education?

9. Describe school bureaucracy.

10. Are U.S. schools effective?

11. Describe higher education in the United States today.

12. Discuss the functionalist, conflict, and interactionist perspectives on education.

13. Define medicine and describe the U.S. health care system.

14. What is managed care? How does it work in the United States?

15. Compare the U.S. health care system with that from another country.

16. How do the functionalist, conflict, and interactionist perspectives on medicine differ?

Internet Connection

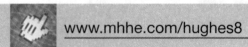 www.mhhe.com/hughes8

Choose any one of the three institutions discussed in this chapter. Using a search engine such as google.com, enter the term "religion," "medicine," or "education" in the search window and conduct a search. Follow the links you find. What do the resources you discover tell us about the nature of this institution in our society? Write a short report, describing the picture you form of the institution from the information available on the Internet and discussing whether it is possible to fully understand the institution using only the material and information you can find on the Internet.

POPULATION AND ENVIRONMENT

World population reached 6 billion before the end of the 20th century and stood at 6.48 billion, with a 1.2 percent growth rate, in 2005 (Haub, 2005). The effects of a world so populated with humans are evident everywhere: global warming, depleted water supplies, mass extinctions, the destruction of the world's rain forests, the spread of deserts, air and water pollution, famine. By the year 2025 more than 60 percent of the world's population will be concentrated in cities (Gottdiener and Hutchison, 2000), where many of our most serious pollution problems already are to be found.

In the coming decades, population increases will occur almost entirely in developing countries. Industrialized countries, including the United States, will be affected more by migration than by internal population increases, with many countries actually experiencing population declines. But industrialized nations consume the vast majority of the world's resources, so even without substantial population increases

they play a major role in resource consumption, pollution, and habitat destruction—and a major role in providing direction and assistance to developing countries.

In this chapter we provide the basics for an understanding of population, the environment, and life in cities. First, some definitions: The **environment** consists of all the surrounding conditions and influences that affect an organism or a group of organisms—a *population*. Among the chief adaptive mechanisms of human populations are social organization and technology; sociologists are interested in how these two mechanisms will be employed to deal with the population and environment problems we face. **Ecology** is the study of the interrelations between the living and nonliving components of an ecosystem. In 1921 two Chicago sociologists, Robert Park and Ernest Burgess, originated the term *human ecology*. They applied theories of plant and animal ecology to the study of human communities (Palen, 1997).

In examining the relationship between humans and their environment, sociologists look not at individuals but at populations of humans.

Ecologists typically study smaller ecosystems, but the earth itself also can be considered an ecosystem. An **ecosystem** is a relatively stable community of organisms that have interlocking relationships and exchanges with one another and their environment. While biologists focus on plant and animal species, sociologists find ecosystem analysis a useful way to view the environments humans inhabit. How important are other species and the environment to humans? Beyond aesthetics, nature provides many services to humans: the raw materials for foods, medicines, building materials, and energy; the production of oxygen, without which people cannot live; the filtering and detoxifying of pollutants; the provision of fresh water; and much more (Wilson, 2002). Humankind cannot afford not to take care of it.

Population

Demography is the science dealing with the size, distribution, composition, and changes in population. Demographic data show that population growth is at once both awesome and sobering. The world's population has passed 6 billion; during the last century, major improvements in nutrition, health care, and education resulted in people living longer lives and being more likely to live to reproduce. Both these contributed to very large increases in population growth rates: Many more humans were born than died. More than half the people in the world live in six nations: China, India, the United States, Indonesia, Brazil, and Russia.

It is estimated that some 40,000 years ago the world population stood at about 3 million. At 8000 B.C., the dawn of agriculture, it was 5 million. At the time of Christ, it was 200 million. By 1650 it had climbed to 500 million, and by 1830 to 1 billion. At the end of World War II

and the advent of the nuclear age, world population stood at 2.3 billion. It took nearly 200,000 years (White et al., 2003) for humankind to reach 1 billion in number, but within a century it had reached 2 billion, and within an additional quarter-century, 4 billion (see Figure 12.1).

Demographic studies help us to see that where population growth is occurring is critical to our understanding of the future. Most industrialized nations now have population declines, no population growth, or very slow population growth. The enormous increases in population expected to occur in the next decades will take place almost entirely in African, Asian, and South American countries. Although these developing nations currently use only about a quarter of the earth's resources, their rapid population growth and industrialization may combine to dramatically change that. In this section we will look at the basics of population change.

Elements in Population Change

All population change within a society can be reduced to three factors: the birth rate, the death rate, and the migration rate into or out of the society. In 2005 the population of the United States stood at 296.5 million, with a projected population of 349.4 million in 2025 and 419.9 million in 2050 (Haub, 2005).

▲ Birth Rate

The **crude birth rate** is the number of live births per 1,000 members of a population in a given year. In 2005 the crude birth rate for the United States was 14.0 per 1,000, while in the countries where population growth is increasing rapidly it is much higher. In western Africa, Niger has a crude birth rate of 56 per 1,000, and Uganda in eastern Africa has a crude birth rate of 47 (Haub, 2005). The measure is called "crude" because it obscures important differences among races, ethnic groups, classes, age groups, and other categories within the population by lumping all births within a single figure.

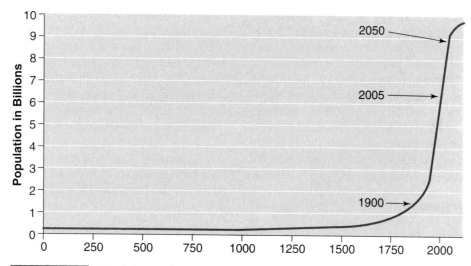

Figure 12.1 World Population Growth Data (from the United Nations) with Projections to 2150

For most of human history, population growth was very slow. During the 20th century, however, rates of growth were extraordinarily high. World population reached 6 billion in 1999, growing from 1 billion to 6 billion in less than 200 years. Demographers predict that rapid growth in world population will continue during most of the 21st century, will begin to taper off slightly by 2050, and may slow considerably in the 22nd century, with total world population size leveling off somewhere between 8.5 and 12 billion people (McFalls, 2003).

Sources: Figure generated by the authors using population data and historical estimates of world population growth from United Nations (1999), available at http://www.un.org/esa/population/publications/sixbillion/sixbilpart1.pdf; and the U.S. Bureau of the Census, available at http://www.census.gov/ipc/www/worldpop.html and http://www.census.gov/ipc/www/worldhis.html.

The **general fertility rate** indicates the annual number of live births per 1,000 women age 15 to 44. Demographers also calculate **age-specific fertility,** or the number of live births per 1,000 women in a specific age group. Fertility rates provide us with information regarding the actual reproductive patterns of a society. By contrast, the potential number of children that could be born if every woman of childbearing age bore all the children she possibly could is called **fecundity.**

The annual number of births among women in the United States fell from just over 4.0 million in 1964 to 3.1 million in 1973 and then began rising again in the late 1970s. In 1990, 4,179,000 babies were born in the United States, more than the 4.15 million born in 2005. The number of births rose as the large generation born during the baby boom of the 1950s reached adulthood. However, the average number of children born to women of childbearing age in recent years has been nearly half of what it was three decades earlier. Childbearing is also up sharply among women in their 30s who postponed having babies until their schooling was completed and their careers were begun.

It takes an average of 2.1 children per woman of childbearing age for a modern population to replace itself without immigration; this is the level of **zero population growth** (ZPG). In 1990, for the first time since 1971, births in the United States surpassed the population-replacement rate of 2.1. The nation's birth rates would be lower if all births represented planned births; some 35 percent of all births to currently and formerly married women, however, are unintended.

▲ Death Rate

The rapid world population growth we are currently experiencing is not caused by any dramatic increase in birth rate; rather, it is caused by dramatic decreases in death rate. The **crude death rate** is the number of deaths per 1,000 members of a population in a given year. In 2005 the crude death rate for Americans was 8 per 1,000. Death rates vary substantially around the world, from 2 per 1,000 in Kuwait to 20 per 1,000 in Mozambique in 2005 (Haub, 2005). Death rates primarily reflect the age distribution of a country's population, although the infection of more than 30 million people in sub-Saharan Africa with HIV, the virus that causes AIDS, has dramatically increased death rates and decreased life expectancies in those countries (McFalls, 2003). As in the case of birth rates, demographers are interested in **age-specific death rate,** or the number of deaths per 1,000 individuals in a specific age group. At ages 24 to 45, the disparity in death rates between minorities and whites is highest: 2.5 times greater for African Americans, 1.8 times higher for Native Americans, and 1.25 times greater for Hispanics. The major reason is that homicide and accidental death rates are substantially higher for these minorities than for whites.

The **infant mortality rate** is the number of deaths among infants under one year of age per 1,000 live births. In 2005 the infant mortality rate in the United States was 6.6 per 1,000 (Haub, 2005), approximately 5.8 deaths per

1,000 live births for whites versus 14.6 deaths for African Americans (U.S. Census Bureau, 2003). Many industrialized nations report even lower infant mortality rates: Iceland, 2.4; Hong Kong, 2.5; Japan, 2.8; Finland, 3.1; Sweden, 3.1; Norway, 3.2; France, 3.9; and others. We have mentioned that a decrease in the death rate results in population increases; likewise, as the infant mortality rate of developing nations drops, population growth increases rapidly. A high birth rate does not add a large number of people to the population if many of those born do not live past their first birthdays. When the number of surviving babies increases, so does the number of children who grow up to have children themselves.

The life expectancy of Americans reached 78 years in 2005 (see Figure 12.2). White men born in 1999 could expect to live 74.6 years, compared with a life expectancy of 67.8 years for African-American men. The life expectancy for white women born in 1999 is 79.9 years, and for African-American women, 74.7 years (U.S. Census Bureau, 2003). Overall, human life expectancy is nearly twice as long as it was in 1840, and research done in Sweden shows that the rate of increase in maximum life span has accelerated from 0.44 years per decade before 1969 to 1.11 years per decade since then (Wilmoth et al., 2000). A number of other developed nations have higher average life expectancies than the United States. Japan, with a life expectancy of 82 years, holds the lead among large developed countries, closely followed by Iceland, Sweden, and Hong Kong (81 years); Australia, Canada, Italy, and Switzerland (80 years); France and Spain (79 years); and Belgium and the United Kingdom (78 years) (Haub, 2005). Some of the lowest life expectancy figures are for African countries, for example, Botswana, Lesotho, and Swaziland, 35 years; Zambia, 37; Angola, 40; Zimbabwe, 41; and Ethiopia, 42. The spread of AIDS has drastically reduced life expectancy in some countries. In general, life expectancy and population growth

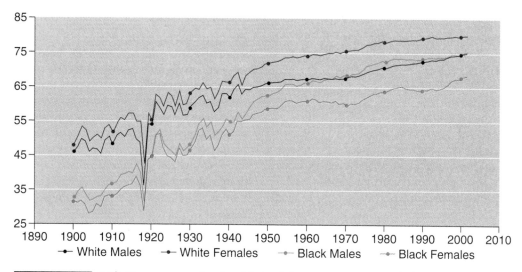

Figure 12.2 Life Expectancy in the United States, 1900–2004, by Gender and Race

Life expectancy has increased significantly over the past century, but significant gender and race differences remain. The dip in 1918 was due to the Great Flu Epidemic.

Source: Figure generated by the authors using data from the National Center for Health Statistics (2003), available at http://www.cdc.gov/nchs/data/hus/hus03.pdf; and Arias (2002), available at http://www.cdc.gov/nchs/data/hus/tables/2003/03hus027.pdf; Miniño, Heron, and Smith (2006), available at http://www.cdc.gov/nchs/products/pubs/pubd/hestats/prelimdeaths04/preliminarydeaths04.htm#fig2; and Hoyert, Kung, and Smith (2005), available at http://www.cdc.gov/nchs/data/nvsr/nvsr53/nvsr53_15.pdf.

rates increase in developing nations along with improvements in education, nutrition, sanitation, income, and medicine (Oeppen and Vaupel, 2002).

▲ Migration Rate

The **net migration rate** is the increase or decrease per 1,000 members of the population in a given year that results from people entering (immigrants) or leaving (emigrants) a society. Migration is the product of two factors. There are forces—*push* factors—that encourage people to leave a habitat they already occupy. And there are other forces—*pull* factors—that attract people to a new habitat. Before people actually migrate, they usually compare the relative opportunities offered by the present and the anticipated habitats. If the balance is on the side

of the anticipated habitat, they typically migrate unless prevented from doing so by government action, immigration quotas, lack of financial resources, or some other compelling barrier. In the 1840s the push of the potato famine in Ireland and the pull of employment opportunities in the United States made this country appear attractive to many Irish people. Both push and pull factors are contributing to the entry into the United States of large numbers of illegal immigrants from Mexico. Low agricultural productivity and commodity prices in Mexican agriculture have served as a push factor, and high American wages have served as a pull factor, with illegalities an insufficient barrier to prevent migration.

Other factors also influence migration patterns. For example, the U.S. military presence in

Korea and the Philippines has meant that potential immigrants from these nations have been partially Americanized even before leaving their homeland; successful immigrants in turn pave the way for additional arrivals by supplying them with information, employment, and financial assistance (Suro, 1991).

Because migration is usually a burden of some kind involving costs of transportation, setting up a new household, and loss of social networks in one's community, migrants are usually people who have the resources to bear such burdens. Consequently, migrants usually have better social, economic, and personal characteristics than those who are left behind (Chiswick, 1979). Migrants are younger, have more education, and are more ambitious than others.

Movement of people from one nation to another is called **international migration.** Only a small percentage of the world's population ever moves across national boundaries. In only a few nations, including Cuba, Afghanistan, Haiti, and El Salvador, have as much as one-tenth of a national population emigrated in recent decades (Kalish, 1994). The United States was the destination for 849,800 immigrants in 2000 (U.S. Census Bureau, 2003). Regulations instituted after the September 11, 2001, terrorist attacks dissuaded thousands of foreign students, scholars, businesspeople, and tourists from coming to the United States (Hockstader, 2003), a trend that has begun to reverse (Bhattacharjee, 2005).

People also move about within a nation. **Internal migration** has resulted in a majority of the U.S. population residing in the South and West, with population increases continuing in those regions. In 2003 Arizona, Nevada, Florida, Texas, and Idaho were the fastest-growing states in terms of percent growth (State Demographics, 2004). Boom states gain political clout nationally because congressional seats are allocated on the basis of population. And although rapid population growth often fuels economic growth, it simultaneously strains municipal and state services.

▲ Growth Rate

The **growth rate** of a society is the difference between births and deaths, plus the difference between immigrants and emigrants, per 1,000 population. In recent years the growth rate of the United States has been roughly 1 percent. The **rate of natural increase** is simply the difference between the birth and death rates. For world population growth, we look only at the rate of natural increase, as immigration and emigration do not affect the total world population. It takes a population with an annual rate of increase of 1 percent 69 years to double its population; a 4 percent annual rate of increase leads to a doubling of the population in 17 years. In 2005 the rate of natural increase for the world was 1.2 percent (Haub, 2005). Although that rate is lower than it had been previously, world population will expand enormously in coming years. This "momentum of population growth" is fueled by the huge population of children approaching their childbearing years. The United Nations has projected that world population will be 8.9 billion by 2050, assuming continued declines in fertility (McFalls, 2003).

The rate of natural increase is now negative for a number of countries, including Germany, Romania, Russia, Hungary, Bulgaria, and Ukraine. This means that the number of deaths in these countries exceeds the number of births. Without immigration, the population of these countries will decrease.

Population Composition

Births, deaths, and migration affect population *size*. Sociologists are also interested in the *composition* or characteristics of a population. Among these characteristics are gender, age, rural or urban residence, race, religion, national origin, marital status, income, education, and occupation. The sex composition of a population is measured by the *sex ratio*—the number of males per 100 females. At birth, there are roughly 105 males for every 100 females.

Demographers are interested in population composition, including the sex ratio. The imbalanced sex ratio at retirement centers is produced by large gender differences in life expectancy.

However, males have higher mortality rates than females. During childhood and adolescence this differential is primarily due to accidents, homicide, and suicide, which are more common among males. The result is that at around age 21 or so, women begin to outnumber men, and the trend accelerates as people grow older because men also have higher rates of illness for disorders that are the leading causes of death, such as cancer, heart disease, and stroke.

The greater longevity of women in the United States has resulted in a ratio of three women for every two men over the age of 65; in the over-85 bracket, the margin is higher than two to one. Why are sex ratios of interest to sociologists? Let's take a look at India, where sex-selective abortions have resulted in a ratio of

874 females for every 1,000 males in the northwestern state Punjab (Naqvi, 2005). Marriage brokers buy brides from neighboring states or Bangladesh and Nepal and sell them to men in Punjab. China also has many more male than female children, and finding a wife will be a serious problem for men in the future. And because marriage is one of the main ways societies have of controlling the behavior of males, China and India may face serious social problems resulting from so many unattached males.

Another important population characteristic is age composition. A population heavily concentrated in the 20- to 65-year range has a large labor force relative to its nonproductive population. Its dependency burdens tend to be light. In contrast, a population concentrated at either extreme of the age distribution—either under 20, over 65, or both—has a heavy dependency ratio (a large number of nonproductive individuals relative to its productive population). We can gain an appreciation for the social significance of sex and age composition by examining population pyramids.

▲ Population Pyramids

The age and sex composition of a population can be portrayed by a **population pyramid.** It is based either on absolute numbers or on proportions. Age groupings are placed in order on a vertical scale, with the youngest age group located at the bottom and the oldest age group at the top of the pyramid. The numbers or proportions that each specified age group represents of

the total are plotted on the horizontal axis. The sum or portion corresponding to the male segment is placed to the left of the central dividing line and that comprising the female segment is placed to the right of it. The pyramid itself represents the entire population. Demographers use population pyramids to visualize age and gender distributions. Sociologists use them to analyze trends in fertility, mortality, and migration. Businesses often use them to gain a better understanding of their markets.

The 2002 Mexican population pyramid shown in Figure 12.3 has the shape of a true pyramid. It is typical of a population that is growing by virtue of a high birth rate and a declining death rate. The U.S. pyramids shown in Figure 12.4 reveal a quite different picture.

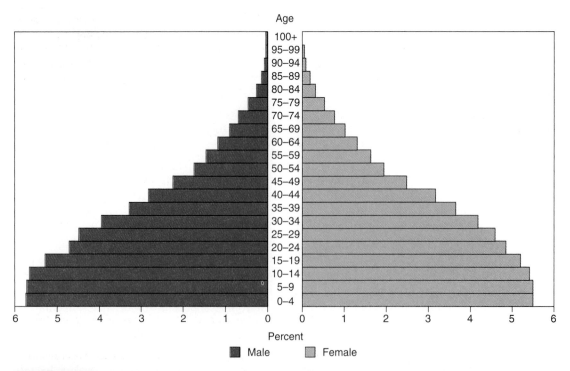

Figure 12.3 **Population Pyramid of Mexico, 2002**
The pyramid reflects a young and growing population.

Source: Population Pyramid, Mexico, 2002: U.S. Census Bureau, International Data Base, available at http://www.census.gov/ipc/www/idbnew.html.

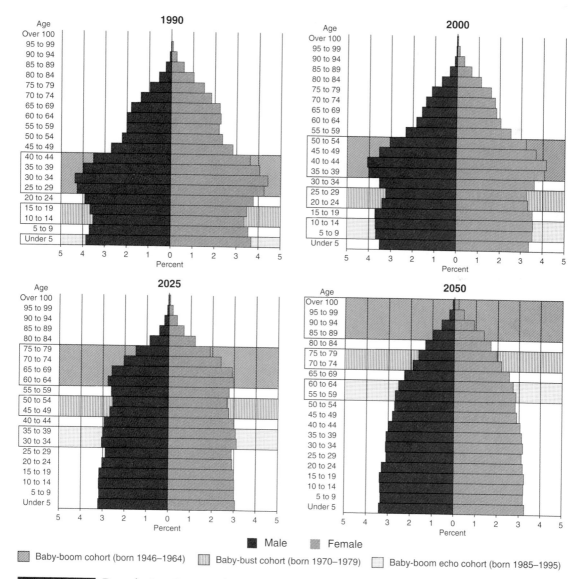

1990

2000

2025

2050

■ Male   ■ Female

▨ Baby-boom cohort (born 1946–1964)   ⫴ Baby-bust cohort (born 1970–1979)   ▢ Baby-boom echo cohort (born 1985–1995)

Figure 12.4 **Population Pyramids in the United States 1990–2050**

The pyramids trace the demographic impact of the baby boom cohort (born 1946–1964), the baby-bust cohort (born 1970–1979), and the baby-boom echo cohort (born 1985–1995).

Sources: For 1990, National Estimates Program; for 2000, 2025, and 2050, National Projections Program, Population Division, U.S. Census Bureau, available at http://www.census.gov/population/www/projections/natchart.html.

They illustrate the projected shape of the age structure of the United States from 1990 through 2050 as the baby-boom generation grows older; the size of future cohorts can only be estimated.

The population projections contained in Figure 12.4 presume fluctuating fertility patterns characterized by "booms" and "busts." The complicating ramifications of migration are not considered here. Let's look at some specific aspects of these pyramids:

1. The *baby-boom cohort* can be seen in all the pyramids. Demographers use the term "baby boom" to refer to the 19-year period (1946–1964) of high fertility following World War II. In 1990 the cohort extends across the middle section (ages 25 to 44); and by 2025 it constitutes the protruding bands of individuals age 60 to 79.

   The baby-boom generation has had an enormous impact upon American life. In the 1950s the baby boomers made the United States a child-oriented society of new schools, suburbs, and station wagons. They watched *The Mickey Mouse Club*, listened to rock and roll, went to Woodstock and Vietnam, and fueled the student, civil rights, and peace movements of the 1960s and early 1970s. By the year 2030 one out of every five Americans will be 65 years of age or older and dependent on a Social Security and Medicare system that must be supported by the smaller generations behind them. The Social Security dependency ratio—the number of workers compared with the number of recipients—was five to one in 1965, but it will drop to two to one by 2035.

2. The *baby-bust cohort* stands in sharp relief to the baby boomers. The baby bust began in the early 1970s when fertility dropped rapidly, reaching its lowest level in 1976 and remaining very low until the mid-1980s. This cohort can be seen in the indentation just above the base of the 1990 pyramid.

3. It in turn is succeeded by the *baby-boom-echo*, sometimes called the "echo boom" or "baby boomlet." These are the children of the baby boomers. Not until 2025 when a rising mortality rate takes its toll of baby boomers will the echo cohort catch up to the baby-boom cohort in size.

4. If we can use past fertility to predict future fertility, we might predict that a baby-bust echo will follow the baby-boom echo, but we won't know for sure about this until it occurs.

▲ Smaller Cohort, Higher Fertility Rates

Much of the demographic theory dealing with U.S. fertility levels has been stimulated by the work of Richard A. Easterlin (1961, 1987), who has charted regular cycles that rise and fall about every 20 years. He suggested that small generations typically produce large ones and large generations produce small ones. Easterlin conjectured that smaller cohorts have less competition for jobs as they enter the workforce, thereby encouraging early marriage and childbearing. This results in rising birth rates that produce a baby boom. Large generations confront the opposite situation when they reach adulthood. They delay marriage and have fewer children, contributing to a baby bust.

If Easterlin is correct, the total fertility rate in the United States should rise above the replacement level as members of the baby-bust cohort start their families. They should have a higher relative income and a more traditional family structure; as members of a small cohort they will have less difficulty finding jobs, allowing them to marry and start their families earlier (Pampel and Peters, 1995).

Malthus and Marx: Two Views of Population Growth

The relationship between population growth and the level of a nation's welfare has long been a central concern for those interested in population problems. In this section we will consider two classic arguments, those of Thomas Robert Malthus and Karl Marx. In the environment section of this chapter we will discuss other views.

▲ Malthus

In 1798 the English economist and cleric Thomas Malthus (1766–1834) published *An Essay on the Principle of Population*. Many of the issues he raised are still debated today. Malthus asserted that human populations tend to increase at a more rapid rate than the food supply needed to sustain them. Human beings, Malthus said, confront two unchangeable and antagonistic natural laws: (1) the "need for food" and (2) the "passion between the sexes." He contended that, whereas agricultural production tends to increase in arithmetic fashion (1-2-3-4-5-6-7-8), population has a tendency to increase in geometric fashion (1-2-4-8-16-32-64-128). Population will invariably catch up with progress and literally "eat away" higher levels of living. Malthus considered famine, war, and pestilence to be the chief deterrents to excessive population growth. As an ordained minister, Malthus either did not consider that people might use birth control, or he viewed birth control as a sin and beneath human dignity. But he did believe people could use what he called "moral restraint," postpone marriage, and refrain from sexual relations when not married.

▲ Was Malthus Right?

Malthus failed to appreciate the full possibilities of the Industrial Revolution and its ability to expand productive capacities to an extent unknown in his time. We now know that it is not true that food always and everywhere can increase only at an arithmetic rate. For example, within the United States the application of technology—farm machinery, irrigation, fertilizers, pesticides, and hybrid plants and animals—has resulted in the food supply growing faster than the population. And as previously noted, Malthus

did not foresee the possibility of new birth control methods or their application within the context of a value system favoring small families.

Those who agree with many of Malthus's ideas but who disagree with his "moral restraint" approach to population control—they favor contraception instead—are termed neo-Malthusians. Like Malthus, they believe that ultimately population will be limited in one of two ways: decreasing births or increasing deaths. They recognize that economic growth has sustained larger populations in some parts of the world in recent times, but they predict that population growth will eventually wipe out these economic gains.

In the 1970s neo-Malthusian and biologist Paul Ehrlich made some central points in his book *The Population Bomb:* There are too many people in the world, there is too little food, and the environment is being degraded. He reminded readers that those who have enough food still suffer the effects of ecosystem destruction and pollution. Neo-Malthusians point out that 0.5 million people are chronically undernourished and that people die of hunger every day; that is, there is already not enough food now (Weeks, 1989).

▲ Marx

Karl Marx (1867/1906) took issue with many Malthusian notions and formulations. He insisted that an excess of population, or more particularly of the working class, depends on the availability of employment opportunities, not a fixed supply of food. Marx believed that a deepening crisis of the capitalist system would inevitably force increasing numbers of workers into the ranks of the unemployed, leading some individuals to conclude that society is overpopulated. Indeed, Marx believed there was enough wealth to go around; it merely needed to be redistributed.

Under socialism, Marx argued, there would be no population problem because all workers would be integrated into the economy and there would be no unemployment. Through proper use of technology, a socialist economy would produce enough food for all. Thus, he traced the problems associated with population growth to capitalist society and sought cures in a fundamental restructuring of the social and economic order. In sum, whereas Malthus looked primarily to the individual to restrain population growth through self-control, Marx looked to collective action to refashion institutional life.

Demographic Transition

A number of social scientists have employed the idea of demographic transition to map out the population growth characteristic of the modern era (Davis, 1945; Chesnais, 1992). Viewed as history, the notion seeks to explain what has happened in European nations over the past 200 years. Viewed as theory, it has been used to predict what will happen in developing nations in the future. **Demographic transition theory** holds that the process of modernization is associated with three stages in population change (see Figure 12.5).

▲ Stage 1: High Potential Growth
Societies untouched by industrialization and urbanization are characterized by a high birth rate and a high death rate. As a result the population remains relatively stable. The stage is described as having "high potential growth" because once

the societies gain control over their death rates, their growth is likely to be rapid.

▲ Stage 2: Transitional Growth
Modernization has its initial impact on mortality levels. Improved housing, better levels of nutrition, and improvements in health and sanitary measures bring about a steady decline in death rates. Since a decisive reduction in the death rate has traditionally been associated with a marked drop in the infant mortality rate, a larger proportion of the huge yearly crop of babies survives and in time themselves become parents. Thus, a drop in the death rate, while the birth rate of a population remains unchanged, results in a marked increase in the rate of population growth. As time passes, however, couples begin to realize that with lower infant mortality rates, fewer births are required to produce the same number of surviving children, and they adjust their fertility accordingly. Moreover, the costs and benefits associated with children change as modernization progresses, making small families economically advantageous. The second stage ends when the birth rate sinks toward the death rate.

▲ Stage 3: Population Stability
Modernization both provides effective birth control techniques and undermines religious proscriptions against their use. The result, according to demographic transition theorists, is

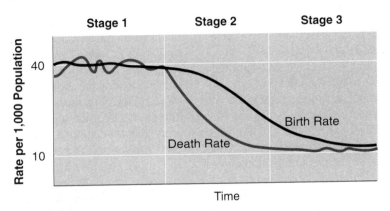

Figure 12.5   Trends in Birth and Death Rates according to Demographic Transition Theory

China's one-child policy is stipulated by law, enforced by the government, and encouraged by propaganda.

that modern societies come to be characterized by low mortality and low fertility, a situation approximating zero population growth.

▲ Demographic Transition Theory Evaluated

Social scientists are not sure that the stages represent an accurate portrayal of European demographic history; the theory also may have limited usefulness in predicting population change in developing nations. Declines in infant mortality and increases in life expectancy can develop very rapidly in today's technologically advanced world and outpace a society's evolution of new attitudes about family size. When children have always been considered an economic asset, it may take a significant period of time to decrease a country's average family size. Although demographic transition theory has a number of underlying problems that are explored in Box 12.1, recent research provides some qualified support for the theory. Crenshaw, Christenson, and Oakey (2000)

studied determinants of fertility in 64 developing countries from 1965 to 1990. Consistent with demographic transition theory, they found that reductions in child mortality were related to decreased fertility. They also found that growth of a service economy was related to fertility decline. Service sector dominance tends to reduce fertility because it employs many women and because complex service jobs are not appropriate for children, thus reducing the economic value of large families. Crenshaw, Christenson, and Oakey (2000) also found that independent of the effects of child mortality, service sector dominance, and other variables, family planning programs played an important role in reducing fertility in developing countries over the 1965 to 1990 period.

Population Policies

For countries that want to control population growth, what are the alternatives? There are three basic schools of thought relating to fertility

Is Development the Best Contraceptive?

A basic principle in demographic transition theory is that there is a general inverse relationship between development and birth rate—that is, as development increases, the birth rate of an area decreases. This idea—that parents adjust their fertility when they see that large numbers of offspring are no longer needed to support their labor-intensive lifestyles—has been used to justify a hands-off policy toward population control in Third World countries. As development proceeds, family size will naturally decrease, without any programs to provide contraceptives or other incentives to reduce the number of offspring per family.

Does any evidence support this notion? Demographers John Knodel and Etienne van de Walle (1979) undertook extensive archival research to determine the accuracy of the "general inverse relationship" in the historical record of European fertility. In general, Europe's change from an agricultural to an industrial society was accompanied by a drop in fertility. But two types of demographic studies, along with qualitative historical analysis, provided them with a better picture of changes in European fertility.

First, microlevel family studies based on church registers of baptisms, burials, and marriages allowed researchers to determine village populations during the preindustrial period. The information gleaned from genealogies and church records can be used to look at changes in reproductive behavior over a long span of time.

Second, macrolevel studies based on data from published censuses and vital statistics can be used to analyze changes in fertility patterns over time for particular geopolitical units.

Knodel and van de Walle also found a third type of study useful: qualitative historical analysis, in which letters, novels, contemporary commentaries, and physicians' reports can be used to gain a sense of how much people knew about birth control and what their attitudes toward children and reproduction were at various times in history.

What did Knodel and van de Walle conclude from their assessment of so many sources of information?

First, sometimes birth rates declined as development increased, but just as often the two were *not* associated. Indeed, fertility declines took place under a wide variety of social, economic, and demographic conditions, not simply in inverse relationship to development.

Second, although a significant number of births may have been unwanted before fertility rates declined, taking action to limit one's family size was essentially unheard of among broad segments of the population.

Third, once people began to limit family size, increases in the practice of family limitation and the decline of marital fertility were basically irreversible.

Last, cultural setting influenced the onset and spread of fertility decline; the fertility rates of areas with similar socioeconomic conditions but dissimilar cultures began to decrease at different times, but the fertility rates of areas with different socioeconomic conditions and similar cultures began to fall at the same time.

In other words, the researchers found that *in addition to* a loose relationship between socioeconomic development and a decline in fertility, many other factors were linked to the decrease in family size in Europe. They proposed that introducing the concept of family planning (and providing means for controlling fertility), along with "the diffusion of tastes for modern consumer goods, higher material aspirations, and an awareness of alternative roles for women" (1979: 239), could have a significant impact on modern populations in the developing world.

Knodel's and van de Walle's findings suggest that population policies can be implemented in overpopulated countries *before* industrialization and modernization occur. They also suggest that simply waiting for industrialization and modernization to take care of fertility is foolish; development may in fact have no effect on the fertility rates of various countries or areas.

Questions for Discussion

1. Based on the findings presented here, what effect would you expect increased educational and employment opportunities for women to have on fertility rates in developing countries?

2. Which of the population policies discussed in the text are supported by the research findings of Knodel and van de Walle?

reduction policies. In this section we will discuss family planning, the developmentalist strategy, and the societalist perspective. We will consider the use of coercion to control fertility and the problems faced by countries whose population is decreasing instead of increasing.

▲ Family Planning

Proponents of *family planning* contend that if contraceptives are made readily available and information regarding the value and need for birth planning is disseminated throughout a society, people will reduce their fertility. In turn, a reduction in fertility will allow investment in economic development. Contemporary Bangladesh provides a good illustration of a nation that is cutting its birth rate significantly by aggressively promoting the adoption of modern contraceptive methods—without first waiting for the reduction that customarily comes with higher living standards.

But even the best family planning technique will not be employed unless people want to use it. For people in many parts of the world, children are still their chief protection against the buffetings of life, providing care when they are unemployed, sick, or elderly.

▲ The Developmentalist Strategy

A second approach entails a *developmentalist* strategy, based on demographic transition theory. According to this school of thought, fertility is a pattern of behavior tied closely to the institutional and organizational structure of society. "Development is the best contraception" was a popular slogan of the 1970s. Although modernization has often been associated with a decline in fertility, as we discussed in the section on demographic transition theory, the relation is not clear-cut enough to justify a simple causal link between industrialization and smaller families (see Box 12.1).

▲ The Societalist Perspective

A third approach involves a *societalist* perspective in which the government fashions policies designed to produce changes in demographic behavior. Demographer Kingsley Davis (1971:403) suggested a number of social reforms that would reduce fertility by rewarding low fertility and penalizing high fertility, including tax, housing, and other advantages for single people; education and career opportunities for women; and free birth control and abortion services.

▲ Coercion

Another approach to population control is coercion. China introduced family planning policies about 30 years ago and has reduced its total fertility rate to 1.6 percent and its rate of natural increase to 0.6 percent (Haub, 2005). China's Population and Family Planning law imposes economic penalties on citizens who have more children than permitted by their area's regulations (Huiting, 2002). The general goal is one child per family, but regulations vary depending on whether a couple lives in a rural or urban area, grew up in one-child families, or are members of ethnic minority groups. Couples can apply for permission to have a second child under certain circumstances (Huiting, 2002). In the 1990s Chinese officials reported an abortion rate of 50 abortions for every 100 births (Tien, 1992). Because male children are valued more highly than female children in China, as in many other countries, the one-child policy has resulted in an imbalance in the sex ratio. In China there are now many more male children than female children.

For the most part population planners in many nations have focused on how to keep the world's poorest women from having more babies. Some women's groups argue that birth rates in poorer nations will decline only after the status, health, education, and economic opportunities for women improve—in brief, when women gain more control over their lives (Chira, 1994). Overall, it is clear that programs for reducing fertility remain controversial, both in terms of their effectiveness and their morality.

▲ Population Loss

In some nations population loss is of more concern than population growth. In Spain and Italy, traditionally nations of large families, the fertility rate has fallen to 1.3 children per woman, and population growth has dropped accordingly. The fertility rate for all of Europe is only 1.4, and its rate of natural increase is −0.1 percent. That is, without immigration, the European population is decreasing. Deaths exceeded births in 14 European countries in 2005 (Haub, 2005). In some countries fertility rates have been below replacement level for so long that the countries have negative growth momentum—even if fertility should rise to two children per woman, the population will continue to decline for decades.

Loss of population can create problems in the specific countries in which it occurs. For example, as the population ages, there may not be a sufficiently large cohort of workers to maintain the institutions of society and to support the retired and elderly cohort.

The Urban Environment

Cities are one of the most striking features of our modern era. A **city** is a relatively dense and permanent concentration of people who secure their livelihood chiefly through nonagricultural activities. The influence of the urban mode of life extends far beyond the immediate confines of a city's boundaries. Many of the characteristics of modern societies, including the problems, derive from an urban existence.

In this section we will consider the origin and growth of cities, patterns of city growth, ecological processes at work in cities, urban crisis, and urban sprawl.

The Origin and Evolution of Cities

Cities constitute a relatively recent development in human history. The domestication of plants and the husbandry of animals were critical innovations that allowed human beings to live together in larger groups. When human beings could "produce" food, population expanded in settled communities.

We will examine the earliest preindustrial cities, move on to industrial-urban centers, discuss metropolitan cities, and conclude with a look at global cities.

▲ Preindustrial Cities

Early Neolithic communities were more small villages than cities. A number of innovations were required for towns to evolve. Between 6000 and 4000 B.C., the invention of the ox-drawn plow, the wheeled cart, the sailboat, metallurgy, irrigation, and the cultivation of new plants allowed for new ways of living. These innovations resulted in an economy that could sustain the concentration of people in one place.

Among the early centers of urban development were Mesopotamia, the Nile River valley of Egypt, the Indus River valley of India, and the Yellow River basin of China (Davis, 1955, 1967). However, a productive economy was not by itself sufficient to bring about the growth of cities. New forms of social organization also were required. Bureaucratic structures and stratification systems arose that enabled government officials, religious personnel, merchants, and artisans to appropriate for themselves part of the produce grown by cultivators (see Chapters 4 and 6).

For the most part, preindustrial cities did not exceed 10 percent of the population of an area. Their sizes were limited by poor transportation, the difficulty of securing larger areas from outside threats, unsanitary conditions, and a feudal social structure that tied potential migrants to the land. Cities of 100,000 or more were rare, although under favorable social and economic conditions some cities surpassed this size.

▲ Industrial-Urban Centers

Urbanization has proceeded quite rapidly during the past two centuries. In 1800, 3 percent of the world's population lived in urban areas; 100 years later, 14 percent of the world's population was urban, and 100 years beyond that brings us to the present, with almost half of the world's population living in urban areas (Population Reference Bureau, 2003). In 1950, just eight urban agglomerations had populations of 5 million or more (see Figure 12.6); this number had jumped to 41 by 2000 and was projected to be 59 by 2015. Most early urban communities were city-states, from which many modern nations have evolved.

Both social factors and technological innovations contributed to the acceleration of urban growth. Organizational changes permitted greater complexity in the division of labor (see Chapter 4). The use of steam as a source of energy promoted the widespread use of machines. Widespread by the mid- to late-19th century, power-driven machines accelerated social

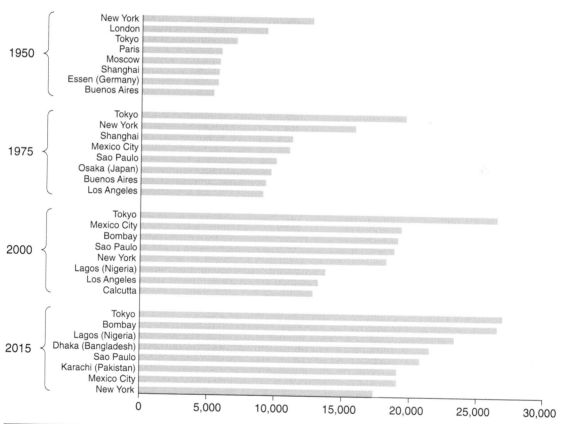

Figure 12.6   **Population Size (in 1000s) of the Eight Largest Urban Agglomerations in the World, in 1950, 1975, and 2000, with Projections to 2015**

In the 1950s, most of the largest urban agglomerations in the world were European and North American metropolitan cities that evolved out of industrial urban centers of the 19th century. By 2000, more than half of the largest areas were in the developing world, a trend that urban demographers expect will continue into the 21st century. [The United Nations defines an agglomeration as "the population contained within the contours of a contiguous territory inhabited at urban density levels without regard to administrative boundaries" (United Nations, 2001); that is, it is essentially equivalent to what we have defined as a metropolitan city.]

Source: Figure generated by the authors using data from United Nations (2001), available at http://www.un.org/esa/population/publications/wup1999/wup99.htm.

trends that were moving manufacturing out of the home into centralized factories. As the factory system expanded, increasing numbers of people moved to cities to find jobs. This Industrial Revolution is a part of American and European history and is now occurring elsewhere around the world.

▲ Metropolitan Cities

Industrial-urban centers typically had only tenuous economic and social relations with the surrounding areas. More recently, metropolitan cities—central cities and suburbs—have emerged. This phase in urban development represents a widening and deepening of urban influences in every area of social life.

Steam and belt-and-pulley power techniques had produced great congestion in urban areas by the beginning of the 20th century. A movement outward was made technologically possible by electric power, rapid transit, the automobile, and the telephone. The result has been the development of satellite and suburban areas—broad, ballooning urban bands linked by beltways—that constitute cities in their own right. In population, jobs, investment, construction, and shopping facilities, the suburbs rival the old inner cities. They are the sites of industrial plants, corporate offices and office towers, fine stores, independent newspapers, theaters, restaurants, superhotels, and big-league stadiums.

In many cases the rural interstices between metropolitan centers have filled with urban development, making a "strip city" or **megalopolis.** The northeastern seaboard is a good illustration of this process. A gigantic megalopolis lies along a 600-mile axis from southern New Hampshire to northern Virginia, encompassing 10 states, 117 counties, 32 cities larger than 500,000 people, and embracing nearly a fifth of the U.S. population. Urban projections suggest that by the year 2050, if not sooner, another urbanized strip will extend from New York State through Pennsylvania, Ohio, northern Indiana and Illinois to Green Bay, Wisconsin, and Minneapolis–St. Paul.

▲ The Global City

For most of the past 200 years, the largest cities in the world have been industrial urban centers in Europe and North America. By 1950 most of the largest urban agglomerations were still in Europe and America, but there had been significant urban growth in Asia and Latin America (United Nations, 2001). Urban demographers predict that by 2015, this situation will have completely changed, and most of the largest urban areas will be in the developing world (see Figure 12.6).

These changes have the potential to affect the rate of development in the now underdeveloped world as long as urbanization is accompanied by continued progress in education and in the development and diffusion of technology.

Sociologist and urban planner Saskia Sassen (1991) contended that changes in the world economy transformed major urban centers into what she called the "global city." Major urban centers are now central marketplaces for financial trading and investment banking and the kind of higher value-added activities (legal and accounting firms, advertising agencies, and management consultants) upon which contemporary corporations rely. New York, London, and Tokyo are prime examples of the global city; Amsterdam, Hong Kong, São Paulo, Sydney, and Toronto are others.

The critical processes fostering the development of the global city are dispersal and concentration. Advanced technology and telecommunications mean that manufacturing and production activities need not be concentrated in a few places, resulting in the transfer of routine jobs to low-wage areas of the world. At the same time, however, this worldwide dispersal of production and manufacturing requires the centralization of a variety of managerial and financial operations and services. These functions tend to cluster in big cities, and the cities in turn become centers for control and coordination of the global economy.

Clustered in big cities are "transnational spaces"—the locations of high-rolling finance and service corporations—that to one degree or another are outside the purview of any state or national government. They have evolved a kind of "global culture" so that the airports, hotels, restaurants, and high-price, high-prestige locations are more or less alike from one global city to another.

But unless attention is paid to the problem of inequality, the benefits of development made possible by the global city may make little difference to the lives of the poor. According to Sassen, the global economy and its cities have contributed to the emergence of a new urban class structure. The growth of transnational financial and service sectors has created a class of highly paid managers and professionals. But their success relies on a large, low-wage, insecure labor force—for example, the cleaning crew that comes in after hours and the truck drivers who deliver the office supplies. The global city becomes the terrain of the affluent and the poor, with the middle class all but disappearing (Sassen and Portes, 1993).

Patterns of City Growth

Human ecologists and urban sociologists are interested in understanding the spatial patterning of people's relationships and activities. They provide a number of models that attempt to capture the ecological patterns and structures of city growth. Here we present three classic models: the concentric circle model, the sector theory, and the multiple nuclei theory (see Figure 12.7). Probably no city has grown in exactly the way any of these models suggest. However, each model emphasizes important processes that help us understand city growth.

▲ Concentric Circle Model

In the period between the two world wars sociologists at the University of Chicago viewed

Concentric Zone Theory

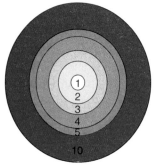

Sector Theory

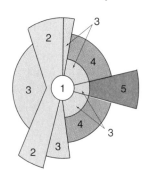

Multiple Nuclei Theory

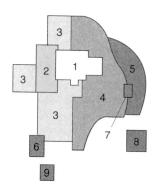

1. Central Business District
2. Wholesale Light Manufacturing
3. Low-Class Residential

4. Medium-Class Residential
5. High-Class Residential
6. Heavy Manufacturing

7. Outlying Business District
8. Residential Suburb
9. Industrial Suburb
10. Commuters' Zone

Figure 12.7   **Theoretical Patterns of Urban Structure**

Urban areas (numbered 1 through 10) are indicated in each structure.

Source: Reprinted from "The Nature of Cities" by Chauncey D. Harris and Edward L. Ullman from *The Annals of the American Academy of Political and Social Science*, vol. 242, 1945. Reprinted by permission.

Chicago as a social laboratory and subjected it to intensive study. The **concentric circle model** enjoyed a prominent place in much of this work (Park, Burgess, and McKenzie, 1925). The Chicago group held that the modern city assumes a pattern of concentric circles, each with distinctive characteristics. At the center of the city—the *central business district*—are retail stores, financial institutions, hotels, theaters, and businesses. Next is an area of residential deterioration caused by the encroachment of business and industry—the *zone in transition*. The zone in transition shades into the *zone of workingmen's homes* that contains two-flats, old single dwellings, and inexpensive apartments inhabited largely by blue-collar workers and lower-paid white-collar workers. Beyond the zone occupied by the working class are *residential zones* composed primarily of small business proprietors, professional people, and managerial personnel. The outermost ring is small cities, towns, and hamlets, the *commuters' zone*.

Critics point out that the approach is more descriptive of cities at the beginning of the 20th century and that many cities have never approximated the concentric circle pattern (Davie, 1937).

▲ The Sector Model

Homer Hoyt (1939) portrayed large cities as made up of a number of sectors rather than concentric circles—the **sector model** (see Figure 12.7). Low-rent districts often assume a wedge shape and extend from the center of the city to its periphery. In contrast, as a city grows, high-rent areas move outward, although remaining in the same sector. Districts within a sector that are abandoned by upper-income groups become obsolete and deteriorate. Thus, instead of forming a concentric zone around the periphery of the city, Hoyt contended that the high-rent areas typically locate on the outer edge of a few sectors. Furthermore, industrial areas evolve along river valleys, watercourses, and railroad lines rather than forming a concentric circle

around the central business district. But the sector model, like the concentric circle model, does not fit a number of urban communities.

▲ The Multiple Nuclei Model

Another model—the **multiple nuclei model**—depicts the city as having not one center but several (Harris and Ullman, 1945). Each center specializes in some activity and gives its distinctive cast to the surrounding area. For example, the central business district has as its focus commercial and financial activities. Other centers include the "bright lights" (theater and recreation) area, "automobile row," a government center, a wholesaling center, a heavy-manufacturing district, and a medical complex. Multiple centers evolve for a number of reasons. First, certain activities require specialized facilities; for example, the retail district needs to be accessible to all parts of the city. Second, similar activities often benefit from being clustered together; for example, a retail district profits by drawing customers for a variety of shops. Third, dissimilar activities are often antagonistic to one another; for example, affluent residential development tends to be incompatible with industrial development. Finally, some activities (e.g., bulk wholesaling and storage) cannot afford high-rent areas and hence locate in low-rent districts. The multiple nuclei model is less helpful in discovering universal spatial patterns in all cities than in describing how unique patterns in particular communities developed.

Ecological Processes: Segregation and Gentrification

Some sociologists have applied the theories and vocabulary of ecology to human populations. "Human ecology" looks at the relationships between humans and their human environment and institutions. City development can be seen as the result of economic and social competition for urban space.

▲ Segregation

One "ecological" process sociologists are interested in is **segregation**—a process of clustering wherein individuals and groups are sifted and sorted out in space based on their sharing of certain traits or activities in common. This clustering takes place voluntarily when people find that close spatial proximity is advantageous, and the resulting segregated areas have been termed **natural areas** because they do not result from any official planning by government units. For example, the multiple nuclei model of city growth suggests that certain similar activities profit from the cohesion provided by a segregated district.

Of course segregation may also be involuntary. Residential neighborhoods frequently attempt to exclude incompatible commercial and industrial activities through zoning ordinances. Ethnic and racial groups may systematically exclude other groups from their neighborhoods. These processes have produced an urban America that is highly segregated racially. African Americans are the most segregated minority group in the United States, followed in turn by Hispanics, Asians, and Native Americans. While racial and ethnic segregation is declining over time, the changes from 1980 to 2000 were very small (Iceland, Weinberg, and Steinmetz, 2002).

Racial segregation supports continuing segregation, as the quantity and quality of white contacts with blacks are determined primarily by physical proximity: If whites don't live near blacks, they simply don't interact, and thus have no opportunity to discard negative stereotypes and build positive attitudes (Sigelman et al., 1996).

Class segregation—the separation of the rich from the poor—increased about 26 percent from 1970 to 1990 (Morin, 1998). The poor in the United States are increasingly concentrated in high-poverty city neighborhoods. Between 1970 and 1990 the number of Americans living in poverty increased by 50 percent, but the number of poor neighborhoods has more than doubled (Jargowsky, 1997). At the same time,

affluent people are increasingly living in affluent neighborhoods (Morin, 1998). Local politics are significantly affected by such segregation, with entire political jurisdictions increasingly becoming "poor" or "rich" and providing services accordingly.

▲ Invasion and Succession

Invasion and succession are critical ecological processes and are concepts that have been "borrowed" by sociologists and applied to urban development. **Invasion** takes place when a new type of people, institution, or activity encroaches on an area occupied by a different type. Should the invasion continue until the encroaching type displaces the other, **succession** is said to have occurred. When people with very different backgrounds come to share or compete for urban neighborhoods, issues of race, class, and culture often become highlighted and lead to social conflict (Winnick, 1991; Wysocki, 1991).

Urban gentrification—the return of the middle class, usually young, white, childless professionals (sometimes called "yuppies," for young urban professionals) to older neighborhoods—is happening in large cities throughout the United States: Haight-Ashbury in San Francisco, Queen Village in Philadelphia, Mount Adams in Cincinnati, New Town in Chicago, German Village in Columbus, Ohio, and the East Village and Soho in New York. Gentrification typically culminates in the displacement of the poor and minorities from these neighborhoods by upwardly mobile whites with financial resources and clout. Many older cities count on urban gentrification to counteract their eroding population and tax bases. However, gentrification also adds to urban problems when it displaces the poor and pushes them into adjoining neighborhoods.

Urban Crisis: Cities in Decline

The long-term trend toward urbanization continues. More than half of all Americans now live in 49 large metropolitan areas, each with a population of more than 1 million (U.S. Census Bureau, 2003). What is happening in these large cities? Let's take a closer look at urban crisis in the United States.

▲ "Doughnut" Development

The "doughnut structure" is an apt description of the course of metropolitan development in many U.S. cities since World War II. The hole in the doughnut is the decaying central city, and the ring is a prosperous and growing suburban and exurban (beyond the city and suburbs) region. In some cases, such as New York City's Manhattan, the hole is a core area that is being revitalized, and the ring is a surrounding part of the city that is becoming progressively blighted. A number of trends have contributed to the phenomenon, including the rapid growth of suburbs and exurbs and the return of urban growth to coastal regions. People tend to follow jobs and migrate to areas where they believe better employment opportunities exist.

▲ Descriptive and Functional Decline

Urban decline can be descriptive or functional. *Descriptive decline* has to do with the loss of population or jobs. It occurs as people who have the resources to leave the city do, while those who are poor have little choice but to remain. The proportion of poor residents increases as their number is swelled by recent migrants who also are poor. Urban ills are thus aggravated and require an increasing share of a city's resources. Life in the city then becomes less agreeable and more costly for middle- and upper-income residents, who move out of the city. This cycle hurts the city and complicates its ability to be responsive to people's needs and results in increasing isolation of poor and immigrant populations.

Functional decline refers to a deterioration in city services and the social amenities of urban life. It is reflected in the decay of the urban infrastructure in older industrial cities—the network of roads, bridges, sewers, rails, and mass transit systems. Currently half of all U.S. communities cannot expand because their water

As populations increase, cities grow, and urban infrastructures decay, repair and construction projects cause major disruptions in traffic flows.

treatment systems are at or near capacity. According to the Environmental Protection Agency, many of the nation's water and wastewater facilities have water quality or public health problems; additionally, some cities lose as much as 30 percent of their daily water supply as a result of leaky pipes. Many roads and bridges are bearing far greater burdens than they were designed to accommodate, and many are deteriorating. Increases in population lead to increases in traffic, with heavier use of roads that are already in poor condition. In response to the fiscal crises of past decades, many local and state officials balanced budgets by canceling preventive maintenance and deferring necessary repairs of public works, adding to the functional decline of cities.

Sprawling Urban Growth: The Rise of "Edge" Cities

Some observers argue that a new form of urban organization has emerged in the United States. Growing American metropolitan areas appear to be sprouting multiple "outer cities," "minicities," or "edge cities" (Suro, 1990; Garreau, 1991). Whereas several decades ago a central city was relatively compact, now everything is spread over a much larger crescent of development. The transition has been facilitated by the development of a service-based economy in which telecommunications allow service-sector firms to locate anywhere. Shopping malls or clusters of office buildings, warehouses, or factories are scattered around at interchanges along the broad, ballooning bands of interlinked beltways. These centers of development generate other development. The typical dwelling units are the condominium, the large apartment complex, and the celebrated suburban home.

In most cases government structures and policies have yet to adapt to the new patterns of growth. Regional approaches may be required to deal with issues such as taxation, highways, parks, water, and waste disposal. Not all urban planners view urban sprawl in a negative light. Robert Bruegmann (2005) argues that urban sprawl is a normal part of urban growth and has been going on for thousands of years. People and businesses move out of center cities because outer areas provide more space, privacy, and other benefits.

The Ecological Environment

Humans have an enormous impact on the environment. Indeed, most of earth's ecosystems are now dominated by humans. By living beyond their means, people have changed the atmosphere, depleted fisheries, jeopardized water supplies, reduced soil fertility, and scattered

pollutants everywhere (McMichael, Butler, and Folke, 2003). A quarter of the planet's mammals are currently endangered (Dirzo and Loreau, 2005), more than 100 species of frogs have become extinct in the past 30 years (Pounds et al., 2006), and commercial fishing has wiped out 90 percent of large predatory fish worldwide (Myers and Worm, 2005). Approximately half of the world's land surface has been transformed by human use (Pielke, 2005), and more than half of all the accessible surface fresh water in the world has been put to use by humans (Vitousek et al., 1997). The debate about global warming has shifted from one about its existence to one about whether we have passed the "tipping point" beyond which it is too late to act to prevent catastrophic changes (Eilperin, 2006).

The United States bears a heavy share of the responsibility for the fix the world is in. For example, a quarter of the world's carbon dioxide emissions comes from the United States (Eilperin, 2005). Each U.S. citizen daily uses more than *five times* the amount of energy calculated to be the worldwide average per capita. The U.S. population comprises about 4 percent of the world population, yet its citizens are responsible for 25 percent of the total energy consumed worldwide. Likewise, the United States produces more waste and pollutants than other countries, some of which is shipped abroad (see Box 12.2).

Why discuss the environment in a sociology book? Scientists understand the problems the planet faces and, in many cases, what people ought to do to solve them. But implementing solutions is a human and social endeavor. The social sciences can help biologists, engineers, ecologists, and environmental managers to identify socially acceptable and politically feasible solutions to our problems (Hull and Robertson, 2000). As biologists expressed in *Science,* "There is an urgent need to integrate biological and social disciplines in order to generate reliable recommendations for society" (Dirzo and Loreau, 2005).

Toxic Trash? Ship It to Another Country

What do you do with your old electronic equipment when you buy something new? E-waste, or electronic waste, is currently the most rapidly growing waste problem in the world, with amounts of E-waste increasing nearly three times more quickly than amounts of other municipal wastes. And E-waste is toxic waste: computers and other electronic equipment contain lead, mercury, cadmium, barium, chromium, beryllium, PCBs, dioxins, and other pollutants. Consumers and business users have to pay recyclers to take E-waste off their hands.

Recycling materials from electronic equipment is time consuming and unprofitable—at least in industrialized nations. So Americans ship it to other countries. In *Exporting Harm: The High-Tech Trashing of Asia* (Puckett et al., 2002), investigators documented the toxic waste trade that makes Asian countries the recipients of as much as 80 percent of the E-waste collected by recyclers in the United States. Although the export of all hazardous wastes from rich to poor countries was banned through the Basel Convention in

1994, the United States never ratified the treaty and continues to export E-waste, even to China, which passed its own ban on E-waste imports in 2002.

It is environmental, health, and safety regulations that make recycling E-waste unprofitable in the United States. It is the lack of such regulations in other countries that make recycling E-waste profitable—and dangerous. For example, in Guiyu, China, about 100,000 men, women, and children are employed in taking computers apart—mostly by hand—and extracting copper from wiring, gold from capacitors, and other valuable products. Employees work with no protection for their hands, eyes, skin, and respiratory systems. Plastics are burned in the open air, acids are poured into canals and rivers, and lead-laden monitor glass and other components are dumped where heavy metals can leach into groundwater.

Global inequality is at the root of E-waste exportation. In the wealthy industrialized United States, protected by multiple layers of regulations, wastes are generated and exported.

In developing nations with few or no environmental and health regulations, people are willing and eager to work for $1.50 a day to handle toxic materials. As the *Exporting Harm* authors point out, people only do such dangerous work when they have no alternative:

> If left unchecked, the toxic effluent of the affluent will flood towards the world's poorest countries where labor is cheap and occupational and environmental protections are inadequate. A free trade in hazardous wastes leaves the poorer peoples of the world with an untenable choice between poverty and poison—a choice that nobody should have to make (Puckett et al., 2002:1).

Questions for Discussion

1. What policies or strategies might the United States adopt to reduce the export of toxic trash?

2. Does the United States protect itself from pollution by exporting toxic wastes?

Human-Environment Interactions: A Closer Look

One impact of humans on the environment is based on the use of natural resources and the production of wastes and contaminants. Another is based on the space human populations take up; every area taken over by humans is unavailable for use by most of the original plant and animal inhabitants, and land use changes afffect climate change (Pielke, 2005).

Sociologists are interested in the relationships between population size, human organizations, environment, and technology. The management of fisheries provides a good example of human factors in environmental problems (Botsford, Castilla, and Peterson, 1997). A major goal of fisheries is sustainability: to limit catches so that fish populations are never damaged or depleted. Overfishing results in the loss of jobs for the 200 million people employed in fisheries globally and a loss of food for the world's population; fisheries account for 19 percent of the total human consumption of animal protein. But the goal of sustainability has never been reached. Researchers have assessed the sociopolitical pressures that interfere with sound fisheries management (Botsford, Castilla, and Peterson, 1997:512):

Managers, under constant political pressure for greater harvests because of their short-term benefits to society (jobs and profits), allow harvests to increase when fishery scientists cannot specify with certainty that the next increase will lead to overfishing and collapse . . . the burden of proving whether higher harvests are harmful falls on the fishery managers, not the fishing industry. The result is a continuous, unidirectional increase in fishing effort, and in some cases fishery collapse.

The end result? Approximately two-thirds of major marine fisheries have been depleted, overexploited, or fully exploited (Lubchenco, 1998).

Just as humans can overexploit their natural resources, so can they protect them. A number of programs aimed at recovering populations of species at the brink of extinction have been successful; for example, the last six condors living in the wild were captured in 1986, and a captive breeding program has produced 12 to 20 fledglings per year since 1991 (Pimm, 2000). Restoration ecology—restoring land altered by human activity—is increasingly successful and has benefits beyond the reclamation of damaged ecosystems. Restoration projects often involve large groups of volunteers, and those who work to restore ecosystems better understand and respect their complexity (Hull and Robertson, 2000).

The Functionalist Perspective

Functionalist theorists approach the ecological environment by examining the interconnections between the various parts composing the ecosystems (Faia, 1989). They see the ecosystem as exhibiting a tendency toward equilibrium, in which its components maintain a delicately balanced relationship with one another. The perspective is nicely captured by the notion of Spaceship Earth—the idea that our planet is a closed system with finite resources that, if destroyed or depleted, cannot be replaced. Life exists only in the biosphere, a thin skin of air, soil, and water on the surface of the planet. Functionalists stress that our survival depends on our ability to maintain the precarious balance among the living and nonliving components comprising the biosphere. They fear that our pollution of the environment and our depletion of the earth's natural resources are jeopardizing the very environment that is the basis for life.

A graphic example of the reciprocal ties that bind human beings and their physical environment is provided by the sub-Saharan region of Africa. The tragedy of the region has been captured in recent years by television portrayals of deserts haunted by starving people, infant bellies swollen by want, and dead cattle. An estimated 35 million people in Africa live on the interfaces of deserts and arable land and are constantly threatened by hunger.

The desert is growing. Some 95 million hectares of arable land in Africa have been degraded to the point that they can no longer produce crops, and soils in sub-Saharan Africa are losing nutrients faster than anywhere else in the world (Holden, 2006). Much of this "desertification" is attributable to the overworking of marginal lands for crops, grazing, and firewood. The introduction of Western techniques, such as irrigation, deep plowing, and the use of chemical fertilizers, compounded the region's problems (Tucker, Dregne, and Newcomb, 1991). The functionalist approach emphasizes that to avoid this type of damage to the ecosystem, human beings must become more sensitive to both the manifest and latent consequences of their actions on the environment.

The Conflict Perspective

As is true for many other issues, the conflict perspective does not offer a unified point of view on environmental matters. Some conflict theorists depict environmental problems as due more to the distribution of the world's resources than to a limited amount of resources available in the world. They say that the basic issue is not one of how much is available but one of which individuals and groups will secure a disproportionate share of what is available. Hence, the critical decisions that affect the environment are made not in the interests of present and future generations but in the interests of those groups that can impose their will on others.

Conflict theorists also point out that people tend to be separated into two camps on environmental issues. On one side are those who favor economic development and growth even if it results in some measure of environmental damage. On the other side are those who see environmental preservation as their primary goal and who believe that the environment must take precedence over economic goals. The two groups are at odds and contest each other in the political arena.

Conflict theorists see many of the same circumstances in Africa as the functionalists, but come to somewhat different conclusions. Desertification is not blamed for the region's problems; rather, conflict theorists say that growing indebtedness exerted pressure on African governments to promote cash crops for export rather than food crops for their people. Complicating matters, much of the money provided by Western aid agencies was diverted to highly visible projects, such as roads, port facilities, airports, and office buildings, while small African farmers were neglected. Moreover, when Western nations have provided food to African governments, they have found an outlet for surplus food in need of a market, which has benefited U.S. and European farmers. Finally, assistance is often rendered to African governments that are friendly toward the donor nations; in the process the existing regimes are stabilized (Farnsworth, 1990).

The Interactionist Perspective

Symbolic interactionists give environmental issues a somewhat different twist, focusing their sociological eye upon "people behaviors." Here we will look at two issues of interest to interactionists: the difference between people's attitudes and their actions, and the difference between expert and public perceptions of risk.

▲ Are You Ready for Action?

Apparently many Americans believe that they are devoted to preserving the environment. But Americans are deeply divided over how to do it and at what cost to taxpayers, businesses, and national economic interests. Two-thirds of survey respondents say they would avoid using a product that was thought to be the cause of harm to the environment, and three-quarters say they recycle regularly (Public Agenda, 2004). Yet the percent of Americans identifying themselves as "environmentalists" dropped from 73 percent in 1990 to fewer than half in 2000, and in 2002 survey respondents ranked protecting the environment as a lower legislative priority than terrorism, the economy, education, and five other issues (Public Agenda, 2004).

▲ Public versus Expert Perceptions of Risk

Interactionists also have provided significant insight on the socially constructed understandings and myths people have about the environment. For example, a considerable gap often exists between public and expert perceptions of risk. Public opinion surveys show that oil spills, hazardous waste, underground storage tanks, and releases of radioactive materials arouse high public emotions. But in terms of the actual magnitude of the risk they pose, scientists advising the Environmental Protection Agency rate these threats near the bottom. By contrast, global warming ranks relatively low in public concerns, but scientists see it as a top concern because its long-term potential consequences are so damaging and its effects so widespread and difficult to reverse.

We should not conclude that the public necessarily disregards "risk hazards" determined by scientists. Rather, people use the information in combination with information about the social, political, and ethical characteristics of a risk to make decisions about its acceptability, or what have been called "risk outrage" factors. Risks are more acceptable to the public when they are voluntary, natural, familiar, detectable, and fairly distributed among the population. The public's perception of risk, then, is in some ways as important as is the reality of risk.

In sum, symbolic interactionists point out that environmental issues qualify for the adjective "social" because they involve human judgments, decisions, and choices. Environmental issues are also social issues because they entail the exercise of power. For example, the poor and minorities are much more exposed than other citizens to the dangers of natural and technological hazards, or what is termed *environmental racism*. Indeed, much risk is actually politically negotiated—a network of government agencies, corporations, and public-interest groups grapple daily with selected hazards.

The New Millennium

Scientists have been warning for years that human beings are overly dependent on fossil fuels, that people are changing the climate, that they are endangering their own lives as they push more and more species of animals over the brink to extinction, and that human inhabitants must change their ways to survive. Now humankind stands poised to add nearly 3 billion people to the world in the next 50 years—half again as many as currently live on earth—and the race to organize a sustainable society is underway. "For human populations, sustainability means transforming our ways of living to maximize the chances that environmental and social conditions will indefinitely support human security, well-being, and health" (McMichael, Butler, and Folke, 2003).

The most potentially catastrophic problem facing us is global warming. While scientists had known for some time that temperatures were rising, the rate at which ice sheets have begun to melt caught them by surprise (Kerr, 2006). Modelers have revised estimates of the time required for loss of an ice sheet from millennia to centuries:

The greenhouse gases that people are spewing into the atmosphere this century might guarantee enough warming to destroy the West Antarctic and Greenland ice sheets . . . possibly as quickly as within several centuries. That would drive up sea level 5 to 10 meters . . . New Orleans would flood, for good, as would most of South Florida and much of the Netherlands. Rising seas would push half a billion people inland (Kerr, 206:1698).

Loss of shoreline is not the only problem global warming will bring. Some of the milder effects include "scorching summers, fiercer storms, altered rainfall patterns, and shifting species"; more serious effects include complete destruction of coral reefs, the spread of deserts, and major shifts in ocean currents bringing cold weather to warm climates and vice versa (Appenzeller, 2004). Impacts on humans will include adverse changes in the availability of drinking water, fish, and forest and agricultural products, and the most adversely affected will be poorest people in developing countries (Watson, 2003).

Despite the fact that our earth has more greenhouse gases (carbon dioxide) in its atmosphere now than at any time in the past 10 million years (Kennedy and Hanson, 2006), since 1997 the United States has repeatedly refused to participate with other nations to set mandatory reductions in carbon emissions (Eilperin, 2005). The first such agreement was ratified by more than 160 nations.

We may not be ready to work with other nations in setting carbon standards, but we definitely produce lots of carbon. Americans use far more than their "fair share" of energy and other resources and generate more waste and pollutants than people elsewhere in the world. If developing nations model themselves on the United States, complete disaster will result. Look at only a single aspect of U.S. life: Americans love cars. The U.S. car population is 774 vehicles per 1,000 people, the highest rate in the world; the world average is only 176 vehicles per 1,000 people, and the U.S. rate is literally hundreds of times higher than that of many other countries (Nash and De Souza, 2002). A world modeled after the United States would have nearly 7 billion cars by 2050, causing traffic jams, spewing pollutants, and using fossil fuels at an unsupportable rate.

This disparity between wealthy industrialized nations and poor developing nations whose populations are growing rapidly is a critical problem. Though population growth is stable in industrialized nations, the American contribution to environmental problems stems from a wealthy and overconsuming lifestyle. Poor people in developing countries, on the other hand, contribute to environmental problems because they are struggling to survive, and that struggle includes cutting trees, growing crops, and grazing livestock in ecologically vulnerable and unstable environments.

The planet's environmental problems are increasingly global in nature. Climate change, radiation from nuclear reactor accidents, species extinction, depleted fisheries, ocean pollution, drifts of atmospheric particulate matter—all are problems with no political boundaries. It is thus

CALVIN AND HOBBES © 1992 Watterson. Reprinted with permission of UNIVERSAL PRESS SYNDICATE. All rights reserved.

increasingly clear that creating a sustainable world society will require a global effort.

What's less clear is how such a global effort will take shape. The late economist Julian L. Simon represents an optimistic view; the central assertion of Simon's book, *The State of Humanity,* is that things are getting better all the time and will continue to do so (Simon, 1995a). Simon promoted leaving the world more or less to its own devices, especially to the operation of unimpeded market forces. This is a point of view many ecologists would compare to Calvin's "ignorance is bliss" fall off the cliff illustrated in the Calvin and Hobbes cartoon (p. 422). Yet many Americans apparently agree: Between 31 percent and 64 percent (depending on age) of survey respondents say they believe the environment will be better than it is now, or at least the same, in the next century (Public Agenda, 2004).

Other analysts also see a role for market forces. Although environmentalism has been primarily a process of grassroots groups pushing for change and governments following behind (Hertsgaard, 1998), some researchers believe that corporations may now lead the way in reducing resource consumption. Their interest in profit provides a strong motivation to recycle, reduce costs caused by planned obsolescence, trade wastes with other companies, and find alternative energy sources (Gardner and Sampat, 1999).

The ability of various social scientists, biologists, economists, and other experts to arrive at different conclusions leads us again to the insight supplied by symbolic interactionists that social problems (including environmental problems) are matters of social definition. But the views presented above can all be seen as "true": It can be true that humans have dealt successfully with many problems in the past *and* that humans need to work hard to deal with the problems we face now and will be facing in the future. A question of interest to sociologists is, Which individuals and groups will be able to translate their vision of reality into official public policy? The answer may determine much about how we approach the future.

The Chapter in Brief: *Population and Environment*

Human populations must achieve a working relationship with their *environment.* Sociologists have applied theories of *ecology* to the study of human communities, including use of the concept of *ecosystem,* with populations as their unit of study.

Population
Demography is the science dealing with the size, distribution, composition, and changes in population.

■ *Elements in Population Change*   All population change within a society can be reduced to three factors: the birth rate, the death rate, and the migration rate into or out of the society. Demographers look at **crude birth rate, general fertility rate, age-specific fertility, fecundity, zero population growth, crude death rate, age-specific death rates,** and **infant mortality rate.** Migration affects population, and demographers measure the **net migration rate.** Movement may take the

form of **international migration** or **internal migration.** Births, deaths, and migration affect the **growth rate.**

■ *Population Composition*   Sociologists are also interested in the composition of a population, particularly in the sex ratio and age composition. A **population pyramid** is a useful tool for analyzing population change and discerning population trends.

■ *Malthus and Marx: Two Views of Population Growth*   Thomas Malthus held that population increases more quickly than food supply. Karl Marx insisted that an excess of population is related to the availability of employment opportunities, not to a fixed supply of food. Neo-Malthusians are those who agree with many of Malthus's ideas but who favor contraception for population control.

■ *Demographic Transition*   **Demographic transition theory** holds that the process of modernization is associated with three stages in population change: high potential growth, transitional growth, and population stability.

■ *Population Policies*   Fertility reduction policies are based on family planning, a developmentalist strategy, or a societalist perspective.

The Urban Environment

The **city** is one of the most striking features of our modern era, basic to many of the characteristics of modern society.

■ *The Origin and Evolution of Cities*   Preindustrial cities were primarily small affairs. Urbanization has proceeded rapidly during the past 180 years, resulting in industrial-urban centers, metropolitan cities, **megalopolises,** and global cities.

■ *Patterns of City Growth*   Sociologists provide a number of models of city growth: the **concentric circle model,** the **sector model,** and the **multiple nuclei model.**

■ *Ecological Processes: Segregation and Gentrification*   The structural patterning

of cities derives from a number of underlying ecological processes. One process by which **natural areas** are formed is **segregation. Invasion** and **succession** are also critical ecological processes. **Urban gentrification** is the return of middle-class professionals to older urban neighborhoods.

■ *Urban Crisis: Cities in Decline*
Urban decline in many American cities has been both descriptive and functional.

■ *Sprawling Urban Growth: The Rise of "Edge" Cities*   "Outer cities," "minicities," or "edge cities" have been made possible by beltways and expressways, and the development of a service-based economy in which telecommunications allow service-sector firms to locate anywhere.

The Ecological Environment

Humans have transformed half of the world's land surface and use more than half of all the accessible surface fresh water in the world. In addition, they have accelerated the rate of species extinctions, changed the atmosphere, depleted fisheries, jeopardized water supplies, reduced soil fertility, and scattered pollutants everywhere.

■ *Human-Environment Interactions: A Closer Look*   Sociologists are interested in the relationships between population size, politics and economics, environment, and technology. While humans can overexploit natural resources, they can also protect and restore them.

■ *The Functionalist Perspective*
Functionalist theorists see the ecosystem as exhibiting a tendency toward equilibrium in which its components maintain a delicately balanced relationship.

■ *The Conflict Perspective*   Some conflict theorists say that the basic issue is not one of how much is available but which individuals and groups will secure a disproportionate share of what is available.

▌ *The Interactionist Perspective*
Symbolic interactionists focus on "people behaviors" related to environmental issues. Interests include the gap between people's attitudes and actions and the difference between public and expert perceptions of risk.

▌ *Entering the New Millennium*
Scientists warn that the coming increases in population and related increases in energy and raw material consumption and waste and pollutant production will spell disaster if steps are not taken to create a sustainable global society. Climate change can now be avoided only by drastically reducing carbon dioxide emissions, something the United States has shown itself reluctant to do. Economist Julian Simon, in contrast, felt that the free market will result in life improving indefinitely. Others see that we have made progress in solving some environmental problems and could continue to do so.

Glossary

age-specific death rate The number of deaths per 1,000 individuals in a specific age group.

age-specific fertility The number of live births per 1,000 women in a specific age group.

city A relatively dense and permanent concentration of people who secure their livelihood chiefly through nonagricultural activities.

concentric circle model The approach to city growth stating that the modern city assumes a pattern of concentric circles, each with distinctive characteristics.

crude birth rate The number of live births per 1,000 members of a population in a given year.

crude death rate The number of deaths per 1,000 members of a population in a given year.

demographic transition theory A view of population change that holds that the process of modernization passes through three stages: high potential growth, transitional growth, and population stability.

demography The science dealing with the size, distribution, composition, and changes in population.

ecology The study of the interrelations between the living and nonliving components of an ecosystem.

ecosystem A relatively stable community of organisms that have established interlocking relationships and exchanges with one another and their natural habitat.

environment All the surrounding conditions and influences that affect an organism or group of organisms.

fecundity The potential number of children that could be born if every woman of childbearing age bore all the children she possibly could.

general fertility rate The annual number of live births per 1,000 women ages 15 to 44.

growth rate The difference between births and deaths, plus the difference between immigrants and emigrants per 1,000 population.

infant mortality rate The number of deaths among infants under one year of age per 1,000 live births.

internal migration Population movement within a nation.

international migration Population movement between nations.

invasion A new type of people, institution, or activity that encroaches on an area occupied by a different type.

megalopolis A strip city formed when the rural interstices between metropolitan centers fill with urban development.

multiple nuclei model The approach to city growth that assumes a city has several centers, each of which specializes in some activity and gives its distinctive cast to the surrounding area.

natural areas Geographic areas with distinctive characteristics.

net migration rate The increase or decrease per 1,000 members of the population in a given year that results from people entering (immigrants) or leaving (emigrants) a society.

population pyramid The age and sex composition of a population as portrayed in the tree of ages.

rate of natural increase The difference between the birth rate and the death rate.

sector model The approach to city growth that assumes that large cities are made up of sectors—wedge-shaped areas—rather than concentric circles.

segregation A process of clustering wherein individuals and groups are sifted and sorted out in space based on their sharing certain traits or activities in common.

succession Invasion that continues until the encroaching type of people, institution, or activity displaces the previous type.

urban gentrification The return of the middle class—usually young, white, childless professionals—to older urban neighborhoods.

zero population growth The point at which a modern population replaces itself without immigration—2.1 children per woman.

Review Questions

1. What is demography?
2. What three factors account for all population change?
3. Describe the populations depicted in the population pyramids presented in this chapter.
4. Compare the views of Marx and Malthus on population growth.
5. What is demographic transition theory?
6. List and describe three population policies.

7. What is a city? How do cities grow?

8. Describe each of the following urban processes: segregation, gentrification, decline, and the growth of edge cities.

9. How does population growth relate to the natural environment?

10. What does sociology have to offer with regard to environmental problems?

11. How do functionalists, conflict theorists, and interactionists see environmental problems?

12. Describe global warming and U.S. policy on climate change.

Internet Connection

 www.mhhe.com/hughes8

Go to the Web site of the Population Reference Bureau (**www.prb.org**) and browse through several pages. Select a topic of interest that discusses the impact of population growth on the environment. Can you find an example of an environmental problem that affects population growth? Write a short report summarizing your findings.

As an interactive exercise, log into the Census Bureau International Data Base and investigate population distributions and change using population pyramids. Use your Web browser to go to **http://www.census.gov/ipc/www/idbnew.html.** Click on "Population Pyramids." As an initial exercise, select the United States in the "Select one country" box, and right below the box, select "Dynamic" and then click "Submit Query." Watch the U.S. population pyramid change over the years from 1950 to the present, and then by way of projections to 2050. What is that bulge in the pyramid that emerges in the 1950s and then moves up over the years? See if you can locate your own cohort as it appears on the pyramid and then watch its position and size change relevant to other cohorts. Explore other countries using the "Dynamic" button, or in specific years ("Select years"), or examine the "Summary" 2000 pyramid with projections to 2015 and 2050. How different is the United States from other countries? Write a report describing the differences in population dynamics between the United States and other countries (both industrial and developing countries). Using what you have learned in this chapter, what accounts for these differences?

Chapter 13

SOCIAL CHANGE

428

A World of Change

Collective Behavior

Social Movements

Looking to the Future

When the World's Columbian Exposition opened in Chicago in 1893, 74 prominent Americans tried their hands at forecasting the future. What would the world be like 100 years later? One expressed the prevailing view that in 1993 the railroad would still be the fastest means of travel. Another was convinced that mail in 1993 would still travel by stagecoach and horseback rider. A few forecasters enthused about air travel—or, more precisely, "balloon travel." None of the 1893 forecasters apparently anticipated the automobile, let alone the cell phone, the Internet, a world of 6 billion people, the publication of a map of the human genome, or the globalization of both our economy and our environmental problems.

Then, as now, forecasters fell victim to two fundamental problems in attempting to predict the future. First, change is so much a part of our lives that we take it for granted, oblivious to or unimpressed by much of it; during the 1880s a number of Europeans had already produced experimental gasoline-powered cars, but the 1893 forecasters either did not know about the primitive "horseless carriages" or did not think they were important. Second, a "rearview-mirror effect" operates in which recent events color and dominate our thinking about the future; the railroads were developing feverishly in the 1880s and 1890s, so it took little imagination to predict that they would become faster and more widespread in the future (Cornish, 1993).

The study of social change is an attempt to understand and predict changes in the world. In this chapter, we will look at sources of social change and at social change in both the United States and developing countries. We will consider collective behavior, including explanations of crowd behavior. We will examine types and causes of social movements, and we will end with a look into the future.

A World of Change

Sociologists refer to fundamental alterations in the patterns of culture, structure, and social behavior over time as **social change.** It is a process by which society becomes something different while remaining in some respects the same. Consider the enormous transformations that have taken place across American life over the past 70 years. We have restyled many of our most basic values and norms: racial upheaval, a sexual revolution, computer and communications breakthroughs, and a new national identity as a world power have remolded our national life (Manchester, 1993). In the early 1930s, the U.S. population was less than half its present size. Rural America lacked electricity, and its roads were dirt. In foreign affairs we were an insular, second-class power, although Americans themselves were an ardently patriotic people. Welfare and divorce were shameful. Pregnancy made even married women uncomfortably self-conscious, and maternity clothes were designed to "keep your secret." Manliness was prized, and patriarchal authority was vested in men as heads of families. Had there been a watchword then, it would have been "duty."

Today that watchword would more likely be "self" or "identity." This cultural shift from "duty" to "self" produces the contemporary emphasis on self-esteem and ethnic identity and is partly responsible for high rates of divorce and religious switching. People's concerns about what the institutions of marriage and religion can do for them have increased relative to their commitments to the traditional duties prescribed by those institutions.

Social change has a tremendous impact on our lives. Let us begin our discussion of it by examining some of its sources. We will go on to consider perspectives on social change and to describe social change in the United States and developing nations.

Sources of Social Change

Social change confronts people with new situations and compels them to fashion new forms of action. Many factors interact to generate changes in people's behavior and in the culture and structure of their society. Sociologists identify a number of particularly critical factors, the impact of which differs with the situation and the time and place. In this section we will consider the physical environment, population, conflict over resources and values, supporting norms and values, innovation, diffusion, and the mass media.

▲ Physical Environment

If humans are to survive, they must achieve a working relationship with their environment. Among the chief adaptive mechanisms available to a population are social organization and technology. Hunting and gathering, horticultural, agricultural, and industrial societies all represent different types of adaptations. The expansion of desert land in Africa, the loss of ice in northern areas, and the increase in extreme weather events all are environmental changes requiring responses from human populations. Societies must make appropriate institutional changes, fashioning new forms of social organization and new technologies. Droughts, floods, epidemics, earthquakes, and other forces of nature are among the ever-present realities that alter people's lives. Added to them may be rising sea levels and massive loss of inhabitable shoreline.

▲ Population

Changes in the size, composition, and distribution of a population also affect culture and social structure. In Chapter 12 we discussed the implications of population growth. Nearly all such growth will occur in developing nations in the coming decades, with resource use in those parts of the world also increasing astronomically. The graying of the population is a principal factor in the United States, with Social Security, Medicaid, and health care costs soaring; those 85 and over are the fastest-growing part of the population.

▲ Clashes over Resources and Values

Conflict is a basic source of social change. The end result of conflict is not a simple quantitative mixing of the groups in conflict, but a completely new entity. Who can foretell today the ultimate form of the societies that arose in eastern Europe and the former Soviet empire following the collapse of communism? Old orders continually erode and new ones arise. The rapid increase in world population we now face will increase conflicts over drinking water, arable land, and other resources necessary to survival. How societies will evolve and adapt to meet these needs cannot be foretold. The resolution of ethnic and religious conflicts also will be accompanied by social change.

▲ Supporting Values and Norms

A society's values and *norms* act as "watchdogs" or "censors" permitting, stimulating, or inhibiting certain innovations. It is interesting to compare our readiness to accept technological innovations with our resistance to changes in religion or the family. For example, we continuously debate changes in sexual behavior norms, while resistance to the lightbulb, the automobile, and the airplane disappeared almost immediately. Our use of the word *inventor* reflects this cultural bias. The inventor is one who innovates in material things, whereas the inventor of intangible ideas is often called a "revolutionary" or "radical," words with sometimes negative connotations.

▲ Innovation

A **discovery** represents an addition to knowledge, whereas an **invention** uses existing knowledge in some novel form. Thus, a discovery constitutes the perception of a relationship or fact that had not previously been recognized or understood. Einstein's theory of relativity and Mendel's theory of heredity were discoveries. In contrast, the automobile—an invention—was composed of six old elements in a new combination: a liquid gas engine, a liquid gas receptacle, a running-gear mechanism, an intermediate clutch, a driving shaft, and a carriage body.

Innovations—both discoveries and inventions—are not single acts but combinations of existing elements plus new elements. The greater the number of cultural elements from which innovators may draw, the greater the frequency of discovery and invention. For example, glass gave birth to lenses, costume jewelry, drinking goblets, windowpanes, and many other products. Lenses in turn gave birth to eyeglasses, magnifying glasses, telescopes, cameras, searchlights, and so on. Such developments reflect the *exponential principle*—as the cultural base increases, its possible uses tend to grow exponentially.

▲ Diffusion

Diffusion is the process by which cultural traits spread from one social unit to another. Diffusion is a people process and hence is expedited or hindered by the social environment. Simply because a trait is functionally superior does not necessarily ensure that individuals will adopt it. Much depends on the network of relationships that tie people together in patterns of meaningful communication and influence (Strang and Tuma, 1993).

Diffusion is often overlooked. We point with pride to what other societies have acquired from us, but we often neglect to note what we have gained from them. Yet a global economy combined with the fact that our society is composed almost entirely of immigrant groups means that everything we use and do can be traced to other societies or cultures. As an illustration, consider the following now classic account of the cultural content in the life of a "100 percent" American written as satire by anthropologist Ralph Linton (1937:427–29):

[D]awn finds the unsuspecting patriot garbed in pajamas, a garment of East Indian origin; and

The values, behaviors, and expressive symbolism of the hippie movement of the 1960s
diffused quickly from San Francisco throughout the United States by means of media
portrayals, such as this cover story in Time
magazine in 1967, facilitating many social
changes during that era.

*lying in a bed built on a pattern which originated
in either Persia or Asia Minor. He is muffled to
the ears in un-American materials: cotton, first
domesticated in India; linen, domesticated in the
Near East; wool from an animal native to Asia
Minor; or silk whose uses were first discovered
by the Chinese. . . .*

*If our patriot is old-fashioned enough to ad-
here to the so-called American breakfast, his
coffee will be accompanied by an orange, domesticated in the Mediterranean region. He will
follow this with a bowl of cereal made from grain
domesticated in the Near East. . . . As a side dish*

*he may have the egg of a bird domesticated in
Southeastern Asia or strips of the flesh of an
animal domesticated in the same region. . . .*

▲ The Mass Media

Diffusion is facilitated by the instant flooding of
information across national, class, ethnic, and
economic boundaries by means of the mass
media. According to one view, the media functions as a kind of giant hypodermic needle, discharging endless propaganda into the passive
body of the population. Another view depicts
the media as affording a "marketplace of ideas"
in which an enlightened public carefully and rationally sifts and winnows a variety of attitudes
and behaviors. Yet the media is not nearly as simple as the proponents of either view would have
us believe. Most efforts at mass communication
merely confirm the beliefs that people already
hold. People typically expose themselves to mass
communications that are congenial or favorable
to their existing opinions and interests. Selective
perception also operates so that people tend to
misperceive and misinterpret persuasive communications in accordance with their existing
opinions.

Nevertheless, the mass media have not-so-
minimal effects. We typically think of news coverage as the media bringing to public attention
the "important" happenings of the day by
reporting on an objective reality "out there." But
as symbolic interactionists point out, "news" is
constructed—some selected occurrences come
to be translated into "public events" for a mass
constituency while others are ignored (Epstein,
1973). With round-the-clock news channels
and Internet news sites, "news" has become an
always-available commodity. Much of what is
broadcast is repetitive, with little "new news" to
flesh out the stories, yet the mere fact of their repetition lends them a significance beyond their
actual importance. Sensational murders and
celebrity news particularly fall into this category.

The media also perform other functions,
including what social scientists call "agenda

13.1 Students Doing Sociology

The Un-TV Experiment

Sociologist Bernard McGrane (1993) of Chapman University in Orange, California, asks his students to watch television for the purpose of "seeing" television. In what McGrane terms "our un-TV experiment," the students engage in "stopping the world" by "stopping the television." McGrane uses this technique as one means to demonstrate to his students how we go about the "social construction of reality."

In one exercise students are instructed to count "technical events" for 10 minutes on television. The students count the number of times they see or hear a cut, zoom, superimposition, voice-over, fade in/out, and the like. The number of technical events that the students typically report range from about 90 to more than 180—in only 10 minutes of watching.

The counting exercise takes on significance when we realize that we commonly take technical events for granted. This insight leads McGrane to inquire of his students what other social practices and institutions escape our conscious notice as we go about our daily lives.

McGrane also asks his students to watch a television program and a news program each for 10 minutes without turning on the sound. Some students reported that when they watched a program of their choice without sound, they were lulled into "a stupor of passivity." Nor had they previously appreciated how "boring" television can be. News programs also tended to dull their senses with an overloading of the mind with images of death, despair, murder, and sensationalism. Moreover, students often had difficulty recognizing when the news stopped and the commercials began because there were no "borders" between the different types of programming. McGrane observes that from a functionalist perspective such a practice is quite functional because "the first imperative of any institution is its own survival"—in brief, "the medium is the message."

Significantly, many students articulate considerable anger and resentment over having to undertake the experiments (they also are instructed to "write up" their observations). They frequently voice the objection: "I wasted 30 minutes of my time." McGrane relates their experience to Weber's "Protestant ethic" in which time is associated with "being productive," "getting ahead," and "accruing value." In watching television in the manner prescribed by their instructor, students were violating societal expectations—indeed, they were not even being entertained.

Questions for Discussion

1. Architect Frank Lloyd Wright said, "Television is chewing gum for the eyes." What do you think he meant by this? Watch people who are watching TV. Think about your own watching. How accurate is Wright's observation?

2. Try the exercises McGrane's students did, record your results, and write up your interpretations. Are your results the same or different? Explain.

---

setting." The media sets the agenda of issues and concerns we spend our time thinking about and discussing with others. Some communications experts argue that fictional media presentations have a "cultivation effect" in which images are provided that influence public attitudes and behavior about such social policies as crime, violence, and welfare (Gerbner et al., 1978), though it is not always clear exactly what television and other media are cultivating in the minds of viewers (Hughes, 1980). Box 13.1 describes what happens when students watch TV critically.

Perspectives on Social Change

The founders of sociology, particularly Auguste Comte and Herbert Spencer, looked to the grand sweep of history, searching for an understanding of how and why societies change. Many contemporary sociologists continue to be intrigued by these "big questions." The major sociological perspectives on social change, which we will consider in this section, fall within four broad categories: evolutionary perspectives, cyclical perspectives, functionalist perspectives, and conflict perspectives.

▲ Evolutionary Perspectives

The doctrine of social progress and a search for underlying evolutionary laws dominated much sociological thinking during the 19th century. According to Social Darwinists like Spencer, social evolution resembles biological evolution and results in the world's growing progressively better. In his theory of unilinear evolution, Spencer contended that change has persistently moved society from homogeneous and simple units toward progressively heterogeneous and interdependent units. He viewed the "struggle for existence" and "the survival of the fittest" as basic natural laws. Spencer equated this struggle with "free competition." If unimpeded by outside intervention, particularly government, those individuals and social institutions that are "fit" will survive and proliferate, while those that are "unfit" will in time die out.

As we pointed out in Chapter 1, pp. 10–11 Spencer's Social Darwinism mirrored the orientation of laissez-faire capitalism. Social Darwinism was a doctrine well suited to imperialism and provided a justification for Western colonialism. The white race and its cultures were extolled as the highest forms of humanity and civilization. Other peoples and cultures were "lower" in evolutionary development, and so it was only proper that Europeans, being "fitter," should triumph in the struggle for existence. However, such blatant ethnocentrism did not stand the test of scientific research. Anthropologists demonstrated that non-Western societies—and many European nations as well—did not pass through the same sequence of stages. In brief, there is no one scenario, but many scenarios of social change.

Contemporary approaches take a *multilinear* view of evolution. Their proponents recognize that change does not necessarily imply progress, that change occurs in quite different ways, and that change proceeds in many different directions. Talcott Parsons (1966, 1977), a leading structure-function sociologist, suggested that societies tend to become increasingly differentiated in their structures and functions, leading to *adaptive upgrading.*

Sociologist Gerhard Lenski (1966; Lenski and Lenski, 1987) held that evolution depends largely on changes in a society's level of technology and its mode of economic production. These changes in turn have consequences for other aspects of social life, including stratification systems, the organization of *power,* and family structures. According to Lenski, there is an underlying continuum in terms of which all societies can be ranked: hunting and gathering societies, simple horticultural societies, advanced horticultural societies, agrarian societies, and industrial societies. More specialized evolutionary bypaths include herding societies and hybrid societies such as fishing and maritime societies.

▲ Cyclical Perspectives

Cyclical theorists look at the rise and fall of civilizations. Their objective is to predict the course of a civilization or society, including its demise. Cyclical theorists compare societies in a search for generalizations regarding their stages of growth and decline.

The German scholar Oswald Spengler (1880–1936) contended that culture passes through the same stages of growth and decline as individuals: a period of development, followed by maturity, eventual decline, and death. Based on his examination of eight cultures, Spengler said that each culture possesses a life span of approximately 1,000 years. Western culture, he held, emerged about A.D. 900, and therefore its end is close at hand.

English historian Arnold J. Toynbee (1934/1954) also sought to depict uniformities in the growth and decline of civilization and to identify the principles that underlie this development. Toynbee said that civilizations arise in response to some challenge, such as severe climate or warlike neighbors. A civilization grows and flourishes when the challenge is not too severe and when a creative minority (an intelligent elite) finds an adequate response to the challenge. When the creative minority fails to find a response adequate to a challenge, the civilization breaks down and disintegrates.

Archaeologists have previously cited combinations of social, political, and economic factors as the root causes of societal collapse, but new research has allowed researchers to conclude that the primary agent in prehistoric and early historic societal collapses was abrupt and highly disruptive climate change (Weiss and Bradley, 2001). Floods, droughts, and changes in the availability of the resources exploited by hunting and gathering societies have been identified with climate changes that have driven societal collapses. Because human contributions of carbon to the atmosphere have been predicted to cause major climate changes in the future, our own societies may be forced to adapt and change rapidly.

▲ Functionalist Perspectives

As we saw in Chapter 1, the concept of ◄─[p. 19] system is central to the structure-function model of society. A system is a set of elements or components related in a more-or-less stable fashion over a period of time. One of the features of a system stressed by structure-function theorists is its tendency toward *equilibrium.*

As we pointed out earlier in the chapter, structure-function sociologists like Parsons (1966, 1977) have introduced the notion of evolution to the perspective to broaden the concept of equilibrium to include both developing and self-maintaining properties. The social group is portrayed as living in a state of dynamic or moving equilibrium. The equilibrated social system adjusts itself to disturbances that occur, accommodating them within the functioning structure and establishing a new level of equilibrium. Hence, even though society changes, it remains stable through new forms of social integration.

Sociologist William F. Ogburn (1922) drew upon evolutionary models to fashion a functionalist approach to social change. He distinguished between *material* and *nonmaterial* culture

and located the source of change in material invention—tools, weapons, and technical processes. Nonmaterial culture—values, norms, beliefs, and institutions—must adapt or respond to changes in material culture, resulting in an adjustment gap Ogburn called **cultural lag.** Although the notion of cultural lag contains a valuable insight, it vastly oversimplifies matters. No single factor is capable of explaining social change; in real-life situations a vast array of forces converge in complex interaction with one another to give society its dynamic properties.

Social life abounds with examples of an uneven rate of change resulting in social dislocation. For instance, the automobile fostered a whole host of changes. It spurred tremendous growth in the oil, tire, glass, and accident insurance industries. It promoted suburban development, degradation of the natural environment, and an exodus of the central city's affluent population. Cultural lag is evident today in the many problems associated with the use of the Internet, including hacking, the spread of computer viruses, Internet pornography, Internet scams, and the Napster controversy. We can expect that our society also will require a significant amount of cultural adjustment as a result of the sequencing of the human genome (Jeffords and Daschle, 2001).

▲ Conflict Perspectives

Conflict theorists hold that tensions between competing groups are the basic source of social change. Nowhere does one find a clearer exposition of the conflict perspective than that provided by Karl Marx, particularly as it finds expression in his notion of the *dialectic.* As we ◄─[p. 11] saw in Chapter 1, the dialectic depicts the world in dynamic terms as a world of *becoming* rather than *being.* According to Marxian *dialectical materialism,* every economic order grows to a state of maximum efficiency, at the same time developing internal contradictions or weaknesses that contribute to its decay. Class conflict is a particularly powerful source of change, and

Marx saw it as the key to understanding human history. Marx said that all change is the product of a constant conflict between opposites. All development—social, economic, or human—proceeds through the resolution of existing contradictions and the eventual emergence of new contradictions. The outcome of the clash between opposing forces is not a compromise (an averaging out of the differences among them), but an entirely new product, one born of struggle. In this manner both individuals and societies change. It is a dynamic process of complex interchanges between all facets of social life. As Marx (1867/1906) observed, "By acting on the external world and changing it, he [the individual] at the same time changes his own nature."

Not all conflict theorists agree with Marx that "all history is the history of class conflict." Other types of conflict may be equally or in some instances more important than class conflict, including conflict between nations, ethnic groups, religions, and economic interest groups (Coser, 1956, 1957; Dahrendorf, 1958).

Social Change in the United States

In this section we will examine one aspect of change, that associated with the rapid introduction of technology into American life. Sociological models depict technological innovations as a reweaving of the social fabric—a reshaping of the norms, roles, relationships, groups, and institutions that make up society. Today we hear a good deal about the construction of "information highways" and "information infrastructures." The building of another highway system—the interstate system—reminds us of the vast impact that changes can have. The system was inspired by a wish to improve commerce, foster physical and social mobility, and bolster national defense. But the interstate system also had many unanticipated consequences that permanently changed the nation's social landscape. It fostered the rapid growth of strip and edge cities and magnified the split between outlying communities and inner cities. Are "information highways" having both positive and negative effects?

▲ The Information Revolution

The Industrial Revolution was a revolution because the steam engine, the cotton gin, the locomotive and rails, and the power loom were agents for great social change. They took people out of the fields and brought them into factories. They gave rise to mass production and, through mass production, to a society in which wealth was not confined to the few.

In a similar fashion, computers are revolutionizing the structure of American life—what some have termed the *information revolution.* Nearly two-thirds of U.S. households had computers in 2003, up from 8 percent just 20 years earlier, and 54.7 percent had Internet access (Day, Janus, and Davis, 2005). We can read the newspaper, access government data, order books and CDs and groceries, check on class assignments, read lectures, and exchange messages or talk directly with friends or strangers in virtually any part of the world—all on the Internet. Growth in Internet use has been extremely rapid; in 1997 only 18 percent of U.S. households had Internet access, a number that more than tripled in six years (Day, Janus, and Davis, 2005). Children and teenagers were using computers and the Internet more than any other age group, with 90 percent of 5- to 17-year-olds using computers for a variety of purposes, including playing games, doing school assignments, using the Internet, sending e-mail, word processing, and others (Day, Janus, and Davis, 2005).

A number of issues have been repeatedly raised about the social impact of computers. First, the computer automates workplace activities that have been performed by people. The Industrial Revolution centered on the supplementation and ultimate replacement of the muscles of humans and animals by introducing

© 2003 Mike Twohy. Distributed by the Washington Post Writers Group. Reprinted with permission.

mechanical methods. The information revolution goes beyond this to supplement and replace some aspects of the minds of human beings by electronic methods. But it seems that job creation accompanies job destruction, with the highest rates of both occurring in the most technologically advanced sectors of the economy where overall employment is increasing (International Labor Organization, 2001).

Second, information is a source of power, and computers mean information. The centralized accumulation of data permits the concentration of considerable power in those who have access to computers. These are most likely to be people who already have more power and advantages than others. While recent increases have occurred in all economic, racial, and ethnic groups, and the gender gap in Internet use has disappeared, important differences remain (see Figure 13.1). For example, African Americans and Hispanics are less likely than whites and Asian Americans to have household Internet access; female-headed households are less likely to have Internet access than two-parent households; and Internet use is strongly correlated with family income and educational attainment (Day, Janus, and Davis, 2005). But in 2001 Internet use among these lower-use groups was growing more rapidly than among any other group (U.S. Department of Commerce, 2002). And although in the Western world many of us take Internet access for granted, only 6 percent of the world's population has ever logged on (International Labor Organization, 2001).

Third, computers alter the way people relate to one another (see Box 13.2). On a telephone, we hear the other person's voice. In face-to-face contact, we see people smile, frown, and nod. But computer exchanges offer no such feedback. Thus, computers may have consequences for our sense of individuality. Computer exchanges differ in other ways. People are less likely to hold back strong feelings when communicating by computer. And as with any piece of writing, how clearly ideas are communicated depends on the writer's skill.

Fourth, computers have implications for individual privacy and the confidentiality of our communications and personal data. The growing use of computers to collect data and store information provides the technical capability for integrating several information files into networks of computerized data banks. With such networks, personal data that we provide for one purpose can potentially be accessed for other purposes. Thus, as people handle more and more of their activities through electronic instruments—mail, banking, shopping, entertainment, and travel

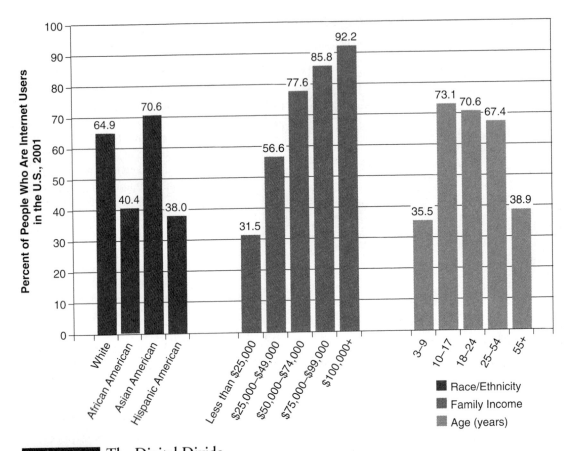

Percent of People Who Are Internet Users in the U.S., 2001

Race/Ethnicity
White — 64.9
African American — 40.4
Asian American — 70.6
Hispanic American — 38.0

Family Income
Less than $25,000 — 31.5
$25,000–$49,000 — 56.6
$50,000–$74,000 — 77.6
$75,000–$99,000 — 85.8
$100,000+ — 92.2

Age (years)
3–9 — 35.5
10–17 — 73.1
18–24 — 70.6
25–54 — 67.4
55+ — 38.9

Figure 13.1   **The Digital Divide**
Although the gender gap in Internet use has disappeared, differences remain in economic, racial, ethnic, and age groups. Data for computer use follow the same patterns.

Source: Figure generated by the authors using data from Day, Janus, and Davis, 2005.

plans—it becomes technically feasible to monitor these activities with unprecedented ease.

Finally, computers and the Internet provide new means and opportunity for crime and deviance. People have found innovative ways to use the Internet to commit fraud and identity theft (O'Harrow, 2003), to solicit for prostitution, to prey upon the vulnerable, and to buy and sell illegal goods and pornography (e.g., Durkin and Bryant, 1995). We should expect more such innovation until means are developed to eliminate or reduce crime and deviance in this new medium of communication.

▲ What the Information Revolution Cannot Do

While the changes to come in this still-very-young revolution will probably be dramatic, there also are clear limits to the impact the Internet will have on our lives. First, as we have mentioned, the "digital divide" effectively

Blogging Our Way to Intimacy

Hey everyone ever. Stop making fun of people. It really is a sucky thing to do, especially if you hate being made fun of yourself . . . This has been a public service announcement. You may now resume your stupid hypocritical, lying lives.

    Blog entry of 15-year-old boy (Nussbaum, 2004)

Web logs, or blogs—online diaries—are growing rapidly in popularity. Free accounts are available, and site design requires almost no technical know-how. Half of all bloggers are 13- to 19-years-old and 90 percent are between 13 and 29. Some 10 million blogs were expected to be broadcasting their users' thoughts, experiences, and feelings by the end of 2004 (Nussbaum, 2004).

    Blogs are one of many ways to communicate that the Internet has made possible. E-mail exchanges, instant messaging, chat rooms on every conceivable interest, and now blogs—a way to post private journal entries for all the world to see. What is the social impact of all this communication? Do we know one another better? Feel closer? Understand and sympathize with the feelings expressed in blogs? Social psychologists Robert Kraut and Sara Kiesler (2003) have spent nearly a decade studying the influence of Internet use on social relationships.

    Kraut and Kiesler began their research in 1995, when in-home Internet access was quite new. Their early studies were primarily descriptive and focused on how people integrated computers and Internet access into their lives. Later they attempted a true experiment, in which they would compare people without Internet access to those with access, but Internet use was growing so rapidly that their "without" group became members of the "with" group even while their study was underway. Nevertheless, they ended up with many years of longitudinal data on Internet use and social relationships. What did they conclude?

    Using the Internet seems to increase the size of people's social circles, their face-to-face (or "offline") communication, and their trust in people. On the other hand, it also seems to increase stress, perhaps by introducing more activities and social obligations into users' lives. It also is associated with a decline in users' knowledge of and commitment to their local area (Kraus and Kiesler, 2003). But these conclusions were not clear-cut. For extraverts, using the Internet was linked to increases in community involvement and self-esteem, while for introverts the opposite was true. And their most recent findings indicate that using the Internet for social purposes is associated with a decline in some measures of social engagement.

    Why such complicated findings? Perhaps their results are complex because it is increasingly difficult to define the nature of the communication made possible by the Internet. As Emily Nussbaum comments in her article on blogging (2004:34), "If this new technology has provided a million ways to stay in touch, it has also acted as both an amplifier and a distortion device for human intimacy. The new forms of communication are madly contradictory: anonymous, but traceable; instantaneous, then saved forever." Kraut and Kiesler see use of the Internet as a continuously evolving phenomenon, and the norms and effects of use change as the purposes of use change (2003:10–11): "The Internet of today is not the Internet of 1996, and the Internet of tomorrow will not be the Internet of today . . . as these changes take place, people will find new ways to use this technology, and its social impact will change once again."

Questions for Discussion

1. How would the structure of young people's lives be different if they did not have access to the Internet, with its chat rooms, instant messaging, e-mail, and blogs?

2. In the early years of Internet use, people thought that the Internet would increase solidarity in towns and communities. Research shows that this has not been a result of Internet use. What do you think accounts for this?

"On the Internet, nobody knows you're a dog."

© The New Yorker Collection, 1993. Peter Steiner from cartoonbank.com. All Rights Reserved.

excludes much of the world, and significant portions of the United States, from participating in Internet-related activities. As the number of people who routinely use the Internet rises, those who have no access are at an increasing disadvantage. Second, how the Internet changes our lives depends entirely on how we use it. In 2003, the biggest use of the Internet was for sending and receiving e-mail (88 percent of users). U.S. citizens also were using it to search for product and service information (78 percent of users), for news, weather, and sports information (67.4 percent of users), to make online purchases (54.2 percent of users) and to play games (36.1 percent of users) (Day, Janus, and Davis, 2005). To the extent that such activities reduce our use of paper, transportation, and other consumers of resources and energy, using the Internet can be seen as environmentally friendly. On the other hand, an assessment of energy consumption concluded that 8 percent of the electricity used in the United States is now attributable to computer use (*The Economist,* 2000b). And when the end result of convenient order placing is increased consumption and delivery of goods, we are not helping the environment.

Neither, some analysts think, are we likely to significantly improve international relations and understanding via the Internet. In the mid-1850s, when the first transatlantic telegraph was sent, technology enthusiasts predicted that it would eradicate "old prejudices and hostilities" (*The Economist,* 2000b). Likewise, the ease of communication offered by the Internet might be thought to have the potential to improve our understanding of those in other cultures. But some pin the blame for war and conflict on human nature, which remains unchanged by the information revolution: "Despite the claims of the techno-prophets, humanity cannot simply invent away its failings. The Internet is not the first technology to have been hailed as a panacea—and it will certainly not be the last" (*The Economist,* 2000b:12). It may be that an intelligently structured and wisely applied computer technology might help a society to raise its standard of literacy, education, and general knowledgeability. But there is no automatic, positive link between knowledge and its enlightened use.

Social Change in Developing Nations

Advances in communications and computer technology have made it possible for workers in developing nations to collaborate and compete in the global economy (Friedman, 2005). Employees in India prepare tax returns for U.S. citizens, American companies have software developers in Bangkok, and computer workers in China do data entry for Japanese medical and law firms. What effect will these and other changes have? Sociologists traditionally have approached social change in developing nations from two somewhat different perspectives: modernization and world system.

▲ Modernization

Modernization describes the process by which a society moves from traditional or preindustrial social and economic arrangements to those characteristic of industrial societies. Implicit in the notion of modernization is the assumption that there is basically one predominant course of development—namely, that followed by advanced Western nations and Japan. Viewed in this manner, modernization entails patterns of convergence in which societies become increasingly urban, industry overshadows agriculture, the population increases in size and density, the division of labor becomes more specialized, and the knowledge base grows larger and more complex. East Asia, including Taiwan, South Korea, Hong Kong (now part of China), and Singapore, is the showcase of modernization theories.

The momentum for change derives from internal forces and processes. The chances that a developing country will evolve in the direction of liberal Western democracies are thought to be enhanced when a nation's economy provides for literacy, education, and communication, creates a pluralistic rather than a centrally dominated social order, and prevents extreme inequalities among the various social strata. Efficient systems of communication and a diversity of social groups and organizations are believed to distribute political resources and skills among multiple segments of the community and provide the foundation of effective opposition parties.

▲ World System or Dependency

World system (and dependency) approaches view the social structures of developing nations as shaped by the historical experience of colonialism, the timing and manner of their incorporation into the global capitalist economy, and the

perpetuation of their dependency through political domination, multinational corporations, and unfavorable exchange arrangements.

According to world system and dependency analysis, developing nations cannot recapitulate the developmental trajectory of Western nations and Japan. An unequal exchange takes place between core and periphery nations (see Chapter 9), with development in core nations occurring at the cost of underdevelopment in periphery nations (London and Williams, 1990; Walton and Ragin, 1990; Chase-Dunn and Hall, 1993). More particularly, specialization in the production and export of raw materials is said to be detrimental to the long-term growth prospects of developing nations. Such specialization distorts these nations' economies because they become responsive to the demands of the world market rather than to internal developmental needs; development is shaped primarily by external forces and processes. Further, investments in the production or mining of raw materials monopolize capital to the detriment of other types of investment. And class formation in the dependent nations results in a small elite whose economic interests are linked to foreign investors in the core countries (Berberoglu, 1987; Bradshaw, 1988). Dependency theorists see Latin America and Africa as affording stark evidence of the limits that dependency imposes on nations.

▲ Is the World "Flat"?

Fast-moving world events have impacted the sociological study of change in developing nations (Firebaugh, 1992; Bollen and Appold, 1993; Moaddel, 1994). The field is in flux because it is confronting a host of new issues: Will an information age enable developing nations to leapfrog stages in economic development? How will rapid population growth, AIDS, and women's issues affect development policies? With India and China moving rapidly in high-technology areas, what changes will occur in these densely populated countries? What effect will the outsourcing of labor and of knowledge work have on these and smaller countries? When the middle and upper classes of previously poor countries expand rapidly, how will societies adapt to changes in the consumption of products, services, and energy?

Thomas Friedman's *The World Is Flat* (2005) describes a world moving toward a single global economy with a playing field "flattened" by technological changes. With a global fiber-optic network in place and an explosion of software, Friedman says, countries, companies, and now even individuals anywhere can compete and collaborate globally. Other analysts see earlier changes in human history as more significant than these most recent ones, arguing that "the increasing facility of communication does not signify a quantum shift in human affairs" and that cultural differences will steer developing nations along different paths, not necessarily toward a single global economy (Gray, 2005).

Collective Behavior

Rapid social change and the upheavals that result from it also make it more likely that people will engage in **collective behaviors**—ways of thinking, feeling, and acting that develop among a large number of people and that are relatively spontaneous and unstructured. And collective behaviors can result in social change. From earliest recorded times people have thrown themselves into a great many types of mass behavior, including social unrest, riots, manias, fads, panics, mass flights, lynchings, religious revivals, and rebellions. Accordingly, no discussion of social change can neglect collective behavior.

Varieties of Collective Behavior

Collective behavior comes in a great many forms. To gain a better appreciation for the impact such behavior has on our lives, let us consider a number of varieties of collective behavior at greater length.

▲ Rumors

A **rumor** is a difficult-to-verify piece of information transmitted from person to person in relatively rapid fashion. We often think of rumors as providing false information, and in many cases this is true. But they also may be accurate or, at the very least, contain a kernel of truth. Rumors typically arise in situations in which people lack information or distrust the official sources of information. Rumors are both a form of collective behavior and an important element in most other forms of collective behavior.

Periods of anxiety and tension provide an environment in which rumors proliferate. After the September 11, 2001, terrorist attacks, rumors flew about a wide range of topics, including the sorts of biological and chemical weapons terrorists might unleash to the best antidotes to such weapons. Official information competed with rapidly circulating advice about sealing doors and windows with duct tape and laying in supplies of gas masks, food, water, and medicines.

Rumors tend to evolve and take on new details as people interact and talk, and with the Internet they can spread around the world in the time it takes to walk to your neighbor's house to gossip. The Internet also can be used to try to control rumors. A high school student who is the subject of gossip may use a Web log—an online journal—to try to set the story straight or at least to provide readers with an alternate view of the story (Nussbaum, 2004).

One type of rumor that is particularly common involves alleged contamination. In 2003 the Centers for Disease Control issued a list of currently circulating hoaxes and rumors that included e-mails about tainted cola products, poisonous perfume samples that arrive in the mail, underarm antiperspirants and deodorants that cause breast cancer, a child who died of a heroin overdose from a needle found on a playground, and online offers for antibiotics that protect users against bioterrorism (Centers for Disease Control, 2003).

▲ Fashions and Fads

The uniformity of dress on college campuses is sometimes so extreme as to make it appear that students are required to wear certain uniforms. Black clunky-heeled platform shoes and black dresses are in for women one year; jeans, hiking boots, and flannel shirts another. Contemporary society is full of both fashions and fads. What is the difference?

A **fashion** is a folkway that lasts for a short time and enjoys widespread acceptance within society. Fashion finds expression in styles of clothing, automobile design, and home architecture.

A **fad** is a folkway that lasts for a short time and enjoys acceptance among only a segment of the population. Fads often appear in amusements, new games, popular tunes, dance steps, health practices, movie idols, and slang. Adolescents are particularly prone toward fads; the fads provide a sense of identity and belonging, with aspects of dress and gesture serving as signs of an *in-group* or *out-group* status (Erikson, 1968).

Some fads become all-consuming passions. Such fads are called **crazes.** Financial speculation at times assumes craze proportions (Chatzky, 1992). In the famous Holland tulip mania in the 17th century, the value of tulip bulbs came to exceed their weight in gold; the bulbs were not planted, but bought and sold among speculators.

▲ Mass Hysteria

Mass hysteria refers to the rapid dissemination of behaviors involving contagious anxiety, usually associated with some mysterious force. For instance, medieval witch hunts rested on the belief that many social ills were caused by witches. Likewise, some "epidemics" of assembly-line illness—*mass psychogenic illness*—derive from hysterical contagion. Fears of terrorism have fueled a number of episodes of mass psychogenic illness in recent years (Bartholomew and Victor, 2004). Close on the heels of the September 11, 2001, terrorist attacks, commuters in both California and Maryland had to be treated for headache, nausea, and sore throats when strange odors—later determined to be harmless—were detected in the subway. Rumors of a bioterror attack in the Philippines resulted in 1,400 students seeking help from physicians. Some turned out to have a mild influenza, while most were suffering psychogenic reactions to the rumors. After the anthrax scare in 2001, mysterious skin rashes that came to be termed "the Bin Laden Itch" were reported by thousands of students in dozens of U.S. schools. The rashes, suspected by students and parents to be anthrax-related, all were diagnosed as having been caused by allergens, insect bites, fungi, fiberglass, and other non-anthrax sources.

▲ Panic

Panic involves irrational and uncoordinated but collective actions among people induced by the presence of an immediate, severe threat. For example, people commonly flee from a catastrophe such as a fire or flood. The behavior is collective because social interaction intensifies people's fright.

As with other forms of collective behavior, panics can be greatly amplified by modern information technologies. When the SARS epidemic spread from China to other countries in 2003, an "information epidemic" fueled a panic that affected the lives of millions of people (Rothkopf, 2003). Although the total number of people who died from SARS worldwide was smaller than the number of people who die from choking on small objects every year in the United States, the panic about the disease resulted in economic losses in Asia of an estimated $30 billion. Rothkopf traces the cause of an information epidemic to mainstream media, specialist media, and Internet sites combined with "informal" media, including pagers, e-mail, faxes, cell phones, and text messaging, all of which may be transmitting rumor, interpretation, propaganda, or fact.

▲ Crowds

The **crowd** is one of the most familiar and at times spectacular forms of collective behavior. It is a temporary, relatively unorganized gathering of people in close physical proximity. Because a wide range of behavior is encompassed by the concept, sociologist Herbert Blumer (1946; see also McPhail, 1989) distinguishes four basic types of crowd behavior. The first, a **casual crowd,** is a collection of people who have little in common except that they may be viewing a common event, such as looking

Although very few people ever contracted SARS, fears of the disease affected millions.

through a department store window, visiting a museum, or attending a movie. The second, a **conventional crowd,** entails a number of people who have assembled for some specific purpose and who typically act in accordance with established norms, such as people attending a baseball game or a concert. The third, an **expressive crowd,** is an aggregation of people who have gotten together for self-stimulation and personal gratification, such as occurs at a religious revival or a rock festival. And fourth, an **acting crowd** is an excited, volatile collection of people who are engaged in rioting, looting, or other forms of aggressive behavior in which established norms carry little weight.

Although crowds differ from one another in many ways, they also share a number of characteristics:

1. *Suggestibility.* The behavior of crowd members is not guided by conventional norms. Individuals are usually more susceptible to images, directions, and propositions emanating from others.

2. *Deindividualization.* **Deindividualization** is a psychological state of diminished identity and self-awareness (Zimbardo,

1969). People feel less inhibited in committing disapproved acts in a group.

3. *Invulnerability.* In crowd settings individuals often acquire a sense that they are more powerful and invincible than they are in routine, everyday settings. Moreover, they feel that social control mechanisms are less likely to be applied to them as individuals, resulting in an increase in behavior not normally approved by society, such as aggression, risk taking, self-enhancement, stealing, vandalism, and the uttering of obscenities (Dipboye, 1977; Mann, Newton, and Innes, 1982).

We will return to a discussion of crowds shortly, considering several theories of crowd behavior. But first, let us examine a number of preconditions for collective behavior.

Preconditions for Collective Behavior

Sociologist Neil J. Smelser (1963) provided a framework for examining collective behavior based on the value-added model popular among economists. **Value-added** is the idea that each step in the production process—from raw materials to the finished product—increases the economic value of manufactured goods.

As viewed by Smelser, episodes of collective behavior are products of a sequence of steps that constitute six determinants of collective behavior: (1) structural conduciveness, (2) structural strain, (3) growth and spread of a generalized belief, (4) precipitating factors, (5) mobilization of participants for action, and (6) the operation of social control. Each determinant is shaped by those that precede it, and it in turn shapes the ones that follow. Moreover, with the introduction of each successive determinant to the value-added sequence, the range of potential final outcomes becomes progressively narrowed. Smelser contended that each of the six factors in the scheme is a necessary condition for the production of collective behavior, while all six are believed to make collective behavior virtually inevitable. Let us take a closer look at each of the determinants in Smelser's model.

▲ Structural Conduciveness

Structural conduciveness refers to social conditions that permit a particular variety of collective behavior to occur. Before a financial panic is possible, for example, such as the stock-market crash of 1929, there must be a financial market where assets can be exchanged freely and rapidly. This basis does not exist in societies where property can be transferred only to the firstborn son on the father's death because the holders of property lack sufficient maneuverability to dispose of their assets on short notice.

▲ Structural Strain

Structural strain is said to occur when important aspects of a social system are "out of joint." Wars, economic crises, natural disasters, and technological change disrupt the traditional rhythm of life and interfere with the way people normally carry out their activities. As stress accumulates across time, individuals experience *social malaise*—a feeling of underlying and pervasive discontent.

▲ The Growth of a Generalized Belief

Structural strain and a sense of social malaise by themselves are not enough to produce collective behavior. People must define a situation as a problem in need of a solution. In the course of social interaction, they evolve a shared view of reality and common ideas about how they should respond to it. This type of belief regarding Martian invaders precipitated the panic associated with the 1938 Halloween broadcast.

▲ Precipitating Factors

Some sort of event is needed to touch off or trigger collective action. A *precipitating event* creates, sharpens, or exaggerates conditions of conduciveness and strain. Additionally, it provides adherents of a belief with explicit evidence of the workings of evil forces or greater promise of success. Revolutions, for example, are often precipitated in this manner: the March 11, 1917, tsarist decrees against Petrograd strikers precipitated the Russian Revolution.

▲ The Mobilization of Participants for Action

Collective behavior requires participants. Sociologists use the concept "critical mass" to refer to the threshold or number of participants that must be reached before collective behavior erupts or explodes (Oliver and Marwell, 1988; Macy, 1991). Recruitment to religious *sects* and to *social movements* typically occurs through lines of preexisting social relationships; for example, among relatives, neighbors, friends, and work associates (Gould, 1991; Opp and Gern, 1993). In turn, intense and sustained social action is mediated through integration into organizational and personal networks of individuals (McAdam and Paulsen, 1993).

▲ Operation of Social Control

The sixth factor in Smelser's scheme is the operation of *social control,* a counterdeterminant that prevents, interrupts, deflects, or inhibits the accumulation of the other factors. Social control typically takes two forms. First, there are controls designed to prevent the occurrence of an episode of collective behavior by lessening conduciveness and strain (e.g., welfare programs that seek to pacify the underclasses). Second, there are controls that attempt to repress an episode of collective behavior after it has begun (e.g., police measures and curfews).

In some instances, however, the activities of the agents of social control precipitate collective behavior and even violence (Waddington, Jones, and Critcher, 1989). A good illustration of this occurred in the spring of 1963 when the Reverend Martin Luther King, Jr., took the civil rights fight to Birmingham, Alabama, alleged to be the most segregated large city in the South. The brutal social control brought to bear on Birmingham African Americans gave impetus to some 1,122 civil rights demonstrations in the following four months in cities throughout the nation.

▲ Assessing the Value-Added Model

Smelser's value-added model provides a useful tool for grasping the complexity of collective behavior, but the approach does have serious limitations. In some cases of collective action, all six stages do not occur, or they do not take place in the sequence Smelser specified (Milgram, 1977). Additionally, some forms of crowd behavior are better explained by other perspectives, to which we turn next.

Explanations of Crowd Behavior

Although crowd members differ in a great many ways, their behavior seems to derive from a common impulse and to be dominated by a single spirit. What happens in the course of crowd behavior? What processes fashion people's behavior under crowd conditions? Three somewhat different answers have been supplied by sociologists to these questions.

▲ Contagion Theory

Contagion theory emphasizes the part that rapidly communicated and uncritically accepted

feelings, attitudes, and actions play in crowd settings. Its proponents assume that unanimity prevails within a crowd; crowd members often seem to act in identical ways and to be dominated by a similar impulse. Thus, a crowd is often spoken of in the singular, as if it were a real thing—"the crowd roars" and "the angry mob surges forward." This view of the crowd is embodied in the influential work of the 19th-century French writer Gustave Le Bon (1896:23–24), who set forth the "law of the mental unity of crowds."

Le Bon's contagion theory depicted the crowd as characterized by a "mob mind" that overpowers and submerges the individual. A uniform mood and imagery evolve contagiously through three mechanisms: *imitation*—the tendency for one person to do the same thing that others are doing; *suggestibility*—a state in which individuals become susceptible to images, directions, and propositions emanating from others; and *circular reaction*—a process whereby the emotions of others elicit the same emotions in oneself, in turn intensifying the emotions of others in a reciprocal manner. However, Le Bon's concept of the crowd mind as some sort of supraindividual entity—one that is endowed with thinking processes and a capacity for feeling and believing—is rejected by most social scientists (Milgram and Toch, 1969). Only individual human beings are capable of thought and emotion.

▲ Convergence Theory

Whereas contagion theorists see normal, decent people being transformed under crowd influence, **convergence theory** proposes that a crowd consists of a highly unrepresentative body of people who assemble because they share the same predispositions. For instance, social psychologist Hadley Cantril (1941) studied a Leeville, Texas, lynching and contended that the active members came chiefly from the lowest economic bracket and several had previous police records. As a class, poor whites were most likely to compete for jobs with African Americans and were most likely to find their own status threatened by the presence of successful African Americans. These individuals provided a reservoir of people who were ready for a lynching with a minimum of provocation.

▲ Emergent-Norm Theory

The **emergent-norm theory** stresses the lack of unanimity in many crowd situations and the differences in motives, attitudes, and actions that characterize crowd members. They may be impulsive, suggestible, opportunistic, passive supporters, cautious activists, or passers-by. The approach denies that people find themselves spontaneously infected with the emotions of others to the extent that they want to behave as others do (Turner, 1964; Turner and Killian, 1972; Shibutani, 1986).

Instead, emergent-norm theory draws upon the work of psychologists Muzafer Sherif (1936) and Solomon Asch (1952) that deals with social conformity in ambiguous situations (see Chapter 4). Collective behavior ◄— pp. 112–113 entails an attempt by people to find meaning in an uncertain social setting (Turner and Killian, 1972). Individuals search for cues to appropriate and acceptable behavior. Like the subjects in Sherif's experiments, who developed group norms that were different from the standards they developed when they were alone, crowd members collectively evolve new standards for behavior. Crowd members then proceed to enforce the norm: They reward behavior consistent with it, inhibit behavior contrary to it, justify proselytizing, and institute actions that restrain dissenters. Since the new behavior differs from that in noncrowd situations, the norm must be specific to the situation—hence, an *emergent* norm.

▲ Assessing the Perspectives

The three perspectives provide differing views of crowd behavior. Even so, they are not mutually exclusive. Consider what happens at a homecoming football game. Contagion contributes to the excitement through a process of circular reaction. Convergence operates since loyal alumni and football enthusiasts are selected out from the larger population and come together in the stadium. Finally, an emergent norm defines what constitutes an appropriate response to a particular event and suppresses incongruous behavior. Each perspective affords a useful tool for understanding crowd behavior.

Social Movements

Sociologists view a **social movement** as a more-or-less persistent and organized effort on the part of a relatively large number of people to bring about or resist change. The civil rights movement mobilized 200,000 people to march in Washington, D.C., in 1963 and many more to demonstrate across the country and resulted in an end to segregated schools and other public facilities. The women's movement has transformed our society from one in which women are relegated to the kitchen to one in which women work alongside men in almost every type of career. Like collective behavior, social movements often appear in times of rapid social change. Both frequently provide an impetus to social change. Indeed, both occur outside the institutional framework that forms everyday life and break through the familiar web of ordered expectations. But while collective behavior is characterized by spontaneity and a lack of internal structure, social movements possess a considerable measure of internal order and purposeful orientation. This organizational potential allows social movements to challenge established institutions.

Central to the concept of social movement is the idea that people intervene in the process of social change. Rather than responding passively to the flow of life or to its troubling aspects, people seek to alter the course of history. Of equal significance, they undertake joint activity. Individuals consciously act together with a sense of engaging in a common enterprise. Christianity, the Crusades, the Reformation, the American Revolution, the antislavery movement, the labor movement, Zionism, and fascism—like other social movements—have profoundly affected the societies they have touched.

Causes of Social Movements

What social factors produce social movements, and what leads people to join and persist in social movements? Social movements may arise from social misery and, more particularly, from social and economic deprivation. They also require resources and organizations.

▲ Deprivation Approaches

As noted in earlier chapters, Karl Marx held that capitalist exploitation leads to progressive impoverishment of the working class. He expected that over time conditions would become so abominable that workers would be compelled to recognize the social nature of their misery and overthrow their oppressors. However, Marx also recognized that the suffering of the underclasses can be so intense and their resulting alienation so massive that all social and revolutionary consciousness is deadened. Marx also recognized a type of **relative deprivation,** a discontent associated with the gap between what people actually have and what they have come to expect and feel to be their just due. He foresaw that the working class could become better off as capitalism advanced, but the gap between owners and workers would widen and produce among the latter deepening feelings of comparative disadvantage (Giddens, 1973; Harrington, 1976).

A number of sociologists have suggested that a major factor in the evolution of the African-American protest in the 1960s was the emergence among African Americans of a growing sense of relative deprivation (Geschwender, 1964; Gurr, 1970). The prosperity of the 1950s and 1960s gave many African Americans a taste of the affluent society. They gained enough to arouse realistic hopes for more. Hence, grievances related to squalid housing, limited job opportunities, persistent unemployment, low pay, and police brutality were felt as severely frustrating. The civil rights movement arose not so much as a protest fed by despair as one fed by rising expectations.

Sociologist James Davies (1962, 1969, 1974) found that relative deprivation may also be fostered under another condition—that characterized by his "rise-and-drop," or "J-curve," hypothesis (see Figure 13.2). He contended that revolutions are most likely to take place when a prolonged period of social and economic betterment is followed by a period of sharp reversal. People fear that the gains they achieved with great effort will be lost, and their mood becomes revolutionary.

▲ Resource Mobilization Approaches

According to the resource mobilization school, social discontent is more or less constant and thus endemic within all modern societies (Tilly, 1978; Taylor, 1989; Walton and Ragin, 1990). They emphasize the importance of structural factors, such as the availability of resources for pursuing particular goals and the network of interpersonal relationships that serve as the focus for membership recruitment. People are seen as participating in a social movement not as the result of deprivation but as a response to a rational decision-making process whereby they weigh the costs and benefits of participation. Consequently, conditions of political opportunity—for instance, support from established elites, contemporary models of successful political activism, and preexisting organizational networks and organizations—play a critical part in the development of social movements.

In many cases, resources and organizations outside the protest group are crucial in determining the scope and outcomes of collective action. External support is especially critical for movements of the poor. Sociologist J. Craig Jenkins (1985) contrasted the unsuccessful attempt to organize farmworkers by the National Farm Labor Union from 1946 to 1952 with the

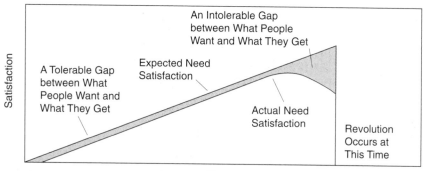

Figure 13.2 Davies's *J*-Curve Theory of Revolution

The figure illustrates Davies's theory that revolutions are often fostered when a period of social and economic betterment is succeeded by sharp reversals, fueling concern that the gains will be lost.

Source: Adapted from James C. Davies, "Toward a Theory of Revolution," *American Sociological Review,* vol. 27, February 1962, fig. 1, p. 6.

successful organization of Mexican farmworkers by the United Farm Workers from 1965 to 1972. Jenkins argued that the United Farm Workers succeeded because internal divisions in government neutralized opposition elites, while the support of the liberal-labor coalition during the reform years of the 1960s and early 1970s turned the tide in favor of the farmworkers. Hence, the success or failure of a social movement derives from strategic factors and the political processes in which it becomes enmeshed (Burstein, 1991b; Morris, 1993).

What keeps people involved in social movements? The rational choice model suggests that people get involved because of what they perceive the movements can do for them (Hechter, 1987). But once people are involved, how should leaders of the movements keep members actively participating and contributing and prevent them from engaging in "free ridership"; that is, being members in name but not actually contributing anything to the cause?

One answer is that leaders must get members and potential members to believe in the cause, to be committed to it out of personal, fervent belief. In addition, social mechanisms are required to control behavior and to maintain commitment to the movement for reasons beyond personal belief in its inherent worth.

Rosabeth Kanter (1968) showed that successful communal groups were more likely to have used mechanisms promoting commitment than unsuccessful groups. John Hall found that four factors were strongly associated with a group's long-term success (1988):

- A common ethnic background and/or a foreign language spoken by the group's members.

- A spiritual hierarchy, with those in authority being of higher moral status than other members.

- Obligatory confession, in which one's transgressions might be pointed out before confession by other members or leaders.

- The wearing of uniforms, or special clothes that set group members apart from the rest of society.

An example might help make those characteristics more concrete: The Amish, a group that speaks German, has church leaders and elders, and dresses very differently than the "English," as Amish call non-Amish persons. Children are not taught to speak English until they attend school. If one transgresses in Amish society, the punishment can be shunning, in which the transgressor is cast out from Amish society and cut off from friends and family.

Hall found that in the groups that were the oldest and survived intact the longest, researchers found continuing high levels of control mechanisms. Hall's study shows that the mechanisms of social control are more important than other factors in maintaining group solidarity and promoting the longevity of social movements and groups.

Types of Social Movements

A set of ideas—an **ideology**—is critical to a social movement. An ideology provides individuals with conceptions of the movement's purposes, its rationale for existence, its indictment of existing conditions or arrangements, and its design for action (Moaddel, 1992). It functions as a kind of glue that joins people together in a fellowship of belief. But an ideology not only binds together otherwise isolated and separated individuals, it unites them with a cause. In so doing it prepares them for self-sacrifice on behalf of the movement—at times even to lay down their lives for the "True God," "the New Nation," or "the Revolution."

Some movements pursue objectives that aim to change society through challenging fundamental values; others seek modifications within the framework of the existing value scheme. In the former case, **revolutionary movements** advocate replacement of the existing value scheme; in the latter, **reform movements** pursue changes that will implement the existing value scheme more adequately. The civil rights movement identified with the leadership of the Reverend Martin Luther King, Jr., had a reform emphasis. It sought to extend values already acknowledged as inherent in political democracy to the African-American population of the United States. In contrast, a number of African-American nationalist groups that arose in the late 1960s had a revolutionary emphasis. They sought to institute basic changes in the republican form of government in the United States, to rearrange the class structure, and to inaugurate a system of greater African-American autonomy.

Organized efforts called **resistance movements** arise not only for the purpose of instituting change but also to block change or to eliminate a previously instituted change. Thus, the movement for civil rights in the South unleashed a white counterattack beginning in the 1950s that found expression in the organization of white citizens' councils and Ku Klux Klan groups (Vander Zanden, 1965, 1983).

Still other types of movements—**expressive movements**—are less concerned with institutional change than with a renovating or renewing of people from *within,* frequently with the promise of some future redemption. Pentecostal and holiness religious sects are the most common examples of expressive movements. Less common are expressive movements that appeal primarily to the middle class, such as Zen Buddhism and *est* (Erhard Seminars Training) that were popular in the United States in the 1970s and 1980s (Tipton, 1982). Although most expressive movements arise among the underprivileged, they do not seek comprehensive social change nor do they aim to save the world. Their goal is to save individuals from a world that is becoming progressively degenerate or oppressive.

Social Revolution

A **social revolution** involves the overthrow of a society's state and class structures and the creation of new social arrangements. Revolutions are most likely to occur under certain conditions. First, a good deal of political power is concentrated in the state, so there is a centralized governing apparatus. Accordingly, the state can become the focus for collective anger and attack. Second, the military's allegiance to the established regime is weakened so that the army is no longer a reliable tool for suppressing domestic disorder. Where army officers are drawn from elites in conflict with the central government, or when troops sympathize with their civilian counterparts, the unreliability of the army increases the vulnerability of the state. Third, political crises—often associated with long-term international conflicts that result in military defeat—weaken the existing regime and contribute to the collapse of the state apparatus. And fourth, a substantial segment of the population must mobilize in uprisings that bring a new elite to power. Peasant revolts usually stem from landlords' taking over peasant lands, substantial increases in taxation or rents, or famines. Urban uprisings commonly derive from sharp jumps in food prices and unusually high levels of unemployment (Skocpol, 1979; Goldstone, 1991).

A number of historians and sociologists have surveyed important Western revolutions in search of common stages and patterns in their development. From this work have stemmed a number of observations regarding the sequence of events that typically unfold in the course of major social revolutions, an approach called the **natural history of revolutions.**

Prior to the revolution, intellectuals—journalists, poets, playwrights, essayists, lawyers, and others—withdraw support from the existing regime and demand major reforms. Under increasing attack, the state attempts to meet the criticisms by instituting a number of reforms (e.g., the reforms of Louis XVI in France). The onset of the revolution is heralded by a weakening or paralysis of the state, usually brought on by the government's inability to deal with a major military, economic, or political problem. The collapse of the old regime brings to the forefront divisions among conservatives who attempt to minimize change, radicals who seek fundamental change, and moderates who try to steer a middle course. Coups or civil war often

ensue. The first to gain the reins of power are usually moderate reformers.

The moderates seek to reconstruct governmental authority on the basis of limited reform, often employing organizational structures left over from the old regime. Simultaneously, radical centers of mass mobilization spring up with new organizations. The moderates, saddled with the same problems and liabilities that felled the old regime, are replaced by the radicals. The disorder that follows the revolution and the seizure of power by the radicals results in coercive rule. This is the stage of "terror" that characterized the guillotine days of the French Revolution. Turmoil persists and allows military leaders to move into ascendancy. Finally, radicalism gives way to a phase of pragmatism and the consolidation of a new status quo. The "excesses" of the revolution are condemned, and the emphasis falls on the fashioning of stable institutions. Although not all revolutions pass through the identical sequence of stages, there are recurrent patterns in the unfolding of revolutionary activity.

Terrorism

The September 11, 2001, attacks in New York City and Washington, D.C., alerted the United States to its vulnerability to terrorists. Although no one definition of **terrorism** is universally accepted, the U.S. Department of State offers this: "premeditated, politically motivated violence perpetrated against noncombatant targets by subnational groups or clandestine agents, usually intended to influence an audience" (Atran, 2003). The U.S. Congress defines acts of terror as acts that appear to be intended "(i) to intimidate or coerce a civilian population; (ii) to influence the policy of a government by intimidation or coercion; or (iii) to affect the conduct of a government by assassination or kidnapping." Familiar to all of us in the 21st Century is suicide terrorism, the use of self-destructing humans to commit terrorist acts.

U.S. interest in and concern about terrorism accelerated rapidly with the September 11, 2001, attacks on Washington, D.C., and New York City.

In practice, what constitutes terrorism is a matter of social definition, with one side labeling people as "terrorists" while another side labels the same people "freedom fighters." Similarly, whether an action is "aid to terrorists" as opposed to "covert support of friendly forces" is a matter of perspective, as illustrated by the Reagan administration's controversial support of the Nicaraguan contras, or counter-revolutionary fighters, in the mid-1980s.

▲ A Media Event

Very often terrorism is aimed at a media audience, not the actual victims. The "theater of terror" becomes possible only when the media afford the stage and access to a worldwide audience. The act of media coverage also often enhances the importance of the issue that allegedly led to the terrorist activities. Newspaper readers and television viewers see the issue as of

substantially greater importance and as justifying resolution by national or international action. As one analyst noted, "The primary target is not those actually killed or injured in the attack, but those made to witness it. The enemy's own information media amplify the attack's effects to the larger target population" (Atran, 2003).

▲ Terrorists and Social Change

Although terrorists have sometimes been profiled as poor, uneducated, and politically powerless, research has shown that suicide terrorists are as educated and economically well-to-do as those in the surrounding populations (Atran, 2003). And although political and social change may be what the terrorists' leaders are seeking, those who carry out the missions are motivated primarily by their group commitment. According to psychologists who studied the September 11 attacks, the 19 men who carried out the plans of Al-Qaida were motivated less by religious zeal and hatred for the United States than by peer pressure—the commitment each had made to the others to go forward with the plan (Vedantam, 2001).

With terrorism a grim fact of contemporary life, some analysts are calling for incorporating the potential for terrorist acts into disaster planning. Although the causes of disaster differ, plans for relief, development of backup systems, and the incorporation of disaster resistance into new communication, energy, water supply, and other systems are equally useful for dealing with natural disasters and large-scale acts of terrorism (Kennedy, 2002).

In an assessment of the root causes of and preventive measures for suicide terrorism, Scott Atran (2003) recommends sociological and psychological research on how terrorist institutions form and on recruitment and retention procedures. The first line of defense, he says, is to reduce the receptivity of potential recruits to recruiting organizations—but that cannot be done until planners understand more about the mix of community and institutional factors that make so many people eager to take part in terrorist groups. Atran also recommends that the United States respond to terrorist acts by addressing the grievances of terrorist organizations: "Our society can ill afford to ignore either the consequences of its own actions or the causes behind the actions of others" (Atran, 2003).

Looking to the Future

We undertake many of our daily activities in anticipation of the future. We carry out our job responsibilities in the expectation that we will be paid at the end of the week or the month. We invest our money, energy, and time in an education based on the assumption that there will be a job payoff down the road. We involve ourselves in environmental, civil rights, antinuclear, or women's movements to have a voice in the shaping of tomorrow's world.

And yet we can only speculate on what the future will bring; see Box 13.3, for example, about the future of same-sex marriages in the United States. We will probably have little more success anticipating the century ahead than did our compatriots 100 years ago at the future-oriented World's Columbian Exposition in Chicago, which we discussed in the introduction to the chapter. For the most part the forecasts provided by 74 prominent Americans not only turned out to be wrong but hilariously wrong.

However, some social phenomena can be predicted fairly accurately. Selling insurance is based on mostly accurate estimates of the risk of loss the company will incur due to illness, death, accidents, crime, and other things. Economists can predict that if the price of a product is doubled, fewer people will buy it. Sociologists can predict the persistence of educational inequality. But social scientists do not do well in predicting major social changes (Hechter, 1995).

Many years ago philosopher Karl Popper distinguished between *scientific predictions*, which are conditional (e.g., a prediction that specific changes in a system will result in specific changes in outcomes), and *unconditional historical prophecies*. The characteristics required to make accurate predictions for a system are that it be well isolated, stationary, and recurrent—characteristics that simply do not apply to societies. Societies can change, new social situations that we have never experienced before can arise, the growth of technology and knowledge can shift things in directions we are unable now to anticipate (Hechter, 1995).

As a consequence, social scientists cannot predict with any accuracy major social phenomena such as revolution. But as Hechter pointed out, the utility of the physical and social sciences "may not rest in their ability to accurately forecast events"; rather, as Karl Popper said (Popper, 1963:343), the role of science in social life is "the modest one of helping us to understand even the more remote consequences of possible actions, and thus of helping us to choose our actions more wisely."

Futurists—individuals who specialize in the study of the future, seeking to understand, predict, and plan the future of society—have identified two broad trends that seem to be central to contemporary social life (Coates and Jarratt, 1990; Halal and Nikitin, 1990). First, the United States is being restructured from an industrial to an information society. Second, modern societies are increasingly shifting from a national to a global economy.

For 300 years technology has been cast in a mechanical model, one based on combustion processes. The steam engine opened the

When Will Same-Sex Marriages Become "the Norm"?

Not long ago, most gay and lesbian people kept their sexual orientation a secret from most people, often even—or perhaps especially—from their families. As we launch a new century, there is increasing acceptance of people who are openly gay or lesbian and live together in same-sex couples. But different elements of society and culture often change at different rates, and in this case what people are willing to tolerate in the sexual behavior patterns of others has changed more rapidly than the societal institutions that have traditionally legitimated and controlled sexual behavior.

Marriage and family, two major American institutions, appear to be in the early stages of including same-sex unions in their definitions. Increased societal acceptance of homosexual lifestyles was one step. Legalization of same-sex unions is another. Although Americans became increasingly supportive of civil liberties for homosexuals over the last quarter of the 20th century (Loftus, 2001), the country's first civil-union law was not passed until 2000, when Vermont extended to gay and lesbian couples the same rights as heterosexual couples. Some cities and counties also have provisions for unmarried couples to register as domestic partners, but by 2003 only Massachusetts had joined Vermont in legalizing same-sex unions (Von Drehle, 2003).

An obvious third step is religious sanction of same-sex unions. But in 2003, when the Episcopal Church gave its bishops the option to allow priests to bless committed homosexual relationships, public outrage was immediate and loud. Polls showed that "a strong majority" of the public disapproved, especially frequent churchgoers (Morin and Cooperman, 2003). Some say that the reaction comes from the extension of the word *marriage*—something Americans see as essentially a religious institution—to same-sex unions. Sociologist Norval Glenn commented, "I know a lot of people who want to give all the rights and privileges to gay couples that married people have, but they don't want to change the traditional meaning of the term marriage" (Bumiller, 2003). The number of people opposed to same-sex unions actually increased after the Episcopal Church controversy, and at the end of 2003 a *New York Times/ CBS News* poll found that 55 percent of Americans favored a constitutional amendment that would ban homosexual marriage (Seelye and Elder, 2003).

Why are Americans able to tolerate gays and lesbians in their communities, but unable to tolerate homosexual marriage? The answer is that social institutions change much more slowly than do patterns of behavior and tolerance. Anthropologist Marvin Harris (1987) argued that both the practice and tolerance of homosexuality and other forms of nonprocreative sexual activity increased over the past 200 years as high birth rates declined. The major function of sexuality in people's lives shifted away from procreation and toward quality of life. But the institutions of religion and marriage have been slower to change. Both institutions legitimate and encourage sexuality because of its link to procreation, and they are not structured to support or to provide a positive moral understanding of homosexual or other nonprocreative sexual behaviors. Simply put, many people have great difficulty accepting homosexual unions as legitimate because neither religion nor traditional marriage provides a way to conceptualize homosexual behavior as morally correct.

It is not clear that same-sex marriage will ever be legitimate in the United States. Legally recognized domestic partnerships may increasingly be seen as the equivalent of civil marriage, as the line between the two kinds of unions slowly disappears. Legitimization of these unions by most mainstream religious bodies, if it occurs, will probably require more than a change of civil procedure: It will require a major change in underlying religious beliefs and ideas.

Questions for Discussion

1. In modern society people engage in sexual activity for purposes other than producing children. What are these?

2. How likely do you think it is that homosexual marriage will be legitimated in U.S. society? When and by what process do you think it will happen?

THE REAL PROBLEM WITH GAY MARRIAGE

Ante up, Mom and Dad. It's tradition.

YOU EITHER END UP WITH TWO WEDDINGS AND **NO** REHEARSAL DINNER, OR TWO REHEARSAL DINNERS AND **NO** WEDDING!

IF THAT DOESN'T MERIT A CONSTITUTIONAL AMENDMENT, I DON'T KNOW WHAT DOES.

rhymeswithorange.com
HILARY B. PRICE 4-20

The appearance of cartoons about gay marriage, such as this one that appeared in the comics pages of *The Washington Post,* suggest that it is becoming a topic of conventional discourse in the United States.

© 2004 Hilary B. Price. Distributed by King Features Syndicate, Inc. Reprinted with permission.

mechanical age, which reached its apex with the discovery of nuclear fission and nuclear fusion. Now high-tech industries are becoming information-intensive rather than energy- or materials-intensive. The shift to an information economy may improve our ability to forecast the future. Crisis forecasting, a technique now being developed at Los Alamos National Laboratory, uses computer models to predict such things as the path and behavior of a wildfire or the spread of biological toxins (Lane, 1998). The method may be extended to human events; researchers are close to being able to track in a computer model all 6 billion people on Earth, and very fast computers already are used to detect suspicious patterns in data that lead to identifying fraudulent tax returns and Medicare claims (Lane, 1998). Similar methods are being developed to use new information technologies to assess the future and develop long-term planning strategies to deal with the emerging challenges facing humankind (Lempert, Popper, and Bankes, 2003).

Global factors influencing our future are many. The rapid population growth that we cannot avoid in the next 50 years will test our abilities to adapt and change. We can expect increased conflicts over resources to be added to worldwide religious, ethnic, and nationalist conflicts. The AIDS epidemic in Africa, now spreading in Asia, has changed the demographics of a number of countries, and scientists predict that other diseases also may challenge our health care delivery systems. The collapse of the communist bloc and the transformation of eastern European and Asian nations into market economies are a few of the political and economic changes underway. And the planet's environmental problems, particularly climate change, provide an unprecedented opportunity to work together: "We must . . . design strategies that minimize the impact of climate change on societies that are at greatest risk. This will require substantial international cooperation, without which the 21st century will likely witness unprecedented social disruptions" (Weiss and Bradley, 2001:610).

As we have noted throughout this textbook, sociology invites us to scrutinize our prosaic world and notice what we otherwise often ignore, neglect, or take for granted. It looks behind the outer reaches of the social experience and discerns its inner structure and processes— suspending the belief that things are simply as they seem. As such, sociology is uniquely suited to fostering the skills necessary for living in an ever-changing world filled with countless choices and seemingly endless uncertainty. The challenges we confront in the 21st century may well inspire you to pursue a sociological career.

The Chapter in Brief: *Social Change*

▌A World of Change

Sociologists refer to fundamental alterations in the patterns of culture, structure, and social behavior over time as **social change.** It is a process by which society becomes something different while remaining in some respects the same.

▌*Sources of Social Change*   Many

factors interact to generate changes in people's behavior and in the culture and structure of their society, including the physical environment, population, clashes over resources and values, supporting values and norms, innovation (**discoveries** and **inventions**), **diffusion,** and the mass media.

▌*Perspectives on Social Change*

Evolutionary theorists, particularly those with a unilinear focus, depict history as divided into sequential stages characterized by an underlying trend. Cyclical theorists look to the course of a civilization or society, searching for generalizations regarding their stages of growth and decline. Functionalist theorists see society as a system that tends toward equilibrium, with **cultural lag** an important factor in social change. Conflict theorists hold that tensions between competing groups are the basic source of social change.

▌*Social Change in the United States*

Computers have consequences for the use and manipulation of social power. They alter the manner in which people relate to one another, and they have implications for individual privacy, the confidentiality of communications and personal data, and employment.

▌*Social Change in Developing Nations*

The **modernization** approach sees development as entailing a pattern of convergence as societies become increasingly urban, industry comes to overshadow agriculture, and other changes occur. According to **world system** and dependency analysis, an unequal exchange takes place between core and periphery nations, with development in core nations occurring at the cost of underdevelopment in periphery nations.

▌Collective Behavior

Collective behavior is not organized in terms of established norms and institutionalized lines of action.

▌*Varieties of Collective Behavior*

Collective behavior comes in many forms, including **rumors, fashions** and **fads** (which can turn into **crazes**), **mass hysteria, panic,** and **crowds.** Types of crowds include the **acting crowd,** the **casual crowd,** the **conventional crowd,** and the **expressive crowd.** These crowd types share three characteristics: suggestibility, **deindividualization,** and invulnerability.

▌*Preconditions for Collective Behavior*   One framework for examining

collective behavior is based on the **value-added** model popular among economists and specifies six determinants of collective behavior.

▌*Explanations of Crowd Behavior*

Sociologists offer three approaches to crowd behavior: **contagion theory, convergence theory,** and **emergent-norm theory.**

Social Movements

Social movements are vehicles whereby people collectively seek to influence the course of human events through formal organizations.

▌ *Causes of Social Movements*   Some sociologists seek the roots of social movements in social and economic deprivation; others look to the resources and organizations aggrieved persons can muster as providing the key to an understanding of social movements.

▌ *Types of Social Movements*   An **ideology** is critical to a social movement. Common forms of social movements include **revolutionary, reform, resistance,** and **expressive movements.**

▌ *Social Revolution*   **Social revolutions** are most likely to occur when: (1) a good deal of political power is concentrated in the state, (2) the military is no longer a reliable tool for suppressing domestic disorders, (3) political crises weaken the existing regime, and (4) a substantial segment of the population mobilizes in uprisings.

▌ *Terrorism*   Although what constitutes **terrorism** is a matter of social definition, sociologists have come to see terrorism as a new mode of warfare with far-reaching implications.

Looking to the Future

Futurists have identified two changes that seem to be central to contemporary social life: the United States is being restructured from an industrial to an information society and modern societies are increasingly shifting from a national to a global economy.

Glossary

acting crowd   An excited, volatile collection of people who are engaged in rioting, looting, or other forms of aggressive behavior in which established norms carry little weight.

casual crowd   A collection of people who have little in common with one another except that they may be viewing a common event, such as looking through a department store window.

collective behavior   Ways of thinking, feeling, and acting that develop among a large number of people and that are relatively spontaneous and unstructured.

contagion theory   An approach to crowd behavior that emphasizes the part played in crowd settings by rapidly communicated and uncritically accepted feelings, attitudes, and actions.

conventional crowd   A number of people who have assembled for some specific purpose and who typically act in accordance with established norms, such as people attending a baseball game or concert.

convergence theory   An approach to crowd behavior stating that a crowd consists of a highly unrepresentative body of people who assemble because they share the same predispositions.

craze   A fad that becomes an all-consuming passion.

crowd   A temporary, relatively unorganized gathering of people who are in close physical proximity.

cultural lag The view that immaterial culture must constantly "catch up" with material culture, resulting in an adjustment gap between the two forms of culture.

deindividualization A psychological state of diminished identity and self-awareness.

diffusion The process by which culture traits spread from one social unit to another.

discovery An addition to knowledge.

emergent-norm theory An approach to crowd behavior stating that crowd members evolve new standards for behavior in a crowd setting and then enforce the expectations in the manner of norms.

expressive crowd An aggregation of people who have gotten together for self-stimulation and personal gratification, such as occurs at a religious revival or a rock festival.

expressive movement A movement that is less concerned with institutional change than with a renovating or renewing of people from within.

fad A folkway that lasts for a short time and enjoys acceptance among only a segment of the population.

fashion A folkway that lasts for a short time and enjoys widespread acceptance within society.

futurists Individuals specializing in the study of the future; they seek to understand, predict, and plan the future of society.

ideology A set of ideas that provides individuals with conceptions of the purposes of a social movement, a rationale for the movement's existence, an indictment of existing conditions, and a design for action.

invention The use of existing knowledge in a new form.

mass hysteria The rapid dissemination of behaviors involving contagious anxiety, usually associated with some mysterious force.

modernization The process by which a society moves from traditional or pre-industrial social and economic arrangements to those characteristic of industrial societies.

natural history of revolutions The view that social revolutions pass through a set of common stages and patterns in the course of their development.

panic Irrational and uncoordinated but collective action among people that is induced by the presence of an immediate, severe threat.

reform movement A social movement that pursues changes that will implement the existing value scheme of a society more adequately.

relative deprivation Discontent associated with the gap between what people actually have and what they believe they should have.

resistance movement A social movement that arises to block change or eliminate a previously instituted change.

revolutionary movement A social movement that advocates the replacement of a society's existing value scheme.

rumor A difficult-to-verify piece of information that is transmitted from person to person in relatively rapid fashion.

social change Fundamental alterations in the patterns of culture, structure, and social behavior over time.

social movement A more-or-less persistent and organized effort on the part of a relatively large number of people to bring about or resist change.

social revolution The overthrow of a society's state and class structures and the fashioning of new social arrangements.

structural conduciveness Social conditions that permit a particular variety of collective behavior to occur.

structural strain   A condition in which important aspects of a social system are "out of joint."

terrorism   The use of force or violence against persons or property to intimidate or coerce a government, a formal organization, or a civilian

population in furtherance of political, religious, or social objectives.

value-added   The idea that each step in the production process—from raw materials to the finished product—increases the economic value of manufactured goods.

world system   An approach that views development as involving an unequal exchange between core and periphery nations, with development at the former end of the chain coming at the cost of underdevelopment at the other end.

Review Questions

1. What is social change? Give one example of a major social change that has taken place in the past 100 years. What were some of the factors responsible for that change?
2. Describe the major theories of social change.
3. How have computer use and Internet access affected life in the United States?
4. Compare the modernization and world system approaches to social change in developing nations.
5. What is collective behavior? List and define some of its forms.
6. What are the major explanations of crowd behavior?
7. What is a social movement? What causes a social movement?
8. What are the differences among revolutionary, reform, resistance, and expressive movements?
9. How does a social revolution occur?
10. What is terrorism?

Internet Connection

 www.mhhe.com/hughes8

Select a social movement that you support or that is of interest to you—the women's movement, gun control, pro-life, pro-choice, rain forest preservation, etc.—and use a search engine such as google.com to find information about this movement.

Write a short report about the movement. Is it a reform, resistance, or revolutionary movement? Which approach to social movements—deprivation or resource mobilization—best accounts for it?

A

Abbott, Pamela, and **Claire Wallace.** 1997. *An Introduction to sociology: Feminist perspectives.* London: Routledge.

Acker, Joan. 1992. Gendered institutions. *Contemporary Sociology,* 21:565–69.

Adam, Barbara, and **Stuart Allan,** eds. 1995. *Theorizing culture: An interdisciplinary critique after post-modernism.* New York: New York University Press.

Adams, Mary. 1998. *Marital status and happiness, 1972–1996.* Paper presented in the Colloquium Series. Department of Sociology, Virginia Polytechnic Institute and State University, Blacksburg, VA 24060-0137, September 1998.

Adler, Freda, Gerhard O. W. Mueller, and **William S. Laufer.** 2004. *Criminology and the criminal justice system.* New York: McGraw-Hill.

Adler, Patricia A., and **Peter Adler.** 1989. The gloried self: The aggrandizement and the constriction of self. *Social Psychological Quarterly,* 52:299, 310.

Adler, Stephen J. 1991. Suits over sexual harassment prove difficult due to issue of definition. *Wall Street Journal* (October 9): B1.

Agger, Ben. 1991. Critical theory, poststructuralism, postmodernism: Their sociological relevance. *Annual Review of Sociology,* 17:105–31.

Ahlburg, Dennis, and **Carol J. De Vita.** 1992. New realities of the American family. *Population Bulletin,* 47: No. 2.

Akard, Patrick J. 1992. Corporate mobilization and political power: The transformation of U.S. economic policy in the 1970s. *American Sociological Review,* 57:597–615.

Alba, Richard D. 1990. *Ethnic identity: The transformation of white America.* New Haven, CT: Yale University Press.

Allport, Gordon W. 1954. *The nature of prejudice.* Boston: Beacon Press.

Altschiller, David. 1988. Selling the presidency: More dollars equal less message. *New York Times* (March 20): F3.

Alwin, Duane, F., and **Jon A. Krosnick.** 1991. Aging, cohorts, and the stability of sociopolitical orientations over the life span. *American Journal of Sociology,* 97:169–95.

Amato, Paul R., and **Alan Booth.** 1997. *A generation at risk: Growing up in an era of family upheaval.* Cambridge, MA: Harvard University Press.

Amato, Paul R., and **Juliana M. Sobolewski.** 2001. The effects of divorce and marital discord on adult children's psychological well-being. *American Sociological Review,* 66:900–21.

American Academy of Pediatrics. 2001. Childhood, adolescents, and television. *Pediatrics,* 107(2):423–26.

American Anthropological Association. 1997. *American Anthropological Association response to OMB Directive 15: Race and ethnic standards for federal statistics and administrative reporting.* Arlington, VA: American Anthropological Association.

American Sociological Association. 1989. Code of ethics. Washington, DC: American Sociological Association.

Amnesty International. 2004. *Starved of rights.* http://www .amnesty.org/library/Index/ ENGASA240032004?open&of= ENG-PRK

Andersen, Margaret L., and **Patricia Hill Collins.** 2004. *Race, class, and gender: An anthology.* Belmont, CA: Wadsworth.

Anderson, Craig A., and **Brad J. Bushman.** 2002. The effects of media violence on society. *Science,* 295:2377–79.

Anderson, Elijah. 1978. *A place on the corner.* Chicago: University of Chicago Press.

Anderson, Elijah. 1990. *Streetwise: Race, class, and change in an urban community.* Chicago: University of Chicago Press.

Anderson, Elijah. 1994. The code of the streets. *Atlantic Monthly,* (May):81–94.

Anderson, Elijah. 1999. *The code of the street: Decency, violence, and the moral life of the inner city.* New York: W.W. Norton.

Anderson, Elijah. 2001. Urban ethnography. *International encyclopedia of social sciences.* New York: Elsevier.

Anderson, Robert, and **Betty L. Smith.** 2005. Deaths: Leading Causes 2002. National Vital Statistics Reports, Vol. 53, No. 17. Hyattsville, MD: National Center for Health Statistics.

Appenzeller, Tim. 2004. The case of the missing carbon. *National Geographic* (February):88–117.

Apple, Michael W. 1982. *Education and power.* London: Routledge & Kegan Paul.

Appy, Christian G. 1993. *Working-class war: American combat soldiers and Vietnam.* Chapel Hill: University of North Carolina Press.

Argetsinger, Amy. 2003. Legacy students pose challenge to affirmative action. *Washington Post* (March 12):A6.

Arias, Elizabeth. 2002. United States life tables, 2000. *National*

Vital Statistics Reports,
51(3):December.

Ariès, Philippe. 1962. *Centuries of childhood.* Trans. R. Baldick. New York: Random House.

Armas, Genaro C. 2003. Study: Rents up by one-third. Associated Press (September 9).

Aronson, Eliot. 1994. *The social animal.* New York: W. H. Freeman.

Arrillaga, Pauline. 2000. Putting polygamy on trial in Utah. *Washington Post* (December 8): A49.

Arrow, Kenneth, Samuel Bowles, and **Steven Durlauf,** eds. 2000. *Meritocracy and economic inequality.* Princeton, NJ: Princeton University Press.

Asch, Solomon. 1952. *Social psychology.* Englewood Cliffs, NJ: Prentice Hall.

Ascher, Marcia. 2002. *Mathematics elsewhere: An exploration of ideas across cultures.* Princeton: Princeton University Press.

Ashford, Lori. 2002. *Hidden suffering.* Washington, DC: Population Reference Bureau.

Associated Press. 2003a. Gay-rights group compares gay couples to others. *Washington Post* (May 18):A7.

Association of American Medical Colleges. 2003. www.aamc.org/data/facts/2003/2003school.htm

Atran, Scott. 2003. Genesis of suicide terrorism. *Science,* 299:1534–39.

Axelrod, Robert, 1984. *The evolution of cooperation.* New York: Basic Books.

Axinn, William G., and **Jennifer S. Barber.** 1997. Living arrangements and family formation attitudes in early adulthood. *Journal of Marriage and the Family,* 59:595–611.

B

Bachu, Amara. 1997. Fertility of American women: June 1995 (update). *Current Population Reports,* P20-499, Washington, DC: U.S. Bureau of the Census.

Baer, Ellen D. 1991. The feminist disdain for nursing. *New York Times* (February 23): 17.

Baker, Beth. 2003. Dead wrong: Most want to die at home. Here's why they don't succeed. *Washington Post* (May 13):F1.

Baker, Stephen. 1993. The owners vs. the boss at Weirton Steel. *Business Week* (November 15):38.

Bales, Robert F. 1970. *Personality and interpersonal behavior.* New York: Holt, Rinehart and Winston.

Bales, Robert F., and **Edgar F. Borgatta.** 1955. Size of group as a factor in the interaction profile. In A. P. Hare, E. F. Borgatta, and R. F. Bales, eds., *Small groups: Studies in social interaction.* New York: Knopf.

Bandura, Albert. 1965. Influence of models reinforcement contingencies on the acquisition of imitative responses. *Journal of Personality and Social Psychology,* 1:589–95.

Bandura, Albert. 1971. *Psychological modeling: Conflicting theories.* Chicago: Aldine-Atherton.

Bandura, Albert. 1973. *Aggression: A social learning analysis.* Englewood Cliffs, NJ: Prentice Hall.

Bane, Mary Jo. 1997. Welfare as we might know it. *The American Prospect,* No. 30 (January February): 47–53.

Bane, Mary Jo, and **David T. Ellwood.** 1994. *Welfare realities: from rhetoric to reform.* Cambridge, MA: Harvard University Press.

Bank, Lew, Marion S. Forgatch, Gerald R. Patterson, and **Rebecca A. Fetrow.** 1993. Parenting practices of single mothers: Mediators of negative contextual factors. *Journal of Marriage and the Family,* 55:371–84.

Banks, James, Michael Marmot, Zoe Oldfield, and **James P. Smith.** 2006. Disease and disadvantage in the United States and England. *Journal of the American Medical Association,* 295:2037–2045.

Barak, Gregg, ed. 1991. *Crimes by the capitalist state. An introduction to state criminality.* Albany: State University of New York Press.

Barber, Bonnie L., Jacquelynne S. Eccles, and **Margaret R. Stone.** 2001. Whatever happened to the Jock, the Brain, and the Princess? Young adult pathways linked to adolescent activity involvement and social identity. *Journal of Adolescent Research,* 16(5):429–55.

Barber, Elizabeth. 1994. *Women's work, the first 20,000 years.* New York: Norton.

Barenboim, Carl. 1981. The development of person perception in childhood and adolescence. *Child Development,* 52:129–44.

Barkey, Karen, and **Sunita Parikh.** 1991. Comparative perspectives on the state. *Annual Review of Sociology,* 11:523–49.

Barnes, Jessica S., and **Claudette Bennett.** 2002. The Asian Population 2000. U.S. Census Bureau C2KBR/01-16. Washington, DC: U.S. Government Printing Office.

Barnet, Richard J., and **John Cavanagh.** 1994. *Global dreams: Imperial corporations and the new world order.* New York: Simon and Schuster.

Barringer, Felicity. 1993. Sex survey of American men finds 1% are gay. *New York Times* (April 15): A1, A9.

Barrow, Clyde W. 1990. *Universities and the capitalist state: Corporate liberalism and the reconstruction of American higher education, 1894–1928.* Madison: University of Wisconsin Press.

Bartholomew, Robert E., and **Jeffrey S. Victor.** 2004. A social-psychological theory of collective anxiety attacks: The "Mad Gasser" reexamined. *The Sociological Quarterly,* 45(2):229–48.

Bartol, Kathryn M., and **David C. Martin.** 1998. *Management.* 3rd ed. New York: McGraw-Hill.

Bartollas, Clemens. 2003. *Juvenile delinquency.* Boston: Allyn and Bacon.

Bass, Bernard M. 1981. *Stogdill's handbook of leadership.* New York: Free Press.

Baudrillard, Jean. 1983. *Simulations.* New York: Semiotext(e).

Baudrillard, Jean. 1990. *Fatal Strategies.* New York: Semiotext(e).

Baxter, Janeen. 1994. Is husband's class enough? Class location and class identity in the United States, Sweden, Norway, and Australia. *American Sociological Review,* 59:220–35.

Baydar, Nazli, and **Jeanne Brooks-Gunn.** 1991. Effects of maternal employment and child-care arrangements on preschoolers' cognitive and behavioral outcomes. Evidence from the children of the National Longitudinal Survey of Youth. *Developmental Psychology,* 27:932–45.

Bean, Frank D., and **Marta Tienda.** 1987. *The Hispanic population of the United States.* New York: Russell Sage Foundation.

Beck, E. M., Patrick Horan, and **Charles Tolbert.** 1980. Social stratification in industrial society: Further evidence for a structural alternative. *American Sociological Review,* 45:712–19.

Beck, E. M., and **Stewart E. Tolnay.** 1990. The killing fields of The Deep South: The market for cotton and the lynching of blacks, 1882–1930. *American Sociological Review,* 55:526–39.

Becker, Howard S. 1963. *Outsiders: Studies in the sociology of deviance.* New York: Free Press.

Beeghley, Leonard. 2000. *The structure of social stratification in the United States.* Boston: Allyn and Bacon.

Beer, William. 1988. New family ties: How well are we coping? *Public Opinion,* 10 (March–April): 14, 15, 57.

Begley, Sharon. 2003. Scientifically, race is only skin deep and not very useful. *Wall Street Journal* (August 1):B1.

Beisel, Nicola, and **Tamara Kay.** 2004. Abortion, race, and gender in nineteenth-century America. *American Sociological Review,* 69:498–518.

Beirne, Piers. 1979. Empiricism and the critique of Marxism on law and crime. *Social Problems,* 26:373–85.

Bell, Alan P., and **Martin S. Weinberg.** 1978. *Homosexualities: A study of diversity among men and women.* New York: Simon and Schuster.

Bell, Alan P., Martin S. Weinberg, and **Sue K. Hammersmith.** 1981. *Sexual preference: Its development in men and women.* Bloomington: Indiana University Press.

Bellah, Robert N. 1970. *Beyond belief.* New York: Harper & Row.

Bellah, Robert N., and **Phillip E. Hammond.** 1980. *Varieties of civil religions.* New York: Harper & Row.

Belsky, Jay. 1990. Parental and non-parental child care and children's socioemotional development: A decade in review. *Journal of Marriage and the Family,* 52:885–903.

Belsky, Jay, and **Michael Rovine.** 1990. Patterns of marital change across the transition to parenthood: Pregnancy to three years postpartum. *Journal of Marriage and the Family,* 52:5–19.

Bem, Sandra. 1981. Gender schema theory: A cognitive account of sex typing. *Psychological Bulletin,* 88:354–64.

Bendix, Reinhard. 1977. Bureaucracy. *International encyclopedia of the social sciences.* New York: Free Press.

Bennett, Amanda. 1990. Quality programs may be shoddy stuff. *Wall Street Journal* (October 4):B1.

Berberoglu, Berch. 1987. *The internationalization of capital: Imperialism and capitalist development on a world scale.* New York: Praeger.

Berger, Peter L. 1963. *Invitation to sociology.* Garden City, NY: Anchor Books.

Berger, Peter L. 1967. *The sacred canopy: Elements of a sociological theory of religion.* Garden City, NY: Doubleday.

Berger, Peter L., and **Brigitte Berger.** 1972. *Sociology: A biographical approach.* New York: Basic Books.

Berger, Suzanne. 2005. *How we compete: What companies around the world are doing to make it in the global economy.* New York: Doubleday.

Bergesen, Albert J. 2004. Durkheim's theory of mental categories: A review of the evidence. *Annual Review of Sociology,* 30:395–408.

Bergman, Mike. 2003. Women edge men in high school diplomas, breaking 13-year deadlock. *U.S. Department of Commerce News* (March 21). U.S. Census Bureau.

Berk, Richard A., and **Phyllis J. Newton.** 1985. Does arrest really deter wife battery? An effort to replicate the findings of the Minneapolis spouse abuse experiment. *American Sociological Review,* 50:253–62.

Berke, Richard L. 1990. Study confirms interest groups' pattern of giving. *New York Times* (September 16):18.

Berkowitz, Leonard. 1989. Frustration-aggression hypothesis: Examination and reformulation. *Psychological Bulletin,* 106:59–73.

Berle, Adolph, Jr., and **Gardner C. Means.** 1932. *The modern corporation and private property.* New York: Harcourt, Brace & World.

Bernard, Jessie. 1987. *The female world from a global perspective.* Bloomington: Indiana University Press.

Bernstein, Aaron. 2003. Waking up from the American Dream: Dead-end jobs and the high cost of college could be choking off upward mobility. *Business Week online* Dec. 1.

Bernstein, Ilene N., William R. Kelly, and **Patricia A. Doyle.** 1977. Social reactions to deviants: The case of criminal defendants. *American Sociological Review,* 42:743–55.

Bernstein, Nina. 2002. Side effect of welfare law: The no-parent family. *New York Times* (July 29).

Bertrand, Marianne, and **Sendhil Mullainathan.** 2001. Are CEOs rewarded for luck? The ones without principles are. *Quarterly Journal of Economics,* 116:910–31.

Bertrand, Marianne, and **Sendhil Mullainathan.** 2003. Are Emily and Greg more employable than Lakisha and Jamal? A field experiment on labor market discrimination. *National Bureau of Economic Research.* Working Paper No. w9873.

Best, Steven, and **Douglas Kellner.** 1991. *Postmodern theory: Critical interrogations.* New York: Guilford Press.

Beylotte, Frank. 2003. Genes and behavior take center stage. *Psychological Science Agenda,* 16(3):14.

Bhattacharjee, Yudhijit. 2005. Schools cheer rise in foreign students. *Science,* 310:957.

Bianchi, Suzanne M. 1999. Feminization and juvenilization of poverty: Trends, relative risks, causes, and consequences. *Annual Review of Sociology,* 25:307–33.

Biderman, Albert D., and **James P. Lynch.** 1991. *Understanding crime incidence statistics: Why the UCR diverges from the NCS.* New York: Springer-Verlag.

Bielby, Denise D., and **William T. Bielby.** 1988. She works hard for the money: Household responsibilities and the allocation of work effort. *American Journal of Sociology,* 93:1031–59.

Bielby, William T., and **Denise D. Bielby.** 1992. I will follow him: Family ties, gender-role beliefs, and reluctance to relocate for a better job. *American Journal of Sociology,* 97:1241–47.

Bierstedt, Robert. 1950. An analysis of social power. *American Sociological Review,* 15:730–38.

Biersteker, Thomas J. 1987. *Multinationals, the state and control of the Nigerian economy.* Princeton, NJ: Princeton University Press.

Billings, Dwight B. 1990. Religion as opposition: A Gramscian analysis. *American Journal of Sociology,* 96:131.

Bimber, Bruce. 2000. Measuring the gender gap on the Internet. *Social Science Quarterly,* 81(3):868–76.

Birdwhistell, Raymond L. 1970. *Kinesics and context.* Philadelphia: University of Pennsylvania Press.

Birkett, Dea. 1997. *Serpent in paradise: Among the people of the Bounty.* New York: Doubleday.

Bittman, Michael, Paula England, Liana Sayer, Nancy Folbre, and **George Matheson.** 2003. When does gender trump money? Bargaining and time in household work. *American Journal of Sociology,* 109(1):186–214.

Blackwell, Brenda Sims. 2000. Perceived sanction threats, gender, and crime: A test and elaboration of power-control theory. *Criminology,* 38(2):439–88.

Blasi, Joseph R. 1988. *Employee ownership: Revolution or rip-off?* Cambridge, MA: Ballinger.

Blau, Judith R., and **Eric S. Brown.** 2001. Du Bois and diasporic identity: The *Veil* and the *Unveiling* project. *Sociological Theory,* 19:219–33.

Blau, Peter M., and **Otis Dudley Duncan.** 1972. *The American occupational structure.* 2nd ed. New York: John Wiley.

Blau, Peter M., and **Richard A. Schoenherr.** 1971. *The structure of organizations.* New York: Basic Books.

Blau, Peter, and **Richard Scott.** 1962. *Formal organizations.* San Francisco: Chandler.

Blauner, Robert. 1964. *Alienation and freedom.* Chicago: University of Chicago Press.

Block, N. J., and **Gerald Dworkin,** eds. 1976. *The IQ controversy: Critical readings.* New York: Pantheon.

Bluhm, Carey, Thomas A. Widiger, and **Gloria M. Miele.** 1990. Interpersonal complementarity and individual differences. *Journal of*

Personality and Social Psychology, 58:464–71.

Blum, Deborah. 1997. *Sex on the brain: The biological differences between men and women.* New York: Viking Penguin.

Blum, Robert W., Trisha Beuhring, Marcia L. Shew, Linda H. Bearinger, Renee E. Sieving, and **Michael D. Resnick.** 2000. The effects of race/ethnicity, income, and family structure on adolescent risk behaviors. *American Journal of Public Health,* 90:1879–84.

Blumer, Herbert. 1946. *Collective behavior.* In A. M Lee, ed., *New outline of the principles of sociology.* New York: Barnes & Noble.

Blumer, Herbert. 1958. Race prejudice as a sense of group position. *Pacific Sociological Review,* 1:3–7.

Blumer, Herbert. 1969. *Symbolic interaction: Perspective and method.* Englewood Cliffs, NJ: Prentice Hall.

Blumstein, Philip, and **Pepper Schwartz.** 1983. *American couples.* New York: Morrow.

Blumstein, Philip, and **Pepper Schwartz.** 1991. Money and ideology: Their impact on power and the division of household labor. In Rae Lesser Blumberg, ed., *Gender, family, and economy: The triple overlap.* Newbury Park, CA: Sage.

Bobo, Lawrence. 1983. Whites' opposition to busing: Symbolic racism or realistic group conflict. *Journal of Personality and Social Psychology,* 45:1196–210.

Bobo, Lawrence, and **James R. Kluegel.** 1993. Opposition to race-targeting: Self-interest, stratification ideology, or racial attitudes? *American Sociological Review,* 58:443–64.

Bobo, Lawrence, James R. Kluegel, and **Ryan A. Smith.** 1997. Laissez-faire racism: The crystallization of a kinder, gentler, antiblack ideology. In Steven A. Tuch and Jack Martin, eds., *Racial attitudes in the 1990s: Continuity and change.* Westport, CT: Praeger.

Boesch, Christophe. 2003. Is culture a golden barrier between human and chimpanzee? *Evolutionary Anthropology* 12:82–91.

Bohannan, John. 2005. Disasters: Searching for lessons from a bad year. *Science,* 310:1883 (December 23).

Bohannon, Paul, and **Rosemary Erickson.** 1978. Stepping in. *Psychology Today,* 11 (January):53–59.

Bok, Derek. 1993. *The cost of talent: How executives and professionals are paid and how it affects America.* New York: Free Press.

Bollen, Kenneth A., and **Stephen J. Appold.** 1993. National industrial structure and the global system. *American Sociological Review,* 58:283–301.

Bonacich, Edna. 1972. A theory of ethnic antagonism: A split-labor market. *American Sociological Review,* 37:547–59.

Bonacich, Edna. 1975. Abolition, the extension of slavery, and the position of free blacks: A study of split-labor markets in the United States, 1830–1863. *American Journal of Sociology,* 81:601–28.

Bonacich, Edna, and **John Modell.** 1980. *The economic basis of ethnic solidarity.* Berkeley: University of California Press.

Bonczar, Thomas P., and **Allen J. Beck.** 1997. Lifetime likelihood of going to state or federal prison. Washington, DC: U.S. Department of Justice. NCJ-160092.

Bonczar, Thomas P., and **Tracy L. Snell.** 2004. Capital Punishment, 2003. Washington, DC: U.S. Department of Justice (NCJ 206627; http://www.ojp.usdoj.gov/bjs/pub/pdf/cp03.pdf).

Bond, James T., Ellen Galinsky, and **Jennifer E. Swanberg.** 1998. *The 1997 national study of the changing workforce.* Washington, DC: Families and Work Institute.

Bonger, William A. 1936. *An introduction to criminology.* London: Methuen.

Boodman, Sandra G. 2000. Second thoughts: Think the arrival of your first child changed your life? Just wait until number two joins the family. *Washington Post Health Magazine* (November 28):6.

Boraas, Stephanie, and **William M. Rodgers III.** 2003. How does gender play a role in the earnings gap? An update. *Monthly Labor Review* (March:9–15).

Boroughs, Don L. 1992. *U.S. News & World Report* (May 4):50–52.

Boswell, Terry. 1989. Colonial empires and the capitalist world-economy: A time series analysis of colonization, 1640–1960. *American Sociological Review,* 54:180–96.

Boswell, Terry, and **William J. Dixon.** 1993. Marx's theory of rebellion: A cross-national analysis of class exploitation, economic development, and violent revolt. *American Sociological Review,* 58:681–702.

Botsford, Louis W., Juan Carlos Castilla, and **Charles H. Peterson.** 1997. The management of fisheries and marine ecosystems. *Science,* 277:509–15.

Bouchard, Thomas J. 1994. Genes, environment, and personality. *Science,* 264:1700–1.

Bouchard, Thomas J., David T. Lykken, Matthew McGue, Nancy L. Segal, and **Auke Tellegen.** 1990. Sources of human psychological differences. The Minnesota study of twins reared apart. *Science,* 250:223–28.

Bound, John, Greg J. Duncan, Deborah S. Laren, and **Lewis Oleinick.** 1991. Poverty dynamics in widowhood. *Journal of Gerontology,* 46:S115–24.

Bourdieu, Pierre. 1994. Rethinking the state: Genesis and structure of the bureaucratic field. *Sociological Theory,* 12:118.

Bowles, Samuel, and **Herbert Gintis.** 1976. *Schooling and capitalist America.* New York: Basic Books.

Bowles, Samuel, and **Herbert Gintis.** 2000. Does schooling raise earnings by making people smarter? In Kenneth Arrow, Samuel Bowles, and Steven Durlauf, eds., *Meritocracy and economic inequality.* Princeton, NJ: Princeton University Press.

Bradburn, Norman M., and **Seymour Sudman.** 1988. *Polls and surveys: Understanding what they tell us.* San Francisco: Jossey-Bass.

Braddock, Jomills Henry, III, and **James M. McPartland.** 1987. How minorities continue to be excluded from equal employment opportunities: Research on labor market and institutional barriers. *Journal of Social Issues,* 43:5–39.

Bradley, Harriet. 1989. *Men's work, women's work: A sociological history of the sexual division of labour in employment.* Minneapolis: University of Minnesota Press.

Bradshaw, York W. 1988. Reassessing economic dependency and uneven development: The Kenyan experience. *American Sociological Review,* 53:693–708.

Brand-Williams, Oralandar. 1997. Tiger's comments stir up racial-designation debate. *Detroit News* (April 25):Metro.

Braxton, John M., and **Alan E. Bayer.** 1999. *Faculty misconduct in collegiate teaching.* Baltimore: The Johns Hopkins University Press.

Brazelton, T. Berry, and **Stanley I. Greenspan.** 2000. *The irreducible needs of children: What every child must have to grow, learn, and flourish.* Cambridge, MA: Perseus Publishing.

Breen, Richard, and **Jan O. Jonsson.** 2004. Inequality of opportunity in comparative perspective: Recent research on educational attainment and social mobility. *Annual Review of Sociology,* 31:223–43.

Breines, Wini. 1980. Community and organization: The New Left and Michels' "iron law." *Social Problems,* 27:419–29.

Brenner, Lynn. 2003. How did you do? *Parade: The Sunday Newspaper Magazine* (March 2):4–7.

Bridges, George S., Robert D. Crutchfield, and **Edith E. Simpson.** 1987. Crime, social structure and criminal punishment: White and non-white rates of imprisonment. *Social Problems,* 34:345–61.

Briggs, Pam. 2002. Learning from *The Experiment. The Psychologist,* 15(7):344–45.

Brody, Elaine M. 1990. *Women in the middle: Their parent-care years.* New York: Springer.

Brody, Elaine M., Sandra J. Litvin, Steven M. Albert, and **Christine J. Hoffman.** 1994. Marital status of daughters and patterns of parent care. *Journal of Gerontology,* 49:S95–S103.

Brouillette, John R., and **Ronny E. Turner.** 1992. Creating the sociological imagination on the first day of class: The social construction of deviance. *Teaching Sociology,* 20:276–79.

Brown, David. 1999. U.S. cancer rates are in decline. *Washington Post* (April 21):A2.

Brown, Dee. 1971. *Bury my heart at Wounded Knee.* New York: Holt, Rinehart, and Winston.

Browne, Irene, and **Joya Misra.** 2003. The intersection of gender and race in the labor market. *Annual Review of Sociology,* 29:487–513.

Brown, Kathryn. 2003. The medication merry-go-round. *Science,* 299:1646–49.

Brown, Lester R., and **Christopher Flavin.** 1999. A new economy for a new century. In *state of the world 1999: A Worldwatch Institute report on progress toward a sustainable society.* New York: Norton.

Brownmiller, Susan. 1975. *Against our will: Men, women, and rape.* New York: Simon and Schuster.

Bruegmann, Robert. 2005. *Sprawl: A compact history.* Chicago: University of Chicago Press.

Brummett, Beverly H., John C. Barefoot, Ilene C. Siegler, Nancy E. Clapp-Channing, Barbara L. Lytle, Hayden B. Bosworth, Redford B. Williams, Jr., Daniel B. Mark. 2001. Characteristics of socially isolated patients with coronary

artery disease who are at elevated risk for mortality. *Psychosomatic Medicine,* 63:267–72.

Bruno, Rosalind R. 1996. *Postsecondary school financing.* Washington, DC: U.S. Bureau of the Census.

Bryson, Bethany. 1996. Anything but heavy metal: Symbolic exclusion and musical dislikes. *American Sociological Review,* 61:884–99.

Buchmann, Marlis. 1989. *The script of life in modern society: Entry into adulthood in a changing world.* Chicago: University of Chicago Press.

Bucks, Brian K., Arthur B. Kennickell, and **Kevin B. Moore.** 2006. Recent changes in U.S. family finances: Evidence from the 2001 and 2004 Survey of Consumer Finances. *Federal Reserve Bulletin,* 92: A1–A38.

Budig, Michelle J., and **Paula England.** 2001. The wage penalty for motherhood. *American Sociological Review,* 66:204–25.

Budros, Art. 2004. Social shocks and slave social mobility: Manumission in Brunswich County, Virginia, 1782–1862. *American Journal of Sociology,* 110:539–79.

Buechler, Steven M. 1990. *Women's movements in the United States: Woman suffrage, equal rights, and beyond.* New Brunswick, NJ: Rutgers University Press.

Bumiller, Elisabeth. 2003. Why America has gay marriage jitters. *New York Times* (August 10): Week in Review.

Bumpass, L. L., and **H.-h Lu.** 2000. Trends in cohabitation and implications for children's family contexts in the United States. *Population Studies,* 54:19–41.

Bumpass, Larry L., James A. Sweet, and **Andrew Cherlin.** 1991. The role of cohabitation in declining rates of marriage. *Journal of Marriage and the Family,* 53:913–27.

Bunzel, John H. 1988. Choosing freshmen: Who deserves an edge? *Wall Street Journal* (February 1):22.

Burawoy, Michael. 1979. *Manufacturing consent.* Chicago: University of Chicago Press.

Burbank, Victoria Katherine. 1988. *Aboriginal adolescence: Maidenhood in an aboriginal community.* New Brunswick, NJ: Rutgers University Press.

Burchard, Esteban Gonzalez, Elad Ziv, Natasha Coyle, Scarlett Lin Gomez, Hua Tang, Andrew J. Kartner, Joanna L. Mountain, Eliseo J. Perez-Stable, Dean Sheppard, and **Neil Risch.** 2003. The importance of race and ethnic background in biomedical research and clinical practice. *New England Journal of Medicine,* 348:1170–75.

Bureau of Justice Statistics. 2003. U.S. Department of Justice Office of Justice Programs. Available at: www.ojp.usdoj.gov/bjs/correct.htm.

Burke, Peter J. 2004. Identities and social structure: The 2003 Cooley-Meade Award address. *Social Psychology Quarterly,* 67:5–15.

Burkett, Steven R., and **Mervin White.** 1974. Hellfire and delinquency: Another look. *Journal for the Scientific Study of Religion,* 13:455–62.

Burnham, James. 1941. *The managerial revolution.* New York: John Day.

Burns, Peter F., Peter L. Francia, and **Paul S. Herrnson.** 2000. Labor at work: Union campaign activities and legislative payoffs in the U.S. House of Representatives. *Social Science Quarterly,* 81(2):507–22.

Burr, Chandler. 1996. *A separate creation: The search for the biological origins of sexual orientation.* New York: Hyperion.

Burris, Val. 1988. The political partisanship of American business. *American Sociological Review,* 52:732–44.

Burstein, Paul. 1991a. Policy domains: Organization, culture, and policy outcomes. *Annual Review of Sociology,* 17:327–50.

Burstein, Paul. 1991b. Legal mobilization as a social movement tactic: The struggle for equal employment opportunity. *American Journal of Sociology,* 96:1201–25.

Bushman, Brad J., and **Craig A. Anderson.** 2001. Media violence and the American public: Scientific facts versus media misinformation. *American Psychologist,* 56(6/7):477–89.

Butterfield, Fox. 1986. Why Asians are going to the head of the class. *New York Times* (August 3): Educ 18–23.

Butterfield, Fox. 1992. Studies find a family link to criminality. *New York Times* (January 31):A1, A8.

Buzawa, E. S., and **C. G. Buzawa.** 1990. *Domestic violence.* Newbury Park, CA: Sage.

Byfield, Joanne. 2001. Home is where the smarts are. *Report/ Newsmagazine,* 28(23):43–4.

C

Cacioppo, John T., Gary G. Bernston, John F. Sheridan, and **Martha K. McClintock.** 2000. Multilevel integrative analyses of human behavior: Social neuroscience and the complementing nature of social and biological approaches. *Psychological Bulletin,* 126:829–43.

Calasanti, Toni, and **Anna M. Zajicek.** 1997. Gender, the state, and constructing the old as dependent: Lessons from the economic transition in Poland. *The Gerontologist,* 37:452–61.

Calasanti, Toni M., and **Kathleen R. Slevin.** 2001. *Gender, social inequalities, and aging.* Walnut Creek, CA: AltaMira Press.

Calavita, K., R. Tillman, and **H. N. Pontell.** 1997. The savings and loan debacle, financial crime, and the state. *Annual Review of Sociology,* 23:19–38.

Campbell, Donald T. 1965. Ethnocentric and other altruistic motives. In Robert Levine, ed., *Nebraska Symposium on motivation.* Lincoln: University of Nebraska Press.

Cantril, Hadley. 1941. *The psychology of social movements.* New York: John Wiley.

Caplow, Theodore, Howard M. Babr, Bruce A. Chadwick, Reuben Hill, and **Margaret H. Williamson.** 1982. *Middletown families: Fifty years of change and continuity.* Minneapolis: University of Minnesota Press.

Cardozo, Arlene Rossen. 1996. *Sequencing.* Minneapolis: Brownstone Books.

Carley, Kathleen. 1991. A theory of group stability. *American Sociological Review,* 56:331–54.

Carmichael, Stokely, and **Charles Hamilton.** 1967. *Black power.* New York: Random House.

Carmona, Richard. 2003. A preventive defense. *Washington Post* (March 11):F1.

Carruthers, Bruce G. 1994. When is the state autonomous? Culture, organization theory, and the political sociology of the state. *Sociological Theory,* 12:19–44.

Case, J., and **R. C. R. Taylor.** 1979. *Co-ops, communes, and collectives: Experiments in social change in the 1960s and 1970s.* New York: Pantheon.

Caspi, Avshalom, Joseph McClay, Terrie E. Moffitt, Jonathan Mill, Judy Martin, Ian W. Craig, Alan Taylor, and **Richie Poulton.** 2002. Role of genotype in the cycle of violence in maltreated children. *Science,* 297:851–54.

Cassel, Carol A. 1999. Voluntary associations, churches, and social participation theories of turnout. *Social Science Quarterly,* 80(3):504–17.

Cast, A. D., and **P. J. Burke.** 2002. A theory of self-esteem. *Social Forces* 80(3):1041–1068.

Castro, Janice. 1991. Watching a generation waste away. *Time* (August 26):10, 12.

Catalano, Shannan. 2005. Criminal Victimization 2004. Washington, DC: U.S. Department of Justice

(NCJ 210674; http://www.ojp.usdoj .gov/bjs/ pubalp2.htm#cv).

Catalyst. 2003. *Women in U.S. Corporate Leadership: 2003.* www.catalystwomen.org

Catalyst. 2005. 2005 Catalyst census of women corporate officers and top earners of the *Fortune* 500. Available online at: http://www.catalyst.org/ files/full/2005%20COTE.pdf.

Centers for Disease Control. 2003. Health related hoaxes and rumors. Available at: www.cdc.gov/ hoax_rumors.htm.

Cernkovich, Steven A., and **Peggy Giordano.** 1987. Family relationships and delinquency. *Criminology,* 25:295–319.

Cernkovich, Steven A., and **Peggy Giordano.** 1992. School bonding, race, and delinquency. *Criminology,* 30:261–91.

Chafetz, Janet Saltzman. 1990. *Gender equity: An integrated theory of stability and change.* Newbury Park, CA: Sage.

Chafetz, Janet Saltzman. 1997. Feminist theory and sociology: Underutilized contributions for mainstream theory. *Annual Review of Sociology,* 23:97–120.

Chafetz, Janet Saltzman, and **Anthony Gary Dworkin.** 1986. *Female revolt: Women's movements in world and historical perspective.* New York: Rowman & Allanheld.

Chambliss, William J. 1973. The Saints and the Roughnecks. *Society,* 2 (November):24–31.

Chambliss, William J., and **Robert B. Seidman.** 1971. *Law, order and power.* Reading, MA: Addison-Wesley.

Charles, Camille Zubrinsky. 2000. Neighborhood racial-composition preferences: Evidence from a multiethnic metropolis. *Social Problems,* 47(3):379–407.

Chase, Susan E., and **Colleen S. Bell.** 1990. Ideology, discourse, and gender: How gatekeepers talk about women school superintendents. *Social Problems,* 37:163–86.

Chase-Dunn, Christopher. 1989. *Global formation: Structure of the world-economy.* Cambridge, MA: Blackwell.

Chase-Dunn, Christopher, and **Thomas D. Hall.** 1993. Comparing world-systems: Concepts and working hypotheses. *Social Forces,* 71:851–86.

Chatzky, Jean Sherman. 1992. A brief history of stock fads. *Forbes* (September 14):253–68.

Chaves, Mark. 1994. Secularization as declining religious authority. *Social Forces,* 72:749–74.

Chen, M. Keith, and **Jesse M. Shapiro.** 2004. Does prison harden inmates? A discontinuity-based approach. *Journal of Economic Literature.* July 30, 2005 (available online at www.reentry.net/library .cfm?fa=download&resourceID= 78811&appView=folder&folderID= 88047&print).

Chen, Li-Hui, Susan P. Baker, Elisa R. Braver, and **Guohua Li.** 2000. Carrying passengers as a risk factor for crashes fatal to 16- and 17-year-old drivers. *Journal of the American Medical Association,* 283:1578–82.

Cheng, Lucie, and **Edna Bonacich.** 1984. *Labor immigration under capitalism.* Berkeley: University of California Press.

Cherlin, Andrew. 1978. Remarriage as an incomplete institution. *American Journal of Sociology,* 84:634–50.

Cherlin, Andrew J. 1997. A reply to Glenn: What's most important in a family textbook. *Family Relations,* 46:209–11.

Cherlin, Andrew J. 1999. *Public and private families: An introduction.* New York: McGraw-Hill.

Cherlin, Andrew J. 2002. *Public and private families: An introduction.* New York: McGraw Hill.

Chesnais, Jean-Claude. 1992. *The demographic transition: Stages, patterns and economic implications: A longitudinal study of sixty-seven countries.* Trans. Elizabeth and Philip Kreager. New York: Clarendon.

Chesney-Lind, Meda, and **Randall G. Shelden.** 1998. *Girls, delinquency, and juvenile justice.* Belmont, CA: West-Wadsworth.

Child Policy. 2004. New 12 country study reveals substantial gaps in U.S. early childhood education and care policies. www.childpolicyintl.org/ issuebrief1.

Childe, V. Gordon. 1941. *Man makes himself.* London: Watts.

Chira, Susan. 1994. Study confirms worst fears on U.S. children. *New York Times* (April 12):A1, A11.

Chiricos, Theodore, and **Gordon Waldo.** 1975. Socioeconomic status and criminal sentencing: An empirical assessment of a conflict proposition. *American Sociological Review,* 40:753–72.

Chiswick, Barry. 1979. The economic progress of immigrants: Some apparently universal patterns. In William Felner, ed. *Contemporary economic problems.* Washington, DC: American Enterprise Institute.

Chomsky, Noam. 1957. *Syntactic structures.* The Hague: Mouton.

Chomsky, Noam. 1980. *Rule and representations.* New York: Columbia University Press.

Chubb, John E., Williamson E. Evers, Chester E. Finn, Jr., Eric A. Hanushek, Paul T. Hil, E. D. Hirsch, Jr., Caroline M. Hoxby, Terry M. Moe, Paul E. Peterson, Diane Ravitch, and **Herbert J. Walbert.** 2003. Our schools, our future: Are we still at risk? *Education Next,* Spring:9–15.

Clark, Kenneth B. 1965. *Dark ghetto.* New York: Harper & Row.

Clawson, Dan, Alan Neustadtl, and **Denise Scott.** 1992. *Money talks: Corporate PACs and political influence.* New York: Basic Books.

Clayton, Obie, ed. 1996. *An American dilemma revisited: Race relations in a changing world.* New York: Russell Sage Foundation.

Clearinghouse on International Developments in Child, Youth and Family Policies. 2003. *Maternity, paternity, parental and family leave policies.* Columbia University. Available at: www.childpolicyintl .org/maternity.html.

Clinard, Marshall B. 1990. *Corporate corruption: The abuse of power.* New York: Praeger.

Clinard, Marshall B., and **Robert F. Meier.** 1995. *Sociology of deviant behavior,* 9th ed. Fort Worth, TX: Harcourt Brace.

Clinard, Marshall B., and **Robert F. Meier.** 2003. *Sociology of deviant behavior.* 12th ed. Belmont, CA: Wadsworth Publishing Co.

Clinard, Marshall B., and **Peter C. Yeager.** 1980. *Corporate crime.* New York: Free Press.

Coates, Joseph F., and **Jennifer Jarratt.** 1990. What futurists believe: Agreements and disagreements. *The Futurist* (November–December):22–28.

Cochran, John K., Mitchell B. Chamlin, Peter B. Wood, and **Christine S. Sellers.** 1999. Shame, embarrassment, and formal sanction threats. Extending the deterrence/ rational choice model to academic dishonesty. *Sociological Inquiry,* 69(1):91–105.

Cockerham, William C. 2006. *Sociology of mental disorder.* 7th ed. Upper Saddle River, NJ: Prentice-Hall.

Cockerham, William C. 2007. *Medical sociology.* 10th ed. Upper Saddle River, NJ: Prentice-Hall.

Cockerham, William C. 2006. *Sociology of mental disorder.* Upper Saddle River, NJ: Prentice Hall.

Cohen, Albert K. 1955. *Delinquent boys.* New York: Free Press.

Cohen, Albert K. 1965. The sociology of the deviant act: Anomie theory and beyond. *American Sociological Review,* 30:5–14.

Cohen, Jean L., and **Andrew Arato.** 1992. *Civil society and political theory.* Cambridge, MA: MIT Press.

Cohen, Jere. 1980. Rational capitalism in Renaissance Italy. *American Journal of Sociology,* 85:1340–55.

Cohen, Jordan J. 2003. The consequences of premature abandonment of affirmative action in medical school admissions. *Journal of the American Medical Association,* 289(9):1143–48.

Colasanto, Diane, and **Linda Williams.** 1987. The changing dynamics of race and class. *Public Opinion,* 9 (January–February): 50–53.

Cole, Stephen. 1972. *The sociological method.* Chicago: Markham.

Coleman, James S., et al. 1966. *Equality of educational opportunity.* Washington, DC: U.S. Government Printing Office.

Coleman, James S. 1988. Social capital in the creation of human capital. *American Journal of Sociology,* 94:S95–S120.

Coleman, James S. 1990. *Foundations of social theory.* Cambridge, MA: Belknap Press.

Coleman, James S., Thomas Hoffer, and **Sally Kilgore.** 1982a. *High school achievement: Public, Catholic, and other private schools compared.* New York: Basic Books.

Coleman, James S., Thomas Hoffer, and **Sally Kilgore.** 1982b. Cognitive outcomes in public and private schools. *Sociology of Education,* 55:65–76.

Coleman, James W. 1987. Toward an integrated theory of white-collar crime. *American Journal of Sociology,* 93:406–39.

Coleman, Richard D., and **Lee Rainwater.** 1978. *Social standing in America.* New York: Basic Books.

Collier, Jane Fisburne. 1988. *Marriage and inequality in classless societies.* Stanford. CA: Stanford University Press.

Collins, Nancy L., and **Stephen J. Read.** 1990. Adult attachment, working models, and relationship quality in dating couples. *Journal of Personality and Social Psychology,* 58:644–63.

Collins, Patricia Hill. 2000. *Black feminist thought.* New York: Routledge.

Collins, Randall. 1975. *Conflict sociology.* New York: Academic Press.

Collins, Randall. 1976. Review of "Schooling in capitalist America." *Harvard Educational Review,* 46:246–51.

Collins, Randall. 1977. Some comparative principles of educational stratification. *Harvard Educational Review,* 47:1–27.

Collins, Randall. 1979. *Credential society.* New York: Academic Press.

Collins, Randall. 1981. *Sociology since midcentury: Essays in theory cumulation.* New York: Academic Press.

Collins, Randall. 1988a. *Sociology of marriage and the family.* 2nd ed. Chicago: Nelson Hall.

Collins, Randall. 1988b. *Theoretical sociology.* San Diego: Harcourt Brace Jovanovich.

Collins, Randall. 2000. Situational stratification: A micro-macro theory of inequality. *Sociological Theory,* 18:17–43.

Collins, W. Andrew, Eleanor E. Maccoby, Laurence Steinber, E. Mavis Hetherington, and **Marc H. Bornstein.** 2000. Contemporary research on parenting: The case for nature *and* nurture. *American Psychologist,* 55:218–32.

Comery, Thomas A., Reena Shah, and **William T. Greenaugh.** 1995. Differential rearing alters spine density on medium-sized spiny neurons in the rat corpus striatum: Evidence for association of morphological plasticity with early response gene expression. *Neurobiology of Learning and Memory,* 63:217–19.

Conger, Rand D., Frederick O. Lorenz, Glen H. Elder, Jr., Ronald L. Simons, and **Xiaojia Ge.** 1993. Husband and wife differences in response to undesirable life events. *Journal of Health and Social Behavior,* 34:71–88.

Connelly, Marjorie. 2000. Who voted: A portrait of American politics, 1976–2000. *New York Times* (November 12): IV-4.

Connolly, Ceci. 2005. Study paints bleak picture of immigrant health care. *Washington Post* (July 26):A11.

Conrad, Peter, and **Deborah Potter.** 2000. From hyperactive children to ADHD adults: Observations on the expansion of medical categories. *Social Problems,* 47(4):559–82.

Conrad, Peter, and **Joseph Schneider.** 1980. *Deviance and medicalization: From badness to sickness.* St. Louis: Mosby.

Cooley, Charles Horton. 1902/1964. *Human nature and the social order:* New York: Scribner's.

Coontz, Stephanie. 1992. *The way we never were: American families and the nostalgia trap.* New York: Basic Books.

Cooper, Richard S., Jay. S. Kaufman, and **Ryk Ward.** 2003. Race and genomics. *New England Journal of Medicine,* 348:1166–70.

Copp, Terry, and **Bill McAndrew.** 1990. *Battle exhaustion: Soldiers and psychiatrists in the Canadian army, 1939–1945.* Montreal and Kingston: McGill–Queen's University Press.

Corcoran, Mary, Sandra K. Danziger, Ariel Kalil, and **Kristin S. Seefeldt.** 2000. *Annual Review of Sociology,* 26:241–69.

Cornish, Edward. 1993. 1993 as predicted in 1893: If they could see us now! *The Futurist* (May–June): 41–42.

Corsaro, William A., and **Donna Eder.** 1995. Development and socialization of children and adolescents. In Karen S. Cook. Gary Alan Fine, and James S. House, eds., *Sociological perspectives on social psychology.* Boston: Allyn and Bacon.

Coser, Lewis A. 1956. *The functions of social conflict.* New York: Free Press.

Coser, Lewis A. 1957. Social conflict and the theory of social change. *British Journal of Sociology,* 8:170–83.

Coughlin, Ellen K. 1988. Worsening plight of the "underclass" catches attention of researchers. *Chronicle of Higher Education* (March 30): A1.

Cox, Oliver C. 1948. *Caste, class, and race.* Garden City, NY: Doubleday.

Crane, Jonathan. 1991. The epidemic theory of ghettos and neighborhood effects on dropping out and teenage childbearing. *American Journal of Sociology,* 96:1226–59.

Creighton, Linda L. 1993. Kids taking care of kids. *U.S. News & World Report* (December 20):26–33.

Crenshaw, E. M., M. Christenson, and **D. R. Oakey.** 2000. Demographic transition in ecological focus. *American Sociological Review,* 65(3):371–91.

Crispell, Diane. 1993. Sex surveys: Does anyone tell the truth? *American Demographics,* 15 (July):9–10.

Crittenden, Ann. 2001. *The price of motherhood. Why the most important job in the world is still the least valued.* New York: Henry Holt and Company.

Crocker, Jennifer, and **Rila Luhtanen.** 1990. Collective self-esteem and ingroup bias. *Journal of Personality and Social Psychology,* 58:60–67.

Cross, Susan E., and **Laura Madson.** 1997. Models of the self: Self-construals and gender. *Psychological Bulletin,* 122:5–37.

Crosset, Todd W., J. Ptacek, M. A. McDonald, and **J. R. Benedict.** 1996. Male student-athletes and violence against women: A survey of campus judicial affairs offices. *Violence Against Women,* 2:163–79.

Crutchfield, Robert D., and **Susan R. Pitchford.** 1997. Work and crime: The effects of labor stratification. *Social Forces,* 76:93–118.

D

Dahl, Robert. 1961. *Who governs? Democracy and power in an American city.* New Haven, CT: Yale University Press.

Dahrendorf, Ralf. 1958. Toward a theory of social conflict. *Journal of Conflict Resolution,* 2:170–83.

Dahrendorf, Ralf. 1959. *Class and class conflict in industrial society.* Stanford, CA: Stanford University Press.

D'Alessio, Stewart J., and **Lisa Stolzenberg.** 1995. Unemployment and the incarceration of pretrial defendants. *American Sociological Review,* 60:350–59.

Dana, Rebecca. 2003. To fight music piracy, industry goes to schools. *Washington Post* (August 28):A1.

Danaei, Goodarz, Stephen Vander Hoorn, Alan D. Lopez, Christopher J. L. Murray, Majid Ezzati, and the **Comparative Risk Assessment collaborating group** (Cancers). 2005. Causes of cancer in the world: Comparative risk assessment of nine behavioural and environmental risk factors. *Lancet,* 366:1784–93.

Dandeker, Christopher. 1990. Surveillance, power and modernity: Bureaucracy and discipline from 1700 to the present day. New York: St. Martin's Press.

Daniels, Arlene Kaplan. 1987. Invisible work. *Social Problems,* 34:403–15.

Darnton, Nina. 1991. The pain of the last taboo. *Newsweek* (October 7): 70–72.

Davidow, William H., and **Michael S. Malone.** 1993. *The virtual corporations: Structuring and revitalizing the corporation for the 21st century.* New York: Harper Business.

Davie, Maurice R. 1937. The patterns of urban growth. In George P. Murdock, ed., *Studies in the science of society.* New Haven, CT: Yale University Press.

Davies, James. 1962. Toward a theory of revolution. *American Sociological Review,* 27:5–19.

Davies, James. 1969. The *J*-curve of rising and declining satisfactions as a cause of some great revolutions and a contained revolution. In H. D. Graham and T. R. Gurr, eds., *The history of violence in America.* New York: Bantam.

Davies, James. 1974. The *J*-curve and power struggle theories of collective violence. *American Sociological Review,* 39:607–10.

Davis, Allison, B. B. Gardner, and **M. R. Gardner.** 1941. *Deep South.* Chicago: University of Chicago Press.

Davis, F. James. 1991. *Who is black? One nation's definition.* University Park: Pennsylvania State University Press.

Davis, James. 1982. Up and down opportunity's ladder. *Public Opinion,* 5 (June–July):11–15ff.

Davis, James Allan, Tom W. Smith, and **Peter V. Marsden.** 2003. *General social surveys, 1972–2002: Cumulative codebook.* Chicago: National Opinion Research Center.

Davis, James Allan, Tom W. Smith, and **Peter V. Marsden.** 2005. *General social surveys, 1972–2004: Cumulative Codebook.* Chicago: National Opinion Research Center.

Davis, Kingsley. 1945. The world demographic transition. *Annals of the American Academy of Political and Social Science,* 237:1–11.

Davis, Kingsley. 1949. *Human society.* New York: Macmillan.

Davis, Kingsley. 1951. Introduction. In William J. Goode, *Religion among the primitives.* New York: Free Press.

Davis, Kingsley. 1955. The origin and growth of urbanization in the world. *American Journal of Sociology,* 60:429–37.

Davis, Kingsley. 1959. The myth of functional analysis as a special method in sociology and anthropology. *American Sociological Review,* 24:757–72.

Davis, Kingsley. 1967. The urbanization of the human population. In *Cities.* New York: Knopf.

Davis, Kingsley. 1971. The world's population crisis. In Robert K. Merton and Robert A. Nisbet, eds., *Contemporary social problems,* 3rd ed. New York: Harcourt Brace Jovanovich.

Davis, Kingsley, and **Wilbert Moore.** 1945. Some principles of stratification. *American Sociological Review,* 10:242–49.

Davis, Nancy J., and **Robert V. Robinson.** 1988. Class identification of men and women in the 1970s and 1980s. *American Sociological Review,* 53:103–12.

Davis-Kimball, Jeannine. 1997. Warrior women of the Eurasian steppes. *Archaeology* (January–February):44–48.

Dawidowicz, Lucy S. 1975. *The war against the Jews 1933–1945.* New York: Holt, Rinehart, and Winston.

Dawson, R. J. M. 1995. The "unusual episode" data revisited. *Journal of Statistics Education* [Online], 3(3) www.amstat.org/publications/jse/ v3n3/datasets.dawson.html.

Day, Jennifer Cheeseman, Alex Janus, and **Jessica Davis.** 2005. *Computer and Internet use in the United States: 2003.* U.S. Census Bureau Current Population Reports, P23–208 (October 2005).

Deane, Claudia. 1998. Husbands and wives. *Washington Post* (March 25):A14.

Deaux, Kay, and **Lawrence S. Wrightsman.** 1984. *Social psychology in the 80s.* 4th ed. Monterey, CA: Brooks/Cole.

Debold, Elizabeth, Marie Wilson, and **Idelisse Malave.** 1993. *Mother daughter revolution: From betrayal to power.* Reading, MA: Addison-Wesley.

DeBruine, Lisa. 2002. Facial resemblance enhances trust. *Proceedings of the Royal Society of London B,* 269:1307–12.

Decoo, Wilfried. 2002. *Crisis on campus: Confronting academic misconduct.* Cambridge, MA: MIT Press.

Deegan, Mary Jo. 1988. *Jane Addams and the men of the Chicago school, 1892–1918.* New Brunswick, NJ: Transaction.

Deegan, Mary Jo. 1991. *Women in sociology: A bio-bibliographical sourcebook.* Westport, CT: Greenwood Press.

Deegan, Mary Jo. 2003. Textbooks, the history of sociology, and the sociological stock of knowledge. *Sociological Theory,* 21:298–305.

Deininger, Klaus, and **Lyn Squire.** 1996. A new data set measuring income inequality. *World Bank Economic Review,* 10(3):565–91.

DeMaris, Alfred, and **Monica A. Longmore.** 1996. Ideology, power, and equity: Testing competing explanations for the perception of fairness in household labor. *Social Forces,* 74(3):1043–71.

DeMaris, Alfred, and **K. Vaninadha Rao.** 1992. Premarital cohabitation and subsequent marital stability in the United States: A reassessment. *Journal of Marriage and the Family,* 54:178–90.

Demos, Vasilikie. 1990. Black family studies in the *Journal of Marriage and the Family,* and the issue of distortion: A trend analysis. *Journal of Marriage and the Family,* 52:603–12.

DeNavas-Walt, Carmen, Bernadette D. Proctor, and **Cheryl Hill Lee.** 2005. *Income, poverty, and health insurance coverage in the United States: 2004.* U.S. Census Bureau, Current Population Reports, P60–229. Washington, DC: U.S. Government Printing Office. (available online at: http://www .census.gov/prod/2005pubs/ p60-229.pdf).

Denton, Nancy A., and **Douglas S Massey.** 1989. Racial identity among Caribbean Hispanics: The effect of double minority status on residential segregation. *American Sociological Review,* 54:790–808.

DePalma, Anthony. 1991. How undergraduates can succeed: Study together, and in small classes. *New York Times* (November 6):B8.

DeParle, Jason. 2004. *American dream: Three women, ten kids, and a nation's drive to end welfare.* New York: Viking/Penguin.

Desai, Sonalde, and **Linda J. Waite.** 1991. Women's employment during pregnancy and after the first birth: Occupational characteristics and work commitment. *American Sociological Review,* 56:551–66.

DeVault, Marjorie L. 1996. Talking back to sociology: Distinctive

contributions of feminist methodology. *Annual Review of Sociology,* 22:29–50.

Devine, Patricia G. 1989. Stereotypes and prejudice: Their automatic and controlled components. *Journal of Personality and Social Psychology,* 56:518.

DeVoe, J. F., K. Peter, P. Kaufman, S. A. Ruddy, A. K. Miller, M. Planty, T. D. Snyder, and **M. R. Rand.** 2003. *Indicators of School Crime and Safety: 2003.* Washington, DC: U.S. Departments of Education and Justice. NCES 2004–004/NCJ 201257.

De Vries, Raymond G. 1981. Birth and death: Social construction of the poles of existence. *Social Forces,* 59:1074–93.

Dewandre, Nicole. 2002. European strategies for promoting women in science. *Science,* 295:278–279.

Dignan, Joe, and **Amy Argetsinger.** 2005. Calif. Senate passes gay marriage bill; move is the first by a state legislative body without a court order. *Washington Post* (September 2):A2.

Dillman, Don A. 2000. *Mail and Internet surveys: The tailored design method.* 2nd ed. New York: John Wiley.

Dillman, Don A., and **Lisa R. Carley-Baxter.** 2001. *Structural determinants of mail survey response rates over a 12-year period, 1988–1999.* 2000 Proceedings of American Statistical Association Survey Methods Section, Alexandria, VA.

Dionne, E. J., Jr. 1980. Abortion poll: Not clear-cut. *New York Times* (August 10):A15.

Dipboye, Robert L. 1977. Alternative approaches to deindividualization. *Psychological Bulletin,* 84:1057–75.

Dirzo, Rodolfo, and **Michel Loreau.** 2005. Biodiversity science evolves. *Science,* 310:943.

Dixit, Avinash K., and **Barry J. Nalebuff.** 1991. *Thinking strategically.* New York: Norton.

Dixon, William J., and **Terry Boswell.** 1996. Dependency, disarticulation, and denominator effects: Another look at foreign capital penetration. *American Journal of Sociology,* 102:543–62.

Djilas, Milovan. 1957. *The new class.* New York: Praeger.

Domhoff, G. William. 1983. *Who rates America now? A view for the '80s.* Englewood Cliffs, NJ: Prentice Hall.

Domhoff, G. William. 1990. *The power elite and the state: How policy is made in America.* New York: Aldine de Gruyter.

Dorsey, Tina L., Marianne W. Zawitz, and **Priscilla Middleton.** 2003. Drugs and crime facts. NCJ 165148. Washington, DC: U.S. Department of Justice, Bureau of Justice Statistics.

Dubin, Robert. 1976. Work in modern society. In Robert Dubin, ed., *Handbook of work, organization, and society.* Chicago: Rand McNally.

Du Bois, W. E. B. 1903/1990. *The souls of black folk.* New York: Vintage.

Dugger, Celia W. 1992. U.S. study says Asian-Americans face widespread discrimination. *New York Times* (February 29):1, 5.

Duncan, Greg. 1984. *Years of poverty, years of plenty.* Ann Arbor: Institute for Social Research, University of Michigan.

Duncan, Greg J. 1987. On the slippery slope. *American Demographics,* 9 (May):30–35.

Duncan, Greg J., Martha S. Hill, and **Saul D. Hoffman.** 1988. Welfare dependence within and across generations. *Science,* 239:467–71.

Duneier, Mitchell. 1992. *Slim's Table.* Chicago: University of Chicago Press.

Dunn, Ashley. 1994. Southeast Asians highly dependent on welfare in U.S. *New York Times* (May 19): A1, A13.

Dunn, J. R., and **M. V. Hayes.** 2000. Social inequality, population health, and housing: a study of two Vancouver neighbourhoods. *Social Science and Medicine,* 51(4):563–587.

Dunn, William. 1993. Educating diversity. *American Demographics,* 15 (April):38–43.

Durkheim, Émile. 1893/1964. *The division of labor in society.* New York: Free Press.

Durkheim, Émile. 1895/1938. *The rules of sociological method.* Glencoe, IL: Free Press.

Durkheim, Émile. 1897/1951. *Suicide.* New York: Free Press.

Durkheim, Émile. 1912/1965. *The elementary forms of religious life.* New York: Free Press.

Durkin, Keith F., and **Clifton D. Bryant.** 1995. "Log on to sex": Some notes on the carnal computer and erotic cyberspace as an emerging research frontier. *Deviant Behavior,* 16:179–200.

Durr, Virginia Foster. 1985. *Outside the magic circle: The autobiography of Virginia Foster Durr.* Tuscaloosa: University of Alabama Press.

Dwyer, Jeffrey W., and **Raymond T. Coward.** 1991. Multivariate comparison of the involvement of adult sons versus adult daughters in the care of impaired parents. *Journal of Gerontology,* 46:S259–S269.

E

Eagly, A. H., M. C. Johannesen-Schmidt, and **M. L. van Engen.** Transformational, transactional, and Laissez-Faire leadership styles: A meta-analysis comparing women and men. *Psychological Bulletin,* 129(4):569–591.

Easterlin, Richard A. 1961. The American baby-boom in historical perspective. *American Economic Review,* 51:869–911.

Easterlin, Richard A. 1987. *Birth and fortune: The impact of numbers on personal welfare.* Chicago: University of Chicago Press.

Economist, The. 2000a. The disaffected. (December 23): 9.

Economist, The. 2000b. What the Internet cannot do. (August 19):11–12.

Edin, Kathryn. 2000. What do low-income single mothers say about marriage? *Social Problems,* 47(1), 112–33.

Edwards, Richard. 1978. The social relations of production at the point of production. *Insurgent Sociologist,* 8:109–25.

Edwards, Richard. 1979. *Contested terrain.* New York: Basic Books.

Eichar, Douglas M. 1989. *Occupation and class consciousness in America.* New York: Greenwood Press.

Eilperin, Juliet. 2005. U.S. is dissenter on global warming; Kyoto parties near deal on new talks. *Washington Post* (December 10):A1.

Eilperin, Juliet. 2006. Scientists debate issue of climate's irreparable change; some experts on global warming foresee 'tipping point' when it is too late to act. *Washington Post* (January 29):A1.

Eisenberg, David M., Ronald C. Kessler, Cindy Foster, Frances E. Norlock, David R. Calkins, and **Thomas L. Delbanco.** 1993. Unconventional medicine in the United States: Prevalence, costs, and patterns of use. *New England Journal of Medicine* (January 28):246–53.

Ekman, Paul, Wallace V. Friesen, and **John Bear.** 1984. The international language of gesture. *Psychology Today,* 18 (May):64–67.

Ekman, Paul, Wallace V. Friesen, and **Maureen O'Sullivan.** 1988. Smiles when lying. *Journal of Personality and Social Psychology,* 54: 414–420.

Elder, Glenn H., Jr. 1983. Families, kin, and the life course. In R. Parke, ed., *The family.* Chicago: University of Chicago Press.

Elder, Glenn H., Jr., and **Elizabeth C. Clipp.** 1988. Wartime losses and social bonding: Influences across 40 years in men's lives. *Psychiatry,* 51:177–97.

Elias, Marilyn. 1994. Poverty impacts children's IQ. *USA Today* (May 9):D1.

Elliot, Gregory C., Morris Rosenberg, and Michael Wagner. 1984. Transient depersonalization in youth. *Social Psychology Quarterly,* 47:115–28.

Ellyson, Steve I., John F. Dovidio, Randi L. Corson, and Debbie L. Vinicur. 1980. Visual dominance behavior in female dyads. *Social Psychology Quarterly,* 43:328–36.

Elman, Cheryl, and Angela M. O'Rand. 2004. The race is to the swift: Socioeconomic origins, adult education, and wage attainment. *American Journal of Sociology,* 110:123–60.

Emerson, Richard M. 1962. Power-dependence relations. *American Sociological Review,* 27:31–41.

Engels, Friedrich. 1884/1902. *The origin of the family, private property, and the state.* Chicago: Kerr.

England, Paula. 1993a. Sociological theories and the study of gender. In Paula England, ed., *Theory on gender/ feminism on gender.* New York: Aldine de Gruyter.

England, Paula. 1993b. Work for pay and work at home: Women's double disadvantage. In *Social Problems- Primis.* Craig Calhoun and George Ritzer, eds., McGraw-Hill. Revised version published 1997.

England, Paula. 2000. Marriage, the costs of children, and gender inequality. In Linda J. Waite, ed., *The ties that bind: Perspectives on marriage and cohabitation.* New York: Aldine de Gruyter.

Epstein, Edward J. 1973. *News from nowhere.* New York: Random House.

Epstein, Noel. 2004. The American Kibbutz. In Noel Epstein, ed. *Who's in charge here? The tangled web of school governance and policy.* Brookings Institution Press and Education Commission of the States.

Erickson, Bonnie H. 1996. Culture, class, and connections. *American Journal of Sociology,* 102:217–51.

Erikson, Erik. 1963. *Childhood and society.* New York: Norton.

Erikson, Erik. 1968. *Identity: Youth and crisis.* New York: Norton.

Erikson, Kai T. 1962. Notes on the sociology of deviance. *Social Problems,* 9:307–14.

Erikson, Kai T. 1966. *Wayward Puritans: A study in the sociology of deviance.* New York: Wiley.

ESOP Association. 2003. ESOP facts and figures. Available at: www.esopassociation.org/pubs/stats.html.

Espiritu, Yen Le. 1992. *Asian American panethnicity: Bridging institutions and identities.* Philadelphia: Temple University Press.

Esposito, John L. 1992. *The Islamic threat: Myth or reality.* New York: Oxford University Press.

Etzioni, Amitai. 1975. *A comparative analysis of complex organizations.* New York: Free Press.

Evenson, Ranae J., and Robin W. Simon. 2005. Clarifying the relationship between parenthood and depression. *Journal of Health and Social Behavior,* 46(4):341–58.

Ezzati, Majid, Alan D. Lopez, Anthony Rodgers, Stephen Vander Hoorn, and Christopher J. L. Murray. 2002. Selected major risk factors and global and regional burden of disease. *The Lancet,* 360:1347–1360.

F

Fagot, Beverly I., Mary D. Leinbach, and Cherie O'Boyle. 1992. Gender labeling, gender stereotyping, and parenting behaviors. *Developmental Psychology,* 28:225–30.

Faia, Michael A. 1989. Cultural materialism in the functionalist mode. *American Sociological Review,* 54:658–60.

Faludi, Susan. 1991. *Backlash: The undeclared war against American women.* New York: Crown Publishers, Inc.

Farkas, George, Robert P. Grobe, Daniel Sheehan, and Yan Shuan. 1990. Cultural resources and school success. Gender, ethnicity, and poverty groups within an urban school district. *American Sociological Review,* 55:127–42.

Farkas, Steve, Jean Johnson, Tony Foleno, Ann Duffett, and Patrick Foley. 2000. For goodness' sake. *Public Agenda.*

Farnsworth, Clyde H. 1990. Report by World Bank sees poverty lessening by 2000 except in Africa. *New York Times* (July 16):A3.

Farnsworth, Clyde H. 1991. Economic woes force Canada to re-examine medical system. *New York Times* (November 24):7.

Fassinger, Polly A. 1989. Becoming the breadwinner: Single mothers' reactions to changes in their paid work lives. *Family Relations,* 38:404–11.

Fay, R. E., Charles F. Turner, A. D. Klassen, and John H. Gagnon. 1989. Prevalence and patterns of same-gender contact among men. *Science,* 243:338–48.

Federal Bureau of Investigation. 2005. Crime in the United States, 2004. Washington, DC: U.S. Government Printing Office.

Feingold, Alan. 1988. Matching for attractiveness in romantic partners and same-sex friends: A meta-analysis and theoretical critique. *Psychological Bulletin,* 104:226–35.

Feingold, Alan. 1990. Gender differences in effects of physical attractiveness on romantic attraction: A comparison across five research paradigms. *Journal of Personality and Social Psychology,* 59:981–93.

Feldman, Marcus W., Richard C. Lewontin, and Mary-Clare King. 2003. A genetic melting-pot. *Nature,* 424:374.

Feldman, Marcus W., Sarah P. Otto, and Freddy B. Christiansen. 2000. Genes, culture and inequality. In Kenneth Arrow, Samuel Bowles, and Steven Durlauf, eds., *Meritocracy and economic inequality.* Princeton, NJ: Princeton University Press.

Felson, Richard B., and Mark D. Reed. 1986. Reference groups and self-appraisals of academic ability and performance. *Social Psychology Quarterly,* 49:103–9.

Fennema, Meinhert. 1982. *International networks of banks and industry.* Boston: Martinius Nijhoff.

Ferree, Myra Marx. 1990. Beyond separate spheres: Feminism and family research. *Journal of Marriage and the Family,* 52:866–84.

Ferree, Myra Marx, and **Elaine J. Hall.** 2000. Gender stratification and paradigm change. *American Sociological Review,* 65(3):475–81.

Fetissov, S. O., J. Hallman, L. Oreland, B. af Klinteberg, E. Grenback, A. Hulting, and **T. Hokfelt.** 2002. Autoantibodies against—MSH, ACTH and LHRH in anorexia and bulimia nervosa patients. *Proceedings of the National Academy of Sciences,* 99:17155–160.

Fiedler, Fred E., and **Joseph E. Garcia.** 1987. *New approaches to effective leadership: Cognitive resources and organizational performance.* New York: John Wiley.

Field, Tiffany. 1991. Quality infant day-care and grade school behavior and performance. *Child Development,* 62:863–70.

Fields, Jason. 2003. *Children's living arrangements and characteristics: March 2002.* Current Population Reports, P20-547. Washington, DC: U.S. Census Bureau.

Fields, Jason, and **Lynne M. Casper.** 2001. America's families and living arrangements. *Current Population Reports: Population Characteristics,* P20-537. Washington, DC: U.S. Census Bureau.

Fields, Suzanne. 1993. Rape as sport: The culture is at the root. *Insight on the News,* 9 (May 3): 19–20.

Fine, Gary Alan. 1993. The sad demise, mysterious disappearance, and glorious triumph of symbolic interactionism. *Annual Review of Sociology,* 19:61–87.

Fine, Mark A., and **Lawrence A. Kurdek.** 1992. The adjustment of adolescents in stepfather and stepmother families. *Journal of Marriage and the Family,* 54:725–36.

Finke, Roger, and **Rodney Stark.** 1992. *The churching of America, 1776–1990: Winners and losers in our religious economy.* New Brunswick, NJ: Rutgers University Press.

Finkelhor, David. 1979. *Sexually victimized children.* New York: Free Press.

Firebaugh, Glenn. 1992. Growth effects of foreign and domestic investment. *American Journal of Sociology,* 98:105–30.

Firebaugh, Glenn. 1996. Does foreign capital harm poor nations? New estimates based on Dixon and Boswell's measures of capital penetration. *American Journal of Sociology,* 102:563–75.

Firebaugh, Glenn, and **Kevin Chen.** 1995. Vote turnout of nineteenth amendment women: the enduring effect of disenfranchisement. *American Journal of Sociology,* 100(4):972–96.

Firebaugh, Glenn, and **Kenneth E. Davis.** 1988. Trends in anti-black prejudice, 1972–1984: Region and cohort effects. *American Journal of Sociology,* 94:251–72.

Fischer, Claude S., Michael Hout, Martin Sanchez Jankowski, Samuel R. Lucas, Ann Swidler, and **Kim Voss.** 1996. *Inequality by design: Cracking the bell curve myth.* Princeton, NJ: Princeton University Press.

Fisher, Bonnie S., Franels T. Cullen, and **Michael G. Turner.** 2000. *The sexual victimization of college women.* National Institute of Justice. Bureau of Justice Statistics.

Fitzpatrick, Ellen. 1990. *Endless crusade: Women social scientists and progressive reform.* New York: Oxford University Press.

Fletcher, Michael A. 2002. Rocky start in "cyber" classrooms. *Washington Post* (February 26):A1.

Fligstein, Neil. 1990. *The transformation of corporate control.* Cambridge, MA: Harvard University Press.

Fligstein, Neil, and **Peter Brantley.** 1992. Bank control, owner control, or organization dynamics: Who controls the large modern corporation? *American Journal of Sociology,* 98:280–307.

Flynn, James R. 2000. IQ trends over time: Intelligence, race, and meritocracy. In Kenneth Arrow, Samuel Bowles, and Steven Durlauf, eds., *Meritocracy and economic inequality.* Princeton, NJ: Princeton University Press.

Ford, C. S., and **F. A. Beach.** 1951. *Patterns of sexual behavior.* New York: Harper & Row.

Forgette, Richard, and **Glenn J. Platt.** 1999. Voting for the person, not the party: Party defection, issue voting, and process sophistication. *Social Science Quarterly,* 80(2):409–21.

Fossett, Mark S., and **K. Jill Kiecolt.** 1989. The relative size of minority populations and white racial attitude. *Social Science Quarterly,* 70:820–35.

Fost, Dan. 1992. Education to back up affirmative action. *American Demographics,* 14 (April): 16–17.

Foster, Terry. 1997. Woods correctly pays tribute to his heritage, but still has much to learn as a minority trailblazer. *Detroit News* (June 12): Sports.

Fowler, Floyd J., Jr. 2001. *Survey research methods.* Thousand Oaks, CA: Sage.

Fox, Isabelle, and **Norman M. Lobsenz.** 1996. *Being there: The benefits of a stay-at-home parent.* Hauppage, NY: Barron's Educational Series.

France, David. 2006. "And then he hit me": Too ashamed or too scared to speak up, tens of thousands of 50-plus victims of domestic violence suffer in silence. *AARP,* Jan/Feb 80-85/112.

Freadhoff, Chuck. 1992. America goes back to school. *Investor's Business Daily* (August 28):1–2.

Freud, Sigmund. 1930/1961. *Civilization and its discontents.* London: Hogarth.

Freud, Sigmund. 1938. *The basic writings of Sigmund Freud.* Trans. A. A. Brill. New York: Modern Library.

Friedman, Andrew. 1977. *Industry and labor: Class struggle at work and monopoly capitalism.* New York: Macmillan.

Friedman, Thomas L. 2005. *The world is flat: A brief history of the twenty-first century.* New York: Farrar, Straus and Giroux.

Fuhrman, Ellsworth R. 1980. *The sociology of knowledge in America, 1883–1915.* Charlottesville: University of Virginia Press.

Fuller, C. J. 1976. *The Nayars today.* Cambridge, MA: Cambridge University Press.

Furstenberg, Frank F., Jr., and **Andrew J. Cherlin.** 1991. *Divided families.* Cambridge, MA: Harvard University Press.

G

Gaertner, Lowell, and **Chester A. Insko.** 2000. Intergroup discrimination in the minimal group paradigm: Categorization, reciprocation, or fear? *Journal of Personality and Social Psychology,* 79:77–94.

Gaither, Avalaura L., and **Eric C. Newburger.** 2000. The emerging American voter: An examination of the increase in the black vote in November 1998. U.S. Census Bureau Population Division Working Paper No. 44. Washington, DC: U.S. Government Printing Office.

Gallup, George, Jr. 1997. Many women cite spousal abuse; job performance affected. *Gallup Poll.*

Gans, Herbert J. 1972. The positive functions of poverty. *American Journal of Sociology,* 78:275–89.

Gans, Herbert J. 1979. Symbolic ethnicity: The future of ethnic groups and cultures in America. *Racial and Ethnic Studies,* 2:1–20.

Garcia-Moreno, Claudia, Lori Heise, Henrica A.F.M. Jansen, Mary Ellsberg, and **Charlotte Watts.** 2005. Violence against women. Science, 310:1282–1283.

Gardner, Gary, and **Payal Sampat.** 1999. Forging a sustainable materials economy. In *State of the world 1999: A Worldwatch Institute report on progress toward a sustainable society.* New York: Norton.

Gardner, LeGrande, and **Donald J. Shoemaker.** 1989. Social bonding and delinquency: A comparative analysis. *Sociological Quarterly,* 30:481–500.

Garfinkel, Harold. 1974. The origins of the term "ethnomethodology." In R. Turner, ed., *Ethnomethodology.* Harmondsworth, Eng.: Penguin Books.

Garland, David. 2003. *The culture of control: Crime and social order in contemporary society.* Chicago: University of Chicago Press.

Garreau, Joel. 1991. Edge cities. *American Demographics,* 13 (September):24–31ff.

Gastil, John. 2000. The political beliefs and orientations of people with disabilities. *Social Science Quarterly,* 81(2):588–603.

Gecas, Viktor, and **Michael L. Schwalbe.** 1983. Beyond the looking-glass self: Social structure and efficacy-based self-esteem. *Social Psychology Quarterly,* 46:77–88.

Gecas, Viktor, and **Monica A. Seff.** 1990. Families and adolescents: A review of the 1980s. *Journal of Marriage and the Family,* 52:941–58.

Gelles, Richard J., Murray A. Strauss, and **John W. Harrop.** 1988. Has family violence decreased? *Journal of Marriage and the Family,* 50:286–91.

Gerald, Debra E., and **William J. Hussar.** 2002. *Projections of education statistics to 2012* (NCES 2002–030). Washington, DC: U.S. Department of Education, National Center for Education Statistics. Available at: http://nces.ed.gov/pubs2002/2002030.pdf.

Gerbner, George, Larry Gross, Michael F. Eleey, Marilyn Jackson-Beeck, Suzanne Jeffries-Fox, and **Nancy Signorielli.** 1978. Cultural indicators: Violence profile no. 9. *Journal of Communication,* 28:176–207.

Geschwender, James A. 1964. Social structure and the Negro revolt: An examination of some hypotheses. *Social Forces,* 43:248–56.

Geschwender, James A. 1978. *Racial stratification in America.* Dubuque, IA: William C. Brown.

Gibbs, Jack P. 1989. *Control: Sociology's central notion.* Urbana: University of Illinois Press.

Giddens, Anthony. 1973. *The class structure of the advanced societies.* New York: Harper & Row.

Giddens, Anthony. 1985. *A contemporary critique of historical materialism.* Vol. 2: *The nation-state and violence.* Berkeley: University of California Press.

Gilbert, Jess, and **Carolyn Howe.** 1991. Beyond "state vs. society": Theories of the state and New Deal agricultural policies. *American Sociological Review,* 56:204–20.

Gilligan, Carol. 1982. *In a different voice: Psychological theory and women's development.* Cambridge, MA: Harvard University Press.

Gilligan, Carol, J. V. Ward, and **J. M. Taylor,** eds. 1989. *Mapping the moral domain.* Cambridge, MA: Harvard University Press.

Ginsberg, Benjamin, and **Martin Shefter.** 1990. *Politics by other means: The declining importance of elections in America.* New York: Basic Books.

Gittleman, Maury, and **Mary Joyce.** 1995. Earnings mobility in the United States, 1967–91. *Monthly Labor Review,* September 3–11.

Glanville, Jennifer L. 1999. Political socialization or selection? Adolescent extracurricular participation and political activity in early adulthood. *Social Science Quarterly,* 80(2):279–90.

Glass, Jennifer, and **Valerie Camarigg.** 1992. Gender, parenthood, and job-family compatibility. *American Journal of Sociology,* 98:131–51.

Glassman, Ronald M., William H. Swatos, Jr., and **Paul L. Rosen,** eds. 1987. *Bureaucracy against* *democracy and socialism.* Westport, CT: Greenwood Press.

Gledhill-Hoyt, J., H. Lee, J. Strote, and **H. Wechsler.** 2000. Increased use of marijuana and other illicit drugs at U.S. colleges in the 1990s: Results of three national surveys. *Addiction,* 95(11): 1655–67.

Glenn, Norval D. 1992. What does family mean? *American Demographics,* 14 (June): 30–37.

Glenn, Norval D. 1997. A critique of twenty family and marriage and family textbooks. *Family Relations,* 46:197–208.

Glenn, Norval D., and **C. N. Weaver.** 1981. The contribution of marital happiness to global happiness. *Journal of Marriage and the Family,* 43:161–68.

Glenn, Norval D., and **Charles N. Weaver.** 1988. The changing relationship of marital status to reported happiness. *Journal of Marriage and the Family,* 50:317–24.

Glick, Clarence. 1980. *Sojourners and settlers: Chinese immigrants in Hawaii.* Honolulu: University of Hawaii Press.

Goffman, Erving. 1959. *The presentation of self in everyday life.* Garden City, NY: Doubleday.

Goffman, Erving. 1961a. *Encounters.* Indianapolis: Bobbs-Merrill.

Goffman, Erving. 1961b. *Asylums: Essays on the social situation of mental patients and other inmates.* Garden City, NY: Anchor Books.

Goldberg, Jeffrey. 2003. The Unknown: The C.I.A. and the Pentagon take another look at Al Qaeda and Iraq. *The New Yorker* (February 10):40–47.

Goldhagen, Daniel Jonah. 1996. *Hitler's willing executioners: Ordinary Germans and the Holocaust.* New York: Knopf.

Goldin-Meadow, Susan, and **Carolyn Mylander.** 1984. Gestural communication in deaf children. *Monographs of the Society for Research in Child Development,* 49, no. 207.

Goldstein, Joshua R., and **Catherine T. Kenney.** 2001. Marriage delayed or marriage forgone? New cohort forecasts of first marriage for U.S. women. *American Sociological Review,* 66:506–19.

Goldstein, Sidney. 1992. Profile of American Jewry: Insights from the 1990 National Jewish Population Survey. In *American Jewish Yearbook 1992.* New York: American Jewish Committee.

Goldstone, Jack A. 1991. *Revolution and rebellion in the early modern world.* Berkeley: University of California Press.

Goleman, Daniel. 1991. Doctors find comfort is a potent medicine. *New York Times* (November 26): B5.

Goleman, Daniel. 1992. Family rituals may promote better emotional adjustment. *New York Times* (March 11):B6.

Goleman, Daniel. 1994. Mental decline in aging need not be inevitable. *New York Times* (April 26): B5, B7.

Goodall, Jane. 1990. *Through a window: My thirty years with the chimpanzees of Gombe.* Boston: Houghton Mifflin.

Goode, Erica E. 1993. The culture of illness. *U.S. News & World Report* (February 15): 74–76.

Goode, William J. 1959. The theoretical importance of love. *American Sociological Review,* 24:38–47.

Goode, William J. 1972. The place of force in human society. *American Sociological Review,* 37:507–19.

Gordon, Milton M. 1964. *Assimilation in American life: The role of race, religion, and national origins.* New York: Oxford University Press.

Gordon, Suzanne. 1997. *Life support: three nurses on the front lines.* Boston: Little, Brown.

Gornick, Vivian, and **B. K. Moran.** 1971. *Women in sexist society.* New York: New American Library.

Gottdiener, Mark, and **Ray Hutchison.** 2000. *The new urban sociology.* Boston: McGraw-Hill.

Gould, Roger V. 1991. Multiple networks and mobilization in the Paris Commune, 1871. *American Sociological Review,* 56:716–29.

Gove, Walter R. 1970. Societal reaction as an explanation of mental illness: An evaluation. *American Sociological Review,* 35:873–84.

Gove, Walter R. 1987. Sociobiology misses the mark: An essay on why biology but not sociobiology is very relevant to sociology. *American Sociologist,* 18:258–77.

Gove, Walter R. 1994. Why we do what we do: A biopsychosocial theory of human motivation. *Social Forces,* 73:363–94.

Gove, Walter R., and **Michael Hughes.** 1980. Reexamining the ecological fallacy: A study in which aggregate data are critical in investigating the pathological effects of living alone. *Social Forces,* 58:1157–1177.

Gove, Walter R., Michael Hughes, and **Michael Geerken.** 1985. Are Uniform Crime Reports a valid indicator of the index crimes? An affirmative answer with minor qualifications. *Criminology,* 23:451–500.

Gove, Walter R., Michael Hughes, and **Carolyn Briggs Style.** 1983. Does marriage have positive effects on the psychological well-being of the individual? *Journal of Health and Social Behavior,* 24(June):122–31.

Gove, Walter R., Carolyn Briggs Style, and **Michael Hughes.** 1990. The effect of marriage on the well-being of adults. *Journal of Family Issues,* 11(March):4–35.

Graff, E.J. 2005. Too pretty a picture. *Washington Post* (November 13):B1.

Granados, Christine. 2000. "Hispanic" vs. "Latino": A new poll finds that the term "Hispanic" is preferred. *Hispanic Magazine* (December). Available at: www.hispanicmagazine.com/2000/dec/Features/latino.html.

Grann, David. 1999. Back to basics in the Bronx. *New Republic* (October 4):24–26.

Grant, Don Sherman, and **Ramiro Martinez.** 1997. Crime and the restructuring of the U.S. economy: A reconsideration of the class linkages. *Social Forces,* 75:769–99.

Granström, K. and **D. Stiwne.** 1998. A bipolar model of groupthink: An expansion of Janis's concept. *Small Group Research,* 29:32–56.

Gray, Bradford H. 1991. The profit motive and patient care: The changing accountability of doctors and hospitals. Cambridge, MA: Harvard University Press.

Gray, John. 2005. The world is round. *New York Review of Books,* 52(13):13–15.

Greeley, Andrew M. 1974. *Ethnicity in the United States: A preliminary reconnaissance.* New York: Wiley.

Greeley, Andrew M. 1977. *The American Catholic: A social portrait.* New York: Harper and Row.

Greeley, Andrew M. 1989. *Religious change in America.* Cambridge, MA: Harvard University Press.

Greenhouse, Linda. 2003. U. of Michigan ruling endorses the value of campus diversity. *New York Times* (June 24):A1.

Greenspan, Stanley J. 1997. The reason why we need to rely less on day care. *Washington Post* (October 19):C1.

Greenstein, Theodore N. 1996. Gender ideology and perceptions of the fairness of the division of household labor: Effects on marital quality. *Social Forces,* 74(3):1029–42.

Greenstein, T. N. 2000. Economic dependence, gender, and the division of labor in the home: A replication and extension. *Journal of Marriage and the Family,* 62(2):322–335.

Greenwald, A. G., and **A. R. Pratkanis.** 1984. The self. In R. S. Wyer and T. K. Srull, eds., *Handbook of social cognition.* Hillsdale, NJ: Erlbaum.

Greenwood, Peter W. 1982. *Selective incapacitation.* Santa Monica, CA: Rand Corporation.

Grimes, Michael D. 1991. *Class in twentieth-century American sociology: An analysis of theories and measurement strategies.* New York: Praeger.

Grimsley, Kirstin Downey. 1997. Avon calling . . . on a man: Board bypasses staff, names former Duracell chief next CEO. *Washington Post* (December 12):G1.

Grob, Gerald N. 1983. *Mental illness and American society, 1875–1940.* Princeton, NJ: Princeton University Press.

Groopman, Jerome. 2002. Dying words: How should doctors deliver bad news? *The New Yorker* (October 28):62–70.

Gross, Paul R., Ursula Goodenough, Lawrence S. Lerner, Susan Haack, Martha Schwartz, Richard Schwartz, and **Chester E. Finn.** 2005. The state of state science standards 2005. Washington, DC: Thomas B. Fordham Institute.

Groves, Robert M., Don A. Dillman, John Eltinge, and **Roderick J. A. Little,** eds. 2002. *Survey nonresponse.* New York: Wiley-Interscience.

Gubrium, Jaber F., and **James A. Holstein.** 1990. *What is family?* Mountain View, CA: Mayfield.

Guelzow, Maureen, Gloria W. Bird, and **Elizabeth H. Koball.** 1991. An exploratory path analysis of the stress process for dual-career men and women. *Journal of Marriage and the Family,* 53:151–64.

Guo, G. 1998. The timing of the influences of cumulative poverty on children's cognitive ability and achievement. *Social Forces,* 77(1):257–287.

Guo, Guang. 2005. Twin studies: What can they tell us about nature and nurture? *Contexts,* 4:43–47.

Gurerk, Ozgur, Bernd Irlenbusch, and **Bettina Rockenbach.** 2006. The competitive advantage of sanctioning institutions. *Science,* 312:108–11.

Gurr, Ted R. 1970. *Why men rebel.* Princeton, NJ: Princeton University Press.

H

Hacker, Helen Mayer. 1951. Women as a minority group. *Social Forces,* 30:60–69.

Hacker, Helen Mayer. 1974. Women as a minority group: Twenty years later. In Florence Denmark, ed., *Who discriminates against women?* Beverly Hills, CA: Sage.

Hadaway, D. Kirk, Penny Long Marler, and **Mark Chaves.** 1993. What the polls don't show: A closer look at U.S. church attendance. *American Sociological Review,* 58:741–52.

Hadden, Jeffrey K. 1987. Toward desacralizing secularization theory. *Social Forces,* 65:587–611.

Hadden, Jeffrey K., and **Anson Shupe.** 1988. *Televangelism, power, and politics in God's frontier.* New York: Henry Holt.

Hagan, John. 1980. The legislation of crime and delinquency: A review of theory, method, and research. *Law and Society Review,* 14:603–28.

Hagan, John. 1989. *Structural criminology.* New Brunswick, NJ: Rutgers University Press.

Hagan, John, Ilene N. Bernstein, and **Celesta Albonetti.** 1980. The differential sentencing of white-collar offenders. *American Sociological Review,* 42:587–98.

Hagan, John, and **Alberto Palloni.** 1999. Sociological criminology and the mythology of Hispanic immigration and crime. *Social Problems,* 46(4):617–32.

Hahn, Robert, and **Scott Wallsten.** 2003. Whose life is worth more? (And why is it horrible to ask?) *Washington Post* (June 1):B3.

Halal, William E., and **Alexander I. Nikitin.** 1990. One world. *The Futurist* (November–December):8–14.

Hall, Edward T. 1966. *The hidden dimension.* Garden City, NY: Doubleday.

Hall, John R. 1988. Social organization and pathways of commitment: Types of communal groups, rational choice theory, and the Kanter Thesis.

American Sociological Review, 53:679–92.

Hamburg, David A., and **Ruby Takanishi.** 1989. Preparing for life: The critical transition of adolescence. *American Psychologist,* 44:825–27.

Hamilton, Richard F. 1972. *Class and politics in the United States.* New York: John Wiley.

Hamper, Ben Rivethead. 1991. *Tales from the assembly line.* New York: Warner.

Haney, C., C. Banks, and **Phillip Zimbardo.** 1973. Interpersonal dynamics in a simulated prison. *International Journal of Criminology and Penology,* 1:69–97.

Hanley, Ruth. 1988. Students hesitant about teaching other races. *Columbus* (Ohio) *Dispatch* (February 4):2.

Hardin, Garrett J. 1968. The tragedy of the commons. *Science,* 162:1243–48.

Hare, A. Paul. 1976. *Handbook of small group research.* 2nd ed. New York: Free Press.

Hareven, Tamara K. 1982. *Family time and industrial time.* New York: Cambridge University Press.

Harkins, Stephen G., and **Kate Szymanski.** 1989. Social loafing and group evaluation. *Journal of Personality and Social Psychology,* 56:934–41.

Harper, Shannon, and **Barbara Reskin.** 2005. Affirmative action at school and on the job. *Annual Review of Sociology,* 31:357–79.

Harrington, Michael. 1976. *The twilight of capitalism.* New York: Simon and Schuster.

Harris, Chauncey D., and **Edward L. Ullman.** 1945. The nature of cities. *Annals of the American Academy of Political and Social Science,* 242:7–17.

Harris, Judith Rich. 1998. *The nurture assumption: Why children turn out the way they do.* New York: Free Press.

Harris, Marvin. 1987. *Why nothing works.* New York: Simon and Schuster.

Harsanyi, Zsolt, and **Richard Hutton.** 1979. Those genes that tell the future. *New York Times Magazine* (November 18):194–205.

Hartjen, Clayton A., and **Sesbarajani Kethineini.** 1993. Culture, gender, delinquency: A study of youths in the United States and India. *Women and Criminal Justice,* 5:37–69.

Hartman, Curtis, and **Steven Pearlstein.** 1987. The job of working. *INC.* (November):61–71.

Hartmann, Heidi, and **Vicky Lovell.** 2003. *The gender wage gap: Progress of the 1980s fails to carry through.* Institute for Women's Policy Research IWPR #C353.

Haslam, S. Alexander, and **Stephen Reicher.** 2002. *A user's guide to* The Experiment—*Exploring the psychology of groups and power: Manual to accompany the BBC video.* London: BBC Worldwide.

Haub, Carl. 2005. *2005 World Population Data Sheet.* Washington, DC: Population Reference Bureau.

Hauser, Marc D., Noam Chomsky, and **W. Tecumseh Fitch.** 2002. The faculty of language: What is it, who has it, and how did it evolve? *Science,* 298:1569–79.

Hawkins, Darnell F. 1987. Beyond anomalies: Rethinking the conflict perspective on race and criminal punishment. *Social Forces,* 65:719–45.

Hayford, Sarah R. 2005. Conformity and change: Community effects on female genital cutting in Kenya. *Journal of Health and Social Behavior,* 46:121–40.

Haynie, Dana L. 2003. Context of risk? Explaining the link between girls' pubertal development and their delinquency involvement. *Social Forces,* 82(1):355–97.

Haynie, Dana L., and **Bridget K. Gorman.** 1999. A gendered context of opportunity: Determinants of poverty across urban and rural labor markets. *Sociological Quarterly,* 40(2):177–97.

Haynie, D. L. 2001. Delinquent peers revisited: Does network structure matter? *American Journal of Sociology,* 106(4):1013–1057.

Hays, Laurie. 1987. Pay problems: How couples react when wives out-earn husbands. *Wall Street Journal* (June 19):19.

Health and Human Services. 2000. *Blueprint for action on breastfeeding.* Washington, DC: U.S. Government Printing Offices.

Hechter, Michael. 1987. *Principles of group solidarity.* Los Angeles: University of California Press.

Hechter, Michael. 1995. Symposium on prediction in the social sciences: Introduction: Reflections on historical prophecy in the social sciences. *American Journal of Sociology,* 100(6):1520–27.

Heckathorn, Douglas D. 1988. Collective sanctions and the emergence of prisoner's dilemma. *American Journal of Sociology,* 94:535–62.

Heckathorn, Douglas D. 1990. Collective sanctions and compliance norms: A formal theory of group-mediated social control. *American Sociological Review,* 55:366–84.

Heilbroner, Robert. 1993. *21st century capitalism.* New York: Norton.

Helmuth, Laura. 2003. The wisdom of the wizened. *Science,* 299:1300–02.

Hepworth, Joseph T., and **Stephen G. West.** 1988. Lynchings and the economy: A time-series reanalysis of Hovland and Sears (1940). *Journal of Personality and Social Psychology,* 55:239–47.

Herberg, Will. 1955. *Protestant-Catholic-Jew.* Garden City, NY: Doubleday.

Herman, Judith, and **Lisa Hirschman.** 1981. Families at risk for father-daughter incest. *American Journal of Psychiatry,* 138:967–70.

Herring, Cedric, and **Karen Rose Wilson-Sadberry.** 1993. Preference or necessity? Changing work roles of black and white women, 1973–1990. *Journal of Marriage and the Family,* 55:314–25.

Herrnstein, Richard J., and **Charles Murray.** 1994. *The bell curve: intelligence and class structure in American life.* New York: Free Press.

Hersey, Paul, and **Kenneth H. Blanchard.** 1988. *Management of organizational behavior: Utilizing human resources.* Englewood Cliffs, NJ: Prentice Hall.

Hertsgaard, Mark. 1998. *Earth odyssey: Around the world in search of our environmental future.* New York: Broadway Books.

Hertzler, J. O. 1961. *American social institutions.* Boston: Allyn and Bacon.

Hewitt, John P. 2003. *Self and society.* Boston: Allyn and Bacon.

Heymann, Jody, Alison Earle, Stephanie Simmons, Stephanie M. Breslow, and **April Kuehnhoff.** 2004. The work, family, and equity index: Where does the United States stand globally? The Project on Global Working Families, www.globalworkingfamilies.org.

Hibbing, John R., and **Elizabeth Theiss-Morse.** 2002. *Stealth democracy: Americans' beliefs about how government should work.* Cambridge: Cambridge University Press.

Higginbotham, Elizabeth, and **Lynn Weber.** 1992. Moving up with kin and community: Upward social mobility for black and white women. *Gender & Society,* 6(3):416–40.

Hill, Martha S., and **W. Jean Young.** 1999. How has the changing structure of opportunities affected transitions to adulthood? In Alan Booth, Ann C. Crouter, and Michael J. Shanahan, eds., *Transitions to adulthood in a changing economy: No work, no family, no future?* Westport, CT: Praeger.

Hilts, Philip J. 1994. 6% of pregnant women say they were battered. *New York Times* (March 4):A8.

Hinden, Stan. 2001. For women, social security safety net is frayed. *Washington Post* (February 4):H1.

Hinkle, Roscoe. 1980. *Founding theory of American sociology: 1881–1915.* London: Routledge & Kegan Paul.

Hirschi, Travis. 1969. *Causes of delinquency.* Berkeley: University of California Press.

Hirschi, Travis, and **Rodney Stark.** 1969. Hellfire and delinquency. *Social Problems,* 17:202–13.

Hirschman, Charles, and **Morrison G. Wong.** 1986. The extraordinary educational attainment of Asian Americans: A search for historical evidence and explanations. *Social Forces,* 65:1–27.

Hitlin, Steven, and **Jane Allyn Piliavin.** 2004. Values: Reviving a dormant concept. *Annual Review of Sociology,* 30:359–93.

Hochschild, A. R. 1990. *The second shift.* New York: Avon Books.

Hochschild, Arlie Russell. 1997. *The time bind: When work becomes home and home becomes work.* New York: Metropolitan Books, Henry Holt.

Hockstader, Lee. 2003. Post-9/11 visa rules keep thousands from coming to U.S. *Washington Post* (November 11):A1.

Hodge, Robert, and **Donald Treiman.** 1968. Class identification in the United States. *American Journal of Sociology,* 73:535–47.

Hoebel, E. A. 1958. *Man in the primitive world.* 2nd ed. New York: McGraw-Hill.

Hoecker-Drysdale, Susan. 1994. *Harriet Martineau: First woman sociologist.* New York: Berg Press.

Hoffman, Curt, and **Nancy Hurst.** 1990. Gender stereotypes: Perception or rationalization? *Journal of Personality and Social Psychology,* 58, 197–208.

Hoffman, John P. 2003. A contextual analysis of differential association, social control, and strain theories of delinquency. *Social Forces,* 81(3): 753–785.

Hoffman, Lois. 1989. Effects of maternal employment in the two-parent family. *American Psychologist,* 44:283–92.

Holden, Constance. 2002. Last word on El Dorado. *Science,* 297:333.

Holden, Constance. 2003. Data points. *Science,* 299:1011.

Holden, Constance. 2006. African soil exhaustion. *Science,* 312:31.

Holder, Kelly. 2006. *Voting and registration in the election of November 2004.* U.S. Census Bureau, Current Population Reports, Series P20-556. Washington, DC.

Hondagneu-Sotelo, Pierrette. 2001. *Domestica: Immigrant workers cleaning and caring in the shadows of affluence.* Berkeley: University of California Press.

Horowitz, Carl. 1994. What's environmental racism? *Investor's Business Daily* (March 2):1–2.

Horowitz, Helen Lefkowitz. 1987. *Campus life: Undergraduate cultures from the end of the eighteenth century to the present.* New York: Knopf.

Hostetler, John A. 1980. *Amish society.* Baltimore: Johns Hopkins University Press.

House, James S., Karl R. Landis, and **Debra Umberson.** 1988. Social relationships and health. *Science,* 241:540–5.

House, James. 1995. Introduction: Social structure and personality: Past, present, and future. In Karen S. Cook, Gary Alan Fine, and James S. House, eds., *Sociological Perspectives on Social Psychology.* Boston: Allyn and Bacon.

Hout, Michael, and **Claude S. Fischer.** 2002. Why more Americans have no religious preference: Politics and generations. *American Sociological Review,* 67:165–90.

Hoyert, D. L., H. C. Kung, and **B. L. Smith.** 2005. Deaths: Preliminary data for 2003. National vital statistics reports; vol. 53 no. 15. National Center for Health Statistics, Hyattsville, MD.

Hoyt, Homer. 1939. *The structure and growth of residential neighborhoods in American cities.* Washington, DC: Federal Housing Administration.

Hsu, Frances L. K. 1943. Incentives to work in primitive communities. *American Sociological Review,* 8:638–42.

Huesmann, L. Rowell, Jessica Moise-Titus, Cheryl-Lynn Podolski, and **Leonard D. Eron.** 2003. Longitudinal relations between children's exposure to TV violence and their aggressive and violent behavior in young adulthood: 1977–1992. *Developmental Psychology,* 39(2):201–21.

Huey, John. 1994. The new post-heroic leadership. *Fortune* (February 21): 42–50.

Hughes, Charles C. 1968. Medical care: Ethnomedicine. In D. Sills, ed., *International Encyclopedia of Social Sciences,* Vol. 10. New York: Macmillan.

Hughes, Michael. 1980. The fruits of cultivation analysis: A reexamination of some effects of television watching. *Public Opinion Quarterly,* 44:289–302.

Hughes, Michael. 1989. Parenthood and psychological well-being among the formerly married: Are children the primary source of psychological distress. *Journal of Family Issues,* 10:163–81.

Hughes, Michael. 1997. Symbolic racism, old fashioned racism, and whites' opposition to affirmative action. In Steven A. Tuch and Jack K. Martin, eds., *Racial attitudes in the 1990s: Continuity and change.* Westport, CT: Praeger.

Hughes, Michael, and **David H. Demo.** 1989. Self-perceptions of black Americans: Self-esteem and personal efficacy. *American Journal of Sociology,* 95:139–59.

Hughes, Michael, and **Walter R. Gove.** 1981. Living alone, social integration, and mental health. *American Journal of Sociology,* 87:48–74.

Hughes, Michael, and **Bradley R. Hertel.** 1990. The significance of color remains: A study of life chances, mate selection, and ethnic consciousness among black Americans. *Social Forces,* 68:1105–20.

Hughes, Michael, and **Melvin E. Thomas.** 1998. The continuing significance of race revisited: A study of race, class, and quality of life in America, 1972–1996. *American Sociological Review,* 63:785–95.

Huiting, Hu. 2002. Family planning law and China's birth control situation. www.china.org.cn/english/ 2002/Oct/46138.htm.

Hull, R. Bruce, and **David P. Robertson.** 2000. Which nature? In Gobster, Paul H., and R. Bruce Hull, eds., *Restoring nature: Perspectives from the social sciences and humanities.* Washington, DC: Island Press.

Hummer, R. A., R. G. Rogers, S. H. Amir, D. Forbes, and **W. P. Frisbie.** 2000. Adult mortality differentials among Hispanic subgroups and non-Hispanic whites. *Social Science Quarterly,* 81(1):459–76.

Humphrey, John A., and **Timothy J. Fogarty.** 1987. Race and plea-bargained outcomes: A research note. *Social Forces,* 66:176–82.

Hunter, James Davison. 1983. *American evangelicalism: Conservative religion and the quandary of modernity.* New Brunswick, NJ: Rutgers University Press.

Hunter, James Davison. 1987. *Evangelicalism: The coming generation.* Chicago: The University of Chicago Press.

Hurst, Charles E. 1998. *Social inequality: Forms, causes, and consequences.* Boston: Allyn and Bacon.

Hutter, Mark. 1998. *The changing family.* 3rd ed. Boston: Allyn and Bacon.

Hyde, Janet Shibley. 2005. The gender similarities hypothesis. *American Psychologist,* 60(6):581–592.

Hyman, Herbert H., and **Eleanor Singer.** 1968. Introduction. In H. H. Hyman and E. Singer, eds., *Readings in reference group theory and research.* New York: Free Press.

I

Iannoccone, Laurence R. 1994. Why strict churches are strong. *American Journal of Sociology,* 99:1180–1211.

Iannoccone, Laurence R., Daniel V. A. Olson, and **Rodney Stark.** 1995. Religious resources and church growth. *Social Forces,* 74:705–31.

Iceland, John. 2003. *Dynamics of economic well-being: Poverty 1996–1999.* U.S. Census Bureau Current Populantion Reports, P70-91. Washington, DC: U.S. Government Printing Office (available online at: http://www.bls.census.gov/sipp/p70s/ p70-91.pdf).

Iceland, John, Daniel H. Weinberg, and **Erika Steinmetz.** 2002. *Racial and ethnic residential segregation in the United States: 1980–2000* (U.S. Census Bureau, Series CENSR-3). Washington, DC: U.S. Government Printing Office.

Ingham, Alan G. 1974. The Ringelmann effect: Studies of group size and group performance. *Journal of Experimental Social Psychology,* 10:371–84.

Inglehart, Ronald, et al. 2000. *World values surveys and European values surveys, 1981–1984, 1990–1993, and 1995–1997* [Computer file]. ICPSR version. Ann Arbor, MI: Institute for Social Research.

Inkeles, Alex. 1968. Society, social structure, and child socialization. In John Clausen, ed., *Socialization and society.* Boston: Little, Brown.

Institute of Medicine. 2003. *Hidden costs, value lost: Uninsurance in America.* National Academies of Sciences.

International Labor Organization. 2001. *World Employment Report 2001: Life at work in the information economy.* International Labor Organization website www.ilo.org.

Intons-Peterson, Margaret Jean. 1988. *Gender concepts of Swedish and American Youth.* Hillsdale, NJ: Erlbaum.

Ishida, Julie. 2003. The scramble for care. *Washington Post* (September 9):F1.

Iyengar, Shanto. 1991. *Is anyone responsible? How television frames political issues.* Chicago: University of Chicago Press.

J

Jackendoff, Ray. 2002. *Foundations of language: Brain, meaning, grammar, evolution.* New York: Oxford University Press.

Jackman, Mary R., and **Robert W. Jackman.** 1983. *Class awareness in the United States.* Berkeley: University of California Press.

Jackson, Philip W. 1968. *Life in classrooms.* New York: Holt, Rinehart and Winston.

Jackson, Walter A. 1990. *Gunnar Myrdal and America's conscience: Social engineering and racial liberalism, 1938–1987.* Chapel Hill: University of North Carolina Press.

Jacobs, David, and **Jason T. Carmichael.** 2002. The political sociology of the death penalty: A pooled time-series analysis. *American Sociological Review,* 67:109–31.

Jacobs, David, and **Ronald E. Helms.** 1996. Toward a political model of incarceration: A time-series examination of multiple explanations for prison admission rates. *American Journal of Sociology,* 102:323–57.

Jacobs, David, and **Ronald E. Helms.** 1997. Testing coercive explanations for order: The determinants of law enforcement strength over time. *Social Forces,* 75:1361–92.

Jacobson, Robert L. 1992. Professors who teach more are paid less, study finds. *Chronicle of Higher Education* (April 15):A17.

Jaffee, David. 2001. *Organization theory: Tension and change.* New York: McGraw-Hill.

James, John. 1951. A preliminary study of the size determinant in small group interaction. *American Sociological Review,* 16:474–77.

Jamieson, Amie, Hyon B. Shin, and **Jennifer Day.** 2002. *Voting and registration in the election of November 2000.* U.S. Census Bureau Current Population Reports P20-542 (February 2002).

Janis, Irving. 1972. *Victims of groupthink.* Boston: Houghton Mifflin.

Janis, Irving L. 1982. *Groupthink.* 2nd ed. Boston: Houghton Miffin.

Janis, Irving L. 1989. *Crucial decisions: Leadership in policy-making and crisis management.* New York: Free Press.

Jargowsky, Paul A. 1997. *Poverty and place.* New York: Russell Sage Foundation.

Jaynes, Gerald D., and **Robin M. Williams,** eds. 1989. *A common destiny: Blacks and American society.* Washington, DC: National Academy Press.

Jeffords, James M., and **Tom Daschle.** 2001. Political issues in the genome era. *Science,* 291:1249–251.

Jencks, Christopher. 1992. *Rethinking social policy: Race, poverty, and the underclass.* Cambridge: Harvard University Press.

Jencks, Christopher, and **Meredith Phillips.** 1998. *The black-white test score gap.* Washington, DC: Brookings Institution Press.

Jenkins, J. Craig. 1985. *The politics of insurgency: The farm worker movement in the 1960s.* New York: Columbia University Press.

Jenness, Valerie. 2004. Explaining criminalization: From demography and status politics to globalization and modernization. *Annual Review of Sociology,* 30:147–71.

Jensen, Gary F., and **Dean G. Rojek.** 1992. *Delinquency and youth crime.* Prospect Heights, IL: Waveland.

Johnson, Hayes. 1988. Hispanics, blacks are dropping out. *USA Today* (March 23):D3.

Johnson, James Weldon. 1927/1989. *The autobiography of an ex-coloured man.* New York: Vintage Books.

Johnson, Jeffrey G., Patricia Cohen, Elizabeth M. Smailes, **Stephanie Kasen,** and **Judith S. Brook.** 2002. Television viewing and aggressive behavior during adolescence and adulthood. *Science,* 295:2468–471.

Johnson, Miriam. 1993. Functionalism and feminism: Is estrangement necessary? In Paula England, ed., *Theory on gender/ feminism on gender.* New York: Aldine de Gruyter.

Johnson, Robert. 1990. Heavenly gifts: Preaching a gospel of acquisitiveness, a showy sect prospers. *Wall Street Journal* (December 11):A1, A6.

Johnston, David Cay. 2003. Very richest's share of wealth grew even bigger, data show. *New York Times* (June 26):A1.

Jones, Arthur F., and **Daniel H. Weinberg.** 2000. The changing shape of the nation's income distribution. *Current Population Reports* P60-204 (June). Washington, DC: U.S. Census Bureau.

Jones, Jacqueline. 1992. *The dispossessed: America's underclasses from the Civil War to the present.* New York: Basic Books.

Jordan, Winthrop D. 1969. *White over black: American attitudes toward the Negro, 1550–1812.* Baltimore: Penguin Books.

Josephy, Alvin M., Jr. 1991. *The Civil War in the American West.* New York: Knopf.

K

Kagan, Jerome, Richard B. Kearsley, and **Philip R. Zelazo.** 1978. *Infancy: Its place in human development.* Cambridge, MA: Harvard University Press.

Kain, Edward L. 1984. Surprising singles. *American Demographics,* 6 (August):16–19ff.

Kain, Edward L. 1990. *The myth of family decline: Understanding families in a world of rapid social change.* Lexington, MA: Lexington Books.

Kalish, Susan. 1994. International migration: New findings on magnitude, importance. *Population Today,* 22:1–3.

Kamolnick, Paul. 1988. *Classes: A Marxist critique.* Dix Hills, NY: General Hall.

Kanazawa, Satoshi. 2000. A new solution to the collective action problem: The paradox of voter turnout. *American Sociological Review,* 65:433–42.

Kanter, Rosabeth M., 1968. Commitment and social organization: A study of commitment mechanisms in utopian communities. *American Sociological Review,* 46:141–58.

Kaplan, Howard B., Robert J. Johnson, and **Carol A. Bailey.** 1987. Deviant peers and deviant behavior: Further elaborations of a model. *Social Psychology Quarterly,* 50:277–84.

Karau, Steven J., and **Kipling D. Williams.** 1993. Social loafing: A meta-analytic review and theoretical integration. *Journal of Personality and Social Psychology,* 65:681–706.

Karen, David. 1990. Toward a political-organizational model of gatekeeping. The case of elite colleges. *Sociology of Education,* 63:227–40.

Kaufman, Marc, and **Rob Stein.** 2006. Record share of economy spent on health care. *Washington Post* (January 10):A1.

Keister, Lisa A., and **Stephanie Moller.** 2000. Wealth inequality in the United States. *Annual Review of Sociology,* 26:63–81.

Keita, Gwendolyn Puryear, and **Steven L. Sauter,** eds. 1992. *Work and well-being: An agenda for the 1990s.* Washington, DC: American Psychological Association.

Keller, Helen. 1904. *The story of my life.* Garden City, NY: Doubleday.

Kelly, Joe, and **Stacy L. Smith.** 2006. Where the girls aren't: Gender disparity saturates G-rated films. A research brief commissioned by the See Jane Program at Dads and Daughters. www.seejane.org.

Kelly, Raymond C. 1976. Witchcraft and sexual relations: An exploration in the social and semantic implications of the structure of belief. In Paula Brown and Georgeda

Buchhinder, eds., *Man and woman in the New Guinea highlands,* a special publication of the American Anthropological Association, no. 8. Washington, DC: American Anthropological Association.

Kendall-Tackett, Kathleen A., Linda Meyer Williams, and **David Finkelhor.** 1993. Impact of sexual abuse on children: A review and synthesis of recent empirical studies. *Psychological Bulletin,* 113:164–80.

Kennedy, Donald. 2002. Science, terrorism, and natural disasters. *Science,* 295:405.

Kennedy, Donald, and **Brooks Hanson.** 2006. Ice and history. *Science,* 311:1673.

Kennedy, Edward M. 2002. America's growing wage-rent disparity. *National Low Income Housing Coalition.*

Kennelly, Ivy, Sabine N. Merz, and **Judith Lorber.** 2001. Comment: What is gender? *American Sociological Review,* 66:598–605.

Kennickell, Arthur B. 2000. An examination of changes in the distribution of wealth from 1989 to 1998. Evidence from the Survey of Consumer Finances. *Summary* 9 (Fall) Working Paper No. 307, www.levy.org/docs/summary/sumfall00.html.

Kennickell, Arthur B. 2003. A rolling tide: changes in the distribution of wealth in the U.S., 1989–2001. Board of Governors of the Federal Reserve System (March 3). Available at: www.federalreserve.gov/pubs/oss/oss2/scfindex.html.

Kepel, Gilles. 2002. *Jihad: The trail of political Islam.* Cambridge, MA: Belknap.

Kerbo, Harold R. 2006. *Social stratification and inequality* (6th ed.). New York: McGraw-Hill.

Kerr, Norman L. 1983. Motivation losses in small groups: A social dilemma analysis. *Journal of Personality and Social Psychology,* 45:819–28.

Kerr, Richard A. 2006. A worrying trend of less ice, higher seas. *Science,* 311:1698–1701.

Kertzer, David. 1991. Household history and sociological theory. *Annual Review of Sociology,* 17:155–79.

Kessler, Ronald C., James S. House, A. Regula Herzog, and **Pamela Webster.** 1992. The relationship between age and depressive symptoms in two national surveys. *Psychology and Aging,* 7:119–26.

Kessler, Ronald C., and **James A. McRae, Jr.** 1981. Trends in sex and psychological distress. *American Sociological Review,* 46:443–52.

Kessler, Ronald C., Amanda Sonnega, Evelyn Bromet, Michael Hughes, and **Christopher B. Nelson.** 1995. Posttraumatic stress disorder in the National Comorbidity Survey. *Archives of General Psychiatry,* 52:1048–60.

Kessler-Harris, Alice. 1990. *A woman's wage: Historical meanings and social consequences.* Lexington: University Press of Kentucky.

Kett, J. F. 1977. *Rites of passage: Adolescence in America, 1870 to the present.* New York: Basic Books.

Kiecolt, K. Jill. 1994. Stress and the decision to change oneself: A theoretical model. *Social Psychology Quarterly,* 57:49–63.

Kiecolt, K. Jill. 2003. Satisfaction with work and family life: No evidence of a cultural reversal. *Journal of Marriage and Family,* 65:23–35.

Kilborn, Peter T. 1992. Sad distinction for the Sioux: Homeland is no. 1 in poverty. *New York Times* (September 20):1, 14.

Kim, Jae-On. 1987. Social mobility, status inheritance, and structural constraints: Conceptual and methodological considerations. *Social Forces,* 65:783–805.

Kinder, Donald R., and **Lynn M. Sanders.** 1996. *Divided by color: Racial politics and democratic ideals.* Chicago: University of Chicago Press.

Kinder, Donald R., and **David O. Sears.** 1981. Prejudice and politics. Symbolic racism versus racial threats to the good life. *Journal of*

Personality and Social Psychology, 40:414–31.

Kinsey, Alfred C., Wardell B. Pomeroy, and **Clyde E. Martin.** 1948. *Sexual behavior in the human male.* Philadelphia: Saunders.

Kirkpatrick, R. C. 2000. The evolution of human homosexual behavior. *Current Anthropology,* 41(3):385–413.

Kitson, Gay C., and **William M. Holmes.** 1992. *Portrait of divorce: Adjustment to marital breakdown.* New York: Guilford.

Klass, Perri. 1987. When the doctor-patient relationship breaks down. *Discover,* 8(March):16.

Klaus, Patsy A. 2002. Crime and the nation's households, 2000. Washington, DC: U.S. Department of Justice. NCJ-194107.

Klein, Katherine J. 1987. Employee stock ownership and employee attitudes: A test of three models. *Journal of Applied Psychology,* 72:319–32.

Klineberg, Otto. 1986, SPSSI and race relations in the 1950s and after. *Journal of Social Issues,* 42:53–59.

Kluckhohn, Clyde. 1960. *Mirror for man.* Greenwich, CT: Fawcett.

Knodel, John, and **Etienne van de Walle.** 1979. Lessons from the past: Policy implications of historical fertility studies. *Population and Development Review,* 5:217–45.

Knottnerus, J. David. 1991. Status attainment's image of society: Individual factors, structural effect, and the transformation of the class structure. *Sociological Spectrum,* 11:147–76.

Koch, Jeffrey W. 1999. Candidate gender and assessments of senate candidates. *Social Science Quarterly,* 80(1):84–96.

Kohlberg, Lawrence. 1966. A cognitive-developmental analysis of children's sex-role concepts and attitudes. In Eleanor F. Maccoby, ed., *The development of sex differences.* Stanford, CA: Stanford University Press.

Kohlberg, Lawrence. 1969. Stage and sequence: The cognitive-developmental approach to

socialization. In D. A. Goslin, ed., *Handbook of socialization theory and research.* Chicago: Rand McNally.

Kohlberg, Lawrence. 1981. *The philosophy of moral development.* San Francisco: Harper and Row.

Kohlberg, Lawrence, and **D. Z. Ullian.** 1974. Stages in the development of psychosexual concepts and attitudes. In R. C. Friedman, R. N. Richart, and R. L. Van de Wiele, eds., *Sex differences in behavior.* New York: John Wiley.

Kohn, Melvin L., Atsushi Naoi, Carrie Schoenbach, Carmi Schooler, and **Kazimierz M. Slomczynski.** 1990. Position in the class structure and psychological functioning in the United States, Japan, and Poland. *American Journal of Sociology,* 95:964–1008.

Kohn, Melvin L., and **Carmi Schooler.** 1973. Occupational experience and psychological functioning: An assessment of reciprocal effects. *American Sociological Review,* 38:97–118.

Kohn, Melvin L., and **Carmi Schooler.** 1982. Job conditions and personality: A longitudinal assessment of their reciprocal effects. *American Journal of Sociology,* 87:1257–86.

Kohn, Melvin L., and **Carmi Schooler.** 1983. *Work and personality: An inquiry into the impact of social stratification.* Norwood, NJ: Ablex.

Kollock, Peter. 1993. "An eye for an eye leaves everyone blind": Cooperation and accounting systems. *American Sociological Review,* 58:768–86.

Komarovsky, Mirra. 1991. Reflections on feminist scholarship. *Annual Review of Sociology,* 17:1–25.

Konner, Melvin. 1993. *Medicine at the crossroads: The crisis in health care.* New York: Pantheon.

Kornhauser, William. 1959. *The politics of mass society.* New York: Free Press.

Koss, Mary P. and **J. A. Gaines.** 1993. The prediction of sexual aggression by alcohol use, athletic

participation and fraternity affiliation. *Journal of Interpersonal Violence,* 8:94–108.

Koss, Mary, Christine A. Gidycz, and **Nadine Wisniewski.** 1987. The scope of rape: Incidence and prevalence of sexual aggression and victimization in a national sample of higher education students. *Journal of Consulting and Clinical Psychology,* 55:162–70.

Kraar, Louis. 1990. The U.S. mood: Ever optimistic. *Fortune* (March 26): 19–26.

Krafft, Susan. 1994. Why wives earn less than husbands. *American Demographics,* 15 (January):16–17.

Krasikov, Sana. 2001. Group recalculates living wage. *Cornell Daily Sun* (March 12).

Kraut, Robert, and **Sara Kiesler.** 2003. The social impact of Internet use. *Psychological Science Agenda,* 16(3):8–11.

Krivo, Lauren J., and **Ruth D. Peterson.** 1996. Extremely disadvantaged neighborhoods and urban crime. *Social Forces,* 75:619–50.

Krivo, Lauren J., and **Ruth D. Peterson.** 2000. The structural context of homicide: Accounting for racial differences in process. *American Sociological Review,* 65:547–59.

Kruetzen, Michael, Janet Mann, Michael R. Heithaus, Richard C. Connor, Lars Bejder, and **William B. Sherwin.** 2005. Cultural transmission of tool use in bottlenose dolphins. *Proceedings of the National Academy of Sciences,* 102(25): 8939–43.

Kruglanski, Arie W. 1986. Freeze think and the Challenger. *Psychology Today,* August:48–49.

Kruttschnitt, Candace, Rosemary Gartner, and **Amy Miller.** 2000. Doing her own time? Women's responses to prison in the context of the old and the new penology. *Criminology:* 38(3), 681–717.

Krymkowski, Daniel H. 1991. The process of status attainment among men in Poland, the U.S., and West Germany. *American Sociological Review,* 56:46–59.

Kübler-Ross, Elisabeth. 1969. *On death and dying.* New York: Macmillan.

Kübler-Ross, Elisabeth. 1981. *Living with death and dying.* New York: Macmillan.

Kuhn, Manford. 1964. Major trends in symbolic interaction theory in the past twenty-five years. *Sociological Quarterly,* 5:61–84.

Kurdek, Lawrence A. 1993. The allocation of household labor in gay, lesbian, and heterosexual married couples. *Journal of Social Issues,* 49:127–39.

Kuttner, Robert. 1994. Pat Moynihan's blarney on health care. *Business Week* (February 14):18.

L

Labich, Kenneth. 1994. Class in America. *Fortune* (February 7): 114–26.

Lachman, Richard. 1988. Graffiti as career and ideology. *American Journal of Sociology,* 94:229–50.

LaFree, Gary. 1999. Declining violent crime rates in the 1990s: Predicting crime booms and busts. *Annual Review of Sociology,* 25: 145–68.

Lamptey, Peter R., Jami L. Johnson, and **Marya Khan.** 2006. The global challenge of HIV and AIDS. Population Bulletin 61(1). Population Reference Bureau.

Lane, Charles. 2003a. Ruling is landmark victory for gay rights. *Washington Post* (June 27):A1.

Lane, Charles. 2003b. U-Michigan gets broad support on using race. *Washington Post* (February 11):A11.

Lane, Earl. 1998. Crisis forcasting offers new ways to predict natural or human events. *Washington Post* (January 2):A16.

Langan, Patrick A., and **David J. Levin.** 2002. Recidivism of prisoners released in 1994. Washington, DC: U.S. Department of Justice. NCJ-193427.

Lantz, Paula M., James S. House, James M. Lepkowski, David R. Williams, Richard P. Mero, and

Jieming Chen. 1998. Socioeconomic factors, health behaviors, and mortality: Results from a nationally representative prospective study of US adults. *Journal of the American Medical Association,* 279(21):1703–1708.

Lareau, Annette. 2002. Invisible inequality: Social class and childrearing in black families and white families. *American Sociological Review,* 67(5): 747–776.

Lareau, Annette. 2003. *Unequal childhoods: Class, race, and family life.* California: University of California Press.

Larson, Jan. 1992. Understanding stepfamilies. *American Demographics,* 14 (July):36–40.

Laslett, Peter. 1974. *Household and family in past time.* New York: Cambridge University Press.

Laslett, Peter. 1976. Societal development and aging. In R. Binstock and E. Shanas, eds., *Handbook of aging and the social sciences.* New York: Van Nostrand/Reinhold.

Lasswell, Harold. 1936. *Politics: Who gets what, when and how.* New York: McGraw-Hill.

Lauer, Robert H., and **Jeanette C. Lauer.** 2000. *Marriage and family: The quest for intimacy.* New York: McGraw-Hill.

Laumann, Edward O., John H. Gagnon, Robert T. Michael, and **Stuart Michaels.** 1994. *The social organization of sexuality: Sexual practices in the United States.* Chicago: University of Chicago Press.

Lawler, Edward J. 1992. Affective attachments to nested groups: A choice-process theory. *American Sociological Review,* 57:327–39.

Lawler, Edward J., Cecilia Ridgeway, and **Barry Markovsky.** 1993. Structural social psychology and the micro-macro problem. *Sociological Theory,* 11:269–90.

Lawler, Edward J., and **Jeongkoo Yoon.** 1993. Power and the emergence of commitment behavior in negotiated exchange. *American Sociological Review,* 58:465–81.

Leary, Mark R., and **Robin M. Kowalski.** 1990. Impression management: A literature review and two-component model. *Psychological Bulletin,* 107:34–47.

Le Bon, Gustav. 1896. *The crowd: A study of the popular mind.* London: Ernest Benn.

LeClere, F. B., R. G. Rogers, and **K. D. Peters.** 1997. Ethnicity and mortality in the United States: Individual and community correlates. *Social Forces,* 76(1):169–98.

Lee, Felicia R. 1990. "Model minority" label adds to the burdens of Asian students. *New York Times* (March 20):A14.

Lee, Gary R. 1977. *Family structure and interaction: A comparative analysis.* Philadelphia: Lippincott.

Lee, Jennifer, and **Frank D. Bean.** 2004. America's changing color lines: Immigration, race/ethnicity, and multiracial identification. *Annual Review of Sociology,* 30:221–42.

Lee, Valerie, E., and **Anthony S. Bryk.** 1989. A multi-level model of the social distribution of high school achievement. *Sociology of Education,* 62:172–92.

Lehman, Edward W. 1988. The theory of the state versus the state of theory. *American Sociological Review,* 53:807–23.

Lehrer, Evelyn L. 1999. Married women's labor supply behavior in the 1990s: Differences by life-cycle stage. *Social Science Quarterly,* 80(3):574–90.

Leitenberg, H., and **H. Saltzman.** 2000. A statewide survey of age at first intercourse for adolescent females and age of their male partners: Relation to other risk behaviors and statutory rape implications. *Archives of Sexual Behavior,* 29(3):203–15.

Lengermann, Patricia Madoo, and **Jill Niebrugge.** 2007. Contemporary feminist theories, in George Ritzer, *Contemporary sociological theory and its classical roots.* New York: McGraw-Hill.

Lekuton, Joseph Lemasolai. 2003. *Facing the lion: Growing up Maasai on the African savanna.* Washington, DC: National Geographic.

Lemert, Charles. 2002. *Social things.* Lanham, MD: Rowman & Littlefield.

Lemert, Edwin M. 1951. *Social pathology: A systematic approach to the theory of sociopathic behavior.* New York: McGraw-Hill.

Lemert, Edwin M. 1972. *Human deviance, social problems and social control.* 2nd ed. Englewood Cliffs, NJ: Prentice Hall.

Lempert, Robert J., Steven W. Popper, and **Steven C. Bankes.** 2003. *Shaping the next one hundred years: New methods for quantitative, long-term policy analysis.* Santa Monica, CA: RAND.

Lengermann, Patricia Madoo, and **Jill Niebrugge-Brantley.** 2000a. Early women sociologists and classical sociological theory: 1830–1930, in George Ritzer, *Classical Sociological Theory.* Boston: McGraw-Hill.

Lengermann, Patricia Madoo, and **Jill Niebrugge-Brantley.** 2000b. Contemporary feminist theory, in George Ritzer, *Sociological theory.* Boston: McGraw-Hill.

Lenski, Gerhard E. 1966. *Power and privilege.* New York: McGraw-Hill.

Lenski, Gerhard E., and **Jean Lenski.** 1987. *Human societies: An introduction to macrosociology.* 5th ed. New York: McGraw-Hill.

LeVay, Simon. 1991. A difference in hypothalmic structure between heterosexual and homosexual men. *Science,* 253:1034–37.

LeVay, Simon. 1996. *Queer science: The use and abuse of research into homosexuality.* Cambridge, MA: MIT Press.

Levine, Daniel U., and **Robert J. Havighurst.** 1992. *Society and education.* Boston: Allyn and Bacon.

Levinson, Daniel J. 1986. A conception of adult development. *American Psychologist,* 41:3–13.

Levinson, Daniel J., et al. 1978. *The seasons of a man's life.* New York: Knopf.

Levinson, Harry. 1964. Money aside, why spend life working? *National Observer* (March 9):20.

Levi-Strauss, Claude. 1956. The family. In Harry L. Shapiro, ed., *Man, culture and society.* New York: Oxford University Press.

Levitt, Steven D. 2004. Understanding why crime fell in the 1990s: Four factors that explain the decline and six that do not. *Journal of Economic Perspectives,* 18: 163–90.

Lewin, Kurt, Ronald Lippitt, and **Ralph K. White.** 1939. Patterns of aggressive behavior in experimentally created "social climates." *Journal of Social Psychology,* 10:271–99.

Lewis, Jone Johnson. 2006. Women's history. http://womenshistory.about.com/od/rulers20th/a/women_heads.htm

Lewis, Michael, Margaret Wolan Sullivan, Catherine Stanger, and **Maya Weiss.** 1989. Self-development and self-conscious emotions. *Child Development,* 60:146–56.

Lewis, Oscar. 1966. *La vida: A Puerto Rican family in the culture of poverty, San Juan and New York.* New York: Random House.

Lewontin, R. C., Steven Rose, and **Leon J. Kamin.** 1984. *Not in our genes.* New York: Pantheon.

Lichter, Daniel T., and **Rukamalie Jayakody.** 2002. Welfare reform: How do we measure success? *Annual Review of Sociology,* 28:117–41.

Lichter, Daniel T., Deborah Roempke Graefe, and **J. Brian Brown.** 2003. Is marriage a panacea? Union formation among economically disadvantaged unwed mothers. *Social Problems,* 50(1):60–86.

Lieberson, Stanley, and **Mary C. Waters.** 1988. *From many strands: Ethnic and racial groups in contemporary America.* New York: Russell Sage.

Lieberson, Stanley, and **Mary C. Waters.** 1993. The ethnic responses of whites: What causes their instability, simplification, and inconsistency? *Social Forces,* 72:421–50.

Liebow, Elliot. 2003/1967. *Tally's corner.* Lanham, MD: Rowman & Littlefield Publishers.

Liker, Jeffrey K., Carol J. Haddad, and **Jennifer Karlin.** 1999. Perspectives on technology and work organization. *Annual Review of Sociology,* 25:575–96.

Lindblom, Charles E. 1990. *Inquiry and change: The troubled attempt to understand and shape society.* New Haven: Yale University Press.

Lindorff, Dave. 1992. *Marketplace medicine: The rise of the for-profit hospital chains.* New York: Bantam Books.

Lindsey, Robert. 1987. Colleges accused of bias to stem Asians' gain. *New York Times* (January 19):8.

Link, Bruce G., Francis T. Cullen, Elmer Struening, Patrick E. Shrout, and **Bruce P. Dohrenwend.** 1989. A modified labeling theory approach to mental disorders: An empirical assessment. *American Sociological Review,* 54:400–23.

Link, Bruce G., Jerrold Mirotznik, and **Francis T. Cullen.** 1991. The effectiveness of stigma coping orientations: Can negative consequences of mental labeling be avoided? *Journal of Health and Social Behavior,* 32:302–20.

Link, Bruce G., and **Jo C. Phelan.** 1995. Social conditions as fundamental causes of disease. *Journal of Health and Social Behavior* (extra issue):80–94.

Linton, Ralph. 1937. One hundred per cent American. *American Mercury,* 40 (April):427–29.

Lipset, Seymour Martin. 1987. Blacks and Jews: How much bias? *Public Opinion,* 10 (July–August): 4–5, 57–58.

Lipset, Seymour Martin. 1993. Reflections on capitalism, socialism and democracy. *Journal of Democracy,* 4:43–53.

Lipset, Seymour Martin. 1994. The social requisites of democracy revisited. *American Sociological Review,* 59:1–22.

Lipset, Seymour Martin, Martin A. Trow, and **James S. Coleman.** 1956. *Union Democracy.* New York: Free Press.

Liska, Allen E. 1986. *Perspectives on deviance.* Englewood Cliffs, NJ: Prentice Hall.

Liska, Allen E., and **Steven F. Messner.** 1999. *Perspectives on crime and deviance.* Upper Saddle River, NJ: Prentice Hall.

Litan, Robert E., and **Alice M. Rivlin.** 2000. The economy and the Internet: What lies ahead? Internet Policy Institute Briefing Paper (November), http://www. internetpolicy.org/briefing/ litan_rivlin.html.

Litan, Robert E., and **Alice M. Rivlin.** 2001. *Beyond the dot.coms: The economic promise of the Internet.* Washington, DC: Brookings.

Lizotte, Alan J. 1978. Extra-legal factors in Chicago's criminal courts: Testing the conflict model of criminal justice. *Social Problems,* 25:564–80.

Lizotte, Alan J., Marvin D. Krohn, James C. Howell, Kimberly Tobin, and **Gregory J. Howard.** 2000. Factors influencing gun carrying among young urban males over the adolescent-young adult life course. *Criminology,* 38(3):811–34.

Locke, John L. 1993. *The child's path to spoken language.* Cambridge: Harvard University Press.

Loftus, Jeni. 2001. America's liberalization in attitudes toward homosexuality, 1973–1998. *American Sociological Review,* 66:762–82.

London, Bruce, and **Bruce A. Williams.** 1990. National political, international dependency, and basic needs provision: A cross-national analysis. *Social Forces,* 69:565–84.

Loomis, Carol J. 1988. The new J. P. Morgans. *Fortune* (February 29): 44–52.

Lopata, Helena Zuaniecki. 1973. *Widowhood in an American city.* Cambridge, MA: Schenkman.

Lopata, Helena Z. 1981. Widowhood and husband satisfaction.

Journal of Marriage and the Family, 43:439–50.

Lopez, Julie Amparano. 1992. Study says women face glass walls as well as ceilings. *Wall Street Journal* (March 3):B1.

Lopez Pintor, Rafael, and **Maria Gratschew.** 2002. Voter turnout since 1945: A global report. Stockholm, Sweden: International Institute for Democracy and Electoral Assistance (International IDEA). Available at http://www.idea/ int.publications/voterturnout.html

Lorber, Judith. 1994. *Paradoxes of gender.* New Haven, CT: Yale University Press.

Lubchenco, Jane. 1998. Entering the century of the environment: A new social contract for science. *Science,* 279:491–97.

Lucal, Betsy. 1994. Class stratification in introductory textbooks: Relational or distributional models? *Teaching Sociology,* 22:139–50.

Lugaila, Terry A. 2003. *A child's day: 2000 (Selected indicators of child well-being).* Current Population Reports P70-89. Washington, DC: U.S. Census Bureau.

Lukacs, Georg. 1922/1968. *History and class consciousness.* Cambridge, MA: MIT Press.

Lukes, Steven. 1977. Alienation and anomie. In *Essays in social theory.* New York: Columbia University Press.

Lundman, Richard J., and **Robert L. Kaufman.** 2003. Driving while black: Effects of race, ethnicity, and gender on citizen self-reports of traffic stops and police actions. *Criminology,* 41(1):195–220.

Luo, Michael. 2006. Evangelicals debate the meaning of "Evangelical." *New York Times* (April 16): Section 4:5.

Ly, Phuong. 2003. Girls teach teen cyber gab to FBI agents: MD students help catch pedophiles on the Internet. *Washington Post* (June 4):A1.

Lyman, Peter, and **Hal R. Varian.** 2000. "How big is the information explosion?" iMP magazine (November). Available at:

http:// www.cisp.org/imp/november_2000/ 11_00lyman.htm.

Lynd, Robert S., and **Helen Merrill Lynd.** 1929. *Middletown: A study in American culture.* New York: Harcourt, Brace & World.

Lynd, Robert S., and **Helen Merrill Lynd.** 1937. *Middletown in transition: A study in cultural conflicts.* New York: Harcourt, Brace & World.

M

Maccoby, Eleanor E., and **Carol N. Jacklin.** 1974. *The psychology of sex differences.* Stanford, CA: Stanford University Press.

MacCoun, Robert J. 1993. Drugs and the law: A psychological analysis of drug prohibition. *Psychological Bulletin,* 113:497–512.

MacCoun, Robert, and **Peter Reuter.** 1997. Interpreting Dutch cannabis policy: Reasoning by analogy in the legalization debate. *Science,* 278:47–52.

MacDorman, Marian F., and **Gopal K. Singh.** 1998. Midwifery care, social and medical risk factors, and birth outcomes in the USA. *Journal of Epidemiology and Community Health,* 52(5):310–317.

MacKinnon, Carol E., and **Donna King.** 1988. Day care: A review of literature, implications for policy, and critique of resources. *Family Relations,* 37:229–36.

Macy, Michael W. 1991. Chains of cooperation: Threshold effects in collective action. *American Sociological Review,* 56:730–47.

Mahoney, James. 2004. Comparative-historical methodology. *Annual Review of Sociology,* 30:81–101.

Malinosky-Rummell, Robin, and **David J. Hansen.** 1993. Long-term consequences of childhood physical abuse. *Psychological Bulletin,* 114:68–79.

Manchester, William. 1993. A world lit only by change. *U.S. News & World Report* (October 25):69.

Manis, Jerome G., and Bernard N. Meltzer. 1994. Chance in human affairs. *Sociological Theory*, 12:45–56.

Mann, Arnold. 2003. Relationships matter: Impact of parental, peer factors on teen, young adult substance abuse. *NIDA Notes*, 18(2):11–13.

Mann, James. 1983. One-parent family: The troubles and the joys. *Newsweek* (November 28): 57–62.

Mann, Leon, James W. Newton, and J. M. Innes. 1982. A test between deindividuation and emergent norm theories of crowd aggression. *Journal of Personality and Social Psychology*, 12:260–72.

Maranto, Robert. 2003. Lobbying in disguise: The American Federation of Teachers "studies" charter schools. *Education Next*, Winter:79–84.

Marger, Martin N. 2006. *Race and ethnic relations: American and global perspectives*. 7th ed. Belmont, CA: Wadsworth/Thompson.

Marks, Carole. 1991. The urban underclass. *Annual Review of Sociology*, 17:445–66.

Marsh, Herbert W. 1986. Global self-esteem: Its relation to specific facets of self-concept and their importance. *Journal of Personality and Social Psychology*, 51:1224–36.

Martin, Carol Lynn, and Jane K. Little. 1990. The relation of gender understanding to children's sex-typed preferences and gender stereotypes. *Child Development*, 61:1427–39.

Martin, Laura. 1983. "Eskimo words for snow": A case study in the genesis and decay of an anthropological example. *American Anthropologist*, 88:418–23.

Martin, Patricia Yancey. 2004. Gender as a social institution. *Social Forces*, 82:1249–73.

Martin, Patricia Yancey, and Robert A. Hummer. 1995. Fraternities and rape on campus. In Alex Thio and Thomas C. Calhoun, eds., *Readings in deviant behavior*. New York: HarperCollins.

Marty, Martin E., and R. Scott Appleby. 1992. *The glory and the power: The fundamentalist challenge to the modern world*. Boston: Beacon Press.

Marx, Karl. 1844/1960. Estranged labour: Economic and philosophic manuscripts of 1844. In C. W. Mills, ed., *Images of man*. New York: Braziller.

Marx, Karl. 1867/1906. *Capital*. Vol. 1. New York: Modern Library.

Marx, Karl. 1970. *Critique of Hegel's "philosophy of right."* Trans. A. O'Malley and J. O'Malley. London: Cambridge University Press.

Marx, Karl, and Friedrich Engels. 1848/1955. *The communist manifesto*. S. H. Beer, ed. New York: Appleton Century Crofts.

Massey, Douglas S. 1990. American apartheid: Segregation and the making of the underclass. *American Journal of Sociology*, 96:329–57.

Massey, Douglas S., and Nancy A. Denton. 1993. *American apartheid: Segregation and the making of the underclass*. Cambridge, MA: Harvard University Press.

Massey, Douglas S., and Mitchell L. Eggers. 1990. The ecology of inequality: Minorities and the concentration of poverty. *American Journal of Sociology*, 95:1153–88.

Mathews, Jay. 2003. Colleges' admissions policies to be studied. *Washington Post* (September 7):A10.

Matsueda, Ross L. 1988. The current state of differential association theory. *Crime and Delinquency*, 34:277–306.

Matsueda, Ross L., and Karen Heimer. 1987. Race, family structure, and delinquency: A test of differential association and social control theories. *American Sociological Review*, 52:826–40.

Maxwell, Sheila Royo, and Christopher D. Maxwell. 2000. Examining the "criminal careers" of prostitutes within the nexus of drug use, drug selling, and other illicit activities. *Criminology*, 38(3):787–809.

Maynard, Douglas W., and Steven E. Clayman. 1991. The diversity of ethnomethodology. *Annual Review of Sociology*, 17:385–418.

Mazur, Allan. 1985. A biosocial model of status in face-to-face primate groups: Social groups. *Social Forces*, 64:377–402.

McAdam, Doug, and Ronnelle Paulsen. 1993. Specifying the relationship between social ties and activism. *American Journal of Sociology*, 99:640–67.

McCarthy, Bill. 2002. The new economics of sociological criminology. *Annual Review of Sociology*, 28:417–42.

McCauley, Clark. 1989. The nature of social influence in groupthink: Compliance and internalization. *Journal of Personality and Social Psychology*, 57:250–60.

MCCD. 2003. Housing costs climb in Maryland. *Maryland Center for Community Development*. Available at: www.mccd.org.

McConahay, John B. 1986. Modern racism, ambivalence, and the modern racism scale. In John F. Dovidio and Samuel Gaertner, eds., *Prejudice, discrimination, and racism*. Orlando, FL: Academic Press.

McFalls, Joseph A., Jr. 2003. *Population: A lively introduction*. Washington, DC: Population Reference Bureau.

McGee, Reece. 1975. *Points of departure*. Hinsdale, IL: Dryden Press.

McGeehan, Patrick. 2003. Executive pay: A special report; again, money follows the pinstripes. *New York Times* (April 6):C1.

McGrane, Bernard. 1993. Zen sociology. The un-TV experiment. *Teaching Sociology*, 21:85–89.

McGuire, Meredith B. 1981. *Religion: The social context*. Belmont, CA: Wadsworth.

McKinnon, Jessie. 2003. *The black population in the United States: March 2002*. Current Population Reports P20-541. Washington, DC: U.S. Census Bureau.

McLanahan, Sara, and **Julia Adams.** 1987. Parenthood and psychological well-being. *Annual Review of Sociology,* 13:237–57.

McLaughlin, Steven D., Barbara D. Melber, John O. G. Billy, Denise M. Zimmerle, Linda D. Winges, and **Terry R. Johnson.** 1988. *The changing lives of American women.* Chapel Hill: University of North Carolina Press.

McLaurin, Melton. 1992. Songs of the South: The changing image of the South in country music. In Melton McLaurin and Richard A. Peterson, eds., *You wrote my life: Lyrical themes in country music.* Philadelphia: Gordon and Breach.

McManus, Patricia A., and **Thomas A. DiPrete.** 2001. Losers and winners: The financial consequences of separation and divorce for men. *American Sociological Review,* 66:246–68.

McMichael, A. J., C. D. Butler, and **Carl Folke.** 2003. New visions for addressing sustainability. *Science,* 302:1919–1920.

McMillen, Matt. 2003. Knowing, not doing: Study measures gap between medical knowledge, practice. *Washington Post* (September 30):F1.

McPhail, Clark. 1989. Blumer's theory of collective behavior: The development of a non-symbolic interaction explanation. *Sociological Quarterly,* 30:401–23.

Mead, George Herbert. 1934/1962. *Mind, self, and other.* Chicago: University of Chicago Press.

Mead, Lawrence M. 1992. *The new politics of poverty: The nonworking poor in America.* New York: Basic Books.

Medlin, Richard G. 2000. Home schooling and the question of socialization. *Peabody Journal of Education,* 75:107–24.

Mehan, Hugh. 1992. Understanding inequality in schools: The contribution of interpretive studies. *Sociology of Education,* 65:1–20.

Mehrabian, Albert. 1968. Communication without words. *Psychology Today,* 2 (September):53–55.

Meier, Ann M. 2003. Adolescents' transition to first intercourse, religiosity, and attitudes about sex. *Social Forces,* 81(3):1031–52.

Melloan, George. 1993. Why America tops Europe in job creation. *Wall Street Journal* (December 13): A15.

Menaghan, Elizabeth G. 1991. Work experiences and family interaction processes: The long reach of the job? *Annual Review of Sociology,* 17:419–44.

Merton, Robert. 1968. *Social theory and social structure.* Rev. ed. New York: Free Press.

Merton, Robert K. 1995. The Thomas Theorem and the Matthew Effect. *Social Forces,* 74:379–422.

Messner, Steven F., and **Marvin D. Krohn.** 1990. Class, compliance structures, and delinquency: Assessing integrated structural-Marxist theory. *American Journal of Sociology,* 96:300–28.

Messner, Steven F., and **Richard Rosenfeld.** 1997a. *Crime and the American dream.* 2nd ed. Belmont, CA: Wadsworth.

Messner, Steven F., and **Richard Rosenfeld.** 1997b. Political restraint of the market and levels of criminal homicide: A cross-national application of institutional-anomie theory. *Social Forces,* 75:1393–1416.

Michael, Robert T., Victor R. Fuchs, and **Sharon R. Scott.** 1980. Changes in the propensity to live alone: 1950–1976. *Demography,* 17:39–56.

Michael, Robert T., John H. Gagnon, Edward O. Laumann, and **Gina Kolata.** 1994. *Sex in America.* Boston: Little, Brown.

Michaels, James W., and **Terance D. Miethe.** 1989. Applying theories of deviance to academic cheating. *Social Science Quarterly,* 70:870–85.

Michels, Robert. 1911/1966. *Political parties.* New York: Free Press.

Mickelson, Roslyn Arlin. 1990. The attitude-achievement paradox among black adolescents. *Sociology of Education,* 63:44–61.

Middleton, Russell. 1962. A deviant case: Brother-sister and father-daughter marriage in ancient Egypt. *American Sociological Review,* 27:603–11.

Milgram, Stanley. 1963. Behavioral study of obedience. *Journal of Abnormal and Social Psychology,* 67(4):371–78.

Milgram, Stanley. 1964. Group pressure and action against a person. *Journal of Abnormal and Social Psychology,* 69(2):137–143.

Milgram, Stanley. 1977. *The individual in a social world.* Reading, MA: Addison-Wesley.

Milgram, Stanley, and **Hans Toch.** 1969. Collective behavior: Crowds and social movements. In G. Lindzey and E. Aronson, eds., *The handbook of social psychology.* 2nd ed., Vol. 2. Reading, MA: Addison Wesley.

Miller, Eleanor M. and **Carrie Yang Costello.** 2001. Comment: The limits of biological determinism. *American Sociological Review,* 66:592–98.

Miller, Judith. 1992. The Islamic wave. *New York Times Magazine* (May 31):23–42.

Mills, C. Wright. 1956. *The power elite.* New York: Oxford University Press.

Mills, C. Wright. 1959. *The sociological imagination.* New York: Oxford University Press.

Milner, Murray, Jr. 1987. Theories of inequality: An overview and a strategy for synthesis. *Social Forces,* 65:1053–89.

Mincy, Ronald B. 2006. *Black males left behind.* Washington, DC: Urban Institute Press.

Miniño, A. M., M. Heron, and **B. L. Smith.** 2006. Deaths: Preliminary data for 2004. Health E-Stats. Released by National Center for Health Statistics, April 19.

Mintz, Beth, and **Michael Schwartz.** 1985. *The power of American business.* Chicago: University of Chicago Press.

Mirowsky, John, and **Catherine E. Ross.** 2003. *Education, social status, and health.* New York: Aldine de Gruyter.

Mischel, Walter. 1970. Sex-typing and socialization. In P. H. Mussen, ed., *Carmichael's manual of child psychology,* 3rd ed., Vol. 2. New York: John Wiley.

Moaddel, Mansoor. 1992. Ideology as episodic discourse: The case of the Iranian revolution. *American Sociological Review,* 57:353–79.

Moaddel, Mansoor. 1994. Political conflict in the world economy: A cross-national analysis of modernization and world-system theories. *American Sociological Review,* 59:276–303.

Moen, Phyllis, and **Yan Yu.** 2000. Effective work/life strategies: Working couples, work conditions, gender, and life quality. *Social Problems,* 47(3):291–326.

Moffatt, Michael. 1989. *Coming of age in New Jersey.* New Brunswick: Rutgers University Press.

Moffitt, Terrie. 2005. The new look of behavioral genetics in developmental psychopathology: Gene-environment interplay in antisocial behaviors. *Psychological Bulletin,* 131:533–54.

Moffitt, Terrie E., Robert F. Krueger, Avshalom Caspi, and **Jeff Fagan.** 2000. Partner abuse and general crime: How are they the same? How are they different? *Criminology,* 38(1):199–232.

Moller, Stephanie, Evelyne Huber, John D. Stephens, David Bradley, and **Francois Nielsen.** 2003. Determinants of relative poverty in advanced capitalist democracies. *American Sociological Review,* 68:22–51.

Molm, Linda D. 1991 Affect and social exchange: Satisfaction in power-dependence relations. *American Sociological Review,* 56:475–93.

Molnar, Stephen. 1997. *Human variation.* Upper Saddle River, NJ: Prentice Hall.

Money, John, and **P. Tucker.** 1975. *Sexual signatures: On being a man or a woman.* Boston: Little, Brown.

Moody, James, and **Douglas R. White.** 2003. Structural cohesion and embeddedness: A hierarchical concept of social groups. *American Sociological Review,* 68:103–27.

Moore, David W. 1997. Today's husband more involved in household duties than post-WWII generation. *Gallup Poll* (December 31).

Morin, Richard. 1998. The new great divide: More and more, where you live depends on what you're worth. *Washington Post Magazine* (January 18): 14.

Morin, Richard, and **Alan Cooperman.** 2003. Majority against blessing gay unions. *Washington Post* (August 14):A1.

Morrill, Calvin, Mayer N. Zald, and **Hayagreeva Rao.** 2003. Covert political conflict in organizations: Challenges from below. *Annual Review of Sociology,* 29:391–415.

Morris, Aldon D. 1993. Birmingham confrontation reconsidered: An analysis of the dynamics and tactics of mobilization. *American Sociology Review,* 58:621–36.

Morrison, Donna Ruane, and **Amy Ritualo.** 2000. Routes to children's economic recovery after divorce: Are cohabitation and remarriage equivalent? *American Sociological Review,* 65:560–580.

Mortimer, Jeylan T., and **Roberta G. Simmons.** 1978. Adult socialization. *Annual Review of Sociology,* 4:421–54.

Moskowitz, Breyne Arlene. 1978. The acquisition of language. *Scientific American,* 239 (November):92–108.

Mouzelis, Nicos. 1992. The interaction order and the micro-macro distinction. *Sociological Theory,* 10:122–28.

Moynihan, Daniel Patrick. 1985. *Family and nation.* Cambridge, MA: Harvard University Press.

Moynihan, Ray, and **Alan Cassels.** 2005. *Selling sickness: How the world's biggest pharmaceutical companies are turning us all into patients.* Nation Books.

Mura, David. 1992. Bashed in the U.S.A. *New York Times* (April 2): A15.

Murdock, George P. 1934. *Our primitive contemporaries.* New York: Macmillan.

Murdock, George P. 1935. Comparative data on the division of labor by sex. *Social Forces,* 15:551–53.

Murdock, George Peter. 1949. *Social structure.* New York: Macmillan.

Murdock, George P. 1950. Feasibility and implementation of comparative community research. *American Sociological Review,* 15:713–20.

Murdock, George Peter. 1967. *Ethnographic atlas.* Pittsburgh: University of Pittsburgh Press.

Murphy, Caryle. 1997. U.S. Catholic bishops urge acceptance of gay orientation. *Washington Post* (October 1):A1.

Murray, Charles. 1994. Does welfare bring more babies? *American Enterprise,* 5 (January–February):52–59.

Murray, Sandra L., Dale W. Griffin, Paul Rose, and **Gina M. Bellavia.** 2003. Calibrating the sociometer: The relational contingencies of self-esteem. *Journal of Personality and Social Psychology,* 85(1):63–84.

Murstein, Bernard I. 1972. Physical attractiveness and marital choice. *Journal of Personality and Social Psychology,* 22:8–12.

Murstein, Bernard I. 1976. *Who will marry whom?* New York: Springer.

Musick, Kelly, and **Larry Bumpass.** 1999. How do prior experiences in the family affect transitions to adulthood? In Alan Booth, Ann C. Crouter, and Michael J. Shanahan, eds. *Transitions to adulthood in a changing economy: No work, no family, no future?* Westport, CT: Praeger.

Musto, David F. 1987. *The American disease: Origins of narcotic control.* New York: Oxford University Press.

Myers, Ransom A., and **Boris Worm.** 2005. Extinction, survival or recovery of large predatory fishes. *Philosophical Transactions of the Royal Society B-Biological Sciences,* 360(1453):13–20.

Myrdal, Gunnar. 1944. *An American dilemma.* New York: Harper.

N

Nagel, Joane. 1994. *American Indian ethnic renewal: Red power and the transformation of identity and culture.* New York: Oxford University Press.

Naimi, Timothy S., Robert D. Brewer, Ali Mokdad, Clark Denny, Mary K. Serdula, and **James S. Marks.** 2003. Binge drinking among US adults. *Journal of the American Medical Association,* 289(1):70–75.

Nanda, Serena, and **Richard L. Warms.** 2002. *Cultural anthropology.* 7th ed. Wadsworth: Thomson Learning.

Naqvi, Muneeza. 2005. Short of brides, Indians turn to brokers: In rural Punjab province, preference for sons has led to population imbalance. *Washington Post* (December 5):A15.

Nash, J. Madeleine. 1997. Fertile minds: From birth a baby's brain cells proliferate wildly, making connections that may shape a lifetime of experience. The first three years are critical. *Time* (February 3): 49–56.

Nash, Jonathan G., and **Roger-Mark De Souza.** 2002. *Making the link: Population, health, environment.* Washington, DC: Population Reference Bureau.

National Center for Health Statistics. 1996. *Health, United States, 1995.* Hyattsville, MD: Public Health Service.

National Center for Health Statistics. 2003. *Health, United States, 2003.* Hyattsville, MD: National Center for Health Statistics.

National Center for Health Statistics. 2005. *Health, United States, 2005, with chartbook on trends in the health of Americans.* Hyattsville, Maryland.

Nazario, Sonia L. 1992. Medical science seeks a cure for doctors suffering from boorish bedside manner. *Wall Street Journal* (March 17):B1.

Needleman, Herbert L., and **David Bellinger,** eds. 1994. *Prenatal exposure to toxicants: Developmental consequences.* Baltimore, MD: Johns Hopkins University Press.

Neil, Cecily C., and **William E. Snizek.** 1988. Gender as a moderator of job satisfaction: A multivariate assessment. *Work and Occupations,* 15:201–19.

Nelson, Mariah Burton. 1994. *The stronger women get, the more men love football: Sexism and the American culture of sports.* New York: Harcourt Brace.

Nelson, Sandi, Rebecca L. Clark, and **Gregory Acs.** 2001. *Beyond the two-parent family: How teenagers fare in cohabiting couple and blended families.* Washington, DC: The Urban Institute. New Federalism: National Survey of America's Families, No. B-31.

Nelson, Toben F., and **Henry Wechsler.** 2001. Alcohol and college athletes. *Medicine and Science in Sports and Exercise,* 33:43–47.

Nestler, Eric J. 2001. Total recall—the memory of addiction. *Science,* 292:2266–67.

Neugarten, Bernice L., and **Dail A. Neugarten.** 1987a. *Forum,* 62:25–27.

Neugarten, Bernice L., and **Dail A. Neugarten.** 1987b. The changing meanings of age. *Psychology Today,* 21 (May):29–33.

Neuhouser, Kevin. 1992. Democratic stability in Venezuela: Elite consensus or class compromise? *American Sociological Review,* 57: 117–35.

Newcomb, Theodore M. 1950. *Social Psychology.* New York: Holt, Rinehart and Winston.

Newman, Katherine S. 2003. *A different shade of gray: Midlife and beyond in the inner city.* New York: The New Press.

Newport, Frank. 1997. Americans' relationship with their children: Much remains the same. *Gallup Poll* press release, March 15, 1997.

Newport, Frank, and **Lydia Saad.** 1997. Religious faith is widespread but many skip church. *Gallup Poll* press release, March 29, 1997.

Newton, Michael. 2002. *Savage girls and wild boys: A history of feral children.* New York: St. Martin's Press (Thomas Dunne Books).

NICHD Early Child Care Research Network. 2003. Does amount of time spent in child care predict socioemotional adjustment during the transition to kindergarten? *Child Development,* 74(4):976–1005.

Nielsen, Joyce McCarl, Glenda Walden, and **Charlotte A. Kunkel.** 2000. Gendered heteronormativity: Empirical illustrations in everyday life. *The Sociological Quarterly,* 41(2):283–96.

NIEHS. 2005. Lead and your health. National Institute of Environmental Health Sciences. www.niehs.nih.gov.

Nisbett, Richard E. 1998. Race, genetics, and IQ. In Christopher Jencks and Meredith Phillips, eds., *The black-white test score gap.* Washington, DC: Brookings Institution Press.

Niven, David. 1999. Partisan bias in the media? A new test. *Social Science Quarterly,* 80(4):847–57.

Noble, Kenneth B. 1989. Low commodity prices vex life in Ivory Coast. *New York Times* (November 19):6.

Noel, Donald L. 1968. A theory of the origin of ethnic stratification. *Social Problems,* 16:157–62.

Noel, Donald M. 1972. *The origins of American slavery and racism.* Columbus, OH: Charles E. Merrill.

Nolan, Martin F. 1997. Tiger's racial multiplicity. *Boston Globe* (April 26):A11.

Nolan, Patrick, and **Gerhard E. Lenski.** 2005. *Human societies: An introduction to macro sociology.* Boulder, CO: Paradigm Publishers.

Noonan, Mary C., Mary E. Corcoran, and **Paul N. Courant.** 2005. Pay differences among the highly trained: Cohort differences in the sex gap in lawyers earnings. *Social Forces,* 84:853–72.

Normile, Dennis. 2002. Japanese societies tackle gender issues. *Science,* 298:36.

Normile, Dennis, Gretchen Vogel, and **Jennifer Couzin.** 2006. South Korean team's remaining human stem cell claim demolished. *Science,* 311:156–57.

Nottelmann, Editha D. 1987. Competence and self-esteem during transition from childhood to adolescence. *Development Psychology,* 23:441–50.

Nuland, Sherwin B. 1994. *Reflections on life's final chapter.* New York: Knopf.

Nussbaum, Emily. 2004. My so-called blog. *The New York Times Magazine* (January 11):32–37.

O

O'Connor, Alice. 2000. Poverty research and policy for the post-welfare era. *Annual Review of Sociology,* 26:547–62.

O'Connor, James. 1973. *The fiscal crisis of the state.* New York: St. Martin's Press.

O'Dell, Jerry W. 1968. Group size and emotional interaction. *Journal of Personality and Social Psychology,* 8:75–78.

Oeppen, Jim, and **James W. Vaupel.** 2002. Broken limits to life expectancy. *Science,* 296:1029–1031.

Ogburn, William F. 1922. *Social change.* New York: Hoebsch.

Ogunwole, Stella U. 2002. *The American Indian and Alaska Native population: 2000.* U.S. Census Bureau C2KBR/01–15. Washington, DC: U.S. Government Printing Office.

Ogunwole, Stella. 2006. *We the people: American Indians and Alaska Natives in the United States.* U.S. Census Bureau, Census 2000 Special Reports, CENSR-28. Washington DC: U.S. Government Printing Office. (available online at: http://www.census.gov/prod/2006pubs/censr-28.pdf).

O'Hare, William P., and **Judy C. Felt.** 1991. Asian Americans: America's fastest growing minority group. *Population Trends and Public Policy.* Population Reference Bureau, no. 19.

O'Harrow, Robert, Jr. 2003. Identity crisis. *Washington Post Magazine* (August 10):14–18, 23–29.

Oliver, Pamela E., and **Gerald Marwell.** 1988. The paradox of group size in collective action: A theory of the critical mass. II. *American Sociological Review,* 53:1–8.

Olsen, Marvin E. 1970. *Power in societies.* New York: Macmillan.

Olson, Daniel V. A., and **Jackson W. Carroll.** 1992. Religiously based politics: Religious elites and the public. *Social Forces,* 70:765–86.

Olson, David H., and **John DeFrain.** 1997. *Marriage and the family: Diversity and strengths.* 2nd ed. Mountain View, CA: Mayfield Publishing.

Olson, David J., and **Philip Meyer.** 1975. *To keep the republic.* New York: McGraw-Hill.

Olzak, Susan. 1990. The political context of competition: Lynching and urban racial violence, 1882–1914. *Social Forces,* 69:395–421.

Olzak, Susan. 1992. *The dynamics of ethnic competition and conflict.* Stanford, CA: Stanford University Press.

Omi, Michael, and **Howard Winant.** 1994. *Racial formation in the United States from the 1960s to the 1990s* (2nd ed.). New York: Routledge.

Opp, Karl-Dieter, and **Christiane Gern.** 1993. Dissident groups, personal networks, and spontaneous cooperation: The East German revolution of 1989. *American Sociological Review,* 58:659–80.

Orcutt, James D. 1987. Differential association and marijuana use: A closer look at Sutherland (with a little help from Becker). *Criminology,* 25:341–58.

Oreskes, Michael. 1990. America's politics loses way as its vision changes world. *New York Times* (March 18):1, 16.

Orfield, Gary. 2004. *Dropouts in America: Confronting the graduation rate crisis.* Cambridge, MA: Harvard Education Press.

Ortner, Sherry. 1996. *Making gender: The politics and erotics of culture.* Boston: Beacon Press.

Osgood, D. Wayne, Janet K. Wilson, Patrick M. O'Malley, Jerald G. Bachman, and **Lloyd D. Johnston.** 1996. Routine activities and individual deviant behavior. *American Sociological Review,* 61:635–55.

P

Packer, George. 2005. *The Assassins' Gate: America in Iraq.* New York: Farrar, Straus, and Giroux.

Page, Clarence. 1997. Grappling with the "one-drop" rule. *Chicago Tribune* (April 27):C19.

Page, Jake. 2003. *In the hands of the Great Spirit: The 20,000 year history of American Indians.* New York: Free Press.

Pager, Devah. 2003. The mark of a criminal record. *American Journal of Sociology,* 108(5):937–75.

Paisano, Edna L. 2003. *The American Indian, Eskimo, and Aleut population.* Available at: www.census.gov/population/www/pop-profile/amerind.html.

Palen, J. John. 1997. *The urban world.* New York: McGraw-Hill.

Paley, Amit R. 2006. A positive prison experience: Inmate offers herself as proof of Md. program's effectiveness. *Washington Post* (March 8):B1.

Palmer, Louann Bierlein, and **Rebecca Gau.** 2003. *Charter school authorizing: Are states making the grade?* Thomas B. Fordham Institute.

Pampel, Fred. 2000. *Sociological lives and ideas: An introduction to the classical theorists.* New York: Worth.

Pampel, Fred C., and **H. Elizabeth Peters.** 1995. The Easterlin effect. *Annual Review of Sociology,* 21:163–94.

Parcel, Toby L., and **Elizabeth G. Menaghan.** 1994. Early parental work, family social capital, and early childhood outcomes. *American Journal of Sociology,* 99:972–1009.

Park, Robert E., Ernest W. Burgess, and **Roderick D. McKenzie.** 1925. *The city.* Chicago: University of Chicago Press.

Parker, Stephen. 1990. *Informal marriage, cohabitation and the law, 1750–1989.* New York: St. Martin's Press.

Parkinson, C. Northcote. 1962. *Parkinson's law.* Boston: Houghton Mifflin.

Parsons, Talcott. 1940. An analytical approach to the theory of social stratification. *American Journal of Sociology,* 45:841–62.

Parsons, Talcott. 1949. *The structure of social action.* 2nd ed. New York: McGraw-Hill.

Parsons, Talcott. 1951. *The social system.* New York: Free Press.

Parsons, Talcott. 1953. A revised analytical approach to the theory of social stratification. In Reinhard Bendix and Seymour M. Lipset, eds., *Class status and power: A reader in social stratification.* Glencoe, IL: Free Press.

Parsons, Talcott. 1966. *Societies: Evolutionary and comparative perspectives.* Englewood Cliffs, NJ: Prentice Hall.

Parsons, Talcott. 1977. On building social system theory: A personal history. In Talcott Parsons, ed., *Social systems and evolution of action theory.* New York: Free Press.

Parsons, Talcott, and **Robert F. Bales.** 1955. *Family socialization and interaction process.* New York: Free Press.

Passell, Peter. 1992. Twins study shows school is sound investment. *New York Times* (August 19): A14.

Pastore, Ann L., and **Kathleen Maguire,** eds. 2003. *Sourcebook of criminal justice statistics.* Available at: http://www.albany.edu/ sourcebook/[Access date].

Pastore, Ann L., and **Kathleen Maguire.** 2005. *Sourcebook of criminal justice statistics, 2003.* Washington, DC: Superintendent of Documents (available online at http://www.albany.edu/sourcebook/).

Paternoster, Raymond. 1989. Absolute and restrictive deterrence in a panel of youth: Explaining the onset, persistence/desistance, and frequency of delinquent offending. *Social Problems,* 36:289–309.

Patterson, Orlando. 1991. *Freedom.* Vol. 1: *Freedom in the making of western culture.* New York: Basic Books.

Paulus, P. B. 1998. Developing consensus about groupthink after all these years. *Organizational Behavior and Human Decision Processes,* 73(2–3):362–74.

Paxton, Pamela, and **Sheri Kunovich.** 2003. Women's political representation: The importance of ideology. *Social Forces,* 82(1):87–114.

Perrow, Charles. 1982. Disintegrating social sciences. *Phi Delta Kappan,* 63:684–88.

Perrow, Charles. 1986. *Complex organizations.* New York: Random House.

Perry, Bruce D., Ronnie A. Pollard, Toi L. Blakley, William L. Baker, et al. 1995. Childhood trauma, the neurobiology of adaptation, and "use-dependent" development of the brain: How "states" become "traits." *Infant Mental Health Journal,* 16:271–91.

Perry, Susan, and **Joseph H. Manson.** 2003. Traditions in monkeys. *Evolutionary Anthropology,* 12:71–81.

Petersen, Trond. 1992. Individual, collective, and systems rationality in work groups: Dilemmas and market-type solutions. *American Journal of Sociology,* 98:469–510.

Peterson, Paul E. 2003. Ticket to nowhere. *Education Next,* Spring:39–46.

Peterson, Richard A. 1979. Revitalizing the culture concept. *Annual Review of Sociology,* 5:137–66.

Peterson, Richard A. 1982. Five constraints on the production of culture: Law, technology, market, organizational structure and occupational careers. *Journal of Popular Culture,* 16:143–53.

Peterson, Richard A., and **N. Anand.** 2004. The production of

culture perspective. *Annual Review of Sociology,* 30:311–34.

Peterson, Ruth D. 1992. Rape and dimensions of gender socioeconomic inequality in U.S. metropolitan areas. *Journal of Research on Crime and Delinquency,* 29:162–77.

Peterson, Ruth D., and **Lauren J. Krivo.** 2005. Macrostructural analyses of race, ethnicity, and violent crime: Recent lessons and new directions for research. *Annual Review of Sociology,* 31:331–56.

Petterson, Stephen M. 1997. Are young black men really less willing to work? *American Sociological Review,* 62:605–13.

Pettigrew, Thomas F., and **Joanne Martin.** 1987. Shaping the organizational context for black American inclusion. *Journal of Social Issues,* 43:41–78.

Pettigrew, Thomas J. 1967. Social evaluation theory: Convergences and applications. *Nebraska Symposium on Motivation.*

The Pew Research Center for the People and the Press. 2001. Interdiction and incarceration still top remedies: 74% say drug war being lost. Washington, DC: The Pew Research Center for the People and the Press (March 21; available online at http://people-press.org/reports/ display.php3?ReportID=16).

The Pew Research Center for the People and the Press. 2005. Public more critical of press, but goodwill persists: Online newspaper readership countering print losses. Survey Report, June 26th. Washington, DC: The Pew Research Center for the People and the Press (available at: http://people-press.org/reports/ display.php3?ReportID=248).

Phelan, Jo C., Bruce G. Link, Ana Diez-Roux, Ichiro Kawachi, and **Bruce Levin.** 2004. "Fundamental causes" of social inequalities in mortality: A test of the theory. *Journal of Health and Social Behavior,* 45:265–85.

Piaget, Jean. 1926/1955. *The language and thought of the child.* New York: New American Library.

Pielke, Roger A. 2005. Land use and climate change. *Science,* 310:1625.

Pierre, Robert E., and **Kari Lydersen.** 2003. Illinois death row emptied: Citing "demon of error," Ryan commutes sentences. *Washington Post* (January 12):A1.

Piketty, Thomas, and **Emmanual Saez.** 2001. *Income inequality in the United States, 1913–1998.* National Bureau of Economic Research Working Paper No. 8467. Available at: http://papers.nber.org/papers/w8467.

Pill, Cynthia J. 1990. Stepfamilies: Redefining the family. *Family Relations,* 39:186–93.

Pimm, Stuart L. 2000. Against triage. *Science,* 289:2289.

Pinker, Steven. 2002. *The blank slate: The modern denial of human nature.* New York: Viking.

Pipher, Mary. 1994. *Reviving Ophelia: Saving the selves of adolescent girls.* New York: Ballantine Books.

Pipher, Mary. 1997. *The shelter of each other.* New York: Ballantine Books.

Plumb, J.H. 1972. *Children.* London: Penguin Books.

Pomer, Marshall I. 1986. Labor market structure, intragenerational mobility, and discrimination: Black male advancement out of low-paying occupations, 1962–1973. *American Sociological Review,* 51:650–59.

Pope, Whitney. 1976. *Durkheim's suicide: A classic analyzed.* Chicago: University of Chicago Press.

Popenoe, David. 1993. American family decline, 1960–1990: A review and appraisal. *Journal of Marriage and the Family,* 55:527–55.

Popper, Karl. 1963. *Conjectures and refutations: The growth of scientific knowledge.* London: Routledge & Kegan Paul.

Population Reference Bureau. 2002b. *Women of our world.* Washington, DC: Population Reference Bureau.

Population Reference Bureau. 2003. *Human population: Fundamentals of growth patterns of world urbanization.* Washington, DC: Population Reference Bureau.

Population Reference Bureau. 2005. 2005 World Population Data Sheet. Washington, DC: Population Reference Bureau.

Portes, Alejandro. 1987. The social origins of the Cuban enclave economy in Miami. *Sociological Perspectives,* 30:340–72.

Portes, Alejandro, and **Robert L. Bach.** 1985. *Latin journey: Cuban and Mexican immigrants in the United States.* Berkeley: University of California Press.

Portes, Alejandro, and **Leif Jensen.** 1989. The enclave and the entrants: Patterns of ethnic enterprise in Miami before and after Mariel. *American Sociological Review,* 54:929–49.

Portes, Alejandro, and **Kenneth L. Wilson.** 1976. Black-white differences in educational attainment. *American Sociological Review,* 41:414–31.

Poulton, R., A. Caspi, B. Milne, W. Thomson, A. Taylor, M. Sears, T. Moffitt. 2002. Association between children's experience of socioeconomic disadvantage and adult health: a life-course study. *The Lancet,* 360:1640–1645.

Pounds, J. Alan, Martin R. Bustamante, Luis A. Coloma, Jamie A. Consuegra, Michael P. L. Fogden, Pru N. Foster, Enrique La Marca, Karen L. Masters, Andres Merino-Viteri, Robert Puschendorf, Santiago R. Ron, G. Arturo Sanchez-Azofeifa, Christopher J. Still, and **Bruce E. Young.** 2006. Widespread amphibian extinctions from epidemic disease driven by global warming. *Nature,* 439:161–67.

Poundstone, William. 1992. *Prisoner's dilemma.* Garden City, NY: Anchor Books.

Pressler, Margaret. 2003. Cost and robbers: Shoplifting and employee thievery add dollars to price tags. *Washington Post* (February 16):H5.

Princeton Religion Research Center. 1994. Religion index hits all-time low mark. *PRRC Emerging Trends,* 16 (March): 1–2.

Princiotta, Daniel, Stacey Bielick, and **Christopher Chapman.** 2006. *Homeschooling in the United States: 2003 Statistical analysis report.* Washington, DC: National Center for Education Statistics.

Proctor, Bernadette D., and **Joseph Dalaker.** 2003. *Poverty in the United States: 2002.* U.S. Census Bureau, Current Population Reports, P60-219. Washington, DC: U.S. Government Printing Office.

Public Agenda. 2000. Necessary compromises: How parents, employers and children's advocates view child care today. Available at: www.publicagenda.org/specials/childcare/childcare.htm.

Public Agenda. 2001. *Child care issue guide.* www.publicagenda.com.

Public Agenda. 2004. The environment: people's chief concerns. Available at: www. publicagenda.org/issues/pcc.cfm? issue_type=environment.

Puckett, Jim, Leslie Byster, Sarah Westervelt, Richard Gutierrez, Sheila Davis, Asma Hussain, and **Madhumitta Dutta.** 2002. *Exporting harm: The high-tech trashing of Asia.* The Basel Action Network and Silicon Valley Toxics Coalition (www.svtc.org).

Putka, Gary. 1991. Education reformers have new respect for Catholic schools. *Wall Street Journal* (March 28):A1, A8.

Q

Quadagno, Jill S. 1982. *Aging in early industrial society.* New York: Academic Press.

Quadagno, Jill S. 1984. Welfare capitalism and the Social Security Act of 1935. *American Sociological Review,* 49:632–47.

Quadagno, Jill. 2005. *One nation uninsured: Why the U.S. has no national health insurance.* Oxford: Oxford University Press.

Quillian, Lincoln. 1995. Prejudice as a response to perceived group threat: Population composition and anti-immigrant and racial prejudice in Europe. *American Sociological Review,* 60:586–611.

Quillian, Lincoln. 1996. Group threat and regional change in attitudes toward African Americans. *American Journal of Sociology,* 102:816–60.

Quinn, Thomas C., and **Julie Overbaugh.** 2005. HIV/AIDS in women: An expanding epidemic. *Science,* 308:1582–1583.

Quinney, Richard. 1974. *Criminal justice in America.* Boston: Little, Brown.

Quinney, Richard. 1980. *Class, state, and crime.* New York: Longman.

R

Radelet, Michael L., and **Marian J. Borg.** 2000. The changing nature of death penalty debates. *Annual Review of Sociology,* 26:43–61.

Rahav, Giora. 1976. Family relations and delinquency in Israel. *Criminology,* 14:259–70.

Ramirez, Roberto R., and **G. Patricia de la Cruz.** 2002. *The Hispanic population in the United States: March 2002.* Current Population Reports, P20-545. Washington, DC: U.S. Census Bureau.

Ramirez, Roberto R. 2004. *We the people: Hispanics in the United States.* U.S. Census Bureau, Census 2000 Special Reports, CENSR-18. Washington, DC: U.S. Government Printing Office (available online at: http://www.census.gov/prod/ 2004pubs/censr-18.pdf).

Rank, M. R., and **T. A. Hirschl.** 2001. Rags or riches? Estimating the probabilities of poverty and affluence across the adult American life span. *Social Science Quarterly,* 82(4):651–69.

Rank, M. R., and **T. A. Hirschl.** 2002. Welfare use as a life course event: Toward a new understanding of the U.S. safety net. *Social Work,* 47(3):237–48.

Rank, Mark R. 2003. As American as apple pie: Poverty and welfare. *Contexts* 2:41–49.

Rank, Mark Robert. 2004. *One nation, underprivileged: Why American poverty affects us all.* New York: Oxford University Press.

Raphael, Ray. 1988. *The men from the boys: Rites of passage in male America.* Lincoln: University of Nebraska Press.

Raspberry, William. 2002. Why black kids lag. *Washington Post* (December 9): A23.

Reckless, Walter C. 1961. A new theory of delinquency and crime. *Federal Probation,* 25:42–46.

Reckless, Walter C. 1967. *The crime problem.* 4th ed. New York: Appleton-Century-Crofts.

Rector, Robert. 1990. Poverty in U.S. is exaggerated by census. *Wall Street Journal* (September 25):A18.

Reed, Susan E. 2005. Lawsuits won't break that glass ceiling. *Washington Post* (August 21):B3.

Reeves, Terrance, and **Claudette Bennett.** 2003. *The Asian and Pacific Islander population in the United States: March 2002.* Current Population Reports, P20-540. Washington, DC: U.S. Census Bureau.

Reeves, Terrance J., and **Claudette E. Bennett.** 2004. *We the people: American Indians and Alaska Natives in the United States.* U.S. Census Bureau, Census 2000 Special Reports, CENSR-17. Washington DC: U.S. Government Printing Office (available online at: http://www.census.gov/prod/ 2004pubs/censr-17.pdf).

Regoli, Robert M., and **John D. Hewitt.** 2000. *Delinquency in society.* New York: McGraw-Hill.

Reicher, Stephen, and **Alex Haslam.** 2002. Ethics and "The Experiment." *The Psychologist,* 15(6):282.

Reicher, Stephen D., and **S. Alexander Haslam.** 2003a. Social psychology, science, and surveillance: Understanding The Experiment. *Social Psychology Review,* 5:7–17.

Reicher, Stephen D., and **S. Alexander Haslam.** 2003b. A new look at the psychology of tyranny: The BBC prison study. Unpublished paper.

Rennison, Callie. 2002a. Criminal victimization 2001: Changes 2000-01 with trends 1993–2001. Washington, DC: U.S. Department of Justice. NCJ-194610.

Reno, Raymond R., Robert B. Cialdini, and **Carl A. Kallgren.** 1993. The transsituational influence of social norms. *Journal of Personality and Social Psychology,* 64:104–12.

Reynolds, J. R. and **C. E. Ross.** 1998. Social stratification and health: Education's benefit beyond economic status and social origins. *Social Problems,* 45(2): 221–47.

Rheingold, Harriet L., Dale F. Hay, and **Meredith J. West.** 1976. Sharing in the second year of life. *Child Development,* 47:1148–58.

Richardson, Laurel. 1987. *The dynamics of sex and gender: A sociological perspective.* New York: Harper and Row.

Richardson, Laurel, Verta Taylor, and **Nancy Whittier.** 1997. *Feminist frontiers IV.* New York: McGraw-Hill.

Richburg, Keith. 1997. North Korea near economic collapse: Spreading famine and hardship reflect system no longer functioning. *Washington Post* (October 19):A1.

Richburg, Keith. 2003. Gay marriage becomes routine for Dutch. *Washington Post* (September 23):A20.

Richmond, Julius B., and **Rashi Fein.** 2003. Health insurance in the USA. *Science,* 301:1813.

Ridgeway, C. L., and **L. Smith-Lovin.** 1999. The gender system and interaction. *Annual Review of Sociology,* 25:191–216.

Riesman, David. 1953. *The lonely crowd.* Garden City, NY: Doubleday.

Risman, Barbara J. 2001. Comment: Calling the bluff of value-free science. *American Sociological Review,* 66:605–11.

Ritch, Ellie. 2002. Prison experiment repeated for ratings. *The Stanford Daily* (February 5). Available at www.stanforddaily.com.

Ritzer, George. 1995. *Expressing America: A critique of the* *increasingly global credit card society.* Thousand Oaks, CA: Sage.

Ritzer, George. 1997. *Postmodern social theory.* New York: McGraw-Hill.

Ritzer, George. 2000. *Sociological theory,* 5th ed. New York: McGraw-Hill.

Ritzer, George, and **Douglas J. Goodman.** 2004. *Sociological theory.* 6th ed. New York: McGraw-Hill.

Ritzer, George. 2007. *Contemporary sociological theory and its classical roots.* New York: McGraw-Hill.

Roberts, Brent W., Kate E. Walton, and **Wolfgang Viechtbauer.** 2006. Patterns of mean-level change in personality traits across the life course: A meta-analysis of longitudinal studies. *Psychological Bulletin,* 132:1–25.

Roberts, Felicia. 2000. The interactional construction of asymmetry: The medical agenda as a resource for delaying response to patient questions. *Sociological Quarterly,* 41(1):151–70.

Roethlisberger, Fritz J., and **William J. Dickson.** 1939. *Management and the worker.* Cambridge, MA: Harvard University Press.

Rohan, Meg J. 2000. A rose by any name: The values construct. *Personality and Social Psychology Review,* 4:255–77.

Roig-Franzia, Manuel. 2003. In Miami, a bus stop for broken marriages. *Washington Post* (May 4):D1.

Rokeach, Milton, and **Sandra J. Ball-Rokeach.** 1989. Stability and change in American value priorities, 1968–1981. *American Psychologist,* 44:775–84.

Rooney, James F. 1980. Organizational success through program failure: Skid Row rescue missions. *Social Forces,* 58:904–24.

Roper Starch Worldwide. 2000. Roper Reports Worldwide Global Consumers 2000 Study.

Rosecrance, Richard. 1990. Too many bosses, too few workers. *New York Times* (July 15):F11.

Rosen, George. 1963. The hospital: Historical sociology of a community institution. In E. Freidson, ed., *The hospital in modern society.* New York: Free Press.

Rosenberg, Morris. 1973. Which significant others? *American Behavioral Scientist,* 16:829–60.

Rosenberg, Morris. 1981. The self-concept: Social product and social force. In Morris Rosenberg and Ralph H. Turner, eds., *Social psychology: Sociological perspectives.* New York: Basic Books.

Rosenberg, Morris. 1986. Self-concept from middle childhood through adolescence. In J. Suls and A. Greenwald, eds., *Psychological perspectives on the self,* Vol. 3. Hillsdale, NJ: Erlbaum.

Rosenberg, Morris. 1989. *Society and the adolescent self-image.* Rev. ed. Middletown, CT: Wesleyan University Press.

Rosenberg, Noah A., Jonathan K. Prichard, James L. Weber, Howard M. Cann, Kenneth K. Kidd, Lev A. Zhivotovsky, and **Marcus W. Feldman.** 2002. Genetic structure of human populations. *Science,* 298:2381–85.

Ross, Andrew. 2003. *No-Collar: The humane workplace and its hidden costs.* New York: Basic Books.

Ross, Catherine E., John Mirowsky, and **Joan Huber.** 1983. Dividing work, sharing work, and in-between: Marriage patterns and depression. *American Sociological Review,* 48:809–23.

Rossi, Alice S. 1973. *The feminist papers.* New York: Columbia University Press.

Rossi, Alice S., and **Peter H. Rossi.** 1990. *Of human bonding: Parent child relations across the life course.* New York: Aldine de Gruyter.

Rothbart, Myron, and **Oliver P. John.** 1993. Intergroup relations and stereotype change: A social cognitive analysis and some longitudinal findings. In Paul M. Sniderman, Philip E. Tetlock, and Edward G. Carmines, eds., *Prejudice, politics, and the American dilemma.* Stanford, CA: Stanford University Press.

Rothchild, John. 1993. Sacred cows. *Worth* (December–January):55–58.

Rothkopf, David J. 2003. When the buzz bites back. *Washington Post* (May 11):B1.

Rothschild, Joyce, and **Raymond Russell.** 1986. Alternatives to bureaucracy: Democratic participation in the economy. *Annual Review of Sociology,* 12:307–28.

Roy, Oliver. 1998. *The failure of political Islam.* Cambridge, MA: Harvard University Press.

Rubenstein, Carin. 1982. Real men don't earn less than their wives. *Psychology Today,* 16 (November):36–41.

Ruef, Martin. 2004. The demise of an organizational form: Emancipation and plantation agriculture in the American South, 1960–1880. *American Journal of Sociology,* 109: 1365–1410.

Ruggles, Patricia. 1992. Measuring poverty. University of Wisconsin, Institute for Research on Poverty, *Focus,* 14:2.

Ruggles, Steven. 1987. *Prolonged connections: The rise of the extended family in nineteenth-century England and America.* Madison: University of Wisconsin Press.

Russakoff, Dale. 2006. In Motor City, anger yields to pragmatism. *Washington Post* (March 26): A1.

Rutter, Michael. 1979. *Fifteen thousand hours: Secondary schools and their effects on children.* Cambridge, MA: Harvard University Press.

Ruth, Henry, and **Kevin R. Reitz.** 2003. *The challenge of crime: Rethinking our response.* Cambridge, MA: Harvard University Press.

Ryan, John. 1985. *The production of culture in the music industry: The ASCAP-BMI controversy.* Lanham, MD: University Press of America.

S

Saad, Lydia. 1996. Americans growing more tolerant of gays. *Gallup Poll.*

Sagarin, Edward. 1975. *Deviants and deviance.* New York: Praeger.

Sakamoto, Arthur, and **Meichu D. Chen.** 1991. Inequality and attainment in a dual labor market. *American Sociological Review,* 56:295–308.

Sampson, Robert J., and **W. Byron Groves.** 1989. Community structure and crime: Testing social-disorganization theory. *American Journal of Sociology,* 94:774–802.

Samuelsson, Kurt. 1961. *Religion and economic action: A critique of Max Weber.* Trans. E. G. French. New York: Harper Torchbooks.

Sanchez, Rene. 1996. Math-science study faults U.S. teaching, curricula. *Washington Post* (November 21):A1.

Sanchez, Rene. 1997. Popularity grows for alternatives to public schools: Some districts reacting to threat of competition. *Washington Post* (October 1):A1.

Sanchez, Sandra. 1993. Equality of sexes? Give it 1,000 years. *USA Today* (February 5):A1.

Sanday, Peggy Reeves. 1981. The socio-cultural context of rape: A cross-cultural study. *Journal of Social Issues,* 37:5–27.

Sanday, Peggy Reeves. 1996. Rape-prone versus rape-free campus cultures. *Violence Against Women,* 2:191–208.

Sapir, Edward. 1949. *Selected writings in language, culture, and personality.* Berkeley: University of California Press.

Saporito, Bill. 1986. The revolt against "working smarter." *Fortune* (July 21):58–65.

Sassen, Saskia. 1991. *The global city: New York, London, Tokyo.* Princeton, NJ: Princeton University Press.

Sassen, Saskia, and **Alejandro Portes.** 1993. Miami: A new global city? *Contemporary Sociology,* 22:471–77.

Satchell, Michael. 1993. Trashing the reservations? *U.S. News & World Report* (January 11):24–25.

Savin-Williams, R. C., and **K. G. Esterberg.** 2000. Lesbian, gay, and bisexual families. In Demo, K. R.

Allen & M. A. Fine, eds., *Handbook of family diversity* (pp. 197–215). New York: Oxford University Press.

Savin-Williams, Ritch C., and **David H. Demo.** 1984. Developmental change and stability in adolescent self-concept. *Developmental Psychology,* 20:1100–10.

Sawa, Akira, and **Solomon H. Snyder.** 2005. Two genes link two distinct psychoses. *Science,* 310:1128–29.

Scales-Trent, Judy. 1995. *Notes of a white black woman: Race, color, and community.* University Park: Pennsylvania State University Press.

Scanzoni, John. 1997. A reply to Glenn: Fashioning families and policies for the future—not the past. *Family Relations,* 46:213–17.

Scanzoni, John, Karen Polonko, Jay Teachman, and **Linda Thompson.** 1989. *The sexual bond: Rethinking families and close relationships.* Newbury Park, CA: Sage.

Schaeffer, Nora Cate, and **Stanley Presser.** 2003. The science of asking questions. *Annual Review of Sociology,* 29:65–88.

Schlenker, Barry R., Michael F. Weigold, and **John R. Hallam.** 1990. Self-serving attributions in social context: Effects of self-esteem and social pressure. *Journal of Personality and Social Psychology,* 58:855–63.

Schoen, Robert, and **Robin M. Weinick.** 1993. Partner choice in marriages and cohabitations. *Journal of Marriage and the Family,* 55:408–14.

Schnittker, Jason, Jeremy Freese, and **Brian Powell.** 2003. Who are feminists and what do they believe? The role of generations. *American Sociological Review,* 68:1–17.

Schor, Juliet B. 1993. All work and no play: It doesn't pay. *New York Times* (August 29):F9.

Schorr, Alvin L. 1984. Redefining poverty levels. *New York Times* (May 9):27.

Schuman, Howard, Charlotte Steeh, Lawrence Bobo, and

Maria Krysan. 1997. *Racial attitudes in America.* Cambridge, MA: Harvard University Press.

Schur, Edwin. 1965. *Crimes without victims.* Englewood Cliffs, NJ: Prentice Hall.

Schwartz, Martin D. 1995. Date rape on college campuses. In Alex Thio and Thomas C. Calhoun, eds., *Readings in deviant behavior.* New York: HarperCollins.

Schwartz, Martin D., and **Walter S. DeKeseredy.** 1997. *Sexual assault on the college campus: The role of male peer support.* Thousand Oaks, CA: Sage.

Schwendinger, Julia R., and **Herman Schwendinger.** 1983. *Rape and inequality.* Beverly Hills, CA: Sage.

Scott, Janny, and **David Leonhardt.** 2005. Shadowy lines that still divide. In *Class Matters.* New York: Henry Holt and Company.

Scott, Janny. 2005. Life at the top in America isn't just better, it's longer. In *Class Matters.* New York: Henry Holt and Company.

Scott, W. Richard. 2004. Reflections on a half-century of organizational sociology. *Annual Review of Sociology,* 30:1–21.

Searle, John R. 1995. *The construction of social reality.* New York: Free Press.

Sears, David O., Jim Sidanius, and **Lawrence Bobo,** eds. 2000. *Racialized politics: The debate about racism in America.* Chicago: University of Chicago Press.

Seelye, Katharine Q., and **Janet Elder.** 2003. Strong support is found for ban on gay marriage. *New York Times* (December 21).

Seeman, Melvin. 1959. On the meaning of alienation. *American Sociological Review,* 24:783–91.

Selin, Helaine. 2002. An inclusive perspective. *Science,* 298:969–70.

Selltiz, Claire, Lawrence S. Wrightsman, and **Stuart W. Cook.** 1981. *Research methods in social relations.* New York: Holt, Rinehart and Winston.

Selz, Michael. 1994. Testing self-managed teams, entrepreneur hopes to lose job. *Wall Street Journal* (January 11):B1–B2.

Serbin, Lisa A., and **Carol Sprafkin.** 1986. The salience of gender and the process of sex typing in three- to seven-year-old children. *Child Development,* 57:1188–99.

Sewell, William H., Jr. 1992. A theory of structure: Duality, agency, and transformation. *American Journal of Sociology,* 98:1–29.

Sewell, William H., Archibald O. Haller, and **George W. Ohlendorf.** 1970. The educational and early occupational status attainment process: Replication and revision. *American Sociological Review,* 35:1014–27.

Sewell, William H., and **Robert M. Hauser.** 1975. *Education, occupation, and earnings: Achievement in early career.* New York: Academic Press.

Shaw, Clifford R. 1930. *Natural history of a juvenile career.* Chicago: University of Chicago Press.

Shaw, Clifford R., and **Henry McKay.** 1942. *Juvenile delinquency in urban areas.* Chicago: University of Chicago Press.

Shea, John C. 1984. *American government: The great game of politics.* New York: St. Martin's Press.

Shellenbarger, Sue. 1992. Flexible policies may slow women's careers. *Wall Street Journal* (April 22):B1.

Shelton, Beth Anne. 2000. Understanding the distribution of housework between husbands and wives. In Linda J. Waite, ed., *The ties that bind: Perspectives on marriage and cohabitation.* New York: Aldine de Gruyter.

Sherif, Muzafer. 1936. *The psychology of social norms.* New York: Harper & Row.

Sherif, Muzafer, O. J. Harvey, B. Jack White, William R. Hood, and **Carolyn W. Sherif.** 1961. *Intergroup conflict and cooperation: The Robbers' Cave experiment.* Norman: University of Oklahoma Book Exchange.

Sherkat, Darren E., and **Christopher G. Ellison.** 1999. Recent developments and current controversies in the sociology of religion. *Annual Review of Sociology,* 25:363–94.

Sherman, Lawrence W., Douglas A. Smith, Janell D. Schmidt, and **Dennis P. Rogan.** 1992. Crime, punishment, and stake in conformity: Legal and informal control of domestic violence. *American Sociological Review,* 57:680–90.

Shibutani, Tamotsu. 1986. *Social processes: An introduction to sociology.* Berkeley: University of California Press.

Shibutani, Tamotsu, and **Kian M. Kwan.** 1965. *Ethnic Stratification.* New York: Macmillan.

Shils, Edward A., and **Morris Janowitz.** 1948. Cohesion and disintegration in the Wehrmacht in World War II. *Public Opinion Quarterly,* 12:280–315.

Shoemaker, Donald J. 2000. *Theories of delinquency.* New York: Oxford University Press.

Shoemaker Donald J. 2005. *Theories of Delinquency: An Examination of Explanations of Delinquent Behavior* 5th ed. New York: Oxford University Press.

Sica, Alan. 1996. Review essay: Sociology as worldview. *American Journal of Sociology,* 102:252–55.

Siegel, Larry J., and **Brandon C. Welch.** 2005. *Juvenile delinquency: The core* 2nd ed. Belmont, CA: Thompson Wadsworth.

Sigelman, Lee, Timothy Bledsoe, Susan Welch, and **Michale W. Combs.** 1996. Making contact? Black-white social interaction in an urban setting. *American Journal of Sociology,* 101:1306–32.

Sills, David. 1957. *The volunteers.* New York: Free Press.

Simmel, Georg. 1908/1955. *Conflict and the web of group affiliations.* New York: Free Press.

Simmel, Georg. 1908/1959. How is society possible? In Kurt Wolff, ed., *Essays in sociology, philosophy, and aesthetics.* New York: Harper & Row.

Simmel, Georg. 1950. *The sociology of George Simmel.* Ed. and trans. Kurt Wolff. New York: Free Press.

Simon, David R., and **D. Stanley Eitzen.** 1993. *Elite deviance.* Boston: Allyn and Bacon.

Simon, Julian, ed. 1995. *The state of humanity.* Cambridge, MA: Blackwell.

Simon, Rita J. 1996. Transracial adoptions: Experiences of a twenty-year study. *The American Sociologist,* 27:79–89.

Simon, Rita J., and **Gloria Danziger.** 1991. *Women's movements in America: Their successes, disappointments, and aspirations.* New York: Praeger.

Simon, Robin W. 1998. Assessing sex differences in vulnerability among employed parents: The importance of marital status. *Journal of Health and Social Behavior,* 39:38–54.

Simon, Viviana. 2005. Wanted: Women in clinical trials. *Science,* 308:1517.

Simons, Ronald L., Jay Beaman, Rand D. Conger, and **Wei Chao.** 1993. Stress, support, and antisocial behavior trait as determinants of emotional well-being and parenting practices among single mothers. *Journal of Marriage and the Family,* 55:385–98.

Singer, Eleanor. 1981. Reference groups and social evaluations. In Morris Rosenberg and Ralph H. Turner, eds., *Social psychology: Sociological perspectives.* New York: Basic Books.

Skinner, B. F. 1953. *Science and human behavior.* New York: Macmillan.

Sklair, Leslie. 1991. *Sociology of the global system.* Baltimore: Johns Hopkins University Press.

Skocpol, Theda. 1979. *States and social revolution.* Cambridge, MA: Cambridge University Press.

Skocpol, Theda. 1980. Political response to capital crisis: Neo-Marxist theories of the state and the case of the New Deal. *Politics and Society,* 10:155–201.

Skocpol, Theda, and **Edwin Amenta.** 1986. States and social politics. *Annual Review of Sociology,* 12:131–57.

Skolnick, Arlene. 1991. *Embattled paradise: The American family in an age of uncertainty.* New York: Basic Books.

Skolnick, Arlene. 1997. A reply to Glenn: The battle of the textbooks: Bringing in the culture war. *Family Relations,* 46:219–22.

Slotkin, James S. 1955. Culture and psychopathology. *Journal of Abnormal and Social Psychology,* 51:269–75.

Small, Stephen A., and **Dave Riley.** 1990. Toward a multidimensional assessment of work spillover into family life. *Journal of Marriage and the Family,* 52:51–61.

Smedley, Brian D., Adrienne Y. Stith, and **Alan R. Nelson,** eds. 2003. *Unequal treatment: Confronting racial and ethnic disparities in health care.* National Academies of Sciences.

Smelser, Neil J. 1963. *Theory of collective behavior.* New York: Free Press.

Smith, Althea, and **Abigail J. Steward.** 1983. Approaches to studying racism and sexism in black women's lives. *Journal of Social Issues,* 39:1–15.

Smith, Dita. 2001. Women and power. *Washington Post* (January 6):A14.

Smith, Ryan A. 1999. Racial differences in access to hierarchical authority: An analysis of change over time, 1972–1994. *Sociological Quarterly,* 40(3):367–95.

Smock, Pamela J. 2000. Cohabitation in the United States: An appraisal of research themes, findings, and implications. *Annual Review of Sociology,* 26:1–20.

Snell, Tracy L., and **Laura M. Maruschak.** 2002. Capital punishment 2001. NCJ 197020. Washington, DC: U.S. Department of Justice.

Snipp, C. Matthew. 1989. *American Indians: The first of this land.* New York: Russell Sage Foundation.

Snipp, C. Matthew. 2003. Racial measurement in the American census: Past practices and implications for the future. *Annual Review of Sociology,* 29:563–88.

Snizek, William E. 1994. Survivors as victims: Some little publicized consequences of corporate downsizing. Address delivered to cabinet members of the Dutch Ministry of Government, The Hague, July 1994.

Snizek, William E. 1995. Virtual offices: Some neglected considerations. *Communications of the ACM,* 38:15–17.

Snowden, Frank M., Jr. 1983. *Before color prejudice: The ancient view of blacks.* Cambridge, MA: Harvard University Press.

Snyder, Thomas D., and **Charlene M. Hoffman.** 2003. *Digest of Education Statistics.* U.S. Department of Education: National Center for Education Statistics (NCES 2003-060).

Sobel, Richard. 1989. *The white-collar working class: From structure to politics.* New York: Praeger.

Solomon, Patrick. 1992. *Black resistance in high school: Forging a separatist culture.* Albany: State University of New York Press.

Solomon, Zahava, Marion Mikulincer, and **Steven E. Hobfoll.** 1986. Effects of social support and battle intensity on loneliness and breakdown during combat. *Journal of Personality and Social Psychology,* 51:1269–76.

Sommer, Robert. 1969. *Personal space.* Englewood Cliffs, NJ: Prentice Hall.

Songer, Donald R., and **Kelley A. Crews-Meyer.** 2000. Does judge gender matter? Decision making in state supreme courts. *Social Science Quarterly,* 81(3):750–62.

Sørensen, Aage B. 2000. Toward a sounder basis for class analysis. *American Journal of Sociology,* 105:1523–58.

Sorokin, Pitirim. 1959. *Social and cultural mobility.* New York: Free Press.

Soupiset, Mark F. 2003. Striking back at fraud. *USAA Magazine* (August):14–18.

South, Scott J., and **Glenna Spitze.** 1994. Housework in marital and nonmarital households. *American Sociological Review,* 59:327–47.

South, Scott J., and **Katherine Trent.** 1988. Sex ratios and women's roles: Cross-national analysis. *American Journal of Sociology,* 93:1096–1115.

Southern School News. 1954. Segregation. 1 (November):3.

Span, Paula. 1998. Taking a wife, and her name. *Washington Post* (January 4):F1.

Spates, James L. 1983. The sociology of values. *Annual Review of Sociology,* 9:27–49.

Sperber, Murray. 2000. *Beer and circus: How big-time college sports is crippling undergraduate education.* New York: Henry Holt.

Spiegel, David. 1994. Compassion is the best medicine. *New York Times* (January 10):A11.

Spohn, Cassia C. 2000. Thirty years of sentencing reform: The quest for a racially neutral sentencing process. *Criminal Justice 2000* 3 (National Institute of Justice).

Spraggins, Renee E. 2003. Women and men in the United States: March 2002. U.S. Census Bureau. Washington, DC: Government Printing Office.

Sprague, Joey, and **Mary K. Zimmerman.** 1993. Overcoming dualisms: A feminist agenda for sociological methodology. In Paula England, ed., *Theory on gender/ feminism on theory.* New York: Aldine de Gruyter.

Sprey, Jetse. 1979. Conflict theory and the study of marriage and the family. In Wesley R. Burr, Reuben Hill, F. Ivan Nye, and Ira L. Reiss, eds., *Contemporary theories about the family,* Vol. 2. New York: Free Press.

St. John, Craig, and **Robert Clymer.** 2000. Racial residential segregation by level of socioeconomic status. *Social Science Quarterly,* 81(3):701–15.

Stacey, Judith. 1996. *In the name of the family: Rethinking family values in the postmodern age.* Boston: Beacon Press.

Stacey, Judith, and **Timothy J. Biblarz.** 2001. (How) does the sexual orientation of parents matter? *American Sociological Review,* 66:159–83.

Stack, John F., Jr., ed. 1986. *The primordial challenge: Ethnicity in the contemporary world.* Westport, CT: Greenwood Press.

Stark, Rodney. 1996. *Sociology.* 6th ed. Belmont, CA: Wadsworth.

Stark, Rodney, and **William S. Bainbridge.** 1979. Of churches, sects, and cults: Preliminary concepts for a theory of religious movements. *Journal for the Scientific Study of Religion,* 18:117–33.

Stark, Rodney, and **William S. Bainbridge.** 1987. *A theory of religion.* New York: Peter Lang.

Starr, Paul. 1982. *The social transformation of American medicine.* New York: Basic Books.

State Demographics. 2004. Available at: http://demog.state.nc.us/demog/stgr13b.html.

Stearns, Peter N. 1977. *Old age in European society.* London: Croom Helm.

Steffensmeier, Darrell, and **Emilie Allan.** 1996. Gender and crime: Toward a gendered theory of female offending. *Annual Review of Sociology,* 22:459–87.

Steffensmeier, Darrell, and **Dana Haynie.** 2000. Gender, structural disadvantage and urban crime: Do macrosocial variables also explain female offending rates? *Criminology,* 38(2):403–38.

Steinberg, Stephen. 1989. *The ethnic myth: Race, ethnicity, and class in America.* Updated and expanded ed. New York: Atheneum.

Steinmetz, George, and **Erik Olin Wright.** 1989. The fall and rise of the petty bourgeoisie: Changing patterns of self-employment in the postwar United States. *American Journal of Sociology,* 94:973–1018.

Stephens, William N. 1963. *The family in cross-cultural perspective.* New York: Holt, Rinehart and Winston.

Stepp, Laura Sessions. 2000. New study questions teen risk factors: School woes, peers are stronger clues than race, income. *Washington Post* (November 30): A1.

Stets, Jan E., and **Michael M. Harrod.** 2004. Verification across multiple identities: The role of status. *Social Psychology Quarterly,* 67:155–71.

Stevenson, David Lee. 1991. Deviant students as a collective resource in classroom control. *Sociology of Education,* 64:127–33.

Stevenson, Harold W., Chuansheng Chen, and **Shi-Ying Lee.** 1993. Mathematics achievement of Chinese, Japanese, and American children: Ten years later. *Science,* 259:53–58.

Stevenson, Harold W., and **James W. Stigler.** 1992. *The learning gap: Why our schools are failing and what we can learn from Japanese and Chinese education.* New York: Summit.

Stinchcombe, Arthur L. 1983. *Economic sociology.* New York: Academic Press.

Stockard, Jean, and **Robert M. O'Brien.** 2002. Cohort effects on suicide rates: International variations. *American Sociological Review,* 67: 854–72.

Stokes, Randall G. 1975. Afrikaner Calvinism and economic action: The Weberian thesis in South Africa. *American Journal of Sociology,* 81:62–81.

Stokes, Randall G., and **Andy B. Anderson.** 1990. Disarticulation and human welfare in less developed countries. *American Sociological Review,* 55:63–74.

Stone, Arthur A., Jaylan S. Turkkan, Christine Bachrach, Jared B. Jobe, Howard S. Kurtzman, and **Virginia S. Cain,** eds. 1999. *The science of self-report: Implications for research and practice.* Mahwah, NJ: Lawrence Erlbaum Associates.

Stone, Katherine. 1974. The origins of job structures in the steel industry. *Review of Radical Economics,* 6:61–97.

Stone, Richard, and **Richard A. Kerr.** 2005. Girding for the next killer wave. *Science,* 310:1602–05 (December 9).

Strang, David, and **Nancy Brandon Tuma.** 1993. Spatial and temporal heterogeneity in diffusion. *American Journal of Sociology,* 99:614–39.

Straus, Murray A., and **Richard J. Gelles.** 1986. Societal change and change in family violence from 1975 to 1985 as revealed by two national surveys. *Journal of Marriage and the Family,* 48:465–79.

Straus, Murray A., and **Richard J. Gelles.** 1990. *Physical violence in American families: Risk factors and adaptations to violence in 8,145 families.* New Brunswick, NJ: Transaction.

Straus, Murray A., David B. Sugarman, and **Jean Giles-Sims.** 1997. Spanking by parents and subsequent antisocial behavior of children. *Archives of Pediatrics and Adolescent Medicine,* 151:761–67.

Strauss, Anselm, Leonard Schatzman, Rue Bucher, Danuta Ehrlich, and **Melvin Sabshin.** 1964. *Psychiatric ideologies and institutions.* New York: Free Press.

Stryker, Sheldon. 1980. *Symbolic interactionism: A social structural version.* Menlo Park, CA: Benjamin/Cummings.

Stryker, Sheldon. 1987. The vitalization of symbolic interactionism. *Social Psychology Quarterly,* 50:83–94.

Substance Abuse and Mental Health Services Administration. 2005. *Results from the 2004 National Survey on Drug Use and Health: National Findings* (NSDUH Series H-28, DHHS Publication No. SMA 05-4062). Rockville, MD: Substance Abuse and Mental Health Services Administration, Office of Applied Studies.

Sudnow, David. 1967. *Passing on: The social organization of dying.* Englewood Cliffs, NJ: Prentice Hall.

Sullivan, Kevin, and **Mary Jordan.** 2002. U.S. called the loser in war on drugs. *Washington Post* (October 31):A1.

Sumner, William Graham. 1906. *Folkways.* Boston: Ginn.

Sunstein, Cass R. 2003. Sober lemmings. *The New Republic* (April 14):34–37.

Super, David A., Sharon Parrott, Susan Steinmetz, and **Cindy Mann.** 1996. *The new welfare law—summary.* Washington, DC: Center on Budget and Policy Priorities.

Suro, Roberto. 1990. Where America is growing: The suburban cities. *New York Times* (February 23):1–10.

Suro, Roberto. 1991. Your tired, your poor, your masses yearning to be with relatives. *New York Times* (January 6):4E.

Sutherland, Edwin H. 1939. *Principles of criminology.* Philadelphia: Lippincott.

Sutherland, Edwin H. 1949. *White-collar crime.* New York: Dryden Press.

Sutton, John R. 1991. The political economy of madness: The expansion of the asylum in progressive America. *American Sociological Review,* 56:665–78.

Sutton, John R. 2000. Imprisonment and social classification in five common-law democracies, 1955–1985. *American Journal of Sociology,* 106:305–86.

Swedberg, Richard. 1991. *Joseph A. Schumpeter: His life and work.* Princeton, NJ: Princeton University Press.

Swedberg, Richard. 2003. The changing picture of Max Weber's sociology. *Annual Review of Sociology,* 29:283–306.

Szymanski, Albert. 1976. Racial discrimination and white gain. *American Sociological Review,* 41:403–14.

Szymanski, Albert. 1981. *The logic of imperialism.* New York: Praeger.

T

Tanioko, Ichiro, and **Daniel Glaser.** 1991. School uniforms, routine activities, and the social control of delinquency in Japan. *Youth and Society,* 23:50–75.

Taylor, Verta. 1989. Social movement continuity: The women's movement in abeyance. *American Sociological Review,* 54:761–75.

Teachman, J. 2003. Premarital sex, premarital cohabitation, and the risk of subsequent marital dissolution among women. *Journal of Marriage and the Family,* 65(2):444–455.

Tetlock, P. E., R. S. Peterson, C. McGuire, S. Chang, and **P. Feld.** 1992. Assessing political group dynamics: A test of the groupthink model. *Journal of Personality and Social Psychology,* 63:403–25.

Thio, Alex. 1998. *Deviant behavior.* 5th ed. New York: Longman.

Thistle, Susan. 2000. The trouble with modernity: Gender and the remaking of social theory. *Sociological Theory,* 18:275–88.

Thoits, Peggy A. 1995. Identity-relevant events and psychological symptoms: A cautionary tale. *Social Forces,* 36:72–82.

Thomas, William I., and **Dorothy S. Thomas.** 1928. *The child in America: Behavior problems and programs.* New York: Knopf.

Thrasher, Frederic M. 1927. *The gang.* Chicago: University of Chicago Press.

Tice, Dianne M. 1992. Self-concept change and self-presentation: The looking glass self is also a magnifying glass. *Journal of Personality and Social Psychology,* 63:435–51.

Tien, H. Yuan. 1992. China's demographic dilemmas. *Population Bulletin,* 47(1) (June).

Tierney, Patrick. 2000. *Darkness in El Dorado: How scientists and journalists devastated the Amazon.* New York: Norton.

Tilghman, Shirley M. 1993. Science vs. women: A radical solution. *New York Times* (January 26): A19.

Tilly, Charles. 1978. *From mobilization to revolution.* Reading, MA: Addison-Wesley.

Tilly, Charles. 1990. *Coercion, capital, and European states, AD 990–1990.* Cambridge, MA: Blockwell.

TIMSS. 2006. Trends in international mathematics and science study 2003. http://nces.ed.gov/pubs2005/timss03.

Tipton, Steven M. 1982. *Getting saved from the sixties.* Berkeley and Los Angeles: University of California Press.

Tittle, Charles R., and **Raymond Paternoster.** 2000. *Social deviance and crime: An organizational and theoretical approach.* Los Angeles, CA: Roxbury Publishing Company.

Tittle, Charles R., and **Alan R. Rowe.** 1974. Certainty of arrest and crime rates: A further test of the deterrence hypothesis. *Social Forces,* 52:455–62.

Tittle, Charles R., and **Michael R. Welch.** 1983. Religiosity and deviance: Toward a contingency theory of constraining effects. *Social Forces,* 61:653–82.

Tong, Rosemarie P. 1998. *Feminist thought: A more comprehensive introduction.* 2nd ed. Boulder, CO: Westview Press.

Toossi, Mitra. 2005. Labor force projections to 2014: retiring boomers. *Monthly Labor Review* (November):25–44 (available at: http://www.bls.gov/opub/mlr/2005/11/art3full.pdf).

Toynbee, Arnold J. 1934/1954. *A study of history.* 10 vols. New York: Oxford University Press.

Tracy, Paul E., Marvin E. Wolfgang, and **Robert M. Figlio.** 1990. *Delinquency careers in two birth cohorts.* New York: Plenum.

Trafford, Abigail. 2001. The hill tunes in to nurses' lament. *Washington Post* (February 27):8.

Trost, Cathy. 1990. Census survey on child care increases concern about how much poor can pay. *Wall Street Journal* (August 15): A10.

Tuch, Steven A., and Michael Hughes. 1996. Whites' racial policy attitudes. *Social Science Quarterly,* 77:723–45.

Tucker, Compton J., Harold E. Dregne, and Wilbur W. Newcomb. 1991. Expansion and contraction of the Sahara Desert from 1980 to 1990. *Science,* 253:299–301.

Tucker, Joan S., Joseph E. Schwartz, Carol Tomlinson-Keasey, Howard S. Friedman, Michael H. Criqui, Deborah L. Wingard, and Leslie R. Martin. 1997. Parental divorce: Effects on individual behavior and longevity. *Journal of Personality and Social Psychology,* 73(2):381–91.

Tucker, Neely. 2000. A matter of violent death and little girls. *Washington Post* (December 31):C1.

Tumin, Melvin M. 1953. Some principles of stratification: A critical analysis. *American Sociological Review,* 18:387–94.

Turkheimer, Eric, and Mary Waldron. 2000. Nonshared environment: A theoretical, methodological, and quantitative review. *Psychological Bulletin,* 126:78–108.

Turner, Bryan S. 1987. *Medical power and social knowledge.* Beverly Hills, CA: Sage.

Turner, Jonathan H. 1990. Émile Durkheim's theory of social organization. *Social Forces,* 68:1089–103.

Turner, Ralph H. 1964. Collective behavior. In R. E. L. Faris, ed., *Handbook of modern sociology.* Chicago: Rand McNally.

Turner, Ralph H. 1968. The self-conception in social interaction. In C. Gordon and and K. J. Gergen, eds., *The self in social interaction.* New York: John Wiley.

Turner, Ralph H., and Lewis M. Killian. 1972. *Collective behavior,* 2nd ed. Englewood Cliffs, NJ: Prentice Hall.

Tyler, Tom R. 1990. *Why people obey the law.* New Haven, CT: Yale University Press.

U

Udry, J. Richard. 1995. Sociology and biology: What biology do sociologists need to know? *Social Forces,* 73:1267–78.

Udry, J. Richard. 2000. Biological limits of gender construction. *American Sociological Review,* 65:443–57.

Udry, Richard. 2001. Reply: Feminist critics uncover determinism positivism, and antiquated theory. *American Sociological Review,* 66:611–18.

Uggen, Christopher. 2000. Class, gender, and arrest: An intergenerational analysis of workplace power and control. *Criminology,* 38(3):835–62.

Uggen, Christopher, and Jeff Manza. 2002. Democratic contraction? Political consequences of felon disenfranchisement in the United States. *American Sociological Review,* 67:777–803.

Uggen, Christopher, and Amy Blackstone. 2004. Sexual Harassment as a gendered expression of power. American Sociological Review, 69:64–92

Ulrich, Laurel Thatcher. 1990. *A midwife's tale.* New York: Random House.

UNESCO. 2006 Illiteracy rates by gender in the Arab states and North Africa 2000–2004. www.uis.unesco.org.

United Nations Conference on Trade and Development. 2005. Information economy report 2005. New York and Geneva: United Nations (available at: http://www.unctad.org/en/docs/sdteedc20051_en.pdf).

United Nations. 1999. *The world at six billion.* New York: United Nations. Available at: http://www.un.org/esa/population/publications/sixbillion/sixbilpart1.pdf.

United Nations. 2001. *World urbanization prospects: The 1999 revision.* New York: United Nations.

United Nations. 2003. *The world's women 2000: Trends and statistics.* Available at: http:unstats.un.org/unsd/demographics/ww2000.

U.S. Census Bureau. 1995. *Getting a helping hand: Long-term participants in assistance programs.* Bureau of the Census Statistical Brief, SB/95-27 (available online at: http://www.census.gov/apsd/www/statbrief/sb95_27.pdf).

U.S. Census Bureau. 1996. *Statistical abstract of the United States.* Washington, DC: U.S. Government Printing Office.

U.S. Census Bureau. 1999. *Statistical abstract of the United States: 1999.* Washington, DC: U.S. Government Printing Office.

U.S. Census Bureau. 2000b. *Coming from the Americas: A profile of the nation's Latin American foreign born.* Census Brief CENBR/00-3. Washington, DC: U.S. Government Printing Office.

U.S. Census Bureau. 2003. *Statistical abstract of the United States: 2002.* Washington, DC: U.S. Government Printing Office.

U.S. Census Bureau. 2004a. "U.S. Interim Projections by Age, Sex, Race, and Hispanic Origin," <http://www.census.gov/ipc/www/usinterimproj/>.

U.S. Census Bureau. 2006. *Statistical abstract of the United States: 2006.* Washington, DC: U.S. Government Printing Office.

U. S. Census Bureau. 2006. Quarterly retail e-commerce sales, 4th quarter 2005. *U.S. Census Bureau News,* February 17 (available at: http://www.census.gov/mrts/www/data/pdf/05Q4.pdf).

U.S. Commission on Civil Rights. 1988. *The economic status of Americans of Asian descent: An exploratory investigation.* Washington, DC: Clearinghouse Publication.

U.S. Department of Commerce. 2002. *A nation online: How Americans are expanding their use of the Internet.* Washington, DC: U.S. Government Printing Office.

U.S. Department of Health and Human Services. 1996. *Vital statistics of the United States 1988: Volume III—marriage and divorce.* Hyattsville, MD: U.S. Department of Health and Human Services.

U.S. Department of Health and Human Services. 2000. *Healthy people 2010: Understanding and improving health.* 2nd ed. Washington, DC: U.S. Government Printing Office.

U.S. Department of Health and Human Services. 2003. *Child maltreatment 2001.* Washington, DC: Government Printing Office.

U.S. Department of Health, Education, and Welfare. 1973. *100 years of marriage and divorce statistics: United States, 1867–1967.* Rockville, MD: Health Resources Administration, National Center for Health Statistics.

U.S. Department of Labor. 2006. www.dol.gov/wb/stats/main.htm

U.S. State Department. 2006. Country reports on human rights practices. www.state.gov/g/drl/rls

U.S. National Center for Educational Statistics. 1995. *Statistics in brief,* October 1995 (NCES 95-824), Washington, DC: U.S. National Center on Health Statistics.

Useem, Michael. 1983. *The inner circle.* New York: Oxford University Press.

V

Vago, Steven. 2003. *Law and society.* 7th ed. Upper Saddle River, NJ: Prentice Hall.

Valente, Judith. 1991. A century later, Sioux still struggle, and still are losing. *Wall Street Journal* (March 25):A1, A12.

Valentine, Charles. 1968. *Culture and poverty.* Chicago: University of Chicago Press.

Valentino, Nicholas A., and **David O. Sears.** 2005. Old times there are not forgotten: Race and partisan realignment in the contemporary

South. *American Journal of Political Science,* 49:672–88.

Van Creveld, Martin. 1982. *Fighting power: German and U.S. Army performance, 1939–1945.* Westport, CT: Greenwood Press.

van den Berg, Axel. 1988. *The imminent utopia: From Marxism of the state to the state of Marxism.* Princeton, NJ: Princeton University Press.

van den Berghe, Pierre. 1963. Dialectic and functionalism: Toward a theoretical synthesis. *American Sociological Review,* 28:695–705.

Vander Zanden, James W. 1965. *Race relations in transition.* New York: Random House.

Vander Zanden, James W. 1983. *American minority relations.* 4th ed. New York: Knopf.

Vander Zanden, James W. 1993. *Human development.* 5th ed. New York: McGraw-Hill.

Vannoy, Dana, and **William W. Philliber.** 1992. Wife's employment and quality of marriage. *Journal of Marriage and the Family,* 54:387–98.

Van Schaik, Carel P., Marc Ancrenaz, Gwendolyn Borgen, Birute Galdikas, Cheryl D. Knott, Ian Singleton, Akira Suzuki, Sri Suci Utami, and **Michelle Merrill.** 2003. Orangutan cultures and the evolution of material culture. *Science,* 299:102–05.

Veblen, Thorstein. 1899. *The theory of the leisure class.* New York: Viking.

Veblen, Thorstein. 1921. *Engineers and the price system.* New York: Viking.

Vedantam, Shankar. 2001. Peer pressure spurs terrorists, psychologists say. *Washington Post* (October 16): A16.

Ventura, Stephanie J., and **Christine A. Bachrach.** 2000. Nonmarital childbearing in the United States, 1940–99. *National Vital Statistics Reports,* 48(16):October 18. Atlanta: Centers for Disease Control.

Visgaitis, Gary. 1994. A look at Native Americans across the USA. *USA Today* (April 28):7A.

Visher, Christy A., and **Jeremy Travis.** 2003. Transitions from prison to community: Understanding individual pathways. *Annual Review of Sociology,* 29:89–113.

Vitousek, Peter M., Harold A. Mooney, Jane Lubchenco, and **Jerry M. Melillo.** 1997. Human domination of Earth's ecosystems. *Science,* 277:494–99.

Vobejda, Barbara. 1997. Who's minding the children? Quality of day care is often a casualty of the booming economy. *Washington Post* (October 22):A1.

Vogel, Lise. 1983. *Marxism and the oppression of women.* New Brunswick, NJ: Rutgers University Press.

von Drehl, David. 2003. Gay marriage is a right, Massachusetts court rules. *Washington Post* (November 19):A1.

Vroom, Victor H., and **Arthur G. Jago.** 1988. *The new leadership: Managing participation in organizations.* Englewood Cliffs, NJ: Prentice Hall.

W

Waddington, David, Karen Jones, and **Chas Critcher.** 1989. *Flashpoints: Studies in disorder.* New York: Routledge.

Waddoups, Jeffrey, and **Djeto Assane.** 1993. Mobility and gender in a segmented labor market: A closer look. *American Journal of Economics and Sociology,* 52:399–411.

Wadman, Meredith K. 1992. Mothers who take extended time off find their careers pay a heavy price. *Wall Street Journal* (July 16):B1–B2.

Wagley, Charles, and **Marvin Harris.** 1964. *Minorities in the New World.* New York: Columbia University Press.

Waite, Linda J., and **Maggie Gallagher.** 2000. *The case for marriage: Why married people are happier, healthier, and better off financially.* New York: Doubleday.

Waitzkin, Howard. 1983. *The second sickness: Contradictions of* *capitalist health care.* New York: Free Press.

Waldo, Gordon P., and **Theodore G. Chiricos.** 1972. Perceived penal sanction and self-reported criminality: A neglected approach to deterrence research. *Social Problems,* 19:522–40.

Wallerstein, Immanuel. 1974. *The modern world-system: Capitalist agriculture and the origins of the European world economy in the 16th century.* New York: Academic Press.

Wallerstein, Immanuel. 1980. *The modern world-system II: Mercantilism and the consolidation of the European world-economy, 1600–1775.* New York: Academic Press.

Wallerstein, Immanuel. 1989. *The modern world-system III: The second era of great expansion of the capitalist world-economy, 1730–1840.* New York: Academic Press.

Walmsley, Roy. 2003. *World prison population list.* 5th ed. United Kingdom Home Office Research, Development and Statistics Directorate.

Walmsley, Roy. 2005. *World prison population list.* 6th ed. London, UK: International Centre for Prison Studies, King's College, London (available at http://www.prisonstudies.org).

Walton, John, and **Charles Ragin,** 1990. Global and national sources of political protest: Third World responses to the debt crisis. *American Sociological Review,* 55:876–90.

Warner, R. Stephen. 1993. Work in progress toward a new paradigm for the sociological study of religion in the United States. *American Journal of Sociology,* 98:1044–93.

Warner, W. Lloyd. 1949. *Democracy in Jonesville.* New York: Harper & Row.

Warner, W. Lloyd, and **Paul S. Lunt.** 1941. *The social life of the modern community.* New Haven, CT: Yale University Press.

Warner, W. Lloyd, and **Paul S. Lunt.** 1942. *The status system of a modern community.* New Haven, CT: Yale University Press.

Warren, John Robert, Robert M. Hauser, and **Jennifer T. Sheridan.** 2002. Occupational stratification across the life course: Evidence from the Wisconsin Longitudinal Study. *American Sociological Review,* 67:432–55.

Washington Post. 2001. Paying the price for "disengaged" workers. (March 2):E2.

Washington Post. 2004. Canadian government proposes bill offering definition of marriage. (July 18):A15.

Waters, Mary C. 1990. *Ethnic options: Choosing identities in America.* Berkeley: University of California Press.

Waters, Mary C., and **Tomas R. Jimenez.** 2005. Assessing immigrant assimilation: New empirical and theoretical challenges. *Annual Review of Sociology,* 31:105–25.

Watson, Robert T. 2003. Climate change: The political situation. *Science,* 302:1925–26.

Weber, Max. 1904/1958. *The Protestant ethic and the spirit of capitalism.* New York: Scribner's.

Weber, Max. 1916/1964. *The religion of China: Confucianism and Taoism.* New York: Macmillan.

Weber, Max. 1917/1958. *The religion of India: The sociology of Hinduism and Buddhism.* New York: Free Press.

Weber, Max. 1921/1968. *Economy and society.* 3 vols. Totowa, NJ: Bedminster Press.

Weber, Max. 1946. *The theory of social and economic organization.* Ed. and trans. A. M. Henderson and Talcott Parsons. New York: Macmillan.

Weber, Max. 1947. *From Max Weber: Essays in sociology.* Ed. and trans. Hans H. Gerth and C. Wright Mills. New York: Oxford University Press.

Wechsler, Henry, Meichun Kuo, Hang Lee, and **George W. Dowdall.** 2000. Environmental correlates of underage alcohol use and related problems of college students.

American Journal of Preventative Medicine, 19:24–29.

Wechsler, Henry, Jae Eun Lee, Meichun Kuo, and **Hang Lee.** 2000. College binge drinking in the 1990s: A continuing problem. Results of the Harvard School of Public Health 1999 College Alcohol Study. *Journal of American College Health,* 48: 199–210.

Weeden, Kim A. 2002. Why do some occupations pay more than others? Social closure and earnings inequality in the United States. *American Journal of Sociology,* 108(1):55–101.

Weeden, Kim A., and **David B. Grusky.** 2005. The case for a new class map. *American Journal of Sociology,* 111:141–212.

Weeks, John R. 1989. *Population: an introduction to concepts and issues.* Belmont, CA: Wadsworth.

Weeks, Linton. 2006. The cheapest shot: The sociology of spitting. *The Washington Post.* (January 10):C1.

Weiss, Gregory L., and **Lynne E. Lonnquist.** 1994. *The sociology of health, healing and illness.* Englewood Cliffs, NJ: Prentice Hall.

Weiss, Harvey, and **Raymond S. Bradley.** 2001. What drives societal collapse? *Science,* 291:609–10.

Weiss, Rick. 1997. Psychologists' society adopts resolution seeking to limit gay "conversion" therapy. *Washington Post* (August 15):A14.

Wells, Thomas. 1999. Changes in occupational sex segregation during the 1980s and 1990s. *Social Science Quarterly,* 80(2):370–80.

Welsh, Sandy. 1999. Gender and sexual harassment. *Annual Review of Sociology,* 25:169–90.

Werschkul, Misha, and **Erica Williams.** 2004. The 2004 national overview report: The status of women in the states. www.iwpr.org/states2004.

Western, Bruce. 2002. The impact of incarceration on wage mobility and inequality. *American Sociological Review,* 67:526–46.

Wethington, Elaine, Hope Cooper, and **Carolyn S. Holmes.** 1997. Turning points in midlife. In Ian Gotlib and Blair Wheaton, eds., *Stress and adversity over the life course: Trajectories and turning points.* New York: Cambridge University Press.

White, Lynn, and **John N. Edwards.** 1990. Emptying the nest and parental well-being: An analysis of national panel data. *American Sociological Review,* 55:235–42.

White, Ralph K., and **Ronald O. Lippitt.** 1960. *Autocracy and democracy.* New York: Harper & Row.

White, T. D., B. Asfaw, D. DeGusta, H. Tilbert, G. D. Richards, G. Suwa, and **F. C. Howell.** 2003. Pleistocene Homo sapiens from Middle Awash, Ethiopia. *Nature,* 423:742–47.

Whitson, John. 2006. College costs hit where it hurts. *Union Leader* (May 1):www.unionleader.com.

Whitt, J. Allen. 1979. Toward a class-dialectical model of power: An empirical assessment of three competing models of political power. *American Sociological Review,* 44:81–100.

Whitt, J. Allen. 1982. *Urban elites and mass transportation: The dialectics of power.* Princeton, NJ: Princeton University Press.

WHO. 2000. Database on violence against women, 2000. In *The World's Women 2000: Trends and Statistics* (United Nations). http://unstats.un.org/unsd/demographic/ww2000/table6c.htm

Whorf, Benjamin L. 1956. *Language, thought, and reality.* Cambridge, MA: MIT Press.

Whyte, Martin King. 1990. *Dating, mating, and marriage.* New York: Aldine de Gruyter.

Wiesel, Elie. 1961. *Night.* Trans. Stella Rodway. New York: Hill & Wang.

Wiggins, James A., Beverly B. Wiggins, and **James Vander Zanden.** 1994. *Social psychology.* New York: McGraw-Hill.

Wilke, John R. 1993. Computer links erode hierarchical nature of workplace culture. *Wall Street Journal* (December 9): A1, A7.

Williams, Kipling, Stephen Harkins, and **Bibb Latané.** 1981. Identifiability as a deterrent to social loafing: Two cheering experiments. *Journal of Personality and Social Psychology,* 40:303–11.

Williams, Redford B. 1998. Lower socioeconomic status and increased mortality. Early childhod roots and the potential for successful interventions. *Journal of the American Medical Association,* 279(21):1745–46.

Williams, Rhys H., and **N. J. Demerath III.** 1991. Religion and political process in an American city. *American Sociological Review,* 56:417–31.

Williams, Robin M., Jr. 1964. *Strangers next door.* Englewood Cliffs, NJ: Prentice Hall.

Williams, Robin M., Jr. 1970. *American society,* 3rd ed. New York: Knopf.

Willie, Charles V. 1979. *Caste and class controversy.* New York: General Hall.

Willie, Charles V. 1991. Universal programs are unfair to minority groups. *Chronicle of Higher Education* (December 4):B1, B3.

Wilmoth, J. R., L. J. Deegan, H. Lundstrom, and **S. Horiuchi.** 2000. Increase of maximum life-span in Sweden. 1861–1999. *Science,* 289:2366–68.

Wilson, Bryan R. 1990. *The social dimensions of sectarianism: Sects and new religious movements in contemporary society.* New York: Oxford University Press.

Wilson, Edward O. 2002. *The future of life.* New York: Knopf.

Wilson, James Q. 1990. *What government agencies do and why they do it.* New York: Basic Books.

Wilson, James Q. 1993. Mr. Clinton, meet Mr. Gore. *Wall Street Journal* (October 28):A18.

Wilson, James Q. 1997. Hostility in America. *New Republic* (August 25): 38–41.

Wilson, Peter J. 1988. *The domestication of the human species.* New Haven, CT: Yale University Press.

Wilson, Scott. 2000. Web of resistance rises in Cuba: Rebels defy government ban on Internet, link up with world. *Washington Post* (December 26):A1.

Wilson, William Julius. 1978. *The declining significance of race.* Chicago: University of Chicago Press.

Wilson, William Julius. 1987. *The truly disadvantaged: The inner city, the underclass, and public policy.* Chicago: University of Chicago Press.

Wilson, William Julius. 1991. Studying inner-city social dislocations: The challenge of public agenda research. *American Sociological Review,* 56:1–14.

Wilson, William J. 1996. *When work disappears.* New York, Knopf.

Wilson, William Julius. 2003. Introduction to the 2003 edition. In Elliot Liebow, *Tally's corner.* Lanham, MD: Rowman & Littlefield Publishers.

Wilson, William Julius, and **Robert Aponte.** 1985. Urban poverty. *Annual Review of Sociology,* 11:213–58.

Winch, Robert F. 1958. *Mate selection: A study of complementary needs.* New York: Harper & Row.

Winnick, Louis. 1991. *New people in old neighborhoods.* New York: Russell Sage Foundation.

Wirt, John, Susan Choy, Stephen Provasnik, Patrick Rooney, Anindita Sen, Richard Tobin, Barbara Kridl, and **Andrea Livingston.** 2003. *The Condition of Education 2003.* U.S. Department of Education: National Center for Education Statistics (NCES 2003–067).

Wiseman, Alan E. 2000. *The Internet economy: Access, taxes, and market structure.* Washington, DC: Brookings Institution Press.

Witt, Linda, Karen M. Paget, and **Glenna Matthews.** 1993. *Running as a woman: Gender and power in American politics.* New York: Free Press.

Wolf, Naomi. 1991. *The beauty myth: How images of beauty are used against women.* New York: Doubleday Anchor Books.

Wolfe, Tom. 1968. *The pump house gang.* New York: Farrar, Straus and Giroux.

Wolfers, Justin, and **Betsey Stevenson.** 2006. Bargaining in the shadow of the law: Divorce laws and family distress. *Quarterly Journal of Economics,* 121(1).

Wolff, Edward N. 1995. *Top heavy: A study of the increasing inequality of wealth in America.* New York: Twentieth Century Fund Press.

Wolff, Edward N. 1996. International comparisons of wealth inequality. *Review of Income and Wealth.* Series 42, No. 4 (December):433–51.

Wolfinger, Nicholas H. 1999. Trends in the intergenerational transmission of divorce. *Demography,* 36:415–420.

Wolfinger, Nicholas H. 2003. Parental divorce and offspring marriage. Early or late? *Social Forces,* 82(1):337–53.

Wolfgang, Marvin E., Robert M. Figlio, and **Thorsten Sellin.** 1972. *Delinquency in a birth cohort.* Chicago: University of Chicago Press.

Woodard, Michael D. 1987. Voluntary association membership among black Americans: The post-civil-rights era. *Sociological Quarterly,* 28:285–301.

Woolhandler, Steffie, Terry Campbell, and **David U. Himmelstein.** 2003. Costs of health care administration in the United States and Canada. *New England Journal of Medicine,* 349:768–75.

World Health Organization. 2003. Suicide rates (per 100,000), by country, year, and gender (data table). Geneva: World Health Organization (available at: http://www.who.int/ mental_health/prevention/suicide/ suiciderates/en/).

Wright, Erik Olin. 1985. *Classes.* New York: Schocken.

Wright, Erik Olin. 1993. Typologies, scales, and class analysis: A comment on Halaby and Weakliem's "Ownership and authority in the earnings function." *American Sociological Review,* 58:31–34.

Wright, Erik Olin. 2000. Working-class power, capitalist-class interests, and class compromise. *American Journal of Sociology,* 105:957–1002.

Wright, Erik Olin. 2002. The shadow of exploitation in Weber's class analysis. *American Sociological Review,* 67:832–53.

Wright, John Paul, and **Francis T. Cullen.** 2000. Juvenile involvement in occupational delinquency. *Criminology,* 38(3):863–96.

Wrigley, Julia. 1995. *Other people's children.* New York: Basic Books.

Wrigley, Julia. 2003. Review of "Domestica: Immigrant workers cleaning and caring in the shadows of affluence." *Gender and Society,* 17:326–28.

Wrigley, Julia, and **Joanna Dreby.** 2005. Fatalities in child care in the United States, 1985–2003. *American Sociological Review,* 70:729–57.

Wysocki, Bernard, Jr. 1991. Influx of Asians brings prosperity to Flushing, a place for newcomers. *Wall Street Journal* (January 15):A1, A10.

Y

Yablonsky, Lewis, and **Martin R. Haskell.** 1988. *Juvenile delinquency.* 4th ed. New York: Harper & Row.

Yamagishi, Toshio. 1995. Social dilemmas. In Karen S. Cook, Gary Alan Fine, and James S. House, eds., *Sociological perspectives on social psychology.* Boston: Allyn and Bacon.

Yamaguchi, Kazuo, and **Yanatao Wang.** 2002. Class identification of married employed women and men in America. *American Journal of Sociology,* 108(2):440–75.

Yamamoto, Akiko, and **Doug Struck.** 2002. Pressured pregnancy in Japan: To get affordable day care, women must carefully plan due date. *Washington Post* (November 14):A20.

Yans-McLaughlin, Virginia. 1982. *Family and community: Italian immigrants in Buffalo, 1880–1930.* Urbana: University of Illinois Press.

Yinger, J. Milton. 1965. *Toward a field theory of behavior.* New York: Macmillan.

Young, Robert L. 2004. Guilty until proven innocent: Conviction orientation, racial attitudes, and support for capital punishment. *Deviant Behavior,* 25:151–67.

Yount, Kathryn M. 2002. Like mother, like daughter? Female genital cutting in Minia, Egypt. *Journal of Health and Social Behavior,* 43:336–58.

Z

Zigli, Barbara. 1984. Asian-Americans beat others in academic drive. *USA Today* (April 25): D1.

Zimbardo, Philip G. 1969. The human choice: Individuation, reason, and order versus deindividualization, impulse, and chaos. In W. Arnold and D. Levine, eds., *Nebraska Symposium on Motivation,* 17:237–307.

Zimmerman, Don H. 1971. The practicalities of rule use. In Jack Douglas, ed., *Understanding everyday life.* Chicago: Aldine.

Zimring, Franklin E., and **Gordon Hawkins.** 1997. *Crime is not the problem: Lethal violence in America.* New York: Oxford University Press.

Zingraff, Matthew T., Jeffrey Leiter, Matthew C. Johnson, and **Kristen A. Myers.** 1994. The mediating effect of good school performance on the maltreatment-delinquency relationship. *Journal of Research in Crime and Delinquency,* 31:62–91.

Zuckerman, Miron, M. H. Kernis, S. M. Guarnera, J. F. Murphy, and **L. Rappoport.** 1983. The egocentric bias: Seeing oneself as cause and target of others' behavior. *Journal of Personality,* 51:621–30.

photo credits

name index